Identification

Investigation, Trial and Scientific Evidence

Second Edition

Paul Bogan QC is a barrister at 23 Essex Street Chambers in London. He represents those accused of serious or organised crime, from murder to drugs trafficking and serious fraud. He undertakes appellate work, both in the Court of Appeal and Privy Council, reviewing trial evidence and examining the safety of convictions. He sits on the Law Reform Committee of the Bar Council for whom he regularly drafts responses to proposed changes in criminal law.

Andrew Roberts is a Senior Lecturer in the Law School at the University of Melbourne. He previously held positions at the Universities of Warwick and Leeds, and a Visiting Senior Fellowship in the Faculty of Law at the University of New South Wales, where he remains an Associate of the Program for Expertise, Evidence and Law. He is the Case Note Editor and a member of the editorial board of the *International Journal of Evidence and Proof*, and provides commentary on cases reported in the *Criminal Law Review*. He has published widely on various aspects of criminal procedure, particularly eyewitness identification and expert evidence.

Identification

Investigation, Trial and Scientific Evidence

Second Edition

Paul Bogan QC
23 Essex Street

Andrew Roberts
Senior Lecturer in Law, University of Melbourne

Published by
Jordan Publishing Limited
21 St Thomas Street
Bristol BS1 6JS

British Library Cataloguing-in-Publication Data

A catalogue record for this book is available from the British Library.

ISBN 978 1 84661 236 7

Typeset by Letterpart Ltd, Reigate, Surrey

Printed in Great Britain by CPI Antony Rowe, Chippenham and Eastbourne

CONTRIBUTORS

DNA

Dr Georgina Meakin BSc (Hons), MSc, PhD
Carrie Mullen BSc (Hons), MSc
Both of The Forensic Institute, Glasgow

Fingerprints

1st Edition

Catherine Tweedy HNC, BSc(Hons), CBiol, AIBMS, MRSH, MIBiol
Forensic Scientist with Keith Borer Consultants in Durham

2nd Edition

Paul Newsham
Formerly, Head of Fingerprint Bureau, Staffordshire Police

Handwriting

Mike Allen BA (Hons), MSc
Consultant on all aspects of forensic documentation examination

Facial Mapping

Richard Neave
Medical Artist and Partner in RN-DS Partnership

Voice

Professor Francis Nolan
Department of Phonetics, University of Cambridge

Dog Tracking

Alan Gerrish

PREFACE TO THE SECOND EDITION

Though the legal landscape is much changed in the 7 years since publication of the first edition of this book, one thing has not – the volume of cases heard by the Court of Appeal in which convictions are challenged on grounds of slender or flawed identification evidence, non-observance of Code D procedural requirements and errors or defects in jury directions. That these appeals represent a significant proportion of appellate business and their fair share of unsafe convictions undoubtedly reflects the special place identification evidence occupies in both the investigation and prosecution of crime.

The second edition of the book is similar in scheme to the first: an introduction followed by Parts on Investigation, Trial and Scientific Evidence. The scope of the text on the psychology of identification evidence in the Introduction is much expanded, providing in-depth analysis and reference to a great deal of academic research. The changes to Part 1 and Code D (Appendix A) reflect the fact that we have moved on from the 5th Edition of the Code to a 7th Edition. The principal change concerns the provision of more detailed guidance on the procedures for obtaining evidence of recognition from images. The on-going jurisprudential saga concerning the retention and use of fingerprint and DNA samples of unconvicted suspects is brought up to date, and an outline of prospective legislative reform has been provided.

The Criminal Justice Act 2003 provisions relating to hearsay and bad character have required wholesale reworking of the main chapter in Part 2 on the admissibility and exclusion of evidence at trial. A mass of appeals relating to bad character in particular have been digested, their dicta rationalised and refined so as to concentrate the reader on the implications for identification evidence.

Lastly, where advances in forensic science have been made or judgments on admissibility been given, the chapters in Part 3 have been revised and updated. In particular the text of the DNA chapter has been entirely rewritten to provide the practitioner with a greater understanding of the science, the forensic techniques, the statistical analysis of the findings and the potential shortcomings of this evidence.

We hope that the book has been improved by the contribution of two minds rather than one and the combination of academic and practical expertise in the field. We are grateful to Tony Hawitt at Jordan Publishing for his patience and guidance during the months in which the manuscript of this second edition took shape, and to Gillian Wright for her diligent editorial work. The Law is stated as at 3 June 2011.

Paul Bogan QC

Andrew Roberts

PREFACE TO THE FIRST EDITION

The identification of an offender is necessary in every criminal trial. In many it is admitted; but in the substantial number of cases where identity is a live issue, it must be proved by eyewitness or scientific evidence. The purpose of this book is, first, to provide an analysis of the powers and duties of police in the collection of identification evidence in a criminal investigation; second to provide a guide to the various sources of identification evidence and to consider how they are treated in the trial process; finally it is to supply an insight into the methodology and admissibility of scientific and other expert means of personal identification.

In the view of the Devlin Committee in 1976, whose object was to propose reforms for the avoidance of miscarriages of justice in visual identification cases, 'identification ought to be specially regarded by the law simply because it is evidence of a special character in that its reliability is exceptionally difficult to assess.' Special rules govern the investigation of offences involving visual identification, a discrete standard exists for stopping cases at the close of the prosecution case and judges are obliged to give juries strong warnings about the dangers of misidentification. Police practice and criminal law in this field are now highly developed. Yet, as the abundance of identification cases in the Court of Appeal each year attests, they continue to generate controversy and debate.

Part one of the book is concerned principally with Code D of the Police and Criminal Evidence Act 1984, which governs police practice in the investigation of identification cases. The Code is currently in its fifth edition. It has been considerably refined since its introduction and reflects the fact that video identification is now used in all but the rarest cases. The identification parade has become a relic of the past, likely only to be seen in old movies. The present rules concerning the mandatory requirement for an identification procedure when identity is disputed are more sophisticated than in earlier editions and, for street identifications, the procedure is vastly more comprehensive than hitherto. Code D also governs police powers to take fingerprints and samples from suspects. Those powers have been increased substantially in recent years, notably by provisions brought into force under the Criminal Justice Act 2003. Their use must now also be considered against European Convention jurisprudence.

The second part of the book considers identification evidence at trial: its sources, its deployment, its admissibility and exclusion, its probative impact, its sufficiency and the corresponding warnings and directions which it is necessary to give to a jury. Where certain topics are much broader than identification alone, such as similar fact, the aim is to restate the general principles in broad terms and to concentrate upon the application of those principles to identification evidence. Once again the spectre of the Criminal Justice Act 2003 hangs over this part. Wholesale reform of bad character and hearsay evidence have been introduced by the Act. There is no doubt that the effect of these provisions will be to allow a far greater degree of latitude in the admission of evidence previously considered in decades of common law jurisprudence to be unreliable or unfair. Those likely to affect evidence of identity are reviewed in Appendix F. At the date of publication it is understood that the reforms are to be brought into force in April 2005.

Part three of the book is concerned with scientific and other forms of personal identification. Scientific evidence of one sort or another has played an increasingly important role in criminal trials in recent years. DNA evidence which was reserved for the more illustrious cases little more than a decade ago is now routine. The science of DNA profiling has advanced considerably in that period, permitting ever greater levels of discrimination between individuals and creating novel forms of detection. Other methods of identification have also been substantially developed in that period: facial mapping, voice identification and earprints are topical examples. This part seeks to explain in rudimentary terms the science of each subject whilst also providing sufficient information to enable the inquisitive mind to ask an expert witness some challenging questions. As indicated, Part three is confined to subjects involving personal identification, that is to say the means of identifying an individual rather than any object, such as clothing, by which an incriminatory link might be made. Hence topics such as fibre, glass, firearm residue transference or footwear analysis are not the subject of this book.

It is hoped that the content of this book will assist those who seek a better understanding of the law and practice relating to identification evidence. I can only hope that if in places it serves to confound, responsibility lies with draftsmen and judgments. Where it does not, responsibility for errors or omissions lie exclusively with the author. The law is stated as at 28 June 2004.

Paul Bogan
July 2004

CONTENTS

TABLE OF CASES

References are to paragraph numbers.

TABLE OF STATUTES

References are to paragraph numbers.

TABLE OF STATUTORY INSTRUMENTS

References are to paragraph numbers.

Chapter 1

INTRODUCTION

LESSONS FROM HISTORY

The case of Adolf Beck

1.1 A little over a 100 years ago a confidence trickster operating in London relieved several women of jewellery, money and other belongings. His inimitable modus operandi was to pose as the wealthy but fictitious Lord Willoughby and find an excuse to engage a woman in conversation in the street, suggesting that he was looking for a housekeeper. So lured, he would arrange to visit his gullible victim at her dwelling to discuss the appointment. On accepting his generous terms the woman was told that she needed a wardrobe and jewellery to match her status. The bogus aristocrat would then generously hand over a worthless cheque with which to purchase the clothes. However, he required a ring from his new employee in order to obtain the measurement for a new ring, promising its return by his non-existent one-armed servant. In some instances, while the victim's back was turned, the sham Lord managed to steal a number of other items.

1.2 On 16 December 1895, two weeks after she had been unburdened of two rings and two watches, one victim claimed to recognise the swindler in the street. She summoned the police and so launched one of the most extraordinary cases of mistaken identification ever to be tried. In the weeks after his first identification Adolf Beck,[1] a Norwegian by birth, was identified by no less than 10 other women who had been swindled in almost identical fashion. Handwriting contained in notes to several of the women served to

---

1 *The Trial of Adolf Beck* (Notable British Trials series. William Hodge & Company Ltd, 1924).

confirm, if further proof was needed, that the same man was responsible for all offences. Indeed that was not in dispute. To compound the mistaken visual identifications of the victims, the prosecution handwriting expert erroneously identified Beck as the author of notes written to the victims. Beck was convicted and sentenced to 7 years' penal servitude. He made several attempts both as a prisoner and after his release to establish his innocence but to no avail.

1.3 The identifications by the other women occurred, by today's standards, in far from ideal circumstances. They were generally from among several other men of whom few, if any, resembled Mr Beck. Nevertheless 11 people who had spent at least an hour or two in the close company of Lord Willoughby identified Adolf Beck with varying degrees of certainty. By contrast the Committee of Enquiry[2] which subsequently examined the case found that he bore only a 'slight resemblance' to the true culprit – a man named William Wyatt.

1.4 William Wyatt had in fact been convicted of identical offences some 15 years earlier in the name of John Smith. Indeed the handwriting in both sets of offences bore the same authorship. Though not advanced at trial, two police officers who had investigated and given evidence in the trial of Smith purported to recognise Beck as Smith. However Beck was not permitted to call evidence of the earlier 'similar fact' offences. Had he done so, he may successfully have shown that he couldn't have committed the crimes 15 years earlier because he was abroad at the time. Moreover, at the time of his trial he was not, himself, permitted to give evidence in his own defence.[3] This desultory sequence of blunders, coincidences and evidential prohibitions would be incomplete if it was not revealed that the Common Serjeant who presided over the Beck trial was none other than the prosecution counsel in the Smith trial.

1.5 In 1904, 2 years after Beck's release, the unthinkable happened. Wyatt was at it again but, needless to say, it was the usual hapless suspect Adolf Beck who was arrested. This time he was identified by four women who had been swindled. He was prosecuted again and convicted again. Mercifully, within days Wyatt was caught in flagrante delicto, whereupon it was realised that Adolf Beck was perfectly innocent of every single charge that he had faced and was given free pardons in respect of his convictions in both cases. The shockwaves of this cause celèbre led directly to the establishment, for the first time, of the Court of Criminal Appeal.[4]

1.6 The Committee of Inquiry, chaired by the Master of the Rolls, considered that:

---

2 Report by Committee of Inquiry, 14 November 1904. Cmd 2315.

3 The Criminal Evidence Act 1898, enacted 2 years later, enabled defendants to give evidence in their own defence.

4 Criminal Appeal Act 1907 – before its enactment the only redress against a miscarriage of justice was a pardon.

'... evidence as to identity based upon personal impressions, however bona fide, is perhaps of all classes of evidence the least to be relied upon, and therefore, unless supported by other facts, an unsafe basis for the verdict of the jury. These elements of uncertainty cannot be eliminated from any system of jurisprudence.'[5]

Devlin Committee

1.7 In the years succeeding the Beck case, rules governing formal identification procedures were introduced and it became generally acknowledged that confrontation and dock identification evidence was unreliable. However, the use of unsupported visual identification evidence as a basis for conviction continued. It was reconsidered by the Devlin Committee in 1976.[6] This followed miscarriages of justice in the cases of Luke Dougherty and Laszlo Virag. In the former case, one of theft, two witnesses identified the defendant first from an album of photographs and secondly at court. In fact he had been on a coach trip with some 40 other people at the time of the offence. Mr Virag was accused of several thefts, use of a firearm with intent to resist arrest and of wounding a police officer on 3 days over a 5-week period. In all, nine witnesses identified him. He was sentenced to a term of 10 years' imprisonment. A year later Georges Payen was arrested for other offences. It gradually became clear that he and not Mr Virag had been responsible for the offences of which the latter had been convicted. Having served about 5 years of his sentence he was granted a free pardon.

1.8 In addition to reviewing these cases in detail, the Devlin Report considered a number of other cases. It explored both pre-trial investigative identification procedures and evidence of identification at trial. It also took evidence from a number of interested parties and looked at psychological research into identification. Among its many conclusions the Committee believed that a conviction could not be regarded as safe unless the circumstances of the identification were exceptional or that it was supported by substantial evidence of another sort. Within 3 months the Devlin Committee report had been digested by the Court of Appeal in the landmark case of *R v Turnbull and others*.[7]

1.9 The Court expressly recognised public disquiet about miscarriages of justice resulting from mistaken identification. Though it gave guidance about withdrawal of weak cases from the jury and the directions necessary to educate juries in the dangers of misidentification, the judgment fell short of imposing the full force of the Committee's conclusion on inferior courts. In a more recent example of a miscarriage of justice, *R v Fergus*,[8] the Court of Appeal echoed previous concerns, stating:

---

5 Cmd 2315, at p vii.

6 Report to the Secretary of State for the Home Department of the Departmental Committee on Evidence of Identification in Criminal Cases, 26 April 1976 (the 'Devlin Report').

7 [1977] 1 QB 224, (1976) 63 Cr App R 132, CA. See **11.2** for the guidance on withdrawing the case from the jury and **12.3–12.30** for directions to the jury.

8 (1994) 98 Cr App R 313, CA, at 317. The identification evidence was of such poor quality that the case should have been stopped by the judge: see **11.4**.

'The issue of the identification of an offender is possibly one of the commonest questions of fact that juries have to consider. It is also one of the issues most susceptible to error. Visual identification of an offender not known to the observer is a particularly fallible process.'

THE PSYCHOLOGY OF VISUAL IDENTIFICATION

1.10 Eyewitness identification evidence, which accounts for much of the subject matter of this book, is both a commonplace and problematic feature of criminal trials. Although eyewitnesses are an important source of evidence,[9] as noted above, it is now widely acknowledged that their attempts to identify others, even those with whom they are relatively familiar, are particularly prone to error.[10] Any attempt to develop procedures that adequately address the risk of error must proceed from an understanding of memory and its vulnerabilities.

1.11 An eyewitness's claim that a suspect or defendant is the person he saw engaged in some prior act of alleged wrongdoing is the product of a series of cognitive processes. In *Craig v R*, these were described by the High Court of Australia in the following terms:

'An honest witness who says "the prisoner is the man who drove the car" whilst appearing to affirm a simple, clear and impressive proposition, is really asserting: (i) that he observed the driver; (ii) that the observation became impressed upon his mind; (iii) that he still retained the original impression; (iv) that such impression has not been affected, altered, or replaced ... and; (v) that the resemblance between the original impression, and the prisoner is sufficient to base a judgment not of resemblance, but of identity.'[11]

---

9 An analysis of arrests at 10 police stations across England and Wales in a study conducted by C Phillips. and D Brown *Entry into the Criminal Justice System: a survey of police arrests and their outcomes*, Home Office Research Study 185 (Home Office, 1998), disclosed that: eyewitness evidence was provided by a police officer in 40% of all offences resulting in an arrest; in 23% of all cases eyewitness identification evidence was provided by an independent witness, the victim providing it in 18% of all cases and security personnel in 10% of cases; in sexual offences, and offences involving the use of violence against the person, the eyewitness testimony of the victim was the main source of evidence. A survey of those involved in Crown Court trials conducted by M Zander and P Henderson, *The Royal Commission on Criminal Justice*, Crown Court Study, Research Study No 19, (HMSO, 1993), suggested that in 25% of contested cases, eyewitness identification evidence formed an important element of the prosecution case.

10 See E Connors et al 'Convicted by Juries, Exonerated by Science: Case Studies in the Use of DNA Evidence to Establish Innocence after Trial' (National Institute of Justice, 1996); the Devlin Report op cit; Law Commission of New Zealand *Evidence: Total Recall? The Reliability of Witness Testimony*, Miscellaneous Paper 13 (NZLC, 1999); Australian Law Reform Commission, Report No 26 *Evidence (Interim)*, vol 2 (ALRC, 1985), ch 11; Australian Law Reform Commission, Report No 38, *Evidence (Final)*, (ALRC, 1987), ch 15; Scottish Home and Health Department *Identification Procedure under Scottish Criminal Law* (HMSO, 1978); N Brooks, Law Reform Commission of Canada Study Paper, *Pretrial Eyewitness Identification Procedures* (LRCC, 1983).

11 (1933) 49 CLR 429, at 446.

1.12 This remarkably perceptive judgment, delivered almost 80 years ago, reflects contemporary understanding of memory function. Information perceived by our senses is stored briefly in short-term memory, before being encoded and then stored in long-term memory. When required, various cues are used to retrieve the information, and when presented with an identification task the appearance of the suspect is compared with information about the appearance of the person seen on an earlier occasion which is recalled from memory. These processes are commonly referred to in the psychological literature as *perception, encoding, retention, retrieval and comparison*. There is a substantial body of empirical research,[12] much of it conducted over the past three decades, which has revealed that the integrity of these processes (and a witness's capacity to provide reliable identification) can be adversely affected by various attendant circumstances.

Perception and encoding

1.13 The most obvious impediments to a witness's perception of events and persons are the distance from which the event is observed, the lighting conditions, and the existence of some physical obstruction. However, it is also recognised that even in the absence of such impediments, when observing an event of any complexity, a witness may encode and store in long-term memory only a relatively small proportion of the amount of information that is perceived. Perception and encoding are also selective and detail may go unnoticed or indeed be distorted. What we 'see', or fail to see, may be coloured by what we would expect to occur in the type of situation that is observed. The expectation may be the result of cultural stereotyping, personal prejudice or past experience. The characteristics with which we associate those from particular cultural, racial, age or gender groupings – such as aggressiveness or docility, lawlessness, integrity or dishonesty – may affect our perception of events involving a member of these social groups. Equally, a person used to seeing an object of a particular appearance or the repetition of the same event may be influenced by experience rather than the observation itself.

1.14 Among the characteristics of an event that might undermine the capacity of a witness to provide a complete and accurate account or a reliable

---

[12] The authors of a Home Office study review of the psychological research on eyewitness memory found that by 1999 there had been over 700 scholarly articles published on the subject: M Kebbel and G Wagstaff *Face Value? Evaluating the Accuracy of Eyewitness Information*, Police Research Series Paper 102 (Home Office, 1999). There are a number of texts and edited collections that provide a review of the psychological literature on various aspects of eyewitness identification, see, eg R Wilcock, R Bull and R Milne *Witness Identification in Criminal Cases: Psychology and Practice*, (OUP, 2008); E Loftus *Eyewitness Testimony* (Harvard University Press, 1979); P Ainsworth *Psychology, Law and Eyewitness Testimony*, (Wiley, 1988); S Lloyd-Bostock and B Clifford (eds) *Evaluating Witness Evidence* (Wiley, 1985); D Ross, D Read and M Toglia (eds) *Adult Eyewitness Testimony: Current Trends and Developments* (CUP, 1994); R Lindsay, D. Ross, D. Read and M. Toglia (eds) *The Handbook of Eyewitness Psychology*, vol 2, Memory for People (Lawrence Erlbaum Associates, 2007); B Cutler and S Penrod *Mistaken Identification: The Eyewitness, Psychology and the Law*, (CUP, 1995).

identification is the amount of time that the witness is able to observe the relevant event. In general, the greater the period of time a witness is exposed to an event, the more detail is likely to be perceived and encoded. Likewise, for identification purposes, the longer the observation, the more facial and other features will have been perceived by the witness.[13] However, relying on witnesses' own estimates as to how long an offender was under observation or of the duration of an event is problematic. In *R v Huntley*,[14] it was observed that 'it is notorious that no eyewitnesses of this sort of incident [a violent assault in the street] can give an accurate description of time'.[15] This is supported by empirical research, which demonstrates that estimates of time are almost invariably over-estimated rather than underestimated by witnesses.[16] Similarly, the more frequently we observe an object or person, the more information we are likely to perceive and encode.[17] This is thought to be the reason that our attempts to identify persons with whom we are familiar are generally more accurate than our attempts to identify strangers.

1.15 Empirical studies have demonstrated the dangers of eyewitness identification based upon a 'fleeting glance' encounter. Buckhout, for example, conducted a study with the co-operation of a New York television station.[18] Viewers of a news programme were shown a brief clip of a purse snatch in which the robber's face was revealed for a second or two. Thereafter viewers were shown a parade of six men, told that the assailant might or might not be among them and invited to telephone with an identification. Of over 2,000 respondents, only 14% were correct, in other words about the same proportion that would have been expected if viewers had selected randomly. Fifty-eight per cent of respondents selected foils, of whom two achieved greater purported recognition than the correct mugshot. A quarter stated that the assailant was not shown on the parade. The ability to recognise may depend upon the expression worn by the person viewed. A subsequent change in expression may hinder recognition. Thus, having observed a struggle in which a person's face was contorted in anger, a witness may have difficulty matching the same individual's expressionless face at a formal procedure. Likewise recognition may be affected by the angle at which the person was observed. A profile alone may be insufficiently revealing or positively impair later recognition of a frontal facial view.

1.16 The nature of the incident observed will also affect the witness's powers of perception. In an incident involving a significant amount of activity, a witness's attention is likely to be drawn to salient features.[19] Many will go

---

13 Loftus, op cit, at p 23; Ainsworth, op cit, at p 36.
14 [2006] EWCA Crim 1709.
15 Ibid, at [6].
16 E Loftus, J Schooler, S Boone and D Kline "Time went by so slowly: over-estimation of event duration by males and females" (1986) 1 *Applied Cognitive Psychology* 3.
17 Loftus, op cit, at p 24.
18 R Buckhout, 'Nearly 2000 witnesses can be wrong', (1975) 2 *Social Action and the Law* 7.
19 Loftus, op cit, at p 25; Wilcock et al, op cit, at p 38.

unnoticed while others w. [20] It may be that during observation of a sir. ıs concentrated on details, which though signific. do not necessarily correspond to the details sough ,es. This may explain some research findings that appe. police officers generally recall more relevant detail about a. ... ıer witnesses.[22] However, it is interesting that contrary to the assump. ..ns of some courts,[23] it seems that police officers are no more reliable in their attempts to identify offenders than lay witnesses.[24]

1.17 Much of the above might be thought by many to be common knowledge. However, it seems that perception may be adversely affected in ways that appear counterintuitive. It might generally be thought that we would be much more likely to remember the appearance of a person who threatens us with a gun (and so be able to identify him) than we would the appearance of someone with whom we have some significant but non-threatening encounter. However, empirical research has consistently demonstrated that a witness's ability to make an accurate identification is likely to be diminished where the crime observed was one in which the offender brandished a weapon.[25] Psychologists have attributed this reduced capacity to a 'weapon focus effect', the witness's attention being drawn to the weapon rather than other aspects of the event including the appearance of the person holding it, which results in impaired perception of such information. Similarly, the findings of a number of studies suggest that the memory of a witness may be significantly less accurate and

---

20 It also appears that consumption of alcohol, even in moderate amounts may adversely effect the amount of information about an event that witnesses perceive and encode; D Reid, J Yuille and P Tollestrup 'Recollections of a robbery: effects of arousal and alcohol upon recall and person identification' (1992) 16 *Law and Human Behavior* 425; J Yuille and P Tollestrup, 'Some effects of alcohol on eyewitness memory' (1990) 75 *Journal of Applied Psychology* 268.

21 For example, the stereotype of male interest in cars and female interest in fashion may, if true of the individual, mean that their respective perceptions for each will be superior and that they are likely to recall more information about these matters. See generally, R Milne and R Bull *Investigative Interviewing: Psychology and Practice* (Wiley, 1999), who suggest that various factors including interests, expectations, past experience, attitudes and training may determine the aspects of an event to which a witness's attention will be drawn.

22 S Christianson, I Karlsson and L Persson 'Police personnel as eyewitnesses to a violent crime' (1998) 3 *Legal and Criminological Psychology* 59; T Lindholm, S Christianson and I Karlsson 'Police officers and civilians as witnesses: inter-group biases and memory performance' (1997) 11 *Applied Cognitive Psychology* 431.

23 In *McKenna v DPP* [2005] EWHC 677 (Admin), for example, the Divisional Court suggested, at [16]: 'The recognition was made by a special constable, someone involved in the criminal justice system who is likely to have a greater appreciation of the importance of identification, by an honest officer, where it can be inferred it is likely to be more reliable than otherwise, and where training of police officers is something which is relevant to be taken into account.'

24 Christianson et al (1998) op cit found that although police officers were more likely to identify the culprit from an identification procedure than were lay witnesses, the difference in their performance was not statistically significant.

25 For a recent review of the relevant research see K Pickel 'Remembering and identifying menacing perpetrators: exposure to violence and the weapon focus effect', in R Lindsay, D Ross, D Read and M Toglia (eds), *The Handbook of Eyewitness Psychology*, vol. 2, Memory for People, (Lawrence Erlbaum, 2007).

complete when the event observed involves violence.[26] Whereas a mild level of emotional arousal can produce alertness and facilitate perception, intense arousal seems to be counterproductive in this respect.[27]

1.18 Notwithstanding the substantial accumulated findings of psychological research it is impossible to predict the accuracy of individual witnesses. The ability of one witness accurately to acquire and store information compared to another may vary enormously.[28] Insofar as it is possible to make generalisations, the perceptions of very young and very old people are likely to be less accurate than others.[29] The young may lack cognitive ability, both may need greater time for assimilation of information, and the hearing and eyesight of the elderly may be impaired. Though one might predict that nervous or anxious people are unlikely to perform as well as those used to stress, the evidence for this is inconclusive. Many studies have considered whether gender affects perception performance. However these have not established with any certainty a discernible trend. The same cannot be said, however, of the effect on a witness's capacity to make an accurate identification in circumstances in which an offender is not of the same racial appearance as the witness. It appears that our attempts to identify persons from other racial groups are likely to be significantly less accurate than attempts to identify those of a similar racial appearance.[30]

Retention and retrieval

1.19 Most people will probably be aware that memory deteriorates over time. However, research suggests that the rate at which memory decay occurs is not linear. Much of the information about an event that is stored in the memory is lost within a relatively short period following observation, after which the rate of deterioration slows, resulting in a 'forgetting curve'. Studies have also demonstrated that memory is malleable and reconstructive rather than fixed and immutable. Expectation, past experience and stereotyping may not only distort our perception of events, but also fill the inevitable gaps in our memory for events that we are asked to recall. Under certain conditions information provided by third parties can supplement or supplant original memories of event, and later be recalled (with great confidence) as information acquired during observation of that event.[31]

---

26 Loftus, op cit, at p 31, Ainsworth, op cit, Wilcock et al, op cit, at pp 37–38.

27 Loftus, op cit, at p 33; Wilcock et al, op cit, at pp 75–76.

28 Ainsworth, op cit, at p 41.

29 See, eg J Searcy, J Bartlett and A Memon 'Influence of post-event narratives, line-up conditions and individual differences on false identification by young and older eyewitness' (2000) 5 *Legal and Criminological Psychology* 219.

30 For a review of the research on this effect see C Meissner and J Brigham 'Thirty Years of investigating the own-race bias in memory for faces' (2001) 7 *Psychology, Public Policy and Law* 3.

31 There is a vast literature on these issues. See, eg E Loftus 'Make-believe memories', *American Psychologist*, November 2003, 867. E Loftus and G Hoffman 'Misinformation and memory: the creation of new memories', (1989) 118 *Journal of Experimental Psychology: General* 100; A Scoboria et al 'Immediate and persisting effects of misleading questions and hypnosis on

1.20 It seems that error in identifying the original source of information that is retrieved from memory can lead witnesses to provide quite vivid, coherent and detailed accounts constructed from information cobbled together from various sources, and rationalised as a recollection of an event witnessed first-hand. Crombag and colleagues, for example, conducted a study in which the participants were a number of people who had been present and witnessed a cargo plane crash into a block of apartments in Amsterdam.[32] When interviewed during the course of the study, 60% of the witnesses stated that they had seen the plane colliding with the building on television and provided answers to detailed questions about the broadcast material, despite the fact that no footage of the crash existed. The witnesses appeared to have pieced together what they heard about the crash from various sources, constructed a composite mental image of events surrounding the disaster and were subsequently confident (and probably convincing) in their claims to have watched it on television.

1.21 A related problem is a phenomenon which psychologists refer to as 'unconscious transference'. An example of this is a situation in which a witness identifies a face that he or she has seen before, but does not correctly recall the context in which it was previously observed. Many of us may have experienced this phenomenon when feeling that we have previously met a person who passes by in the street, later realising that he or she is an actor or presenter who we have only seen on the television. In the context of identification evidence, transference may typically occur when a witness identifies a person in an identification procedure who appears familiar. That familiarity is wrongly assumed by the witness to have been the result of seeing the person committing the crime that is being investigated when, in fact, the person was observed in some other context or on the periphery of the criminal event.[33]

1.22 It appears that vivid memories of a fictitious event (or fictitious detail about some event that did, in fact, occur) can be created simply through the use of imagination.[34] Similarly, those who speculate about a course of events or state of affairs can recall the subject-matter of their speculation as something that they have experienced. Testimony from those who have undergone hypnosis to assist recall is treated with great caution by the courts for just this reason.[35] The fragile nature of human memory is best summed up in Loftus' claim that 'memories are not only the sum of what [subjects] have done [or seen] ...[they] are also the sum of what they have thought, what they have been

---

memory reports' (2002) 8 *Journal of Experimental Psychology: Applied* 26; R Belli 'Influences of misleading postevent information: misinformation interference and acceptance' (1989) 118 *Journal of Experimental Psychology: General* 72.

[32] H Crombag, W Wagenaar and P van Koppen 'Crashing memories and the problem of "source monitoring"' (1996) 10 *Applied Cognitive Psychology* 95.

[33] Loftus, op cit, at p 142; Ainsworth, op cit, at p 72.

[34] E Loftus and G Hoffman, op cit; D Lindsay, L Hagan, K Wade and M Garry, 'True photographs and false memories' (2004) 15 *Psychological Science* 149.

[35] A Scoboria et al 'Immediate and persisting effects of misleading questions and hypnosis on memory reports' (2002) 8 *Journal of Experimental Psychology: Applied* 26; see *R v Trochym* [2007] 1 SCR 239, 2007 SCC 6, in which the Supreme Court of Canada held post-hypnosis

told, what they believe'.[36] Questions remain as to whether, once a witness's memory has been distorted by the provision of 'misinformation' following observation of an event, the unadulterated memory of the original event can be retrieved. The view adopted in some quarters is that some memories undergo irreversible transformations.[37]

1.23 Memory distortion can also be caused by the language that a questioner employs to elicit information from a witness. Answers to the questions 'how *tall* was the person?' and 'how *short* was the person?' have been shown to lead to different responses according to the implied suggestion of height. In a well-known study, subjects viewed a videotape of a traffic accident.[38] Of those asked to estimate the speed at which one vehicle *made contact* with the other, the average estimate was 30.8 mph. Those asked the speed at which one car *smashed* into the other estimated an average of 40.8 mph. Similarly the question 'did you see *the* ...?' tends to be answered affirmatively with greater frequency than the neutral question 'did you see *a* ...?'. Kohnken has suggested that this might occur because the interviewee who has experienced an event is unlikely to be able to perceive and encode all available information.[39] Additional information acquired from an interviewer may, therefore, be used by the witness, along with general knowledge and social expectations, to fill 'gaps' in his or her recollection of events.

IDENTIFICATION, EMPIRICAL RESEARCH AND THE CRIMINAL PROCESS

1.24 Two broad conclusions might be drawn from the empirical research on eyewitness memory. The first is one that appears to be widely accepted; the vulnerability of human memory is such that there is a significant risk of error in an eyewitness's attempts at identification. The second is that satisfactory

---

evidence to be inadmissible on the grounds that the effect of hypnosis on the memory was not understood well enough for testimony obtained by means of it to be considered sufficiently reliable.

36 E Loftus 'Make-believe memories', *American Psychologist*, November 2003, 867, at 872.

37 See E Loftus and G Loftus, 'On the permanence of stored information in the human brain' (1980) 35 *American Psychologist* 409; also D Hall, E Loftus and J Tousignant 'Post-event information and changes in recollection for a natural event' in E Loftus (ed) *Eyewitness Testimony* (CUP, 1984).

38 Loftus, op cit, p 96. E Loftus and J Palmer 'Reconstruction of automobile destruction: an example of the interaction between language and memory' (1974) 13 *Journal of Verbal Learning and Verbal Behavior* 585. See also E Loftus and G Zanni 'Eyewitness testimony: the influence of the wording of a question' (1975) 5 *Bulletin of Psychonomic Science* 86. R Christiansen, J Sweeney and K Ochalek 'Influencing eyewitness descriptions' (1983) 7 *Law and Human Behavior* 59 who conducted a study in which one group of witnesses were told by the interviewer that the man was a truck driver while another group were told that he was a dancer. Those who were told he was a truck driver estimated his weight to be significantly greater than those who were informed that he was a dancer. Similarly, where interviewers described the stranger as a 'man' estimates of his age were significantly higher than when he was referred to as a 'young man'.

39 See G Kohnken 'Interviewing Adults' in R Bull and D Carson (eds) *Handbook of Psychology in Legal Contexts* (Wiley, 1st edn, 1995), at p 218.

evaluation of the witness's claim that the suspect is the person he or she saw engaged in the alleged wrongdoing presents a formidable forensic challenge.

1.25 In most cases the trial is the culmination of a legal process comprising a series of decisions and interactions engaged in by various parties to the proceedings. Twining notes that:

> '... by the time a witness comes to testify at the trial he has typically 'presented' at least some of his information on several occasions, for example in informal conversation, in interviews with the police, with one or more lawyers ... [t]his is why it is useful to think in terms not merely of witnesses testifying ... but of the creating and processing of information.'[40]

1.26 These encounters will not necessarily constitute the one-way flow of information from witness to other parties on matters relating to the relevant event that is suggested in this passage. Police officers might have seen the person suspected of committing the offence; spoken to other witnesses who have provided information about the event and offender; formed their own views as to the guilt of the suspect; spoken to other officers who have done either of these things, etc. These activities may well be necessary during the course of an investigation, nevertheless the potential for cross-pollination of inaccurate information, the drawing of false inferences, and the resultant risk of error is manifest. Nor are the potential risks restricted to encounters between witness and police officers. Conversations between lawyers who might have seen statements provided by other witnesses, rumours recounted by friends and relatives of the witness regarding what may have happened, and who the culprit may be, all give rise to danger that his or her subsequent recollection of events will be coloured by information (and misinformation) acquired from others.

1.27 As the pre-trial process draws out, the opportunities for encounters that distort the witness's memory increase and the task of establishing whether such distortion has occurred (even establishing whether such encounters have occurred) becomes increasingly difficult. Moreover, the systemic positioning of the trial, typically occurring many months after the events in question, leaves open the possibility that the witness may acquire information that might appear to him to corroborate the correctness of the identification he has made and inflate his confidence in its accuracy.[41]

---

40 W Twining *Rethinking Evidence: Exploratory Essays* (Northwestern University Press, 1994), at p 165.

41 This risk has been judicially acknowledged; see, for example, *R v Johnson* (unreported) 24 October 2000 (2000 WL 1675176), at [18]: '... it has been the courts' experience that identification evidence should be subject to particularly careful scrutiny. The reason for that is because a perfectly honest witness could believe, and become increasingly convinced that they were right in so believing that they had identified the right person when subsequently it could be shown in other ways that they had in fact made a mistake and identified the wrong person.'

Cross-examination

1.28 Although some courts have taken the view that cross-examination provides an adequate means of testing the reliability of an eyewitness's identification of the defendant,[42] there is long-standing acceptance of its limitations in relation to this type of evidence. The Devlin Committee considered it to be ineffectual.[43] It noted that where a witness's testimony comprises a narrative of some external event, cross-examination might impugn it by exposing inconsistencies and any unwarranted assumptions that have been made by the witness. But the Committee pointed out that identification evidence is a bare assertion, which is the product of a series of inscrutable internal processes; there is no story to dissect.[44] Cross-examination may reveal circumstances that cast doubt on the reliability of a witness's identification of the defendant, for example, that the light was poor or the witness had consumed alcohol, or found the event stressful, but empirical research suggests that it offers little assistance to the jury in determining the accuracy of a witness's identification.[45] Indeed some studies have demonstrated that the manner in which eyewitnesses are cross-examined may lead to the introduction of inaccurate details in a witness's account of events.[46]

Expert testimony

1.29 It has been suggested that greater use could be made of the knowledge that has been derived from empirical research on eyewitness identification by permitting psychologists to provide expert testimony concerning the manner in which the memory functions and the sources of potential error in witnesses' attempts at identification.[47] Arguments for the reception of such testimony are

---

42 See *US v Thevis* (1982) 459 US 825; *US v Langan* (2001) 263 F.3d 613.

43 Report to the Secretary of State for the Home Department of the Departmental Committee on Evidence of Identification in Criminal Cases, (HMSO, 1976), at para 4.25; see also J Jackson 'The insufficiency of identification evidence based on personal impression' [1986] Crim LR 203; T Dillickrath 'Expert testimony on eyewitness identification: admissibility and alternatives' (2001) 55 *University of Miami Law Review* 1059, at p 1094; R Wise, K Daupinais and M Safer 'A tripartite solution to eyewitness error' (2007) 97 *Journal of Criminal Law and Criminology* 807, at pp 828–830.

44 The limitations of cross-examination have also been judicially acknowledged; see *US v Downing* (1985) 753 F.2d 1224, 1231, note 6: 'To the extent that a mistaken witness may retain great confidence in an inaccurate identification, cross-examination can hardly be seen as an effective way to reveal weaknesses in a witness's recollection of an event.'

45 See G Wells, R Lindsay and T Ferguson 'Accuracy, confidence and juror perceptions in eyewitness identifications' (1979) 64 *Journal of Applied Psychology* 440; R Lindsay, G Wells and F O'Connor 'Mock juror belief of accurate and inaccurate eyewitnesses: a replication and extension' (1989) 13 *Law and Human Behaviour* 333; J Devenport, V Stinson, B Cutler and D Kravitz 'How effective are the cross-examination and expert testimony safeguards? jurors' perceptions of the suggestiveness and fairness of biased line-up procedures' (2002) 87 *Journal of Applied Psychology* 1042.

46 T Valentine and K Maras 'The effect of cross-examination on the accuracy of adult eyewitness testimony', *Applied Cognitive Psychology* (forthcoming).

47 See generally, B Cutler (ed), *Expert Testimony on the Psychology of Eyewitness Identification* (OUP, 2009).

usually advanced on one of two grounds.[48] The first is that it will better enable juries to distinguish identification evidence that is reliable from that which is not. The second, and less ambitious, claim is that the provision of this kind of evidence will counteract juries' tendencies to attach too much weight to eyewitness identification evidence.

1.30 The admissibility of expert testimony on the reliability of eyewitness identification is an issue that is not covered in the chapters that follow. These are concerned with the law in England and Wales and, at the time of writing, there is no authority on its admissibility in this jurisdiction. When the Court of Appeal is provided with an opportunity to consider admissibility, its conclusion is likely to be determined by application of the principle expressed in *R v Turner* (often referred to as the common knowledge rule):[49]

> 'An expert's opinion is admissible to furnish the court with scientific information which is likely to be outside the experience and knowledge of a judge or jury. If on the proven facts a judge or jury can form their own conclusions without help then the opinion of an expert is unnecessary.'[50]

1.31 The nature of the common knowledge rule is such that it tends to be applied in rather arbitrary fashion, a problem that is evident in divergent conclusions on the admissibility of expert evidence that have been reached by courts in the United States.[51] In *People v McDonald*,[52] the Supreme Court of California, having observed that various factors bearing on reliability 'may be known only to some jurors, or may be imperfectly understood by many, or may be contrary to the intuitive beliefs of most' held that in 'appropriate cases' such testimony may be admissible. It suggested that jurors would not be aware of what has become apparent through research – that there is little correlation between the confidence of a witness and the accuracy of the identification that he or she has made. Similarly, in *Arizona v Chapple*,[53] in which the Supreme Court of Arizona found that expert testimony had been wrongly excluded, it

---

48 D Yarmey 'Expert testimony: does eyewitness memory research have probative value for the courts?' (2001) 42 *Canadian Psychology* 92.

49 [1975] 1 All ER 70. See M Redmayne, *Expert Evidence and Criminal Proceedings* (OUP, 2001), at p 187, suggesting that expert evidence on the reliability of eyewitness identification would be caught by the rule in *R v Turner*. Support for this view is drawn from the Court of Appeal's ruling in *R v Browning* [1995] Crim LR 227 that the rule in *Turner* rendered expert testimony on memory decay inadmissible.

50 [1975] 1 All ER 70, at 74. This passage in *Turner* has also been cited as authority for what some have referred to as the 'helpfulness principle'. Clearly expert evidence on matters that can be assumed to be part of the stock of knowledge possessed by a jury will not be helpful: see, e g *Barings Plc v Coopers & Lybrand (No.2)* [2001] Lloyd's Rep Bank 85, for example, in which the Court of Appeal explained that expert evidence 'will not be helpful where the issue to be decided is … one on which the Court is able to come to a fully informed decision without hearing such evidence' and as a consequence, would be inadmissible. But the question of the helpfulness of expert evidence must encompass a broader range of issues including reliability. The common knowledge rule in *Turner* ought to be viewed, therefore, as an instantiation of a broader helpfulness principle.

51 For a thorough review of the jurisprudence in this jurisdiction see Dillickrath, op cit.

52 37 Cal.3d 351, 368 (1984).

53 135 Ariz 281 (1983).

was suggested that while most jurors would appreciate that memory fades over time, few would appreciate that the rate at which it deteriorates is not uniform and that forgetting occurs initially at a rapid rate and then tails off.

1.32 However, the views expressed in these cases lie in stark contrast to the conclusion in *US v Hudson*[54] that expert evidence on the reliability eyewitness identification would not aid the jury 'because it addresses an issue of which the jury is generally aware, and it will not contribute to their understanding'.[55] Likewise, in *US v Langan*,[56] the Court of Appeals, while acknowledging that an expert might be able to inform the jury of the intricacies of the cognitive processes that are used by an eyewitness in order to make an identification, concluded that the 'hazards of eyewitness identification are within the ordinary knowledge of most lay jurors'.[57] Such views have been expressed by courts in other jurisdictions; in *R v Fong*[58] for example, the Queensland Court of Criminal Appeals endorsed the trial judge's view that:

> 'what a person remembers and how they are likely to remember and the manner in which human memory works by reconstruction or suggestion or otherwise, are everyday matters well within the field of knowledge of juries.'[59]

1.33 The suggestion that an expert will be unable to provide a jury with knowledge that it does not already possess about these matters, or the ways in which the integrity of the cognitive processes that a witness relied upon to make an identification might be undermined, appears implausible. In application, the common knowledge rule might simply be an instantiation of the general principle that requires the exclusion of evidence the probative value of which is outweighed by its prejudicial effect. But what is the value of this kind of evidence?

1.34 Typically, an expert's testimony on the reliability of eyewitness identification will consist of general observations derived from empirical research. Usually, such research will have been conducted in a laboratory under conditions that enable the particular variables to be isolated and their effect measured. The expert may be able to inform the tribunal of fact, for example, that research suggests the presence of a weapon tends to have an adverse effect on the accuracy of witness identifications. But it will usually be the case that some of those who took part in the experiments from which this generalisation is derived will have made an accurate identification notwithstanding the presence of a weapon. The basis of the generalisation will be a higher rate of inaccuracy among the members of the group who observed an event in which a weapon was brandished than was found in a control group who witnessed an event in which no weapon could be seen. The question for a tribunal of fact is

---

54 884 F.2d 1016 (1989).
55 Ibid, at 1024.
56 263 F.3d 613 (2001).
57 At 623.
58 [1981] Qd. R. 90.
59 [1981] Qd. R. 90, 95.

whether the identification made by a witness in the proceedings is reliable, and as the Supreme Court of Victoria observed in *R v Smith*,[60] expert testimony of this nature does not appear to be particularly helpful:

> '... the [expert] evidence which it is desired to adduce in the present matter is directed to the question of the possible unreliability of identification in a general sense although consideration would presumably be given to observation made in particular circumstances, for example in a state of stress, apprehension or excitement.
>
> The evidence challenged ... is that of individual witnesses who have expressed opinions of identity, and it is the reliability of those witnesses which must be considered by the jury. There are many persons in the community who possess acute powers of observation and considerable ability to recall precisely what was observed, and accordingly whose evidence may be very reliable, whilst there are clearly many others of whom this statement could not be made.
>
> It is doubtful in the extreme that expert evidence concerned with eyewitness identification generally will assist a jury in determining whether or not it would be safe to act upon the evidence of any particular eyewitness ...'[61]

1.35 In a trial for armed robbery, for example, the difficulty for the fact-finder will be to determine how the case at hand fits with the generalisation that the presence of a weapon will tend to have an adverse effect on the witnesses' abilities to make an accurate identification. In other words, is the witness who has identified the defendant as the robber, one of those whose accuracy will have been adversely affected by the presence of a weapon, or is he someone whose capacity to make an accurate identification will be unaffected by this? However, these are not the only uncertainties that the tribunal of fact must deal with. There might be doubts as to whether the conditions that were established for the purposes of experimental study reflect those that are experienced by a witness's real crimes. Additionally, it may not be possible to predict with any accuracy what effect the infinite combination of variables that attend real criminal events will have on identification accuracy. Given these uncertainties, it might be reasonable to take the view that the costs associated with the reception of expert evidence – the prolonging of the trial, the risk that the jury will become confused or distracted from the main issues, or that the trial might descend into a battle between opposing experts – outweigh its limited probative value, and justifies exclusion.[62]

---

60 [1987] VR 907.

61 *R v Smith* [1987] VR 907, 911. Similarly in *Gage v HM Advocate* [2011] HCJAC 40, the Scottish Appeal Court, High Court of Justiciary, in holding expert evidence on the reliability of eyewitness identification, observed at [36] that the expert had 'conducted no case-specific tests or research. He [could] only alert the court to some of the factors that might in general affect the reliability of identification evidence. Much of his report has no bearing on the facts of this case.'

62 *Gage v HM Advocate* [2011] HCJAC 40.

Psychology and pre-trial procedure

1.36 The fundamental problem facing a tribunal of fact charged with the task of evaluating a witness's identification is one that Stone has referred to as the 'privacy of psychological facts'.[63] The reliability of the witness's identification will depend on the integrity of the cognitive processes that he or she has relied upon for that task. At trial, cross-examination might reveal the existence of some of the factors that are known to adversely affect identification accuracy, and experts could be called to explain the findings of research into such matters. Judicial warnings may be issued admonishing fact-finders of the need for caution in convicting on the basis of eyewitness identification evidence or directing their attention to any of the surrounding circumstances that suggest that the witness might be mistaken.

1.37 None of these measures can tell us much about the state of the witness's memory. Much more can be achieved in this respect through the use of formal pre-trial identification procedures. The outcome of well-designed procedures, which establish conditions that are intended to control the risk of suggestion and require the witness to make choices about a number of individuals of similar appearance, all of whom (apart from the suspect) are known to be innocent, may provide some indication of the quality of the witness's memory. Where the witness identifies the suspect during such a procedure, there appears to be a satisfactory basis for inferring both that the witness's memory is accurate, and consequently, that the suspect is the person that the witness saw on the earlier relevant occasion. That inference may be more reliable where procedures are conducted at the earliest opportunity. The shorter the period between a witness's perception of the offender and any procedure designed to elicit reliable identification evidence, the less likely it is that a witness will have been exposed to situations which give rise to a risk of memory contamination or distortion.

1.38 Although the findings of psychological research might be of limited value in the courtroom, such research has informed the design of procedures that are used to obtain identification evidence from eyewitnesses prior to trial. Unlike the problems encountered in attempting to stage realistic criminal events to measure the effect on certain variables on witnesses' accuracy, the controlled conditions under which evidence is obtained from eyewitnesses in pre-trial procedures can be replicated in laboratory-based studies with considerable accuracy. Empirical studies have led, for example, to the development of the cognitive interview, which enables greater amounts of accurate information to be obtained from eyewitnesses.[64] Such research has also pointed to various ways in which the accuracy of identification procedures might be improved.

---

63 M. Stone, *Proof of Fact in Criminal Trials*, (Green & Son, 1984).

64 See generally, S Henderson and L Taylor, 'Nothing but the truth: achieving best evidence through interviewing in the forensic setting', in B Brooks-Gordon and M Freeman (eds) *Law and Psychology, Current Legal Issues*, Vol 9, (OUP, 2006); R Wilcock et al, op cit at pp 44–48; G Davies and H Westcott 'Investigative interviewing with children: progress and pitfalls', in A

1.39 Identification procedures should be composed of people who resemble the suspect,[65] and researchers have devised various means of testing the fairness of procedures in this respect. One method of revealing any bias in the images or persons selected for use in an identification procedure is to provide volunteers who have no connection with the events being investigated with a description of the suspect and invite them to attempt to identify him or her.[66] Indeed this is the technique advised for voice identification procedures.[67] If all of those selected for a procedure bear a sufficient resemblance to the suspect, the odds of any one of them being chosen by someone who has not seen the suspect before but has been given a description of him should be around chance – for a nine-person procedure, odds of 1 in 9. However, if some of those selected are picked out much more frequently than this it would suggest that the other persons appearing in the procedure do not sufficiently resemble the suspect. If, for example, three people including the suspect were picked out by a disproportionately high number of persons who were provided with the description of the suspect, there would be good grounds for concluding that the *functional size* of the procedure (three persons sufficiently resembling the suspect) is far smaller than its *nominal size* (the nine persons appearing in the procedure).[68] The results of the exercise would suggest that six persons appearing in the procedure do not constitute effective choices.

1.40 For some time, those engaged in empirical research have been advocating the adoption of 'sequential line-ups' rather than more traditional procedures in which the subjects are presented simultaneously. In addition to the individual presentation of subjects, the sequential lineup differs fundamentally from traditional simultaneous procedures by requiring the witness to make a decision in relation to one person appearing in the procedure before being shown the next. As soon as the witness makes an identification, the procedure is concluded and he or she is not permitted to see the remaining images. Those who argue that this form of procedure ought to be adopted point to research that suggests its use will lead to fewer instances of 'false positive' identification. In other words, it appears that innocent suspects are less likely to be mistakenly identified in a sequential procedure than in a traditional simultaneous procedure.[69] Although this finding has been replicated across a number of

---

Heaton-Armstrong, E Shepherd, G Gudjonsson and D Wolchover (eds) *Witness Testimony: Psychological, Investigative and Evidential Perspectives* (OUP, 2006); A Kapardis *Psychology and the Law* (CUP, 3rd edn, 2010), at pp 98–108. C Dando, R Wilcock, R Milne and L Henry 'A modified Cognitive Interview procedure for frontline police investigators' (2009) 23 *Applied Cognitive Psychology* 698.

65 PACE, Code D, Annex A.2 provides that the foils must, as far as possible, resemble the suspect in age, height, general appearance and position in life. See **5.34** et seq.

66 A Doob and H Kirshenbaum 'Bias in police lineups: partial remembering' (1973) 1 *Journal of Police Science and Administration* 287.

67 See **8.14**.

68 R Malpass, 'Effective size and defendant bias in eyewitness identification lineups'", (1981) 5 *Law and Human Behavior* 299. For a review of the relevant research see R Malpass, C Tredoux and D McQuiston-Surrett 'Lineup Construction and Lineup Fairness', in R Lindsay et al, op cit.

69 See N Steblay et al, 'Eyewitness accuracy rates in sequential and simultaneous lineup presentations: a meta analytic comparison' (2001) 25 *Law and Human Behavior* 459. For a

studies, findings concerning the effect that the use of sequential procedures has on the rate of accurate identifications (that is, the identification of the culprit) is rather more inconsistent. Much of the research suggests that the use of this form of procedure has a negligible effect on the rate of accurate identification, but there are some studies in which its use has been found to significantly reduce the rate of such outcomes.[70]

1.41 In the United States, publication by the National Institute of Justice of guidelines for conducting pre-trial identification procedures[71] has been instrumental in the move towards the use of sequential procedures in some US jurisdictions.[72] The guide prescribes model procedures, which were drafted by a working group comprising psychologists, prosecutors and police officers. Although the document contains instructions for conducting both simultaneous and sequential procedures, it expresses a preference for neither. However, some have argued that the US constitutional Due Process clause requires exclusive use of the sequential line-up procedure on the grounds that it reduces the incidence of false positive identification.[73]

1.42 One explanation of the significant reduction in the rate of false positive identification produced by sequential lineups when compared with simultaneous presentation concerns the judgment strategy that the witness may use in the respective procedures. Simultaneous presentation of subjects allows the witness to compare the persons appearing in the procedure to one another. It is suggested that this might lead to the witness selecting the subject who bears the *closest* resemblance to the culprit, though that resemblance may not, in fact, be particularly close. The suspect may be identified on the basis that he is the 'best candidate'.

1.43 Because in the sequential lineup the witness is shown only one image at a time and is required to make a decision in relation to each image before the next is shown, the opportunity to compare subjects does not arise. Because intra-subject comparison is not possible, any identification is more likely to be based on there being a close similarity in the suspect's appearance and the witness's recollection of the culprit. It has been suggested that, as identification

---

review of the relevant research findings and the limitations of the procedure, see P Dupuis and R Lindsay, 'Radical alternatives to traditional lineups', in R Lindsay et al, op cit.

70 See, e g T Valentine, S Darling and A Memon 'Do strict rules and moving images increase the reliability of sequential identification procedures?' (2007) 21 *Applied Cognitive Psychology* 933.

71 *Eyewitness Evidence: A Guide for Law Enforcement*, (National Institute of Justice, 1999).

72 Eg Wisconsin: 2005 Wisconsin Act 60; New Jersey, see Attorney General's Guidelines, http://www.state.nj.us/lps/dcj/agguide/photoid.pdf (accessed March 2010). For a sceptical report on the effectiveness of the procedure, see S Mecklenburg, *Report to the Legislature of the State of Illinois: The Illinois Pilot Program on Sequential Double Blind Identification Procedures* (2006); http://www.chicagopolice.org/IL%20Pilot%20on%20Eyewitness%20ID.pdf (accessed 26 May 2011). However, see D Schacter et al 'Policy Forum: Studying Eyewitness Investigations in the Field', (2007) 32 *Law and Human Behavior* 3; K Findley 'Innocents at risk: adversary imbalance, forensic science, and the search for truth', (2008) 38 *Seton Hall Law Review* 893, at pp 958–964 for a critical analysis of the methodology employed in this research.

73 M R Headley 'Long on Substance, Short on Process: An Appeal for Process Long Overdue in Eyewitness Lineup Procedures', (2002) 53 *Hastings Law Journal* 681.

of a suspect through a shallow relative judgment may amount to no more than speculation on the part of the witness, a higher rate of false identification might be expected. This kind of speculation on the part of the witness might be expected to lead to identification of suspects from time to time and if the opportunity to speculate is removed then the rate of accurate identification may fall.

1.44 The principal identification procedure in England and Wales, the video identification, is not a strict sequential procedure. Although it involves the sequential presentation of single images, the witness is not required to make a decision in respect of one image before being permitted to view the next. Indeed, the provisions of Code D require the witness to view the entire set of images at least twice before making any identification, and directs officers conducting the procedures to inform witnesses that there is no limit on the number of times that they may see the sequence, or part of the sequence, of images.[74] Nevertheless, there is evidence suggesting that the use of this form of procedure leads to a higher rate of correct identification than the strict sequential procedure, while bringing about no change in the number of incorrect identifications.[75]

1.45 Some psychologists have suggested the use of procedures that do not require witnesses to make binary decisions about those appearing in the procedure; that is, to choose either to identify or reject an individual. It is inevitable that a witness's memory of the person observed on the relevant earlier occasion will be deficient. Changes (perhaps quite subtle) in the physical appearance of the culprit, failure to perceive all relevant information during observation of the earlier event, deterioration of the memory, and the impossibility of recreating the conditions in which the culprit was originally observed, mean that any 'positive identification' of the suspect will involve some degree of speculation on the part of the witness. As the High Court of Australia observed in *Craig v R* (see **1.11**), a witness's assertion that the defendant was the person seen on the previous relevant occasion is a consequence of the witness being satisfied that there is *sufficient similarity* in the defendant's appearance and the witness's recollection of the culprit's appearance. If the High Court's analysis is accepted, and what we now know about memory and its shortcomings provide good grounds for doing so, forcing witnesses to make binary choices appears undesirable. The diligent fact-finder would want to know how closely the witness believes the suspect to resemble the culprit.

1.46 Studies have been conducted which suggest that asking witnesses to state how strongly they believe each participant in a procedure to be the culprit, and measuring the time it takes a witness to reach a decision on each produces more reliable evidence than can be obtained from a procedure that requires binary

---

[74] Code D, Annex A, para 11.

[75] See R Wilcock and W Kneller 'A comparison of presentation methods of video identification parades', *Applied Cognitive Psychology* (forthcoming).

decisions.[76] There have also been proposals for a modified sequential procedure in which the witness is shown a larger number of images and is permitted to select any number of persons who he believes might be the culprit.[77] A witness who has a poor memory of the culprit, or is more inclined to overlook disparities in the appearance of those presented and memory of the culprit's appearance, might be expected to select more individuals than a witness who has a good memory and exercises more rigorous judgment when making comparisons. If a witness selects only the suspect from a procedure that permits multiple choices from a large number of images, it might reasonably be concluded that the suspect is likely to be the culprit. The weight that ought to be placed on such evidence will vary according to the size of the pool of images of similar looking people from which the suspect's image is selected. However, as the number of images selected by the witness increases, the probative value of the witness's selection of the suspect will diminish.

Empirical research and legal decision-making

1.47 Empirical research has provided us with considerable understanding of the manner in which witnesses' memory functions and of its vulnerabilities. It has also been of value in the development of pre-trial procedures that are likely to produce reliable identification evidence. But there remain many aspects of procedure that have been largely ignored by empirical researchers. There have been surveys of various actors' knowledge of the factors that might affect a witness's capacity to make an accurate identification. There is also a significant body of research on the manner in which juries approach the evaluation of eyewitness identification evidence. However, little is known about the decision-making processes that police, prosecutors and judges undertake in relation to such evidence.[78] It will be seen in Chapter 3 that whether a suspect is afforded the protection offered by a formal pre-trial identification procedure conducted under controlled conditions, or is the subject of a rather more crude and suggestive ad hoc procedure carried out in the street during the early stages of an investigation will depend on whether the police officers concerned conclude that there is sufficient information available to justify an arrest without resorting to the street identification. There has been no empirical research on the manner in which these procedures are conducted; what we little know about their use is provided by the descriptive accounts in the judgments of appellate courts.

---

76 See J Sauer, N Brewer and N Weber 'Multiple confidence estimates as indices of eyewitness memory' (2008) 137 *Journal of Experimental Psychology: General* 528; N Brewer and N Weber 'Eyewitness Confidence and Latency: Indices of Memory Processes not just Markers of Accuracy' (2008) 22 *Applied Cognitive Psychology* 827; J Sauer, N Brewer and G Wells 'Is there a magical time boundary for diagnosing eyewitness identification accuracy in sequential line-ups?' (2008) 13 *Legal and Criminological Psychology* 123.

77 A Levi 'An analysis of multiple choices in MSL lineups, and a comparison with simultaneous and sequential ones' (2006) 12 *Psychology, Crime and Law* 273.

78 See A Roberts 'Towards a broader perspective on the problem of mistaken identification: legal decision-making and identification procedures' in B Brooks-Gordon and M Freeman (eds), *Current Legal Issues*, vol. 9, *Law and Psychology*, (OUP, 2006), at pp 182–202.

1.48 Empirical researchers have not yet studied the way in which trial judges in England and Wales (or it appears, in any other jurisdiction) make decisions about the admissibility of disputed identification evidence. Observations on the exercise of judicial discretion made by the Australian Law Reform Commission are interesting in this respect:[79]

> 'A reading of reported Australian cases leaves the impression of a reluctance on the part of trial judges to exclude eyewitness identification evidence, however unreliable or weak it may seem. Instead reliance is placed on the warning to the jury and appellate courts give lengthy statements about the appropriate detail of such warnings. So, even evidence of identification which is so liable to being mistaken that it would be "extremely dangerous for a jury to assign any probative value to it" may be properly admitted as long as a jury is given a warning in such terms.'[80] [Internal references omitted]

1.49 Although concerned with the exercise of discretion by Australian judges, these observations may have a salience that extends beyond the boundaries of that jurisdiction. In England and Wales, trial judges have discretion to exclude prosecution evidence where its reception would have an adverse effect on the fairness of proceedings. While failure to follow the provisions of the code of practice that regulates the use of pre-trial procedures might lead to the exclusion of identification evidence on which the prosecution proposes to rely (see Chapter 10), there is no empirical research on trial judges use of this discretion in such circumstances. Similarly, despite the perceived importance of the various duties that are imposed on trial judges as a consequence of the Court of Appeal's judgment in *R v Turnbull*[81] (see Chapter 12), there has been no systematic study of whether these duties are discharged satisfactorily. Nothing is known of the criteria that trial judges employ in order to determine whether disputed identification is of 'poor quality' and consequently whether or not the case should be withdrawn from the jury. *Turnbull* also requires trial judges to point out to the jury the weaknesses in the identification evidence tendered by the prosecution. Likewise, but little is known about how this task is performed.

1.50 The Australian Law Reform Commission's concerns about trial judges' reluctance to exclude poor quality identification evidence led to a proposal for a more rigorous approach to admissibility, which now forms part of the Uniform Evidence Acts. The broad position is that admissibility of 'visual identification'[82]is predicated on there having been an 'identification parade' held prior to trial. This position is, however, qualified. Evidence is admissible notwithstanding the failure to conduct an identification parade where it would not have been reasonable to conduct one,[83] or where the defendant refused to

---

79 Australian Law Reform Commission, *Evidence*, Report No 26. Interim, (ALRC, 1985).

80 Ibid, at [424].

81 (1976) 63 Cr App R 132, [1977] 1 QB 224, CA.

82 'Visual identification' is defined in s 114(1) as 'identification evidence relating to an identification based wholly or partly on what a person saw but does not include picture identification evidence'.

83 Section 114(2)(b).

participate in one.[84] The statute provides a non-exhaustive list of factors which the court is required to take into account in determining the reasonableness of a failure to conduct an identification parade.[85] These include: the nature and gravity of the offence concerned; the importance of the evidence; the defendant's failure to co-operate in the parade, and the practicality of conducting a parade in view of the relationship between the witness and defendant. Among the virtues of this approach is that it establishes a prima facie presumption of exclusion where eyewitness identification evidence has been obtained through the use of an informal procedure that does not offer the degree of accuracy that might be provided by a formal identification parade.

1.51 However, the approach adopted in the Uniform Evidence Act appears flawed. It makes reception of visual identification evidence conditional on a procedure – 'an identification parade' – having been conducted, but fails to define what is meant by that term. This failure undermines the purpose of the adoption of an exclusionary approach; that of ensuring that the evidence presented to the tribunal of fact is as reliable as possible. This is because it is possible for a procedure which has the appearance of an 'identification parade' and might be appropriately described as such, to be conducted in a manner that produces evidence of little, if any, probative value.[86]

1.52 A similar exclusionary approach governs the admissibility of eyewitness identification evidence in New Zealand, but differs significantly from that which is provided by the Australian uniform legislation. Section 45(2) of the Evidence Act 2006 establishes a presumption that visual identification evidence will be excluded where: (i) it was obtained through means other than a 'formal procedure', and (ii) there was no 'good reason' for not following such a procedure. The Act differs from the Australian legislation in a number of respects. First, it provides an exhaustive list of reasons that constitute 'good reasons' for not following a formal procedure.[87] However, where identification evidence has been obtained by means other than a formal procedure, and there is no good reason for the failure to conduct such a procedure, the prosecution may still be able to rely on the evidence if it is able to prove beyond reasonable doubt that the evidence is reliable.

1.53 Some of the characteristics of such a procedure are prescribed in s 45(3) of the New Zealand Evidence Act and these may be supplemented by further prescription in secondary legislation. In this event, compliance with any such regulation also becomes a condition of admissibility. Defining or prescribing elements of formal procedures in primary legislation is not without its

---

84 Section 114(2)(c).

85 Section 114(3).

86 It has been suggested that the characteristics of 'an identification parade' may be determined by recourse to other bodies of law, common law and statute; see J Anderson, J Hunter and N Williams, *The New Evidence Law* (Butterworths, 2002), at pp 389–391. However, the nature of the common law judicial legislating process is unlikely to lead to procedures which are grounded in the relevant scientific findings.

87 Section 45(4).

problems. Prescription contained in primary legislation is likely to become much more entrenched than that provided in delegated legislation and statutory codes. Ensuring that procedures set out in primary legislation reflect developments in empirical research is likely to be a more difficult task than it would be if those procedures were set out in sub-ordinate legislation. Under s 45 of the Act, evidence obtained through a sequential lineup appears to be presumptively inadmissible. Section 45(3)(b) provides that a 'formal procedure' is one in which 'the person to be identified is *compared to* no fewer than seven other persons who are similar in appearance to the person to be identified' [emphasis added]. What distinguishes a sequential lineup from the more traditional forms of identification procedure, such as a parade, is that it is designed to prevent the witness comparing those who appear in the procedure to one another.

1.54 Although the legislative approaches to the issue of admissibility of eyewitness identification evidence in Australia and New Zealand that are described above mark a radical departure from preceding practice in those jurisdictions, whether they have had the effect that the legislature desired remains unclear.

Part I

INVESTIGATION

Chapter 2

INTRODUCTION TO CODE D

INTRODUCTION

2.1 Sections 60 and 66 of the Police and Criminal Evidence Act 1984 (PACE) impose on the Secretary of State, a duty to issue Codes of Practice that are intended to regulate the exercise of certain police powers.[1] The Codes issued by virtue of these provisions now number eight, Code D governing 'the Identification of Persons by Police Officers'.[2] The first version of the Code was published in 1985,[3] and was effective from 1 January 1986. Prior to Code D, rules regarding identification parades and the use of photographs were contained in Home Office Circulars.[4] Code D, though much refined, echoed many of the provisions of its forerunner. It has been revised on seven occasions. The second edition came into force on 2 April 1991. The third edition came into force on 10 April 1995 and temporary modifications to it were introduced on 1 April 2002. The fourth edition came into force on 1 April 2003 with further editions published in 2004, 2005 and 2008. The current edition came into force on 7 March 2011.

THE FUNCTION OF THE CODE

2.2 The Code has been described as existing 'to provide standards which can be applied to police conduct and to ensure, as far as it is practicable to do so, the quality and reliability of the evidence collected by police officers and used in criminal proceedings'.[5] Though the focus of Code D is upon the procedures for visual identification, it also contains the procedures for the taking of fingerprints, photographs, body samples and for body searches for identifying

---

1 Section 60 establishes a duty to issue a Code of Practice concerning the tape-recording of interviews with suspects, while section 66 requires the promulgation of Codes relating to the exercise of powers of arrest, search of persons, vehicles and premises, and the seizure of property from such premises, and the detention, treatment, questioning and identification of persons by police officers.

2 The current Code D is set out in full at Appendix A.

3 Pursuant to PACE, s 66(1)(b).

4 Home Office Circular (HOC) 109/1978.

5 *R v Popat* [1998] 2 Cr App R 208 at 212, CA.

features such as scars and tattoos.[6] A relatively recent addition to the provisions of the Code is a general statement concerning the function of the procedures that it establishes.[7] It is explained in para D1.2 that the 'eyewitness identification procedures are designed to: (i) test the witness' ability to identify the suspect as the person they saw on a previous occasion, and (ii) provide safeguards against mistaken identification.'[8] This is, however, an inadequate statement of the ends that ought to be served by the procedures.

2.3 It was explained in *R v Nicholson*[9] that, although identification procedures are administered by the police, the courts have taken the view that the Code should not be perceived only as a set of procedures which enable the police to obtain reliable identification evidence for the prosecution case. Rather, they provide a means of securing evidence that might assist either party:

> 'Despite what might at first be thought to be the purpose of an identification parade, namely that it is a method or procedure by which the police seek to obtain evidence for the purposes of prosecuting suspects, as opposed to a service performed impartially for prosecution and defence, this court in various of its previous decisions, leaned towards the latter view on the basis, it seems, that a parade may produce negative evidence favourable to an accused which the defence are incapable of generating for themselves.'[10]

2.4 In general terms, the identification procedures set out in the Code provide a means of obtaining *any* evidence that is relevant to the issue of identity (in a manner that optimises its potential probative value). In view of the fact that those who administer the procedures, and whom the Code addresses, have an adversarial interest in the outcome of procedures, it might be thought preferable that purpose of the identification procedures established by the Code be expressed in terms that are clearer than those currently used. In particular, it ought to be explained, as was pointed out in *Nicholson*, that the procedures also provide a means of securing reliable evidence that supports a suspect's claim that he was not the offender. The guidelines published by the US Department of Justice,[11] for example, state that the function of identification procedures is to provide for 'accurate identification or non-identification.'[12]

2.5 The value of a satisfactory statement of the purpose of the Code should not be overlooked. The Court of Appeal appears on occasion to have lapsed

---

6 See Chapter 6.

7 First included in the version of the Code issued in 2005.

8 See *R v Ball* [2006] EWCA Crim 1048, at [31]: 'The main mischief behind Code D is to prevent the possibility of contamination of the witness's identification evidence . . .'

9 [2000] 1 Cr App R 182.

10 *Ibid*, at 188–189. See also, S. Charman and G. Wells, 'Applied Lineup Theory', in R. Lindsay, D. Ross, D. Read and M. Toglia (eds.), *Handbook of Witness Psychology*, vol. 2, *Memory for People*, (London, Lawrence Erlbaum, 2006), who suggest that the function of an identification procedure is to test the hypothesis that the suspect is the offender.

11 *Eyewitness Evidence: A Guide for Law Enforcement*, (Washington DC; US Department of Justice, National Institute of Justice, 1999).

12 *Eyewitness Evidence: A Guide for Law Enforcement*, at p 29, n 34.

into thinking that identification procedures serve only the ends of the prosecution. In *R v Thomas*,[13] at the defendant's trial for armed robbery the prosecution relied on facial mapping evidence to prove identity. Although there were a number of eyewitnesses who had observed the culprit, the police failed to arrange any identification parades. In respect of this failure the Court of Appeal observed:

> 'There appears to us to be a distinction between a case where the Crown relies for identification on a witness who could have taken part in an identification parade, and cases, such as the present, where the Crown does not rely on an identification by any such witness and seeks to identify the defendant by other evidence. The advantage to a defendant in the former situation, of having a relevant witness fail to pick him out in an identification parade, is greater than any advantage in the latter situation of having a person, who *might* have been an identifying witness but on whom the Crown is *not* relying for identification, fail to identify the defendant on a parade.'[14] (original emphasis)

2.6 What the Court appears to suggest is that the probative value of a witness's failure to pick out the suspect on an identification parade is affected by a prosecution decision not to rely on that witness in its case. Of course, a witness's failure to make an identification provides the defendant with an opportunity to invite the tribunal of fact to infer that the reason for the failure was that the culprit did not appear in the procedure.

2.7 The provisions of the Code also fail to give effect to the 'impartial service' conception of the Code. Prior to taking part in a procedure, the Code requires the identification officer to instruct the witness that 'the person they saw on a specified earlier occasion may, or may not, appear in the images they are shown and that if they cannot make a positive identification they should say so.'[15] However, this is at odds with the suggestion in *Nicholson*, that the identification procedures in Code D constitute a service that is to be performed impartially for the prosecution and the defence. An instruction that invites a witness to provide a positive identification, or alternatively, to offer an equivocal response – 'I cannot make a positive identification' – does not sit well with the idea of an impartial procedure. There seems to be no good reason why the witness should not also be invited to state that the person they observed on an earlier relevant occasion does not appear in the procedure.[16]

2.8 The Court of Appeal has emphasised that the detailed regime contained in Code D is to be followed without variation or substitution of any other system.[17] In *R v Forbes*[18] the House of Lords held that:

---

[13] (Unreported), November 22, 1999.

[14] Ibid, at [43].

[15] Code D, Annex A, para 11.

[16] The guidelines issued by the US National Institute of Justice, *Eyewitness Evidence: A Guide for Law Enforcement*, op cit, note 11, suggest that the witness be instructed that 'it is just as important to clear innocent persons from suspicion as to identify guilty parties'.

[17] *R v Quinn* [1995] 1 Cr App R 480, CA.

[18] [2001] 1 AC 473, [2001] 1 Cr App R 430 at [26], HL.

> 'Code D is intended to be an intensely practical document, giving police officers clear instructions on the approach that they should follow in specified circumstances. It is not old-fashioned literalism but sound interpretation to read the Code as meaning what it says.'

2.9 Nevertheless a failure to follow the procedures does not, of itself, render a positive identification inadmissible. The principal significance of breaches at trial lies in the question, asked under PACE, s 78, whether the evidence so obtained 'would have such an adverse effect on the fairness of the proceedings that the court ought not to admit it'.[19] In considering that issue the Code is admissible in evidence and, where 'relevant to any question in the proceedings shall be taken into account in determining that question'.[20] In short, while it must be taken into account, it is ultimately the test of fairness that determines admissibility.

2.10 In broad outline, the Code comprises three categories of provisions: those that prescribe the procedures that are to be used to procure identifications from witnesses (formal identification procedures); those that prescribe the circumstances in which these procedures are to be conducted; and those that establish a hierarchy among them. The following chapter deals with the provisions concerning the circumstances in which identification procedures are to be conducted. Those that establish the procedural hierarchy and regulate the manner in which the various identification procedures are to be conducted are covered in Chapters 4 and 5 respectively.

2.11 The Annexes to Code D which make detailed provision for the conduct of formal identification procedures carry the same weight as the Code itself. By contrast the 'Notes for Guidance' are, as their title suggests, guidance as to the interpretation and application of the Code.[21] Though no breach might be occasioned by a failure to follow the guidance, the notes may nevertheless be cited and relied upon in argument, and could influence a decision concerning the fairness of the procedure. In deciding whether to exclude evidence, a court can take into account the terms of a revised Code which, while not in force at the time of the conduct of the procedure, reflect current thinking as to what is fair.[22]

2.12 The Code does not impose on police officers a statutory duty. Thus a breach of Code D would not of itself render a police officer liable to criminal or civil proceedings.[23] It may, however, be relevant and probative in deciding liability in civil actions such as proceedings for malicious prosecution or misfeasance in public office.[24]

---

[19] The exclusion of evidence under PACE, s 78 is considered in Chapter 10.

[20] PACE, s 67(11).

[21] Code D2.2.

[22] *R v Ward* (1994) 98 Cr App R 337, CA.

[23] PACE, s 67(10).

[24] The provision in PACE, s 67(8) which automatically rendered a police officer liable to disciplinary proceedings for any breach has been repealed: Police Act 1996, Sch 2.

APPLICATION TO INVESTIGATORS OTHER THAN POLICE OFFICERS

2.13 The Code is concerned primarily with the use of investigative powers by police officers. However, others who possess such powers are also bound to 'have regard to any relevant provision' of the Code. They include, under PACE, s 67(9A), police authority employees and accredited community safety officers;[25] and under PACE, s 67(9), 'persons other than police officers who are charged with the duty of investigating offences and charging offenders'. Officers of Customs and Excise[26] and officers of the Serious Fraud Office (SFO)[27] have been held to be within the latter category in the context of Code C (for the detention, treatment and questioning of persons). There can be little doubt these prosecuting authorities would also be bound by Code D. There are a wide variety of other bodies whose statutory responsibilities include the detection of offences and prosecution of offenders. These range from government departments and local authorities, for example in the context of benefit fraud,[28] to lesser known organisations such as the Medicines Control Agency. In their role as prosecutors they too are subject to PACE, s 67(9). In *R v Tiplady*[29] it was accepted by all parties and the Court of Appeal that local government trading standards officers prosecuting under the Trades Descriptions Act 1968 fell within it. Similarly, in *Royal Society for the Prevention of Cruelty to Animals v Eager*,[30] though not argued, the Divisional Court proceeded on the basis that the RSPCA inspector's conduct was governed by PACE, s 67(9). Whether a person has a duty to investigate offences is an issue of fact, not law, and may turn on the extent to which the discovery of criminal conduct is the objective of an inquiry or is ancillary to another purpose.[31]

2.14 The phrase 'charged with the duty' is not confined to those who have a 'quasi official statutory duty' but is to be construed as embracing 'any type of

---

25 The role of civilian support staff in identification procedures is considered at 4.6.

26 *R v Okafor* (1994) 99 Cr App R 97, CA; *R v Weerdesteyn* [1995] 1 Cr App R 405, CA. In *R v Gill* [2003] EWCA Crim 2256, the Court of Appeal held that the provisions of Code C applied to Revenue officers when conducting Hansard interviews.

27 *R v Director of the Serious Fraud Office ex p Saunders* [1998] Crim LR 837, CA.

28 In *R v South Central Division Magistrates' Court ex p Secretary of State for Social Security* 23 October 2000 (unreported), DC, Code C was assumed to apply.

29 [1995] Crim LR 651, CA.

30 [1995] Crim LR 59, CA.

31 See *R v Seelig and Spens* (1992) 94 Cr App R 17, CA ('the *Guinness* case') in which it was held that the primary purpose of a Department of Trade and Industry (DTI) investigation under the Companies Acts 1985 was to investigate the affairs of the company and report to the Secretary of State. See also *R v Smith* (1994) 99 Cr App R 233, CA, in which the court distinguished the supervisory role of the Bank of England under the Banking Act 1987 from an investigative role. In *R v Ristic* [2004] EWCA Crim 2107, the court concluded that a prison officer who was responsible for searching those attending prison to visit inmates but would not take part in any investigation that might be conducted as a consequence of a search was not subject to the provisions of the Codes of Practice. The headteacher of a school is not 'charged with the investigation of offences and prosecution of offenders' and so not subject to Code D when making arrangements for the victim of a robbery to attempt to identify which students were responsible; *R v I* [2007] EWCA Crim 923; *R v Hussein* [2007] EWCA Crim 1842.

legal duty, whether imposed by statute or by the common law or by contract': *Joy v Federation against Copyright Theft*.[32] The investigator in that case was employed by the Federation. Its work involved the investigation of offences under the Copyright, Design and Patents Act 1988 on behalf of its members whose financial interests it aimed to protect. He was held to be subject to PACE, s 67(9). The existence of a duty to investigate offences must be decided on a case-by-case basis and in doing so it may be necessary to explore in evidence the contractual arrangements of the employee investigator. In *R v Bayliss*,[33] the Court of Appeal accepted that a store detective, whose job entailed the detection of theft, might come within the scope of the duty. However, in the absence of clear evidence at first instance as to the terms of the store detective's employment, the court declined to make such a finding. By contrast, in *R v Twaites and Brown*[34] the trial judge misdirected himself in failing to address the issue of whether the duty imposed by PACE, s 67(9) applied to two investigators employed by a firm of bookmakers. This failure vitiated his decision not to exclude an interview by them of the defendant.

2.15 Unlike the police, who are under a duty to comply with the Code, the duty of other persons is to 'have regard to any relevant provision'. The degree of compliance required will be determined by what is reasonable and practicable in the circumstances. What is appropriate to the police, Customs and Excise or the SFO may not be appropriate to a store detective. There is, for example, no impediment to employed investigators cautioning before interview in strict compliance with Code C. Conversely, they are unlikely to have the facilities for implementing an identification procedure under Code D. However that analysis may not necessarily be an end to the matter for two reasons. First, there may be circumstances in which it would be appropriate, in 'having regard to' the principles of Code D, to hand over an investigation to the police for the purposes of formal identification. Liaison with statutory or employed investigators is not uncommon, for example, where police give assistance for the purposes of making an arrest and search.[35] Secondly, the fact that Code D may not apply does not preclude the exclusion of an identification on the ground of unfairness under PACE, s 78.[36] An absence of fairness and the danger of misidentification may exist regardless of whether the person responsible for an identification is bound by Code D procedures.

---

32 [1993] Crim LR 588, CA.
33 (1994) 98 Cr App R 235, CA.
34 (1991) 92 Cr App R 106, CA.
35 For example, Department of Social Security investigators.
36 See *R v Hickin and others* [1996] Crim LR 584, CA and generally on PACE, s 78 in Chapter 10.

Chapter 3

VISUAL IDENTIFICATION PROCEDURES AND THEIR APPLICATION

INTRODUCTION

3.1 Sections 1–3 of Code D prescribe the procedures that are to be used to obtain visual identification evidence from eyewitnesses and other persons. Paragraph D1.2 explains that 'eyewitnesses' are those who have 'seen the offender committing the crime'. The reference to having 'seen the offender committing the crime' must be read as having been physically present when the crime was committed and observed the offender committing it.[1] Otherwise

[1] There may be circumstances when an eyewitness was not physically present, for example, a security guard who witnesses a theft occurring while monitoring contemporaneously broadcasted CCTV images.

those who were not present but have seen an incident reported on the news or have been shown other images would fall within the Code's definition of an 'eyewitness.' In respect of such witnesses, Code D makes a fundamental distinction between 'Cases when the suspect's identity is not known' and 'Cases when the suspect is known'. The principal effect of the distinction is, in respect of a known suspect, to prohibit the use of street identification and (unless a suspect is unavailable) the showing of photographs. If there is no known suspect, the Code is not directory as to the method of identification that may be used. By contrast, if there is a known suspect, the Code regulates which of a number of procedures may be used and includes a further category of 'Cases when the suspect is known but not available'. The procedures relating to these circumstances are dealt with at **3.3** ff.

3.2 Where film or photographs of an incident exist, they may be used for identification by persons who were not present to witness the criminal event but may be able to identify the offender in images. Such images may be shown whether or not the identity of a suspect is 'known'. The procedures to be followed in such circumstances are set out at **3.89** ff.

EYEWITNESSES: SUSPECT'S IDENTITY NOT KNOWN

Street identification

3.3 Street identification[2] generally occurs when, in the immediate aftermath of an offence, it is believed that the perpetrator may still be in the vicinity and takes two broad forms. It is common practice for police officers, together with potential identifying witnesses, to conduct a search of the area in order to identify the perpetrator. It may be the only realistic means of apprehending an offender. In *R v Brown,*[3] for example, the victim of a robbery was taken in a police vehicle on a tour of nearby streets and, after 5 or 10 minutes, made a positive identification of the appellant who was walking along the street. Unless the offender bears some unusual physical or sartorial feature, the ability of a witness or victim to recognise that person is likely to prove far more effective than merely giving a description for which a police officer must try to find a match. The alternative form occurs in circumstances in which a witness has provided a description, and soon after the commission of the offence police officers not accompanied by the witness come across a person who matches the description. That person may be detained and presented to the witness with a view to establishing whether he or she is the perpetrator.

3.4 The importance of immediate identification is increased if the witness's ability to identify is dependent upon recognition of the clothing worn by the offender rather than physical features. Street identifications have also been justified on the ground that where there are many people in the vicinity to whom a description might apply, it would make criminal investigations quite

---

2 The procedure for street identifications is set out Code D3.2 and is considered at **5.11**.

3 [1991] Crim LR 368, CA.

impossible if the police had to arrest everybody who might answer the description, and thereafter arrange identification procedures for each.[4]

3.5 Though overwhelmingly used shortly after an offence, the street procedure might also be employed some days or weeks after the commission of an offence where it was believed that the offender would return to the place where it was committed. That might be the case if, for example, the offender is believed to make the same journey regularly or to frequent the same public house.[5] The witness in these circumstances might be taken to the place by a police officer to await discreetly the anticipated attendance of the offender.

3.6 Although the arrest and detention of a perfectly innocent person may be avoided by an immediate procedure, the dangers inherent in a street identification, in particular when it amounts to no more than a confrontation rather than a true test of the witness's ability to recognise the offender, are manifold.[6] While the forensic value of a more formal procedure such as a parade may be diminished where delay in arranging one results in some deterioration of a witness's memory, the controlled conditions under which it is conducted and other safeguards attached to it, including legal representation, provide a significantly higher degree of protection from mistaken identification.

3.7 Consequently Code D3.2 sanctions this means of investigation only when the suspect's identity is not known:

> 'In cases when the suspect's identity is not known, a witness may be taken to a particular neighbourhood or place to see whether they can identify the person they saw.'

But once the person becomes a known suspect, witnesses may not be permitted to take part in a street identification and only those procedures authorised for known suspects are allowed.[7]

Photographs and other images

3.8 The practice of showing photographs[8] or other images of suspects who are 'not known' is likely to occur in cases where, perhaps because of the location of the offence or the method of its commission, the number of possible suspects is thought to be limited to persons already known to police – the 'usual suspects'. Examples include local burglars or confidence tricksters with a distinctive modus operandi. In such situations the code permits the

---

4 *R v Rogers* [1993] Crim LR 386, CA; *R v Hickin* [1996] Crim LR 584, CA, See **3.28** for a discussion of the case.

5 See for example *R v Popat* [1998] 2 Cr App R 208, CA, and *R v Jones and others* (1994) 158 JP 293, CA.

6 For these, see **5.12**.

7 Code D3.2(d).

8 The procedure for showing photographs is set out in Annex E to Code D and is considered at **5.112**.

showing of police photographic records to a victim or witness to discover whether the perpetrator is among them.

3.9 Though the format for this procedure is controlled and structured, it remains a less transparent test than a video identification and may suffer from a lack of real choice in the physical appearance of those depicted in the photographs. Thus Code D3.3 allows photographs to be shown only 'if the suspect's identity is not known'. It expressly prohibits this method of identification:

> '... if the identity of the suspect is known to the police and the suspect is available to take part in a video identification, an identification parade or a group identification.'

The prohibition extends to computerised or artist's composite likenesses or similar likenesses or pictures including e-fit images.

3.10 Code D3.3 excludes the use of this procedure if the suspect is known and available[9] but is permissive if the suspect's identity is not known. In other words it is not expressly permissive if the suspect is known but not available. In *R v Kitchen*[10] the suspect had escaped from custody and was therefore unavailable. The provision in force at the time,[11] materially the same as Code D3.3, was held to allow an identification by photographic procedure. However the modifications to Code D since then suggest that if photographs are to be used, the appropriate procedure should be video identification by use of stills, permitted under Code D3.21 when a suspect is not available.[12]

EYEWITNESSES: SUSPECT'S IDENTITY KNOWN

3.11 The procedures permitted by Code D if the identity of the suspect is known are video identification, identification parade, group identification and confrontation,[13] depending upon whether the suspect is available,[14] or not available.[15] The factors which determine the selection of the procedure, the use of covert procedures and, as a last resort, confrontations are considered in Chapter 5. In practice, video identification is now the procedure overwhelming used by police.

---

9 See *R v Dixon* [2005] EWCA Crim 3409, in which the showing of a set of photographs which included the appellant to a woman after her husband had picked out the appellant from the same set of photographs was held to be a breach of the Code.

10 *R v Kitchen* [1994] Crim LR 684, CA.

11 The procedure was under Code D2.18 of the second edition of Code D.

12 See **4.25**.

13 The conduct of these procedures are laid out in Annex A: video identification (see **5.29**); Annex B: identification parade (see **5.66**); Annex C: group identification (see **5.91**); Annex D: confrontation (see **5.104**).

14 Code D3.4–3.10.

15 Code D3.21–3.23.

When is a person a known suspect?

3.12 One of the most commonly disputed issues under Code D is whether the defendant was a known suspect. There are an infinite variety of ways in which a person may become a known suspect for an offence. These include being named or described by an eyewitness; by confession; by association with other accused persons; by possession of incriminating articles; by comparison of fingerprints, handwriting or DNA sample; by motive or opportunity; by elimination of other candidates.

3.13 The term 'known' is defined in Code D3.4. It reproduces the definition in earlier editions of the Code;[16] however its status was enhanced in the 2004 version of the Code from a mere Note for Guidance to part of the Code. A suspect is 'known' if:

> '... there is sufficient information known to the police to justify the arrest of a particular person for suspected involvement in the offence.'[17]

3.14 A person does not become a known suspect merely because he or she voluntarily remains with a police officer having been stopped or 'detained'. Where, by contrast, a person has been arrested it might be thought that, short of asserting the arrest to be unlawful, the detainee must have assumed the status of 'known suspect'.[18]

3.15 The evidential threshold for an arrest by a constable under PACE is reasonable grounds for suspecting a person to be guilty of an offence.[19] The grounds for suspicion have been held to import both an objective and subjective element, namely reasonable grounds to suspect and the officer's actual suspicion.[20] However, the wording of the Code D3.4, 'sufficient information known to police to justify the arrest', suggests that the test to be applied in order to establish the existence of an obligation to conduct a formal procedure is purely objective. Such an approach was adopted in *R v Kitchen*[21] where a police officer had seen the defendant in the vicinity of a robbery 2 hours before it was committed and subsequently learnt that he fitted the description of one of the robbers. The victim was later shown photographs including that of the defendant and it was contended that there had been a breach of the prohibition against showing photographs because the defendant

---

16 See third edition, Note for Guidance, 2E.

17 The same definition is used in the context of a street identification. 'Once there is sufficient information to justify the arrest of a particular individual' the procedures for known suspects apply to other potential witnesses: Code D3.2(d). See **3.23**.

18 See *R v Williams* [2003] EWCA Crim 3200; (2003) SJ 1305, for a case in which a person was detained in circumstances which clearly amounted to an arrest, albeit possibly unlawful. The Court of Appeal side-stepped the issue of whether he was a known suspect. For a trenchant criticism of the judgment see [2003] 42 CLW 3.

19 PACE, s 24(5)(b).

20 *O'Hara v Chief Constable of the Royal Ulster Constabulary* [1997] AC 286; [1997] 1 Cr App R 447, HL; *Chapman v DPP* (1988) 89 Cr App R 190, CA; *Castorina v Chief Constable of Surrey* [1996] LGRR 241, CA.

21 [1994] Crim LR 684, CA.

was a known suspect. The argument was rejected on the ground that the police officer's suspicion that the defendant was one of the robbers was based upon instinct rather than reasonable evidential grounds. Thus there was insufficient information to justify an arrest.

3.16 A similar view was taken in *R v Rogers*.[22] The appellant was alleged to have damaged cars on an industrial estate. Two witnesses who approached noted that his speech was slurred and that he was wearing a pullover. Shortly afterwards police heard movement inside a warehouse and on entering found the appellant. His speech was slurred but he was not wearing the pullover described by the witnesses. It was held that there was at that stage insufficient evidence to make an arrest because of the discrepancy in the clothing. Consequently there was no known suspect and when, shortly after he was found, the witnesses attended at the warehouse, the street identification was permitted. On the facts the appellant was what might be described as a 'possible suspect'.[23]

3.17 In *R v El Hannachi and others,*[24] it was held that the duty to conduct a formal procedure had not arisen even though the police believed that there had been sufficient grounds to justify the arrest of a suspect prior to the street identification that occurred. After a disturbance in the car park of a public house, a witness was taken in a police car and invited to say whether she saw anyone she recognised. On passing a police van at which police officers had detained a group of people, she identified the four defendants. One of the police officers gave evidence that they would have been arrested even if the witness had not identified them and it was therefore argued that they were known suspects. The Court of Appeal rejected this submission holding on the facts that there was plainly insufficient information available to the police to justify their arrest.

3.18 In many cases the conscientiously exercised judgment of a police officer as to whether to arrest or to refrain from making an arrest may help to inform whether there was sufficient information for an arrest. However, by parity of reasoning with *R v Kitchen* and *R v El Hannachi,* a court should acknowledge the status of a known suspect where there was, objectively, ample information to justify an arrest despite a police officer refraining from doing so. So it was in *K v DPP*[25] that the Divisional Court substituted its own judgment for that of the police officer. The appellant had been detained shortly after a robbery in the early hours of the morning. He broadly matched the victim's description and had been tracked from the scene by a police dog. It was held that there was sufficient evidence to have arrested the appellant. In consequence, a formal

---

22 [1993] Crim LR 386, CA. The criterion was applied although the second edition of the Code in force at the time did not then include the definition of 'known' suspect.

23 See also *R v Bush* (unreported) 27 January 1997, CA, in which the assailant was known to be within a nightclub sealed off by the police. Fitting the description with long hair and tattoos, he was asked to step aside from the crowd, whereupon he was identified by the victim.

24 [1998] 2 Cr App R 226, CA.

25 [2003] EWHC 351 (Admin); [2003] 4 *Archbold News* 1.

identification procedure should have been held at some later stage rather than the street identification that, in fact, took place.

3.19 Any claim that it was necessary to conduct a street identification or some other informal identification procedure in order to establish the grounds required to arrest the individual concerned, involves two competing procedural safeguards. Predicating the power of arrest on the existence of reasonable suspicion provides suspects with some degree of protection against the risk of arbitrary detention. The requirement that formal identification procedures be used where there is sufficient information known about a person to justify his arrest is intended to ensure that a suspect benefits from procedures that are designed to mitigate, in various ways, the risk of error that attends a witness's attempt to identify an offender. These procedural requirements cannot properly be said to conflict or to give rise to any tension, both are intended to safeguard the suspect's interests. While a suspect who is wrongly arrested might suffer some inconvenience and anxiety, damage to reputation, and a relatively short period of detention, a suspect who is wrongly identified in a street identification might suffer all of these misfortunes in addition to conviction and punishment. Where a question arises as to whether a suspect is 'known' it might be that the suspect's interests are better served by a strict approach to determining whether there were sufficient grounds to justify the arrest of the suspect when he or she was subject to a street identification or other informal procedure.[26]

3.20 There are, however, cases which suggest that the courts are prepared to take a relatively generous approach to determining whether there were sufficient grounds to justify the arrest of a suspect prior to informal identification.[27] In *R v Toth*,[28] Customs and Excise officers had two vehicles under observation in the car park of a fast-food restaurant. The driver of a vehicle of which the appellant was the registered keeper was seen to pull up next to a second vehicle and transfer a number of holdalls from the boot of the appellant's car into the boot of the second car. Both cars sped off and were pursued by Customs officers. The appellant's car was lost, but the second vehicle crashed after the driver lost control. Although the occupants made off, officers recovered the holdalls from the boot, which were found to contain a large quantity of cocaine having a street value in excess of £2 million. One of the officers who had observed events in the car park subsequently visited the address of the registered keeper to see whether he could make an identification for the purpose of arresting him. The appellant was duly arrested and subsequently picked out at identification parade by the officer. It was submitted on appeal following his conviction, that the identification of the appellant at his home address prior to his arrest was a breach of the Code. The fact that the

26 See further A. Roberts, 'Pre-trial Defence Rights and the Fair Use of Eyewitness Identification Procedures', (2008) 71 *Modern Law Review* 33.

27 See, eg *R v Gornall* [2005] EWCA Crim 668, in which the Court of Appeal concluded that twin brothers who were the only males found in a house which the victim of a burglary saw the man who had burgled her house enter, were not known suspects.

28 [2005] EWCA Crim 754.

appellant was the registered keeper of the vehicle provided sufficient grounds to justify his arrest for suspected involvement in the transaction that had been observed. This being so, it was argued, he was a 'known suspect' before the confrontation occurred at his home address. Rejecting this submission, the Court of Appeal took the view that the fact that appellant was the registered keeper did not make him a known suspect, and that a necessary pre-requisite to his being arrested was an 'identification link' between him and the driving of the vehicle on the relevant occasion. With respect, the fact that the appellant was the registered keeper of the vehicle, provides such a link, albeit circumstantial. The inferences that might be drawn from this fact – that the driver was likely to be the registered keeper or someone known to him – would seem to provide reasonable grounds for suspecting the registered keeper to have been in some way involved in the offence. The questionable nature of the court's conclusion is perhaps, more apparent when one considers whether the arrest of a registered keeper of a vehicle, the driver of which was observed delivering a large consignment of illegal drugs, would be unlawful for want of reasonable grounds to suspect him of some form of involvement in the offence.

3.21 It has been suggested that a witness who might be able to identify by clothing falls outside the ambit of the prohibition of a street identification for known suspects on the ground that a later procedure in which the suspect wore different clothing might be valueless.[29] However, as the known suspect is by definition likely to have been arrested or at least liable to arrest, there is no impediment to the seizure of his or her clothing for the evidential purpose of comparison with the witness's recollection.

3.22 Neither Code D nor the arrest conditions under PACE preclude the possibility of two persons becoming known suspects for the activities of one individual.[30] However the more suspects there are, the less likely it is in practice that each would be classified as a known suspect. Thus where the perpetrator could only come from a class of persons, for example every white male in a nightclub or every Asian female employee of a large company, it would be unrealistic to suggest that each was a known suspect.

Prohibition on street procedure for known suspect

3.23 Code D3.2 permits a police officer to carry out a street identification procedure if the suspect's identity is not known. Once a person becomes a known suspect a street identification is prohibited by Code D3(2)(d). Code D3.4 provides that where 'the suspect's identity is known to the police and they are available, [a video identification, identification parade or group identification] may be used'. The apparently permissive wording of this provision is rather misleading. If the conditions in Code D3.12 are satisfied,

---

29 *R v Oscar* [1991] Crim LR 778, CA, and see also *R v Hickin* [1996] Crim LR 584, CA.

30 *Cumming and others v Chief Constable of Northumbria Police* [2003] EWCA Civ 1884. It was held, in the context of an action for wrongful arrest, that 'there can be nothing wrong with arresting more than one person even if the crime can only have been committed by one person'.

giving rise to a duty to conduct a formal procedure, Code D3.14–3.16 require the use of a video identification, identification parade or group identification in respect of a suspect who is 'available'. The true nature of Code D3.4, therefore, is directive rather than permissive. Once a suspect is known and available the *only* procedures that may be used are a video identification, identification parade or group identification. Note for guidance 3F specifically draws attention to the fact that the admissibility and value of street identification evidence may be compromised if the suspect's identity becomes known before the procedure. It may result in the exclusion of the street identification and contaminate a later formal procedure.[31] Even if not excluded, a breach will call for appropriate directions in the summing up.[32]

3.24 The prohibition of a street identification procedure for a known suspect came under scrutiny in *R v Hickin and others*.[33] The facts of the case provoked the Court of Appeal to take a pragmatic approach, prompting the observation that 'Code D is not to be interpreted in such a way as to require the police to act in a manner which would be an affront to common sense'. The case concerned a violent gang attack on two people. Shortly afterwards police arrested a large group of people. Within a few minutes two witnesses were taken by a police officer to the group with the result that they identified seven of the members. The Court of Appeal found it unnecessary to decide whether the situation confronting the police was one which was governed by the Code but inclined to the view that it was not.[34] The Court accepted that the high watermark of the submission that it was catered for in the Code was that the defendants were arrested suspects at the time of the identifications; thus it was a case where the identity of the suspects was 'known' and therefore appropriate to proceed only by way of identification parade. Nevertheless the Court was reluctant slavishly to follow the Code.

> 'There is, we recognise, a powerful argument that these men were 'known' suspects. What though were the realities of the situation? Following serious disorder in the streets of Blackpool a large group of men is arrested soon afterwards by officers who have information that two men had been seriously injured. Another officer, knowing of certain arrests and having been approached by witnesses who saw the attacks, decides to enlist their assistance in identifying the actual assailants. This is still minutes after the assaults. In our judgment there can be no objection in principle to such a course being taken ... Setting up fourteen identification parades that night was clearly impracticable. The passage of time clouds the clarity of recollection. The recognition of clothing can be a valuable aid to identification. We see no reason in principle why the police and the witnesses

---

31 See **10.46** for exclusion of evidence.

32 See **12.105** for summing up.

33 [1996] Crim LR 584, CA, followed in *R v Bush* (unreported) 27 January 1997.

34 In considering whether the Code applied, the reliance was placed on *R v Oscar* [1991] Crim LR 778, CA and *R v Rogers* [1993] Crim LR 386, CA. That seems misplaced. *R v Oscar* was concerned with the obligation to hold a parade after a street identification and, being a case of identification of clothing as distinct from that of a person, it was held that a later parade was pointless. *R v Rogers* was decided on the basis that there was insufficient evidence to arrest at the time of the identification.

should be deprived of that assistance as they might have been were the law, in circumstances such as these, to oblige the police to hold identification parades.'[35]

3.25 The conundrum which faced the Court in *R v Hickin* is not uncommon.[36] On the one hand is the urgency of a difficult situation faced by police who seek an immediate identification, sometimes compounded by the large number of people arrested. On the other hand are the dangers of misidentification, the safeguards against it of a formal procedure, and the plain words of Code D. The point that *R v Hickin* confronted but did not resolve was this: is Code D's prohibition of the street identification procedures for known suspects of universal application or may it be disapplied in an emergency or where strictly to adhere to the letter of the Code would 'require the police to act in a manner which would be an affront to common sense'?

3.26 Though the House of Lords in *R v Forbes*[37] was considering a different issue – whether an identification parade was mandatory – the dicta concerning the construction and application of Code D are informative. It was held that Code D was intended to give 'police officers clear instructions on the approach that they should be following in specified circumstances. It is not old-fashioned literalism but sound interpretation to read the correct Code as meaning what it says'. No reading of the Code suggests that the prohibition of street identifications for known suspects may not apply to situations such as in *R v Hickin.*

3.27 To apply the Code according to the number of known suspects and other prevailing circumstances would be a capricious interpretation. Moreover the definition of 'known suspect', which at the time that *R v Hickin* was decided was contained in the Notes for Guidance, has now been incorporated into the substantive provisions of the Code. The better approach, it is submitted, is to apply the meaning of known suspect literally and to concentrate upon the question under PACE, s 78 whether the street identification resulted in unfairness. Indeed the Court of Appeal in *R v Hickin* ultimately concluded, in considering admissibility, that the question of the fairness of the procedure was the same regardless of whether there had been a breach or not.[38] The literal approach to the meaning of a known suspect does not prevent a court, on the question of admissibility, from considering 'the circumstances in which the

---

35 Transcripts 95/7025/Y5, 95/7027/Y5, 95/7029/Y5, 95/7031/Y5, 95/7033/Y5, 95/7034/Y5, 95/7121/Y5 for full judgment.

36 The real problem may have been the assumption, created by the arrests, that there was sufficient information to justify the arrests thereby rendering those arrested as 'known suspects'. The group was arrested en masse because 'they were obvious candidates for rounding up'. The problem for the prosecution was that to have argued that they were not known suspects would have been to concede that the arrests were unlawful.

37 [2001] 1 AC 473; [2001] 1 Cr App R 430, CA, see **3.34–3.37** for further discussion of the case.

38 A similar pragmatic approach was adopted in *R v Vaughan* (unreported) 30 April 1997, CA in which the Court of Appeal was reluctant to criticise officers' on the spot decision to hold a street identification despite its own view that there was quite enough evidence to arrest. Nevertheless the procedure was held to be unfair and ought to have been excluded. See also *R v Williams* (2003) SJ 1305, [2003] EWCA Crim 3200, CA in which the precise nature of the breach was regarded as less important than its effect.

evidence was obtained' under PACE, s 78 which may include the practical demands of a situation facing the police at the time of a street identification. Certainly the arguments for street identification based upon the impracticability of arranging identification procedures may be of significantly less force with the advent of video identification.[39]

3.28 A literal approach was taken in *R v Nunes*.[40] A police officer observed a burglar in a house and circulated a description but could not arrest him. Shortly thereafter other officers arrested the appellant who broadly fitted the description. He immediately denied having done anything. The eyewitness officer then attended the scene of the arrest in order to confirm that the suspect was the person he had seen earlier and positively identified the appellant. It was submitted that at the time of arrest the police were dealing with a known suspect and accordingly the street identification was not permitted. The Court of Appeal expressed some doubt as to whether the Code's draftsman could have intended such a restriction to be placed upon the conduct of the police in confirming that the correct person had been apprehended. However, citing the above dicta in *R v Forbes*, it was held that there was 'no escape from the conclusion that [the] identification of this appellant did amount to a breach of the Code'.[41] In *R v Lennon*[42] the prevailing circumstances were not dissimilar to those in *R v Hickin*. The defendant was alleged by two constables to have thrown a bottle during a demonstration. His description was circulated and he was later arrested. Whilst held in a police van, the constables attended and purported to identify him. No later formal procedure was held. Despite the suggestion made by the trial judge that the street identification was justified by the particular situation, the Court of Appeal found that it was a flagrant and gross breach of the Code. A similar conclusion was arrived at in *R v Preddie*,[43] in which the victim of a violent robbery was taken by police officers to a location at which their colleagues were struggling with the appellant as they arrested him. The Court of Appeal found that the officers effecting the arrest clearly entertained reasonable suspicion, therefore, the appellant was a known suspect. The correct course of action would have been for the officers who were in the company of the victim to have left him with the attendant paramedics while they went to the assistance of the arresting officers.

Identification procedure sought by police

3.29 In many investigations it will be the police who seek confirmation of the identity of an offender by one of the prescribed methods the visual identification. Code D3.13 confers a discretionary power that enables an

---

39 See David Wolchover and Anthony Heaton-Armstrong 'Ending the farce of staged street identifications' [2004] 3 *Archbold News* 5 for a trenchant criticism of street procedures and the argument in favour of immediate video identification.

40 [2001] EWCA Crim 2283; [2001] 10 *Archbold News* 1.

41 See *Coulman v DPP* [1997] COD 91, DC for a different conclusion on similar facts, although decided before *R v Forbes*.

42 (1999) 63 JCL 459, CA.

43 [2011] EWCA Crim 312.

identification procedure to be conducted if the officer in charge of the investigation considers it would be useful. Where, for example, a witness asserts that he or she would not recognise the culprit if they were to see them again, from the prosecution perspective there may be little to lose in conducting an identification procedure. The witness's failure to make any identification will merely confirm what he or she has asserted. It neither advances the defence case nor undermines the prosecution case. There may be some advantage to the prosecution, however, were the witness to make an identification of the suspect, notwithstanding the witness's prior misgivings about his or her ability to do so.

Duty to conduct an identification procedure for a known suspect

3.30 An identification procedure is more than an investigative and evidential tool for the police. It is also provides the opportunity of testing a witness's accuracy and reliability and, for a defendant who is not selected by a witness, the means to challenge the correctness of identification or other incriminatory evidence. It may prevent a miscarriage of justice.[44] Code D therefore grants a suspect, subject to being available,[45] the right to an identification procedure in certain circumstances. The extent of this right and the corresponding duty has, over many years, been the most problematic and controversial aspect of the Code. The difficulties that the courts have encountered are evident in three important judgments that are considered in some detail in the following section.

A purposive or literal interpretation of the Code?

3.31 Although the question addressed in *Popat* and *Forbes* was whether the police were required to conduct a formal procedure in respect of a witness who had already made a street identification of the suspect, the decisions raise broader issues regarding the general nature of the provisions in Code D.[46] The relevant provision of the version of the Code in force at the time, Code D2.3, provided that 'whenever a suspect disputes an identification an identification parade shall be held', subject to the suspect's consent to and it being practicable to arrange one. It appeared, therefore, to require a formal identification procedure in circumstances in which a suspect had been identified in an informal street identification, which was disputed. Nevertheless, in *R v Popat*[47] the Court of Appeal concluded that the provision did not apply where 'the witness has already made an actual and complete identification of that individual', which it explained was a confrontation conducted under good

---

44 *R v Graham* [1994] Crim LR 414, CA.

45 See **3.85**.

46 The question is not limited to circumstances in which the suspect has been the subject of a street identification, it also arises, for example, where the witness claims to have recognised the culprit; where the witness has identified the suspect from a photograph, and; where there is circumstantial evidence that might be used to prove identity.

47 [1998] 2 Cr App R 208, [1998] Crim LR 825, CA. This was followed faithfully in a number of subsequent cases including *R v El Hannachi and others* [1998] 2 Cr App R 226, [1998] Crim LR 881, CA, where the judgment of Hobhouse LJ in *R v Popat* was described as the definitive analysis and *R v Bell* [1998] Crim LR 879, CA.

conditions with no risk of corruption of the witness's memory. The Court reviewed a number of cases in which faithful application of this provision would have required the police to conduct an identification parade where doing so would have served no useful purpose. It concluded that the provisions of the Code were not 'all-embracing' and that there may be situations that fell outside them.[48] It was therefore suggested that in interpreting and applying the Code's provisions it was *always necessary* to have regard to the purposes of Code D.[49] In particular, if an informal street identification had yielded reliable and accurate evidence, the purposes served by the relevant provision of the Code would have been fulfilled and a formal identification procedure would not be required.

3.32 There is, however, a problem with the internal logic of the judgment in *Popat*. The Court issued an admonishment to those to whom the Code is addressed, by stating that nothing in the judgment was to be taken as detracting from the importance of complying with the provisions of the Code.[50] At the same time it permitted (perhaps required) the addressee to use his or her own judgment in determining whether any course of action prescribed by the provisions should be followed in any particular circumstances. This approach, referred to as the *purposive approach*, treats the relevant provision of the Code as a mere 'rule of thumb'; a general guide to action that could be disregarded where following it seemed to be at odds with the ends that the relevant provision of the Code was intended to serve.

3.33 Shortly after *Popat* was decided, the Court of Appeal revisited the issue in *R v Forbes*.[51] On this occasion a differently constituted Court adopted what has been referred to as a 'literal' approach, treating the provision as a strict rule that precluded those to whom it was addressed from exercising their own judgment on the merits of pursuing the course of action that it appears to require in the particular circumstances. Although the terms purposive and literal have been used as convenient labels to distinguish the two approaches, the real issue was the extent to which the police were permitted to act on their judgment of the merits of conducting a procedure. In *Forbes* the Court considered the Code to be 'plainly mandatory', and that the provision setting out the circumstances in which a procedure should be conducted was subject only to those exceptions set out in the provision, i e where a procedure was impracticable or the suspect did not consent.[52] As to the over-inclusiveness of the provision, the Court observed:

> 'so far as it imposes a requirement for an identification parade which applies in circumstances where there is no point in one, it is for those having the

---

48 *R v Popat* [1998] 2 Cr App R 208, CA, at 223.
49 Ibid, at 224.
50 Ibid, at 224.
51 [1999] 2 Cr App R 501.
52 Ibid, at 516.

responsibility under statute to draft or revise the Code to consider whether [it] might be amended to introduce some greater element of flexibility.'[53]

3.34 The decision in *Forbes* prompted the Criminal Cases Review Commission to refer *Popat* back to the Court of Appeal.[54] On this occasion, the Court rejected the approach in *Forbes* and approved its original decision in *Popat*. There followed a renewed appeal to the House of Lords by the appellant in *Forbes*.[55] Their lordships took the view that the requirement of a parade 'whenever a suspect disputes an identification' imposed a *mandatory* obligation on the police and that there was 'no warrant for reading additional conditions into this simple text'. However, their Lordships appeared to proceed to do just this. It was suggested that the approach in *Popat* had been correct insofar as the 'rule' was not applicable to all cases that appeared to fall within its scope. Lord Bingham identified three situations in which it would not be necessary to conduct a formal identification procedure, as the Code appeared to require. These were: (i) where a witness claimed that he would not be able to identify the culprit; (ii) if the witness is only able to identify the clothing worn by the culprit; and (iii) where the case is one of recognition of someone well-known to the witness.

3.35 Recognition of these exceptions amounted to judicial modification of the relevant provision of the Code. If the police were faced with circumstances in which there was a dispute over identity, it was practicable to arrange a formal procedure, the suspect consented, and none of the exceptions identified by Lord Bingham applied, they would be obliged to conduct one. Unfortunately, Lord Bingham went further, suggesting that there might be other 'exceptional circumstances' in which the obligation to conduct a formal procedure would not arise. But it was not made clear with whom the authority to determine what amounted to 'exceptional circumstances' resided. If it was for the police to determine whether the particular circumstances were 'exceptional' and the course of action prescribed by the provision was to be disregarded, the provision could not properly be described as mandatory. The position would be broadly consistent with that adopted in *Popat*.

3.36 But that approach had been firmly rejected by Lord Bingham:

> 'Such an approach in our opinion subverts the clear intention of the Code. First, it replaces an apparently hard-edged mandatory obligation by an obviously judgmental decision. Such decisions are bound to lead to challenges in the courts and resulting appeals. Second, it entrusts that decision to a police officer whose primary concern will (perfectly properly) be to promote the investigation and prosecution of the crime rather than to protect the interests of the suspect. An identification parade, if held, may of course strengthen the prosecution, but it may also protect the suspect against the risk of mistaken identification, and a suspect should not save in circumstances which are specified or exceptional be denied his prima facie right to such protection on the decision of a police officer. Third, this

---

53 [1999] 2 Cr App R 501, at 516.

54 *R v Popat (No.2)* [2000] 1 Cr App R 387.

55 *R v Forbes* [2001] 1 All ER 686, HL.

approach overlooks the important fact that grave miscarriages of justice have in the past resulted from identifications which were 'fully satisfactory', 'actual or complete' and 'unequivocal' but proved to be wholly wrong. It is against such identifications, as well as against uncertain and equivocal identifications that paragraph 2.3 is intended to offer protection to the suspect.'[56]

3.37 The better view of *Forbes* might be that it establishes that the authority to determine the extent of the class of 'exceptional circumstances' lies with the courts and not with those who are required to follow the Code's provisions. On this view, the assertion that the provision is mandatory rests on firmer conceptual grounds, although the issue would only fall to be determined by the courts where the police had failed to follow the course of action prescribed by the Code.

3.38 The relevance of the preceding analysis becomes apparent when the terms of the provision of the current version of the Code that corresponds with that considered in *Popat* and *Forbes*, Code D3.12, are considered. It was introduced during the first substantive revision of the Code following the House of Lords judgment in *Forbes* and is the result of considerable refinement and change in order to resolve some of the lacunae and uncertainties thrown up by the authorities under earlier versions:

'Circumstances in which an eyewitness identification procedure must be held

3.12Whenever:

(i) an eyewitness has identified a suspect or purported to have identified them prior to any identification procedure set out in paragraphs 3.5 to 3.10 [Video identification, identification parade and group identification] having been held; or
(ii) there is a witness available, who expresses an ability to identify the suspect, or where there is a reasonable chance of the witness being able to do so, and they have not been given an opportunity to identify the suspect in any of the procedures set out in paragraphs 3.5 to 3.10,

and the suspect disputes being the person the witness claims to have seen, an identification procedure shall be held unless it is not practicable or it would serve no useful purpose in proving or disproving whether the suspect was involved in committing the offence, for example:

- if the suspect admits being at the scene of the crime and gives an account of what took place and the eyewitness does not see anything which contradicts that.
- when it is not disputed that the suspect is already well known to the witness who claims to have recognised them when seeing them commit the crime.'

3.39 There are two generic exceptions to the requirement to hold a procedure. These exceptions, considered in detail in later sections of this chapter, are:

---

56 *R v Forbes* [2001] 1 All ER 686, HL, at [26].

(1) that a procedure is not practicable;

(2) that a procedure would serve no useful purpose in proving or disproving whether the suspect was involved in committing the offence.

3.40 The specific exceptions to the duty to conduct an identification procedure identified by the House of Lords in *Forbes* are encompassed by the second of the generic exceptions in Code D3.12. But the exception invites the police, in explicit terms, to consider the ultimate purpose served by the provision and the Code generally – that of establishing whether or not the suspect committed the offence. In this respect it is resonant with the approach adopted by the Court of Appeal in *Popat*. This part of the provision appears, at first sight, to confer a broad discretion on the police.

3.41 The introduction of the 'no useful purpose' purpose exception has been the source of considerable uncertainty[57] and sits awkwardly with Lord Bingham's suggestion that 'Code D is intended to be an intensely practical document, giving police officers clear instructions on the approach that they should follow in specified circumstances'.[58] Moreover, it is vulnerable to the various criticisms that were directed at the approach adopted by the Court of Appeal in *Popat* (see **3.36**). The extent of the discretion conferred on the police by virtue of the 'no useful purpose' exception is determined in part by the manner in which the appellate courts interpret these words and their conclusions on the value of a procedure in particular circumstances that fall for their consideration. The cases that have determined the scope of this exception are considered later in this chapter.

The circumstances in which an obligation to conduct formal procedures arises under D3.12

3.42 The first version of the Code, published in 1986, required an identification parade to be conducted in a cases involving 'disputed identification evidence' only if the suspect asked for one and it was practicable to hold one.[59] This evolved to a requirement that 'whenever a suspect disputes an identification, an identification parade shall be held if the suspect consents'.[60] Consent as a condition of the duty to conduct a formal procedure

---

57 It has been suggested that this provision reverses *R v Forbes* and reinstates the *R v Popat* position. See David Wolchover and Anthony Heaton-Armstrong 'Farewell to Forbes' [2003] 7 *Archbold News* 4. However it appears simply to acknowledge, as did R v Forbes, that there are exceptional cases where a procedure would be futile. See Paul Bogan, 'Forbes alive and well' [2003] 9 *Archbold News* 6 for a critique of the article and 'A reply to Forbes alive and well' by the same authors which follows.

58 *R v Forbes* [2001] 1 AC 473, [2001] 1 Cr App R 430, at [26], HL; cf the draft provision suggested by A. Roberts and S. Clover, 'Managerialism and Myopia: The Government's Draft Consultation on Code D', [2002] Crim LR 873, on which Code D3.12 appears to have been largely based, which contained no general exception allowing the police to consider the purposes served by the Code.

59 D2.1 (1st edn, 1986).

60 C2.3 (3rd edn, 1995). It was subject to a number of practical exclusions.

is omitted from the corresponding provision of the current version of the Code, Code D3.12. Consequently, the means of justifying a decision not to conduct a procedure on the grounds that the suspect does not consent to one is less straightforward. If the suspect refuses to participate in a procedure, he or she will become 'unavailable'.[61] In such circumstances, paragraph D3.21 provides that an 'identification officer *may* make arrangements for a video identification' (emphasis added) using covertly obtained video recording or other suitable images. If neither the suspect nor investigating officer seeks an identification procedure, this provision confers on the police the discretion to give effect to the suspect's preference. The duty to conduct a procedure under Code D3.12 should only be lifted in circumstances where the police are able to demonstrate that positive steps have been taken to ascertain whether or not the suspect is willing to take part in an identification procedure, and the suspect has clearly indicated that he or she will not do so.

3.43 However, in *R v French*,[62] a police officer attended a police custody suite and identified the appellant as the driver of a stolen vehicle that he had been pursuing. No identification procedure was held subsequently. The issue on appeal was whether there had been a breach of the Code. Although no request had been made for the appellant to take part in an identification procedure, his legal representative indicated during the appeal hearing that had such a request been made he would have advised the appellant against taking part. The Court concluded that this indicated that this was a situation in which a formal procedure was not appropriate. This reasoning appears unsatisfactory. The appellant's legal representative's *ex post facto* remarks as to what he may, or may not, have advised had the police taken steps to arrange an identification procedure during the investigation does not appear to be a logical basis for determining the existence of a duty to conduct a procedure at that time. On the facts that existed at the relevant time, the failure to make any attempt to arrange a formal procedure amounted to a breach of the Code. The legal representative's remarks regarding the advice that he would have given had he been it been sought is relevant only to consideration of the consequences of the breach.

3.44 The obligation created by D3.12 relates to an 'identification procedure', whereas earlier editions of the Code referred to the primary requirement to hold 'an identification parade.' This reflects Code D's preference for the use of video identification at the expense of the traditional parade. The selection of the appropriate procedure is governed by Code D3.14–3.16.[63]

3.45 Code D3.12 is the lynchpin of the Code and can be analysed as follows:

(1) The *eyewitness conditions,* of which there are two alternatives:

(i) the witness has identified or purported to identify the suspect, or

---

61 Code D3.4.

62 [2004] EWCA Crim 88.

63 See **4.18**.

(ii) the witness expresses an ability to identify the suspect or there is a reasonable chance of the witness being able to do so.

(2) The *suspect condition:* that the suspect disputes being the person the witness claims to have seen.

(3) The *mandatory procedure:* an identification procedure shall be held.

(4) The *exceptions*, if a procedure:

(i) is not practicable,
(ii) would serve no useful purpose in proving or disproving whether the suspect was involved in committing the offence.

The eyewitness conditions

3.46 The requirement to hold a parade depends in the first instance on one of two alternative qualifying conditions relative to the eyewitness. The first is the existence of an eyewitness who has identified a suspect or purports to have done so. It covers situations such as a street identification, an identification as the result of showing photographs, and the purported recognition or naming of a suspect by a witness.

3.47 The qualifying condition is also met if an available eyewitness expresses an ability to identify the suspect, or there is a reasonable chance of the witness being able to do so[64] and has not yet been given the chance of making an identification in one of the procedures for known suspects.[65] The wording of this sub-paragraph is unfortunate and it is submitted that for 'suspect' should be read 'perpetrator' or 'person seen on the relevant earlier occasion'.[66] This interpretation is reinforced by the use of the later phrase 'the person the witness claims to have seen'.

3.48 A description of an offender will not, by itself, amount to an identification. In *R v Byron*[67] the witness described a man with a tattoo on his left arm. It was held that this did not amount to an identification and hence no identification parade was required. That decision was made under the 3rd

---

64 This adopts almost verbatim the dicta in *R v Rutherford and Palmer* (1994) 98 Cr App R 191, CA that, notwithstanding the narrow literal construction of the early Code, it should apply 'where a witness has indicated he or she would be able to identify the offender or there is a reasonable chance of him or her doing so'.

65 This limb effectively overturns the dicta in *R v Nicholson* [2000] Cr App R 182, CA, which implied into the words 'whenever a suspect disputes an identification' in the third edition of the Code the prerequisite of an identification having already taken place.

66 To profess an ability to identify a suspect who, unlike in the first alternative, has not previously been identified by the witness, would require prophetic qualities. See A. Roberts and S. Clover, 'Managerialism and Myopia: The Government's Draft Consultation on PACE – Code D' [2002] Crim LR 873 for an alternative drafting proposal which uses the word 'culprit' instead of suspect.

67 (Unreported) 12 February 1999, CA.

edition of Code D. However, the fact that the witness had expressed an ability to recognise the offender would, under the present Code, render an identification procedure necessary. Where, as in *R v Montgomery*,[68] there is no reasonable possibility of making an identification, the witness condition is not met. In that case the witness gave police a description which did not fit that of the defendant and she doubted that she would be able to recognise the man again.

3.49 The passage of time or the suspect's change in appearance may adversely affect the ability of a witness to make an identification.[69] In *R v Murhaba*,[70] for example, the passengers in a taxi were assaulted by the driver following a dispute over the fare. The victims noted the registration number of the vehicle which led the police, some 3 months after the incident, to the registered keeper. He denied involvement and claimed that the victims must have made a mistake when making a note of the registration number. No identification procedure was arranged as the victims stated that, due to the period that had elapsed since the assault, they did not think that they would be able to pick the assailant out. The Court of Appeal found that there had been no breach of Code D3.12, the issue 'was not whether they would have been able to identify the assailant, but whether they had expressed an ability to do so'.[71] Equally, there may be no reasonable prospect of an eyewitness identifying a suspect where the witness's observation and description or even street identification was of the suspect's clothing. An identification parade involving a suspect in different clothing would be futile.[72]

3.50 The decision in *Murhaba* suggests that where a witness claims that he or she would not recognise the culprit if seen again the duty to conduct a procedure is lifted notwithstanding that objective consideration of the circumstances might lead to the conclusion that there must be some possibility of the witness being able to make an identification. There is nothing unsatisfactory about this position. It was explained above that paragraph D3.12 is concerned with ensuring that an identification procedure is conducted where it might produce an outcome useful to the defence; paragraph D3.13 provides the police with the discretion to conduct one wherever they consider that it might be useful. If the witness claims not to be able to recognise the culprit, the defence case cannot be advanced by a failure to make an identification.

3.51 The duty to conduct a formal procedure is not lifted, however, where the witness is ambivalent or makes no statement as to his or her ability to identify the culprit.[73] It may be assumed that the police will have some responsibility for

---

68 [1996] Crim LR 507, CA.

69 For an extreme example see *R v Folan* [2003] EWCA Crim 908; (2003) 147 SJ 477.

70 [2006] EWCA Crim 1491.

71 Ibid at [10].

72 *R v Oscar* [1991] Crim LR 778, CA and D v DPP (1998) *The Times* 7 August, DC. See also **3.57** and the dicta in *R v Forbes* [2001] 1 AC 473; [2001] 1 Cr App R 31, HL at [27].

73 See *R v Toussaint-Collins* [2009] EWCA Crim 316. The witness to a murder identified the

inquiring whether a witness is likely to be able to identify a suspect. The importance of this responsibility lies in the fact that the police alone may have access to the witness and indeed at the early stages of a case the existence of the witness may be unknown to the suspect. Moreover a person can become a suspect for any number of different reasons unconnected with the witness's observation and may do so a considerable time after the crime. Thus the responsibility of making the relevant inquiry should continue.

3.52 Similarly, there may be no obligation to conduct a procedure where a witness observes a culprit at some distance and, as a result, can provide only limited detail regarding the person's physical appearance. In *R v Gayle*[74] a handbag was stolen from within a school. The caretaker was able to give a general description of the perpetrator fitting many people – colour, approximate age, height and build – but because of the distance between them at the moment of observation he did not see any facial features. He had initially said in his statement that he might be able to identify the person but later indicated that he would not be able to and in evidence thought that the chances were 2 per cent. It was held that it would have been pointless to have conducted a parade. There would not have been, in the words of Code D3.12(ii) 'a reasonable chance' of an identification.

Suspect disputes being the person seen by witness

3.53 The direction that 'an identification procedure shall be held' is contingent upon the suspect disputing being the person the eyewitness claims to have seen. The fact disputed by the suspect is that he is the same person as the offender the witness claims to have seen. It is not confined to a dispute about an identification already made by the witness. The drafting of the present Code D3.12 appears to have resolved a difficulty encountered with the early versions of the Code, which required a parade 'whenever a suspect disputes an identification'.[75] This led to a straining of language in *R v Rutherford and Palmer*.[76] Within a few hours of a robbery the appellant was arrested in a vehicle containing much of the proceeds. In interview he denied participation and expressed his willingness to stand on an identification parade. One witness claimed to be able to recognise one of the robbers but no parade was held. On

---

appellant in a video identification procedure as being the person who had been sitting in the passenger seat of a vehicle, the driver of which she had observed as he crossed a residential street and shot the deceased. In a police interview prior to the identification procedure she had been asked whether she would recognise either of the men again, to which she replied 'I think I would probably the darker man', referring to the alleged gunman. The Court of Appeal took the view (at [41]–[42]) that it could be inferred from the circumstances that there was a reasonable chance of the witness being able to identify the passenger and that it was 'quite unnecessary for the witness to express an ability to identify the suspect before it becomes a requirement to hold an identification procedure'.

74 [1999] 2 Cr App R 130, CA. See also *D v DPP* (1998) *The Times* 7 August, DC.

75 Para 2.3 of the third edition of Code D. The present provision effectively overturns the dicta in *R v Nicholson* [2000] Cr App R 182, CA, which held that there could be no dispute if there had been no identification.

76 (1994) 98 Cr App R 191, CA.

a literal construction, as the trial judge held, there was no disputed identification evidence because there had been no identification and thus the obligation to hold a parade was not engaged. The Court of Appeal, in order to give the provision a 'sensible and purposive meaning' was forced to interpret the right to a parade as occurring where a disputed identification 'might reasonably be anticipated'.

3.54 This drafting lacuna was remedied in a subsequent revision of the Code. In effect, the suspect may dispute being the person seen by the witness without even knowing of the witness's existence. Provided the police are aware both of a potential identification witness and the suspect's denial of presence, the need for an identification procedure arises. For example, a person is arrested as a consequence of a scientific link to the scene of a burglary and raises alibi in interview. A witness later comes forward with evidence of a sighting of the burglar. At that stage the suspect will, by implication, dispute being the person the witness claims to have seen.

3.55 In deciding whether there is an identification issue or not it will be necessary for the police to consider all the information available to them, and evaluate the suspect's defence against the evidence of prosecution witnesses.[77] In doing so, care must be taken in examining whether a suspect's account amounts to a disputed identification. In *R v Emiku*[78] the defendant was accused of attempted kidnapping. It was alleged by the victim that a man had tried to force her into his car at around 10.15 to 10.30pm. The defendant's vehicle was identified and a description of him was given. In interview he accepted that he had stopped at the place of the alleged abduction because of mechanical trouble and spoken to a woman but stated that this had taken place some 2 hours earlier. He denied that he had made any attempt to force her into his car. At first instance the judge, like the police, concluded that the defendant had admitted some form of association with the victim which left only the question of what had occurred to be decided by the jury. The Court of Appeal disagreed and held that in essence he was asserting that he had been wrongly identified and accordingly that there ought to have been an identification parade.

3.56 The dispute about identification may be brought to the attention of the police by a suspect's response to arrest, in interview, by letter from the defence solicitor, or by service of a defence statement or alibi notice. On the other hand a failure to indicate that identification is in dispute, for example by giving a 'no comment' interview and making no request for a procedure, will not trigger the requirement to hold an identification procedure.[79] The Code does not provide for a specific time-limit, rather it imposes a duty to conduct an identification procedure as soon as practicable. In practice, some procedures may be conducted within hours of a suspect's arrest and others well after charge. In *R v*

---

77 *R v Lambert and others* [2004] EWCA Crim 154.

78 [2003] EWCA Crim 2237.

79 *R v Meredith and Cowan* [2001] EWCA Crim 1415; *R v McCartney and others* [2001] EWCA Crim 2283; [2003] 6 *Archbold News* 2; *R v Lambert* [2004] EWCA Crim. 154.

B (Darren),[80] for example, the prosecution was informed only at a Plea and Case Management Hearing that identification would be disputed. Notwithstanding the relatively late stage at which this notice was given, the Court of Appeal concluded that a video identification procedure ought to have been conducted and that failure to do so amounted to a breach of Code D.[81] However, the later the prosecution become aware that identification is in dispute the less practicable and, given deterioration of memory, less useful a procedure may become. Thus it would be almost inconceivable that there would be an obligation to hold a procedure where a defendant announced his defence of mistaken identity for the first time at trial.

Exceptions to the duty to conduct an identification procedure for a known suspect

3.57 There are two generic exceptions to the duty to conduct a formal identification in respect of a known suspect. The first is where it is impracticable to do so, and the second arises where conducting a procedure would serve no useful purpose in proving or disproving whether the suspect was involved in committing the offence.

Practicability

3.58 An identification procedure is not required under Code D3.12 where it is not practicable to conduct one. This exception (or the requirement of practicability) is common to each of the procedures in the selection process.[82] It therefore appears to add little save to emphasise that *a* procedure is not practicable under Code D3.12 only if it can be concluded that *no* procedure is practicable.

3.59 A procedure will not be impracticable simply because it is inconvenient. All reasonable efforts to achieve a procedure should be made before it might be regarded as impracticable.[83] Impracticability might be the result of the difficulty in assembling sufficient people of comparable appearance to the suspect,[84] though many problems of the past will not have survived the present use of video identification with its extensive databases. Difficulties may persist if the suspect is of an ethnic background little represented in the United Kingdom or of wholly unusual appearance which cannot be disguised by some

---

80 [2005] EWCA Crim 438.

81 See also *R v Gojra* [2010] EWCA Crim 1939 in which, notwithstanding that the appellant gave a no comment interview and did not explicitly dispute identification while at the police station, the Court of Appeal suggested that it must have been obvious to the police when his counsel made a bail application that he was disputing identification. The failure to invite the witness to attend an identification procedure at this point amounted to a breach of Code D.

82 Code D3.14–3.16. See **4.18** for the selection process.

83 *Tomkinson v DPP* [1995] Crim LR 60, DC; and *R v Gaynor* [1988] Crim LR 242; *R v Britton and Richards* [1989] Crim LR 144, both first instance decisions.

84 *R v Joseph* [1994] Crim LR 48, CA. See **5.34** and **5.72** for requirements of resemblance and **4.23** for further consideration of the practicability of achieving it.

artifice. Delay might also render a procedure impracticable.[85] However, the mere fact that a procedure is impracticable on one day does not mean that it is impracticable if it could be achieved on another.[86] Again, with the advent of video identification, a procedure can generally be conducted within a short time frame.

Procedure serving no useful purpose

3.60 It was noted above that Code D3.12 provides that an identification procedure need not be held if:

> '... it would serve no useful purpose in proving or disproving whether the suspect was involved in committing the offence. For example, when it is not disputed that the suspect is already well known to the witness who claims to have seen them commit the crime.'

The scope of this exception is potentially broad, its terms redolent of those used by the Court of Appeal in *Popat.* On its face, it would appear to permit the kind of evaluative inquiry suggested by the Court of Appeal in that case, lifting the duty to conduct a formal procedure, for example, in circumstances where some prior informal identification of the suspect is considered to be reliable. It also seems open to an interpretation that would permit the police to decline to conduct a formal procedure where the case against the suspect appears to them to be so overwhelming that no reasonable jury would acquit, notwithstanding a failure by a witness to identify him in any formal procedure that might be conducted.[87] However, it was noted by Lord Bingham in *Forbes* that the primary concern of the police is to promote the investigation of crime and the prosecution of offenders, rather than to protect the interests of suspects. The implication of this appeared to be that the police should not enjoy the kind of broad discretion conferred by the decision in *Popat* as it might not be exercised as it ought to be; to ensure that a procedure is conducted where it might produce an outcome that would assist the defence.

3.61 The 'no useful purpose' exception in paragraph D3.12 might give rise to similar concerns. However, it was made clear in *R v Callie*[88] that those words are to be taken literally:

---

85 *R v Jamel* [1993] Crim LR 52, CA. A procedure should be held as soon as practicable: Code D3.11.

86 *R v Penny* [1992] 94 Cr App R 345; [1992] Crim LR 184, CA.

87 However, it is now clear that failure to conduct a procedure on such grounds would be a breach of the Code. See *R v Gojra* [2010] EWCA Crim 1939, in which a police officer gave evidence that a defendant had not been invited to attend an identification procedure because it was felt that there was already enough evidence against him. Finding a breach of Code D, the Court of Appeal suggested that the officer had not understood the nature of the obligation imposed by the Code.

88 [2009] EWCA Crim 283.

> 'Those words "no useful purpose" are strong and the Code is mandatory. They do not allow a proportionality exercise so that the Code, as a matter of construction, would not apply if some, but very limited, purpose would be served.'[89]

Consequently, the scope of the exception is, in practice, rather narrow. It does not apply to circumstances in which there is a possibility that a formal identification procedure will produce evidence that might assist the defence, even if the possibility is a remote one and any evidence that might be produced may be of low probative value, viewed either in isolation or in the context of the case as a whole. In other words, the 'no useful purpose' exception extends only to those circumstances in which it can be said, either as a matter of logic or empirical certainty, that a formal procedure will not produce evidence that is relevant to a fact in issue. As the Privy Council observed in *Pipersburgh & Robateau v The Queen*,[90] 'in a serious case … where the identification of the perpetrators is plainly going to be an issue at any trial, the balance of advantage will almost always lie with holding an identification parade.'[91]

3.62 As a formal identification procedure is intended and designed to procure identification evidence that is based primarily on the facial features of a suspect, it would serve no useful purpose where, for example, a previous street identification was made on the basis of clothing alone or the witness is able to recognise only the clothing worn by the culprit.[92] Similarly, a procedure serves no useful purpose where the offender was wearing a mask that covered most or all of his or her face.[93]

3.63 A change in a suspect's appearance might also render a procedure ineffective, depending upon the extent of the difference and the clarity of the witness's recollection of the person seen. Where there has been a quite dramatic change in his or her appearance, the witness's failure to identify might be thought to lack the probative value that would be required for its reception as evidence relevant to the issue of identity. However, it is submitted that, given the difficulty that those responsible for administering formal identification procedures might have in determining the point at which a change in appearance is such that a failure to identify is devoid of the necessary probative value, the most appropriate course of action would be to conduct the procedure and leave issues of probative value and relevance to be determined at trial.

---

89 [2009] EWCA Crim 283, at [22].

90 [2008] UKPC 11.

91 Ibid, at [6].

92 *R v Forbes* [2001] 1 AC 473; [2001] 1 Cr App R 430; *R v Oscar* [1991] Crim LR 778, CA; *R v Haynes* [2004] EWCA Crim 390.

93 See *R v Abbott* [2006] EWCA Crim 151. The offenders wore masks during an armed robbery. Consequently, the witness was only able to describe what she could see through the eye holes in the mask, namely eye colour and skin tone. The Court of Appeal concluded that given the limited descriptions provided by the witnesses and the fact that they wore garments that hid the entirety of their faces, there would have been no point in conducting an identification procedure.

Previous informal identification

3.64 The results of empirical studies suggest that a witness who has identified a suspect in a street identification procedure is likely to identify the same person in a video identification procedure.[94] However, a formal procedure may provide a witness who has had time to reflect on events and is unsure of the correctness of his or her original identification of the suspect with an opportunity to resile from it by declining to identify the suspect in the subsequent procedure. In *R v Harris*,[95] the Court of Appeal suggested that denying the suspect a procedure in such circumstances 'ignores the possibility of a change of mind and/or failure to identify the appellant at the identification parade' from which the suspect might benefit. The question of whether a formal procedure is required following an identification of a suspect in an informal procedure such as a street identification has been a vexed one. However, the issue now appears to be settled. The duty to conduct a formal procedure extends to such circumstances, provided the informal identification of the suspect is based on physical appearance.

3.65 In *R v Brown*,[96] for example, the victim of a robbery was taken in a police vehicle on a tour of neighbouring streets. After a few minutes she made a positive identification of a pedestrian. He was arrested and denied the offence. At first instance it was held that a parade was not practicable, the street identification rendering a subsequent identification redundant. The Court of Appeal disagreed. The trial judge was not entitled to predict that a subsequent identification procedure in more formal conditions and with no prompts (intended or otherwise) would have resulted in the same outcome. The victim may have had doubts when faced with several men of similar appearance. The loss of the defendant's opportunity to test the original identification was considered to be a breach of the Code. A similar conclusion was reached in *R v Wait*[97] where the victim of an attack saw two of his assailants some days later. He flagged down a police vehicle and they were arrested. It was suggested that because the victim was present at the arrest, any subsequent positive identification would have been criticised as a recognition of the person arrested and therefore a pointless exercise. That proposition was rejected. The police, it was held, had ignored the fact that identification procedures are for the benefit of the defence as well as the prosecution. The failure to hold a parade was a breach of Code D.

---

94 For empirical research carried out using a methodology based on the requirements of Code and using VIPER video identification equipment, see T. Valentine, J. Davis, A. Memon and A. Roberts, 'Showups and their influence on subsequent video lineup' *Applied Cognitive Psychology* (forthcoming).

95 [2003] EWCA Crim 174, at [15].

96 [1991] Crim LR 368, CA. The facts of *R v Forbes* are indistinguishable.

97 [1998] Crim LR 68, CA. See also *R v McMath* [1997] Crim LR 586, CA and *R v O'Leary and Lloyd-Evans* [2002] EWCA Crim 2055, 67 JCL 115, CA.

3.66 The situation in *R v Brown* was distinguished in *R v Anastasiou*,[98] in which two police officers observed the assailant commit the offence, gave chase and eventually found him on a rooftop. He was arrested and one of the officers escorted him to the police station. The Court of Appeal upheld the trial judge's ruling that conducting a parade in such circumstances would have been a farce, achieving no more than an identification of the man arrested. *R v Brown* was distinguished on the ground that, there, a lay witness made the street identification and played no further part in events whereas the police officers in *R v Anastasiou* had made the arrest and remained with the suspect, in one case, all the way to the police station. The decision in *Anastasiou* can be contrasted with that reached in *R v Nunes.*[99] In this case a police officer observed the offence and, after an arrest by others, made a street identification. The Court of Appeal concluded that the appellant was wrongly denied the chance 'however unlikely that might be thought to be' that the officer would fail to select him at a subsequent identification procedure.

3.67 Each of the cases discussed above predates publication of the version of the Code in which the 'no useful purpose' exception was introduced. There has been some debate as to effect of the exception, the view being canvassed (with some justification)[100] that its effect in respect of the duty to conduct a formal procedure following the identification of the suspect in a street identification was to reinstate the approach adopted by the Court of Appeal in *Popat*.[101] The outcome of a formal procedure cannot be predicted with absolute certainty. It would seem, therefore, that the effect of the Court of Appeal's judgment in *Callie* (see **3.61**), subject to satisfaction of the other conditions discussed in this section, is to require a formal procedure *whenever* a suspect has been identified in a prior informal procedure on the basis of his physical appearance.[102]

3.68 It is doubtful whether *Anastasiou* could now be relied on in support of a submission that no formal procedure is required where a police officer, having identified the suspect in an informal procedure, accompanies him to the police station and is engaged in further dealings with him.[103] It should be noted that Note for Guidance 3A explicitly states that a police eyewitness is subject to the same principles as a civilian witness. In this respect, the observations of the

---

98 [1998] Crim LR 67, CA. This case was decided under the third edition of the Code which did not contain the 'no useful purpose' exclusion, hence the critical commentary, and before *R v Forbes* in the House of Lords.

99 [2001] EWCA Crim 2283; [2001] 10 *Archbold News* 1.

100 See **3.41**.

101 See David Wolchover and Anthony Heaton-Armstrong 'Farewell to Forbes' [2003] 7 *Archbold News* 4 and Paul Bogan 'Forbes alive and well' [2003] 9 *Archbold News* 5 for a critique of the article and the following 'Reply to Forbes alive and well' by the same authors.

102 For cases in which the failure to conduct a formal identification was found to be a breach of Code D3.12 see, *R v Callie* [2009] EWCA Crim 283; *R v Msimanga* [2007] EWCA Crim 297.

103 However, see *R v Noonan* [2003] EWCA Crim 3869, in which police officers had been provided with good quality photographs of the defendants in order to carry out observations on them. They duly observed those depicted in the photographs who were, in consequence arrested. The 'no useful purpose' exception was upheld. It is submitted, however, that in light of the subsequent authority discussed in this section, the duty to conduct a formal procedure would arise in similar circumstances.

Privacy Council in *Nyron Smith v The Queen*[104] are significant. The witness had seen a fatal stabbing in the street where a party was taking place. He was able to keep the assailant under observation and attract the attention of police who were nearby. He provided them with a brief description and directed them to a person who was among a crowd that was present at the scene. The witness went to check the victim and then followed officers to a location at which another officer had detained the appellant. Both the witness and the appellant were then taken to the police station where the witness was asked to confirm whether the appellant was the man he had observed stabbing the victim, which he duly did. Lord Carswell, delivering the opinion of the Committee, concluded that while the value of an identification parade might have been limited, if there was a possibility of it producing evidence that would assist the defence, arrangements should have been made to conduct one:

> 'By the stage when an identification parade could have been held it would have had limited usefulness, for it was a case akin to recognition. If a parade had been held and the appellant picked out, the defence would have been able to maintain that [the witness] was identifying him as the man whom he had seen in police custody, at the scene and in the police station, not as the man whom he had seen committing the crime. Holding a parade would, however, have conferred on the appellant the potential advantage, limited though it may have been in practice, that the witness might have failed to pick the appellant out.'[105]

3.69 Although street identification is probably the most common form of informal or *ad hoc* procedure, the duty to conduct a formal procedure extends to situations in which the suspect is identified in circumstances other than a street identification. In *Wellington v DPP*,[106] police officers stopped a vehicle and asked the driver to provide his name and date of birth. While the officers carried out checks on the Police National Computer, the man fled the scene. Some 2 weeks later one of the officers attended a briefing at which a photograph of the appellant was shown. The officer believed that the appellant was the person who 2 weeks earlier had fled the scene when stopped. Around 2 months later the officer encountered the appellant in the custody suite of Kentish Town Police Station and again identified him as the person who had been stopped. The appellant was arrested for driving offences relating to the initial encounter and for obstructing a police officer in the execution of his duty. He responded by denying any knowledge of the incident. No formal identification procedure was conducted. While acknowledging that the police officer may well have identified the appellant had a formal procedure been conducted, the failure to do so amounted to a breach of Code D3.12.

Recognition

3.70 Though less common than in witnesses' attempts to identify strangers, mistakes where a witness purports to have recognised an offender as someone

---

104 23 June 2008; Privy Council Appeal No.102 of 2006; 2008 WL 2443251.

105 Ibid, at [25]. See also *Goldson & McGlashan v R* [2000] UKPC 9; *Pop v R* [2003] UKPC 60.

106 [2007] EWHC 1061 (Admin).

with whom he or she is familiar can occur, hence confirmation by formal procedure may be necessary to ensure the reliability of an identification which is based on recognition.[107] However an identification procedure involving a witness who undoubtedly knows a suspect well is likely to be futile in the sense that the witness is bound to choose the suspect. In such circumstances conducting a procedure will not assist that person's defence. However, the Code's example of an identification procedure serving no useful purpose when 'it is not disputed that the suspect is already well known to the witness' gives more complete expression to the proviso in *R v Forbes* of a case 'of pure recognition of someone well-known to the eyewitness'.

3.71 The applicability of the 'recognition exception' in D3.12 turns on two questions: (i) is the suspect, in fact, well-known to the witness? and (ii) does the suspect dispute that he or she is well-known to the witness? If the first question is answered in the negative then the exception does not apply and a formal procedure must be conducted, provided the other conditions on which the duty is predicated are satisfied. If an objective evaluation of the circumstances leads to the conclusion that the suspect *is* well-known to the witness, then the duty to conduct an identification procedure arises only if the suspect disputes this state of affairs.

3.72 The phrase 'well known' was considered in *R v Williamson.*[108] After an arson attack at a house, a witness saw a man leave the premises carrying a petrol can. The witness said in her statement that she had seen him on a number of occasions over the previous 3 years but she did not know his name. Though the description did not entirely match the defendant the trial judge found that the case was one of recognition which rendered the holding of a parade useless. The Court of Appeal very much doubted whether the witness's acquaintance with this man, or indeed any based upon casual observations on a number of occasions, could properly be characterised as one in which the suspect was 'well known' to the witness.

3.73 It seems that a suspect is unlikely to be considered 'well-known' to a witness where there is some period of familiarity between witness and suspect in the distant past, but little contact in the years immediately preceding the witness's claim to have recognised the suspect as being the person engaged in the relevant criminal conduct. In *McKenna v DPP*,[109] an off-duty special constable observed someone she believed to be the appellant, who she knew to be disqualified from driving, at the wheel of a motor vehicle. Around 14 years previously she had dealings with him on a couple of occasions while working for a firm of solicitors. However, she had seen him only once in the 10 year period prior to the incident in question and had not spoken to him on that occasion. The Divisional Court found the degree of knowledge and familiarity that the constable had with the appellant 'failed to establish a basis of contact which entitled the fact-finder to reach the conclusion that the suspect was

---

[107] *R v Pop* (2003) SJ 692, PC.

[108] [2002] EWCA Crim 1809.

[109] [2005] EWHC 677 (Admin).

well-known to the witness'.[110] It was suggested that the position may have been different had the period between the witness's previous contact with the suspect and the incident not been so long.

3.74 Even frequent contact, if it occurred some years prior to the events in question, might not be sufficient to establish that the suspect was well-known to the witness. In *R v B (Darren)*,[111] it was found that the trial judge had erred in finding that the appellant was well-known to the witness notwithstanding that she had known him since childhood and had met him on occasions subsequently. The appellant had been in a relationship with the witness's cousin for a period of 3 years, during which the witness had been between the ages of 7–9 years. This relationship had ended some 10 years prior her purported recognition of him as the person who had robbed her. The witness had seen the appellant on a number of occasions subsequently, the most recent of which had been 18 months prior to the robbery. The Court concluded that the trial judge had been wrong to elevate the appellant to the category of someone who was 'well-known' to the witness on the basis of his admission in interview that he knew her.

3.75 The example in Code D3.12 anticipates the possibility of a witness purporting to have a familiarity which is not accepted by the suspect. It reminds those applying the Code that the utility of a procedure should be viewed from the suspect's perspective as well as from that of the prosecution. A person's familiarity with another can be measured in degrees. There is no bright line separating those cases involving 'recognition' of someone with whom the witness is familiar, from those involving identification of someone with whom he or she is 'unfamiliar'. Thus where a suspect disputes a claim that he or she is well known to a witness, an identification procedure is likely to serve a useful purpose in testing that contested claim.[112] The possibility that a witness may purport to recognise a person and yet, for example, be mistaken about the person's name further demonstrates the need to consider the integrity of the recognition when it is disputed. An identification procedure in those circumstances would prevent the perpetuation of a mistake. This approach is illustrated in two cases. In *R v Conway*[113] a mother and son purported to recognise the attacker of another person. They knew his first name only and had later learnt the surname from a neighbour. They claimed to have seen him in a public house on a number of occasions and that he had been to their house for a meal. The defendant maintained that he had no previous acquaintance of any sort with either. It was held that the failure to allow him an identification parade had:

---

[110] Per Newman J, at [13].

[111] [2005] EWCA Crim 438.

[112] See for example *Goldson and McGlashan v R* [2000] UKPC 9. Though the Code was of no application in this Jamaican case, the Privy Council held that a parade would have tested the assertion by a witness that she knew one of the defendants, a claim denied by him.

[113] (1990) 91 Cr App R 143, CA.

> '... deprived him of the opportunity of properly putting to the test the crucial issue of whether or not the witnesses knew him. Had they failed at such a parade to identify him, the case would have inevitably collapsed. Conversely, had they identified him, their evidence that he was the assailant would have been immensely strengthened.'[114]

3.76 *R v Harris*[115] provides another example of the need to consider the utility of an identification from the defence perspective. Two teenagers were assaulted and robbed. They named one of the robbers as Tristan, a boy who they claimed to recognise as having attended the same school as them some 2 years previously. Both had had little to do with him at school and had not seen him since he had left. The headmaster testified that all three were at school contemporaneously and that the defendant was the only pupil named Tristan at that time. The defendant raised an alibi and said he did not know the complainants. The Court of Appeal found that the trial judge had erred in discounting the possibility that the defendant would not have been selected and therefore the deprivation of a formal identification procedure was a breach of the Code.

3.77 It appears that the dispute need not be explicit for the obligation to conduct a formal procedure to arise. In *R v Merchant*,[116] the appellant had been identified in a video identification procedure by the witness to an armed robbery. On appeal, it was submitted that as it was not in dispute that the two were already acquainted with one another, the video identification procedure had no probative value and that by placing evidence of the witness's identification of the appellant before the jury it was likely that they would place disproportionate weight on it. Rejecting the submission, the Court of Appeal observed that there was a substantial difference in the accounts given by the witness and suspect as to the degree of familiarity between them. While it was not disputed that there was some prior level of acquaintance, the disparities in their accounts were such that it could be inferred that a dispute as to whether the suspect was already well-known to the witness existed, and in such circumstances, it could not be said that no useful purpose would be served by conducting a formal procedure.

Disputed identification or participation?

3.78 It is not uncommon that a suspect accepts the correctness of a witness's observation of him or herself at the scene of an offence, but denies participation in it. This often occurs where a group of people are alleged to be responsible for an outburst of violence. In the pell-mell of fighting, the danger of a mistaken identification by a witness, who may fail to describe individuals or fail to ascribe particular conduct to them, is obvious. A mistake as simple as

---

114 (1990) 91 Cr App R 143, CA, at 147.

115 [2003] EWCA Crim 174; (2003) 147 SJ 237. The modifications to the third edition of the Code were in force at the time. The relevant part of Code D2.15 which then applied contains similar wording to the current Code D3.12. See also *R and others v DPP* [2003] EWHC 3074 (Admin).

116 [2005] EWCA Crim 1195.

an incorrect number count of participants may wrongly incriminate a person present but uninvolved. The question arises whether Code D3.12, which demands an identification procedure if 'the suspect disputes being the person the witness claims to have seen', applies to the issue of participation.[117] In other words can Code D3.12 be interpreted as 'the suspect disputes being the person the witness claims to have seen *doing what is alleged*'?[118]

3.79 In the version of the Code issued in 2011, paragraph 3.12 was amended, so as to provide a second specific example of the application of the 'no useful purpose' exception. It explains that an identification procedure would serve no useful purpose:

> '... where the suspect admits being at the scene of the crime and gives an account of what took place and the eyewitness does not see anything that contradicts that.'

The wording of this part of the paragraph is unfortunate. It appears to be a rather convoluted means of stating that a procedure is to be conducted whenever a suspect admits presence but disputes the role attributed to him in an identifying witness's account of events.[119] In other words, a dispute relating to participation or the particular role of a suspect is to be treated as a 'disputed identification' and will trigger the obligation to conduct a formal procedure under paragraph D3.12.

3.80 If this correctly reflects the drafter's intention, the duty to conduct a procedure appears to be over-inclusive. If the identities of all who were present at the scene of the alleged offence are known to the police, and the question is which of those persons was responsible for particular acts, putting any of the suspects in a procedure with eight persons who were known not to have been present can throw no light on the fact in issue; which of the persons who were

---

117 For a discussion of this topic see A. Roberts, 'Questions of "Who was there?" and "Who did what": the application of Code D in cases of dispute as to participation but nor presence' [2003] Crim LR 709.

118 A similar point may arise in relation to the question whether a Turnbull directions is necessary; see **12.48–12.53** and *R v O'Leary and Lloyd Evans* 67 JCL 115, [2002] EWCA Crim 2055, CA; *R v Skeetes* (unreported) 5 March 1998, CA and *R v Thornton* [1995] 1 Cr App R 578, CA.

119 In some respects the exception appears superfluous. If the suspect admits to playing a particular part in the alleged wrongdoing, and the witness claims to have seen him engaged in the activity to which he admits, it is difficult to see how any issue of dispute as to identification might occur; see for example, *R v Muradi* [2005] EWCA Crim 2089, in which the appellant conceded that he was found in the driver's seat of a vehicle which had been involved in a collision with another vehicle, but claimed not to know how he came to be there and stated that he had not been driving. The driver of a third vehicle witnessed the collision but had not seen who was driving at the time. After stopping his vehicle he saw two other men attempting to help the appellant out of the vehicle. The witness had pointed the appellant out to police at a scene. The issue on appeal was whether a formal procedure should have been conducted subsequently. The Court of Appeal noted that while the appellant disputed being the driver of the vehicle he did not contest the witness's account of events, and found that it was a situation in which there was no duty to conduct such a procedure. It appears, therefore, that the dispute was not one on which a formal procedure could throw any light. In other words a procedure could not result in any relevant evidence and so the circumstances in *Muradi* fell within the 'no useful purpose' exception.

known to be present, all of whose identities are known, did what was alleged. In such circumstances, there would appear to be no reason, in principle, why the witness should not be shown images of those eight persons and asked what role each played in events. However, the Code makes no provision for such a procedure. In any case, given the difficulties that are likely to be encountered in establishing with any certainty who was in fact present, over-inclusiveness in the extent of the duty to conduct formal procedures is more desirable than the risks associated with the adoption of this alternative form of procedure. It should be noted that the detailed provisions relating to the conduct of video identification procedures and identification parades require the witness to be asked whether the person they saw on the relevant earlier occasion appeared in the images.[120] These words alone will not elicit from the witness the information that is required where what is disputed is participation or the particular role of the suspect rather than his or her presence. The most satisfactory course of action might be to instruct the witness in accordance with the requirements of Code D at the outset of the procedure, and if the witness makes an identification, to then ask a supplementary open-ended question to establish the role played by that person, ie 'What did you see the person that you have identified do on that occasion?'

3.81 Cases decided under previous versions of the Code, in which the need for an identification parade arose 'where a suspect disputes an identification',[121] indicated that if there was a possibility of a witness having mistaken the suspect for some other person who may have been present, an issue of participation was generally to be regarded as synonymous with an issue of identification, and a procedure was required. In *R v McMath*[122] there was a street identification of a group of three suspects immediately after an assault. The evidence of one witness suggested that each of the group was involved. The appellant admitted presence at the scene but denied participation. The Court of Appeal found that 'it was still an identification case for the reason that there were a fair number of people in the vicinity at the time, and so presence would not necessarily be evidence of identification as a participant'. Likewise in *K v DPP*[123] the appellant was alleged to have been one of a group of four involved in a robbery in which demands were made for the victim's watch and mobile telephone. He was detained shortly afterwards and positively identified in the street. It was alleged that it was he who had made the demands. In interview the appellant admitted being one of the group of four but denied participation, asserting that he was an innocent bystander. The court at first instance decided that the issue was one of participation and not identification and there was thus no requirement for a parade. On appeal it was held that the denial created an issue of identification and the formal procedure should have been held.

---

120 Annex A, para 11 (Video identification); Annex B, para 17 (Identification parade).
121 D2.3 (3rd edn).
122 [1997] Crim LR 586, CA.
123 [2003] EWHC 351 (Admin), [2003] 4 *Archbold News* 1.

3.82 If, objectively, there is no possibility that someone else present might have been responsible for the crime there can be no identification issue.[124] That consideration was decisive in *R v Slater,*[125] a case concerning the analogous identification versus participation debate in the context of whether a *Turnbull* direction was appropriate. A man of unusually large size was convicted of inflicting grievous bodily harm in a club. It was held that a necessary prerequisite for an identification issue to arise was the possibility of mistake. By reason of the appellant's wholly unusual size, and the absence of any suggestion that there might have been another person of similar stature present for whom he might conceivably have been mistaken, there was simply no other candidate for the crime and thus no evidential basis for the possibility of mistake.

3.83 *R v Hope, Limburn and Bleasdale*[126] also considered the possibility of mistake in more controversial circumstances. H (the first appellant), a beggar, demanded money from V. V alleged that, having refused, others of similar appearance gathered and H then punched V on the cheek. This prompted a further attack by the others. Following V's initial description H was arrested the next day and he admitted trying to beg from V but denied participation in any violence, stating that he had seen V fighting with another member of the group. Some days later V was shown photographs of the suspects and described their roles. It was argued that both the showing of photographs and the failure to hold an identification parade were breaches of the Code.[127] On appeal it was stated that the Code did not apply to H because there was no disputed identification. It was held, because of H's admission that he was the person who had begged from V, the question whether V was correct to say his assailant was the same person was a matter for the jury. However, it is difficult to sustain the assertion that H did not dispute V's identification of him as his assailant. The logic of the judgment is successful only on the finding that V was right in stating that the beggar and the assailant were one and the same person – the very issue at trial. If he was wrong the mistake may have been exposed by an identification procedure.

3.84 The question of whether the dispute is one of identification may depend upon the nature of the offence and the period over which it takes place. *R v Chen and others*[128] contrasts with the above cases in that the offences of

---

124 See, for example *R v Muhidinz* [2005] EWCA Crim 2464. Here there was some inconsistency in the statements of a police officer and victim of a robbery as to whether there were two or three people present when the police happened to come across the scene of a street robbery moments after it had occurred. Such circumstances, the Court of Appeal said, rendered the case one involving a dispute as to identification, rather than one in which the dispute was merely as to the role, if any, played by the appellant.

125 [1995] 1 Cr App R 584, CA.

126 [1994] Crim LR 118, CA.

127 A certain amount of extrapolation from the report is necessary. The submission that 'the showing of photographs ... was in breach of Code D2.3' (second edition) combines two breaches: Code D2.3 in the failure to hold a parade and D2.18 in respect of showing of photographs.

128 [2001] 5 *Archbold News* 3, CA.

conspiracy to kidnap and falsely imprison took place over several days. The appellants accepted their presence at various times but claimed that they had either not participated in the conspiracy or were subject to duress. The Court of Appeal held that the dispute related to the role of each defendant and their responsibility for particular acts over a protracted period. Code D therefore did not apply at all. The issue was of participation alone.

Availability of suspect

3.85 The right of the police to seek a procedure under D3.13 and the obligation on them to hold one under D3.12 are contingent upon the availability of the suspect to participate. Both provisions are contained within section (b) of Code D entitled 'Cases when the suspect is known and available'. The meaning of 'available' is given by Code D3.4 and is considered further in the context of the procedure selection process at **4.11**. Where it is the police who seek a procedure under D3.13, the suspect has the right to withhold consent to or co-operation in a procedure,[129] and cannot be physically forced to comply or compelled to do so by threats.[130] But the consequence of a refusal may be an alternative procedure, which has fewer safeguards. A refusal to take part in an identification procedure cannot be inferred, however, from the fact that a suspect has merely refused to accede to a police request for an interview.[131]

3.86 Code D3 Section (c) sets out the alternative methods of identification that may deployed in 'Cases when the suspect is known but not available'. Code D3.21 allows the video identification procedure to be adapted in order to use any moving or still images in the possession of the police. If necessary such images may be obtained covertly. Alternatively a group identification may be held covertly. As a last resort Code D3.23 permits a confrontation. The use of these alternative procedures is further discussed in the context of the procedure selection process at **4.25**.

Eyewitnesses: other situations

3.87 Code D does not purport to contemplate every conceivable situation in which a visual identification issue arises, nor to limit the ability of the police to carry out an investigation in a case not envisaged by the Code. However in assessing the fairness of evidence of visual identification falling outside its ambit a court will have regard to the standards it sets. Two cases illustrate situations not specifically governed by Code D. In *R v Folan*[132] the decomposed remains of the defendant's wife were found during demolition work at a hospital, 20 years after she had disappeared. The defendant was arrested and,

---

129 Code D3.17(iv).

130 *R v Jones and Nelson* (1999) *The Times* 21 April, CA; *R v Harley* (unreported) 22 February 2000, CA. However reasonable force may be used to take photographs pursuant to PACE, s 64: PACE, s 117.

131 *R v Johnson* [1996] Crim LR 504.

132 [2003] EWCA Crim 908, (2003) 147 SJ 477.

though he denied it in interview, the investigating officers believed that he had carried out building work at the hospital at the time of her disappearance. His appearance had changed significantly in the meantime and an identification parade would have been pointless. The only contemporary available image of the defendant was an old passport photograph. Though the Code specifically prohibits the showing of photographs of a known suspect, the police showed it to persons with knowledge of the building works two decades earlier and who recognised the defendant as having worked at the hospital at that time. The Court of Appeal held that in this unusual and possibly unique situation the application of the Code was inappropriate. The Court nevertheless went on to state that even though it did not apply, the procedure of showing a series of photographs should have been followed.

3.88 In *R v Jones and others*[133] disorder in a public house left a doorman with serious injuries. Though he recognised those responsible, he could not identify them by name and thus there were no known suspects. A video camera was installed in the public house some weeks later so that, should they return, they would be recorded and might later be identified. They did return and having seen the recording the doorman was able to point out the offenders to the police who knew them. The procedure was not one specifically contemplated by Code D. However, in finding it comparable to street identification or a group identification by means of the showing of a video recording, the Court of Appeal gauged its fairness by analogy with the Code's requirements for those procedures.

PERSONS OTHER THAN EYEWITNESSES: FILMS AND PHOTOGRAPHS OF INCIDENTS

3.89 Substantial growth in the number of public and private CCTV systems in recent years and the consequent increase in the availability of images of those engaged in criminal acts for identification purposes had led to calls for Code D to provide appropriate procedural guidance. It was noted above that Code D3.28 provides for the publication of such images to the world at large through national or local media, for the purposes of 'recognition and tracing suspects'.[134] However, where such images are shown with the intention of obtaining '*evidence* of recognition', ie an identification that for use in subsequent criminal proceedings, the detailed procedures concerning the conditions in which the images are to be viewed, and various recording requirements, that are set out in Part B of section 3 of the Code must be followed (see **5.122–5.127**).

3.90 The distinction is an unsatisfactory one. The use of images is not limited to cases where the suspect's identity is not known. Publication may take place

---

133 (1994) 158 JP 293; (1994) *The Times* 13 January, CA.

134 Code D3.28 provides: 'Nothing in this Code inhibits showing films or photographs to the public through the national or local media, or to police officers for the purposes of recognition and tracing suspects.'

in order to trace a person whose identity is known, in which case there will be no issue concerning the evidential use of any purported identification of an individual from the images. But images of suspects who are not known may be published to the world at large in an attempt to establish the identity of the person depicted in the images, perhaps in the hope (if not the expectation) that any person who recognises that person will be willing to provide testimony to that effect. The use of any purported identification as evidence may often be contemplated prior to publication, but the kind of regulation that Part B of Section 3 of the Code provides will be impracticable in such circumstances. However, where the images are shown to police officers (or other groups who might be expected to know the identity of the offender) the issues of the contemplated use of any purported identification and regulation of the conditions under which they are viewed and recording requirements may be more problematic.

3.91 In *R v Tucker*,[135] a police inspector was asked to examine CCTV images of a person who was suspected of committing a robbery to see whether he recognised him. The Court of Appeal held that safeguards that are now found in Part B of Section 3 of the Code did not apply as the officer was only asked to see if he could recognise the person in the images, and at that time it was not proposed to call him as a witness in any subsequent trial. However, it seems unlikely that the possibility of a police officer who purports to identify the person depicted, subsequently testifying to that effect, will not have at least been contemplated by those who make a request. It is submitted, that whenever images are shown to police officers, it may be readily inferred that, while the intention may not have been to secure evidence of identification, those making the request will have envisaged this as a possibility and that consequently the procedures set out in Part B of Section 3 of the Code ought to be followed. Of course, no question as to whether this course of action should be followed ought to arise where there is a known suspect and images of the offender are shown to those who are familiar with the suspect. For example, where a person found in possession of stolen property has been arrested on suspicion of theft, CCTV images that show the culprit engaged in the act of stealing might be shown to persons to whom the suspect is known to establish that the suspect is the person depicted in the images, stealing the property.

---

[135] [2008] EWCA Crim 3063.

Chapter 4

IDENTIFICATION OFFICER, NOTICE TO SUSPECT AND PROCEDURE SELECTION

IDENTIFICATION OFFICER AND INVESTIGATING OFFICER

4.1 The arrangements for, and conduct of, video identification, identification parades and group identification procedures are the responsibility of 'the identification officer'.[1] A confrontation must also be arranged by an identification officer.[2]

4.2 The identification officer must be an officer not below the rank of Inspector.[3] In order to guard against the possibility or the appearance of witness contamination, the requirement in Code D3.11 that the identification officer must be unconnected with the investigation is of paramount importance. The provision further demands that:

---

1 Code D3.11.

2 Code D3.23.

3 Proposals to change this position were set out in a Home Office consultation paper, *Modernising Police Powers*, published in 2007. It was suggested that identification procedures could be administered by police civilian staff acting as Designated Identification Officers under the Police Reform Act 2002, Sch 4. Although this proposal attracted significant criticism, see e g D Wolchover, 'PACE Code D Review on Video ID Parades: The Innocuous Cloaking the Insidious', (2007) *Archbold News*, 6, 7–9, also D Wolchover, 'VIPER and the Vanadalizing of PACE' (2009) 173 JPN 5. Nevertheless, the Government indicated that it proposed to effect the necessary legislative amendments to enable Chief Constables to appoint Designated Identification Officers. In 2010 the Home Office published tables of proposed legislative changes, which suggested that those amendments would be made as soon as a 'suitable legislative vehicle' could be found; see *PACE Review: Summary of Responses to the Public Consultation on the Review of the Police and Criminal Evidence Act 1984*, (Home Office, March 2010). At the time of writing, the proposals had been taken no further than this.

'... no officer or any other person involved in the investigation of the case against the suspect, beyond the extent required by these procedures, may take any part in these procedures[4] or act as the identification officer.'

4.3 This prohibition has been interpreted strictly. In *R v Gall*[5] the investigating officer, having escorted a witness to a parade, entered the parade room and had the opportunity of speaking to the witness before the procedure began. Although there was no evidence to suggest that anything untoward had taken place, the Court of Appeal held that the officer had taken part in the conduct of the parade and that the evidence of the parade ought to have been excluded. Similarly in *R v Quinn*[6] where there was no evidence of improper conduct, a breach of Code D was found where an investigating officer had conducted a demonstration of an identification parade to witnesses shortly before the actual procedure. The attendance of investigating officers with the victim of a robbery at the police station where a confrontation was held was described as a 'substantial breach' of the Code.[7] By contrast, simply driving the suspect to the police station for a parade has been held not to form part of the arrangements for the parade.[8] Once the procedure has concluded, there is no prohibition against the investigating officer making contact with a witness.[9] Indeed it will often be necessary for the purposes of taking a statement concerning the procedure.

4.4 Code D3.11 prohibits any officer involved in the investigation of the relevant offence from taking any part in a video identification, identification parade or group identification.[10] It does not extend to confrontations, presumably because the mischief with which it is concerned – the possibility that it will be suggested to the witness who they should identify – is an inherent feature of a confrontation. It also follows that the showing of photographs or recordings of incidents may generally be undertaken by officers other than an identification officer, including investigating officers. However, in *R v Ball*[11] the Court of Appeal agreed with the trial judge's conclusion that the involvement of an officer who had played some part in the investigation in a procedure in which CCTV images were shown to other officers amounted to a breach of Code D3.11. The images had been obtained from a shop in which an armed robbery had been committed. The appellants had been charged with the offence. A police inspector who had conveyed one of the appellants to the police station following his arrest then arranged and conducted a number of

---

4 The procedures described earlier in the provision to which the words 'these procedures' appear to relate are those described in D3.5–3.10, namely, a video identification, identification parade and group identification.

5 [1989] Crim LR 745, CA.

6 [1995] 1 Cr App R 480, CA.

7 *R v Ryan* [1992] Crim LR 187, CA.

8 *R v Jones (Terrence)* [1992] Crim LR 356.

9 *R v Walters* [2001] EWCA Crim 1261. There, the witness had dwelt upon the suspect at a parade, asking him to stand, but did not make a positive identification. Shortly afterwards she met the investigating officer and said that she had been confused by the height from which she had made her original observation and was, on reflection, positive.

10 See note 4.

11 [2006] EWCA Crim 1048.

identification procedures in which local beat officers who knew the appellants were invited to view the images to establish whether they (the appellants) were the persons depicted in the images. The reasoning that led to the conclusion that this amounted to a breach of the Code is not fully articulated in the judgment delivered by the Court of Appeal. The procedures conducted were the type envisaged by D3.28. This provision provides that 'nothing in this Code inhibits showing films or photographs . . . to police officers for the purposes of recognition'. However, it also provides that such material 'shall be shown on an individual basis to avoid the possibility of collusion, and as far as possible, the showing shall follow the principles for video identification if the suspect is known.' In this case the suspects were known, they had been arrested and charged with the offence. Consequently, it is submitted that the principles that applied to the conduct of a video identification procedure should have been followed, including the prohibition on investigating officers taking any part in the procedures.

4.5 Though an investigating officer may not participate in the conduct of an identification procedure, collaboration is necessary for arranging one. Consultation is needed for the decision as to the appropriate procedure,[12] to provide the description of the suspect for comparative purposes and other matters such as dates for witness availability.

Identification officer's delegated powers

4.6 In practice the identification officer might not play a hands-on role in the procedures. Much of the work in arranging and conducting identification procedures, in particular the video procedure, is carried out by subordinate officers and police staff.[13] The Code permits this, provided the identification officer is able effectively to supervise the arrangements for and conduct of the procedures and, where necessary, to intervene or be contacted for advice. Police staff 'must have regard to any relevant provisions of the Codes of Practice'.[14] Compliance remains the responsibility of the identification officer. Thus any failure would be a breach committed vicariously by the identification officer.

INFORMATION AND NOTICE TO SUSPECT

4.7 Code D3.17 entitles the suspect to an explanation of the identification procedure before a video identification, identification parade or group identification is arranged. The same information must also be provided in a written notice handed to the suspect. After the suspect has had an opportunity

---

12 Code D3.14.

13 A member of the police staff to whom identification procedures may be delegated must be employed directly by the police authority and under the direction of the Chief Officer or employed by a person contracted to the police authority: Code D2.21.

14 Code D2.22. Their obligation is the same as non-police investigators who are charged with the duty of investigating offenders: PACE, s 67(9). See **2.13**. However, unlike the latter they will not be able to suggest that they do not possess the means to carry out procedures under the Code.

to read it, the suspect should be asked to sign it indicating a willingness to participate in one of the procedures.[15] It is commonplace for the decision to conduct a procedure to be made while the suspect is under arrest at a police station and it is unlikely that an identification officer will be available to deal with the notice. In order to avoid or reduce delay in arranging an identification procedure the identification officer's duty to provide the information and the notice to the suspect may be performed by a custody officer or other officer not involved in the investigation. The officer concerned must then inform the identification officer of the action taken and hand over the signed copy of the notice.[16]

4.8 The requirement to provide the information contained in the Notice to Suspect under Code D3.17 does not apply if the suspect's lack of co-operation prevents it.[17] Moreover the notice, which includes the warning that a covert procedure may take place in the absence of the consent, may pre-emptively be suspended if both the identification officer and officer in charge of the investigation suspect on reasonable grounds that the suspect would otherwise take steps to avoid an identification procedure.[18]

4.9 A specimen of the Notice to Suspect is set out in Appendix C. The information to be supplied is set out below:

(i) the purposes of the video identification, identification parade or group identification;

(ii) their entitlement to free legal advice; see Code C6.5;

[Note – Code C is the Code of Practice for the detention, treatment and questioning of persons by police officers. Code C6.5 requires the custody officer to secure the provision of free legal advice. In many cases following arrest, the suspect will already have instructed a solicitor. Where not, a duty solicitor may be sought. The important point is that the suspect should understand the procedure and be able to take advice and make an informed decision as to whether to consent to an identification procedure and the consequences of failing to do so.]

(iii) the procedures for holding it, including their right to have a solicitor or friend present;

(iv) that they do not have to consent to or co-operate in a video identification, identification parade or group identification;

(v) that if they do not consent to, and co-operate in a video identification, identification parade or group identification, their refusal may be given in

---

15 Code D3.18.

16 Code D3.19 and Note for Guidance 3C.

17 Code D3.24.

18 Code D3.20. See **4.29**.

evidence in any subsequent trial[19] and police may proceed covertly without their consent or make other arrangements to test whether a witness can identify them, see D3.21;[20]

(vi) whether, for the purposes of the video identification procedure, images of them have previously been obtained, see D3.20, and if so, that they may co-operate in providing further, suitable images to be used instead;

(vii) if appropriate the special arrangements for juveniles;

(viii) if appropriate the special arrangements for mentally disordered or otherwise mentally vulnerable people;

(ix) that if they significantly alter their appearance between being offered an identification procedure and any attempt to hold an identification procedure, this may be given in evidence if the case comes to trial,[21] and the identification officer may then consider other forms of identification, see D3.21[22] and Note 3C;

[Note – Code D3.21 refers to the use of alternative methods, including covertly obtained images. Note for guidance 3C emphasises the importance of issuing the warning at the earliest opportunity and that it may be done by an officer other than the identification officer in order to avoid delay.]

(x) that a moving image or photograph may be taken of them when they attend for any identification procedure;

(xi) whether, before their identity became known, the witness was shown photographs, a computerised or artist's composite likeness or similar likeness or image by the police, see Note 3B;

[Note – The note for guidance 3B places a responsibility on the officer in charge of the investigation to ensure that the identification officer is apprised of any such showing.]

(xii) that if they change their appearance before an identification parade, it may not be practicable to arrange one on the day or subsequently and, because of the appearance change, the identification officer may consider alternative methods of identification, see Note 3C;

[Note – see (ix) above.]

---

19 As to the admissibility of a failure to consent or co-operate in an identification procedure, see **10.26**.

20 The failure to consent or co-operate is tantamount to being unavailable under Code D3.21. See **4.13**.

21 As to the admissibility of a failure to consent or co-operate in an identification procedure, see **10.28**.

22 The significant alteration in appearance is tantamount to being unavailable under Code D3.21. See **4.14**.

(xiii) that they or their solicitor will be provided with details of the description of them as first given by any witnesses who are to attend the video identification, identification parade, group identification or confrontation, see paragraph 3.1.

[Note – Paragraph 3.1 demands a first description of the offender to be taken from the witness.]

PROCEDURE SELECTION

4.10 When the identity of a suspect is known,[23] Code D3 makes the distinction between those who are 'available' to participate in an identification procedure, D3(b), and those who are not available, D3(c). The choice of procedure is circumscribed by the suspect's availability. Video identification, identification parades or a group identification may be used if the suspect is known and available. Alternative and covert procedures may be adopted if the suspect is known but not available.

SUSPECT 'AVAILABLE'

4.11 Availability is defined in D3.4:[24]

> 'A suspect being "available" means they are immediately available or will be within a reasonably short time and are willing to take effective part in at least one of the following which it is practicable to arrange
>
> - video identification;
> - identification parade; or
> - group identification.'

4.12 The first element of the definition, physical availability immediately or within a reasonably short time must be taken as meaning a period beginning with the decision to hold the procedure. This will usually occur on the suspect becoming known and a witness purporting to be able to identify the perpetrator, though the time to be allowed will vary according to the circumstances of the particular offence and police inquiry. The extent to which delay might prejudice the investigation may be an important factor as will the reasons for the suspect's unavailability. An escapee will be considered to be unavailable. Conversely, where a suspect's arrest was likely to be imminent he might be regarded as available.[25]

4.13 The second element of availability, a willingness to take an effective part, is a refinement of the Code which makes clear that the suspect who is physically available but whose conduct frustrates the procedure is deemed unavailable.

---

23 See **3.12**.

24 In the third edition of the Code this was merely a Note for Guidance: 2E.

25 *R v Kitchen* [1994] Crim LR 684, CA.

The identification procedures depend to a large extent upon the willingness of the suspect to submit to the procedure. A suspect has the right to withhold consent to, or co-operation in a procedure[26] and cannot be physically forced to comply or compelled to do so by threats.[27]

4.14 A suspect's decision not to participate in an identification is not irrevocable, but a substantial delay between an initial refusal and a subsequent change of heart may lead to the suspect's request to participate in the type of procedure to which he or she was initially offered being declined. In *R v Nolan*,[28] for example, the appellant had been arrested for assault, and having taken legal advice, declined to answer any questions put to her in a police interview, and refused to participate in a video identification procedure. The police made arrangements for an identification procedure to be conducted using appropriate still images. Around 4 weeks after the initial refusal, the appellant's legal representative was provided with an opportunity to view the still images that had been selected for the procedure. Objection was made to these images and the appellant requested a video identification procedure using moving images. The position of the identification officer was that unless there were good grounds for the initial refusal to participate in a video identification he would not revert to the use of that procedure. A procedure using still images was conducted some 3 weeks later. The Court of Appeal, noting that 4 months had elapsed since the assault, considered the use of still images to be fair given the late stage at which the appellant had indicated a willingness to co-operate in a procedure using moving images. The Court observed, however, that:

> 'the Code of Practice was not provided for this situation and we consider, in appropriate circumstances, the inspector running the procedure should consider carefully any timely and clearly communicated change of mind on the part of the suspect, resulting in an agreement by him or her to co-operate. If it is still reasonably possible to organise a fair video/moving image identification procedure without materially endangering the willingness of the witness to co-operate or otherwise prejudicing the identification procedure, the inspector should consider whether fairness dictates that he should revert to a video/moving image identification. Whether or not he should accede to a request/change of mind of this kind will always depend on the circumstances of the case.'[29]

4.15 A suspect's change in appearance after the time of the witness's observation may nullify the purpose of an identification procedure. If the change in appearance is significant and is effected between the offer of an identification procedure and an attempt to hold one, the identification officer may then consider other forms of identification as permitted when the suspect is not available.[30] Similarly alternatives may be considered if, before an identification parade, a change in appearance (though not necessarily

---

26 D3.17(iv).

27 *R v Jones and Nelson* (1999) *The Times* 21 April, CA; *R v Harley* 22 February 2000 (unreported), CA.

28 [2005] EWCA Crim 3661.

29 At [34].

30 Code D3.17(ix).

significant) renders it impracticable to hold one on the day arranged or thereafter.[31] Some changes in appearance, such as a short haircut, may be remediable by use of video images of volunteers with short hair. Others, so substantial that the witness is unlikely to be able to recognise the suspect, may demand an alternative such as the use of pre-existing images of the suspect.

4.16 The suspect's willingness to take an effective part must relate to at least one of the procedures which it is practicable to arrange. In considering which, reference must be made to the selection criteria in Code D3.14–D3.16, set out at **4.18**. A suspect who is willing only to co-operate with a procedure which is unsuitable or impracticable to arrange will not be considered available.

SUSPECT KNOWN AND AVAILABLE: PROCEDURE HIERARCHY

4.17 Video identification is now the preferred procedure under the current edition of Code D. The advance in technology has resulted in the use of the video procedure in the overwhelming majority of cases. Indeed for some police forces the identification parade is a creature now almost extinct. By comparison with parades the advantages of video identification are the speed and relative ease with which they can be arranged,[32] the facility for finding comparable 'volunteers' from a database and a farewell to aborted procedures when a suspect did not attend. It has also been suggested that witnesses may be less prone to anxiety. Their principal disadvantage is the limitation of the images captured on video. They are of head and shoulders only and allow no movement (other than the turning of the head from side to side) that occasionally a witness might desire to observe at a parade.[33]

4.18 The hierarchy of procedure in 'cases where the suspect is known and available' is set out in Code D3.14 to D3.16:

> D3.14 If, because of paragraph 3.12, an identification procedure is to be held, the suspect shall initially be offered a video identification unless:
>
> (a) a video identification is not practicable; or
> (b) an identification parade is both practicable and more suitable than a video identification; or

---

31 Code D3.17(xii).

32 Most police forces have the ability to respond to the need for a video identification with great rapidity. For example the Metropolitan Police have a mobile unit that in an urgent case can, in the same day, attend a police station in which an arrested person has been detained, set up its equipment and video the suspect, compile a line up from its database and confirm its content with the suspect or solicitor and then attend the witness's home or a hospital to conduct the procedure.

33 On the advantages of video procedures over corporeal procedures generally, see Y Tinsley, 'Even Better Than the Real Thing: The Case for Reform of Identification Procedures', (2001) 5 *International Journal of Evidence and Proof* 99. See also, N Brace et al, 'Eyewitness identification procedures and stress: a comparison of live and video identification procedures' (2009) 11 *International Journal of Police Science & Management* 183.

(c) paragraph 3.16 applies.[34]

The identification officer and the officer in charge of the investigation shall consult each other to determine which option is to be offered. An identification parade may not be practicable because of factors relating to the witnesses, such as their number, state of health, availability and travelling requirements. A video identification would normally be more suitable if it could be arranged and completed sooner than an identification parade.

D3.15 A suspect who refuses the identification procedure first offered shall be asked to state their reason for refusing and may get advice from their solicitor and/or if present, their appropriate adult. The suspect, solicitor and/or appropriate adult shall be allowed to make representations about why another procedure should be used. A record should be made of the reasons for refusal and any representations made. After considering any reasons given, and representations made, the identification officer shall, if appropriate, arrange for the suspect to be offered an alternative which the officer considers suitable and practicable. If the officer decides it is not suitable and practicable to offer an alternative procedure, the reasons for that decision shall be recorded.

D3.16 A group identification may initially be offered if the officer in charge of the investigation considers it is more suitable than a video identification or an identification parade and the identification officer considers it practicable to arrange.'

4.19 The initial part of Code D3.14 invokes the selection process where a procedure 'shall be held' under Code D3.12, but omits reference to its application where a procedure is to be held under Code D3.13 'if the officer in charge of the investigation considers it would be useful'. It is submitted that this should be regarded as a drafting error and that the scheme of Code D3.14 should be applied in both cases to avoid the anomalous situation in which the selection process could be ignored if the procedure was not mandatory.[35]

4.20 The Code requires consultation between the identification and investigating officers in deciding 'which option is to be offered'. The decision is circumscribed by the demand for a video identification to be offered first, subject to its practicability. Only if not practicable, or a parade is both practicable and more suitable, or a group identification is more suitable and is practicable, will an alternative be offered. If a video identification is not practicable, there is no requirement for the identification to consider a parade before resorting to a group identification.[36]

---

34 Group identification more satisfactory – see below.

35 That the selection process should apply in both situations is apparent from the modifications to the third edition of the Code. In that, both the mandatory and discretionary procedure were combined into one paragraph, Code D2.14. In removing the discretionary procedure to its own paragraph the draftsman appears to have forgotten to widen the scope of the selection scheme to both paragraphs.

36 *R v Stott* [2004] EWCA Crim 615.

4.21 Should a suspect seek to persuade the identification officer that a particular identification procedure is preferable to the one first offered, such representations must be considered by the identification officer. If the suspect refuses the procedure first offered the identification officer should ask for the reason and consider the validity of any ground for objection. The basis for it may be a matter outside the knowledge of the identification officer and the officer involved in the investigation. If the reasons for the refusal or preference are justified the identification officer should offer an alternative provided if it is suitable and practicable. The failure to do so where there is no impediment will be a breach of the Code.[37] However, the refusal to participate in a suitable and practicable procedure will render the suspect liable to be treated as if not available and to the use of alternative measures under D3.21.[38]

4.22 Promptness of procedure is an important consideration. D3.11 demands that a procedure is held as soon as practicable in the interests of fairness to suspects and witnesses. D3.14 also indicates video identification to be preferable to a parade if achievable sooner[39] and witnesses' difficulties such as their number, health, availability and travel can be considered when assessing the practicability of a parade. It is difficult to conceive of many situations in which a parade could be organised more quickly and with less inconvenience to witnesses than a video identification.

4.23 The practicability of a video identification or an identification parade is most likely to be affected by any difficulty in assembling a gallery of foils who resemble the suspect. The requirement of resemblance is considered further in the next chapter, which deals with the conduct of the procedures. In most cases the video database of many thousands of volunteers and the facility for searching through it by specified feature will be infinitely more practicable than securing the physical presence appropriate foils.[40] It is particularly advantageous where, perhaps outside a metropolitan area, there are few or no volunteers of the suspect's ethnic background. The greatest difficulty is generally encountered with a suspect of distinctive appearance. Height and build are of less importance in video identification because generally the images will comprise head and shoulders. The use of hats to conceal distinctive hair or the provision of spectacles to parade volunteers have been techniques often used in eliminating a suspect's outstanding appearance. The same effect has been achievable in video identification by the expedient of recording videos of the same volunteer two of three times in various guises. More problematic is the concealment of a facial scar which, in a parade, is customarily performed by use of a plaster. A comparable effect can be achieved by pixillation of the

---

37 *R v Gasper* [2002] EWCA Crim 1764, CA.

38 D3.17(v).

39 The preference for a video identification is already stated in the hierarchy. This part of D3.14 is an incongruous hangover from the modifications to the third edition of Code D in which video identification and parade were ranked equally.

40 There is a likelihood that, with the increased use of video and the infrequent use of parade volunteers, the pool of parade volunteers will become too limited for the assembly of an effective parade.

video, though this technique is in its infancy. There will thus remain cases in which an identification parade will be a more suitable means of eliminating a distinctive feature of a suspect's appearance. A parade may also be more suitable where it is thought that sight of the suspect's overall appearance is important or that the witness may wish to see a certain movement. Even if more suitable, significant delay caused by difficulties in assembling volunteers of similar appearance can render a parade impracticable.[41] However, the mere fact that insufficient volunteers are available on the day of an arranged parade does not of itself render a parade on another day impracticable.[42]

4.24 Code D3.14(c) and D3.16 permit a group identification to be offered initially, subject to practicability, instead of a video identification or identification parade if the officer in charge of the investigation considers it more suitable than those procedures. That decision is subject to the consultation with the identification officer required by D3.14. A decision to favour a group identification might be appropriate if the posture or gait may be an important aid to a witness's identification. Practicability might depend upon the need for a location with a sufficient number of people of similar appearance.[43]

SUSPECT KNOWN BUT NOT AVAILABLE: ALTERNATIVE AND COVERT PROCEDURES

4.25 The alternative procedures are set out in Code D3, section (c) 'Cases when the suspect is known but not available'. Availability is considered at paragraphs 4.10 to 4.14 above. Note for Guidance 3D suggests the use of alternative methods of identification if the suspect deliberately delays or frustrates the arrangements for obtaining identification evidence or refuses or fails to take part in a procedure.

4.26 D3.21 provides that when a suspect is known but not available or has ceased to be available a video identification procedure may be adapted:

> 'If necessary, the identification officer may follow the video identification procedures but using still images. Any suitable moving or still images may be used and these may be obtained covertly if necessary. Alternatively the identification officer may make arrangements for a group identification.'

4.27 As a last resort Code D3.23 provides that:

> 'The identification officer may arrange for the suspect to be confronted by the witness if none of the options referred to in paragraphs 3.5 to 3.10[44] or 3.21 are practicable.'

---

41 *R v Jamel* [1993] Crim LR 52, CA.

42 *R v Penny* 94 Cr App R 345, [1992] Crim LR 184, CA.

43 See **5.93**.

44 Video, parade and group identification.

4.28 A procedure without the suspect's consent might make use of pre-existing images such as photographs taken from criminal records or seized from the suspect's address. Alternatively photographs taken of a suspect while detained at a police station under PACE, s 64A can be used,[45] as might a recording taken from the custody suite of a police station. Code D3.21 also permits the police to obtain images covertly,[46] though such activity should be strictly limited to that necessary to test the ability of the witness to make an identification.[47]

4.29 Covert action may be taken pre-emptively if both the identification officer and the officer in charge of the investigation suspect on reasonable grounds that the suspect would otherwise take steps to avoid an identification procedure. In that situation the identification officer may arrange for images of the suspect suitable for use in a video identification procedure to be obtained before giving the information and notice. If that happens the suspect must then be allowed the opportunity of consenting by providing new images to be used instead.[48] As to the admissibility of covert procedures, see **10.57**.

4.30 The Code also permits the use of a covertly conducted group identification if the suspect is unavailable or has not consented or co-operated.[49] Provided other persons of similar appearance are likely to be present, this method might be appropriate where, for example, the suspect is known to make the same journey each day or frequent the same public house. Finally a confrontation may be used but only if all other procedures including the covert procedures discussed above are not practicable. Clearly a confrontation is the least desirable form of procedure. It provides no real test of the ability to recognise a person seen earlier and the witness will know that the person confronted is already suspected by the police.

DOCUMENTATION

4.31 The documentation of decisions taken by police officers and the responses and representations by suspects is an important part of the identification procedure. It enables a court to monitor compliance with the Code where an issue arises. Code D3.18 requires the identification officer to invite the suspect to sign a second copy of the Notice to Suspect indicating a willingness to co-operate with the making of a video or taking part in an identification parade or group identification. A suspect's reasons for refusing the procedure first offered together with representations for an alternative procedure must be recorded, as must any reasons why the alternative is not suitable or practicable.[50]

---

45 PACE, s 64A(4)(a) specifically permits their use for the investigation of an offence. See **6.15**.
46 For example in *Perry v UK* [2003] Crim LR 281, ECtHR.
47 Code D3.22.
48 Code D3.20.
49 Code D3.21 and Annex C.2.
50 Code D3.15. See Part 2 of the pro-forma Notice to Suspects in Appendix C.

4.32 Code D3.26 requires the identification officer to make a written record of the reasons for the impracticability of a video identification or identification parade. The reasons must also be explained to the suspect. This record and explanation are expressed as requirements if the suspect has requested either of the procedures. However, since it is the Code which formulates the necessity for a procedure and not the request of a suspect, there is no obvious reason why it should be so limited. Equally it would seem appropriate to record and explain a decision that a group identification is more suitable than either a video or parade identification.

4.33 Code D3.27 requires that a written record is made of a suspect's failure or refusal to co-operate in a video identification, identification parade or group identification and, if applicable, of the grounds for obtaining images of the suspect before giving the Notice to Suspect under Code D3.20. Best practice and a caution against a complaint of later rationalisation suggest a contemporary record of all significant decisions should be made.

Chapter 5

CONDUCT OF VISUAL IDENTIFICATION PROCEDURES

INTRODUCTION

5.1 This chapter concerns the conduct of each of the identification procedures governed by Code D. In seeking to secure a fair and valid test of reliability, the principles of each are broadly similar and many of the specific provisions are either identical or adaptations. Much of the case law is concentrated upon identification parades, though the reasoning may be equally applicable to other procedures. In particular the procedure for video identification contains a number of parallel provisions whose interpretation and application can be understood by reference to the corresponding provisions concerning identification parades.

5.2 The ubiquitous phrase 'if practicable' and a variety of exceptions allow a degree of flexibility to accommodate the circumstances of each situation. That flexibility apart, there should be strict adherence to the requirements of the Code. The observations of the Lord Chief Justice in *R v Quinn*[1] should be noted:

> 'We wish to emphasise that where a detailed regime is laid down in a statutory Code, it is not for police either at any one or more police stations to substitute their own procedure and their own rules for that which is laid down … As long as there is a statutory Code, it is there to be observed and not varied at will.'

Whether a failure to adhere to Code D will taint a positive identification and compromise its admissibility will depend upon the court's view of its fairness under PACE, s 78.[2]

5.3 Code D does not prescribe the stage of proceedings at which an identification procedure can or should be held, rather Code D3.11 imposes a duty, in the interest of fairness to suspects and witnesses, to conduct one 'as soon as practicable'. In most cases it forms part of the pre-charge investigation. Usually it is preceded by an interview in which the suspect has denied involvement or made no admissions. If selected at an identification procedure before charge, a further interview is normally held to give the suspect the opportunity to comment on the positive identification. It is by no means unusual for a procedure to be held after charge, particularly where a witness has only become known at that stage.

5.4 Though not an identification procedure, the taking of a first description is of such integral importance to the procedures to warrant separate consideration.

FIRST DESCRIPTION

5.5 The need, at an early stage, to obtain from a witness a description of the person observed is one of the most important aspects of Code D. Quite apart from the benefit to an investigating officer in tracing the perpetrator of the crime, it may afford some protection against misidentification where a defendant does not match the description first given. It provides a:

> '… yardstick for testing the accuracy of any subsequent identification and it precludes the recording in a later witness statement of a description which, may and in reality almost certainly would be based upon (or coloured by) the appearance of the suspect at the time of the identification.'[3]

---

1 [1995] 1 Cr App R 480, CA.

2 See **10.36**.

3 *R v Hickin* [1996] Crim LR 584, CA; similar observations were made in *H v DPP* [2007] EWHC 2192 (Admin), at [14].

5.6 For those reasons the description should be as full as circumstances permit. Code D3.1 demands that:

> 'A record shall be made of the suspect's description as first given by a potential witness. This record must:
>
> (a) be made and kept in a form which enables details of that description to be accurately produced from it, in a visible and legible form, which can be given to the suspect or the suspect's solicitor in accordance with this Code; and
> (b) unless otherwise specified, be made before the witness takes part in any identification procedures under paragraphs 3.5 to 3.10, 3.21 or 3.23.'[4]

5.7 Though not included in this provision, there is no reason in principle why the taking of a first description is any less important where a witness is to be shown photographs under Code D3.3. That this should happen seems to be assumed by Annex E.2 to Code D,[5] which requires the supervising officer to 'confirm the first description of the suspect given by the witness' before the procedure begins. The requirement under Code D3.2(a) to record a first description in street identification cases is limited by practicability in the prevailing situation. This is further considered at **5.19**.

5.8 A record of first description may initially be taken by a police officer in a notebook; sometimes it may be conveyed by radio message and recorded on a police computer system. Usually, it will also be recorded in a crime report.

5.9 Code D3.1 also states that:

> 'A copy of the record shall where practicable, be given to the suspect or their solicitor before any procedures under paragraphs 3.5 to 3.10, 3.21 or 3.23 are carried out.'

The need to supply details of the first description before the procedure is reinforced by the Notice to Suspect requirements in Code D3.17(xiii)[6] and in the rules for each procedure.[7] This enables a suspect to make an informed choice as to whether to consent to an identification procedure and to make representations as to its arrangements and composition. The details of the description to be supplied have been held not to include the circumstances of the observation, such as distance and angle of view.[8]

---

4 These Code D paragraphs are references to video identification, identification parade, group identification, and confrontation.

5 See **5.112** for Annex E.

6 See **4.9**.

7 Street identification: Code D3.2(a); video identification: Annex A.8. Identification parade: Annex B.3; group identification: Annex C.11; confrontation: Annex D.2.

8 *R v Nolan* [2002] EWCA Crim 464.

STREET IDENTIFICATION

5.10 An illustration of a street identification is provided by *R v Brown*.[9] In the immediate aftermath of a robbery the victim was taken in a police vehicle on a tour of nearby streets and, after 5 or 10 minutes, made a positive identification of the appellant who was walking along the street. The procedure may also be used where, as in *Coulman v DPP*,[10] the defendant had already been detained by police when the witnesses attended and identified him. This form of street identification is analogous to a confrontation, an inherently unreliable guide because it suggests the identity of the offender. The case of *R v Popat*[11] provides a more refined example of the use of a street identification. There, a woman who had been attacked subsequently saw her assailant in the same vicinity. Believing that the suspect might return to the vicinity on a later occasion, she kept observation in that area with a police officer over a number of days. Eventually the person she recognised as her assailant came into view and was arrested. In each of these situations, once an identification is made a video identification procedure may then be required if the person identified disputes being the person seen by the witness.[12]

5.11 Code D3.2 sanctions this form of investigation in the following way:

> 'In cases when the suspect's identity is not known, a witness may be taken to a particular neighbourhood or place to see whether they can identify the person they saw.'

Once the suspect is known (that is, there is sufficient information to justify an arrest) a street identification is prohibited and the formal procedures must be followed.[13]

5.12 The paramount consideration of the police shortly after a crime will be a search for the suspect. It may be the only chance of apprehension or identification. The Code understandably does not prescribe a precise formula for the difficult situation immediately following a crime and courts may be slow to challenge tactical policing decisions.[14] Nevertheless a tension exists between the imperative of crime detection and the frailties of a street identification. Lacking the safeguards of the formal methods, the inherent dangers affecting their integrity and reliability include:

(1) the absence of a (thorough) first description if there is no opportunity to take one;

---

9 [1991] Crim LR 368, CA.

10 [1997] COD 91, QBD.

11 [1998] 2 Cr App R 208, CA. Note that the decision itself is no longer good law.

12 Code D3.12. See **3.38**.

13 Code D3.2(d) and 3.4. See **3.13** for the definition of 'known suspect' and **3.23** for the prohibition.

14 *R v Vaughan* (unreported) 30 April 1997, CA, the Court stated that 'we would be reluctant to criticise officers who had to take a decision on the spot in the knowledge that whatever they did they were likely to be criticised by lawyers on one side or the other for not doing the opposite.'

(2) a witness's assured description in a statement or at trial, or any later formal identification, may in fact be based upon the view of a suspect when making the street identification rather than at the time of the offence;

(3) the identification may be unconsciously influenced by the fact that a person has been detained by a police officer;

(4) the identification may be influenced by the fact that the witness's attention was drawn to a person;

(5) the identification may be influenced by information from another source such as a second witness making a positive identification or by some detail of overheard police conversation;

(6) the witness may be inclined to select the first person who bears a passing resemblance to the person actually seen, particularly if it appears there are few or no other potential candidates walking the street at that time;

(7) the distance and lighting and other aspects of the street identification may be less than ideal;

(8) the recording and consequential accuracy of the words and gestures (eg, pointing) of the identification may be open to doubt;

(9) the suspect does not have the opportunity of legal representation to ensure fairness.

5.13 The Code recognises the criticisms of the fairness of the ad hoc nature of street procedures and seeks to mitigate them by requiring the police to have regard to the principles of the formal procedures. Code D3.2 states that:

> 'Although the number, age, sex, race, general description and style of clothing of other people present at the location and the way in which any identification is made cannot be controlled, the principles applicable to the formal procedures under paragraphs 3.5 to 3.10[15] shall be followed as far as practicable.'

5.14 Code D3.2 then sets out examples of the practices that would normally be expected of police officers conducting a street identification, subject to practicability. These are described below.

First description

5.15 The requirement of Code D3.1(a) to record the witness's first description may not always be appropriate very shortly after the commission of an offence. It is therefore qualified by the constraints of practicability.

---

15 Video identification, identification parade and group identification.

> '3.2(a)where it is practicable to do so, a record should be made of the witness's description of the suspect, as in paragraph 3.1(a), before asking the witness to make an identification.'

5.16 This is often the most important safeguard against mistaken street identification. It serves as a comparison with the actual appearance of the suspect, when identified. It was described as 'a very valuable prerequisite' in *R v Hickin*[16] where it was recognised that the failure to take descriptions before street identifications were conducted created difficulties in determining whether descriptions may have been based upon observations at the time of identification rather than at the time of the offence. The risk of this happening, even quite subconsciously, may be heightened if the observation at the time of the offence is for a short period by a frightened victim or an observer at some distance; and where by contrast the later identification provides a better opportunity to view and digest descriptive information about a person who is perhaps static, closer, or in better lighting. A first description may also protect against the risk of suggestion when a suspect has been detained by police especially if the detainee is, in effect, the sole candidate for identification.

5.17 In *R v Vaughan*,[17] the failure to make a record of first description led to the exclusion of the street identification. It was held that:

> 'This provision of the Code is not mere bureaucracy: it affords the best safeguard that has so far been devised against the possibility of auto suggestion when officers on the spot reasonably judge a confrontation to be needed in order to firm up suspicion to the point required for an arrest.'

5.18 In that case the suspect for a robbery was arrested, principally on the basis of a witness's description of a vehicle into which he had apparently fled. The witness was conveyed to the scene. Although he was told that the assailant might or might not be there:

> '… what he was unavoidably shown was the appellant, a young black man, standing between two police officers near a red Datsun Sunny bearing the number which Mr Ali [the witness] had already written down shortly before. That in these circumstances he identified the appellant as the culprit was hardly surprising.'

While not criticising the decision to hold this confrontation, the Court of Appeal recognised its evidential frailty and held that the evidence should have been excluded because the precaution of a record of the witness's pre-identification description was not available.

5.19 Unless it can be shown to have been impracticable to have taken a first description the failure to take one before identification will be a breach of the

---

16 [1996] Crim LR 584, CA.

17 (unreported) 30 April 1997, CA. Also, *R (on the application of Pierre Wellington) v DPP* [2007] EWHC 1061 (Admin), at [21]: 'The breach of paragraph 3.1 which occurred in this case is certainly not a technicality. It is a material matter which weighs against the prosecution . . ..'

Code.[18] However, courts will recognise the realities of what may be 'a volatile situation [in which] the primary need is to identify suspects before they disperse'[19] and where it is thus not practicable to record a description. In *R v Crowe*,[20] where police were summoned to a public house shortly after an assault, the Court of Appeal found that it would have been an affront to common sense to have taken a description during which time the suspect may have made good his escape. In some circumstances, even if the making of a record is impracticable, it will be possible to obtain an oral description which can passed over a police radio or recorded after the identification. In *R v Duggan*[21] the admitted failure to take a first description was compensated for by the description available from the 999 call made by the victim which was an 'incontrovertible record that could carry the greatest weight'. Thus the breach caused no prejudice.[22]

Avoidance of suggestion

5.20 Code D3.2(b) states:

> '... care must be taken not to direct the witness's attention to any individual unless, taking into account all the circumstances, this cannot be avoided. However, this does not prevent a witness being asked to look carefully at the people around at the time or to look towards a group or in a particular direction, if this appears necessary to make sure that the witness does not overlook a possible suspect simply because the witness is looking in the opposite direction and also to enable the witness to make comparisons between any suspect and others who are in the area.'

The importance of this guidance is demonstrated by the accompanying warning in the Notes for Guidance 3F(a) that the admissibility and value of any street identification may be compromised if, before a person is identified, the witness's attention is specifically drawn to that person.

5.21 The witness's attention may be unavoidably drawn to a suspect who is in the company of a police officer, as in *R v Vaughan*.[23] Indeed in some circumstances it may not be possible to conduct a street identification without drawing the witness's attention to certain individuals. In *R v North*,[24] following a robbery late in the evening, a police dog led officers to an unlit park where a

---

18 *Ryan v DPP* (unreported) 10 October 2000, DC; *Marsh v DPP* [2006] EWHC 1525 (Admin), [2007] Crim LR 162.

19 *R v McMath* [1997] Crim LR 586, CA.

20 (Unreported) 6 March 1998, CA. See also *R v El Hannachi and others* [1998] 2 Cr App R 226, CA, where a first description was held to be impracticable due to the urgency of the situation. It was night time and the defendants were departing the scene.

21 (Unreported) 16 June 1998, CA.

22 See also *R v Preddie* [2011] EWCA Crim 312, in which the Court of Appeal found the failure of officers who attended the scene to take a description from the victim to be a breach of the Code, notwithstanding that a 'very brief description' had been recorded on the police computer system by the operator who received the emergency call made by the victim.

23 (Unreported) 30 April 1997, CA. See **5.18**.

24 [2006] EWCA Crim 915.

number of youths were found. The members of the group were escorted out of the park individually and positioned under a street light to enable the victim to see them. The Court of Appeal found that the procedure adopted did not breach Code D3.2, noting that 'if it were otherwise the obvious investigatory step would be denied the officers and it is difficult to see what then would have been open to them.'[25] However, in the absence of such circumstances, pointing to a suspect and asking a witness 'is that the person' is not permissible.[26] In *R v Brizey*[27] the effect of a police officer's words was held merely to have widened the ambit of the victim's attention. Nevertheless the danger of suggestion was recognised in that case when it was said that:

> 'What the police must obviously not do, and this is only, as indeed is much of this Code, a combination of common sense and fairness, is having themselves seen somebody, to say: 'what about him?' Or 'don't you think that looks like the chap you described?' or words to that effect ... Clearly anything which ... really amounts to asking the equivalent of a leading question is to be deprecated.'

5.22 The duty to avoid drawing a witness's attention to particular individuals also extends to procedures that are analogous to street identification. In *R v Smith (Steven Anthony)*,[28] one of a number of police officers attending the scene of an armed robbery conducted a search of the locality. Having found no-one who matched the description provided by the victim, the officer made enquiries with the owners of nearby shops, one of whom stated that someone fitting that description had been in his shop shortly before the robbery. After the officer and the shop reviewed footage from the shop's CCTV system, the witness attended the shop to view the tape, whereupon it was fast-forwarded and she was shown only the section of footage in which the appellant appeared. The Court of Appeal, while acknowledging the difficulties faced by the police in such circumstances, concluded that the witness's identification of the appellant in the CCTV footage was 'highly unsatisfactory'. The manner in which the witness had been invited to view the footage was such as to unnecessarily direct her attention to the appellant in circumstances in which it had been possible to avoid doing so. The guidance in paragraph D3.2(b), that care ought to be taken not to direct the witness's attention to any individual, ought to have been followed. This could have been achieved by inviting the witness to see people who appeared in the footage other than the appellant. The Court observed that the suggestiveness of the procedure had been exacerbated by the fact that the witness had been informed by the officer prior to her identification of the appellant, that footage had been found of a person matching the description that she had provided. Although no reference is made to paragraph D3.28 in the judgment, it should be noted that this provision requires the principles set out in Annex E to be followed (as far as it is possible to do so) when images of suspects who are not known are shown to potential witnesses (see **5.112–5.120**).

---

25 At [14].

26 The danger was understood a century ago in *R v Chapman* [1911] 7 Crim App R 53, CCA.

27 (Unreported) 10 March 1994, CA.

28 [2005] EWCA Crim 3375.

More than one witness

5.23 Code D3.2(c) states:

> '... where there is more than one witness, every effort should be made to keep them separate and witnesses should be taken to see whether they can identify a person independently.'

5.24 This guideline codifies previously expressed concerns that one witness may influence or fortify another's identification.[29] It must be read subject to D3.2(d), that a positive identification by one witness precludes another street identification in respect of a known suspect.[30] The separation of witnesses will enable police to prevent a further street identification occurring. It may also serve to avoid contamination of a later identification procedure by another witness. The practicability of chaperoning witnesses separately will depend upon the number of witnesses, police officers and vehicles, and the urgency of the need to identify suspects before they disperse.[31]

No second street identification

5.25 Code D3.2(d) states:

> '... once there is sufficient information to justify the arrest of a particular individual for suspected involvement in the offence, eg, after a witness makes a positive identification, the provisions set out from paragraph 3.4 onwards[32] shall apply for any other witnesses in relation to that individual ...'

5.26 This provision restates the prohibition on a street identification procedure for a known suspect[33] with the emphasis on the prevention of successive street identifications taking place after a first positive street identification.[34] In *R v Fuller*[35] a suspect was identified by a witness and again

---

29 *R v Hickin* [1996] Crim LR 584, CA; *R v McMath* [1997] Crim LR 586, CA.

30 See **5.25**.

31 'In an ideal world, there would only be one potential witness in each car to preserve the integrity of each and every identification': *R v McMath* [1997] Crim LR 586, CA.

32 Relating to cases when the suspect is known.

33 See Code D3.4, and **3.13** for the definition of a 'known suspect'. See also **3.23** for the prohibition on the street identification of known suspects.

34 In *B v DPP* [2006] EWHC 660 (Admin), the witness was driven, in a police vehicle, past a group of people standing at a bus stop and identified the appellant. At the end of the street the police turned the vehicle around and drove back to the bus stop where the witness again identified the appellant who was this time in the company of police officers. The appellant submitted that when he was identified on the first occasion he became a known suspect and the 'second' street identification of him by the witness was a breach of the Code's requirement to conduct a formal procedure. Rejecting this submission, the Divisional Court took the view that as the witness had the group in his sight at all times, the incident comprised a single transaction, the second identification being merely a confirmation of the first rather than a second street identification.

35 (Unreported) 22 May 2000, CA and see *R v Hickin* [1996] Crim LR 584, CA, and the commentary in *R v Malashev* [1997] Crim LR 587, CA.

shortly afterwards by a second. It was held that the suspect ought to have been arrested after the first identification whereupon a formal procedure should have been conducted for the second witness.

Record of witness's observations

5.27 Code D3.2(e) states:

> '... the officer or police staff accompanying the witness must record, in their pocket book, the action taken as soon as, and in as much detail, as possible. This record should include: the date, time and place of the relevant occasion the witness claims to have previously seen the suspect; where any identification was made; how it was made and the conditions at the time (eg, the distance the witness was from the suspect, the weather and light); if the witness's attention was drawn to the suspect; the reason for this; and anything said by the witness or suspect about the identification or the conduct of the procedure.'

5.28 This guideline requires police to record information which may be of considerable importance later when assessing the reliability of the street identification. In addition to the witness's first description, 3.2(a) above, (see **5.15**) a record of the circumstances of the observation from which the description was derived should be noted. The record of the circumstances of a street identification should include such details as whether the suspect was accompanied by a police officer or other people at the time. A record of the words or gestures by which the identification was made may cast light on the witness's assuredness. It might also assist should any controversy arise as to whether the person identified was the person arrested and, where several people are arrested, the role attributed to a suspect by the witness.

VIDEO IDENTIFICATION – ANNEX A

5.29 Video identification is a procedure by which a witness is shown moving images of a suspect among a series of similar images of others who resemble the suspect.[36] The use of video identification is the preferred procedure under most recent editions of Code D[37] and represents the vast majority of procedures conducted. The principles and many of the provisions of Annex A are identical to those for identification parades, found in Annex B. The principles derived from the case law on identification parades are equally applicable to video identification procedures.

Suspect's representation

5.30 A suspect is entitled to legal representation.[38] The solicitor's role in the procedure concerns the assessment of the suitability of the images and

---

36 Code D3.5.

37 It became the preferred procedure under the previous fourth edition, on 1 April 2003.

38 There is nothing in Annex A corresponding to the explicit provision in the procedure for

observing the conduct of the procedure. The solicitor must be given reasonable notice of the time and place for the procedure. If no solicitor has been instructed, this information must be given to the suspect[39] thus enabling him to instruct one. The requirement to give notice is subject to practicability. However it is likely to be rare and exceptional that sufficient notice is not feasible. An example might be an urgently arranged procedure for a critically ill witness. The prohibition on the presence of the suspect at the viewing procedure[40] heightens the importance of representation. If no solicitor is present the viewing of the video itself must be recorded on video.[41]

First description

5.31 Prior to a video identification a suspect and his solicitor are entitled to know the description first given to police by the witness[42] to enable an informed decision as to the fairness of the compilation and suitability of the volunteers. There will be occasions when a witness may have given a first description to a police officer immediately after a crime and a further description in a witness statement. It is submitted that if there is any material difference or elaboration in the statement, that too should be disclosed. A pro forma record of first description for service on a suspect is contained in Appendix C.

Previous showing of photographs and other images

5.32 A witness's ability to identify may be influenced by other images that the witness has seen. If a witness has previously been shown photographs or a computerised (e-fit) or an artist's composite or similar likeness of the perpetrator of the crime, the suspect and solicitor must be informed. This information should be included in the Notice to Suspect[43] and in any event before the procedure takes place.[44] It is the responsibility of the officer in the case to inform the identification officer of such a showing.[45] This provision is of no application if the image was created and based upon the witness's own description.[46] Though there is no Code requirement, there is no reason that the image itself should not also be disclosed unless it is impracticable.

Previous broadcast or publication of image or description

5.33 A witness might be influenced in making an identification having seen film or photographs of an incident, for example if the image should contain

---

identification parades in Annex B.1. However Code D3.17(ii) requires notification to the suspect of the right to legal advice and Annex A.7, A.8 and A.9 assume a solicitor's involvement.

39 Annex A.9.

40 Annex A.9.

41 Annex A.9.

42 Annex A.8 and the Notice to Suspect, Code D3.17(xiii).

43 Code D3.17(xi).

44 Annex E.9.

45 Annex E.9 and Note for Guidance 3A.

46 *R v Wright* [1994] Crim LR 131, CA.

features of the suspect previously unobserved by the witness. The suspect or solicitor must be allowed to view such material released to the media, provided that is practicable and would not unreasonably delay the procedure.[47] The Code can be read to include images of a suspect released to the media which do not show the incident such as identikit images and descriptions.[48] Curiously, it is only after the procedure has concluded that witnesses are to be asked whether they have seen any broadcast images of the suspects for the offence.[49]

Composition of series of images

5.34 The arrangements for obtaining and ensuring the availability of a suitable set of images to be used in a video identification must be the responsibility of an identification officer with no direct involvement with the case.[50] Annex A.2 makes provision for the composition of the video:

> 'The set of images must include the suspect and at least eight other people who, so far as possible, resemble the suspect in age, height, general appearance and position in life.'

5.35 In *R v Dowling*,[51] the Court of Appeal suggested in respect of arrangements for an identification parade that 'one is not looking for clones or a group of men who are identical. One is looking for people whose general appearance is similar to the person who is being put on the parade as a suspect'. Similarly, in *R v Maughan and Ward*,[52] it was stated that the requirement of resemblance did not impose a duty on the police to 'produce a film of men who are virtually identical to the suspect. The object is to choose men so that the whole procedure will avoid any bias towards the witness focusing on the suspect'.[53]

5.36 Although it was pointed out in *R v Francis*[54] that if the police were required to use individuals who precisely resembled one another, 'there could be no effective identification [procedure]',[55] the need for resemblance is clearly of fundamental importance to the fairness of the procedure.[56] Where the suspect is of singular appearance the procedure would be tantamount to a

---

47 Code D3.29 and Annex A.8.

48 Code D3.29 and Annex A.8 refer back to Code D3.28, the text of which does not limit the provision to images of incidents. The section title embraces 'information' as well as films and photographs.

49 Annex A.14.

50 Annex A.1.

51 (1995) *The Times*, October 20.

52 [2006] EWCA Crim 3301.

53 Ibid, at [26].

54 [2005] EWCA Crim 903.

55 Ibid, at [15]. The Court took the view that the police could not be expected to seek access to databases other than those maintained for the purposes of identification procedures in order to obtain images of people who resembled the suspect.

56 If police officers are used as foils, anything which might identify them as such must be concealed: Annex A.6.

confrontation.[57] In *R v Pecco*,[58] for example, witnesses provided descriptions of the person involved in a robbery. Both witnesses observed that she had tattoos on her neck. At a subsequent video identification procedure, it could clearly be seen that the appellant was the only person who had tattoos in this position. The Court of Appeal found that in such circumstances the value of an identification procedure was 'insignificant.' The decision in *Pecco* can be contrasted with that in *R v Bennett*.[59] Two robbery victims had described the offender as having his hair in 'cane rows'. The appellant was the only person in the video identification procedure who wore his hair in this style. However, the Court of Appeal concluded that the trial judge's decision to allow evidence of the victim's identifications of the appellant in the procedure could not be described as unreasonable or perverse. It seems, however, that an important consideration for the court in reaching this conclusion was that several days before the procedure had been conducted the identification officer had forwarded the set of still images that he proposed to use in the procedure to the appellant's legal representative, who declared herself satisfied with them.

5.37 A particularly egregious breach of the requirement regarding resemblance occurred in *R v Marcus*.[60] Some difficulty was encountered in obtaining images for use in a video identification procedure, the suspect being a black male in his late forties with greying hair and beard. This led to the use of images, some of much younger men, on which the hair around the temples and the lower part of the face were masked. However, when the witnesses were shown the set of masked images, none was able to make an identification. In light of advice obtained from the CPS prior to the identification procedure, the witnesses were then shown a set of unmasked images which resulted in the appellant being identified. The identification officer conceded during a *voir dire* that the defendant had 'blatantly stood out' in the set of unmasked images, and that the procedure adopted had been 'blatantly unfair'. The Court of Appeal considered the use of the unmasked procedures to be a deliberate breach of the Code that ought to have led to the exclusion of the resulting identification evidence.

5.38 Most video identification procedures are arranged with the use of volunteers whose images are stored in computerised databases.[61] The databases enable an operator to recall images of volunteers according to a number of characteristics such as sex, ethnic origin, age, height, build, hair colour and style. Difficulties are sometimes encountered when the suspect is of an appearance which cannot readily be replicated in volunteers. An identification parade in that case may sometimes allow improvisation, such as the use of headgear where the suspect has an unusual hairstyle or colour or a plaster if the suspect has a facial scar.[62] A similar result is achievable in video

---

57 See for example *R v Finlay* [1993] Crim LR 50, CA.

58 [2010] EWCA Crim 972.

59 [2008] EWCA Crim 3043.

60 [2004] EWCA Crim 3387.

61 Different constabularies employ different systems, Promat and Viper the most commonly used.

62 See **5.72**.

identification if volunteers have additionally been filmed with headgear or the technique ??. Distinguishing features such as scars, birth marks and tattoos can either be replicated with the use of suitable software or hidden by means of pixellation. Empirical research suggests that witnesses are more likely to correctly identify the culprit (with no corresponding increase in the likelihood of an innocent suspect being identified) if distinguishing features are replicated rather than concealed.[63] If resemblance is not possible because of the suspect's distinctive appearance, video identification may be impracticable and another procedure may be appropriate.[64]

5.39 The principle of resemblance as a true test of the witness's ability to recognise the person previously seen is occasionally less than straightforward.[65] There may be situations in which the suspect has a distinctive feature to which the witness has made no reference in a first description or statement. This would be particularly problematic if Code D required images to be selected for the procedure on the basis of their similarity with the person described by the witness rather than the appearance of the suspect.[66] The suspect could be justifiably concerned if he was the only person shown with a distinctive feature. The absence from the witness's description of a distinctive feature of the suspect's appearance might be a consequence of a poor initial interview, inadequate recording, or a failure on the part of the witness to mention the feature to the police. In such circumstances, if the suspect is the only person in the procedure who has that feature, there is a risk that at the time he or she is invited to observe those appearing in the procedure, the witness may recall that the culprit also shared that feature.

5.40 The approach adopted in the Code, of requiring those appearing in the procedure to resemble the suspect, is not without problems, particularly where there is some significant dissimilarity between the appearance of the suspect and the description of the witness. The nature of the problem is illustrated in quite dramatic fashion by the facts giving rise to the appeal heard by the South Australian Supreme Court in *R v Kostic & Stefanopoulos*.[67] The prosecution case was that the male appellants had been involved in a joint enterprise in which shop premises were set alight. A local resident had observed two persons in the vicinity of the premises who smelt of paint thinners. He gave a statement to the police in which he stated that he was able to get a good look at one of these people, who he had observed in side-profile. He provided the police with a statement in which he asserted that he was 'positive' from what he had seen that the person was female. K was subsequently arrested and placed on an

---

63 See T Zarkadi, K Wade and N Stewart, 'Creating Fair Line-ups for Suspects with Distinctive Features', (2009) 20 *Psychological Science* 1448.

64 See Selection process, at para 4.18.

65 See the commentary to *R v Knowles* [1994] Crim LR 217, CA.

66 Guidance issued by the US National Institute of Justice recommend the selection of foils who 'generally fit the witness's description of the perpetrator', although where the suspect has significant features that have not been described by the witness, foils should share those features; *Eyewitness Evidence: A Guide for Law Enforcement* (1999, Washington D.C.; US Department of Justice), p 29.

67 [2004] SASC 406.

identification parade from which he was identified by the witness as the person he had described in his statement to the police as a woman. At trial, K's submission that the witness's identification ought to have been excluded on the grounds the parade had consisted entirely of males was rejected. However, the Supreme Court took a rather different view:

> 'By submitting [the witness] to an all male line-up for the purpose of identifying the person that he saw..., the police officer was suggesting to him that the person he saw could not possibly have been a woman, and that it must be the male person in the line-up who looks most like the woman that he claims to have seen. Furthermore, the fact that only males were presented in the line-up suggested to the jury, by that fact, a belief by the police that the suspect must be a man and that [the witness's] earlier statement could not be relied on. It was not for the police to make that assertion directly or indirectly by their choice of persons in the line-up.'[68]

The court observed that compliance with the obligation to use foils who resembled the suspect when composing the parade did not necessarily render admissible any evidence that might be obtained. The witness having described the culprit as a woman should not have been asked to identify anyone from a parade comprising male participants.

5.41 Although the facts in *Kostic & Stefanopoulos* are rather unusual, circumstances in which there is a significant disparity in the description of the culprit provided by the witness and the appearance of the suspect arrested by the police might not be uncommon. At some point the degree of variation must be such that the procedure constitutes not so much a test of the witness's ability to identify a person that he or she might have seen previously, as a procedure in which the witness is being invited by the police to observe and attempt to identify an altogether different person.

5.42 In addition to resemblance of appearance the images should, as far as possible, show the suspect and other people in the same positions or carrying out the same sequence of movements and under identical conditions.[69] This is achieved in most cases by volunteers and suspects recorded seated in the same position against the same backdrop and with the same lighting. Each person faces the camera, turns to the left, then the right and finally faces the camera again. Each movement is timed to last a certain number of seconds. A departure from this requirement is permitted by the Code if the Identification Officer reasonably believes that it is not practicable to obtain images under identical conditions because of the suspect's refusal to co-operate and that any difference would not direct a witness's attention to any individual image. Once suitable images are collated, they are placed in a sequence in which each image in the series is marked with a number for selection purposes.[70]

---

68 [2004] SASC 406, at [34].

69 Annex A.3.

70 Annex A.5. Whether the sequence in which the images are shown can be changed depends upon the system being operated.

Viewing of images by suspect and suspect's objections

5.43 The suspect, solicitor, friend or appropriate adult must be given a reasonable opportunity to see the complete set of images before it is shown. If objection is raised to the set of images or to any of the people depicted in them the reason for it should be requested. If the objection is reasonable the ground of objection should be removed if practicable.[71] If the objection cannot be met the reasons should be explained.[72] A sensible precaution is the availability of a surplus of images so that, as is common with volunteers at a parade, those with the greatest resemblance can be chosen and objections may be met.[73]

5.44 Raising objections may be a crucial point of the procedure. If objections are not made or are unresolved, courts faced with assertions of unfairness in the procedure may be influenced by the attitude of the suspect and legal advisor at the time of the procedure. In *R v Quinn*[74] the Court of Appeal were told that for a number of reasons the appellant stood out like a sore thumb at a parade. He and his solicitor had played an active part in assembling it. However, because no complaint about unfairness was made either before or after the parade the trial judge, whose ruling was upheld, rejected the alleged breach of the Code. The suspect or solicitor may be placed in an unenviable position where there is a lack of resemblance with the volunteers. A refusal to participate may lead to a less desirable procedure whereas even 'a grudging acceptance of the position'[75] might be used to suggest that the parade, though not ideal, was approved.

More than one suspect

5.45 Only one suspect may appear in a series unless there are two suspects of roughly similar appearance. They may then be shown together provided there are at least 12 other people.[76] It is submitted that this provision is directed towards a case in which two people are suspected of being a sole offender and not two suspects each suspected of involvement in a joint offence.[77]

5.46 Commonly a witness who has observed more than one offender will be asked to take part in two or more procedures for different suspects. The set of

---

71 In *R v Middleton* [2005] EWCA Crim 692, the Court of Appeal acknowledged that the purpose of Annex A.2 is to enable the suspect or solicitor to raise any reasonable objection that may exist and, if practicable, to have it removed. However, where such an opportunity had not been provided it would be relevant for the purposes of determining admissibility to consider whether there could have been any reasonable objection.

72 Annex A.7.

73 Whether this is feasible or practicable depends upon the system operated.

74 [1995] 1 Cr App R 480, CA. In that case five volunteers were rejected and clothing was changed to achieve resemblance. Similar observations were also made in *R v Middleton* [2005] EWCA Crim 692.

75 *R v Mendili* [2001] EWCA Crim 757.

76 Annex A.2.

77 See the corresponding provisions relating to identification parades in which there is an additional provision for the parading of two suspects who are members of a group of possible suspects: see **5.76**.

images for each procedure should comprise different foils in order to avoid the witness recognising and thereby eliminating volunteers.[78]

Location

5.47 There is no requirement that a video identification procedure should be held at a specified place. In practice most are held at dedicated identification suites. However, by means of portable equipment they may be conducted at any police station and in some cases, for example, if the witness is frail or injured, at his or her home or in hospital.

Contamination prevention

5.48 There are several procedural restrictions designed to prevent the possibility of contamination of a witness's memory or the corruption of the procedure's integrity. Some of the restrictions are to be met by dedicated identification suites equipped with facilities to segregate witnesses who have not yet viewed a parade from those who have already done so and also from investigating officers. The Code demands the following procedural precautions for which the identification officer is responsible:

(1) no officer involved in the investigation may participate in the conduct of the video identification;[79]

(2) no-one involved in the investigation is permitted to view the images to be used for the procedure before they have been shown to the witness;[80]

(3) before viewing the set of images, witnesses may not communicate with other witnesses about the case or overhear a witness who has already seen the material;[81]

(4) there must be no discussion with the witness about the composition of the set of images;[82]

---

78 There is no requirement for this expedient in Annex A but it may be inferred from the corresponding provision in Annex B.9. See **5.76**.

79 Code D3.11. See **4.2**.

80 Annex A.15. In *R v Ball* [2006] EWCA Crim 1048, the Court of Appeal found the involvement of an officer who had accompanied the defendant to the police station following his arrest, selected the police officers who were to view CCTV footage and administered the showing of the images, to be a breach of the Code's prohibition on the involvement of investigating officers in the conduct of an identification procedure. The Court explained, at [31] that '[t]he main mischief behind Code D is to prevent the possibility of contamination of the witness's identification evidence, which might occur if an officer were to make suggestions to the witness as to who the people on the parade or the video might be.'

81 Annex A.10. See *R v Finley* [1993] Crim LR 50, CA, as an example of a breach of this provision.

82 Annex A.10.

(5) the witness cannot be reminded of any photograph, composite likeness or of any description of the suspect;[83]

(6) only one witness may see the set of images at a time;[84]

(7) the witness must not be told whether a previous witness has made any identification;[85]

(8) care must be taken not to direct the witness's attention to any one individual image or give any indication of the suspect's identity;[86]

(9) no unauthorised people may be present.[87]

5.49 Adherence to these restrictions is not a guarantee of an absence of contamination. Where, for example, witnesses to an incident are members of a family or work colleagues, it may be necessary to consider whether discussion between them outside the formality of the procedure, albeit quite innocent, could have contributed to a positive identification.[88]

Conduct of the video identification

5.50 Unlike an identification parade there is no need for the presence of the suspect. Indeed the presence of the suspect is not permitted when the images are viewed by the witnesses.[89] Before viewing commences the witness must be told that the person he or she saw on an earlier specified occasion may or may not appear in the images and that if no positive identification can be made the witness should say so. This will involve repeating the essential details of time and place of the earlier observation, though no detail of any earlier description. The witness should also be informed that there is no time limit, that images may be viewed as many times as desired and that any part of the set may be frozen if the witness should want to study it. However it must be explained that no identification should be made until the entire set of images has been seen at least twice.[90] Thus even if the witness purports to make an identification before the second viewing is complete, he or she should be asked

---

83 Annex A.13.
84 Annex A.11.
85 Annex A.10.
86 Annex A.13.
87 Annex A.9.
88 *R v Finley* [1993] Crim LR 50, CA.
89 Annex A.9.
90 Annex A.11. In *R v B* [2008] EWCA Crim 1524, the Court of Appeal noted the difference in the wording of the instructions to be given to witnesses in corresponding provisions in Annex A and B. Annex A.11 provides that, prior to viewing a video identification procedure, witnesses 'should be asked not to make any decision as to whether the person they saw is on the set of images until they have seen the whole set at least twice.' Annex B.16, however, provides that witnesses 'must … be told they should not make any decision about whether the person they saw is on the identification parade until they have looked at each member at least twice'. It was suggested that this discrepancy might have been a possible reason for the wording of the proforma used by the police, which failed to fulfil the requirements of either provision.

to continue to view and to make a decision at the conclusion. At that stage the witness should be asked if the person previously seen was among the images viewed and if so to state the number of the image identified. That image should then be re-played to confirm the selection.[91]

5.51 After the procedure has concluded the witness must be asked if he or she has previously seen any broadcast or published film, photograph or description of the suspect.[92] Where one of two persons is suspected of committing an offence involving one offender, and separate video procedures are arranged for each suspect, references to the 'whole set' of images in Annex A should be read as the 'whole of both sets'.[93] In such circumstances, witnesses should be informed that they will be shown two sets of images.[94] Before viewing the images they must be instructed that both sets of images should be viewed at least twice, and that only after viewing both sets of images twice would they be asked whether or not the person seen on the previous relevant occasion appeared in the images.[95]

'Positive identification'

5.52 There is no prohibition on telling a witness whether a positive identification was of the suspect. However, research suggests that a witness's confidence in the accuracy of their identification of an innocent suspect can be bolstered by the provision of post-identification feedback that they identified the suspect.[96] Although not required by Code D, a statement of confidence taken from the witness immediately after the identification is made might assist the fact-finder's evaluation of the witness's evidence at trial.[97] Any apparent increase in confidence may provide counsel with an opportunity to address the jury on the inferences that might be drawn and how this might affect the weight that they attach to the identifying witness's evidence. Similarly, informing a witness of a failure to select the right person may cause an adjustment to the witness's evidence.[98]

5.53 The taking of a statement from a witness regarding the degree of confidence or certainty that he or she has in an identification would address a further problem that lies in the Code's requirement that witnesses be asked

---

91 Annex A.12.

92 Annex A.14.

93 *R v Coddington* [2005] EWCA Crim 197, at [38].

94 Ibid, at [37].

95 Ibid.

96 See A Bradfield Douglass and N Steblay, 'Memory Distortion in Eyewitnesses: A Meta-analysis of the Post Identification Feedback Effect, (2006) 20 *Applied Cognitive Psychology* 859.

97 In *R v Callum* [2010] EWCA Crim 1325, the Court of Appeal noted the impracticability of preventing the possibility that the 'quality' of a witness's identification being affected by the acquisition of information in the period between the witness's identification of a suspect in a pre-trial procedure and the trial.

98 In *R v Willoughby* [1999] 2 Cr App R 82, CA, it was suggested that best practice is for a statement to be taken before the witness is told whether the suspect was identified.

whether they are able to make a 'positive identification'. In *Craig v R*,[99] the High Court of Australia explained that lying behind a witness's simple statement that the defendant was the person he saw engaged in the relevant act are a number of antecedent cognitive processes. In identifying a suspect, the witness is claiming: that he observed the culprit; that he committed information about the culprit to memory; that his memory for the culprit remains good and has not been distorted or supplemented by the acquisition of information from third parties; and that the resemblance between the appearance of the culprit recalled from memory and the appearance of the suspect as presented to him, is a sufficient basis for concluding that the suspect and culprit are the same person. The last process is significant for present purposes.

5.54 Memory is not photographic, it decays, can be distorted and reconstructed. Even identifications made by the most confident of witnesses are likely to have required the witness to have reconciled some disparity in the recalled memories of the culprit and the appearance of the suspect; to have bridged some gap in his or her memory, however slight, in order to make an identification. The degree of disparity that the witness is willing to countenance in order to make an identification can position a positive identification at any point on a spectrum of probability between chance and virtual certainty.[100]

5.55 During a review of the law of evidence undertaken by the Australian Law Reform Commission in the 1980s, consideration was given to limiting evidence given by a witness to the statement that the suspect 'looks like the person who did it'.[101] The suggestion was rejected on the grounds that such a limitation might weaken the force of sound identification evidence, and that it would artificially limit a witness who could properly give more positive identification evidence. Prior to this the Devlin Committee[102] had considered whether it would be appropriate to ask three questions:

(1) Can you positively identify anyone on the parade as the person you saw?

(2) If not, does anyone on the parade closely resemble the person you saw?

(3) If not, can you say that the person you saw is not on the parade?

This proposal was also rejected, principally because of the confusion that the second question might cause to some witnesses.

5.56 Nonetheless, the practice of asking witnesses whether or not they are able to make a 'positive identification' is problematic.[103] It does not allow a

---

99 (1933) 49 CLR 429.

100 A Levi and N Jungman, 'The Police Lineup: Basic Weaknesses, Radical Solutions' (1995), 22 Criminal Justice and Behavior 347, 351.

101 Evidence (Interim), ALRC Report 26, (1985), para 834.

102 Report to the Secretary of State for the Home Department Committee on Evidence of Identification in Criminal Cases, Cmd 338, 1976, paras 5.58–6.62.

103 The compatibility of limiting witnesses to saying whether or not they are able to make a

witness to express any degree of (un)certainty with which the identification is made. Given the frail nature of the cognitive processes that are called upon in order to make an identification it is unsurprising that witnesses may often volunteer expressions that betray some doubt.[104] However, where a witness complies with the instruction to make a positive identification it may be difficult to establish at some later point in the process whether he or she had such thoughts without uttering them. The witness may not in fact be asked any qualitative question until trial, a considerable time later. Slight misgivings at the time may not be recalled, or an identification might be fortified by the knowledge of an identification of the same person by another witness or the witness learning of the existence of other incriminating evidence. The witness may simply feel under pressure to express greater certainty before the jury, especially if the prosecution is dependent on the identification. Instructing a witness that she must say whether or not she can make a positive identification might also deter a reliable but cautious witness from probative evidence.

5.57 Research suggests that there is some correlation between identification accuracy and a witness's confidence in the accuracy of that identification where it is measured immediately after the identification is made.[105] The Code's requirement that witnesses be asked only whether or not they are able to make a positive identification constitutes a rather crude means of obtaining identification evidence that sits awkwardly with contemporary understanding of the nature of the psychological processes involved in making an identification. One alternative might be the use of a simple model of the type of gradations used by scientific experts. Before embarking on the viewing the witness would be told that in the event of identifying someone, the identification officer will ask on a scale of 1–10 how sure the witness is that the person is the same person as previously seen.[106]

5.58 On some occasions where a number of people have been involved in a crime, usually of group violence, it may not be clear which offender the witness is purporting to identify. In those circumstances it is desirable for the witness not merely to identify a person previously seen but, where possible, to ascribe the role alleged to have been played by that person. A failure to do this can mean that the witness is confronted by this question for the first time many months later in court. In the meantime the defendant may have been left

---

positive identification, with the notion that formal identification procedures are an impartial service to be performed for the benefit of prosecution and defence is discussed at **2.3**.

104 See **10.29** for the admissibility of qualified identifications.

105 There is an extensive psychological literature on this issue, a recent and accessible review of which is provided in R Wilcock, R Bull and R Milne *Witness Identification in Criminal Cases: Psychology and Practice* (OUP, 2008), pp 68–71.

106 It may be noted that the procedure for group identification and showing photographs, make provision for a selection by a witness who is unable to confirm the identification. The witness is then to be asked how sure he or she is: Annex C.23 and E.9 respectively. For a proposal for an alternative procedure in which the witness is asked to provide a confidence estimate in relation to each of the persons observed in a procedure see J Sauer, N Brewer and N Weber 'Multiple confidence estimates as indices of eyewitness memory' (2008) 137 *Journal of Experimental Psychology: General* 528.

guessing at his or her alleged participation in the criminal activity suggested by the identification. The risk of leading a witness in a question such as 'Is the person previously seen wielding the knife among the images viewed?' should be avoided. It is preferable to follow the normal procedure of asking whether a person previously seen was among the images viewed, followed by a further question as to what that person did.[107] Where an account is given a further statement may then be taken.

Identification after procedure

5.59 Sometimes a witness may make an identification after the procedure has ended and in the absence of the suspect's solicitor or while the procedure is not captured on video. Annex A contains no procedural guidance as to the steps to be taken in such circumstances. It is submitted that the requirements of Annex B relating to identification parades should be followed. That provides that the suspect or solicitor should be informed and consideration given to conducting a second procedure.[108]

Alternative and covert procedures

5.60 When a suspect is not available any suitable still photograph or moving image may be used including those obtained covertly.[109] These may be photographs taken from criminal records or seized from the suspect's address. Alternatively photographs taken of a suspect while detained at a police station under PACE, s 64A or a CCTV recording taken from the custody suite of a police station might be used.[110] Clearly such images will not conform to the video identification stereotype. However if police 'mugshots' are used there is every chance that all persons will have been photographed in the same position. Even ad hoc photography of a suspect might be recreated with a degree of similarity of movement. In *R v Perry*[111] the police used a video recording of the suspect taken from a CCTV camera installed in the custody suite of a police station. A semblance of the recording was achieved by recordings of volunteers carrying out the same sequence of movements. If it is not practicable to show the volunteers in the same positions and carrying out the same sequence of movements, the conditions in which the suspect and volunteers are shown may be non-identical provided that any difference does not direct a witness's attention to any individual image.[112]

---

[107] See G Cooke 'Identification parades: preparation and procedures' [2000] 5 *Archbold News* 4.

[108] Annex B.20. See **5.86** and the cases cited for what constitutes an identification after the procedure. The imperative of a second procedure immediately is not so great as with a parade because the video identification can be reconstituted with the same volunteers.

[109] Code D3.21. See **4.11–4.16** for the meaning of 'available' and **4.25–4.30** for procedure selection if a suspect is not available.

[110] PACE, s 64A(4)(a) specifically permits their use for the investigation of an offence. Moreover reasonable force may be used to take them: PACE, s 117.

[111] (Unreported) 3 April 2000, CA; *Perry v United Kingdom* [2003] Crim LR 281, ECtHR.

[112] Annex A.3.

5.61 The requirements to provide information to the suspect do not apply if the suspect's lack of co-operation prevents it. Likewise the opportunity to view images before the procedure may be suspended for that reason.[113] If represented, a suspect's lack of co-operation will not necessarily prevent compliance with the formalities in respect of the suspect's solicitor, including presence at the procedure.

Prisoners

5.62 Where a suspect is remanded in custody or serving a custodial sentence it may be possible for a recording of the suspect to take place at the prison. The suspect should not be required to wear prison clothing unless the volunteers are similarly attired.[114] Alternatively, arrangements can sometimes be made for the suspect's release to the identification suite for that purpose.[115]

Documentation and image retention

5.63 A form designed for the purpose must be used to record the conduct of the video identification.[116] A specimen is set out in Appendix C. It must include anything said by the witness about an identification or the conduct of the procedure and the reason for non-compliance with any provision of the Code. If identical conditions for each image are not practicable the reason must be noted on the form.[117] If the suspect or legal representative voices any objections which cannot be met, they should also be recorded together with the reasons why they were not met.[118] The form should also include the names of all those participating in and viewing the images.[119]

5.64 Some constabularies make a video recording of the identification procedure as a matter of routine. If the suspect is unrepresented the procedure must be recorded[120] enabling an analysis of any selection and accompanying speech. This is preferably done by means of a split screen in which the images being shown and the witness's viewing are recorded and displayed simultaneously.

5.65 The set of images used for the procedure must be retained and kept securely[121] for later examination and, if necessary, court use. The images of the suspect may be used or disclosed only for the purposes of the investigation and prosecution of offences. Unless the suspect is charged, prosecuted, cautioned, warned, reprimanded or if the suspect gives consent to its retention, the images

---

113 Code D3.24.
114 Annex A.6.
115 Annex B.4
116 D3.25 and Annex A.18.
117 Annex A.4.
118 Annex A.7.
119 Annex A.17.
120 Annex A.9.
121 Annex A.15

of the suspect must be destroyed save where necessary to retain it pursuant to the Criminal Procedure and Investigations Act 1996.[122]

IDENTIFICATION PARADE – ANNEX B

5.66 Historically, and until the modification to the third edition of Code D, the identification parade was the preferred procedure and in practice the vast majority of identification cases were conducted by parade. As a result of the technology now available and the preference in the present Code D for video identification, identification parades are now little used. They may nevertheless remain more practicable or suitable in some cases; moreover many of the principles which have evolved in the conduct of parades and some of its case law have continuing relevance in relation to video identifications.

Location and video recording

5.67 Most parades are held at dedicated identification suites with one-way screen facilities enabling the witness to view the line-up without being observed or heard by the suspect or volunteers, though a parade in a normal room is still permitted.[123] A video recording must normally be made of the identification parade. All identification suites are equipped with recording facilities. If for some reason a video recording is impracticable a colour photograph of the line-up must be taken.[124] The recording will generally show the preliminary arrangements for the parade and, by split screen, the line-up and the viewing by the witness. All conversation including a positive identification will also be recorded.

Suspect's representation

5.68 A suspect must be given a reasonable opportunity to be represented by a solicitor or have a friend present at a parade. Whether one is requested or not should be recorded on the Notice to Suspect.[125] If a screen is used the parade may only take place if either the suspect is represented or in the presence of the suspect's friend or appropriate adult, or if the parade is recorded on video.[126] After the formation of the parade all conversation with a witness must take place in the presence of the representative. If a room without screen facilities is used everything said and done must take place in the presence and hearing of both suspect and representative.[127]

---

[122] Annex A.16, and Code D3.30 and D3.31.

[123] Annex B.2.

[124] Annex B.23.

[125] Annex B.1 and Code D3.17(ii).

[126] Annex B.2.

[127] Annex B.8.

First description

5.69 Prior to an identification parade the suspect or solicitor is entitled to know the description first given to police by the witness who is to attend,[128] to enable an informed decision as to the fairness of the composition of the parade and the suitability of the volunteers. There will be occasions when a witness may have given a first description to a police officer immediately after a crime and a further description in a witness statement. It is submitted that if there is any material difference or elaboration in the statement, that too should be disclosed.

Previous showing of photographs and other images

5.70 A witness's ability to identify may be influenced by other images that the witness has seen. If a witness has previously been shown photographs or a computerised (e-fit) or artist's composite or similar likeness of the perpetrator of the crime, the suspect and solicitor must be informed. This information should be included in the Notice to Suspect[129] and in any event before the procedure takes place.[130] This provision is of no application if the image was created and based upon the witness's own description.[131] It is the responsibility of the officer in the case to notify the identification officer of such a showing.[132] Though there is no Code requirement, there is no reason that the image itself should not also be disclosed unless it is impracticable.

Previous broadcast or publication of image or description

5.71 In making an identification a witness might be influenced by having seen film or photographs of an incident, for example if it should contain features of the suspect previously unobserved by the witness. The suspect or solicitor must be allowed to view such material released to the media, provided that is practicable and would not unreasonably delay the procedure.[133] The Code can be read to include images of a suspect released to the media which do not show the incident, such as identikit images and descriptions.[134] Curiously, it is only after the procedure has concluded that witnesses are to be asked whether they have seen any broadcast images of the suspect for the offence.[135]

Parade composition

5.72 Annex B.9 states:

---

128 Annex B.3 and the Notice to Suspect, Code D3.17(xiii).
129 Code D3.17(xi).
130 Annex E.9.
131 *R v Wright* [1994] Crim LR 131, CA.
132 Annex E.9 and Note for Guidance 3A.
133 D3.29 and Annex B.3.
134 D3.29 and Annex B.3 refer back to D3.28 – the text of which does not limit the provision to images of incidents. The section title embraces 'information' as well as films and photographs.
135 Annex B.21.

> 'The identification parade shall consist of at least eight people (in addition to the suspect) who, so far as possible, resemble the suspect in age, height, general appearance, and position in life …'

This requirement is of fundamental importance in ensuring that the parade is a genuine test of the witness's ability to recognise the person earlier seen. Normally a surplus of volunteers will attend so that the most suitable may be selected. A parade may be problematic when there are insufficient volunteers of similar appearance available[136] or where the suspect is of singular appearance and a parade would be tantamount to a confrontation. If the problem cannot be resolved, an identification parade may be rendered impracticable.[137]

5.73 Resemblance between those paraded may be achieved by the removal, adjustment or replacement of clothing. Moreover there is provision in the Code for the concealment of a suspect's unusual physical feature, such as a facial scar, tattoo or distinctive hairstyle or colour. Steps may be taken, if the suspect or representative agrees, to conceal the suspect's distinctive feature with a plaster or hat or other artifice and similarly disguise the appearance of volunteers so that the all members of the parade resemble one another.[138] In *R v Wright*[139] tape was applied to the upper lips of the suspect and other members of the parade where the witness had described a moustache. In *R v Marrin*[140] baseball caps were worn back to front and make up was applied to at least two volunteers. Upholding the validity of the parade, the Court of Appeal stated that care needed to be taken with such measures and that the wearing of headgear where the perpetrator did not do so should be avoided unless necessary to achieve a resemblance. However it was held that 'if such steps are taken bona fide to achieve [resemblance so far as possible] and they are sensible and reasonable steps, then there will be no breach'.

5.74 The need to remove a distinctive feature may be regarded as applying even if the feature does not appear to have been originally observed by the witness. If there is a significant dissimilarity between the appearance of the suspect and the description of the witness, the Code demands resemblance with the suspect and not the description.

---

136 In *R v Britton and Richards* [1989] Crim LR 144, a decision at first instance, it was held that where police had difficulties assembling any volunteers resembling the Afro-Carribean suspects they ought to have accepted the solicitor's offer of assistance. *R v Thorne* [1981] Crim LR 702, CA, was distinguished. There, the police had sufficient volunteers and refused the suspect's request to introduce a man he had brought with him.

137 If impracticable, consideration would have to be given to alternative procedures: Code D3.14 and 3.15.

138 Annex B.10. This provision, which was not in previous editions of the Code, recognises the arrangements that were often made by identification officers.

139 [1994] Crim LR 131, CA. In *R v Gall* [1989] Crim LR 745 a plaster was used to cover a scar. In *R v Hutton* [1999] Crim LR 74, CA, each member of the parade wore a baseball cap back-to-front and a scarf obscuring the lower part of their face. It is unclear from the report whether this device was used because the assailant had been so clad when observed by the witness or because he had a very distinctive chin. For that reason the unspecified criticism of the procedure should not be taken as general disapproval of the technique.

140 [2002] EWCA Crim 251.

Suspect's objections

5.75 The suspect should be asked whether he has any objections to the arrangements for the parade or any of the volunteers. If there are reasons for any objection, these should be ascertained and steps should be taken, where practicable, to satisfy any complaint.[141] If impracticable, the suspect should be told the reason which must also be recorded on the parade form. Normally the identification officer will have arranged a surplus of volunteers so that the suspect is able to select those with the greatest likeness to him. The importance of making a complaint at the time and the consequences at trial of failing to do so are considered at **5.43**.

More than one suspect

5.76 Only one suspect may be paraded at one time unless there are two suspects 'of roughly similar appearance' in which case they may be paraded together with at least 12 other persons. No more than two suspects may be paraded together.[142] Though ambiguous, this provision appears to be directed towards a situation where there are two suspects but a sole offender rather than two persons suspected of involvement in a joint offence. A separate provision allows two suspects of roughly similar appearance to be paraded together if they are members of 'a similar group of suspects'.[143] The Code does not provide any guidance as to how the procedure is to be explained to the witness. In practice it is very rare for a parade to contain two suspects, whose interests in its arrangements might conflict. Where a witness is to view separate parades for separate suspects, the parade for each suspect must comprise different volunteers[144] in order to avoid the witness recognising and thereby eliminating volunteers.

Contamination prevention

5.77 There are several restrictions designed to prevent the possibility of contamination of a witness and corruption of the procedure. Some are met by dedicated identification suites equipped with facilities to segregate witnesses who have not yet viewed a parade from those who have already done so and also investigating officers. The Code demands the following precautions against contamination for which the identification officer is responsible:

(1) no officer involved in the investigation may participate in the conduct of the parade;[145]

---

[141] Annex B.12.
[142] Annex B.9.
[143] Annex B.11.
[144] Annex B.9.
[145] Code D3.11. See **4.2**.

(2) before a parade the witness cannot communicate with other witnesses about the case or overhear a witness who has already seen the parade;[146]

(3) before a parade the witness cannot see any volunteer member of the parade;[147]

(4) before a parade the witness cannot see or be reminded of any photograph or description of the suspect or be given any other indication of his identity;[148]

(5) the witness cannot see the suspect before or after the parade;[149]

(6) only one witness shall view the parade at one time;[150]

(7) the person conducting a witness to a parade must not discuss the composition of the parade nor, to prevent pressure on the witness to make a selection, shall it be disclosed whether a previous witness has made an identification;[151]

(8) all unauthorised people must be excluded from the place where the parade is held.[152]

Though these precautionary measures protect against corruption of the procedure they cannot provide a complete guarantee of an absence of contamination.[153]

Caution

5.78 Immediately before the parade the suspect must also be reminded of the procedure governing the conduct of the parade and, somewhat incongruously, cautioned in the terms of the interview caution:[154]

> 'You do not have to say anything. But it may harm your defence if you do not mention when questioned something which you later rely on in Court. Anything you do say may be given in evidence.'[155]

---

146 Annex B.14(i).
147 Annex B.14(ii).
148 Annex B.14(iii).
149 Annex B.14(iv).
150 Annex B.16.
151 Annex B.15.
152 Annex B.7.
153 See **5.49**.
154 Annex B.6.
155 Code C10.5 or 10.6 for the restricted caution.

Conduct of the parade

5.79 Each position in the line should be identified by a numeral placed either at the feet or above the head of each person on the parade. The suspect may choose his or her position. To allay any fear about information being supplied to succeeding witnesses, the suspect is allowed to change position for each witness.[156] Immediately before the inspection of the parade begins the witness should be told that the person he or she saw on a specified earlier occasion may or may not be on the parade and that if no positive identification can be made the witness should say so.[157] This will involve repeating the essential details of time and place of the earlier observation. However care should be taken not to remind the witness of the detail of the description. The witness should be instructed not to make a decision before having looked at each member of the parade at least twice.[158]

5.80 The witness should take as much time and care as needed.[159] When satisfied that the witness has properly looked at each member of the parade, the identification officer should ask whether the person seen on the earlier occasion is on the parade and if so to indicate the number.[160] Where a number of people were involved in the offence, it may be necessary to ask supplementary questions following identification of the suspect in order to establish what role he or she played in events (see **5.58**).

Posture, motion or speech

5.81 In some cases, because of the circumstances of the original observation, the witness may wish to see a member of the parade in a different posture or see that person move or hear their speech. Before any variation to the standard view of parade members is made, the Code requires the identification officer to ask the witness whether an identification can be made on appearance only.[161] If the answer is yes the participant should be identified. It is implicit in the Code, by its silence on the matter, that after a positive identification in those circumstances no further action is to be taken. There should be no need for that witness to be supplied with further visual information at that stage if he is sure that he has made a correct identification. If a positive identification cannot be made, the option exists for the members of the parade to be asked to comply with the request to move, adopt a specified posture or to hear the members of

---

156 Annex B.13.

157 It may be assumed, though it is not explicit in the Code, that if two suspects are paraded, the explanation will be appropriately adapted.

158 Annex B.16.

159 This may seem self-evident but the requirement that the witness is to be so informed did not survive the early editions of the Code, see third edition Annex A.14.

160 Annex B.17. Where at trial a witness can no longer remember the parade number selected, the evidence of the identification officer can be adduced on this point: *R v McKay* (1990) 91 Cr App R 84; [1990] Crim LR 338, CA; *R v Osbourne and Virtue* (1973) Cr App R 297, CA, see **10.151**. See the commentary in **5.58** on the issue of supplementary questions concerning the suspect's participation in the relevant events.

161 Annex B.18.

the parade speak.[162] This may serve to confirm the tentative identification already made; alternatively the further observation may cast more doubt on the identification or even cause it to be withdrawn.

5.82 Whether to allow the further opportunity to examine the participant will depend on the nature of the request. If the witness makes a request for some movement or speech, it may be prudent first to discover what particular feature the witness seeks to recognise, if that is not apparent from the first description or statement, before making a decision. Generally there should be little problem with a request to view a profile. By contrast a request to see a parade member walk where, for example, the person observed committing the offence had a limp, would not be a true recognition of the appearance of an offender. This failing would be accentuated if the request was made in respect of all participants of whom none but the suspect limped. A suspect's limp, if already described by the witness, could if necessary be adduced independently by an investigating officer as could a concealed scar or tattoo.

5.83 If the request is to hear speech, the witness must be reminded that the participants have been selected on the basis of physical appearance alone,[163] whether or not the request is complied with. If the witness had not previously indicated a particular accent or speech pattern it would be preferable to ascertain what the witness sought to recognise, bearing in mind that hearing one person alone would provide no point of comparison. A Londoner robbed in Birmingham and attending a parade there might be persuaded simply by hearing a local regional accent rather than by recognition of the particular voice. Another mischief exists where for example a Scot is paraded in Devon with local volunteers and all are invited to speak. Evidence of the Scottish accent is likely to be independently available to be adduced in evidence. The further difficulty arises in deciding what should be spoken, especially if the request is to hear the words that were allegedly uttered by the offender. The risks associated with voice identification have been recognised by the courts.[164] A dedicated procedure for voice identification now exists. The elaborate arrangements required, involving the assistance of an expert phonetician, demonstrate the need for carefully applied safeguards against error. Those procedures are set out in Chapter 8.

Concealed features

5.84 If some artifice has been used to conceal a feature and the witness requests that a person removes the article used for concealment, the person may be asked to do so.[165] Once again whether that should be done will depend upon the circumstances. Though the Code does not in terms require it, it is submitted that, as with requested movement or speech, the witness should first be asked

---

[162] Annex B.18.

[163] Annex B.18.

[164] *R v Hersey* [1998] Crim LR 281, CA; *R v Roberts* [2000] Crim LR 183, CA. See **10.91** for a review of voice identification evidence.

[165] Annex B.19.

whether an identification can be made from the parade as originally constituted. If the witness can make a positive identification without further assistance, there is no need for further action. By contrast the witness who is simply trying to avoid the artifice in respect of all or most of the members of the parade should not be accommodated. The discretion might properly be reserved for the witness who is not sure of a correct identification, but seeks a degree of certainty.[166] Even then the integrity of the procedure may be risked if the witness is disappointed not to find a feature once the artifice is removed and is thereby encouraged to transfer preference to another candidate.

Conclusion

5.85 After the conclusion of the parade and the witnesses have departed the identification officer must ask the suspect whether he wishes to make any comments on the conduct of the parade.[167] This will normally be done after the suspect has been informed whether or not he has been identified by any witness. Anything said concerning the conduct of the procedure and any identification made must be recorded.[168]

Identification after parade

5.86 Witnesses occasionally may make an identification after the parade has ended[169] in the absence of the suspect and solicitor and while the procedure is not captured on video. In those circumstances the suspect or solicitor, if still present should be informed. Moreover the Code requires consideration to be given to allowing the witness a second opportunity to identify the suspect.[170] If feasible the second parade should take place immediately in order to comprise the same people. A later parade with different volunteers is likely to lead to the witness choosing the person common to both – the suspect.

5.87 The question of what constituted 'an identification after the parade' arose in *R v Willoughby*.[171] There a witness stated at the parade 'It's Number 4 I think. It might be Number 3.' Within 10 minutes she made a statement in which she said that she was now positive that Number 3 was her assailant. The resolution of her initial equivocation was held to be an identification and therefore the failure to reveal this to the suspect or his solicitor straight away was treated as a breach of the Code.[172] In contrast where a witness in the same case merely 'firmed up' her evidence from 'I think it might be Number 3' to

---

166 *R v Marrin* [2002] EWCA Crim 251, CA.

167 Annex B.21.

168 Annex B.28.

169 *R v Creamer* (1985) 80 Cr App R 248, CA is an example in which, in the days before screens, the witness explained that she had been too frightened at the time of parade.

170 Annex B.20.

171 [1999] 2 Cr App R 82, CA. See also *R v Walters* [2001] EWCA Crim 1261.

172 It was argued that this deprived the defendant the opportunity of a second parade immediately. However, no representation was made by the solicitor once the identification was made known some time later that day. The finding that the breach was not such as to require exclusion of the witness's evidence was upheld.

'having now thought about his face … I'm a hundred per cent sure that Number 3 was the man', the Court of Appeal was inclined to view that this was not an identification after the fact because an identification had already been made. It was simply a change in emphasis. Notwithstanding that view, the Court went on to suggest that in the spirit of Code D and in order to avoid later difficulties whenever there was some significant modification it would be desirable to inform the suspect or solicitor as soon as practicable.

Prisoners

5.88 Where a suspect is remanded in custody or serving a custodial sentence arrangements can sometimes be made for the suspect's release to participate in a parade.[173] If release from prison for that purpose is deemed inappropriate a parade may be held at a prison using, so far as is practicable, normal identification rules. Unless there are security objections, the volunteers should be members of the public. Alternatively, other inmates may be used. The suspect should not be required to wear prison clothing unless the volunteers are similarly attired.[174]

Documentation and image retention

5.89 A form designed for the purpose must be used to record the conduct of the identification parade.[175] The procedure should be documented step by step including the information given to the suspect, the previous descriptions of witnesses and the numbering of the parade and position of the suspect. Anything said by the witness or suspect about identifications or the conduct of the parade must be included together with any reason for non-compliance with any provision of the Code. In particular any objection to the arrangements or any of the participants and where appropriate the reason that the objection has not been met should be noted.[176] A record of all people present at the parade and whose names are known to the police shall also be recorded.[177] If a person is excluded because of interference with the conduct of the parade the circumstances shall be recorded.[178]

5.90 A copy of the recording (or photograph) of the identification parade must be provided on request to the suspect or solicitor within a reasonable time.[179] A recording may be used or disclosed only for the purposes of the investigation and prosecution of offences. Unless the suspect is charged, prosecuted, cautioned, warned, reprimanded or if the suspect gives consent to

[173] Annex B.4.
[174] Annex B.5.
[175] Code D3.25 and Annex B.28.
[176] Annex B.13.
[177] Annex B.26 and B.28.
[178] Annex B.25.
[179] Annex B.23.

its retention, the recording must be destroyed save where necessary to retain it pursuant to the Criminal Procedure and Investigations Act 1996.[180]

GROUP IDENTIFICATION – ANNEX C

5.91 Group identification is a procedure in which the witness sees the suspect in an informal group of people.[181] It ranks below that of video identification and identification parade, being generally regarded as a less fair test of a witness's reliability because of the lack of formality and the irregular conduct and appearance of the group among whom the suspect will be viewed. Nevertheless it may be more suitable in some circumstances. Where it is, Annex C demands that the principles and procedures for identification parades should be followed in order to make the conditions as fair a test of the witness's ability to identify as possible.[182]

Suspect's representation

5.92 A suspect must be given a reasonable opportunity of having a solicitor or friend present and asked to indicate on the Notice to Suspect whether or not one is requested.[183]

Location selection and suspect's appearance

5.93 In selecting a location for the procedure, a place must be found at which the suspect is visible to the witness among a group of people but not conspicuously so. Examples of locations provided by the Code divide into two types: moving groups such as people leaving an escalator, pedestrians walking through a shopping centre and passengers at railway and bus stations; and stationary groups such as people waiting in queues and other public places where groups are standing or sitting.[184] The procedure for each (see **5.96** and **5.98**) is slightly different. To some extent the location will be dictated by the suspect's age, race, general description and style of clothing. The identification officer must have regard to the general appearance of others likely to be present at the location and the importance of seeing a number of other people whose appearance is broadly similar to that of the suspect.[185] The suspect or solicitor may very well wish to make representations concerning the location. Though the choice is ultimately that of the identification officer, the representations must be taken into account.[186] If a suspect has refused to consent to or co-operate in a group identification, the procedure may be conducted

---

[180] Annex B.24, Code D3.30, 3.31 and D3.33. The suspect must be given the opportunity to witness the destruction or be provided with a certificate confirming its destruction: Code D3.32.

[181] Code D3.9.

[182] Annex C.1.

[183] Annex C.13.

[184] Annex C.4.

[185] Annex C.6.

[186] Annex C.3.

covertly.[187] If, because of the unusual appearance of the suspect the identification officer believes no suitable location in which other people resembling the suspect can be found, a group identification need not be held.[188]

First description and previous showing, broadcast or publication of images

5.94 The provisions regarding disclosure to a suspect of the witness's first description,[189] any previous viewing by the witness of photographs, computerised or artist's composites of the offender[190] and any previous broadcast or publication of an image or description of the suspect[191] are identical to those relating to the video identification procedure.[192]

Contamination prevention

5.95 In order to avoid compromising the efficacy of the procedure the following precautions, for which the identification officer is responsible, must be taken:

(1) no officer involved in the investigation may participate in the conduct of the group identification;[193]

(2) the person conducting the witness to the group identification must not discuss the group identification and in particular whether a previous witness has made an identification;[194]

(3) the witness may not see or be reminded of any photographs or description of the suspect or be given any other indication of the suspect's identity;[195]

(4) the witness must not be able to see the suspect before the procedure;[196]

(5) witnesses must be brought to the location one at a time;[197]

(6) witnesses are not allowed to communicate with each other about the case or overhear a witness who has already been given the opportunity to see the suspect in the group.[198]

---

[187] Annex C.2. See **5.59**.
[188] Annex C.7.
[189] Annex C.11 and the Notice to Suspect Code D3.17(xiii).
[190] Annex E.9 and Code D3.17(xi).
[191] Annex C.11.
[192] See **5.31–5.33**.
[193] Code D3.11. This prohibition is considered at **4.2**.
[194] Annex C.15.
[195] Annex C.17(iii).
[196] Annex C.17(ii).
[197] Annex C.18.
[198] Annex C.17(i).

Conduct of the group identification

Moving groups

5.96 Where there are two or more suspects and the procedure is to take place within a moving group, such as at a shopping centre, each suspect must be subject to a separate group identification procedure. They may be conducted consecutively on the same occasion.[199] The witness, the identification officer, the suspect's solicitor or friend, appropriate adult and any interpreter present may be concealed from the group if the identification officer considers that such a step will improve the procedure.[200] The witness must first be informed that the person seen on the previous specified occasion may or may not be within the group and that if a positive identification cannot be made the witness should say so.[201] The witness should then be instructed to observe the group and to point out any person thought to be the person seen on the earlier occasion.[202] Once the witness is prepared, the suspect should join the group taking whatever position within it he or she wishes.[203] A suspect who unreasonably delays joining the group or is deliberately concealed from the witness may be treated as refusing to co-operate in the procedure.[204]

5.97 Once an identification is made the witness should, if practicable, take a closer look at the person identified to confirm the identification or not as the case may be. If it is not practicable or confirmation is not forthcoming, the witness must be asked how sure he or she is that the person indicated is the person previously seen.[205] This may be a significant question even if a member of the public has been identified. The procedure should last for so long as the identification officer considers it necessary to enable the witness to make comparisons.[206] Anything said to or by the witness during the procedure should be said in the presence and hearing of the suspect's representative.[207] An explanation should be provided to a member of the public wrongly identified and that person should be asked if he or she would be willing to provide a name and address, though clearly there would be no obligation to do so. At the conclusion of the procedure the suspect should be told whether an identification has been made[208] and asked for any comment on the conduct of the procedure.[209]

---

[199] Annex C.20.
[200] Annex C.14.
[201] Annex C.18.
[202] Annex C.21.
[203] Annex C.22.
[204] Annex C.30.
[205] Annex C.23.
[206] Annex C.24.
[207] Annex C.16.
[208] Annex C.33.
[209] Annex C.32.

Stationary groups

5.98 Most of the features of the group identification are common to both moving and stationary groups. The differences in the conduct of a stationary group procedure, such as a queue, are as follows. Generally one suspect will be viewed at a time, but two or more suspects may participate provided they are of broadly similar appearance. If suspects are to be viewed separately the groups must comprise different people to prevent the witness from recognising and thus eliminating members of the public.[210] If more than one witness is to view the group the suspect must be allowed to change position for each viewing.[211] The witness should be asked to pass along or among the group and to look at each person at least twice, taking as much care and time as is possible in the circumstances before making an identification.

5.99 In *R v Stott*,[212] it was held that where the group is seated, the appellant may be asked to stand where such a request is made by the witness, the court observing that 'the Code does not prevent at a group identification, any more than it does at an identification parade, the officer in charge asking those taking part to adopt particular stances or clothing'. However, there is a fundamental difference in the two procedures that is unlikely to be lost on the witness. Those taking part in an identification parade will be paid volunteers, who can be expected to comply with any such request without hesitation. Most group identifications are conducted in public places where there are likely to be a reasonably large number of people present. The procedure in *Stott*, for example, was conducted in a public bar at Newcastle Airport. Generally, those being observed by the witness in a group identification procedure will not be aware that they are 'taking part' in one, and might be expected to object or question any request to stand or adopt a particular stance. If it were to be met with unquestioned compliance, there may be some force in the assertion made by Stott's counsel that such a request is, 'in effect . . . the same as pointing an arrow at the appellant's head'.[213] The manner in which the request is made, even the fact that it was made at all, may have the same effect.

Covert group identification

5.100 If a suspect is not available or does not consent or co-operate in a group identification, the procedure may be conducted covertly.[214] In such a case the normal rules should apply as far as is practicable.[215] The choice of location will necessarily be limited to those places frequented by the suspect at which other suitable people are likely to be present, such as a location along a routine travel

---

210 Annex C.26.
211 Annex C.27.
212 [2004] EWCA Crim 615.
213 Ibid, at [19].
214 Code D3.21.
215 Annex C.34.

route.[216] Any number of suspects may be viewed simultaneously in a covert group identification.[217] The nature of the procedure naturally precludes the suspect's right to representation.[218]

Group identification in a police station or prison

5.101 A group identification may take place in a police station but only on grounds of safety or because it is not practicable to conduct one elsewhere.[219] A group identification involving a prison inmate may only be held at a police station or at a prison.[220] In either case the procedure may then take place either in a room equipped with a screen through which the group may not see the suspect or some other appropriate place.[221] If it is to take place at a prison other inmates may act as foils. The suspect will not have to wear prison clothing unless other participants do so.[222] Whenever the procedure is held at a police station or prison additional safeguards applicable to identification parades should, if practicable, be followed.[223] These will include the provisions designed to prevent contamination of witnesses by contact with others.

Documentation and recording

5.102 A form designed for the purpose must be maintained to record the conduct of a group identification.[224] It should contain the previous descriptions of witnesses; the place, time and conditions of the group identification; representations made by or on behalf of the suspect concerning the arrangements for the procedure; anything said by the witness or suspect about identifications or the conduct of the procedure. Any reason for non-compliance with any provision of the Code must also be recorded.[225]

5.103 Some visual record of the conditions under which the procedure took place is required. If practicable the procedure may be video-recorded. Alternatively a video recording should be made or colour photograph taken giving a general impression of the scene and the people present immediately after the procedure has concluded.[226] If that is impracticable it may be done at a later time.[227] A recording of the procedure should not be used to improve the quality of the witness's identification evidence by a later showing of it to the witness.[228] A copy of the recording or photograph must be made available to a

---

216 Annex C.5.
217 Annex C.36.
218 Annex C.35.
219 Annex C.37.
220 Annex C.40.
221 Annex C.38.
222 Annex C.41.
223 Annex C.39.
224 Code D3.25 and Annex C.44.
225 Annex C.44.
226 Annex C.8.
227 Annex C.9.
228 *R v Smith and Doe* (1987) 85 Cr App R 197, CA.

suspect or solicitor within a reasonable time on request.[229] The provisions as to the retention and destruction of these images are identical to those relating to identification parades.[230]

CONFRONTATION – ANNEX D

5.104 A confrontation is a procedure whereby a suspect is directly confronted by a witness. It does not require the suspect's consent. It is the identification procedure of last resort and to be used only if the suspect is unavailable[231] and all other procedures, including covert procedures are impracticable.[232] It provides no discriminatory test of the witness's accuracy and Annex D provides few of the safeguards of other procedures. If other methods ought properly to have been used, it is likely to be excluded.

Suspect's representation

5.105 A suspect is permitted to have legal representation. The confrontation should take place in the solicitor's presence unless that would cause unreasonable delay.

First description and previous showing, broadcast or publication of images

5.106 The provisions regarding disclosure to a suspect of the witness's first description,[233] any previous viewing by the witness of photographs, computerised or artist's composites of the perpetrator[234] and any previous broadcast or publication of an image or description of the suspect[235] are identical to those relating to the video identification procedures.[236]

Contamination prevention

5.107 Annex D has none of the measures, common to the other procedures, designed to avoid influencing a witness (or the appearance of it). There is, for example, no express prohibition on an investigating officer conducting the confrontation though this may be regarded as implicit. Nor, save for the requirement that one witness should confront a suspect at a time,[237] is there any express prohibition upon contact between witnesses before or after a confrontation has taken place. Indeed there is no requirement that the

229 Annex C.43.
230 Annex C.44. See **5.90**.
231 See **4.11–4.16**.
232 Code D3.23, **4.27** above.
233 Annex D.2 and the Notice to Suspect Code D3.17(xiii).
234 Annex E.9 and Code D3.17(xi).
235 Annex D.2.
236 See **5.31–5.33**.
237 Annex D.5.

principles of other procedures are considered or followed. Despite that, it is submitted that prudence dictates that they are followed if possible. Because the Code has not formally been breached, it does not follow that the integrity of the identification has not been compromised or that the identification will not be excluded on grounds of unfairness.

Conduct of the confrontation

5.108 A confrontation should normally take place in a police station. It may take place directly between the suspect and witness so that an identification or associated observation by the witness may be seen and heard by the suspect. The suspect is entitled to be represented by a solicitor unless that would cause unreasonable delay. Alternatively the confrontation may be conducted in a room equipped with a one-way screen. If it is, it must be in the presence of the suspect's representative or recorded on video.[238]

5.109 Before the procedure the witness is to be informed that the person to be confronted may or may not be the person previously seen and if not the witness should say so.[239] If there is more than one witness each should confront the suspect independently. The witness should be asked 'Is this the person?' If the witness identifies the suspect he or she should be asked to confirm it. If unable to do so the witness should be asked how sure he or she is that the suspect is the person seen on the earlier occasion.[240] After the confrontation the witness should be asked whether he or she has viewed any broadcast or read any published description of the suspect.[241]

5.110 Since a confrontation will be likely to be the result of a suspect's refusal to co-operate in other procedures, the suspect may be unwilling to co-operate in the procedure. Though consent is not necessary, force may not be used to make the suspect's face visible to the witness.[242] In such circumstances the confrontation could be arranged surreptitiously.

Documentation and recording

5.111 A written record of a confrontation must be maintained on a form designed for the purpose.[243] A video recording must be made of a confrontation which takes place in a room in which the suspect is behind a one-way screen.[244] There is no explicit provision regarding the use, retention and destruction of the recording though it may be assumed that the provisions relating to video identification should apply.[245]

---

[238] Annex D.6.
[239] Annex D.1.
[240] Annex D.5.
[241] Annex D.7.
[242] Annex D.3. See also *R v Jones and Nelson* (1999) *The Times* April 21, CA.
[243] Code D3.25.
[244] Annex D.6.
[245] See **5.90**.

SHOWING PHOTOGRAPHS AND OTHER IMAGES – ANNEX E

5.112 The provisions in Annex E are designed primarily to address circumstances in which photographs from a police library or database are to be shown to a witness where the identity of a suspect is not known. This procedure may be appropriate where the offender is thought to be one of a class of possible suspects with a propensity to commit the offence being investigated. If a positive identification is made the person identified will have become a known suspect. Another witness cannot then participate in the photograph procedure. If the suspect disputes the identification, a video identification or alternative procedure will be required for the identification by other witnesses.[246] The only exception arises when the suspect is not available. This might apply to a suspect who cannot be traced or who has escaped from custody.[247] However in those circumstances the photographs should be shown as stills in the form of a video identification procedure.[248]

Responsibility for conduct of procedure

5.113 Unlike the procedures for video identification, identification parade or group identification, the responsibility for the Annex E procedure need not be that of an identification officer. An officer of the rank of sergeant or above must be responsible for the supervision and direction of the procedure though the actual showing may be done by another officer or civilian support staff.[249] There is no express prohibition against the officer being one who is involved in the investigation, presumably because of the unlikelihood of any influence being exerted if there is no known suspect. However, given that a person might be suspected, but fall short of the 'known suspect' test, any later argument about the propriety of a procedure is more likely to be avoided if someone unconnected with the investigation conducted the procedure. In *R v Kitchen*[250] an officer, who himself gave evidence of the presence of the suspect in the vicinity of the offence some two hours earlier, was present when the victim of a robbery made an identification of the suspect from photographs. Though it was held on the facts that there was no reason to suppose the officer had prompted the witness, the safer course would certainly have been to have absented himself.

First description

5.114 Before the procedure commences the supervising officer must confirm that the first description of the suspect given by the witness has been recorded. The showing of photographs must be postponed until that has been done.[251]

---

246 Annex E.6 and Code D3.3.

247 *R v Kitchen* [1994] Crim LR 684, CA.

248 See **4.26**.

249 Annex E.1.

250 [1994] Crim LR 684, CA.

251 Annex E.2.

The description provided can assist in the compilation of the series of photographs. It also guards against the risk of a witness later adopting a description based upon the photograph rather than the original observation.

Previous broadcast or publication of image or description

5.115 Unlike the procedures for a known suspect, there is no specific requirement in Annex E for the witnesses to be asked whether they have previously seen a broadcast of an incident or some other publication of an image or description.[252] However it is submitted that it is no less important to appreciate the possibility of some subliminal influence in an identification by photographs.

Composition of photographs

5.116 The minimum number of photographs that may be shown at one time is 12, although if the pool of potential suspects is substantial the witness will view several series. The photographs should, as far as possible, all be of a similar type and numbered.[253] As regards the persons depicted in them however there is no stipulation, as with a video identification, that they be of similar appearance. The witness will have provided at least a rudimentary first description enabling the compiler to narrow the photograph gallery to those that accord with the description. This will provide the witness with a genuine choice and deter a selection of an individual whose appearance stands out or, worse, the only person resembling the witness's description. In *R v Finley*[254] the defendant was a blond skinhead whereas the others in the gallery had neither of these features. The Court of Appeal recognised that the fairness of the procedure was compromised. It should be noted that the procedure may relate to a person who is a suspect but who, because of insufficient evidence to make an arrest, could not be classified as a known suspect. In that case even greater caution should be exercised in the photograph selection.

Contamination prevention

5.117 The importance of preventing the possibility of contamination is accentuated by the fact that no solicitor will be present on behalf of the suspect selected. The Code provides that:

(1) only one witness can be shown photographs at a time;[255]

---

252 Code D3.29.
253 Annex E.4 and E.10.
254 [1993] Crim LR 50, CA.
255 Annex E.3.

(2) there should be no communication between witnesses and they should be given as much privacy as practicable;[256]

(3) the witness must not be prompted.[257]

Conduct of the procedure

5.118 Before the viewing takes place the witness must be informed that the person previously seen may or may not be among the photographs and if no positive identification can be made, the witness should say so. The witness must also be instructed to view the entire series of at least 12 before making a decision to ensure that there is a genuine choice.[258] If a selection is made but the witness cannot confirm the identification the officer should ask the witness how sure he is that the photograph is of the person previously seen.[259] Once a positive identification has been made, there will be a known suspect. Hence other witnesses may not be shown the photographs; rather they and the identifying witness should attend a formal procedure if identification is disputed.[260] If there are other potential suspects among the photographs, the viewing may continue with other witnesses provided the photograph of the suspect already identified is removed.[261]

Documentation and retention

5.119 A record of the procedure must also be kept on forms provided for the purpose. It should record anything said about an identification or the conduct of the procedure and any reason why it was impracticable to comply with the Code. Thus any additional descriptive feature remembered by the witness during the course of the showing should be noted; likewise the absence of any feature. The record must also include the name and rank of the supervising officer who, if not conducting the procedure, shall inspect and sign it as soon as practicable thereafter.[262] It would be appropriate for the name and status of the person conducting the procedure to be added in case an issue concerning the integrity of the procedure arose.

5.120 For trial purposes it may be necessary to assess the similarity between the types of photographs used and of the persons depicted in them. It may also be useful to examine the photograph of a defendant shown to a witness who failed to make an identification or that of a person wrongly identified by the witness. Consequently, regardless of whether an identification is made, the

---

256 Annex E.3. In *R v Finley* [1993] Crim LR 50, CA, two witnesses were shown photographs in circumstances where it was found that one must have overheard the other identify the defendant: 'I recognise him by his beady eyes'.

257 Annex E.5.

258 Annex E.5.

259 Annex E.7.

260 Annex E.6.

261 *R v Lamb* (1980) 71 Cr App R 198, CA.

262 Annex E.11 and 12.

photographs shown to the witness must be preserved and available for production in court. If an identification is made, a photograph should be taken of the frame or part of the album from which the selection was made as an aid to its reconstitution.[263]

BROADCASTING, PUBLISHING AND SHOWING IMAGES OF AN INCIDENT

5.121 The police may be in possession of recorded images of the perpetrator at or around the time of the offence which constitute direct evidence of it. The images may be released to the media for broadcast on television or publication in the press in order to obtain information and evidence about the identity of the perpetrator.[264] However, should publication occur after the arrest of a suspect in a case where identification is an issue, it may amount to a contempt of court if it creates a substantial risk of prejudice.[265] An exception would be the release of images for the purpose of tracing a prolific or dangerous offender or an escapee. A copy of the published images must be kept and the suspect or solicitor allowed to view the material before any of the identification procedures takes place, unless it would be impracticable or cause unreasonable delay to the investigation. If images have been published any witness who takes part in a formal identification procedure must, once the procedure has been conducted, be asked whether they have seen any image or description published in the media or on social networking sites.[266] If so, they should be asked to provide details of the circumstances, eg date and place that they saw the image or description.[267] A record must be made of the witness's account.[268]

Showing images to obtain evidence of recognition

5.122 Images of an incident can also be shown to police officers or others who might be considered able to recognise the person depicted.[269] For example, a shoplifter caught on video might be recognised by a local beat officer or company staff might be able to identify an employee committing an offence recorded on CCTV. A recording can also be shown in order to confirm (or otherwise) the likeness of a suspect whose identity is already known. In a series of decisions that preceded publication of the current version of the Code in 2011, the Court of Appeal had concluded that the Code was not directly applicable to the showing of images for such purposes.[270] However, that lacuna has been addressed and the Code now prescribes in some detail, the procedure

---

263 Annex E.10.

264 Code D3.28.

265 Contempt of Court Act 1981, s 2.

266 Code D3.29.

267 Ibid.

268 Ibid.

269 As to the admissibility of a consequential identification, see **10.16**.

270 In *R v Smith* [2008] EWCA Crim 1342, the Court of Appeal left open the question of whether or not the showing of CCTV images to police officers to ascertain whether they are able to

to be followed when showing images 'for the purposes of obtaining evidence of recognition' by any person, including a police officer.[271]

5.123 Where the identity of a person depicted in CCTV images is sought, the circulation of those images among police officers is a perfectly acceptable and desirable practice. However, it is a practice that presents evidential problems. It was suggested in *R v Smith*,[272] that the mischief in cases of recognition from CCTV images is the absence of any objective means of testing the accuracy of the identification. To this end, the court recommended that the police officer's reaction to seeing the image and any words of doubt ought to be recorded, and that a note should be made of what it was about the image that was said to have triggered the recognition. It may frequently be the case that the only person present when an identification is made is the identifying officer and in such circumstances it might be rather difficult to establish the veracity of any record which was made. Further, in *R v Chaney*[273] it was acknowledged that it may be difficult for the person asserting recognition to identify those features of the subject which form the basis of the recognition, an observation that is supported by some psychological theories which suggest that facial recognition is the product of a complex holistic process that draws on various types of encoded information.[274] Research suggests that there is a poor correlation between a witness's accuracy in identifying a face and the completeness of any description that he or she is able to provide.[275] A witness's difficulty in articulating what it is about a face that triggered recognition may have no bearing on identification accuracy.

5.124 The showing of images and recordings for the purposes of obtaining evidence of recognition is now governed by the procedures set out in Part B of Section 3 of the Code. Code D3.34 explains that:

> 'This Part of this section applies when, for the purposes of obtaining evidence of recognition, any person, including a police officer:
>
> (a) views the image of an individual in a film, photograph or any other visual medium; and
> (b) is asked whether they recognise that individual as someone who is known to them.'

---

identify the person depicted was subject to the provisions of Code D. However, in the subsequent case of R v Chaney [2009] EWCA Crim 21, it considered the view that Code D was not directly applicable to be 'well-founded'.

271 Code D3.34.

272 [2008] EWCA Crim 1342.

273 [2009] EWCA Crim 21.

274 See R Wilcock, R Bull and R Milne *Witness Identification in Criminal Cases*, (OUP, 2008), pp.17–22.

275 C Meissner, S Sporer, and K Susa 'A Theoretical Review and Meta-Analysis of the Description-Identification Relationship in Memory for Faces', (2008) 20 *European Journal of Cognitive Psychology* 414.

Showing the images

5.125 Code D3.35 requires images or recordings to be shown on an individual basis 'to avoid collusion and to provide safeguards against mistaken recognition'. Although Code D3.36 requires a record to be made of whether the person to whom the images/recordings were shown was given information concerning the name or identity of any suspect, information about the crime or the offender, it would seem that the provision of such information will usually amount to a breach of the Code. Code D3.35 requires the principles of video identification (Annex A) to be followed where the suspect is known. If the suspect is not known the principles relating to identification by photographs are followed (Annex E). Annex A provides that 'Care must be taken not to . . . give any indication of the suspect's identity'.[276] Similarly, Annex E provides that 'The witness shall not be prompted or guided in any way but shall be left to make a selection without help'.[277] Although these principles are to be followed only so far as it is possible to do so, it will generally be possible to withhold from the person asked to view the recordings/images any information which might suggest the identity of the person depicted – for example, details about suspects, the crime (eg the time, location or modus operandi) or the offender himself. Providing such contextual information will inevitably influence the viewer's perception of the image.[278] Where the person who is invited to view the image is given the name of a suspect, the request takes the form of a leading question and evidence of recognition obtained in such circumstances may be of little or no probative value. As the purpose of showing the image/recording is to establish whether the person to whom they are shown is able to recognise the culprit on the basis of his or her physical appearance alone, there appears to be no good reason why such information should be provided.[279] It is, therefore, regrettable that Part B of section 3 of the Code contains no explicit prohibition on the provision of contextual information.

Recording requirements

5.126 Code D3.36 imposes a general duty to record 'the circumstances and conditions under which a person is given an opportunity to recognise an individual'. The non-exhaustive list of matters that must be recorded includes:

(a) Whether the person knew or was given information concerning the name or identity of any suspect.

---

[276] Annex A, para.13.

[277] Annex E, para.5.

[278] See, for example, studies which suggest that expert analysis of fingerprints can be influenced by the provision of contextual information about an investigation, e g I Drior, D Charlton and A Peron, 'Contextual Information Renders Experts Vulnerable to Making Erroneous Identifications' (2006) 156 *Forensic Science International* 74.

[279] See *R v Jabar* [2010] EWCA Crim 130, in which the Court of Appeal deprecated the use of a procedure in which an officer was asked if she had previously arrested the appellant and was then invited to see whether she could identify anyone in stills taken from CCTV footage depicting a person who it was believed subsequently committed a robbery which was being investigated, a fact which might also have been pointed out to the identifying officer.

(b) What the person has been told *before* the viewing about the offence, the person(s) depicted in the images or the offender and by whom.

(c) How and by whom the witness was asked to view the image or look at the individual.

(d) Whether the viewing was alone or with others and if with others, the reason for it.

(e) The arrangements under which the person viewed the film or saw the individual and by whom those arrangements were made.

(f) Whether the viewing of any images was arranged as part of a mass circulation to police and the public or for selected persons.

(g) The date time and place images were viewed or further viewed or the individual was seen.

(h) The times between which the images were viewed or the individual was seen.

(i) How the viewing of images or sighting of the individual was controlled and by whom.

(j) Whether the person was familiar with the location shown in any images or the place where they saw the individual and if so, why.

(k) Whether or not on this occasion, the person claims to recognise any image shown, or any individual seen, as being someone known to them, and if they do:

 (i) the reason;
 (ii) the words of recognition;
 (iii) any expressions of doubt;
 (iv) what features of the image or the individual triggered the recognition.

5.127 These matters may be recorded by the person who views the image or any officer or police staff who is responsible for showing the image.[280]

---

[280] Code D3.37.

Chapter 6

BODY MARKS, PHOTOGRAPHS, FINGERPRINTS AND SAMPLES

INTRODUCTION

6.1 The acquisition and use of evidence relating to certain personal characteristics for identification purposes is governed by the Police and Criminal Evidence Act 1984 (PACE) and Code D. The relevant sections of PACE may be found at Appendix D below and Code D is reproduced in its entirety at Appendix A. They make provision for:

(1) physical examination for and photography of identifying body marks;

(2) taking of photographs;

(3) fingerprinting;

(4) intimate and non-intimate body samples;

(5) the taking of impressions of footwear.

Separate powers exist under the Terrorism Act 2000, Sch 8 to take steps to identify a detained person and to take fingerprints, intimate and non-intimate samples. See **6.71–6.82**. As this book is concerned with identification of persons from their physical characteristics, the powers to take and retain impressions of footwear are not referred to below but mirror the provisions relating to fingerprints and samples.

6.2 Some terms are mentioned frequently throughout these provisions. They and their meanings are as follows:

- *Detained at a police station*: 'Police detention' is defined by PACE, s 118. It describes the status of a person who has been taken to a police station following arrest or has been arrested there having attended voluntarily. The term has been held to apply to a person remanded in custody and temporarily housed at a police station.[1]

- *Appropriate consent*: Defined by PACE, s 65(1) according to age. If the person to whom the procedure is to be applied is over 17 years of age, the consent of that person is required; in the case of a person aged under 17 that of the person and their parent or guardian; and for a person under 14 years old the consent of a parent or guardian alone.[2]

- *Recordable offence*: All imprisonable offences and certain others, such as soliciting for the purposes of prostitution and improper use of public

---

1 *R v Seymour* [1995] 9 *Archbold News* 1, CA.
2 See Chapter 7 below for consent of a juvenile.

telecommunications systems: PACE, ss 27(4) and 118 and the National Police Records (Recordable Offences) Regulations 2000.[3]

BODY MARKS

6.3 A body mark may assist in identifying an offender where, for example, it matches the description of a witness or CCTV image. Alternatively the absence of such a mark may eliminate a suspect. A mark may also establish a suspect's identity by reference to a description or photograph in pre-existing records.

Power to search, examine and photograph

6.4 PACE, s 54A[4] permits the search and examination of a person to discover a suspected body mark. If found, a photograph may be taken of it. A 'mark' includes features or injuries.[5] Clearly it includes a tattoo, scar or birth mark. A 'feature' taken with the phrase – 'that would tend to identify' – (see **6.5**) appears wide enough to cover a common natural condition such as a hairy chest.

6.5 A search or examination[6] of a person is permitted by PACE, s 54A(1), (2) and (3)[7] when:

(1) the person to be searched is detained at a police station;[8] and

(2) it is authorised by an officer at least the rank of inspector;

(3) it is for the purpose:

- either of ascertaining whether the detainee possesses a mark that would tend to identify him or her in the commission of an offence and either:
  - the detainee withholds appropriate consent to the search; or
  - it is impracticable to obtain it;[9]

---

3 SI 2000/1139. See also; National Police Records (Recordable Offences) (Amendment) Regulations, SI 2003/2823; National Police Records (Recordable Offences) (Amendment) Regulations, SI 2005/3106; National Police Records (Recordable Offences) (Amendment) Regulations, SI 2007/2121.

4 See also Code, D5.1.

5 PACE, s 54A(12).

6 But not an intimate search: PACE, s 54A(8); Code, D5.11.

7 See also Code, D5.1 and 5.2.

8 It does not include someone present at the police station for a stop and search procedure: Code, D5.1.

9 Code D, Note for Guidance 5D provides some examples of impracticability of obtaining consent: a person who is drunk or unfit to give consent; where there are reasonable grounds to suspect that a person may prevent or resist and where, in the case of a juvenile, there has been insufficient time to seek the consent of a parent.

- or of facilitating the ascertainment of the identity[10] of the detainee and either:
  - that person has refused to reveal his or her identity; or
  - the officer has reasonable grounds for suspecting that he or she has given a false name.[11]

If an identifying mark is found it may be photographed with consent and, if consent is withheld or is impracticable to obtain, without it.[12] An identifying mark is one which facilitates the ascertainment of the person's identity or the person's involvement in an offence.[13]

6.6 The search, examination and photography may be carried out by a police officer or designated person[14] who may use reasonable force if consent is withheld.[15] The person searching or taking a photograph must be of the same sex as the detainee.[16] The search for a mark must be limited to what is necessary for the required purpose. One involving the removal of more than outer clothing should be carried out in accordance with the requirements for the conduct of strip searches.[17]

6.7 Police may also carry out a consensual search and take photographs of marks of a person who is not detained but has attended a police station voluntarily provided that there are reasonable grounds to suspect his or her involvement in an offence.[18] However in those circumstances if consent is withheld force may not be used[19] and the person may leave at any time.[20]

Information and documentation

6.8 The provisions relating to the supply and recording of information under PACE, s 54A are mostly identical to those for the taking of photographs under PACE, s 64A. They are set out in **6.13–6.14**.

---

10 The purpose of ascertaining identity includes ascertaining that the suspect is not a particular person: PACE, s 54(11)(a).

11 PACE, s 54A(1) and (3), Code, D5.1 and 5.3.

12 PACE, s 54A(5), Code, D5.4.

13 PACE, s 54A(12).

14 PACE, s 54A(6), Code, D2.19. See Police Reform Act 2002, ss 38 and 47 for 'designated person' and Sch 4, para 27 of the 2002 Act for powers under PACE, s 54A.

15 PACE, s 117, Code, D5.9.

16 PACE, s 54A(7); Code, D5.5.

17 Code, D5.10. They are found in Code C, Annex A.

18 Code, D5.19.

19 Code, D5.21.

20 PACE, s 29.

Use, retention and destruction of photographs

6.9 The provisions relating to the use, retention and destruction of photographs taken pursuant to PACE, s 54A are the same as those applicable to photographs taken pursuant to PACE, s 64A. See **6.15–6.16**.

PHOTOGRAPHS

6.10 Photographs may be useful as a contemporary record of a person's appearance at the time of arrest for establishing identity. They may also be used in checking against pre-existing photographic or descriptive records, and against photographic images of offences.[21] The power under PACE, s 64A, unlike that to search for and photograph body marks, is absolute and not contingent upon an identification purpose. The power is independent of the power to take photographs for the purposes of an identification procedure, though photographs taken under PACE, s 64A may be used for such a procedure in certain circumstances.[22]

Power to take photographs

6.11 PACE, s 64A(1)[23] enables police to photograph a person:

(1) who is detained at a police station;[24]

(2) either:

- with the appropriate consent of the person; or
- without it if it is withheld or it has been impracticable to obtain it.[25]

The photograph may be taken by a police officer or designated person.[26] The detainee can be required to remove anything which obscures the face or head. Failing that, the photographer may remove it.[27] Reasonable force to take the photograph is permitted if consent has been withheld. It may also be used if the request to remove the item obscuring the face has not been met.[28] However,

---

21 Code D, Note for Guidance 5B provides a number of examples of their potential use.

22 See **4.26**.

23 See also Code, D5.12.

24 A photograph of a person may be taken at a location other than a police station (with the appropriate consent or in the absence of it where it is not practicable to obtain it) when (s 64A(1A)): arrested by a constable for an offence (s 64A(1B)(a)); taken into custody having been arrested by a person other than a constable (s 64A(1B)(b)); he or she has been required to wait with a Community Support Officer (s 64A(1B)(c)); he or she has been given a direction to leave a locality under Violent Crime Reduction Act 2006, s 27 (s 64A(1B)(ca)); he or she has been issued with one of a number of specified Fixed Penalty Notices (s 64A(1B)(d)–(g)).

25 See note 7.

26 PACE, s 64A(3); Code, D2.19. See Police Reform Act 2002, ss 38 and s 47 for 'designated person' and Sch 4, para 33 of the 2002 Act for powers under PACE, s 64A.

27 PACE, s 64A(2); Code, D5.13.

28 PACE, s 117; Code, D5.14.

in order to use force to take a suitable photograph, Code D provides that it must not have been reasonably practicable to take one covertly.[29] The Code further states that a copy of an image taken from a camera installed within a police station may be used if consent has been withheld.[30]

6.12 A photograph may also be taken of a person who has attended a police station voluntarily if there are reasonable grounds to suspect his or her involvement in an offence,[31] though force may not be used[32] and the person may leave at any time.[33]

Information and documentation for searches and photographs

6.13 A person who is to be searched, examined or photographed pursuant to the above powers must be informed[34] of:

(1) its purpose;

(2) the grounds on which authority for a search has been given; and

(3) the purposes for which any photograph obtained may be used, disclosed or retained.

The information should be given to the detainee prior to the exercise of the power. The information concerning a photograph may be delayed if it is to be taken covertly or an image is to be extracted from a camera system installed inside the police station.

6.14 A record of any search or photography must be made. It should include:[35]

(1) the identity of the officer conducting the search or taking the photograph;

(2) its purpose;

(3) the consent to it or, if withheld, the reason for the search or photograph without consent;

(4) the authority for a search which, if oral must be confirmed in writing as soon as practicable;

(5) the grounds for the authority to search and the authorising officer;

---

29 Code, D5.14.
30 Code, D5.15.
31 Code, D5.19.
32 Code, D5.21.
33 PACE, s 29.
34 Code, D5.16.
35 (1)–(3) and (5): Code, D5.17; (4): PACE, s 54A(4) and Code D5.17; (6): Code, D5.18.

(6) if force was used to search or take a photograph, the circumstances and the persons present.

Use, retention and destruction of photographs

6.15 Photographs of a person or of a person's body mark may be used by or disclosed to any person for any purpose related to the prevention and detection of crime, the investigation of an offence, the conduct of a prosecution, or the enforcement of a sentence.[36] The reference to crime extends to conduct outside the United Kingdom, which is either a crime in that territory or corresponds to an offence if it had taken place in the United Kingdom; the reference to investigations and prosecutions includes those outside the United Kingdom.[37]

6.16 The persons to whom disclosure may be made and who may use photographs – 'any person' – is widely drawn. It is not confined to those organisations whose purpose is the prevention and detection of crime, provided their use does not extend beyond that necessary to achieve those aims. In *R v Hellewell*[38] police photographs of the 'usual suspects' were passed to an association of local shopkeepers for the use of staff, subject to a prohibition against displaying them. The plaintiff, who had many convictions, was among those whose photographs were provided to the association. His application for an injunction to restrain the Chief Constable failed, the court holding that the disclosure was reasonably directed to the prevention of crime and thus lawful.

6.17 The statutory provisions permit the retention of photographs after use or disclosure, but only for the specified purposes.[39] Thus they may be retained after acquittal and even where there has been no charge. The exception is the case of a person who consented to photographs being taken when attending a police station voluntarily. If that person was not later charged, informed they may be prosecuted, cautioned, warned or reprimanded for a recordable offence the photographs must be destroyed unless consent in writing is given to their retention.[40]

---

[36] PACE, s 64A(4)(a); Code, D3.30 for photographs and PACE, s 54A(9)(a) for body mark photographs.

[37] PACE, s 64A(5) for photographs and PACE, s 54A(10) for body mark photographs.

[38] [1995] 1 WLR 810, QBD. The case was a civil action for breach of confidence prior to the existence of PACE, s 64A when there was no statutory regulation of the use of photographs. However the formula regarding use applied in the judgment is strikingly similar to that in s 64A. See also *R (Ellis) v Chief Constable of Essex* [2003] EWHC 1321 (Admin).

[39] PACE, s 64A(4)(b); Code, D3.30 for photographs and PACE, s 54A(9)(b) for body mark photographs.

[40] Code, D5.22. Copies and negatives are subject to the same requirement and the person photographed is entitled either to witness the destruction of them or to a certificate confirming the destruction. As to admissibility, if wrongly retained, see **10.76**.

FINGERPRINTS

6.18 The identity of a person who has left fingerprints at the scene of a crime may be revealed upon a comparison with those kept on a database of retained fingerprints. A suspect's fingerprints may be compared with scene-of-crime fingerprints for identification or elimination purposes. In some cases a non-suspect may also be asked to provide fingerprints in order to eliminate innocent scene of crime fingerprints. Less commonly, fingerprints may be sought on a voluntary basis from a class of people to whom an offender is thought to belong. The term 'fingerprints' is defined as the skin pattern and other physical characteristics or features of a person's fingers and palms.[41]

Power to take fingerprints

6.19 Fingerprints may be taken with appropriate consent, but may not be taken without it[42] unless one of four separate powers under PACE, s 61 applies. First, a power exercisable after arrest; secondly, after charge; thirdly, in connection with bail; and fourthly, after conviction, caution, warning or reprimand. In each case the power is exercisable by a constable or designated person[43] who may use reasonable force if necessary.[44]

Post-arrest

6.20 A person's fingerprints may be taken without appropriate consent pursuant to PACE, s 61(3)[45] if:

(1) the person is detained at a police station in consequence of an arrest for a recordable offence, or has been released on bail following arrest for a recordable offence;[46] and

(2) fingerprints have not already been taken in the course of the investigation of the offence, unless those already taken do not constitute a complete set or some or all are not of sufficient quality for satisfactory analysis, comparison or matching.

6.21 PACE, Sch 2A provides police officers with a power to direct a person who has been arrested for a recordable offence and released to attend a police station for the purposes of taking his or her fingerprints pursuant to this power.[47] Where a person is directed to attend a police station he or she must be given 7 days' notice and may be required to attend on a specific day or at a

---

41 PACE, s 65(1); Code, D4.1. They may be taken manually or electronically: Code, D4.5.

42 PACE, s 61(1), Code, D4.2.

43 PACE, s 61(8B); Code, D2.19. See Police Reform Act 2002, ss 38 and 47 for 'designated person' and Sch 4, para 29 of the Act for powers under PACE, s 61.

44 PACE, s 117; Code, D4.6.

45 See also Code, D4.3(a).

46 PACE, s 61(5A); Code, D4.3(ca).

47 Code, D4.4(a). Where a person's fingerprints have been taken but are incomplete or not sufficient for satisfactory analysis etc, the direction to attend must be issued within 6 months of

specific time.[48] If a person is attending a police station for some other purpose consideration ought to be given to taking fingerprints on that occasion.[49] The 7-day period may be shortened if there is an urgent need to obtain fingerprints for the investigation of an offence, or where a shorter period is authorised by an officer of the rank of inspector or above.[50] Where such an authorisation is given the reasons are to be recorded as soon as practicable after it has been given.[51] The provisions regarding notice are common to directions to attend to give fingerprints, intimate and non-intimate samples.

Post-charge

6.22 Fingerprints may be taken from a person without appropriate consent, whether or not he or she is detained at a police station,[52] if:

(1) he or she has been charged with, or informed that he or she will be reported for, a recordable offence; and

(2) fingerprints have not already been taken in the course of the investigation of the offence, unless those already taken do not constitute a complete set or some or all are not of sufficient quality for satisfactory analysis, comparison or matching.[53]

PACE, Sch 2A also provides police officers with a power to direct a person who has been charged with, or informed that he or she will be reported for, a recordable offence to attend a police station for the purposes of taking his fingerprints pursuant to this power.[54] See **6.21** for provisions concerning the notice to be given to persons directed to attend for these purposes.

In connection with bail

6.23 Fingerprints may be taken from a person without appropriate consent at a court or police station pursuant to PACE, s 61(4A) and (4B)[55] if:

---

the investigating officer being informed that the original set of fingerprints were incomplete or insufficient: PACE, Sch 2A, para 1(2); Code, D4.4(a)(i).

48 PACE, Sch 2A, para 16(1).

49 PACE, Sch 2A, para 16(2).

50 PACE, Sch 2A, para 16(3).

51 PACE, Sch 2A, para 16(4).

52 PACE, s 61(4) provides a power in relation to persons who are detained at a police station (see also Code, D4.3(b)), and s 61(5B) provides a power in relation to those who are not detained at a police station. See also Code, D4.3(cb).

53 PACE, s 61(3A), (5B).

54 Where a person's fingerprints have been taken but are incomplete or not sufficient for satisfactory analysis etc, the direction to attend must be issued within 6 months of the investigating officer being informed that the original set of fingerprints were incomplete or insufficient in respect of persons who have been charged, and in respect of those who have been informed that they will be reported, within 6 months of the date that they were so informed: Sch 2A, para 2(2).

55 See also Code, D4.3(c).

(1) the person has answered bail to the court or police station;

(2) it is authorised by the court or an officer of at least the rank of inspector; and

(3) the person bailed has previously provided fingerprints; and

(4) either:

- there are reasonable grounds for suspecting that the person answering bail is not the same person as bailed: or
- the person answering bail claims not to be the person bailed.

Post-conviction or caution

6.24 Finally, fingerprints may be taken from a person without appropriate consent pursuant to PACE, s 61(6)[56] once a person has been:

(1) convicted of a recordable offence;

(2) cautioned in respect of a recordable offence and at that time admitted it;

(3) warned or reprimanded[57] for a recordable offence;

(4) convicted of an offence under law in force in a country or territory outside England and Wales, which would constitute a 'qualifying offence'.[58]

PACE, Sch 2A, para 3 provides that following any of the outcomes described above, a police officer may require the person to attend a police station at a specified time for fingerprinting, if (i) he or she has not had his or her fingerprints taken since the relevant outcome, or (ii) fingerprints have been taken but did not constitute a complete set or are insufficient for satisfactory analysis, comparison or matching.[59] In respect of the outcomes described at (1)–(3) above if the offence is a 'qualifying offence' the power is not subject to any time limit.[60] In respect of offences that are not qualifying offences the power must be exercised (i) within 2 years of the date of conviction, caution, warning or reprimand (or of the date that the Schedule came into force if this was later), and (ii) within 2 years of the date that the investigating officer was informed that the original set of fingerprints were insufficient (or of the date

---

56 See also Code, D4.3(d).

57 Pursuant to Crime and Disorder Act 1998, s 65.

58 PACE, s 61(6D). A list of 'qualifying offences' is provided in s 65A. This power may be exercised only where the subject has not had his fingerprints taken previously, or any previously obtained fingerprints are not of sufficient quality to enable comparison, analysis or matching: s 61(6E). The authority of an officer of the rank of inspector is required: s 61(6F).

59 PACE, Sch 2A, para 3(1); and Code, D4.4(b).

60 PACE, Sch 2A, para 3(5). PACE, s 65A provides a list of 'qualifying offences'.

that the Schedule came into force if this is later).[61] The power to direct attendance in respect of a conviction in a jurisdiction other than England and Wales is not subject to any time limit.[62] A power of arrest without warrant exists for failure to comply with any requirement to attend made under Sch 2A.[63]

Information and documentation

6.25 If fingerprinting takes place with consent it must be in writing if given at a police station.[64] A person whose fingerprints are to be taken must be informed of:

(1) the reason for doing so;

(2) the power under which they have been taken; and

(3) where authorisation of the court or a police officer has been required, the fact that the authorisation has been given.

These matters must be recorded as soon as practicable after they have been taken.[65] In bail cases where the authority of a senior police officer is necessary, it may be given orally (but must be confirmed in writing as soon as practicable) or in writing.[66]

6.26 The person from whom fingerprints are to be taken, with or without consent, must be informed before they are taken that they may be retained and subject to a speculative search[67] (see below) unless their destruction is required in which case he or she may witness their destruction.[68] That the person has been informed of the possibility of a speculative search must be recorded as soon as practicable after the fingerprints have been taken.[69] If force has been used to take fingerprints the circumstances must be recorded with details of those present.[70]

---

61 PACE, Sch 2A, para 3(3); Code, D4.4(a)(iii).

62 PACE, Sch 2A, para 13; Code, D4.4(a)(v).

63 PACE, Sch 2A, para 17 and Code, D4.4(b).

64 PACE, s 61(2); Code, D4.2.

65 PACE, s 61(7); Code D4.7(a) and 4.8. The statutory provision is stated to apply to non-consensual post-arrest, post-charge and post-conviction fingerprinting but not in connection with bail. However the Code requires the reason to be given in all cases. The record of the reason under PACE, s 61(7) must be made on the custody record if fingerprints are taken at a police station: PACE, s 61(8).

66 PACE, s 61(5).

67 PACE, s 61(7A); Code, D4.7(b)(i). The statutory provision is stated to apply when fingerprints are taken at a police station. The Code does not apply this limitation.

68 Code, D4.7(b)(ii).

69 PACE, s 61(7A)(b); Code, D4.8. The record must be on the custody record if the fingerprints are taken at a police station: PACE, s 61(8).

70 Code, D4.9.

Use, retention and destruction of fingerprints

6.27 The provisions relating to the use, retention and destruction of fingerprints pursuant to PACE, s 61 are the same as those applicable to samples taken pursuant to PACE, ss 62 and 63. See **6.50–6.52**.

SAMPLES

6.28 The advance of DNA technology allows minute and visually imperceptible traces to be profiled and compared. Samples may also be of value, for example, in hair fibre analysis or the discovery of substances such as skin, clothing, fibres or chemicals under fingernails.

Intimate and non-intimate samples

6.29 There are two classes of samples under PACE: intimate and non-intimate.

6.30 An 'intimate sample' is defined[71] as:

(1) a sample of blood, semen or any other tissue fluid, urine or pubic hair;

(2) a dental impression;

(3) a swab taken from a body orifice other than the mouth.

6.31 A 'non intimate sample' is defined[72] as:

(1) a sample of hair other than pubic hair;

(2) a sample of or from under a nail;

(3) a swab from a person's body including mouth but no other orifice;

(4) saliva;

(5) a skin impression.[73]

6.32 The principal effect of the distinction between the two types of sample is that consent to the taking of an intimate sample may be refused and force may not be used to take one.

---

71 PACE, s 65; Code, D6.1(a).

72 PACE, s 65; Code, D6.1(b).

73 PACE, s 65; Code, D6.1. A skin impression means any record (other than fingerprints) of skin pattern and other physical characteristics of a foot or other part of the body.

Power to take non-intimate samples

6.33 PACE, s 63 governs the taking of non-intimate samples. A non-intimate sample may be taken with consent and, in certain circumstances, without it. The four situations in which no consent is needed are first, after a person's arrest, secondly where a person is held in custody by the police on the authority of a court, thirdly after charge and fourthly after conviction. A non-intimate sample may be taken by a constable or a designated person.[74] If consent is withheld it may be taken by force.[75] Restrictions apply to the unnecessary presence of others, in particular to those of the opposite sex, if the removal of clothing to obtain a sample is likely to cause embarrassment.[76]

Post-arrest

6.34 A non-intimate sample may be taken without appropriate consent:

(1) pursuant to PACE, s 63(2A) if the person is in police detention in consequence of an arrest for a recordable offence;[77] or

(2) pursuant to PACE, s 63(3ZA) if the person has been arrested for a recordable offence and released (whether on bail or otherwise);[78] and

(3) a non-intimate sample of the same type and from the same part of the body has not already been taken in the course of the investigation or, if it has, it proved insufficient.[79]

Police custody on court authority

6.35 A non-intimate sample may be taken without appropriate consent pursuant to PACE, s 63(3)[80] if:

(1) the person is held in custody by the police on the authority of a court; and

(2) a police officer of at least the rank of inspector has authorised it[81] on reasonable grounds:

---

74 PACE, s 63(9ZA); Code, D2.19. See ss 38 and 47 of the Police Reform Act 2002 for 'designated person' and Sch 4, para 31 of the Act for powers under PACE, s 63.

75 PACE, s 117; Code, D6.7.

76 Code, D6.9.

77 PACE, s 63(2A). See also Code, D6.6(a).

78 PACE, s 63(3ZA); Code, D6.6(c).

79 Insufficiency, relative to either quantity or quality, means insufficient to enable information to be produced by analysis of the sample. It includes the frustration of the purpose of obtaining information as a result of the loss, destruction, contamination of, or damage to a sample or part of one, or where the sample produced no result or an unreliable result: PACE, s 65(1) and (2); Code D, Note for Guidance 6B(a).

80 See also Code, D6.6(b).

81 PACE, s 63(4). No authority for a skin impression may be given if one has already been taken of the same part of the body which is not insufficient for its purpose: s 63(5A); Code D6.6(a).

- for suspecting the involvement of that person in a recordable offence;[82] and
- for believing that the sample will tend to prove or disprove that involvement.[83]

Post-charge

6.36 A non-intimate sample may be taken without appropriate consent pursuant to PACE, s 63(3A)[84] if:

(1) the person has been charged with or informed that he or she will be reported for a recordable offence; and

(2) a sample has not already been taken in the course of the investigation, or if it has, it proved to be unsuitable or insufficient for analysis; or[85]

(3) a sample has been taken and destroyed pursuant to the duty to do so as soon as a DNA profile is derived, and there is a dispute as to whether a profile was derived from the sample provided by the person.[86]

Post-conviction

6.37 PACE, s 63(3B), provides the power to take a sample after a person has been convicted, cautioned, warned or reprimanded for a recordable offence.[87] It applies also following a finding of insanity or unfitness to plead.[88] A non-intimate sample may also be taken from anyone convicted of an offence under the law of a jurisdiction outside England and Wales that, if committed in England and Wales, would constitute a qualifying offence.[89]

6.38 Powers to direct persons who have been arrested or charged with a recordable offence and released, or convicted of a recordable offence, to attend a police station for an intimate sample to be taken are provided by PACE, Sch 2A, paras 9–14 which mirror the powers to direct persons to attend for fingerprinting and the associated notice requirements (set out at **6.21**).

---

82 PACE, s 63(4)(a).

83 PACE, s 63(4)(b).

84 See also Code, D6.6(b).

85 An unsuitable sample is one which by its nature is not suitable for a particular form of analysis: Code D, Note for Guidance 6B(b). See note 65 above for the meaning of insufficient.

86 PACE, s 63(3A)(c).

87 Provided no sample has been taken since the person was convicted, cautioned, warned or reprimanded, except where the sample obtained was insufficient for analysis. See also Code, D 6.6(e).

88 PACE, s 63(3C).

89 PACE, s 63(3E). This power is subject to (i) such a sample not having been taken from the person previously, or a previously taken sample being of insufficient quantity or quality to be analysed; (ii) authorisation by an officer of the rank of at least inspector.

Power to take intimate samples

6.39 The circumstances in which intimate samples may be taken is governed by PACE, s 62. Consent is always necessary. Intimate samples may only be taken by a registered medical practitioner or registered nurse or registered paramedic, save in the case of a dental impression which must be taken by a registered dentist.[90] Restrictions apply to the unnecessary presence of others, in particular to those of the opposite sex other than medical practitioners, if the removal of clothing to obtain a sample is likely to cause embarrassment.[91]

6.40 An intimate sample may be taken from a person pursuant to PACE, s 62(1)[92] if:

(1) the person is either:

- in police detention; or
- is not in police detention but from whom two or more non-intimate samples have been taken which have proved insufficient for analysis; and

(2) a police officer of at least the rank of inspector has authorised it on reasonable grounds:

- for suspecting the involvement of that person in a recordable offence; and
- for believing that the sample will tend to prove or disprove that involvement; and

(3) the appropriate consent of that person is given.

6.41 Section 62(2A) provides a power to take an intimate sample where two or more non-intimate samples have been taken from a person convicted of an offence under the law of a jurisdiction other than England and Wales, which if committed in England and Wales would have been a qualifying offence, but have proved insufficient. Consent must be given and authorisation is to be obtained from an officer of the rank of at least inspector.[93]

6.42 Though consent may be refused and force may not be used to take an intimate sample, the Act permits the drawing of an adverse inference against a person who refuses without good cause.[94] The provision does not demand that the authority to take the sample should precede the person's consent. In *R v Butt*[95] consent was obtained before authorisation. It was argued that PACE and

---

90 PACE, s 62(9) and (9A) and Code, D6.4.

91 Code, D6.9.

92 PACE, s 62(1A) and (2) and Code, D6.2.

93 Code, D6.2(c).

94 PACE, s 62(10). See **6.48**.

95 20 February 1998, CA (unreported).

Code D required authorisation to be given first on the ground that only on being given the reasons for it could the defendant make an informed decision. The Court of Appeal acknowledged that the authorisation can affect the basis on which a person has given consent. Consent may, for example, be founded upon some misconception as to the purpose or use of the sample. However on the facts it was held that there had been no breach because the defendant knew the basis upon which the sample had been requested, which was the basis upon which the authorisation was subsequently given.

6.43 Powers to direct persons to attend a police station to provide an intimate sample are provided by PACE, Sch 2A, paras 7 and 8, and are subject to the notice requirements described at **6.21**.

Further powers

6.44 The power to take samples from a person remanded in custody or serving a sentence is exercisable in a prison or other institution to which the Prison Act 1952 applies.[96] A non-intimate sample from a person convicted of an offence may be taken at the hospital at which the person has been detained pursuant to the Mental Health Act 1983. Likewise a non-intimate sample may be taken at a hospital at which a person has been detained following a finding of insanity or unfitness to plead.[97] In the case of a convicted young offender detained under s 92 of the Powers of Criminal Courts (Sentencing) Act 2000, the non-intimate sample may be taken at the place of detention.[98]

6.45 A police officer can order a person to attend a police station for the purpose of taking a sample.[99] The power applies to a person either charged with or informed that he or she will be reported for a recordable offence who has not had a sample taken in the course of an investigation or whose sample previously taken was unsuitable or insufficient.[100] The power also applies in the case of a person convicted of a recordable offence who has not had a sample taken since conviction or who has provided a sample, either before or after conviction, that was unsuitable or insufficient. The power must be exercised within 1 month of charge, conviction or the date on which the appropriate officer[101] was informed that the previous sample was unsuitable or insufficient. Seven days' notice must be given to the person to attend and a particular time may be specified. A person who fails to comply is liable to arrest without warrant. The power to order attendance at a police station does not discriminate between intimate and non-intimate samples. However its application corresponds to non-intimate post-charge and post-conviction

96 PACE, s 63A(3).
97 PACE, s 63A(3A).
98 PACE, s 63A(3B).
99 PACE, s 63A(4), (5), (6) and (7).
100 PACE, s 63(3) and (4); Code, D6.6(a). See note 79.
101 In post-charge cases the requirement must be made by the investigating officer, in post-conviction cases the officer in charge of the police station from which the investigation was conducted: PACE, s 63A(8).

samples. To apply to it intimate samples would be to extend those powers and would not be reconcilable with the requirement of consent.

Information and documentation

6.46 If consent has been obtained to taking an intimate or non-intimate sample it must be given in writing.[102] In the case of a non-intimate sample taken pursuant to the power that exists post arrest, charge or conviction the person from whom the sample is to be taken must be given the reason for taking it[103] and informed of the nature of the offence in which he is suspected of involvement.[104] A record of these matters should be made as soon as practicable after the sample has been taken.[105] If the sample is taken on the authority of a senior police officer, the authority may be given orally or in writing but if oral must be confirmed in writing as soon as practicable.[106] The authorisation, the grounds and, in the case of an intimate sample, the fact of consent must be recorded as soon as practicable after the sample has been taken.[107] If force is used to take a non-intimate sample a record of the circumstances and those present must be made.[108]

6.47 A person from whom a sample is requested is entitled to know of the possibility of a speculative search (see **6.50**) and must be so informed before any sample may be taken, whether with or without consent. The fact that he or she has been informed must be recorded as soon as practicable after the sample has been taken.[109]

6.48 A person from whom an intimate sample is requested must be warned that if consent is withheld an adverse inference may be drawn at trial.[110] The suggested warning is as follows:

> You do not have to provide this sample/allow this swab or impression to be taken, but I must warn you that if you refuse without good cause, your refusal may harm your case if it comes to trial.[111]

A record must be made of the warning.[112] The importance of these provisions is underlined by the requirement that a person who is not legally represented must be told or reminded of his or her entitlement to free legal advice.[113]

---

[102] PACE, s 62(4) and Code, D6.2(a)(ii) for intimate samples; s 63(2) and Code, D6.5 for non-intimate samples.
[103] PACE, s 63(6)(a) for non-intimate samples; s.62(5)(a) for intimate samples.
[104] PACE, s 63(7) for non-intimate samples; s 62(6) for intimate samples.
[105] PACE, s 63(6)(b); Code, D6.10.
[106] PACE, s 62(3) for intimate samples; s 63(5) for non-intimate samples.
[107] PACE, s 62(7) and s 63(8); Code, D6.10.
[108] Code, D6.10.
[109] PACE, s 62(7A) for intimate samples; s 63(8B) and Code, D6.8(b)(i) for non-intimate samples.
[110] Code, D6.3(b).
[111] Code, Note for guidance 6D.
[112] Code, D6.11.
[113] Code, D6.3(b).

6.49 The recording of matters required by PACE must take place on a custody record if the person from whom the sample is to be taken is detained at a police station.[114]

Use, retention and destruction of fingerprints and samples

The current law

6.50 The law concerning the retention of fingerprints, DNA samples and profiles is currently in a state of flux and will, in the near future, be subject to significant amendment, see **6.53–6.70**.The use that can be made of fingerprints and samples, including the information derived from samples such as a DNA profile, stretches beyond the investigation of the offence of which the person is suspected. A 'speculative search' of any database or other records may be conducted to compare the fingerprints, samples or derivative information of a person who has been arrested for, charged with or informed that he or she is to be reported for a recordable offence.[115] The search may include checks against records held by all United Kingdom police forces and other public authorities under a duty to investigate offences, their corresponding agencies in any other countries and other bodies with an investigative role under an international agreement.[116] A speculative search may also be conducted in respect of a person who has not been arrested for or charged with a recordable offence provided he or she has given consent in writing to such use. Once it has been given the consent may not later be withdrawn.[117]

6.51 PACE, s 64 as presently enacted, reverses the previous requirement for destruction of fingerprints and samples in respect of persons who were not prosecuted or were cleared of the offence for which they were investigated.[118] The retention of fingerprints and samples is permitted (save for a limited exception) for the purposes of prevention or detection of crime, the investigation of an offence, the conduct of a prosecution or the identification of deceased persons, including speculative searches of any databases.[119]

---

114 PACE, s 62(8) for intimate samples; s 63(9) for non-intimate samples.

115 PACE, s 63A(1).

116 The compendium of agencies is set out in PACE, s 63A(1A) and (1B). DNA samples lawfully taken by the police, or profiles derived from them cannot be used for purposes that are not set out in PACE, s.64(1A); see *Lambeth LBC v S* [2006] EWHC 326 (Fam), the Court of Appeal finding that a court could not order disclosure of biometric material to enable parentage to be established for the purposes of care proceedings. Also, *London Borough of Lewisham v D* [2010] EWHC 1239 (Fam); the results of any analysis carried out on biometric data cannot be released to the local authority for use in care proceedings by virtue of it being caught by the prohibition on 'information derived from' biometric data in s.64(1A).

117 PACE, s 63A(1C) and (1D).

118 This was the result of two cases, *R v Weir* (2000) *The Times*, June 16, CA and *Attorney-General's Reference (No 3 of 1999)* [2000] 2 Cr App R 416, [2000] Crim LR 994, CA in which an acquittal was directed and a conviction quashed. They concerned the use of samples that should have been destroyed and derivative information that should not have been used. *Attorney-General's Reference (No 3 of 1999)* was reversed in the House of Lords on the PACE, s 78 issue: see **10.59** on this point.

119 PACE, s 64(1A) and (1B).

Fingerprints and samples must be destroyed where the person from whom they were taken is not suspected of having committed the offence under investigation.[120] This duty must also be taken to extend to the destruction of DNA profiles that may have been derived from a sample that is required to be destroyed by virtue of the person's innocence. However, fingerprints and samples may be kept if another person from whom fingerprints or a sample was taken is convicted of the offence.[121] In such an event they may not then be used either for a subsequent investigation of, or in evidence against, the person who would otherwise have been entitled to their destruction.[122]

6.52 The requirement for destruction and the prohibition against use does not apply if consent in writing has been obtained for the retention of the fingerprints or samples because the consent cannot later be withdrawn.[123] Where the destruction of fingerprints is required, copies should also be destroyed and if the information is recorded as computer data, access to it must be rendered impossible.[124] A person whose fingerprints are to be destroyed is entitled to witness the destruction and is entitled to a certificate that the corresponding computer data is inaccessible.[125] Samples for testing for Class A drugs under PACE, s 63B may not be used for identification or investigative purposes.[126] Neither should they be used in evidence against that person.[127] As to the evidential use of samples and fingerprints which should have been destroyed, see **10.59**.

The legislative response to the judgment in S & Marper v United Kingdom

6.53 The provisions permitting retention of samples and biometric data (DNA profiles and fingerprints) taken from those who are arrested for, or charged with, an offence but not subsequently convicted, have been the subject of much criticism.[128] In 2000 the Government launched a 'DNA Expansion Programme', the initial objective being to create a database containing the DNA profiles of every active offender in England and Wales.[129] It was estimated that this would involve taking DNA samples from around 2.5 million individuals. The number of profiles stored on the database reached this figure

---

120 PACE, s 64(3).

121 The preservation of another person's fingerprints or sample might be relevant to the case and therefore to any later appeal.

122 PACE s 64(3), (3AA) and (3AB), Code D Annex F.1.

123 PACE, s 64(3AC).

124 PACE, s 64(5).

125 PACE, s 64(6) and (6A).

126 Code D, Note for Guidance 6F and Code C, 17.14(a).

127 Code C, Note for Guidance 17D.

128 See, eg Nuffield Council on Bioethics, *The Forensic Use of Bioinformation: Ethical Issues* (Nuffield Foundation, 2007); A Roberts and N Taylor, 'Privacy and the DNA Database' [2005] *European Human Rights Law Review* 373; L Campbell, 'A Rights-Based Analysis of DNA Retention: "Non-Conviction" Databases and the Liberal State' [2010] Crim LR 889.

129 See generally, C McCartney, 'The DNA Expansion Programme and Criminal Investigation' (2006) 46 *British Journal of Criminology* 175.

early in 2004. Thereafter the objective was to ensure that the profiles of any 'newcomers to crime' were added to the database.[130] The Criminal Justice Act 2003[131] effected an amendment to PACE, s 63 which extended powers to take DNA samples and fingerprints from any person arrested for a recordable offence. Section 64 had previously been amended to permit the retention of samples taken in the course of an investigation, irrespective of whether or not the persons from whom they were taken were subsequently charged with, or convicted of the offence. Consequently, by 2007, the National DNA Database contained samples taken from over 4.4 million people,[132] 1 million of whom had no criminal conviction.[133] The compatibility of the legislative scheme with the right to respect for private and family life guaranteed by Art 8 of the European Convention on Human Rights was considered by the House of Lords in *R (on the application of S & Marper) v Chief Constable of South Yorkshire*.[134] Their Lordships[135] doubted that retention of fingerprints, DNA samples and profiles interfered with the right, and took the view that even if it did, any interference could be justified for the purposes of the prevention and detection of crime. However, in *S and Marper v UK*,[136] the Grand Chamber of the European Court of Human Rights found that blanket retention of DNA samples, profiles and fingerprints taken from those who had not been convicted of any offence was incompatible with the right provided by Art 8 of the Convention.[137]

6.54 The Court's decision will, in due course, lead to amendment of the provisions of PACE concerning the retention of fingerprints, DNA samples and profiles derived from those samples. The Crime and Security Act 2010 contains provisions that would amend these provisions. However, it seems unlikely that they will take effect. On 11 February 2011, the Protection of Freedoms Bill was presented to Parliament. If enacted, the proposed legislation will repeal the amending provisions found in the Crime and Security Act 2010 and establish a more restrictive retention scheme, with greater external oversight. Given the uncertainty that currently exists, the following sections outline both the framework that is established by the Crime and Security Act 2010, and that which will replace it if the legislative provisions set out in the Protection of Freedoms Bill receive Royal Assent.

---

130 DNA Expansion Programme 2000–2005: Reporting Achievement (Home Office, 2007).

131 PACE, s 10.

132 National DNA Database Annual Report, 2006–2007.

133 *The Forensic Use of Bioinformation: Ethical Issues* (Nuffield Council on Bioethics, 2007), 52.

134 [2004] UKHL 39.

135 With the exception of Baroness Hale.

136 Application nos. 30562/04 and 30566/04 [2008] ECHR 1581 (4 December 2008).

137 In *R (on the application of GC) v The Commissioner of the Police of the Metropolis* [2011] UKSC 21, the Supreme Court, held that it was possible to read and give effect to s.64(1A) PACE in a way which is compatible with Article 8 of the ECHR. However, the ACPO guidelines ('Exceptional Case Procedure for Removal of DNA, Fingerpints and PNC Records'; ACPO, 2006) setting out a policy of retaining data taken from every person who is arrested but not convicted were incompatible with the Convention right and therefore unlawful. In light of impending reform, and the likelihood that the guidance would be withdrawn and revised following enactment of a new legislative regime for the retention of biometric data, relief was limited to a declaration of unlawfulness.

The Crime and Security Act 2010

6.55 The amending provisions of the Crime and Security Act 2010 establish a rather complex set of provisions concerning the retention of DNA profiles and fingerprints taken from those who have not been convicted of any offence. The revised legislative scheme would require DNA samples to be destroyed as soon as a profile is derived from it, and in any case within 6 months of the date on which it was taken,[138] although the provisions do not define what constitutes a 'DNA sample'. Profiles and fingerprints taken from persons who were aged over 18 years at the time of the alleged offence and who have no previous convictions, or only one exempt conviction,[139] and were not subsequently convicted of the offence[140] may be retained for a period of 6 years from the date on which the sample of DNA was taken.[141] Cautions, warnings and reprimands for a recordable offence, are treated as convictions,[142] and convictions for a number offences arising out of a single course of action are treated as a single conviction.[143] An 'exempt conviction' is a conviction for a recordable offence (other than one of a category of offences referred to in the Act as 'qualifying offences' and prescribed in s 65A) which was committed when the person was aged under 18 years.[144] If the person is arrested for, or charged with, a further recordable offence during the 6 year period during which the original profile and fingerprints may be retained, a further 6 year retention period runs from the date of the subsequent arrest.[145]

Juveniles

6.56 The Act makes detailed provision regarding the retention of fingerprints and DNA profiles taken from juveniles. Where a person under the age of 18 is convicted of a qualifying offence, fingerprints and a DNA profile may be retained indefinitely.[146] An exhaustive list of 'qualifying offences' is set out in s 65A and includes serious offences such as murder, manslaughter, kidnapping and false imprisonment, as well as potentially much less serious offences, including burglary and assault occasioning bodily harm.

6.57 Profiles and fingerprints taken from those convicted of a recordable offence, other than a qualifying offence, who were under 18 at the time that the offence was committed and have no previous convictions, may be retained for a period of 5 years from the date on which the fingerprints and profiles were taken.[147] If that person is arrested for, or charged with, a recordable offence before the expiration of this period, the profiles and fingerprints may be

---

[138] PACE, s 64ZA.
[139] PACE, s 64ZD(1).
[140] PACE, s 64ZD(5).
[141] PACE, s 64ZD(3).
[142] PACE, s 64ZI(3).
[143] PACE, s 64ZI(4).
[144] PACE, s 64ZI(2)(b).
[145] PACE, s 64ZD(4).
[146] By virtue of the general power to retain provided by PACE, s 64.
[147] PACE, s 64ZH(3).

retained for a further period, commencing from the date on which the person was arrested or charged. That period is 6 years if:

(1) the person was aged 18 or over at the time that the alleged subsequent offence was committed;[148] or

(2) the person was aged 16 or 17 at that time, and the alleged offence was a qualifying offence.[149]

The period is 3 years if:

(1) the person was under 18 at the time of the subsequent alleged offence, and the offence is not a qualifying offence;[150] or

(2) the person was under 16 years at the time of the subsequent alleged offence and the offence is a qualifying offence.[151]

The limitation on the period for which profiles and fingerprints may be retained ceases to have effect if the person is convicted of a further recordable offence before the relevant period expires.[152]

6.58 Where a juvenile, who has no previous convictions (or one exempt conviction) is arrested or charged with a recordable offence, but not subsequently convicted, the period for which fingerprints and a DNA profile may be retained varies according to his or her age and whether or not the offence is a qualifying offence. DNA profiles and fingerprints taken from those who are under 18 at the time of the alleged offence may be retained for 3 years if the offence is not a qualifying offence.[153]

6.59 If the person was 16 or 17 at the time of the alleged offence and the offence was a qualifying offence, a profile and fingerprints may be retained for 6 years,[154] and if under 16 years for 3 years.[155] The limitation on the period of retention ceases to have effect in each situation where the person:

(1) is convicted of a recordable offence and is over 18 when the alleged offence was committed;

(2) is convicted of a qualifying offence; or

---

148 PACE, s 64ZH(4)(a).
149 PACE, s 64ZH(4)(d).
150 PACE, s 64ZH(4)(b).
151 PACE, s 64ZH(4)(c).
152 PACE, s 64ZH(5).
153 PACE, s 64ZE(3).
154 PACE, s 64ZG(3).
155 PACE, s 64ZF(3).

(3) having a previous exempt conviction is subsequently convicted of a recordable offence.[156]

The provisions relating to the effect of subsequent arrest for a recordable offence during the period in which profiles and fingerprints are retained, mirror the effect of those that relate to retention following the conviction of a person under 18 years for a recordable offence other than a qualifying offence (described at **6.57**).

Persons subject to control orders

6.60 Fingerprints and DNA profiles taken from persons who are the subject of a control order, and who have no previous convictions (or one exempt conviction), must be destroyed within 2 years of the date on which the control order is lifted.[157] The requirement to destroy fingerprints and profiles ceases to have effect if the person is convicted of a recordable offence (or in Scotland, an offence punishable by imprisonment) before the 2 year period expires.[158]

Power to retain for an extended period on the grounds of national security

6.61 DNA profiles and fingerprints taken from those who have not been convicted (or have only one exempt conviction) may be retained beyond the periods set out in ss 64ZD–ZH 'for the purposes of national security'.[159] The initial decision must be reviewed 2 years from the date that the material was taken. This is renewable, subject to review to establish that grounds for retention remain. Where they do not, the material must be destroyed.[160]

Duty to destroy material taken from the persons who have not been convicted

6.62 The power to retain material taken from those who have not been convicted of any offence (or have only one exempt conviction) is qualified by s 64ZI(5). This provides that following its use in any speculative search, DNA profiles and fingerprints must be destroyed if it appears to the Chief Officer that:

(1) the arrest was unlawful; or

(2) the taking of the DNA sample or fingerprints was unlawful; or

(3) the arrest was based on mistaken identity; or

(4) there are other circumstances relating to the arrest or the alleged offence that mean it is appropriate for the material to be destroyed.

---

156 PACE, s 64ZF(5), s 64ZG(5),
157 PACE, s 64ZC(1), (2).
158 PACE, s 64ZC(4).
159 PACE, s 64ZK(1).
160 PACE, s 64ZK(3).

Retention of samples provided voluntarily

6.63 The Crime and Security Act would change the current position whereby persons who provide fingerprints and samples and consent to them being retained cannot revoke that consent. The amendments provided for by the Act require fingerprints and any profiles derived from samples provided voluntarily for the purposes of an investigation, save in certain circumstances, to be destroyed as soon as those purposes have been fulfilled.[161] Such material would not need to be destroyed where the person is convicted of the offence under investigation (or any other offence of which the person is convicted in consequence of providing the material), or where provision of the material leads to the person's arrest for a recordable offence, but no subsequent conviction.[162] The material would not need to be destroyed if the person consented to its retention. Consent must be in writing, and may be given or revoked at any time.[163]

The Protection of Freedoms Bill 2011

6.64 The legislation set out in the Bill would, if enacted in the form that it was presented to Parliament, repeal the provisions of the Crime and Security Act 2010 relating to the retention of biometric data, and replace it with a legislative scheme which is more limited in scope, and based on the equivalent legislation in Scotland.[164] The Bill defines a DNA sample as 'any material that has come from a human body and consists of or includes human cells', and a DNA profile as 'any information derived from a DNA sample'.[165] The requirement for DNA samples to be destroyed as soon as a profile is derived (and in any case within 6 months of it being taken) is retained.[166] Likewise the requirement for DNA profiles and fingerprints to be destroyed where the taking of the fingerprints or the sample from which the profile was derived was unlawful, or where the powers to take samples and fingerprints were exercised by virtue of the person's arrest, and the arrest was unlawful or the result of mistaken identity.[167] The Bill establishes a general requirement to destroy profiles and fingerprints unless one of the various powers of retention that it provides applies.

6.65 The Bill provides for a sample taken from a person who is arrested to be retained until the conclusion of the investigation or subsequent proceedings.[168] It also permits a speculative search to be conducted within a reasonable time using any profile or fingerprints that have been taken during the investigation.[169] If a person has previously been convicted of a recordable

---

161 PACE, s 64ZB(2).
162 PACE, s 64ZB(2)(3).
163 PACE, s 64ZL.
164 Criminal Procedure (Scotland) Act 1995, ss 18–20.
165 Clause 18, amending PACE, s 65(1).
166 Clause 14.
167 Clause 1.
168 Clause 2.
169 Clause 1.

offence, any fingerprints and DNA profiles derived from a DNA sample taken during the investigation of the offence for which the person has been arrested may be retained indefinitely.[170]

6.66 The concepts of qualifying and exempt offences that are established by the provisions of the Crime and Security Act 2010 are retained for the legislative scheme set out in the Bill. The retention of fingerprints and DNA profile derived from a sample taken from a person who has been arrested and charged with a qualifying offence but not convicted of it would be permitted for a period of 3 years from the date on which the fingerprints or DNA sample were taken.[171] However, where a person arrested for a qualifying offence was not subsequently charged, retention of fingerprints and DNA profile is subject to the consent of the Commissioner for the Retention and Use of Biometric Material, a position that is also created by Bill, and other conditions that might be prescribed by the Secretary of State.[172] At the end of the 3 year period of retention the chief officer may apply to a District Judge for an order which would permit the material to be retained for a further period of 2 years. The decision to grant or refuse an order would be subject to a right of appeal to the Crown Court.

Persons under 18 years

6.67 Fingerprints and DNA profiles taken during the investigation of a recordable offence, other than a qualifying offence, taken from a person who was subsequently convicted of the offence and who was under 18 at the time of the offence, may be retained indefinitely if the person was given a custodial sentence of 5 years or more.[173] If sentenced to a custodial sentence of less than 5 years, the fingerprints and DNA profile may only be kept for the period of imprisonment and a further 5 years from the end of that period.[174] If given a non-custodial sentence, the 5 year period of retention will run from the date that the fingerprints and DNA sample were taken.[175] However, if the person is convicted of a further recordable offence before the end of any finite period of retention, material may be retained indefinitely.[176]

National security

6.68 As is the case under the Crime and Security Act 2010, the Bill provides for retention of fingerprints and DNA profiles taken from those who are not convicted of any offence where the chief officer makes a 'national security determination'.[177] The determination has effect for a period of 2 years and may

---

[170] Clause 5.

[171] Clause 3. Material taken from those who are subsequently given a penalty notice for the offence for which they were arrested may be kept for a period of 2 years: clause 8.

[172] Clause 20.

[173] Clause 7.

[174] Clause 7.

[175] Clause 7.

[176] Clause 7.

[177] Clause 9.

be renewed. The Secretary of State is required to issue guidance on making or renewing such determinations,[178] and the Commissioner for the Retention and Use of Biometric Data must review any determination or decision to renew a determination.[179] Where the Commissioner concludes that it is not necessary to retain the material he or she may order its destruction, where there are no grounds for its retention under any other power.[180]

Material given voluntarily and retained with consent

6.69 The provisions regarding material that is given voluntarily mirror those found in the Crime and Security Act 2010.[181]

Use of material retained after its destruction was required

6.70 The Bill will establish a prohibition on the use of DNA profiles and fingerprints in evidence against the person from whom they were taken or for the purposes of investigating any offence, either in England and Wales or another jurisdiction, where they are available for such use only by virtue of having been retained after their destruction was required.[182]

POWERS OF IDENTIFICATION UNDER THE TERRORISM ACT 2000

6.71 Schedule 8 of the Terrorism Act (TA) 2000 specifies the powers for examination, photography, taking of fingerprints and samples of persons arrested under TA 2000, s 41 or detained at ports and borders pursuant to TA 2000, Sch 7. The PACE powers of taking fingerprints and samples do not apply to persons detained under terrorism provisions.[183] However, the definitions of terms such as 'appropriate consent', 'fingerprints', 'insufficient', 'intimate sample', 'non-intimate sample' and 'recordable offence' are those applied under PACE.[184]

Photography and other means of identification

6.72 By TA 2000, Sch 8, para 2, an 'authorised person' meaning a constable, a prison officer, a person authorised by the Secretary of State and additionally, in the case of detention pursuant to TA 2000, Sch 7, an immigration and a customs officer,[185] may take any steps which are reasonably necessary for:

---

[178] Clause 22.

[179] Clause 20.

[180] Clause 20.

[181] Clauses 10 and 11.

[182] Clause 16.

[183] PACE, s 61(9)(b) – fingerprints; PACE, s 62(12) – intimate samples; PACE, s 63(10) – non-intimate samples.

[184] TA 2000, Sch 8, para 15(1).

[185] TA 2000, Sch 8, para 2(2)(d) and Sch 7, para 1(1).

(1) photographing the detained person;

(2) measuring him; or

(3) identifying him.

The unspecified measures for identification under (3) do not include the power to take fingerprints, intimate or non-intimate samples which are considered separately.

Fingerprints

6.73 TA 2000, Sch 8, para 10(2) permits a constable to take fingerprints either:

(1) with the appropriate consent in writing of a person arrested on suspicion of being a terrorist under TA 2000, s 41 or detained under TA 2000, Sch 7; or

(2) without consent if either:[186]

- the suspect is detained at a police station and authorisation is given by an officer of at least the rank of superintendent; or
- the suspect has been convicted of a recordable offence.

6.74 Where authorisation is required it may only be given if either:[187]

(1) in the case of a person arrested under TA 2000, s 41, the officer reasonably suspects the person to have been involved in a terrorist offence within TA 2000, s40(1)(a) and reasonably believes that the fingerprints will tend to confirm or disprove that involvement; or

(2) the officer is satisfied that the fingerprints are necessary to assist in determining whether the person was concerned in the commission, preparation or instigation of acts of terrorism under TA 2000, s 41(1)(b); or

(3) the officer is satisfied that the fingerprints will facilitate the ascertainment of the person's identity in circumstances where the person has refused to identify himself or the officer has reasonable grounds for believing that the person is not the person he or she claims to be.

---

[186] TA 2000, Sch 8, para 10(4).

[187] TA 2000, Sch 8, paras 10(6) and (6A).

Non-intimate samples

6.75 TA 2000, Sch 8, para 10(3) permits a constable to take non-intimate samples either:

(1) with the appropriate consent in writing of a person arrested on suspicion of being a terrorist under TA 2000, s 41 or detained under Sch 7; or

(2) without consent if either:[188]

- the suspect is detained at a police station and authorisation is given by an officer of at least the rank of superintendent; or
- the suspect has been convicted of a recordable offence on or after 10 April 1995.

6.76 Where authorisation is required it may only be given if either:[189]

(1) in the case of a person arrested under TA 2000, s 41 the officer reasonably suspects the person to have been involved in a terrorist offence within TA 2000, s 40(1)(a) and reasonably believes that the sample will tend to confirm or disprove that involvement; or

(2) the officer is satisfied that the sample is necessary to assist in determining whether the person was concerned in the commission, preparation or instigation of acts of terrorism under TA 2000, s 1(1)(b).

Intimate samples

6.77 As under PACE, an intimate sample may only be taken with consent but an adverse inference may be drawn from a failure to consent without good cause.[190] TA 2000, Sch 8, para 10(5) allows an intimate sample to be taken from a detained person if:

(1) detention is at a police station;

(2) appropriate consent is given in writing;

(3) authorisation is given by an officer of at least the rank of superintendent; and

(4) the sample is taken, in the case of urine by a constable, in the case of a dental impression by a registered dentist and in any other case by a registered medical practitioner.[191]

---

188 TA 2000, Sch 8, para 10(4).
189 TA 2000, Sch 8, para 10(6).
190 TA 2000, Sch 8, para 13(1).
191 TA 2000, Sch 8, paras 13(2) and (3).

6.78 An intimate sample may also be taken if two or more non-intimate samples have been taken from a person who has been released from detention and those samples prove to be insufficient, provided conditions (2), (3) and (4) above are met.[192]

6.79 Where authorisation is required it may only be given if either:

(1) in the case of a person arrested under TA 2000, s 41, the officer reasonably suspects the person to have been involved in a terrorist offence within TA 2000, s 40(1)(a) and reasonably believes that the sample will tend to confirm or disprove that involvement; or

(2) the officer is satisfied that the sample is necessary to assist in determining whether the person was concerned in the commission, preparation or instigation of acts of terrorism under TA 2000, s 41(1)(b).

Information and documentation

6.80 If oral authorisation for the taking of fingerprints or samples is given under the above provisions the officer giving it must confirm it in writing as soon as reasonably practicable.[193] The person from whom the fingerprints or samples are to be taken must be informed of the following:

- the purposes for which they may be used (see **6.81**);
- where consensual or pursuant to conviction of a recordable offence the reason for taking them;[194]
- where pursuant to authorisation, that it has been given and the grounds on which it was given; and
- where relevant the nature of the offence of which the person is suspected.[195]

6.81 After fingerprints or samples have been taken, a record must be made of the following, as applicable:

- the grounds for taking them;
- the fact that the detainee has been supplied with the required information;
- the reason for taking the fingerprints or sample;
- the authorisation and the grounds for it; and

192 TA 2000, Sch 8, paras 12(1) and (2).
193 TA 2000, Sch 8, para 10(7).
194 TA 2000, Sch 8, para 11(1).
195 TA 2000, Sch 8, para 11(2).

- the fact that appropriate consent was given.[196]

Use and retention of fingerprints and samples

6.82 Fingerprints, samples and the information derived from the samples may be subject to speculative searches[197] and checked against other fingerprints and samples taken under TA 2000, Sch 10 only for the purposes of a terrorist investigation or those related to the prevention or detection of crime, the investigation of an offence or the conduct of a prosecution.[198] The Crime and Security Act 2010[199] amends TA 2000, Sch 8 to establish a scheme of retention that is broadly similar to that provided by PACE. However, it is doubtful whether these provisions will come into force. The Protection of Freedoms Bill contains provisions that would amend Sch 8 to the TA 2000, establishing a scheme of retention broadly consistent with the amended PACE provisions.

196 TA 2000, Sch 8, para 11(3).
197 See **6.47** for meaning and ambit.
198 TA 2000, Sch 8, para 14.
199 Crime and Security Act 2010, s 17.

Chapter 7

JUVENILE AND OTHER VULNERABLE SUSPECTS

JUVENILE SUSPECTS

7.1 Anyone appearing to be under the age of 17 must be treated for the purposes of Code D as a juvenile unless there is clear evidence to the contrary.[1] Where the Code requires information to be given to or sought from a juvenile, it must be done in the presence of an appropriate adult. If the appropriate adult is not present when the information is given, as for example where it is not at first realised that the suspect is a juvenile, the procedure must be carried out again in the presence of an appropriate adult.[2]

7.2 An appropriate adult will be:

(i) the juvenile's parent or guardian or, if in care of a local authority, voluntary organisation, or if subject to an order under the Children Act 1989, a person representing the authority or organisation;

(ii) a social worker from the social services department of a local authority;

(iii) failing these, some other responsible person aged 18 or over who is not a police officer or employed by the police.[3]

7.3 The consent required for a physical examination for body marks, the taking of photographs, fingerprints and body samples is governed by the relevant sections of PACE. In each case 'appropriate consent' is required.[4] The meaning of that term corresponds to the consent of a juvenile required for the conduct of a Code D identification procedure. Under the Code, the consent of a person under 17 will be valid only if the parent or guardian also consents. If the juvenile is under 14 years of age, the consent of the parent or guardian

---

1 Code D2.4 and Code C1.5.
2 Code D2.14.
3 Code C1.7(a).
4 See **6.2**.

alone will suffice.[5] In the case of a juvenile in the care of a local authority or voluntary organisation, consent may be given by that body.[6] The consent of an appropriate adult who does not fall within these classes of person does not comply. The person consenting need not actually be present to give consent unless that person is also the appropriate adult, provided he or she has been given proper disclosure about the offence, full information about the proposed procedure and has been allowed to speak to the juvenile and appropriate adult. Provided the consent is fully informed and not withdrawn it may be obtained at any time before the procedure takes place.[7]

7.4 Should the necessary consent of the parent or guardian not be given or if reasonable efforts to obtain it have failed, the provisions relating to suspects who are not available, including the use of covertly obtained images, can be applied by the identification officer.[8] A somewhat harsh consequence of this provision is that a juvenile may consent to a video identification but if a parent refuses, the juvenile could then be subjected to a group identification or covert video procedure.

7.5 Any identification procedure involving a juvenile must take place in the presence of an appropriate adult.[9]

MENTALLY DISORDERED SUSPECTS

7.6 If a person is suspected by an officer of being mentally disordered or otherwise mentally vulnerable, or the officer is told so in good faith, unless and until that suspicion is dispelled by clear evidence the suspect must be treated as such when applying the provisions of Code D.[10] 'Mental disorder' bears the same definition as contained in the Mental Health Act 1983.[11] 'Mentally vulnerable' includes a person who, because of their mental state or capacity, may not understand the significance of what is being explained, including questions and their replies[12] or the procedure itself.

7.7 Where the Code requires information to be given to or sought from a mentally disordered or vulnerable suspect, this must be done in the presence of an appropriate adult. If the appropriate adult is not present, for example where it is not at first realised that the suspect has a mental disability, the procedure must be carried out again in the presence of an appropriate adult.[13] The

---

5 Code D2.12.

6 Code D, Note for Guidance 2A.

7 Code D, Note for Guidance 2A .

8 Code D2.12. See Code D3.21.

9 Code D2.15.

10 Code D2.3 and Code C1.4.

11 Code C, Note for Guidance 1G. Section 1(2) of the Act defines it as mental illness, arrested or retarded development of the mind, psychopathic disorder and any other disorder or disability of the mind.

12 Code C, Note for Guidance 1G.

13 Code D2.14.

consent of a mentally disordered or vulnerable person to the conduct of an identification procedure will be valid only if given in the presence of an appropriate adult.[14] Any identification procedure must take place in the presence of the appropriate adult.[15] The procedures themselves set out the degree of participation expected by an appropriate adult, for example the opportunity to see the images to be used in a video identification before the procedure commences.

7.8 'Appropriate adult' for the purposes of a mentally disordered suspect means a relative, guardian or other person responsible for the care of the mentally disordered suspect; or someone experienced in dealing with mentally disordered people such as a psychiatric nurse.[16] A suspect's preference for a relative should be respected.[17] Failing those options the appropriate adult must be a responsible adult over 18 years of age. It may not be a police officer or someone employed by the police.

SUSPECTS WITH VISUAL AND COMMUNICATIVE DIFFICULTIES

7.9 A suspect who appears to be blind, seriously visually impaired, deaf, unable to read or speak or has a difficulty because of a speech impediment shall be treated as such in the absence of evidence to the contrary.[18] If a person suffers serious visual impairment or cannot read the custody officer must ensure that a solicitor, relative, appropriate adult or some other person likely to take an interest in the suspect's welfare is available to check any required documentation. If written consent or the signing of documentation is required the person assisting may sign instead if the suspect prefers.[19] If the suspect appears to be deaf or there is doubt about his or her hearing or speaking ability or ability to understand English and effective communication cannot be established, an interpreter (sign or foreign language) must be instructed to channel the communication.[20]

---

[14] Code D2.12.

[15] Code D2.15.

[16] Code C1.7(b).

[17] Code C, Note for Guidance 1D.

[18] Code D2.5 and Code C1.6.

[19] Code D2.13. This provision seeks to protect the interests of both the suspect and the police if the person with impairments does not wish to sign police documents: Code D, Note for Guidance 2B.

[20] Code D2.14.

Chapter 8

VOICE IDENTIFICATION PROCEDURE

INTRODUCTION

8.1 Code D makes no provision for voice identification procedures by witnesses, though it does not preclude the use of an 'aural identification' procedure where the police judge it to be appropriate.[1] Historically, therefore, the procedures that have been used have either drawn on some of the features of procedures for visual identification or have, in effect, been no more than aural confrontations. However, as the result of concern expressed by researchers and phoneticians about the ability of persons to recognise or identify a voice,[2] the judicial acknowledgement of such concern[3] and the previous ad hoc nature of police procedures in the absence of any formal guidelines, a Home Office Circular[4] (HOC 57/2003) has been issued advising police on the use of voice identification parades.

8.2 The procedure in HOC 57/2003 is not mandatory, but it is recommended that as an 'example of good practice' it should be followed closely.[5] The text of the circular is set out in Appendix E. Although the drafters have not taken the opportunity to do so in the most recent revision, it is anticipated that voice identification may in, due course, be incorporated into Code D.

---

1 Code D1.2.

2 See D Ormerod, 'Sounds Familiar? Voice Identification Evidence' [2001] Crim LR 595, discussing the problems of voice identification and the merits of a variety of formal identification techniques.

3 See *R v Roberts* [2000] Crim LR 183, CA.

4 Home Office Circular 57/2003, issued 5 December 2003.

5 HOC 57/2003, para 5.

WHEN A VOICE IDENTIFICATION PROCEDURE SHOULD BE HELD

8.3 HOC 57/2003 does not specify the circumstances in which a procedure should be held. Hence, though a voice identification procedure may be desirable either where a witness purports to recognise the offender by his or her speech or expresses an ability later to identify the voice, unlike visual identification[6] there is no right to a procedure where identity is in dispute. In *R v Gummerson and Steadman*[7] the victim of a robbery claimed to recognise the voices of his masked attackers. The appellants' defence was that the identification was mistaken and that they were elsewhere at the material time. It was argued on appeal that there should have been a voice identification parade. The Court of Appeal dismissed the submission summarily by asserting that Code D had no application. However, in *R v Hersey,*[8] a voice identification procedure was held. Yielding a positive identification the defence sought to exclude it. The Court of Appeal approved the decision to conduct the procedure. Its propriety was founded upon fairness to a suspect who might be exculpated if the original identification was shown to be erroneous.

8.4 In the absence of any protocol as to the circumstances in which a procedure should be held, it may not be over-cynical to suggest that a voice identification procedure will appeal to an investigating officer when the outcome is likely to be advantageous to a successful prosecution, for example, to supplement an otherwise weak case. Moreover there is no express prohibition on confrontation-like procedures, which have been upheld in the past.[9] However the failure to follow the 'example of good practice' in HOC 57/2003 may found a submission to exclude voice evidence acquired by other means. The admissibility of non-expert voice identification is further considered at **10.102**.

DESCRIPTIVE STATEMENT

8.5 HOC 57/2003 requires the identification officer in charge to obtain a statement from the witness containing as much detail and description of the voice as possible.[10] The descriptive statement should be supplied to the expert instructed in the preparation of the parade and disclosed to the suspect or solicitor prior to the identification procedure. This statement will be additional to any record of 'first description' which may have been given to an investigating officer shortly after the offence.

---

6 Code D3.12.

7 [1999] Crim LR 680, CA. See also *R v Deenik* [1992] Crim LR 578, CA.

8 [1998] Crim LR 281, CA. See **10.67** for facts.

9 *R v Deenik* [1992] Crim LR 578, CA.

10 HOC 57/2003, para 6.

TIMING OF PROCEDURE

8.6 The Circular states that the identification officer should ensure that all the work can be undertaken and completed within a reasonable time. Delay will cause the witness's memory to degrade or fade. It is therefore advised that the procedure should take place within 4 to 6 weeks of the incident in question.[11]

SOURCE OF SAMPLES

8.7 The identification procedure should be carried out by use of recordings. Under no circumstances should a live voice identification be conducted.[12] The identification officer should obtain a representative sample of the suspect's voice. HOC 57/2003 advises that a suitable source for the suspect's sample may be the tape-recorded interview, 'during which the suspect is speaking naturally, responding to questions'.[13] What must not be done is to request the suspect to read a set text. This is unlikely to represent the suspect's natural speech pattern that would have been heard by the witness. Rhythm and tone may well be altered when reading aloud from written material. The challenge in seeking material for a fair voice selection procedure is the procurement of suitable samples which provide no innate clue as to the identity of the suspect.

8.8 The suspect should be informed at the beginning of the interview that a sample from the recording may be used for identification purposes and asked to give his or her consent.[14] Clearly the identification purpose of the recording will be frustrated if the suspect elects not to answer questions or apparently seeks to disguise his or her voice. However, there is no provision in HOC 57/2003 for obtaining a sample without notice, or by covert recording or even deception.[15] No doubt the principles of Code D, PACE, s 78, the common law rules on the privilege against self-incrimination and the suspect's European Convention[16] rights will be considered in determining the lawfulness and admissibility of a recording obtained by some subterfuge.[17]

8.9 In addition to the sample of the suspect's voice the identification officer should obtain no less than 20 samples of speech from persons of similar age, ethnic, regional and social background as the suspect. Once again HOC 57/2003 advises that a suitable source for such material may be the recorded interviews of other suspects unconnected with the case. It is suggested that

---

11 HOC 57/2003, para 10.

12 HOC 57/2003, para 7.

13 HOC 57/2003, para 8.

14 HOC 57/2003, para 8.

15 In *R v Deenik* [1992] Crim LR 578, CA the possibility that a suspect might change his voice was relied upon in the Court's reasoning for allowing an interview to be overheard by a witness for the purpose of voice recognition. See also *R v Colman and Terry* (unreported) 23 July 2003, CA.

16 European Convention on Human Rights.

17 See D Ormerod 'Sounds Familiar? Voice Identification Evidence' [2001] Crim LR 595, at p 611 for a discussion of this topic.

these may be obtained from other police forces if the suspect has a regional accent which differs from that prevalent in the area in which the offence was committed.

COMPILATION OF SAMPLES BY EXPERT AND POLICE

8.10 An approved expert witness in phonetics or linguistics must be instructed to compile the voice samples.[18] All recordings are to be supplied to the expert whose task will be to select comparable samples of speech. The first description should also be supplied.[19] The expert must ensure that the final selection and compilation of speech samples provide a match with the suspect's sample which is as accurate and balanced as possible. The guidance in HOC 57/2003 suggests that each extract should be about one minute long and may comprise various fragments of speech and/or continuous speech. It is irrelevant that the extracts contain different words or topics of conversation. However, in *R v Davies*,[20] a gunman had uttered the words 'Where's Chrissie?' before shooting the witness who claimed to have recognised the gunman's voice. The Court of Appeal noted that the victim and another witness who were both familiar with the person alleged to be the gunman were invited to identify the voice of the gunman in a procedure in which they were presented with relatively long passages of speech. The Court suggested that a more relevant test might have been to establish whether they were able to identify the appellant only on the basis of the two words spoken by the gunman, rather than the recordings used in the procedure that contained far more words.

8.11 The final compilation should comprise nine extracts; a sample of the suspect's voice and a selection of eight foil voices.[21] Each of the eight foil samples must be examined to ensure that the accent, inflection, pitch, tone and speed of the speech provide a fair example for comparison against the suspect.[22] The expert's task in achieving this should eliminate the type of complaint made about the foils not matching the defendant's voice in *R v Hersey*.[23]

8.12 While the subject matter contained in the extract may be immaterial from a phonetic perspective, it may be very revealing in other ways.

---

18 HOC 57/2003, para 11. A member of the International Association of Forensic Phonetics is suggested. However, see *R v Davies* [2004] EWCA Crim 2521, in which the Court of Appeal considered the admissibility of a voice identification procedure in respect of which the recordings used were selected by a police officer. Although this procedure was conducted prior to publication of HOC 57/2003, in concluding that the resultant voice identification evidence was admissible, the Court observed, at [35], that 'even assuming that it would have been best practice in 2000 to involve an expert in phonetics to make the relevant selection … it is not shown that [the police officer's] selection is actually of dissimilar voices or unfair'.

19 HOC 57/2003, para 6.

20 [2004] EWCA Crim 2521.

21 HOC 57/2003, para 13.

22 HOC 57/2003, para 15.

23 [1998] Crim LR 281, CA.

Accordingly, 'the identification officer is responsible for ensuring, as far as is reasonable, that there is nothing within the selected samples which would lead to the identification of any individual or the offence which they were being questioned about'.[24] That may be easier said than done. In the context of an interview whose subject matter is likely to be exclusively connected to the commission of the offence there may be few, if any, entirely innocuous excerpts. Equally, excerpts from the interviews of foils may be indicative of an offence pointing away from the offence with which the witness is concerned. Moreover the identification officer may not be well placed to determine whether the subject matter for the sample is innocuous or not. The suspect may refer to information which, unknown to the identification officer, reveals or hints at a connection with the offender or the offence. The investigating officer is likely to be better qualified to undertake this task.

8.13 HOC 57/2003 has no provision for the involvement of the suspect or solicitor in the process. It notes that the procedure does not offer any opportunity for the suspect to review or reject any of the foil samples.[25] It can be contrasted with the procedure for video identification in which the suspect may view the line up and make representations about its composition. This safeguard would allow further screening of the material to ensure that the suspect's sample contained nothing remotely incriminating.

SAFEGUARDS

8.14 HOC 57/2003 seeks to provide safeguards by strongly advising that control procedures are conducted to assess whether, objectively, the samples are suggestive of the suspect.[26] It is suggested that the expert and identification officer conduct a number of test hearings, utilising mock witnesses, who are neither police officers nor connected with the suspect. These individuals should be given a brief resumé of the case and asked to listen to the samples in controlled conditions. They should then be asked to try to pick out the suspect for the offence. It is assumed that such control tests will identify any suspect bias. Random selection will demonstrate an absence of bias. On the other hand the selection of the suspect, presumably on more than one occasion that might be accounted for by random selection, will show bias. The efficacy of this control depends on several mock procedures being carried out, perhaps the same number as there are samples – nine. It is quite possible that these tests may disclose some unwitting bias towards a foil!

8.15 Once the control tests have been carried out HOC 57/2003[27] contemplates a further examination of the samples against the results of the tests to ensure that:

---

24 HOC 57/2003, para 15.
25 HOC 57/2003, para 15.
26 HOC 57/2003, para 16.
27 At para 17.

(1) there is nothing contained in the words spoken, which would lead to an unfair assumption that one or other of the samples was that of the suspect; and

(2) there is nothing in the manner of the speech, which would lead to an unfair assumption that one or other of the samples was that of the suspect.

EVIDENCE OF PROCEDURE INTEGRITY

8.16 It is anticipated by HOC 57/2003 that the expert will provide evidence in a statement. This will exhibit the nine selected sample tapes and describe the work undertaken in relation to the preparation of the material.[28] Moreover the expert is expected to state the results of the control tests and demonstrate the objectivity of the procedures and the careful, balanced manner in which they were conducted.[29] Whether the compilation represents a fairly constituted procedure may in due course be subject to examination by a defence expert and, where appropriate, determination at trial. The sanction for a procedure which is biased against a defendant will be exclusion under PACE, s 78.

CONDUCT OF THE PROCEDURE

8.17 The procedure should be conducted by use of video recording. Each of the samples is to be recorded on three video cassettes: A, B and C, in random order. The video cassettes should contain three cycles of the samples. A number is attributed to each sample voice. The number of the sample must be recorded and displayed on the screen throughout the playing time of each sample. The identity of each speaker is separately indexed by the identification officer.[30] Provision is made for the continuity and integrity of the samples and recordings.[31]

8.18 The suspect is entitled to be represented by a solicitor at the procedure.[32] The descriptive statement taken from the witness together with any first description must be disclosed to the suspect or solicitor prior to the identification procedure.[33] However, the silence of HOC 57/2003 on the point indicates that, as with video identification, the suspect has no right to be present. The procedure must nevertheless be videotaped and the suspect must later be offered the opportunity of reviewing the recording.[34]

---

28 HOC 57/2003, para 19.
29 HOC 57/2003, para 18.
30 HOC 57/2003, paras 14 and 19.
31 HOC 57/2003, paras 19, 20 and 21.
32 HOC 57/2003, para 22.
33 HOC 57/2003, para 6.
34 HOC 57/2003, para 23.

8.19 The solicitor must be allowed to select which of the three video cassettes is to be used.[35] Before listening to the samples the witness should be told that the voice of the suspect may or may not be on one of the samples to be played. The witness must then be instructed to listen to each sample at least once before making a selection. The witness may be allowed to listen to any or all of the samples as many times as he or she wishes.[36] The identification officer must make a complete record of any comments or selections made by the witness.[37]

8.20 After the conclusion of the procedure a statement should be taken from the witness recording the events and their selection. Once the witness has left the identification room, the identification officer should remove from an envelope within a sealed bag the index to the samples containing the cross-references to the samples of suspect and foils. The solicitor is to be given the opportunity to record these details.[38] All materials relating to the procedure must be retained by the identification officer.[39]

---

35 HOC 57/2003, para 24.

36 HOC 57/2003, para 25. The paragraph appears erroneously to refer to an instruction to listen to each tape at least once rather than each sample. Further, see D Ormerod 'Sounds Familiar? Voice Identification Evidence' [2001] Crim LR 595, at p 617 for criticism of a procedure which allows the witness to hear the suspect more than twice.

37 HOC 57/2003, para 26.

38 HOC 57/2003, para 27.

39 HOC 57/2003, para 28.

Part II

TRIAL

Chapter 9

DISCLOSURE

INTRODUCTION

9.1 The Criminal Procedure and Investigations Act (CPIA) 1996 introduced a statutory disclosure regime applicable to both the prosecution and defence.[1] It is supplemented by a Code of Practice.[2] The prosecution's duties are amplified by the Attorney General's Guidelines on Disclosure (AG Guidelines).[3] The court has further powers to order disclosure in 'serious fraud' and 'long and complex' cases.[4] The aim of this chapter is to draw attention to the disclosure requirements with regard to issues of identification and, in particular, alibi. A comprehensive analysis of the statutory disclosure regime is not within the scope of this book.

9.2 Disclosure to the defence is also necessary under Code D. If there is to be an identification procedure, which will ordinarily have taken place before the

---

1 The rules governing procedure are contained in Part 22 of the Criminal Procedure Rules: Criminal Procedure Rules 2010, SI 2010/60.

2 Code of Practice as to the recording and retention by the police of material obtained during an investigation and its supply to the prosecutor: Criminal Procedure and Investigations Act 1996 (Code of Practice) Order 2005, SI 2005/985.

3 Published in April 2005. Available from www.attorneygeneral.gov.uk/Publications/Pages/AttorneyGeneralsGuidelines.

4 Criminal Justice Act 1988, s 9 for serious fraud and CPIA 1996, s 31 for long and complex cases.

CPIA 1996 obligations arise, first descriptions and material released for broadcast or publication should have been disclosed at that stage.[5]

PROSECUTION

9.3 The Attorney General's guidelines on disclosure remind all concerned that:

> 'A fair trial is the proper object and expectation of all participants in the trial process. Fair disclosure to an accused is an inseparable part of a fair trial.'[6]

9.4 The guidelines emphasise that failure to make disclosure may result in a wrongful conviction.[7] Thus it hardly needs stating that in any case in which identification is in issue, the prosecution is duty bound to disclose all information which might directly or indirectly undermine any visual or scientific identification of a defendant or which might point to another person as having been responsible for the crime.

Investigation, recording and retention

9.5 The concept of disclosure by the prosecution encompasses certain prerequisite obligations relating to the collection of information by the police. A Code of Practice[8] issued under CPIA 1996, s 23 governs the investigation of offences and the obtaining, recording and retention by police[9] of information and material during the course of a criminal investigation. A failure to comply with its provisions may be taken into account where relevant to any issue in a trial.[10] The CPIA Code demands that the investigating officer should pursue all reasonable lines of inquiry 'whether these point towards or away from the suspect'.[11]

9.6 The officer in charge of an investigation is under a duty to record information received if it may be relevant to an investigation.[12] Whether it is relevant might not become clear until the conclusion of the investigation or later, hence prudence would suggest that the provision should be construed widely. For example, notes of observations from potential eyewitnesses or as the result of house to house enquiries should be maintained even if, at first glance, they appear to provide no probative information. A person's non-observation of an event or a suspect at a material time may nevertheless

---

5 See for example **5.31** and **5.33** in relation to video identification.

6 AG Guidelines, para 1.

7 AG Guidelines, para 23.

8 Hereafter referred to as the CPIA Code. See note 2.

9 Others charged with the duty of conducting a criminal investigation must have regard to the Code of Practice: CPIA 1996, s 26(1).

10 CPIA 1996, s 26(4).

11 CPIA Code, para 3.5.

12 CPIA Code, para 4.1.

provide relevant evidence.[13] It follows that names and addresses should be obtained from such people if they are willing to provide them. All material which is potentially relevant must thereafter be retained.[14]

9.7 The records to be kept include internal police records such as 999 calls and entries within computer messaging systems.[15] In the context of identification the CPIA Code specifically demands the retention of

> 'records of the first description of a suspect by each potential witness who purports to identify or describe the suspect, whether or not the description differs from that of subsequent descriptions by that or other witnesses.'

The CPIA Code of Practice also covers material such as draft witness statements which differ from final versions. Where scientific tests are to be conducted, communications between police and forensic scientists should be retained.

9.8 Where the existence of potentially relevant material under the control of another person comes to the attention of the police, that person should be requested to retain it.[16] This might typically apply to a CCTV device on commercial premises. If the police are likely to have greater ease of access to material, the defence could invite their attention to it in an appropriate case. If a government department or other Crown body appears to possess potentially relevant material, reasonable steps should be taken to consider it.[17] If such material is in the possession of a non-government agency or third party, such as a local authority, hospital, school or business and it would be disclosable if in the possession of the prosecution, consideration should be given by the prosecution to seeking access to it. This is especially important if it is thought likely to undermine the prosecution case or assist a known defence, in which case steps should be taken to obtain it. Where necessary, the prosecution should seek a witness summons for the production of the material. In any event the existence of disclosable information held by the third party to the knowledge of the police or prosecution should be recorded.[18]

Disclosure

9.9 In certain circumstances disclosure at an early stage of proceedings before the statutory requirement under the CPIA arises might be necessary. This common law duty exists for example if there are eyewitnesses, known to

---

13 CPIA Code, para 4.3.

14 CPIA Code, para 5.1. It must be kept at least until acquittal or a decision not to proceed has been taken; and in the case of conviction at least until after release from custody or if the sentence was non-custodial at least 6 months; where the conviction is subject to an appeal or an application to the Criminal Cases Review Commission until the appeal is determined or a decision is made not to refer the case to the Court of Appeal: paras 5.7, 5.8, 5.9 and 5.10.

15 CPIA Code, para 5.4.

16 CPIA Code, para 3.6.

17 AG guidelines, para 47.

18 AG guidelines, paras 51–54.

the prosecution but whom they do not intend to use, whose memories are likely to fade over time thereby rendering defence preparation less effective.[19]

9.10 The initial duty to disclose, sometimes referred to as 'primary disclosure', is found in CPIA 1996, s 3. The material to be disclosed to the defence, which includes information,[20] is that which 'might reasonably be considered capable of undermining the case for the prosecution against the accused or assisting the case for the defence'. The obligation relates to material which is either in the prosecutor's possession or has been inspected pursuant to the CPIA Code in connection with the case against the accused. Disclosure of such material or, conversely, a statement that there is no such material is the catalyst for the requirement by a defendant under CPIA 1996, s 5[21] to provide a defence statement. The defence statement may itself trigger an obligation on the prosecution to make further disclosure in accordance with s 7A. That section demands that the prosecutor must keep under review throughout the proceedings, and in particular following service of the defence statement, whether any further material is disclosable. Thus defence disclosure is of obvious importance where details of the defence have not previously been revealed, for example an interview in which a suspect fails to raise the issue of identification. After a defence statement has been served, the defence may apply to the court under CPIA 1996, s 8 if it is thought that material which might assist the defence has not been disclosed.

9.11 The prosecution disclosure obligations under CPIA 1996 are augmented by the Attorney General's Guidelines on Disclosure.[22] Were it not already obvious, disclosure must be applied to all material which might cast doubt upon the accuracy or credibility of any prosecution evidence or point to another person, including a co-accused, having involvement in the offence.[23] It will also include material which might have a bearing upon the admissibility of prosecution evidence,[24] such as breaches of Code D.

9.12 A defence statement will often contain specific requests for disclosure to which the prosecution should be alert and responsive.[25] Information which may potentially, and even speculatively, lead to evidence helpful to the defence should be disclosed. In *R v Heggart and Heggart*[26] the details of 999 callers who reported a public order offence were withheld from the defence. Though it was not known what the witnesses might say, the Court of Appeal construed the information as 'capable of undermining the prosecution case' and regarded it as being 'precisely the sort of material to which the defence is entitled in order to make proper investigations of the circumstances surrounding the offence'.

---

19 *R v DPP ex p Lee* [1999] 2 Cr App R 304, DC.

20 CPIA 1996, s 2(4)(a).

21 CPIA 1996, s 6 applies to voluntary disclosure in summary proceedings.

22 See note 3.

23 AG Guidelines, para 12.

24 AG Guidelines, para 10.

25 AG Guidelines, paras 17–18.

26 [2001] 4 *Archbold News* 2, CA. It was also held that 999 calls did not attract any duty of confidentiality to the caller.

DEFENCE

Defence statement

9.13 The general provisions of defence disclosure under CPIA 1996, ss 5(5) and (6A) require the service of a defence statement which (by reference to the statutory lettering):

(a) sets out the nature of the accused's defence including any particular defences on which he intends to rely;

(b) indicates the matters on which issue is taken with the prosecution;

(c) sets out in respect of each matter why issue is taken;

(ca) sets out particulars of matters of fact on which he intends to rely for the purposes of his defence; and

(d) indicates any point of law he intends to take together with authorities in support.

9.14 Clearly, misidentification is an issue which would need to be asserted. Where a witness description is disputed, strict adherence to these disclosure obligations dictates that a defence statement not only indicates the inaccuracy of that description but, for example, sets out a defendant's true height or build. By contrast, a defence statement may admit presence or participation, or accept the correctness of an identification but rely upon a defence of lack of intent or duress. In that situation, should an attack later be mounted on the admissibility of identification evidence, a court would be entitled to have regard to the content of the statement when determining whether it should be excluded under PACE, s 78.[27]

9.15 A defendant is also required by s 6C to give notice of his intention to call a witness in his defence.[28] The introduction of this provision, combined with s 6A(ca) are likely to have a profound effect upon the case law which has developed on the subject of alibi notices. Accordingly it should be noted that the analysis which follows is subject to the impact of these provisions, discussed at **9.28**.

Notice of alibi

9.16 The purpose of the alibi disclosure provisions is to deter a defendant from ambushing the prosecution with details of an unexpected alibi and to permit the prosecution an opportunity to investigate its integrity. The

---

27 *R v Royes* [2004] EWCA Crim 3470.

28 This provision is substantially the same as that applicable to alibi notices under s 6A(2) – see **9.17**. It was brought into force on 1 May 2010 by the Criminal Justice Act 2003 (Commencement No. 4 and Transitional Provisions) Order, SI 2010/1183.

requirements for notice of alibi were formerly contained in the Criminal Justice Act 1967, s 11. They are now part of the disclosure scheme under the CPIA 1996 and are significantly different.

9.17 The two elements to this disclosure are first, particulars of the alibi and second, details of witnesses. Section 6A(2) provides:

> 'A defence statement that discloses an alibi, must give particulars of it, including –
>
> (a) the name, address and date of birth of any witness the accused believes is able to give evidence in support of the alibi, or as many of those details as are known to the accused when the statement is given;
> (b) any information in the accused's possession which might be of material assistance in identifying or finding any such witness in whose case any of the details mentioned in paragraph (a) are not known to the accused when the statement is given.'

9.18 'Alibi' is not defined but is generally construed to correlate to the meaning of the phrase 'evidence in support of an alibi'. That is defined by CPIA 1996, s 6(3) as follows:

> 'For the purposes of this section evidence in support of an alibi is evidence tending to show that by reason of the presence of the accused at a particular place or in a particular area at a particular time he was not, or was unlikely to have been, at the place where the offence is alleged to have been committed at the time of its alleged commission.'

Place and time of offence and evidence tending to rebut presence

9.19 Where the time or place of an offence is not set out in the indictment, the particulars can often be identified from the prosecution statements if the offence comprises a single act. This is so even if the indictment alleges a day between two dates, provided the evidence itself is specific.[29] However, commonly the evidence may not disclose the time or date, such as a burglary at an uncertain time during the course of a day or over a weekend. Extreme examples are sometimes found in historic sexual abuse cases where the indictment alleges an offence committed between two dates a year apart. In those circumstances, only if the defence rendered the defendant's presence over the entire period impossible or unlikely would alibi disclosure be necessary. That might be the case if the defendant claimed to be abroad throughout the period.

9.20 The time at which the defendant was at a particular place does not have to coincide with the time of the offence, provided it tends to show absence or

---

29 *R v Lewis* (1969) 53 Cr App R 76, CA The indictment alleged receiving stolen goods between two dates but the evidence was of receipt on a specific occasion. See below for facts. Contrast *R v Hassan* [1970] 54 Cr App R 56, CA in which it was reasoned that the notice requirement did not apply because the indictment alleged living off immoral earnings 'in the City of Cardiff' though the evidence appears to have been confined to one address.

unlikelihood of presence on the latter occasion. The example given in *R v Fields and Adams*[30] demonstrates the scope of 'evidence in support of an alibi'. An offence is committed in London at 3.30 pm and the defendant seeks to establish presence in Glasgow at 3.00 pm. Notice of alibi would be required because the evidence tended to show that the defendant was unlikely to have been in London at the material time.

9.21 CPIA 1996, s 6(3) seems clear in its concern with the defendant's whereabouts at the time and place of the offence and not in relation to incriminating conduct on another occasion. In *R v Lewis*[31] the defendant was alleged to have received stolen postal orders. The prosecution adduced evidence that a couple of days after receipt he had cashed some at a post office. The issue arose as to whether an alibi notice was required in respect of the encashment. It was held that:

> '… the only evidence in support of an alibi to which section 11 [now CPIA 1996, s 6(3)] applies is evidence relative to the whereabouts of the accused at the time when the crime is alleged to have been committed. Evidence relative to his whereabouts on another occasion is not subject to the restrictions of the section, however significant that evidence may be to the issues in the case.'

9.22 The court went on to draw the analogy with a defendant accused of robbery which took place on Monday and against whom there was evidence that he was the driver of a van containing the stolen goods on Tuesday. In that case also no notice of alibi was necessary in relation to his whereabouts on Tuesday.

9.23 The decision in *R v Lewis* may be contrasted with *R v Fields and Adams*.[32] In that case a robbery took place at 6.00 pm and the main evidence was that of an eyewitness who later identified the defendants. She stated that she had seen the men in the vicinity of the robbery some 3 hours earlier. The issue arose as to whether one defendant's presence 25 miles away at the earlier time was 'evidence tending to show that … he was not, or was unlikely to have been, at the place where the offence is alleged to have been committed at the time of its alleged commission'. It was held that an assertion of presence elsewhere on the earlier occasion went beyond an attack on the witness's reliability and tended to show he was not present at the time of the robbery. The court drew the analogy of the witness keeping the person under observation throughout the period and found that there was no distinction. However the decision is arguably flawed and has a certain circularity to it.[33] It was an undeniable fact that, as a matter of time and geography, the defendant might have been present both where he claimed 3 hours before the robbery and at the scene of the robbery. Hence the evidence of his presence elsewhere at the

30 [1991] Crim LR 38, CA.

31 (1969) 53 Cr App R 76, CA.

32 [1991] Crim LR 38, CA.

33 See the commentary by Professor Smith. It should be noted that the issue arose in the context of an argument whether a letter sent to the prosecution amounted to an alibi notice and had therefore been properly introduced in evidence by the prosecution.

earlier time did not tend to show absence from the scene of the robbery, but rather that the witness's identification evidence of having seen the same person on both occasions was incorrect. Put another way, it only tended to show absence from the scene of the crime on the assumption that the identification evidence was correct. Taken a logical step further, *R v Field and Adams* would suggest that an alibi notice would be required of a sighting of a person days or weeks before or after an offence if the witness identified the person sighted as the offender.

Continuing offences and conspiracies

9.24 Whether an alibi notice is required for a continuing offence will depend upon its factual circumstances. That an offence is, as a matter of law, a continuing offence will not per se obviate the need for an alibi notice if the allegation is confined to a particular place and time. An offence which continues as a matter of fact may also require an alibi notice if proof of its commission is contingent upon a single identifiable act. Where, by contrast, the offence alleged involves a continuing course of conduct or comprises a series of acts, alibi is unlikely to arise. In *R v Hassan,*[34] the Court of Appeal stated that the definition of 'evidence in support of an alibi' appeared 'to envisage an offence which necessarily involves the accused being at a particular place at a particular time'. The defendant was accused of living off the immoral earnings of prostitution between two dates more than 3 weeks apart. On the day before the end of that period a search warrant was executed at the premises at which the prostitution was taking place. A man was seen to escape through the window. At trial the defendant sought to demonstrate his presence elsewhere at that time. It was held no alibi notice was required of that time because its substantiation did not provide a defence. Even if he was not the person observed escaping, he was still capable of being guilty of the offence charged; and if he was the runaway, that fact did not of itself establish guilt. The incident was only part of the narrative which the prosecution presented and upon which the jury was invited to conclude the defendant's guilt. However the court left open the question whether an alibi notice would be required of a defendant whose case was that he was abroad throughout the entire period of a continuing offence.

9.25 In *R v Beynon (Wasted Costs)*[35] an allegation of repeated indecent assault was reflected in a single specimen count covering a period of a year. The complainant stated that the offences took place on Wednesdays. The defendant stated that he invariably went to the gym on that day. The Court of Appeal regarded the allegation as a continuous offence that could take place at any time on any number of days over a substantial period and doubted that the alibi notice provisions could apply.

---

[34] (1970) 54 Cr App R 56, CA.

[35] [1999] 8 *Archbold News* 1, CA.

9.26 An offence of conspiring to commit an offence is committed at the time and place that the agreement is reached, though it is also a continuing offence. If, unusually, there was direct evidence of the parties making the agreement at a particular time and place there is no reason to think that the alibi provisions would not apply. However most conspiracies are inferred from a course of activity which, like a continuing offence, sits uneasily with the definition of alibi. Whether CPIA 1996, s 6(3) calls for an alibi notice may depend upon the duration of the conspiracy. One comprising a single short-lived activity could be within the purview of the section. That may be contrasted to a conspiracy which encompasses a number of substantive offences over a period of time, for example, a series of robberies or a benefit fraud. It is no doubt possible that a defendant would be able to provide an alibi for one, more or even all of the substantive offences identified within the conspiracy. However such a conspiracy is inconsistent with the literal wording of the section which, as was pointed out in *R v Hassan,*[36] assumes the commission of an offence (in the singular) at a particular place and time.

Uncertainty as to defendant's whereabouts at the time of offence

9.27 CPIA 1996, s 6(3) is engaged where the defendant asserts presence at a particular place and time. Hence, if it is merely asserted that the defendant was absent from the place of the offence, from which it follows that he or she must have been at some other unspecified place, the disclosure requirement is not engaged.[37] That will be the situation where a defendant is unable to recollect his or her whereabouts at the material time. The position may be less clear if the defendant believes that he or she could have been, probably was, or would normally have been present at a particular place at the relevant time. The phrase 'by reason of the presence of the accused' suggests a degree of certainty about the evidence. However courts are likely to apply a qualitative approach to the matter, depending upon the strength of the likelihood and the availability of corroborative evidence. If a defence amounts to no more than a speculative assertion of presence elsewhere, incapable of confirmation, there will be no need for a notice. The opposite may be true of a defendant who claims probable presence at a place say a public house which could be capable of verification by other witnesses or by calling a witness to his 'probable' presence there.

Effect of CPIA 1996, s 6A(ca) and s 6C

9.28 The Impact of successive legislative amendments to the general provisions relating to defence disclosure on the alibi provisions and its case-law is profound. Indeed arguably they have been superseded and are redundant. Evidence of a defendant's presence at a place other than the crime scene at the material time is a fact on which he will seek to rely within s 6A(ca); and a witness the defendant proposes to call who can testify to such a fact falls

---

36 (1970) 54 Cr App R 56, CA.

37 *R v Johnson* [1995] 2 Cr App R 1, CA.

squarely within s 6C. Furthermore, much of the conceptual argument over the meaning of alibi[38] will count for nothing when any fact asserted and relied upon in a defence must be revealed in a defence statement and any witness to such a fact disclosed by notice.

Interviews of defence witnesses

9.29 Investigators may seek to interview persons identified as witnesses a defendant proposes to call at trial. The arrangements and conduct of such interviews are governed by a Code of Practice.[39] It dictates the procedure to be followed, and in particular the need to obtain the witness's consent, his right to representation, provision for the attendance of the suspect's solicitor with the witness's consent, the need to record and prepare written records of the interview and the requirement to serve a copy on the witness and, with his consent, on the accused or his solicitor.

Default in disclosure

9.30 CPIA 1996, s 11 prescribes the circumstances in which sanctions for non-disclosure might arise. These are:

(1) failure to serve or the late service of a defence statement: s 11(2)(a)–(d);

(2) a defence statement with inconsistent defences: s 11(2)(e);

(3) a defence advanced at trial not mentioned in or different from the defence statement: s 11(2)(f)(i);[40]

(4) reliance on matters of fact not mentioned in the defence statement: s 11(2)(f)(ii);

(5) late service of a witness notice: s 11(4)(a); and

(6) calling a witness not included or inadequately identified in a witness notice: s 11(4)(b).

9.31 In the context of an alibi defence the consequences of non-disclosure might be suffered by a defendant who at his trial:

(1) adduces evidence in support of an alibi without having given particulars of the alibi in the defence statement; or

---

38 See **9.19–9.26**.

39 In force 1 May 2010: Criminal Procedure and Investigations Act 1996 (Code of Practice for Interviews of Witnesses Notified by the Accused) Order 2010, SI 2010/1223.

40 The court must have regard to the extent of the difference and any justification for it before allowing adverse comment of inference: CPIA 1996, s 11(8).

(2) calls a witness to give evidence in support of an alibi without having complied with the notice requirements.

9.32 The CJA 1967 alibi provisions prohibited, without leave of the court, a defendant from giving evidence or calling alibi witnesses if a notice had not been served. There is no such prohibition under the CPIA 1996. The court has no power to refuse to hear an alibi witness,[41] nor for that matter any other witness whose identity has not properly been disclosed. The sanction for any failure to comply with the alibi disclosure requirements is set out in CPIA 1996, s 11(5):

> 'Where this section applies: –
>
> (a) the court or any other party may make such comment as appears appropriate; and
> (b) the court or jury may draw such inferences as appear proper in deciding whether the accused is guilty of the offence concerned.'

These sanctions apply similarly to breaches of the general defence disclosure obligations, save that in the case of witness notice requirements, leave of the court is necessary for comment by another party.[42]

---

41 *Tinnion v Reading Crown Court* 174 JP 36, DC; [2009] EWHC 2930 (Admin).
42 CPIA 1996, s 11(7).

Chapter 10

EVIDENCE: ADMISSIBILITY AND EXCLUSION

INTRODUCTION

10.1 This chapter considers the admissibility of both direct identification evidence and other circumstantial forms of evidence capable of supporting the identification of a suspect. The ubiquity of CCTV cameras and the evidential deployment of images depicting crimes or suspects in recent years has been matched by the evolution of now commonplace video identification procedures. More fundamentally, the Criminal Justice Act 2003 has dramatically shifted the law of bad character and hearsay on the evidential landscape. Despite such changes, the basic rule of admissibility remains constant: evidence is admissible if it is relevant to an issue in the case and is probative either of guilt or innocence.

EXCLUSIONARY POWERS: PACE, S 78 AND COMMON LAW

10.2 At common law there exists an inherent power to exclude evidence that unfairly prejudices a defendant's right to a fair trial. The test is usually characterised as a balance between the probative value of the evidence and its prejudicial effect. Where the former is outweighed by the latter the evidence ought to be excluded. Police and Criminal Evidence Act 1984 (PACE), s 78(1) introduced a further exclusionary power, contingent upon the effect of the evidence on the fairness of the proceedings. It provides:

> 'In any proceedings the court may refuse to allow evidence on which the prosecution proposes to rely to be given if it appears to the court that, having regard to all the circumstances, including the circumstances in which the evidence was obtained, the admission of the evidence would have such an adverse effect on the fairness of the proceedings that the court ought not to admit it.'

10.3 The common law power was preserved by PACE, s 82(3) though in most respects it adds little to a submission under s 78. The reference in s 78 to 'the circumstances in which the evidence was obtained' has particular resonance in applications to exclude identification evidence on grounds of breaches of the Code D. Section 78 applies only to evidence the prosecution propose to rely upon. It does not permit a court at the request of one defendant to exclude relevant and probative evidence called by another, notwithstanding that it may have been excluded as against the prosecution. It should be noted that additional exclusionary powers are contained with the statutory hearsay and bad character provisions considered below.

PRESUMPTIONS CONCERNING IDENTITY OF THE PERSON IN THE DOCK

10.4 Most identification cases concern the evidential link between the defendant and the person who committed the crime. Rarely is it questioned whether the person who occupies the dock is the person accused of the crime. Where it does arise, there would appear to be an evidential burden on the defence to raise the issue and the failure to do so will allow presumptions to operate. These might be summarised as:

(1) a presumption that the person appearing in the dock is the person who was charged or summonsed for the offence; and

(2) a presumption that evidence naming a person relates to the defendant bearing the same name.

10.5 In *Allan and others v Ireland*[1] a very large number of football supporters were arrested at Euston Railway Station for public disorder offences. They were

---

1 (1984) 79 Cr App R 206, DC.

tried in batches, the first comprising 11 people. The point was taken that there was no evidence of the arrest of these individuals and therefore no continuity between the persons alleged to have committed the offence and those appearing in the dock. The Divisional Court held that the magistrate was entitled to take judicial notice of the ordinary process of arrest, charge and bail. An inference could be drawn, at least on a prima facie basis, that a person surrendering to bail and answering the name laid in the charge was the same person as had been arrested, charged and bailed in that name.

10.6 Where a person is identified in evidence by name, it will generally be presumed that the reference to that name is a reference to the person in the dock and not some other person by the same name. In *Ellis v Jones*[2] the defendant was charged with making a false declaration in support of a claim for sickness benefit. His employer, in a statement which was read, said 'I know Clive Jones' and proceeded to contradict the declaration that he had not worked. It was submitted that there was no evidence that the employee and the defendant were one and the same Clive Jones. It was held that in the absence of any suggestion made by the defence that they were not, the justices were entitled to assume that they were.

IDENTIFICATION OF PERSON PREVIOUSLY CONVICTED

10.7 When a defendant's previous conviction is admissible, either as an element of the offence or for the purpose of establishing bad character, how is it to be established that the defendant was the person convicted? It is certainly not unprecedented that a person's antecedent criminal record has been incorrectly recorded. Under PACE, s 73 a certificate of conviction is admissible for the purpose of proving that 'the person named in the certificate as having been convicted … is the person whose conviction … is to be proved'. But that does not establish that the person so named and the defendant in the dock are one and the same. Proof of identification of the defendant as the person previously convicted must be to the criminal standard.[3]

10.8 The difficulty in establishing the identity of a person previously convicted has arisen on a number of occasions in the context of charges of disqualified driving, where the conviction and disqualification need to be proved. In *R v Derwentside Justices ex p Heaviside*[4] it was doubted that 'the mere matching of the personal details, whether the name, address or date of birth of a defendant, with those upon a certificate is sufficient to establish the

---

2 [1973] 2 All ER 893, [1973] Crim LR 361, DC. See also *Smith v DPP* [2008] EWHC 771 (Admin).

3 *Olakunori v DPP* [1998] COD 443, DC; *West Yorkshire Probation Board v Boulter* [2005] EWHC 2342 (Admin); *Pattinson v DPP* [2006] 2 All ER 317; *R v Burns* [2006] EWCA Crim 1273, [2006] 1 WLR 1273.

4 [1996] RTR 384, DC. It was followed in *R (Kingsnorth and Denny) v DPP* [2003] EWHC 768 Admin. See also *DPP v Mansfield* [1997] RTR 96, DC.

defendant as the person earlier convicted'. It was suggested that a formal admission,[5] fingerprint evidence or the evidence of a person present at the trial at which the conviction was entered was necessary. However the means of identification suggested in *ex p Heaviside* are not exhaustive of the ways of making the necessary connection; each case will depend upon its own facts.[6] Thus a defendant may be identified as the person arrested for the offence for which he or she was previously convicted[7] or may admit to the past conviction during the investigation.[8] In *R v Sunderland Justices ex p Bate*[9] the connection was established by the evidence of a police officer who had been present at court when a person of the same name as the defendant had been convicted and disqualified. The absence of any suggestion to the witness that the disqualified person was not the defendant allowed the court to assume that he was.

10.9 In deciding whether the defendant's conviction had been established to a prima facie threshold, the court in *Olakunori v DPP*[10] considered that the coincidence of names and dates of birth might be sufficient, though not where the name is common and there was material which indicated the possibility of mistake. The court went on to suggest that if the defendant remained silent at trial, a court might take into account the inference permitted by the Criminal Justice and Public Order Act 1994, s 35. If, on the other hand, all the prosecution are able to muster is the coincidence of name and date of birth and the defendant has given evidence denying that he was previously convicted, the court may well be left in doubt. On the facts it was held that the deliberate lies by the person arrested about his identity was a feature that supported the prosecution case as to the defendant's identity on the earlier occasion.

10.10 *West Yorkshire Probation Board v Boulter*[11] took a further step away from *ex p Heaviside*: it was held that an inference might be drawn from the coincidence of name (which was uncommon), address and date of birth could alone, in the absence of defence evidence, suffice to establish identity beyond reasonable doubt. A variation on this theme emerged in *R v Bailey*[12] in which the defendant made the positive assertion in evidence that the driving conviction in his name had been secured by an imposter adopting his identity. In circumstances where such a claim was credible, it was necessary for the prosecution effectively to rule out that explanation beyond reasonable doubt and, absent evidence doing so, the conviction was quashed.

10.11 The cases thus far cited were tried in the magistrates' court and concerned convictions which were necessary elements of the offences charged.

---

5 Criminal Justice Act 1967, s 10.
6 *R v Burns* [2006] EWCA Crim 1273, [2006] 1 WLR 1273.
7 *DPP v Mansfield* [1997] RTR 96, DC; *R v Derwentside Justices ex p Swift* [1997] RTR 89, DC.
8 *DPP v Mooney* [1997] RTR 434, DC.
9 *R v Sunderland Justices ex p Bate* [1997] RTR 89, DC following *Ellis v Jones* [1973] 2 All ER 893, [1973] Crim LR 361, DC. See **10.6**.
10 [1998] COD 443, DC.
11 [2005] EWHC 2342 (Admin) followed in *Pattison v DPP* [2006] 2 All ER 317, [2006] RTR 13.
12 (1998) 163 JP 518.

The trial in *R v Burns*[13] was on indictment and the convictions adduced were pursuant to the bad character provisions of CJA 2003. The principle that the coincidence of personal details may, depending upon the particular facts and circumstances of the case, suffice to prove identity was constant. In that case however, having ruled that there was sufficient prima facie evidence to establish that the previous convictions belonged to the defendant, the judge failed to leave the ultimate decision for the jury.

PHOTOGRAPHIC, CCTV AND OTHER IMAGES

Sketch, photofit, e-fit and similar images

10.12 The manifestation of a witness's description of a suspect in photofit, sketch or similar form is admissible evidence. The descriptive information given by the witness, through the medium of a person with the requisite skill, is converted into visual form. These images are intended to provide a contemporary record of a person's observation. Provided the witness concurs with the likeness there would be no difference in principle to the witness creating a pictorial image and thus no question of hearsay arises. Further, such images are not to be regarded as statements and therefore cannot offend the rule against previous consistent or self-serving statements. Rather they are a separate species of evidence, akin to a photograph of the offender, albeit imperfect and not contemporaneous with the offence.[14] They may be admissible notwithstanding that the witness later made a less than satisfactory identification,[15] has failed to select the suspect at an identification parade,[16] or where a later positive identification was ruled inadmissible.[17] Their use by the jury for comparison with the defendant, or a contemporary photograph of him,[18] is the same as that for photographs and video recordings of incidents, discussed below.

Photographs, video and other recordings

10.13 Photographs of a suspect probative of guilt have been recognised as admissible evidence since very shortly after photography was invented.[19] There is no distinction in principle between photographs, film, video recordings or audio recordings of relevant events.[20] A recording is not hearsay but direct evidence of the event shown.[21] The best evidence rule does not apply. An

---

13 [2006] EWCA Crim 1273, [2006] 1 WLR 1273.

14 *R v Cook* (1987) 84 Cr App R 369, [1987] Crim LR 402, CA.

15 *R v Cook* (1987) 84 Cr App R 369, [1987] Crim LR 402, CA.

16 *R v Okorudu* [1982] Crim LR 747, CCC; *R v Fletcher* [2009] EWCA Crim 1187. Contrast *R v O'Brien and others* [1982] Crim LR 746, CCC.

17 *R v Constantiniou* (1990) 91 Cr App R 74, CA.

18 *R v Fletcher* [2009] EWCA Crim 1187.

19 *Tolson* (1864) 4 F & F 103, a case of bigamy.

20 *R v Fowden and White* [1982] Crim LR 589, CA, video recording; *R v Maqsud Ali* [1966] 1 QB 688, CCA, audio recording.

21 *Taylor v Chief Constable of Cheshire* (1987) 84 Cr App R 191, DC.

authentic copy can be produced in evidence.[22] If a witness has viewed a recording which subsequently goes missing, oral evidence of what that witness observed on the recording will be admissible without offending the hearsay rule.[23] Whether the evidence should be admitted in those circumstances is a matter for the exercise of the court's judgment under PACE, s 78. In an exceptional case where the loss of a recording prevents a fair trial or it would be unfair to try the defendant the proceedings may be stayed as an abuse of the process of the court.[24]

10.14 It may be necessary or prudent in some cases to call the person responsible for making the recording, but where events speak for themselves it will not always be an essential prerequisite for its admission.[25] Indeed there is no such person where the recording is automated, such as CCTV. However evidential continuity after the recording has been seized may avoid argument as to provenance. Equally, records should be maintained of copying, alteration or enhancement of recorded images, particularly where expert analysis may be necessary.

Identification from photographs and video recordings

10.15 In the leading case of *Attorney General's Reference (No 2 of 2002)*[26] the Court of Appeal, having fully reviewed the authorities on the use to which photographic images could be put in identification cases found that they fell into four categories:

(1) For comparison by a jury with the defendant in the dock (see **10.23**).

(2) Recognition by a person who knows the person shown (see **10.16**).

(3) Recognition by a person who acquires special knowledge of the person shown by repeated viewing and analysis (see **10.21**).

(4) Facial mapping (see Chapter 15).

Recognition by a person who knows the person shown

10.16 Images of a suspect during the commission of an offence or a connected event may be used in order to establish the identity of the person

---

22 *Kajala v Noble* (1982) 75 Crim App R 149, DC.

23 *Taylor v Chief Constable of Cheshire* (1987) 84 Cr App R 191, DC in which a video recording in shop premises was accidentally erased after it had been viewed by police officers.

24 *R (Ebrahim) v Feltham Magistrates' Court* [2001] 1 WLR 1293, DC in which a line of previous cases was reviewed.

25 *Kajala v Noble* (1982) 75 Cr App R 149, DC.

26 [2003] 1 Cr App R 21, CA. For critical comment and a summary of relevant psychological literature see the commentary by A Roberts, 'Identification of Suspects from CCTV and Video Recordings' (2003) 67 *Journal of Criminal Law* 91; R Costigan, 'Identification from CCTV: The Risk of Injustice' [2007] Crim LR 591.

shown. The evidence of a police officer,[27] store detective,[28] friend, relative or acquaintance[29] who purports to recognise and identify the person depicted is admissible. This includes recognition of features other than facial appearance such as build, gait or posture.[30] That a jury may be able to perform the task of comparing the image and the person in the dock is no bar to someone with prior knowledge of the defendant doing so.[31] There is no distinction in principle between the evidence of a person making an identification from a recording and that of a person observing the events actually taking place.[32]

10.17 Typically a CCTV recording will have been seized during an investigation and a witness, often a police officer, will be asked whether he recognises a suspect. It should be recalled that where an identification by recognition from images is sought, D3.35[33] demands that viewing takes place on an individual basis to avoid collusion and that, as far as possible, the principles of video identification should be followed if the suspect is already known or the principles of identification by photographs if not known.[34] Where a breach of the Code or contamination is evident, it may be arguable that procedure is unfair and should be excluded, or at the very least the jury should be given a warning about its potential weaknesses. In *R v Tucker*[35] a police officer viewed some CCTV footage and recognised the defendant who he knew. The defence complained that he had already been informed that it was thought to be the defendant and thus his evidence was contaminated by the expectation of seeing him and the knowledge that he was already a suspect. Though none of the procedures of Code D strictly applied, the spirit of D3.35 seems to have been ignored. Moreover, because the defendant had already been recognised, he appears to have been a 'known suspect' at the time of the viewing. Nevertheless the Court of Appeal held that the viewing could not be faulted because, curiously, at that time it was not proposed to call the officer to give evidence at trial. In *R v Swinscoe*[36] the court found that in similar circumstances it would have been appropriate not to have alerted a police officer to the identity of a named suspect before viewing images of a robbery.

---

27 *Taylor v Chief Constable of Cheshire* (1987) 84 Cr App R 191, DC; *R v Caldwell and Dixon* (1994) 99 Cr App R 73, CA.

28 *R v Fowden and White* [1982] Crim LR 588, CA.

29 *Kajala v Noble* (1982) 75 Cr App R 149, DC; *R v Grimer* [1982] Crim LR 674, CA.

30 *R v Savalia* [2011] EWCA Crim 1334.

31 *R v Caldwell and Dixon* (1994) 99 Cr App R 73, CA; cf *Smith v The Queen* [2001] HCA 50, in which the High Court of Australia considered the admissibility of the evidence of two police officers who, on the basis of some prior dealings with the appellant, purported to recognise him as the person depicted in CCTV images robbing a bank. It concluded, at [11], that the evidence was not relevant (and hence inadmissible) on the grounds that the 'the witness's assertion of identity was founded on material no different from the material available to the jury from its own observation, [therefore] the witness's assertion that he recognised the appellant is not evidence that could rationally affect the assessment by the jury of the question [of identity].'

32 *R v Grimer* [1982] Crim LR 674, CA.

33 Formerly D3.28.

34 See **5.122–5.125** for a fuller analysis of this part of Code D.

35 [2008] EWCA Crim 3063, [2009] Crim LR 441.

36 [2005] EWCA Crim 916.

When viewing takes place D3.36 and D3.37 set out the requirements for a record of the circumstances in which the viewing and any recognition takes place. Where there is no such record the evidence may be challenged as unsafe.[37]

10.18 The weight and reliability of such evidence may also depend upon a number of factors such as the clarity of the recording, its length and the extent of the witness's prior knowledge of the person said to be identified.[38] Plainly the ability to view and re-view will be an advantage not afforded an eyewitness. However, as with any identification case, the tribunal must assess the factors reflected in the *R v Turnbull*[39] guidelines though there may be additional features bearing upon the reliability of an identification such as the position and view of the camera.[40]

10.19 Recognition does not have to be based upon a witness's knowledge of the person prior to the offence or even prior to the suspect's arrest. In *R v Blenkinsop*[41] a violent disorder took place, part of which was recorded on video and by still photographs. The defendant was interviewed by a police officer for a period of 3 minutes. Some 2 months later the officer viewed the stills and purported to recognise the defendant from his association with him in interview. The admissibility of the identification evidence, based upon after-acquired knowledge, was not the subject of argument on appeal. As a matter of principle it would seem that there can be no logical distinction with cases of pre-offence knowledge of the suspect. However, such situations may require a more rigorous and cautious approach, particularly where the person recognising the defendant is a police officer engaged in the investigation of the defendant.

10.20 The defendant has as much right as the prosecution to call witnesses who may be able to say that the person shown is not the defendant, or go further to state that someone other than the defendant can be identified. On the basis of *R v Blenkinsop,* there should be no bar, for example, upon a legal advisor at the 3-minute interview giving evidence that the person shown on video was not the defendant.

Recognition by a person who acquires special knowledge

10.21 The third category of identification evidence from recordings referred to in *Attorney General's Reference (No 2 of 2002)* concerns recognition by a person who acquires special knowledge of the person shown by repeated

---

37 *R v Smith* [2008] EWCA Crim 1342, [2009] 1 Cr App R 521; see by contrast *R v Chaney* [2009] EWCA Crim 21, [2009] 1 Cr App R 512.

38 On the dangers associated with the adduction of this form of evidence see D Elliott, 'Videotape Evidence: The Risk of Over-Persuasion' [1998] Crim LR 159.

39 (1997) 63 Cr App R 132, CA.

40 *Taylor v Chief Constable of Cheshire* (1987) 84 Cr App R 191, DC.

41 [1995] 1 Cr App R 7, CA.

viewing and analysis.[42] A violent disorder at a football match was the subject matter of *R v Clare and Peach*.[43] A black and white video recording captured the fracas. Because of its brevity and the number of participants and onlookers, the scene was confused, making it extremely difficult to discern precisely what was being done and by whom. A police officer viewed and studied it about 40 times. He had examined it in slow motion, frame by frame, to detect the activities of individuals. He also had access to a far better quality colour recording and still photographs of supporters arriving at and leaving the stadium. It was accepted that the defendants were shown on the colour images. By comparing the two he was able to identify people committing acts of violence in the recording of the fracas from the better quality images. He was permitted at trial to perform this task before the jury. It was argued that the officer's commentary ought to have been excluded on the ground that he was not an expert and it should have been left for the jury alone to decide the identities of the participants in the disorder. The Court of Appeal held that by virtue of his 'lengthy and studious' analysis the officer possessed a special knowledge which the court at first instance did not have and his evidence was properly admitted. It would have been impracticable, the court continued, to afford the jury the time and facilities to conduct their own research. The defence were not disadvantaged because recordings were available to the defence for examination, as was the officer for cross-examination.

10.22 *Attorney General's Reference (No 2 of 2002)* illustrated recognition by police officers both from acquaintance and from study. One police officer was a community constable who had known the defendant reasonably well over a period of about 5 years. The second had spent a considerable number of hours viewing a recording of a riot. Unlike the officer in *R v Clare and Peach,* who compared the questioned image with a known image of the defendant, the second officer later by chance saw the defendant. Because of his study of the film the officer purported to identify him as someone shown on the recording. Both identifications were held to have been properly admitted.

IDENTIFICATION BY JURY

10.23 When a witness has given a suspect's description in evidence the jury will inevitably compare it to the defendant's appearance in the dock or witness box, especially where the features described are particularly distinctive. However, unless unique, the features described may do no more than show a consistency of appearance which does not exclude the defendant or is capable of supporting other probative evidence.

---

[42] See R Munday, 'Videotape Evidence and the Advent of the Expert Ad Hoc' (1995) 159 JP 547. For further critical analysis concerning the admissibility of such evidence, see G Edmond and M San Roque, 'Quasi-Justice: Ad hoc experts and identification evidence' (2009) 32 *Criminal Law Journal* 8.

[43] [1995] 2 Cr App R 333, CA. See also *R v Abnett* [2006] EWCA Crim 3320.

10.24 Images of a suspect at the time of an incident have the advantage of allowing repeated study. On the other hand they may suffer the disadvantages of being one dimensional or providing a limited view of the person captured in the image. Juries are entitled to compare the appearance of a defendant with such images provided, importantly, that the images are sufficiently clear to permit a meaningful comparison.[44] They can be shown in order to demonstrate a general consistency in appearance between suspect and defendant which may be used as support for other evidence.[45] Equally, certain features may tend to exclude a defendant. But if they do not attain a threshold of clarity that will enable them positively to make a comparison, the jury should be directed to refrain from doing so.[46] If there has been a change in the defendant's appearance between incident and trial, the jury can be given a photograph that is contemporary with the offence or taken at the time of the defendant's arrest.[47] A comparison of the defendant may also be made with sketches and e-fit images. But a defendant cannot be compelled to 'exhibit' him or herself by standing up in the dock for the jury's inspection. Where a defendant had refused to do so, no adverse inference was permitted.[48] The appropriate jury directions to be given when the jurors are invited to or may themselves assess likeness are discussed at **12.94**.

CODE D IDENTIFICATION PROCEDURES

10.25 Code D is often the battleground over which disputes about compliance and fairness are contested; breaches of it are generally the gateway to the exclusion of identification evidence under PACE, s 78.The Code is itself admissible in evidence when relevant to the determination of any question arising in proceedings.[49]

Refusal of consent and non co-operation

10.26 The Notice to Suspect required to be served before an identification procedure contains a warning that a failure to consent to or co-operate in a procedure may be given in evidence.[50] No doubt a refusal will be admissible if explanatory or probative of an issue in the case, for example if a complaint is made about the absence of a procedure or where the reason for a covert procedure is contested. However the warning is not to be read as allowing an adverse inference to be drawn against a defendant who refuses to co-operate. A

---

44 *Attorney General's Reference (No 2 of 2002)* [2003] 1 Cr App R 21; *R v Dodson and Williams* (1984) 79 Cr App R 220.

45 *R v Williams* [2005] EWCA Crim 2332.

46 For example see *R v Faraz Ali* [2008] EWCA Crim 1522, [2009] Crim LR 40 in which the Court of Appeal expressed doubts about whether the images supplied to the jury were clear enough to make the comparison.

47 *R v Dodson and Williams* (1984) 79 Cr App R 220, CA; *R v Downey* [1995] 1 Cr App R 547, CA.

48 *R v McNamara* [1996] Crim LR 750, CA. See also *Holland v HM Advocate* [2005] UKPC D1.

49 PACE, s 67(11).

50 Code D3.17(v). See **4.9**.

suspect's refusal must be viewed in the context of the privilege against self-incrimination and the right to a fair trial under Article 6 of the European Convention on Human Rights (ECHR). The privilege against self-incrimination protects a suspect from a demand to provide evidential assistance to the state by means of compulsion or coercion.[51] Thus for example in *Holland v HM Advocate*[52] the Privy Council stated that a requirement on a defendant in the dock to assist the prosecution by standing up, turning round or showing part of his body to assist the prosecution in identification was not permitted and would be likely to breach his Article 6 right against self-incrimination.

10.27 What further distinguishes a refusal to co-operate in an identification procedure from a refusal to answer questions under caution or to consent to the taking of an intimate sample is that in the latter instances an adverse inference is permitted by primary legislation.[53] The evidential use to which a refusal to consent to an identification procedure is apparently derived is found only in the warning contained in the Notice to Suspect. It is submitted that in the context of an erosion of the privilege against self-incrimination, an adverse inference should properly be the subject of a statutory exception which sets out the criteria for its application.

10.28 The Notice to Suspect also warns that a change in appearance before an identification procedure may be adduced in evidence.[54] Once again this should not be read as permitting an adverse inference, not least because a prohibition on changing appearance, say by cutting one's hair, is likely to infringe the right to respect for a person's private life under ECHR, Article 8. However the evidence may be admissible in order to explain a discrepancy in appearance between the time of the offence and an identification procedure or trial. It may also be permitted as an explanation for a witness's failure to identify a suspect at an identification procedure.[55]

Qualified and non-identification

10.29 A failure to identify will normally be adduced by the defence as demonstrative of the innocence of the defendant. However, between complete failure and a positive identification there are a wide range of responses. A witness may indicate a person by saying, 'he looks like the person', 'I think that it might be number two' or 'I have a feeling about number six'. A witness may vacillate between two or three candidates before settling on a volunteer. The Court of Appeal considered the admissibility of qualified or non-identification

---

51 *Jalloh v Germany* (2007) 44 EHRR 32. See *R v Kearns* [2003] 1 Cr App R 7 for a review of Strasbourg and domestic authorities and a summary of the general principles to be applied.

52 *Holland v HM Advocate* [2005] UKPC D1, on appeal from the High Court of Justiciary, Scotland. See also *R v McNanmara* [1996] Crim LR 750, CA.

53 See **10.184** and **10.190**.

54 Code D3.17(ix).

55 *R v George* [2002] EWCA Crim 1923, [2003] Crim LR 282, CA. See **10.29**.

evidence in *R v George*.[56] The high profile case concerned the murder of a television presenter. Many witnesses gave descriptions of a person in the vicinity of the victim's address on the evening before and on the morning of the murder. It was accepted that those were admissible regardless of the result of the identification procedure. However the court was invited by the defence to conclude that if a witness failed to make an unqualified positive identification, any uncertain identification or other comment concerning the suspect should be excluded and that the jury should know no more than the witness's failure to make a positive identification. The submission was rejected. It is necessary to consider the decision in the context of the particular circumstances of the challenged evidence.

10.30 It was almost a year before the defendant was arrested and 13 months before he stood on an identification parade. In that time he had grown a full beard. Thereafter he refused to consent to a parade and the remaining procedures were by video procedure. These difficulties were compounded by a further delay before the video parade was prepared and viewed, by then some 16 to 18 months after the original observation. Of the nine witnesses who gave evidence describing the person observed, only one made an unqualified positive identification. However the evidence of the video procedures of three witnesses who either made a qualified identification or hinted at the possibility of recognition was admitted. In each case the defendant was positioned at number 2 in the sequence. The first witness wavered between three persons, numbers 1, 2 and 8 before settling on number 8. The witness said she was 80 to 85% sure. It was apparent that the selection and the defendant were very similar in appearance. In evidence she stated that she found the procedure difficult because of the lapse of time and the fact she could only see the head and shoulders of each person. The second witness also concentrated on numbers 2 and 8. She said it could be either, that she could not tell between them but that her gut feeling was that it was number 2. She concluded by saying 'I would say it was number 2' but refrained from making a positive identification. In her subsequent statement that day she repeated that she could not make a positive identification. In a further statement made the following day she stated that number 2 had 'brought something back' to her as had number 8 though not so strongly and explained that she was hindered by not seeing number 2 stand and hence his build. The third witness likewise concentrated on numbers 2 and 8 but when asked if the person she had previously seen was paraded she said that she did not think so. She explained contemporaneously the difficulty concerning the importance of height and build and that she had not been expecting a moustache or beard.

10.31 The Court of Appeal upheld the decision to admit the evidence. It was acknowledged that a defendant must not be convicted on the evidence of a qualified identification alone, but such evidence might be admissible in some circumstances:

---

[56] [2002] EWCA Crim 1923; [2003] Crim LR 282, CA. For critical comment see A Roberts, 'The Perils and Possibilities of Qualified Identification Evidence: *R v George*', (2003) 7 *International Journal of Evidence and Proof* 130.

'However, there are at least two situations where a qualified identification may in appropriate circumstances be both relevant and probative. First, where although the weight of the evidence will still be less than a positive identification, it supports or at least is consistent with other evidence that indicates the defendant committed the crime with which he is charged. Secondly, the explanation for a non or qualified identification may help to place the non or qualified identification in its proper context and so, for example, show that other evidence given by the witness may still be correct. Otherwise a non or qualified identification could be used to attack the credibility of other evidence given by a witness when the explanation for this may show that such an attack is unjustified.'[57]

10.32 Thus spontaneous explanatory remarks at the procedure concerning the difficulty caused by the lapse of time or the additional facial hair were correctly adduced. However the court warned that:

'... prosecuting counsel must be cautious and avoid conducting his examination of a witness who had failed to make a positive identification in a manner which suggests that but for this fact or that fact the witness would have made a positive identification. An identification which is qualified cannot be transformed into one which is unqualified by careful questioning.'[58]

10.33 The court stated that the admission of qualified identification evidence depended upon the balance between its prejudice and its relevance and probative value, bearing in mind the importance of protecting the defendant from unfairness. A spontaneous remark made at the time of the procedure would be admissible if relevant and probative and subject to the discretion to exclude under PACE, s 78. On the facts of the case the Court of Appeal held that the evidence was properly admitted as supporting an 'underlying unity of description' of the assailant and general consistency of the identification evidence. Moreover it was held to support 'a considerable volume of other circumstantial evidence'.[59]

10.34 A qualified identification in its simplest form occurs where a witness's recognition is expressed as less than absolute, for example in terms such as 'almost sure', '90% certain' or 'looks the same but can't be positive'. It is submitted that, subject to the power to exclude, in principle there is no greater admissibility difficulty than of a witness who expresses less than full certainty about the number of blows struck, the number of people involved, the description of an assailant or even a street identification procedure. Following *R v George*, in *R v Ciantar*[60] the witness made no identification at the procedure but immediately thereafter stated that the defendant's image had reminded her of the assailant. She had said nothing at the time of the procedure because she was nervous and scared, and thought she had to be 100% sure, which she was

57 Ibid, at [35].

58 Ibid, at [34].

59 For confirmation of the dangers of over reliance on qualified identification evidence it is necessary only to refer to *R v George (No. 2)* [2007] EWCA Crim 2722, in which at his second appeal the appellant's conviction was quashed on different grounds, and his subsequent acquittal at his retrial in 2008.

60 [2005] EWCA Crim 3559.

not. The admission of this evidence was upheld on the grounds that it lent support to other identification evidence, it placed the qualification in its context and corrected what would otherwise have been the misleading impression that she had failed to make a positive identification.

10.35 A more arcane identification took place in *R v Gray*,[61] in which none of the singular difficulties thrown up by *R v George* arose. Having viewed the video parade twice the victim of an assault asked to view three of the images again and then two of those, the defendant's image included, a further time. As between the defendant and the volunteer, he finally selected the volunteer. The Court of Appeal rejected the submission that the principle of admitting qualified identification evidence should not apply to a straightforward single witness case. It held that the principle in *R v George* was intended to be of general application and that the request to view the defendant on two further occasions amounted to a qualified identification under the first limb of the dicta. This seems to have come perilously close to the conversion of a non-identification into a positive identification. More persuasively, the court found that because the defence had wanted the jury to know that the witness had failed to identify the defendant the jury were entitled to have the full picture – the second situation cited in *R v George*. The court went on to add that the position might have well have been different if the defence had wanted the jury to know nothing whatsoever about the procedure. That approach may be a sensible compromise in which neither party is prejudiced. It appears not to have been one canvassed in *R v Barrowes*[62] in which the victim of a robbery was asked whether his attacker was among those paraded at a video identification procedure. He indicated that his choice was between the defendant and a volunteer before settling on the latter. The argument at trial seems to have been confined to the admissibility of the material prior to the false identification and accordingly no point was taken on the admission of the whole procedure. Nevertheless the appeal succeeded because the judge fell into the trap identified in *R v George*: in summing up he referred to the case being, in part, an identification case thereby promoting a non-identification into identification evidence, or at the very least leaving the jury in a state of confusion as to how it could be treated.[63]

Code D breaches and PACE, s 78

10.36 The Codes have been described as providing 'a platform of fairness upon which the difficult business of assessing the possible guilt of suspects of crime, not least in relation to identification, may properly be carried out.'[64] PACE, s 78[65] requires the court to have regard to the 'circumstances in which

---

61 [2005] EWCA Crim 3564. See also *R v Brown* [2011] EWCA Crim 80 in which a 'qualified suspicion' concerning the defendant on parade was admitted as a counterpoint to the discrepancies between his appearance and the witness's description.

62 [2010] EWCA Crim 1293

63 As to jury directions, see **12.109**.

64 *R v Fuller* (unreported) 22 May 2000, CA.

65 See **10.2**.

the evidence was obtained' when exercising its judgment about the fairness of the evidence. General guidance as to the relationship between Code D breaches and PACE, s 78 was given in *R v Popat*:[66]

> 'At a trial, the trial judge has to consider any question of compliance with the Code in deciding the question of fairness under section 78. But it is not a simple relationship between a question of compliance and a question of fairness. Even where the Code has been complied with, a proper exercise of the discretion under section 78, or the related inherent discretion that the judge has in relation to prejudicial or inherently unreliable evidence, may require the judge to rule that the evidence should not be admitted. Compliance with the Code is a factor but not the only factor, nor is it a decisive factor. Similarly non-compliance with the Code is not decisive. It is again only a factor, maybe a cogent factor, in the decision to admit or exclude evidence.'

10.37 Phrases such as 'significant and substantial' have been coined to indicate the type of breach which might call for the exclusion of evidence.[67] Such phrases may assist but cannot determine whether evidence should be excluded. Even a 'major' breach or a series of breaches of Code D will not necessarily compel a court to exclude the identification evidence.[68] However, as the judgment in *R v Popat* concluded:

> 'The overall purpose [of Code D] is one of adopting fair identification practices and adducing reliable identification evidence. Where insufficient regard is had to these purposes the discretion to exclude evidence under section 78 is likely to be exercised and convictions will be liable to be treated as unsafe.'[69]

10.38 Equally, it is possible that the admission of identification evidence will result in unfairness where there has been no breach of procedure at all. Thus it has been held that an identification made in 'highly unsatisfactory circumstances' ought to have been excluded notwithstanding that Code D was not engaged.[70] Indeed over-reliance on the question of breaches to determine questions of exclusion may itself be a vice which masks the proper s 78 test. In *R v Hickin*[71] the Court of Appeal found it unnecessary to decide whether Code D applied because the question to be asked under s 78 was precisely the same in either case. In the court's view the examination of the issue conducted at trial was too focused upon whether there had been breaches, with the effect that

---

66 [1998] 2 Cr App R 208 at 212, CA. The case is no longer good law on the interpretation of D3.12: see **3.31–3.41**.

67 *R v Walsh* (1989) 91 Cr App R 161, [1989] Crim LR 822, CA.

68 See *R v Grannell* (1990) 90 Cr App R 149, CA the wholesale failure to provide notice to suspect; *R v Ryan* [1992] Crim LR 187, CA a 'major' and 'substantial breach' in holding a confrontation; *R v Quinn* [1995] 1 Cr App R 480, CA a series of breaches in the procedure for a parade.

69 *R v Popat* [1998] 2 Cr App R 208 at 224, CA.

70 *R v Martin and Nicholls* [1994] Crim LR 218, CA.

71 [1996] Crim LR 584, CA. This case is considered in detail at **3.24**. See also *R v Vaughan* (unreported) 30 April 1997, CA; *R v Williams* [2003] EWCA Crim 3200, (2003) SJ 1305, and *R v Haynes* [2004] EWCA Crim 390. In these cases the Court of Appeal was less interested in whether there had been a breach of Code D, or of precisely what provision, than in the fairness of the procedure.

insufficient attention had been paid to the quality of the evidence, the manner in which it was obtained and its potential for injustice. Similarly in *R v Smith and others*[72] it was held that whether or not Code D was intended to apply to police officers making identifications from CCTV, the principles concerning safeguards for the viewing of photographs were equally important in ensuring that, so far as possible, the accuracy of the identification can later be assessed.

10.39 Some breaches of Code D, such as the failure to achieve a resemblance with volunteers, will have a direct impact upon the fairness of a procedure. In respect of others. the link between the breach and the unfairness will be derivative: for example the remedy sought for the failure to hold a video identification might be the exclusion of street identification evidence, notwithstanding that procedure was compliant with Code D. The unfairness derives from the denial of the defendant's right to test the original identification in controlled circumstances. Hence the dangers of an identification by photograph not followed by a formal procedure has been held to be analogous to those of a dock identification.[73]

10.40 In 'having regard to all the circumstances' under PACE, s 78, a court may take into account the content of a defence statement. Where therefore in *R v Royes*[74] the defendant, facing a charge of violent disorder, sought to exclude police identification evidence on the ground that Code D, Annex E (Showing Photographs) had been infringed, the judge was entitled to consider the acceptance of his presence at the scene in his defence statement.

10.41 In some circumstances it may be necessary to hear evidence on a voir dire to determine admissibility. In *R v Flemming,*[75] a pre-PACE decision, on an application to exclude evidence the trial judge held a trial within a trial to consider whether there had been a breach of the Home Office guidelines on identification parades and the quality of the identification evidence. The Court of Appeal held that in respect of neither issue should a judge have recourse to a voir dire. As to any qualitative analysis of the identification evidence, the position has not changed; submissions and judicial intervention should be based upon the statements or on the evidence once it has been given before the jury. However, it is submitted that *R v Flemming* can no longer be regarded as authoritative where it is necessary to make a factual finding on alleged Code D breaches or in order make a PACE, s 78 ruling.[76] Being a pre-PACE case it was not concerned with the statutory requirements of PACE, s 78, that is to say to consider 'the circumstances in which evidence was obtained' in order to arrive at a conclusion about the impact of the evidence on the fairness of the

---

72 [2009] 1 Cr App R 521 (36).

73 *R v Maynard and others* (1979) 69 Cr App R 309, CA.

74 [2004] EWCA Crim 3470. See also *R v Johnson* [2001] EWCA Crim 2312 in which a defence statement was used to determine a lack of prejudice to the defence in allowing the prosecution to re-open its case to adduce identification evidence. The statement had indicated that the defence was duress.

75 (1986) 86 Cr App R 32, CA.

76 The cases in which evidence has been heard on a voir dire without criticism by the Court of Appeal are too numerous to cite.

proceedings. In many cases a conclusion and the exercise of judgment can only be achieved by hearing evidence to determine the underlying basis of factual claims. Moreover the importance of a full and proper evidential review under s 78 is reinforced by the reliance so often placed on it in European Convention jurisprudence. It is regarded as the safety valve which provides a defendant with the opportunity to challenge the admissibility of prosecution evidence thereby guaranteeing the ECHR, Article 6 right to a fair trial.[77]

10.42 Where an alleged breach of Code D involves a contested issue of fact the judge should explain how it has been resolved. If a ruling in favour of admitting evidence is made despite an admitted or proven breach, the judge must give reasons for doing so.[78] In those circumstances a direction to the jury identifying the breaches and the consequential disadvantage to the defendant will be necessary.[79] The Court of Appeal will be slow to interfere with a decision to admit identification evidence, notwithstanding Code D breaches, provided the decision to do so was not 'Wednesbury' unreasonable,[80] that any unfairness was not irremediable and that the potential impact of the breach was explained by an appropriate jury direction.

10.43 The subjects which follow are no more than a guide to Code D breaches which commonly lead to argument over the exclusion of evidence. They include cases in which evidence ought, in the Court of Appeal's judgment, to have been excluded but which are necessarily anecdotal. They thus provide examples of the application of general principles but of limited value in seeking to deduce rules which could be applied to other circumstances.

Exclusion of description

10.44 Evidence of a description may be challenged if there has been an improper failure to hold an identification procedure resulting in unfairness. In *R v Allen*[81] in the light of non-compliance with the requirement to hold a parade the admission of the victim's description of the woman who had snatched a purse resulted in the trial process being radically flawed.

---

77 See for example *Khan v UK* (2001) 31 EHRR 45.

78 *R v Allen* [1995] Crim LR 643, CA. See also *R v Fuller* (unreported) 22 May 2000, CA for a criticism of the failure to do so.

79 See **12.105** for jury directions.

80 *Associated Provincial Picture Houses Ltd v Wednesbury Corporation* [1948] 1 KB 223. See for example *H v DPP* [2007] EWHC 2192 (Admin) and *R v B* [2008] EWCA Crim 1524. The latter was a prosecution appeal against a terminating ruling. A witness was not asked to refrain from making an identification until he had viewed the parade twice (breach of D.11) and selected the defendant after one viewing. The judge excluded the evidence on the basis of a possibility that a second viewing might have elicited a different response. The Court of Appeal quashed the ruling having stated that it would interfere only if the discretion was 'Wednesbury' unreasonable.

81 [1995] Crim LR 643, CA.

Exclusion of confrontation

10.45 In *R v Jones and Nelson*[82] a confrontation was excluded because police had unlawfully used force to compel a defendant to be confronted by a witness. In *Powell v DPP*[83] a police officer drove alongside a vehicle being driven with faulty lights. The car subsequently crashed and the driver fled. Some hours later the defendant was apprehended and brought to the police station. While in custody the police officer caused him to be brought from the cells for the purpose of viewing him. He there identified the detainee as the driver. The confrontation was held to have created considerable unfairness and that no court, properly directed, could have concluded that it was admissible. In *R v Joseph*[84] an identification by confrontation in the cell area of the court at the beginning of the trial ought to have been excluded even though it was held at the behest of the defence after a ruling that all other procedures had been impracticable. That decision might be contrasted with *R v O'Brien*[85] in which, following a fight at a public house, the defendants insisted on returning with police to exonerate themselves. It was held that there was no breach of Code D or unfairness.

Exclusion of street procedure

10.46 A street identification might be excluded because it should never have taken place (in the case of a known suspect) or because the procedure was inherently flawed and unfair. It may also be excluded as a result of the failure to follow it up by a formal procedure. Moreover, a later formal procedure may be tainted by a flawed street procedure. The Code itself, in Note for Guidance 3F, specifically draws attention to the fact that the admissibility and value of a street identification may be compromised if a witness's attention is specifically drawn to the person identified or where the suspect's identity is already known at the time of the identification. In *R v Nagah*[86] the defendant, accused of rape, was released from a police station while the complainant waited in a car nearby observing people leaving. On seeing him she made an identification. This 'contrived' street identification when there ought to have been an identification parade was found to be a 'complete flouting of the Code' and ought to have been excluded.

10.47 The mere fact that a street identification is not made in ideal circumstances is no reason for excluding it. Neither does the fact alone that a person has been detained (not under arrest) by police compel the exclusion of a

---

82 (1999) Times 21 April, CA.
83 [1992] RTR 270, DC.
84 [1994] Crim LR 48, CA.
85 [2003] EWCA Crim 1370. See also *R v Lamb* (1980) 71 Cr App R 198, CA.
86 (1991) 92 Cr App R 344, CA.

street identification.[87] Where however the circumstances are particularly adverse, the risk of misidentification is that much greater. In *R v Hickin*[88] it was held that:

> 'The answer to the section 78 question required … a detailed consideration of this identification evidence and an assessment of its potential for injustice, having regard to the manner in which it was obtained – in other words having regard to its quality.'

There, witnesses made street identifications in each other's presence allowing the opportunity of cross-pollination of information. No records were made as to which witness had identified which suspect. In the main, no prior descriptions were taken with the result that descriptions in statements were made after the identifications, thus the opportunity to compare first descriptions with the suspect's actual appearance was lost. The Court of Appeal held that the street identification evidence ought to have been excluded regardless of whether breaches of Code D had occurred.

10.48 In *R v Forbes*[89] on the other hand the street identification evidence was 'compelling and untainted … and did not suffer from such problems or weaknesses as sometimes attend evidence of this kind; as for example, where the suspect is already visibly in the hands of the police'. In the circumstances, notwithstanding a breach of the mandatory requirement to hold a later formal procedure, the House of Lords, upholding the Court of Appeal, declined to rule that the street identification ought to have been excluded.

10.49 In *K v DPP*[90] a street identification should have been excluded because the defendant was at the time a known suspect, the witness's attention was drawn to him by police and there was no subsequent formal procedure. In *R v Vaughan*[91] a street identification should have been excluded where there was no record of the witness's first description and the identification was made in circumstances prejudicial to the suspect. Similarly in *Ryan v DPP*[92] where there had been no record of first description and no later parade to test what had been a street identification in adverse circumstances, it ought not to have been relied upon. In *R v Fuller*[93] the police wrongly conducted a street identification in respect of a known suspect and failed to take a record of the witness's first description. It was held that the fairness of the trial was compromised by the admission of identification evidence obtained in 'gross violation' of the Code.

---

87 *R v Rogers* [1993] Crim LR 386, CA.
88 [1996] Crim LR 584, CA. See **3.24**.
89 [2001] 1 AC 473, [2001] 1 Cr App R 31, HL.
90 (Unreported) 11 February 2003, DC.
91 (Unreported) 30 April 1997, CA.
92 (Unreported) 10 October 2000, CA.
93 (Unreported), 22 May 2000, CA.

Exclusion of video, parade and other procedures

10.50 The involvement of an investigating officer in the procedure is prohibited. In *R v Gall*[94] it was held that the identification parade ought to have been excluded notwithstanding that no actual contamination was found. The officer who had escorted a witness to a parade had improperly seen the parade before the viewing began. The Court of Appeal endorsed the view that it should have been excluded because of the appearance of unfairness. In *R v Ryan*[95] by contrast, the admission of a confrontation was upheld, despite the involvement of an investigating officer in the confrontation which was described as a 'major breach'. The judge was satisfied that nothing improper had in fact taken place and the breach was mitigated by precautions taken by the defendant's solicitor. So too in *R v Ball and Ball*[96] the Court of Appeal upheld the admission of identification evidence despite the involvement of an investigating officer on the ground that the breach had not been serious or flagrant, neither did it give rise to a real suspicion that it might have been unfair.

10.51 The risks of contamination between witnesses was considered in *R v Finley*.[97] The trial judge found that one witness to a photographic identification must have overheard the remarks of another when identifying the defendant. Further, there was a grave risk of crosspollination between four witnesses either before or when they attended a parade together. Though there was no evidence that the witnesses had in fact communicated with each other they were plainly in a position where they could have done so. For those and other reasons (set out below) the conviction was quashed.

10.52 Evidence of a procedure may also be excluded if a defendant's appearance among the line up is clearly outstanding. *R v Finley* may also be cited in this context also as a somewhat extreme example in which a photographic procedure was tainted and unfair because the defendant was the sole blond skinhead on display. Similarly in *R v Marcus*[98] the Court of Appeal ruled that the trial judge should have excluded a parade in which the defendant, who was in his forties with a greying beard, was being compared with volunteers in their twenties only two of whom had any sort of facial hair. The defendant in *R v Pecco*[99] had two prominent tattoos on her neck. The witness to a robbery had noticed tattoos on the assailant's neck. Because nothing had been done to conceal these distinguishing features, all or all but one of the volunteers could be excluded. The Court of Appeal found that the parade was therefore valueless and should not have been placed before the jury. By contrast, the fact that in breach of the Code a defendant and his solicitor have not been shown or afforded the opportunity to object to the selection (Annex

94 [1989] Crim LR 745, CA.
95 [1992] Crim LR 187, CA. See also *R v Quinn* [1995] 1 Cr App R 480, CA and *R v Kitchen* [1994] Crim LR 684, CA.
96 [2006] EWCA Crim 1048.
97 [1993] Crim LR 50, CA.
98 [2004] EWCA Crim 3387.
99 [2010] EWCA Crim 972.

A.7) does not create any risk of unfairness where there can be no reasonable objection to the similitude of the persons paraded.[100]

10.53 If a defendant or representative has exercised some control over the composition of the line-up it may be difficult thereafter to substantiate a complaint that it was unfair.[101] The complaint may also be met by the response that the recording can be played to a jury who can consider its merit.

10.54 In *R v Johnson*[102] a robbery victim identified a suspect from a video recording taken near the scene of the offence. There was no identification parade as there might have been. The Court of Appeal held that the identification by video was akin to a confrontation and should have been excluded. In *R v Harley*[103] the defendant was threatened with the use of force to bring about a confrontation if he did not agree to stand on an identification parade. The defendant's consent was vitiated and the parade should have been excluded.

Exclusion of expert evidence

10.55 In *R v Walker*[104] the defendant was identified by facial mapping evidence after he had been wrongly denied an identification parade. The Court of Appeal held that a court should be slow to allow the prosecution to 'fill the gap' by adducing the expert evidence. There might be circumstances in which it was appropriate, but where 'the evidence was called to circumvent a clear breach of the Code', the prosecution should not have been permitted to do so. That decision was considered in *R v Donald*[105] in which the failure to hold identification procedures was characterised as an oversight. In that case no objection was made to the admission of facial mapping evidence but it was claimed thereafter that the prosecution was an abuse of the process of the court. The Court of Appeal, noting that there might be circumstances in which filling the gap was justifiable, distinguished *R v Walker* and upheld the conviction. It did so on the ground that the appellant had failed to overcome the obstacle which an abuse of process argument (rather than a s 78 argument) posed, namely demonstrating that the defendant could not have a fair trial.

UNLAWFULLY OBTAINED EVIDENCE

10.56 PACE, s 78 specifically directs the court's attention to the circumstances in which evidence was obtained when deciding whether evidence should be excluded.[106] Thus the principle that, save for confessions, courts have no

---

100 *R v Middleton* [2005] EWCA Crim 692.
101 *R v Quinn* [1995] 1 Cr App R 480, CA; *R v Mendili* [2001] EWCA Crim 757.
102 [1996] Crim LR 504, CA.
103 (Unreported) 22 February 2000, CA.
104 (Unreported) 14 November 1994, CA.
105 [2004] Crim L R 841, [2004] EWCA Crim 965.
106 See, for example, *R v Nathaniel* [1995] 2 Cr App R 565, CA.

discretion to exclude admissible evidence due to the manner in which it was obtained[107] must be read subject to that provision. Moreover, in disputes over the admission of evidence, the European Court of Human Rights will generally look to the safeguards of the PACE, s 78 procedure to discover whether the defendant's right to a fair trial was properly protected.

Covert procedures

10.57 The covert photography of a suspect is authorised in some circumstances by Code D3.21 for the purposes of a video procedure. Such covert action may amount to an infringement of a suspect's right to respect for private and family life under ECHR, Article 8. However, provided that it is 'in accordance with law', that is to say compliant with PACE and Code D[108] it is likely to be regarded as justified. Whether a failure to adhere to PACE will render a covert photograph or video recording and any consequential identification evidence inadmissible will depend upon the test of fairness under PACE, s 78. In *Perry v United Kingdom*[109] notwithstanding that a covert video of the suspect was made in breach of a number of provisions of Code D and despite the finding of an unjustified interference with the suspect's Article 8 rights, the application to the European Court under Article 6 was held to be inadmissible. The procedural safeguards at trial had been followed and the defendant was able to test the evidence in his defence.

10.58 *R v Loveridge and others*[110] produced a similar result. Covert photography was used in order to obtain images of suspects for expert comparison with CCTV images – an identification procedure outside the scope of Code D. The filming took place within court precincts and therefore contravened the Criminal Justice Act 1925, s 41.[111] The Court of Appeal expressed disapproval of the practice and found it to be a breach of ECHR, Article 8. Neither could the contravention be justified under Article 8(2) since it was not in accordance with law. However it was held that the contravention had not interfered with the fairness of the trial and the judge had been entitled to conclude that the evidence should not be excluded under PACE, s 78.

Unlawfully obtained/retained samples and fingerprints

10.59 Unless there is an express statutory prohibition upon the admission of unlawfully obtained or retained fingerprints, samples or information derived from samples, their use at trial is not prohibited but will be subject to the power to exclude under PACE, s 78. In *Attorney General's Reference (No 3 of 1999)*[112] a sample taken from the defendant in earlier proceedings that should have been

---

[107] *R v Sang* [1980] AC 402; 69 Cr App R 282, HL.

[108] Also, where applicable, the Regulation of Investigatory Powers Act 2000.

[109] [2003] Crim LR 281, CA (on Art 6) and [2003] 7 *Archbold News* 2 (on Art 8), ECtHR.

[110] [2001] Cr App R 29, CA.

[111] It was also argued that the photography fell outside the power to take photographs under PACE and Code D, though the point was not resolved on appeal.

[112] [2001] 2 AC 91; [2001] 1 Cr App R 34; [2001] Crim LR 394, HL.

destroyed was retained. It later led to the identification of the defendant for a rape. After arrest, a further sample was taken from the defendant which, also matching, was adduced in evidence. PACE, s 64 prohibited the use of the first sample and its DNA profile in evidence because it should have been destroyed.[113] Its use for the purposes of an investigation was also prohibited by PACE, s 64, hence the initial matching by which the defendant was identified was unlawful. However the House of Lords held that while the statute expressly prohibited the evidential use of the first sample, it did not do so for the second. The breach of the prohibition against use for investigative purposes did not render the second sample and profile inadmissible. The 'fruits of the poisoned tree' – the second sample – was therefore admissible subject to the trial judge's power under PACE, s 78 to exclude it.

10.60 The s 78 discretion to exclude an unlawfully retained DNA profile was considered in *R v Nathaniel*.[114] The prosecution relied upon a DNA profile taken in relation to another investigation that ought to have been destroyed some years earlier. Consent to the taking of the sample had been given after the defendant had been informed that the sample would be destroyed if he was cleared but that his failure to provide it might later draw an adverse inference. In those circumstances the Court of Appeal held that its unlawful retention must have had an adverse effect upon the fairness of the proceedings and ought to have been excluded. It should be noted that the statutory power to retain fingerprints, samples and derivative profiles has been significantly widened since the decision.[115]

10.61 The effect of the ECHR Article 8 right to respect for private and family life on the power of retention of fingerprints and samples under PACE, s 64 was considered in *R (S) v Chief Constable of South Yorkshire; R (Marper) v Chief Constable of South Yorkshire*.[116] In both cases complaints were made about retention. In one case the defendant was acquitted; in the other the proceedings were discontinued. It was argued that the retention (but not the taking) interfered with their rights under ECHR, Article 8(1) and that it was not necessary in a democratic society for the prevention of crime because it was not proportionate to that legitimate aim under ECHR, Article 8(2). The Court of Appeal accepted that the retention of fingerprints was an interference with the Article 8(1) rights but held that it was justified under Article 8(2) on the grounds that the interference was not significant by comparison with the limited purposes of retention which the Act allowed.[117] The House of Lords doubted that Article 8(1) was engaged at all but that if it was, any interference was very modest and justified.[118] The case was taken to the European Court of

---

[113] PACE, s 64 in its amended form would now have allowed retention and use. See **6.51**.
[114] [1995] 2 Cr App R 565, CA.
[115] See **6.50** for the power to retain fingerprints, samples and profiles, the requirement of destruction and the prohibitions on use.
[116] [2002] EWCA Civ 1275, [2003] 1 Cr App R 247, CA.
[117] A further argument that retention discriminated against those suspected but not convicted and those who had never been suspected was also rejected.
[118] [2004] UKHL 39.

Human Rights in *S and Marper v UK*[119] which held that the retention of fingerprints and DNA samples after discontinuance or acquittal was indeed an interference with Article 8(1) which, by the nature of its indiscriminate application, could not be justified under Article 8(2).

VOICE IDENTIFICATION

10.62 Voice identification evidence is available when, during the course of an offence, either the offender speaks in a witness's presence or the offender's voice is recorded. In the former case, because the speech is transient, the evidence can only be based upon recognition of a known voice or later identification of the suspect as the speaker.[120] Where the voice has been recorded additional identification is available: study of the recording by police, recognition of the recorded voice and by expert analysis and comparison of recordings of the known voice of a suspect with that of the offender.[121] The jury may also have a role in arriving at their own conclusions.

10.63 The admission of voice recognition evidence has been described as controversial.[122] Serious doubts about witnesses' ability to recognise or identify by voice, exposed by academic research, persist.[123] These were acknowledged in *R v Roberts*[124] and subsequent voice identification cases, and they appear to be recognised by the elaborate measures to safeguard against mistaken identification in the guidance for voice identification parades issued in the Home Office Circular.[125]

Factors affecting accuracy and reliability

10.64 The probative value of voice identification will depend upon a variety of factors akin to visual identification. These include:

- audibility and clarity of speech heard at time of offence;
- amount and variety of speech;
- interference by extraneous noise and other environmental factors;
- quality of a recording;
- degree of the witness's familiarity with the suspect's voice;

---

119 (2009) 48 EHRR 50.

120 See Chapter 8 for the conduct of voice identification procedures.

121 Expert voice identification is considered in Chapter 17.

122 *R v Flynn and St. John* [2008] EWCA Crim 970, [2008] 2 Cr App R 20.

123 See **10.65**.

124 [2000] Crim LR 183, CA.

125 HOC 57/2003. See Chapter 8.

- whether offender's speech/voice/accent has positive or lack of distinguishing features;
- witness's familiarity with language and ability to distinguish accent;[126]
- witness's ability to identify voices in general;
- witness's hearing disability, whether natural or induced by intoxication;
- discrepancy between first or other description and offender's voice;
- lapse of time between offence and identification procedure or between hearing known voice and attempt to recognise disputed voice.

10.65 These factors need to be considered against the inherent dangers in voice identification, discussed in research and academic texts for a considerable time.[127] The dangers were given judicial recognition in *R v Roberts,*[128] in which the research evidence of Professor Bull clearly influenced the court in its judgment. His conclusions included the following propositions:

- voice identification is more difficult than visual identification;
- voice identification is more likely to be wrong than visual;
- there exists an even greater danger than in visual identification of the witness believing himself or herself to be right when in fact mistaken;
- voice identification of a stranger's voice is a very difficult task, even where the opportunities to listen to the voice are relatively good;
- the warning given to jurors of the danger of a miscarriage of justice should be even more stringent than that given in relation to visual identification.

Finally it was asserted that the voice identification was so prone to error that without supporting or confirmatory evidence it should not be the sole basis of conviction. Though the last proposition is unlikely ever to be regarded as an evidential principle, its message is apparent in a number of cases.[129] In *R v Flynn and St John*,[130] relying on the evidence of two voice experts, the Court of Appeal confirmed the many difficulties identified in *R v Roberts*.

---

126 See *R v Korgbara* [2007] NSWCCA 75 in which the New South Wales Court of Criminal Appeal held admissible voice recognition evidence, in circumstances in which the identifying witness did not speak the language used in the conversation.

127 See D. Ormerod 'Sounds Familiar? Voice Identification Evidence' [2001] Crim LR 595.

128 [2000] Crim LR 183, CA. See also the evidence of Dr Nolan in *R v O'Doherty* [2003] 1 Cr App R 77, NICA.

129 *R v Devlin* (unreported) 14 March 1997, CA and other cases cited at **11.12–11.14**.

130 [2008] 2 Cr App R 20, [2008] EWCA Crim 970.

Voice recognition

10.66 *R v Gummerson and Steadman*[131] provides a common example of voice recognition at the time of an offence. A man was robbed and beaten by four masked men. He purported to recognise their voices as belonging to the defendants who he had known for some years. One ground of appeal was that there ought to have been a voice identification procedure to test the witness's ability to recognise one of the defendants. It was held that Code D was of no application to voice identification. Unlike visual identification, no obligation is imposed on the police to hold a procedure where a witness purports to recognise a voice even where that may be the sole basis for identifying the defendant.[132] Neither does the Home Office Circular[133] prescribe the circumstances in which a voice identification procedure should be held.

10.67 Though no obligation to hold a voice identification exists, its value was recognised in *R v Hersey*.[134] Two masked men robbed a shop. The shopkeeper claimed to recognise the voice of one of the robbers as a longstanding customer. In that case a voice identification procedure was held and the suspect was identified. At trial the defence submitted that it ought to be excluded under PACE, s 78. One of the grounds for this submission was that the original recognition should have stood alone because the witness was bound to pick the suspect and his voice would be the only voice with which the witness was familiar. In rejecting these arguments the Court of Appeal held that:

> 'One of the purposes of an identification parade is to give the witness an opportunity to test whether his original identification was or was not correct and, even more important, as has been recognised in cases concerning visual recognition, in appropriate circumstances out of fairness to the accused so that he can be excluded if the original identification was erroneous. It is often overlooked that identification parades may be as valuable to an accused as they are to the prosecution.'

As indicated in this dicta, the rationale for testing recognition parallels the reasoning applied in many cases of visual identification.

10.68 By contrast no formal procedure was held in *R v Roberts.*[135] The defendant was identified by the victim of an indecent assault at a street identification shortly after the offence. It emerged that the identification rested almost wholly on the voice of the defendant as he spoke to police officers near the scene. The offender's voice had been heard near to a noisy main road while the complainant was being attacked and in fear. More significantly, the defendant had an unexceptional London accent and, the complainant being Polish, it may have made it difficult for her to distinguish from other such voices. Accordingly the court found the conviction to be unsafe.

---

131 [1999] Crim LR 680, CA.

132 See also *R v Deenik* [1992] Crim LR 578, CA.

133 See **8.3**.

134 [1998] Crim LR 281, CA.

135 [2000] Crim LR 183, CA.

10.69 In *R v O'Doherty*[136] the identification of the defendant rested upon the voice on a 16-second recorded tape of a 999 call. The Northern Ireland Court of Appeal held that in view of the difficulties attending voice identification, a conviction based upon a police officer's purported recognition of the recorded voice could not be regarded as safe. Should the voice identification evidence be poor and unsupported by other evidence the case must be withdrawn from the jury in accordance with the *Turnbull* guidelines.[137]

10.70 Where a recording of the suspect's voice at the time of the offence is available, as with identification from a photograph or video recording, there is no prohibition in principle against a potential witness listening to the recording to see whether the voice is recognisable.[138] However the weight to be attached to an identification might vary according to whether or not there was a known suspect of whom the witness was aware at the time. In *R v Robb*[139] a wealthy businessman was kidnapped and demands for ransom were made by telephone to his wife, some of which were recorded. The defendant was accused of making those calls. During the course of the investigation police officers had a conversation with the defendant lasting several hours. They later heard the recordings and purported to recognise the voice of the person making demands as the defendant. The identification evidence was admissible, albeit the trial judge had properly cautioned that the evidence might be of little evidential value.

Study of covert recordings

10.71 In some cases, mostly where covert bugging evidence is relied upon, it may be necessary to identify and distinguish the parties to conversations. For that purpose transcripts of incriminating conversations can be placed before the jury in which the speaker is named. In addition to voice recognition evidence there may be other indices such as observation or surveillance recordings revealing the identities of those present. The content of the speech itself might indicate the speaker or the person to whom the speech is addressed. Subject to appropriate safeguards, a police officer is entitled to study voice recordings and other material and give evidence of the fact of voice recognition. A parallel is found in the identification from video recordings by an officer who acquires special knowledge by repeated viewings of video recordings.[140]

10.72 In *R v Chenia*[141] the defendant was alleged to have been supplying drugs from a golf club. No less than 179 covert recordings of conversations at the

---

136 [2003] Cr App R 77, [2003] Crim LR 766, NICA.

137 *R v Devlin* (unreported) 14 March 1997, CA. See **11.12**.

138 See **10.15**.

139 (1991) 93 Cr App R 161, [1991] Crim LR 539, CA. See also *R v Deenik* [1992] Crim LR 578, CA. Both are considered further at **10.75** and **10.76**.

140 *Attorney General's Reference (No 2 of 2002)* [2003] 1 Cr App R 21. See **10.21**.

141 [2003] 2 Crim App R 83(6), CA.

club were made. From these a compilation, together with transcripts, were prepared by police and adduced in evidence. The Court of Appeal held that:

> 'The police officers were no doubt doing their best to deduce who was speaking when they named a particular speaker on the transcript. None of them was, however, an expert in voice identification. If the prosecution wished to rely upon the evidence of a particular police officer to identify the particular speaker, we are of the view that the basis of that evidence should have been spelled out in a statement so that the defence could see what it was. For example, in the case of the appellant, was the opinion of the particular officer based on recognition of his voice and, if so, how was it that he was sufficiently familiar with the voice to enable him to recognise it? If it was based upon some other consideration, the statement should have identified that consideration so that the defence, and indeed the court, could form a view as to whether the evidence was admissible and, if admissible, whether it was reliable. It is not at all clear to us what was the basis for each officer's opinion as to who was speaking.'

10.73 In *R v Flynn and St John,*[142] while acknowledging the admissibility of police recognition evidence, the Court of Appeal held minimum safeguards to be necessary. A record of the process is plainly fundamental to ensuring that the identification can later be reviewed. The amount of time spent with the suspect will be relevant to the officer's familiarity with his voice. The dates and times of listening to and compiling transcripts of recordings must also be noted. An officer's annotations of a transcript with views as to the identity of the speakers must be recorded and, in order to avoid contamination, any other officer embarking on the exercise should use an unannotated copy. The Court of Appeal considered it to be highly desirable that an officer unconnected with the investigation should carry out the procedure. It regarded it as 'all too easy for an investigating officer wittingly or unwittingly to be affected by knowledge already obtained in the course of the investigation'. The court went so far as to express the view that 'where the prosecution seek to rely on [lay listener evidence from police officers] it is desirable that an expert should be instructed to give an independent opinion on the validity of such evidence'.

10.74 A different situation confronted the Court in *R v Tamiz and others.*[143] Covertly recorded conversations, in which large scale drug importations were being discussed, took place largely in Arabic, Bengali and a dialect known as Syhleti. The recordings were translated by two interpreters. Additionally they gave evidence that two of the speakers were common to a number of recordings, though the voices were not attributed to any defendants; the speakers were identified by other means. Their evidence was held to be admissible, no expert in phonetics speaking those languages having been available.

---

142 [2008] EWCA Crim 970, [2008] 2 Cr App R 20. See **10.78** for facts.

143 [2010] EWCA Crim 2638.

Exclusion of voice identification

10.75 Voice identification evidence, as with other forms of identification evidence, will be excluded under PACE, s 78 if 'having regard to all the circumstances, including the circumstances in which the evidence was obtained, the admission of the evidence would have such an adverse effect on the fairness of the proceedings that the court ought not to admit it'. It was recognised in *R v Chenia* (see **10.72**) that it may be necessary to examine the reliability of voice identification evidence when assessing admissibility; in *R v Robb* (see **10.70**) that such evidence would be excluded if procured for ulterior motives, or where unfair advantage has been taken of the defendant to strengthen the case against him. Moreover, though no obligation to hold a procedure exists under Code D, its value 'in appropriate circumstances out of fairness to the accused so that he can be excluded if the original identification was erroneous' was confirmed in *R v Hersey* (see **10.67**).

10.76 In *R v Deenik*,[144] the identification was no more than a confrontation. The defendant was alleged to have been engaged in the importation of cannabis resin during the course of which he spoke by telephone to a customs officer who was masquerading as an accomplice's wife. He was arrested and interviewed. During the interview the customs officer was allowed to overhear the defendant speaking and purported to recognise his voice as belonging to the person spoken to on the telephone. It was argued on appeal that the evidence ought to have been excluded on the ground, among others, that no consideration had been given as to how to reduce the chance of mistaken identification. The Court of Appeal dismissed the appeal holding that the scheme for identification parades under Code D (which did not apply) provided little help in the application of the general law and that nothing could have been done to reduce the chance of error. Two decades later, in which the Court of Appeal has acknowledged the difficulties of voice recognition, it must be open to considerable doubt whether the case would be decided in the same way.

10.77 Where recognition of an unrecorded voice is claimed, against the background of an increased awareness of the dangers of misidentification and the introduction of Home Office Circular (HOC) guidelines for fair procedures,[145] courts may be more inclined to question the fairness of voice identification in the absence of a formal procedure. Those guidelines, which reflect current wisdom on the fairest means of conducting voice identification procedures, may render a live procedure or one in which the suspect and volunteers read a set text, both of which occurred in *R v Hersey,* susceptible to challenge under PACE, s 78. Moreover a court is likely to be more sympathetic than it was in that case to the submission that the pitch of the defendant's voice was markedly different to all but one of the volunteers.

10.78 Different considerations are likely to arise where identification is of a recorded voice capable of repeated listening and study. In *R v Flynn & St John*

---

144 [1992] Crim LR 578, CA.

145 See Chapter 8.

(see **10.73**) a bugging device had been placed in a vehicle which was later used in a robbery. Police officers listened to the recordings and purported to identify the appellants. However two experts considered the recording to be of very poor quality, of whom one could not even distinguish the different voices. Moreover the listening equipment used was unsophisticated, the opportunity to acquire familiarity with the defendant's voices had been limited and safeguards the court regarded as necessary had been transgressed. Those factors, together with the problems associated with voice identification by lay listeners, were held to militate powerfully against the admission of the evidence and accordingly the judge ought to have excluded it under PACE, s 78. *R v Flynn & St John* can be contrasted with *R v Tamiz and others* (see **10.74**). In that case, there was both ample quality and quantity of recorded material from which the interpreters could compare voices. No other means of comparison was possible because of the unavailability of a phonetics expert in the relevant language. Moreover, the identification evidence was limited to the assertion that the voices on separate recordings were the same; it did not purport to identify a particular person. The court also considered relevant the fact that admissions made by other defendants confirmed the correctness of other evidence given by the interpreters, thus enhancing their reliability. Notwithstanding the failure of the interpreters to adhere to the practice of making contemporaneous records on the lines set out in *R v Flynn & St John*, which the court held the evidence to have been correctly admitted, such failure going to its weight.

Voice identification by jury

10.79 An incriminating recording may be adduced as evidence of what was said and in what manner, quite apart from any identification purpose. Unless the task would be pure guesswork, a jury would be entitled to decide the content and meaning of the spoken words. But to what identification use may the recording be put by the jury in arriving at their own conclusions? In considering the answer to this question, two distinctions should be noted: (a) that between cases in which the jury are, and are not, being asked to evaluate the evidence of a voice identification witness; (b) that between cases in which the jury have, and have not, heard the defendant give evidence.

10.80 If an expert has given evidence based upon a comparison of a recording of the offender and the defendant's known voice, the jury must be entitled to assess the expert's opinion and conclusion by reference to the recordings.[146] Equally where the identification is the result of a study of recordings by a police officer the jury should be able to form their own view about the accuracy of the conclusions reached. However in *R v Chenia*[147] the judge's invitation to the jury to conduct the exercise themselves was disapproved. In that case there was an issue about the identity of speakers at certain points in a compilation of covert police recordings. The Court of Appeal expressed its view about the propriety of the judge's direction in the following manner:

---

146 *R v Bentum* (1989) 153 JP 538, CA.

147 [2003] 2 Cr App R 83(6), CA.

> 'We question whether it was appropriate to invite the jury to identify who was speaking on the recording by comparing what they could hear on the recording either with another voice on the recording or, say, with the appellant's voice …
>
> … we do not think that a jury should, as it were, be asked to be their own voice expert. We have reached the conclusion, on the particular facts of this case, where the jury were unassisted by expert evidence, they should have been warned that they should not compare one voice with another by comparing the characteristicness of each because of the dangers of doing so.'

10.81 To the extent that *R v Chenia* suggested that jury identification in all circumstances was to be discouraged, it was disapproved in *R v Flynn and St John.*[148] In that case it was held that the jury should be permitted to compare recordings and the live voices of defendants at trial provided the they were directed to consider the guidance of voice recognition witnesses. Likewise *R v O'Doherty*[149] took the view that the jury must be able to evaluate for themselves voice identification evidence. The maker of a 999 call was identified as the defendant by both a police officer who purported to recognise his voice and by an expert who compared it with the defendant's known voice. The court, drawing from authorities concerning visual identification, stated that:

> 'If evidence of voice recognition is relied on by the prosecution, the jury should be allowed to listen to a tape-recording on which the recognition is based, assuming that the jury have heard the accused give evidence.'

10.82 This proposition, suggesting that the jury are entitled to assess the accuracy of a witness's recognition from a recording by reference to the defendant's voice from the witness box must be correct. It applies whether the evidence of voice recognition emanates from an expert or from a non–expert, such as a police officer who purports to recognise the defendant's voice whether from prior acquaintance or special knowledge gained by study of the recordings.[150] Such comparison as the jury themselves make should be subject to a *Turnbull* direction[151] and a warning that they are not trained experts. It may be presumed to follow that if no voice recognition evidence is called, the jury may not themselves conduct the inquiry. The dangers are self evident and may be exacerbated by the exercise becoming a dock voice identification.[152] However there is no absolute rule of prohibition. It may not be possible to be prescriptive about the circumstances in which the jury may rely upon their own opinion, though clearly the length, content and clarity of the recording and opportunity to make a meaningful comparison while the defendant is in the witness box are relevant matters.

---

148 [2008] EWCA Crim 970, [2008] 2 Cr App R 20, and see **10.78**.

149 [2003] Cr App R 77, [2003] Crim LR 766, NICA.

150 *R v Flynn and St John* [2008] EWCA Crim 970, [2008] 2 Cr App R 20.See D Ormerod 'Sounding out Expert Voice Identification' [2002] Crim LR 771 at 787 for a review of the dangers of jury identification.

151 See **12.99**.

152 See D Ormerod 'Sounding out Expert Voice Identification' [2002] Crim LR 771 at 787 for a criticism of the jury conducting a voice identification exercise.

DOCK IDENTIFICATION

Inherent danger

10.83 A dock identification is the identification by a witness from the witness box of a defendant across the courtroom in the dock. As a matter of strict law such evidence is admissible as direct evidence of the guilt of the accused. The inherent dangers of this form of identification evidence stem from the likelihood that a witness will make a positive identification because of the defendant's obvious status. The lure of pointing to the dock may be based upon the presumption that the defendant must be regarded by the police, the CPS and possibly other witnesses as the culprit. The witness, whose memory may have faded since the offence, might be fortified by an awareness of other incriminating evidence against the defendant. Put another way, one might well understand the reluctance of a witness to feel responsible for jeopardising a prosecution by failing to identify the accused in the dock. The Devlin Committee noted 'the root of all objections to dock identification is that it comes as an answer to what is, in effect, if not form, a leading question, that is, a question put in a way which suggests the answer that is expected'.[153] Similarly in *Alexander v R*,[154] the Australian High Court suggested that 'circumstances conspire to compel the witness to identify the accused in the dock'.[155] Some commentators have ventured so far as to assert that dock identification is of no probative value.[156]

On indictment

10.84 The practice of dock identification in a trial on indictment where identity is in issue has all but fallen into disuse. Judicial disapproval of confrontation identification, whether before or at trial, has been voiced since the early twentieth century when the use of identification parades was acknowledged as an infinitely better process.[157] In 1970 the Court of Appeal recognised the prejudice to an accused caused by the ease with which a witness could point to a defendant in the dock;[158] and a year earlier it was held that such identifications should be avoided if possible.[159] At that time the Court of Appeal recognised an exception where the defendant had refused to take part in a parade.[160] In 1976 the Court stated that 'This Court has long appreciated that

---

153 Devlin Report, para.4.99.

154 (1981)145 CLR 395, 427.

155 Ibid, at 427.

156 J Heydon, *Cross on Evidence*, 7th Australian edition, (2004: Butterworths, Chatswood NSW), at p.84.

157 See *R v Cartwight* 12 Cr App R 219, CCA and *R v Williams* 8 Cr App R 84, CCA.

158 *R v Howick* [1970] Crim LR 403, CA.

159 *R v Hunter* [1969] Crim LR 262, CA.

160 *R v John* [1973] Crim LR 113, CA.

dock identifications are unsatisfactory and dangerous.'[161] Following publication of the 'Devlin Report',[162] the Attorney General issued a statement concerning the use of dock identification evidence.[163] It asserted that prosecution counsel would not invite a witness to identity, who has not previously identified the accused at an identification parade, to make a dock identification unless there were exceptional circumstances.

10.85 Since that time, the regulation of pre-trial identification procedures in Code D[164] places a further substantial hurdle in the way of a dock identification. Compliance with the Code should lead to the use of one of the specified procedures. These include the use of covert measures to photograph a recalcitrant suspect and, as a last resort, a regulated confrontation. There are likely to be few situations in which one form of Code D procedure or another is unavailable. Such a situation might exist should a suspect succeed in frustrating all attempts to conduct an identification procedure or if the police have been positively misled by a defendant into believing that identity was not in issue. On the other hand, the lack of Code D identification evidence which is the result of some default in the investigation is likely to be decisive in excluding dock identification evidence.[165]

10.86 A dock identification will not usually of itself amount to a breach of a defendant's right to a fair trial.[166] However in *Constance, Wilson and Lee v The State*[167] the Privy Council warned that it 'is only in the most exceptional circumstances that any form of dock identification is permissible in the trial process'. In that case a first identification in court was regarded as a 'serious irregularity'. The prosecution were criticised for seeking it and the judge for not intervening. That strict approach was expressly disavowed in *Tido v The Queen*[168] in which it was held that 'the admission of such evidence is not to be regarded as permissible only in the most exceptional circumstances'. But the Board, considering the discretion to admit the evidence in the particular circumstances of a case, went onto state that if 'there was no good reason not to hold the parade this will usually militate against the admission of the evidence' and confirmed that even for recalcitrant suspects, dock identification is a rarity because there exists the means to perform variant forms of pre-trial identification procedures. By contrast criticism of a dock identification would

---

161 *R v Tricoglus* (1977) 65 Cr App R 16, CA.

162 Report of the Committee on Evidence of Identification in Criminal Cases, 1976, paras 4.89–4.109. The report dealt with the case of *Dougherty* in which a mistaken dock identification led to a miscarriage of justice.

163 Hansard (Written Answers) 27 May 1976.

164 See Chapter 3.

165 *R v Fergus* [1992] Crim LR 363, CA; *Tido v The Queen* [2011] UKPC 16.

166 *Holland v HM Advocate* [2005] UKPC D1, on appeal from the High Court of Justiciary, Scotland, at [41] 'While one cannot exclude the possibility that, in an extreme case, the judge could conclude that admitting dock identification evidence would inevitably render the trial unfair, normally the requirements of article 6 will not raise any issue of admissibility.' See also *Tido v The Queen* [2011] UKPC 16.

167 Privy Council Appeal No 31 of 1998 (unreported).

168 [2011] UKPC 16.

be inapposite if it was undisputed that a defendant had been well known to the witness over many years, that the defence was that the witness was lying and where, accordingly, a dock identification carried no risk of undue influence.[169] But where the witness purports to know or recognise the defendant, a dock identification should not take place if that is in dispute, especially when there has been no prior identification procedure.[170] *R v Gardner*[171] must be regarded as an exceptional case. The defendant was alleged to have caused a fire which led to the death of an occupant of a block of flats. A local resident claimed to know the defendant as a tenant of the block, having seen him in the vicinity many times over a substantial period. They had acknowledged one another on several occasions and, crucially, some 2 weeks before the fire had had a conversation in which the defendant threatened to burn down the flats. Though it was undeniable that the witness may have seen the defendant on occasions, the defence case was that no such a conversation took place. The Court of Appeal upheld the exercise of the trial judge's discretion to permit a dock identification. With scant attention to authority, its rationale was that the witness was not identifying the perpetrator in the act of committing the crime, that it was clear to the court that he knew the defendant sufficiently well to be sure that had an identification parade been carried out he would have picked out the defendant, that the defence statement had not put the conversation in issue and indeed in an interview which had been excluded, the defendant admitted it.

10.87 A more subtle form of dock identification might occur if a witness, when asked for a description of the suspect, relies on the observation of the defendant in court for the reply. Difficult to prevent or even detect, the possibility underlines the need for compliance with Code D procedures, and in particular obtaining a comprehensive first description from the witness.

10.88 Might there be a variation on the rule applicable to a defendant, not the prosecution, who seeks to implicate a co-defendant by inviting a witness to identify the other? In *R v Robinson*[172] the widow of a murder victim sitting in the public gallery purported to recognise the voice of a defendant when giving evidence as the person who had made threats to her on the telephone shortly before the death of her husband. The prosecution did not seek to deploy the evidence but a co-defendant did. The evidence was held to be admissible: it was relevant, had some probative value and, unlike its powers vis-à-vis the prosecution, the court had no power to exclude it.

Unsolicited dock identification

10.89 On occasion a witness makes an unsolicited dock identification by gesturing towards the dock when being questioned about the offender's

---

[169] *Capron v R* [2006] UKPC 34.

[170] *R v Fergus* [1992] Crim LR 363, CA; *R v Conway* (1990) 91 Cr App R 143, CA.

[171] [2004] EWCA Crim 1639.

[172] [2005] EWCA Crim 1940.

appearance.[173] In those circumstances the judge may either discharge the jury and order a re-trial or allow the trial to continue. Which course is to be taken will depend upon the degree of prejudice. Where there is a risk that the defendant may no longer receive a fair trial the judge will take the former course. Where, on the other hand, the risk of prejudice is small and might be overcome by an appropriately-worded warning to the jury the judge will allow the case to continue. It may be prudent to issue a warning immediately in addition to any direction in the summing up.[174]

Defence inspired dock identification

10.90 There may be situations where the defence seek to establish in cross-examination of a witness that the person in the dock is not the offender. It might be hoped or expected that a witness who has not participated in a pre-trial identification procedure will eliminate the defendant; or that a witness who failed to make a positive pre-trial identification will go a step further by exculpating the defendant. This is undoubtedly a very dangerous strategy[175] though there is no bar to such questioning.[176] Certainly a dock elimination may be deployed in respect of a defence eyewitness who can assert that the defendant was not the perpetrator of the offence.

Summary trial

10.91 The propriety of using this method of identification evidence for offences tried summarily is the subject of conflicting Divisional Court cases. The first case, in 1994, *North Yorkshire Trading Standards Department v Williams*[177] broadly restates the prevailing position in the Crown Court. There, the defendant was charged with an offence of unlawful harassment of a debtor contrary to the Administration of Justice Act 1970, s 40(1). There was no evidence connecting the defendant with the crime and, when the justices refused to allow the victim to identify him in the dock, a submission of 'no case' necessarily succeeded. On appeal by the prosecution it was asserted that numerous attempts to interview the defendant were made but to no avail. It was accepted by the court that because the offence was non-arrestable there was no way, other than the voluntary co-operation of the defendant, to invoke the identification procedures of Code D. A dock identification was therefore the only means at the disposal of the prosecution to enable the victim to make an identification and it was therefore submitted that the justices ought to have allowed it. The Divisional Court held that the justices, having taken into

---

173 See *R v Hope, Limburn and Bleasdale* [1994] Crim LR 118, CA.

174 Jury directions are considered in Chapter 12. See **12.104**.

175 Such a course should never be taken without specific instruction from the defendant.

176 Consider *R v Joseph* [1994] Crim LR 48, CA, in which a confrontation in the cells took place during the course of a trial. Defence counsel, at whose request the confrontation was held, then applied to exclude the positive identification. It was held that the failure to exclude the evidence was a material irregularity.

177 (1995) 159 JP 383, DC.

account the judicial disapproval expressed about this form of evidence, had exercised their discretion correctly. Potts J stated:

> 'In my opinion it would be wrong to apply one approach to dock identification for minor offences and another for more serious offences. Such a course would be likely to lead to injustice.'

Rose LJ acknowledged that magistrates' courts can, as a matter of law, allow a dock identification in their discretion. They were admissible but undesirable. However he stated that he was:

> '... [not able] to conclude that different principles should apply to dock identification in relation to summary non-arrestable offences than those which apply in more serious cases.'

10.92 The issue was revisited in the 1997 Divisional Court case of *Barnes v The Chief Constable of Durham*.[178] It concerned the more commonplace type of proceedings – a failure to provide a blood specimen after a road accident contrary to the Road Traffic Act 1988, s 7. A summons was issued against John William Hawkins, the name given by the person who had been taken to the police station and interviewed and who was allegedly the driver of the vehicle. The non-attendance of the defendant led to the issue of an arrest warrant in the same name. Some two years later, by means undisclosed in the report, it was thought that the true identity of the suspect was in fact John William Barnes. The court granted the prosecution application to amend the summons accordingly. When the trial finally took place a police officer gave evidence that the person in the dock, John William Barnes, was the driver and specimen defaulter. He claimed to remember him because of his attitude in interview. The justices convicted, relying on the identification. In a judgment dictated by expedience, the Divisional Court upheld the admission of the dock identification. Popplewell J stated:

> 'There is no logic in making a distinction in regard to dock identification between the Crown Court and the magistrates' court. However it has to be recognised that every day in a magistrates' court those charged for instance with careless driving, who have made no statement to the police, are entitled to sit back and in the absence of identification to submit that it has not been proven that they are the driver ... If in every case where the defendant does not distinctly admit driving there has to be an identification parade, the whole process of justice in a magistrates' court would be severely impaired.'

In the event it was held 'on the facts of this case as they appeared to the magistrates' it was not unfair to allow a dock identification.

10.93 The departure from the views expressed in the *North Yorkshire* case might be explained by the fact that it does not appear to have been cited to the

---

178 [1997] 2 Cr App R 505, DC.

court. Neither was it cited in the case of *R (Karia) v DPP*[179] which, following *Barnes*, at least has the merit of a detailed analysis of the identification problem. A man was stopped by police for speeding and was reported for that offence and failing to produce driving documents. Police recorded his name as Vijai Kari. When eventually the defendant, whose name was Vijay Karia, appeared at court he pleaded not guilty and the matter was set down for trial. The officer who had stopped him claimed to have seen him in the meantime driving the same car. He purported to recognise him again just before the trial began. At the hearing the officer made a dock identification which led to conviction. The defence sought to distinguish *Barnes* on the basis that there, the defendant had foregone the opportunity to raise identity in interview, whereas in *Karia* the defendant had had no such opportunity. The argument was rejected. It was held that it was not unreasonable to expect a person, who genuinely disputes identity and claims to have been wrongly served with a summons, to respond by indicating just that. The fact that no such indication was given meant that identity was not disputed for the purposes of Code D and therefore there was no requirement or other clue that a procedure should be held. Moreover it was held that the failure to give notification led to a practical problem: if, as on the facts, the issue is raised only after the proceedings have begun the witness will have observed the defendant rendering an identification procedure pointless. The judgment concluded it to be:

> '… fair to permit the prosecution to seek and rely upon the accused as the driver for the purpose, as was stated in *Barnes*, of preventing an unmeritorious, purely formal objection being taken to the prosecution case and an unmeritorious submission of no case to answer.'

10.94 On one view, the decision in *Karia*, like *Barnes*, can be regarded as confined to motoring cases, minor regulatory offences or proceedings which were commenced by summons. To apply it in summary proceedings to an either-way offence, for example theft, would create an obvious anomaly. The decision has been criticised as 'amounting to a charter for the police to cut corners when there are other methods available to identify a driver.'[180] In some summary cases represented defendants will have the advantage of advice about the consequences of a failure to notify the prosecution of an identification issue and appropriate steps can be taken. For example a defence statement claiming mistaken identity might be served. But where unrepresented, the notice requirement suggested in *Karia* may ascribe to defendants an unreasonable degree of insight into the criminal justice process.

10.95 A court has yet to reconcile the conflicting judgments of the Divisional Court. No attempt was made to do so in *Smith v DPP*[181] because it was conceded by the prosecution that a dock identification should not have taken place. The case concerned a Youth Court trial in which the defendant faced a

---

179 [2002] EWCA 2175 (Admin).

180 See T Watkin 'In the Dock – an overview of the decisions of the High Court on Dock Identifications in the Magistrates' Court' [2003] Crim LR 463.

181 [2008] EWCA Crim 771 (Admin).

charge of attempted burglary. The principal witness identified the defendant in the dock after the district judge had asked her the question 'Have you seen him today?'. In quashing the conviction the court agreed that the question should not have been put, particularly having regard to the fact that the defendant faced a serious charge which, but for his age, would have been tried by a jury. Where a dock identification does take place in a summary trial justices must follow the guidance appropriate to juries when evaluating the probative effect of a dock identification.[182]

BAD CHARACTER

Background

10.96 To what extent may the identity of an offender be proved by evidence of a defendant's previous convictions or other misconduct? Prior to the Criminal Justice Act 2003 (CJA 2003), the answer was infrequently and in heavily circumscribed situations. The position was governed by the common law prohibition on the use of a defendant's disposition or propensity to commit offences[183] and the shield provided by the Criminal Evidence Act 1898. That provision protected a defendant from cross examination 'tending to show he has committed or been convicted of or been charged with any offence other than the one with which he is then charged, or is of bad character'[184] unless directly probative of the offence charged. A body of case-law developed in which 'similar fact' evidence was deemed capable of being probative of the offence charged, notwithstanding that it related to other offences or misconduct. Initially, before it could be admitted, it was necessary to satisfy a 'striking similarity' test, for example by demonstrating that the modus operandi bore the offender's 'hallmark' or 'signature'.[185] That test was later relaxed to the point where it was necessary only to establish that its probative force was sufficiently great to make it just to admit it, notwithstanding its prejudicial effect.[186] The underlying premise for its admission was that the unlikelihood of coincidence rendered the similar fact evidence probative of the matter in issue, for example the identity of the offender or his state of mind at the material time.

10.97 The CJA 2003 swept away the statutory shield[187] and the common law similar fact rules.[188] The new bad character provisions have led to the routine introduction of previous convictions and a considerable number of appeals

---

182 *North Yorkshire Trading Standards Department v Williams* (1995) 159 JP 383, DC. See **12.104** for jury directions.

183 *Makin v Attorney General for New South Wales* [1894] AC 57, PC.

184 Section 1(3)(i). Other exceptions related to a defendant advancing good character or making imputations against prosecution witnesses (s 1(3)(ii)) and giving evidence against a co-accused (s 1(3)(iii)).

185 *DPP v Boardman* [1975] AC 421, (1974) 60 Cr App R 165, HL.

186 *DPP v P* [1991] 2 AC 447, (1991) 93 Cr App R 267, HL.

187 Section 331 and Sch 36.

188 Section 99.

traversing their meaning and effect by reference to a variety of factual scenarios. The following paragraphs do not purport to be a comprehensive review of the bad character provisions, a topic beyond the scope of this book; rather they are intended to provide a summary of the current state of the law and an analysis of its impact upon cases in which identity is in dispute. It will be seen that some of the principles behind the abolished common law rules are not entirely obsolete.

CJA 2003

10.98 Bad character is defined by CJA 2003, s 98 as 'evidence of, or a disposition towards, misconduct'. Importantly, it is evidence other than that which 'has to do with the alleged facts of the offence or in connection with the investigation or prosecution of that offence' which is admissible in the ordinary way. Evidence which relates to proof of identity does not per se categorise it as having to do with the facts of the offence. In *R v Tirnaveanu*[189] the defendant was on trial for a variety of offences relating to the illegal entry of Romanian immigrants. He was alleged to have posed as a solicitor. He denied that he was the person responsible. At his address were found documents relating to other illegal immigrants. The prosecution sought to introduce evidence concerning his connection to those other immigrants. The Court of Appeal rejected the submission that the evidence had 'to do' with the facts of the alleged offences any more than it might in any other case (for example one of sexual misconduct) where the prosecution sought to rely upon evidence of other misconduct to prove the identity of the offender. It ought to have been the subject of an application under s 101(1)(d) of the Act (see below).

10.99 Section 101 sets out a number of different gateways through which an application to put a defendant's bad character may pass.

> '(1) In criminal proceedings evidence of the defendant's bad character is admissible if, but only if –
> (a) all parties to the proceedings agree to the evidence being admissible,
> (b) the evidence is adduced by the defendant himself or is given in answer to a question asked by him in cross-examination and intended to elicit it,
> (c) it is important explanatory evidence,
> (d) it is relevant to an important matter in issue between the defendant and the prosecution,
> (e) it has substantial probative value in relation to an important matter in issue between the defendant and a co-defendant,
> (f) it is evidence to correct a false impression given by the defendant,
> (g) the defendant has made an attack on another person's character.
> …
> (3) The court must not admit evidence under subsection (1)(d) or (g) if, on an application by the defendant to exclude it, it appears to the court that the admission of the evidence would have such an adverse effect on the fairness of the proceedings that the court ought not to admit it.'

---

[189] [2007] EWCA Crim 1239, [2007] 2 Cr App R 23.

10.100 In the vast majority of cases the prosecution rely on s 101(1)(d): 'important matter in issue between the defendant and the prosecution'. There is no definition of that phrase but plainly it may include the situation where the issue is the identity of the offender. In addition, by s 103(1), the propensity of a defendant is deemed to be 'a matter in issue'. That section provides:

> '(1) For the purposes of section 101(1)(d) the matters in issue between the defendant and the prosecution include –
> (a) the question whether the defendant has a propensity to commit offences of the kind with which he is charged, except where his having such a propensity makes it no more likely that he is guilty of the offence;
> (b) the question whether the defendant has a propensity to be untruthful, except where it is not suggested that the defendant's case is untruthful in any respect.'

10.101 The leading judgment, particularly as to the application of the propensity provisions, is *R v Hanson*.[190] Where propensity to commit the offence is relied on there are essentially three questions to be considered:

(1) Does the history of conviction(s) establish a propensity to commit offences of the kind charged?

(2) Does that propensity make it more likely that the defendant committed the offence charged?

(3) Is it unjust to rely on the conviction(s) of the same description or category; and in any event will the proceedings be unfair if they are admitted?

10.102 Among the factors to be considered are the number of previous events or convictions. The fewer, the weaker the evidence of propensity is likely to be. A single conviction will often not show propensity, though it may do so where it demonstrates a tendency to unusual behaviour or has particular probative force. The older the conviction, absent some special feature, the less likely it is that a continuing propensity will be established. Where there is no or very little other evidence against a defendant it is unlikely to be just to admit previous convictions.

Identification cases

10.103 An analysis of the particular statutory basis on which it is proposed to introduce bad character evidence is generally necessary, especially in cases which depend upon identification evidence. In *R v Edwards & others*[191] for example, the evidence of an eyewitness to a robbery that the defendant was her heroin supplier was correctly admitted as 'important explanatory evidence'

---

190 [2005] EWCA Crim 824, [2005] 2 Cr App 21.

191 [2006] EWCA Crim 1813, [2006] 1 CR App R 3.

under s 101(1)(c) in order to establish her relationship with him and thus her ability to identify him. The majority of cases, however, are brought within s 101(1)(d): 'an important matter in issue between the defendant and the prosecution', when it will be appropriate to consider whether the evidence goes to the issue of the identity of the offender, whether to the issue of propensity under s 103, or to a combination of the two.

10.104 Whether bad character is probative of identity or propensity may be a fine distinction.[192] The need to distinguish at all would be of semantic interest only but for the additional burden of fulfilling the criteria under s 103 where propensity is relied on and the need for consequential jury directions. It has been suggested that when identity is in issue, bad character may be considered as evidence of both.[193] In the majority of cases bad character has been characterised as evidence of propensity capable of supporting evidence of identification.[194] However there are cases in which bad character goes to the identity of the offender and not to the defendant's propensity to commit offences of the kind with which he is charged.

Identity as an important matter in issue

10.105 An illustration of circumstances in which the issue was exclusively one of identity is *R v Isichea*.[195] The defendant was alleged to have taken two women to a cash dispenser where they were assaulted before being forced to withdraw money. One of the victims identified the defendant at a video identification parade. The defence case was one of mistaken identification. At the time of the offences the assailant was heard to have referred to wanting cocaine. He had a conviction for importation of cocaine. The conviction did not show a propensity to commit either of the offences charged, assault or robbery. However, cocaine being the apparent motive for the offence, the reference to it was held to be a connecting factor in support of the identification.

10.106 The cumulative effect of offences which are linked by modus operandi, geography and time, may be to identify a particular individual as the person responsible. The question whether in such circumstances propensity under s 103(1) is brought into play or whether the evidence of the linked offences merely enables a jury to decide if the sum of offences makes it more likely that the defendant committed the offence(s) has been considered in a series of cases. In *R v Wallace*[196] the defendant was charged with four robberies in the Nottingham area. They were all of small shops in the same area, within 3 weeks of each other and were characterised by the use of balaclavas,

---

192 *R v Randall* [2006] EWCA Crim 1413.

193 *R v Pope* [2010] EWCA Crim 2113; *R v Ali* [2010] EWCA Crim 1619.

194 See for example *R v Blake* [2006] EWCA Crim 871; *R v Randall* [2006] EWCA Crim 1413; *R v Maughan & Ward* [2007] EWCA Crim 3301; *R v Spittle* [2008] EWCA Crim 2537, [2009] RTR 14; *R v Woods and Upson* [2009] EWCA Crim 299; *R v Miller* [2009] EWCA Crim 2890.

195 [2006] EWCA Crim 1815, (2006) 170 JP 753.

196 [2007] EWCA Crim 1760, [2007] 2 Cr App R 30.

handguns and poles. The defendant was linked to each by, variously, DNA, fingerprints, CCTV and his presence near the scene of a crash involving a stolen getaway vehicle. In isolation, there was insufficient on each count to warrant a conviction; but seen as a whole the evidential coincidence of his association with each of the linked offences was powerful. The Court of Appeal concluded:

> 'In our view, the important matter in issue was not whether the appellant had a propensity to commit offences … but whether the circumstantial evidence linking him to the robberies, when viewed as a whole, pointed to his participation in and guilt of each offence. Nevertheless, the definition of 'bad character' in s 98 is in our view sufficiently wide to have triggered the operation of s 101 and in particular s 101(1)(d). Although technically within the definition of bad character, the purpose of the admission of the evidence was not to prove that the appellant was of bad character in the sense that that expression is commonly understood. Once before the jury the evidence was relevant for what it tended to prove, namely that when viewed as a whole the appellant was guilty of each of the offences'.

10.107 A similar approach is evident in *R v McAllister.*[197] The defendant had been tried in Scotland for a robbery in Banff and the jury had returned a verdict of not proven. The prosecution sought to introduce the details of that robbery to identify him as the perpetrator of a very similar robbery in Leeds (robber wearing balaclava and using sawn-off shotgun) three days earlier. Crucially he had been in both places at the material times. The court offered this analysis as to the purpose of such evidence:

> '[a]sking a jury to look at evidence relating to a number of allegations as a whole in order to cast light on the evidence relating to an individual offence is not asking a jury to consider propensity to commit an offence; on the contrary it is merely asking the jury to recognize that the evidence in relation to a particular offence on an indictment may appear stronger and more compelling when all the evidence, including evidence relating to other offences is looked at as a whole.'

10.108 Such reasoning is evident also in *R v Freeman, R v Crawford.*[198] In each of two street robberies committed within a few weeks of each other, the defendant was picked out by the victim in a video identification procedure. It was held the evidence in each 'was admissible in relation to the other … not because they showed propensity. The evidence of each made it more likely that it was the appellant who had committed the other.' The court went further. Three convictions for robbery were also admitted. They too were linked in time, having taken place within the same period of a few weeks, and also by a methodology almost identical. Thus it was said that they formed part of series of similar offences. The Court of Appeal held that their proximity in time and similarity of commission was:

---

[197] [2008] EWCA Crim 1544, [2009] 1 Cr App R 10. The bad character evidence had such an adverse effect on the fairness of the proceedings it ought not to have been admitted.

[198] [2008] EWCA Crim 1863, [2009] 1 Cr App R 15.

'material evidence to support the Crown's case that the appellant was the person who had committed the robberies in question. Although the judge referred to propensity, this is case where the convictions were admissible in themselves as supporting the Crown's case.'

Propensity as an important matter in issue

10.109 Where propensity is relied upon, on the first question posed in *R v Hanson*, the decision whether the history of conviction(s) establishes a propensity is a matter of judgment, not simply the exercise of a judicial discretion: *R v Murphy*.[199] In that case the defendant, who was accused of discharging a firearm towards two cars, was identified at an identification procedure as the culprit. The prosecution succeeded in adducing a conviction recorded 20 years earlier for the possession of a firearm without a certificate. There was no suggestion that it had been used on that occasion. The Court of Appeal found it impossible to accept that one isolated incident of possession of such a weapon when the defendant was aged 28 was capable of establishing a propensity to commit firearms offences when aged 48; absent some very special and distinctive feature it was too slender a basis upon which a propensity could be founded. By contrast in *R v Dobson and Green*[200] more recent convictions for firearms offences were held to be probative of propensity towards gun crime. The two appellants faced a charge of murder in which it was alleged that they were part of a group of four men jointly responsible for the shooting of the victim, albeit another person had fired the fatal shot. Dobson was additionally accused of possessing a second firearm with which he fired a shot into the victim's leg. Both denied presence. However Dobson was named by three eyewitnesses, of whom two picked him out on parade. Two also identified Green. Dobson had a conviction for use of an air pistol during a robbery 6 years earlier. Green had convictions for possession of a loaded semi automatic hand gun and robbery of petrol stations one year earlier. The Court of Appeal confirmed that the convictions demonstrated a propensity to commit gun crime whether as a principal or secondary party. The Court went on to hold that there is no enhanced form of propensity, akin to striking similarity, required for cases in which identity was in issue under s 101(1)(d).

10.110 Propensity evidence is not confined to previous convictions. In *R v Ali*[201] photographs of the defendant holding firearms and the possession of body armour was held to have been rightly admitted on a charge of murder with a firearm. However, focus should be applied to the nature of the propensity asserted. It must relate to a propensity to 'commit offences of the kind with which he is charged'. In *Tully & Wood*[202] the defence to the charge of robbery was alibi. It was held that the decision to admit evidence of a catalogue of previous convictions tending to show a propensity merely to acquire other

---

199 [2006] EWCA Crim 3408.

200 [2008] EWCA Crim 435.

201 [2010] EWCA Crim 1619. See also *R v Smith & others* [2008] EWCA Crim 435, [2009] 1 Cr App R 36.

202 [2006] EWCA Crim 2270, (2006) 171 JP 25, CA.

people's property was flawed. Only those for robbery were found to be of probative force meriting the jury's attention.

10.111 Though, in accordance with *Hanson,* little or no other evidence will militate against admission, there may be extreme cases in which the conduct is so strikingly similar that it bears the hallmark of the defendant, in which case it could be said truly to represent evidence of the offender's identity. No doubt *Straffen,*[203] a pre-CJA 2003 similar fact case, would be decided in then same way today under the propensity provisions. A young girl was murdered and there was no evidence other than opportunity: the defendant was in the area having escaped from Broadmoor Hospital at the time. It was held that his confession to the murder of two other girls in very similar and singular circumstances was admissible to prove that he and no other was responsible. In effect, evidence of propensity and evidence of identity were one and the same thing.

10.112 The second question posed by *R v Hanson* is whether propensity makes it more likely that the defendant committed the offence charged. It has been argued that in the context of an identification case, propensity does not enhance that likelihood. In *Eastlake & Eastlake*[204] two brothers were alleged to have been in a group of three people involved in two assaults. They claimed to have been elsewhere but each was picked out at an identification procedure by a different witness. Both defendants had convictions for common assault, one of which was committed together, which were adduced by the prosecution. It was submitted that, being an identification case in which alibi was raised, the issue and only issue was whether the identifications were accurate and reliable. It was argued that the convictions did not make it any more likely that the defendants were present and were accordingly irrelevant. The argument failed. The admission of the evidence was upheld as capable of lending support to the conclusion that the defendants were responsible. The Court of Appeal held that, particularly by reference to the joint offence, 'the evidence was capable of lending support to the conclusion which the Crown invited the jury to reach, namely that the two appellants were correctly identified as those who committed the attack'.

10.113 Similarly it was argued in *R v Dobson & Green* (see **10.109**) that propensity was irrelevant to the issue in the case, namely identity – whether three eyewitnesses had correctly identified the defendants – but went only to participation once identity was proved.

> 'What was in issue was whether these two applicants were the men (or some of the men) who were there and participating in the way alleged in the murder. That was an important matter in issue. We do not accept that previous convictions showing a particular propensity cannot be relevant to showing that a defendant was the person who committed the crime charged. Merely because identity is put in issue and an alibi raised does not render propensity irrelevant. It will not by itself be

---

203 (1952) 36 Cr App R 132, CCA.

204 [2007] EWCA Crim 603.

enough to establish identity, but it may often be capable of supporting the credibility and reliability of other evidence of identification.'

10.114 The appellants in *R v Smith & others,*[205] faced a charge of joint enterprise murder by shooting a night club doorman. It was held that previous convictions for attempted murder and possession of a handgun and ammunition of one of the appellants who had been identified by a police officer from CCTV footage were 'capable of supporting not only the proposition that he had knowledge of the carrying of guns with the intention that they should be discharged but also they were capable of supporting the proposition that he was present as part of the group at the scene of the shooting'.

10.115 Bad character evidence is as capable of supporting expert identification evidence as it is eyewitness identification. In *R v Ellis*[206] a burglar was captured on CCTV driving away from the crime scene. The defendant's previous convictions were admitted to support facial mapping evidence. In *R v Harding*[207] the defendant's DNA was recovered from a glass at the scene of a robbery. His previous convictions for robbery were capable of supporting the assertion that he was one of the robbers, allowing the jury to assess whether the innocent explanation for the presence of DNA might be true.

Rationale – similarity and coincidence

10.116 In order to consider whether bad character makes it more likely that the defendant committed the offence one need ask why it makes it more likely. Where identity is in issue, it will generally depend upon the degree of similarity and the coincidence in the identification of someone who has a propensity to commit the type of crime with which he is charged.

10.117 As *R v Straffen* (see **10.111**) shows, the degree of similarity and coincidence can be powerful and decisive evidence. So it may have proved in *R v Brisland*[208] in which the defendant was accused of the theft of 45 Dell computers. The modus operandi involved the offender masquerading as the authorised recipient of the goods when delivered to a multi-occupational block of offices. The prosecution relied upon CCTV evidence which, it was suggested, depicted the defendant as the offender. It was buttressed by the coincidence that 6 months later he had committed an almost identical offence in connection with a consignment of 26 Dell computers to a multi occupational office block for which he claimed to have authority to accept delivery. On that occasion, the suspicion of a delivery man was aroused and the defendant fled. In doing so he dropped a mobile phone by which he was linked to the offence and subsequently pleaded guilty. The Court of Appeal found that the similarity of

---

205 [2008] EWCA Crim 435, [2009] 1 Cr App R 36.
206 [2010] EWCA Crim 1893.
207 [2010] EWCA Crim 2145.
208 [2008] EWCA Crim 2773.

the later offence made it more probable that the appellant was the disputed man in the footage, or at least capable of being regarded as such by the jury.

10.118 Most cases do not exhibit such striking similarity between the conduct which is the subject of the offence charged and other bad character and as was the case in *R v Brisland*. Nevertheless the coincidence between identification evidence and the defendant's propensity to commit similar, even generic, offences, may manifest considerable probative force; the more so when the identification is made by someone wholly unconnected to the defendant rendering the coincidence truly random, the less so when the evidence is of recognition by someone familiar with the suspect.[209]

10.119 In *R v Pope*[210] the defendant was alleged to have committed a burglary. He was identified by a witness but denied responsibility, asserting that the case was one of mistaken identity. His bad character was held to strengthen the identification evidence. 'It would be an odd coincidence if the person whom [the witness] identified as the man who came into her grandmother's flat on 2 August turned out to be a man who had a tendency to rob other people of their property on several occasions' the court observed. Similarly In *R v Ali*[211] (see **10.110**) the rationale for allowing bad character evidence was that 'it would have been another unfortunate coincidence that the man identified as the gunman showed an attraction to guns, and body armour at home'.

10.120 The coincidence or probability factor in an identification case is, as a matter of logic, relative to the likelihood of others, possessing similar propensity, being the true culprit. Hence the two questions which should be asked are:

(1) what is the likelihood of someone else having similar propensity; and

(2) in the light of the other evidence implicating the defendant (eg an identification, opportunity), what is the likelihood that the defendant, rather than other candidates suggested by (i) being responsible for the act?

10.121 Such rationale is evident in *Purcell*.[212] The defendant was alleged to have stolen a car. A minor road collision with the loser's car was engineered by the offender and, when she got out of her vehicle to exchange details, her car was stolen and driven off in a dangerous manner. The defendant was picked out at a video identification procedure. The defence was alibi. He had many driving convictions: one for taking without consent, another for dangerous driving and several for driving whilst disqualified. The Court of Appeal held

---

209 See for example *R v Spittle* [2008] EWCA Crim 2537, [2009] RTR 14, in which the purported recognition by a police officer of a disqualified driver driving dangerously is far from random and possibly not coincidental at all.

210 [2010] EWCA Crim 2113.

211 [2010] EWCA Crim 1619. See also *R v Smith & others* [2008] EWCA Crim 435, [2009] 1 Cr App R 36, [2009] Crim L R 440.

212 [2007] EWCA Crim 2604.

that 'the appellant's proven propensity to commit vehicle crime was plainly material as support for the complainant's identification in that it placed the appellant in a limited category of offenders who were substantially more likely to be engaged in stealing cars than would have been other members of the public at large.'

10.122 Plainly the court will not be in a position to embark on any sort of statistical analysis of random occurrence, but will use its judgment as to the degree of coincidence before deciding the admissibility of bad character evidence. However there may be circumstances in which such evidence does not enhance the likelihood of the defendant's guilt at all. The facts of *R v McMinn*[213] provide a useful illustration. The defendant was one of a group of 10 involved in late night city centre public disorder. He was charged with both affray and a specific assault by knocking one of the victims in another group to the ground and kicking her. He accepted presence but denied participation. He was identified as a participant by a taxi driver purporting to recognise him and who thereafter identified him at a video identification parade. Evidence of a previous conviction for an assault was admitted and he was convicted. In accordance with *R v Eastlake & Eastlake* and other authorities cited above, the Court of Appeal held that the evidence potentially had probative force for a jury considering whether the taxi driver's identification evidence was honestly mistaken on the one hand or accurate on the other. Would that conclusion have been the same if each of the others in the group of 10 had similar previous convictions to those of the defendant? The logic of the propensity provisions suggests that his conviction would not make it more likely that he, rather than any other, was responsible for the assault. There would be no coincidence at all. Section 103 of the CJA 2003 deems propensity to be an independent source of evidence probative of a defendant's guilt and capable of supporting other evidence. The point in *Eastlake* was that the defendant's culpability was more likely due to the unfortunate coincidence of the independent evidence that he had committed similar offences in the past and his identification by the witness. But in *McMinn* it would be equally coincidental if the witness had selected any of the group of 10. In other words the taxi driver's identification might have been quite random. Yet the conviction of that randomly selected person would, in the absence of any consideration of the propensity of the other candidates, paint an entirely misleading picture of the likelihood of the correctness of the identification.

10.123 Another example may be used to illustrate the point. A defendant is accused of a glassing during the course of a melee in a pub. He accepts presence but denies being the attacker. He states that there has been a mistaken identification by the eyewitness. He goes further and says it was his brother or another named drinker for whom he has been mistaken. It matters not in principle whether the source of this accusation is the defendant himself, a friend or indeed the pub landlord who might be quite independent. The defendant has a previous conviction for assault which the prosecution seek to

---

[213] [2007] EWCA Crim 3024.

adduce. However the other candidate also has a similar previous conviction. Does the defendant's conviction make it any more likely that he rather than the other was responsible? What if the other candidate has a more substantial record of violence, or his convictions are more recent or factually more similar to the offence charged? As a matter of propensity logic, whereby propensity is a species of probative evidence independent of the facts of the case, the greater nexus between the offence alleged and the other candidate's propensity, the greater the likelihood that the other person, and not the accused, was the culprit.

Identification from patterns of criminal conduct

10.124 In *R v Wilson*,[214] evidence showing the cessation of offences after the defendant's arrest and remand in custody was admitted to prove the identity of the offender. Over a period of 4 days, seven street robberies took place in Islington, London. In each the victim was female, the assailant carried a knife and was masked, allowing only the top of his nose and eyes to be seen. It may be assumed that the mask effectively prevented any visual identification. Discovered in the defendant's flat were items belonging to three of the victims. A search of police computer records for the borough was made, using a number of different combinations of criteria. 'Robber' and 'mask' threw up two other offences, neither similar, and when other criteria were added such as 'knife' no results were produced at all for the period of 6 months after the defendant's arrest. It was held that this data 'was probative on the issue of whether the defendant was the robber'.

10.125 The Court of Appeal in *R v Wilson* went on to state that had evidence of robberies of the kind committed by the defendant continued after his arrest, it would have been relevant and probative. A similar conclusion was reached in *R v Apps.*[215] The defendant was identified by each of three victims of indecent assault. All occurred within a 3-month period in Tunbridge Wells in similar circumstances, namely an approach on a bicycle and indecent grabbing. The jury were entitled to draw the inference that the attacker was the same person in each case. The defence sought to introduce evidence that other similar offences had been committed in the area for which another person was responsible. By reason of their similarity to the indicted offences it was submitted that the evidence was admissible to exculpate the defendant by demonstrating that another person was responsible. The trial judge prohibited this approach. The Court of Appeal, in allowing the appeal, agreed that 'what was sauce for the goose was sauce for the gander' and that the defendant was entitled to use similar fact evidence to undermine the identifications of the victims.

10.126 An altogether different conclusion was reached in *R v Silburn.*[216] The defendant was alleged to be responsible for a series of robberies which place on the same lane in North London over a period of 5 weeks. They were

---

[214] [2008] EWCA Crim 1754.

[215] (Unreported) 10 February 1998, CA.

[216] [2009] EWCA Crim 1946.

characterised by an approach from behind, grabbing of the victim's head or neck and pushing or forcing the victim to the floor. In the first incident, one of the two female victims positively identified the defendant. In the second incident, again one of the two female victims positively identified him. In the final incident, the male victim made a street identification shortly after the defendant's apprehension but then failed to recognise him at the video identification procedure. However, fibres recovered from the defendant's jeans were very strongly associated with the clothing worn by the victim of that robbery. In response to a defence request, the prosecution revealed that there were 40 hits on a search of CRIS reports relating to robbery in the same area after the defendant's remand in custody. They were described as involving a black man of around 5' 10", apparently consistent with the defendant. On a defence application for disclosure of the reports themselves, the judge ruled that the prosecution were entitled to withhold them, finding, it seems without examining them, that there was nothing that could assist the jury in deciding whether the identifications were correct or not. The Court of Appeal agreed with the judge's assessment that there was nothing sufficiently singular in the robberies to warrant the intended trawl. Though neither *R v Wilson* nor *R v Apps* was cited in the judgment, there may have been no departure from the principle of those cases; rather the Court of Appeal implicitly acknowledged its existence. The case was distinguishable on the ground that, as the court stated, there was no very significant area of similarity between the various robberies, nothing which stood out as a striking individual feature.

Identification revealing bad character

10.127 An identification may co-incidentally reveal the bad character of the person identified, for example where it is based upon a criminal records photograph or recognition by a police officer. Where the bad character is to come to the jury's attention it must be the subject to an application under CJA 2003. As in *R v Edwards* (see **10.103**) it is likely to be characterised as 'important explanatory evidence' under s 101(1)(c) but may also be 'relevant to an important matter in issue' namely the identity of the offender. Set out below is a summary of the law as is applied before CJA 2003.

Criminal records photographs

10.128 When a witness has identified a suspect from criminal records photographs (mugshots), the photographs are prima facie admissible to prove the identification.[217] However to allow such photographs to go before the jury will be tantamount to leading evidence of the defendant's bad character. The question of their exclusion may therefore arise. If identity is not in issue an admission by the defence can be made. Further, in normal circumstances a positive photographic identification (at a time when the identity of the suspect is not known) will inexorably lead to a video identification if identity is an

---

[217] *R v Governor of Pentonville Prison ex p Voets* [1986] 1 WLR 470, DC.

issue.[218] Thus the evidence of the photographic identification may become otiose because it will either have been superseded by a positive formal identification, or no identification will have been made in which case the effect of the initial identification will have been nullified. In *R v Lamb*[219] the introduction of a police mugshot led to the quashing of the conviction. It was held that such photographs may be led only where the defence seek their introduction or in other exceptional circumstances, such as the suspect's refusal to co-operate in a subsequent identification procedure. *R v Lamb* was followed in *R v Williams*[220] in which the conviction was likewise quashed despite the attempt to sanitise the mugshot. It was held in that case that even the use of mugshots after a failure to co-operate was now circumscribed by the availability to the police of covert procedures. These cases were followed in *R v Green*[221] in which the appellant was alleged to have committed a robbery. He was identified from an album of police photographs the following day and, some weeks later, at a formal video procedure. Despite objection to the photographic procedure, both identifications were adduced in evidence. The Court of Appeal quashed the conviction on the ground that the jury may have appreciated from the photographic procedure that the defendant had a criminal record and such knowledge compromised the safety of the conviction.

10.129 The proper introduction of a mugshot photograph might be the result of the manner in which the defence is conducted. If, for example, a witness's reliability was attacked on the basis of the lapse of time between the offence and a later video procedure, the prosecution might then be allowed to refer to a photographic identification much closer in time to the offence. In *R v Bleakley*[222] a newsagent's shop assistant identified the defendant as the robber of the shop from police photographs. He later identified him at a parade. However, on the evening before the parade the defendant attended the shop and tried to speak to the witness who recognised him as the robber. At trial it was suggested that the identification at the parade had come about because of the defendant's visit to the shop the evening before. In the circumstances the trial judge had been correct to allow the jury to know of the identification from the mugshot so that they were not misled.

10.130 The defence itself might call for the introduction of a mugshot where, for instance, its purpose was to undermine a later procedure by suggesting that it was no more than a repetition of the photographic identification.[223] This approach might be adopted if the photographic procedure was itself flawed and the identification tainted a later procedure. When a mugshot connoting a

---

218 Code, D3.12.
219 (1980) 71 Cr App R 198, CA.
220 (Unreported) 22 February 2000, CA.
221 [2006] EWCA Crim 776.
222 [1993] Crim LR 203, CA.
223 See for example *R v Kitchen* [1994] Crim LR 684, CA where it was described as an inevitable tactical decision.

defendant's previous criminal record is adduced, the explanation for it should be as neutral and cause as little prejudice as possible to the defendant.[224]

Recognition by police officer

10.131 The recognition of a suspect by a police officer, either from direct observation of an offence or from viewing a recording of an incident, will indicate some previous association between the two. That association, unless otherwise explained, may very well suggest some previous criminality of the suspect. Though the identification is clearly admissible, there may be circumstances in which it ought to be excluded. In *R v Fowden and White*[225] a police officer and a store detective watched a video recording of a person stealing from a shop. They both recognised the defendant and their evidence was admitted. That recognition was founded upon another incident of alleged shoplifting by the defendant a week later. The other misconduct was bound to emerge from any significant challenge to the reliability of the identification and the defence were thus deprived of testing the accuracy of the identification without prejudice and embarrassment. Accordingly it was held on appeal that the evidence ought to have been excluded because the prejudicial effect outweighed the probative value of the evidence.

Bad character of co-defendant

10.132 Section 101(1)(e) permits evidence of bad character where 'it has substantial probative value in relation to an important matter in issue between the defendant and a co-defendant'. This is the gateway to be opened by those engaging in cut throat defences and it applies to issues of identity as it applies to any other important matter in issue.[226]. It often is in the context of the rivalry between co-defendants as to which is to blame. The exclusionary provision of s 101(3) which applies to matters in issue between the prosecution and defence does not apply to matters in issue between co-defendants. Neither does PACE, s 78 which, it will be recalled, is available when applied to 'evidence on which the prosecution proposes to rely'. Accordingly, provided the evidence is relevant and probative the trial judge has no power to exclude it.[227]

Bad character of non–defendant

10.133 Should it be asserted as part of a defence of mistaken identification that a third party was responsible, evidence of that person's bad character may be admissible to demonstrate his propensity or the likelihood that he, rather

---

224 *R v Campbell* [1994] Crim LR 357, CA.

225 [1982] Crim LR 588, CA.

226 See for example *R v Randall* [2003] UKHL 69, [2004] 1 Cr App R 26 which was decided under the common law rules but whose effect is likely to remain unaltered.

227 *R v Robinson* [2005] EWCA Crim 1940. Even the co-defendant's right to a fair trial under ECHR, Art.6 cannot apparently trump his adversary's right to put in his bad character once the criteria of s 100 are satisfied: *R v Musone* [2007] EWCA Crim 1237, [2007] 2 Cr App R 379.

than the defendant on trial, is the offender. In order to introduce the bad character of a non-defendant, one of the conditions of CJA 2003, s 100 would have to be satisfied.

> '(1) In criminal proceedings evidence of the bad character of a person other than the defendant is admissible if and only if –
> (a) it is important explanatory evidence,
> (b) it has substantial probative value in relation to a matter which –
> (i) is a matter in issue in the proceedings, and
> (ii) is of substantial importance in the context of the case as a whole, or
> (c) all parties to the proceedings agree to the evidence being admissible.'

HEARSAY EVIDENCE

CJA 2003

10.134 Save for the retention of certain exceptions, the common law hearsay rules have been replaced by the statutory provisions of CJA 2003. A hearsay statement is defined by s 114(1) and s 115 as a representation of fact or opinion, not made in oral evidence, whose purpose was to cause either another person to believe it or another person or machine to act on it. Hearsay remains inadmissible unless it satisfies one of the categories of evidence under CJA 2003, s 114 and the sections which follow.[228]

10.135 In broad terms these are:

(1) s 114(1)(a) and s 116(2): where a witness is unavailable, because he:

- (a) is dead;
- (b) is unfit because of his bodily or mental condition;
- (c) is outside the jurisdictions and it is not reasonably practicable to secure his attendance;
- (d) cannot be found despite reasonable steps having been taken to find him;
- (e) does not give evidence through fear;

(2) s 114(1)(a) and s 117: business documents;

(3) s 114(1)(a), s 119 and s 120: previous statements of witnesses;

(4) s 114(1)(b): preserved common law rules and s 118:

- (a) rule 1: public information;
- (b) rule 2: reputation as to character;
- (c) rule 3: reputation or family tradition;

---

[228] The provisions are set out in full in Appendix F.

(d) rule 4: res gestae;
(e) rule 5: confessions;
(f) rule 6: common enterprise;
(g) rule 7: expert evidence;

(5) s 114(1)(c): all parties agree to the admission of the evidence;

(6) s 114(1)(d): the court is satisfied that it is in the interests of justice to admit the evidence; s 114(2) lists, non exhaustively, the factors to which a court must have regard.

10.136 It should be noted that unlike previous hearsay legislation[229] there are no requirements for statements to be in documents. Further, in respect of witness unavailability, except for the witness in 'fear' ground which requires the court's leave,[230] once the fact of the ground is proved there is no judgment or discretion involved; the hearsay is admissible. However the court retains the power to exclude hearsay evidence under PACE, s 78 and has an additional exclusionary power under CJA 2003, s 126 if satisfied that the case for excluding the hearsay statement substantially outweighs the case for its admission. The 'interests of justice' gateway in s 114(1)(d) is sometimes described as the 'safety valve'. It is noteworthy that the nature and provenance of hearsay admitted in the interests of justice are not circumscribed, though the court must take account of a number of factors set out in s 114(2) when deciding whether to admit the statement. The Act makes provision for multiple hearsay (s 121), the non admission of hearsay if the statement maker lacked capacity (s 122), the admission of evidence as to the statement maker's credibility (s 124), and stopping the case where the hearsay evidence is unconvincing (s 125). The focus of the following paragraphs is identification evidence, the content of which is hearsay. They are not intended to be a substitute for more general works on the subject of hearsay.

Hearsay identification and previous statements

10.137 The common law rule permitting a dying declaration to be adduced as an exception to the hearsay rule has not been preserved for the very simple reason that once the death of the statement maker is established, the hearsay is automatically admissible under s 116(2)(a), subject to an exclusionary power. In *R v Musone*[231] the deceased was stabbed to death in his prison cell. Two prisoners heard him name the defendant as his assailant before he collapsed and died. In respect of the first, the evidence was admitted and the trial judge was held correctly to have declined to exclude the evidence under PACE, s 78. The second prisoner refused to testify. He had made no statement but there existed a record of a conversation in which he informed an investigating police officer of the dying declaration identifying the defendant. The admission of

229 Section 23 of the Criminal Justice Act 1988.

230 *R v Sullivan* [2010] EWCA Crim 2676 provides an example of a witness whose selection of the defendant at an identification procedure was read on grounds that he was in fear.

231 [2007] EWCA Crim 1237, [2007] 2 Cr App R 29.

that too was upheld, the enhanced test of multiple hearsay under s 121, ('the value of the evidence … is so high that the interest of justice require [it] to be admissible') having been satisfied.

10.138 The majority of cases in which a witness, whose evidence would otherwise be given orally, is absent will fall within one of the species of unavailability in s 116. However, there may be rare circumstances in which, despite a lack of explanation for a witness's refusal to testify, reliance on the interests of justice provisions, s 114(1)(d), can be placed. In *R v Sadiq and Hussein*[232] the victim of an attempted murder by shooting had been rendered unable to communicate other than by alphabet board, the means by which he gave evidence. At trial, he gave crucial evidence identifying the defendants as his attackers. The trial ended with the jury hung, and thereafter he refused to give evidence at the re-trial or to explain the reasons for his refusal. Despite this, the evidence he had given at the first trial was admitted in the second 'in the interests of justice'. The appellants submitted that there ought to have been a good and identifiable reason for his refusal before s 114(1)(d) could be invoked. The court agreed that it:

> 'cannot be seen as regarding it as normally in the interests of justice that an important witness's evidence should be given under the hearsay provisions … when he simply refuses to testify and will not provide a good reason for his refusal when he is available and capable of giving evidence'.

However the unique reasons for upholding the judge's decision to admit the testimony were that his credibility and reliability had already been explored in the course of examination at the first trial and that, because of his disability, the jury would get very little assistance by studying his demeanour, thus greatly reducing any potential prejudice to the defence.

10.139 Business and other documentary records, including police records, are admissible subject to the requirements of s 117. In *Wellington v DPP*[233] the driver of a vehicle was stopped by police but, having provided personal details, he fled the scene. He was identified under a different name by one of the police officers some time later and denied having been the driver of the vehicle that had been stopped. However a PNC record purported to show that he had previously used the name given by the driver as an alias. The Administrative Court held that the magistrates' court were entitled to rely upon the hearsay contained within the PNC record, there being an inescapable inference that the information had been supplied by a person with knowledge of the fact that the defendant had previously used the alias.

10.140 Previous statements made by a witness called to give evidence may, under ss 119 and 120, assume the status of evidence in the trial despite the witness not adopting or even refuting its accuracy or truth. Thus where a witness retracts an identification contained in a statement or claims to have a

---

[232] [2009] EWCA Crim 712, (2009) 1732 JP 471.

[233] *Wellington v DPP* [2007] EWHC 1061 (Admin), (2007) JP 497.

failure of recollection, the statement may be deployed to prove its content. In *R v Joyce and Joyce*[234] three witnesses to a firearms incident identified the defendants in their statements. However they retracted their identifications before and at trial. Their statements were adduced under s 119 and the defendants were convicted. The Court of Appeal upheld the judge's decision to admit the statements stating that it:

> 'would have been astonished if the judge had reached any other conclusion. The shootings took place in broad daylight … The defendants were known to all three witnesses, who had unobstructed views of them, over a significant period of time … In the circumstances, the suggestion that all three witnesses were initially confused or mistaken in the statements which they made on the day of these events strains credulity.'

The jury were accordingly entitled to decide between the account given in evidence and that contained within the witness statement.

Incrimination and identification by accomplice

10.141 Not uncommonly a defendant will be identified by an accomplice in a police interview or other out-of-court statement. At common law as it is under CJA 2003, such a statement is hearsay and admissible against its speaker alone and not against any other defendant in the trial. The principal reason for this rule is that, by contrast to a confession which is admissible because generally it can be said to be inherently reliable, an accusation against another person may be quite the opposite where the speaker has an incentive to exculpate himself and blame another. In addition it is said that the person accused, not being present, has no opportunity to contradict the accusation. Accordingly in a joint trial the jury is given a standard direction to ignore the accusation and to dispel from their minds its prejudicial effect. Of course this is otiose if the accomplice accuser repeats the evidence on oath.

10.142 The general rule must now be considered subject to modification by virtue of s 114(1)(d). An out-of-court statement by an accomplice, whether contained in a confession, police interview or made in any other manner is now capable of being deployed against the person accused if it satisfies the 'interests of justice' test. In principle such evidence is capable of admission whether at the behest of the prosecution or a co-defendant, and whether the statement maker is a co-defendant or an accomplice not being tried with the defendant incriminated by his statement. In *R v McClean*[235] one of three defendants accused of murder who did not give evidence at trial was said to have told a prison officer that a second defendant had fatally stabbed the deceased. The prosecution did not seek to rely upon it but the third defendant, who was accused of the stabbing by the second defendant, sought to call the evidence of the prison officer. It was that the trial judge had incorrectly ruled that the

---

[234] [2005] EWCA Crim 1785. Other examples can be found in *R v Hallam* [2007] EWCA Crim 966 and *R v Bennett and Turner* [2008] EWCA Crim 248.

[235] [2007] EWCA Crim 219, [2008] 1 Cr App R 11.

common law prohibition on the use of the co-defendant's out-of-court statement prevailed. The Court of Appeal was not required to consider the merits of a ruling that might otherwise have been made, but nevertheless considered the s 114(2) factors 'likely to be critical' to the decision had the court at first instance not debarred itself from exercising its judgment. These included the circumstances in which the statement was made and its reliability. The prejudice to the person accused and the difficulty in challenging the statement where the maker has chosen not to give evidence were factors of 'very great importance' requiring 'very careful evaluation'. The problem in reconciling a direction as to how to approach the evidence with an adverse inference against its maker under the Criminal Justice and Public Order Act (CJPOA) 1994 s 35 was another factor requiring careful reflection.

10.143 In *R v Y*,[236] s 114(1)(d) was considered from a different perspective: the use by the prosecution of an out-of-court statement by an accomplice who, having pleaded guilty to murder in earlier proceedings, was not on trial. In a confession to his girlfriend, the accomplice revealed that the defendant was the other attacker. That confession was the only evidence capable of establishing the identity of the second attacker. The prosecution sought to adduce her statement on the ground that it was in the interests of justice under s 114(1)(d). It was submitted by the defendant that the common law exception to the hearsay rule relating to confessions had been preserved by s 114(1)(b) and s 118 rule 4 and that the confession was therefore admissible only against its maker. The Court of Appeal ruled that the common law rule could not preclude the operation of the 'interests of justice' test and that accordingly a confession by one offender was capable of admission against another. *R v Y* was an interlocutory appeal and, as in *R v McLean*, the Court of Appeal was not asked to consider the merits of such an application against the factors listed in s 114(2). However the court once again took the opportunity of restating the degree of caution that is required when considering hearsay applications which comprise accusations by one alleged offender against another.

> 'Absent inducement, mental instability or perhaps an incentive to protect someone else, it can no doubt normally be said that a person is unlikely to confess to a serious crime unless he did it. Precisely the reverse may well be true of an accusation against someone else, whether it is combined with a reliable confession or not.'

The court also took the opportunity to consider the status of police interviews. It held that:

> 'S 114(1)(d) does not make police interviews routinely admissible in the case of persons other than the interviewee, and that the reasons why they are not ordinarily admissible except in the case of an interviewee are likely to continue to mean that in the great majority of cases it will not be in the interests of justice to admit them in the case of any other person.'

---

[236] [2008] EWCA Crim 10, [2008] 1 Cr App R 34.

10.144 Where a defendant does not repeat an earlier accusation against his co-defendant in evidence, absent a hearsay ruling, the jury will be directed to dispel from their minds the prejudicial effect of the statement on the co-defendant. Evidential blindness of this nature may require of a jury a considerable degree of mental acuity. Can the interview or its offending part be excluded at the request of the prejudiced co-defendant? The answer depends upon the nature of the statement or interview and may be subject to a number of competing interests.[237] An interview which is wholly incriminating and one in which a suspect makes a mixed statement[238] (part admission, part denial) are both prima facie admissible against the interviewee, subject to challenges under PACE, ss 76 and 78. Where there is consensus between the defendants, the prosecution may agree to omit references implicating another defendant which do not detract from its case against the interviewee.[239] Where there is consensus between the defendants, the judge may exclude material from a co-defendant's interview which is of greater prejudice to another defendant than probative of the prosecution case. If the sense of an interview is not lost, one possible means of remedying the prejudice to a co-defendant may be to denote the person named in the interview by letter so that he is not identified.[240] However, if there is no agreement between defendants, normally because the interview is helpful to the defence of the interviewee, he or she has an inalienable right to rely on it despite its prejudicial effect on another.[241] The prejudiced co-defendant has no basis under PACE, s 78 or at common law for applying to exclude the part not admissible against him or her. The Privy Council in *Loban v R*[242] disapproved 'a tenuous line of authority' suggesting that there was a discretion to edit according to the relative prejudice to co-defendants.[243]

10.145 As a matter of practice, wholly exculpatory interviews are generally adduced by the prosecution as part of their case although they are not strictly admissible at common law unless to show a suspect's attitude or reaction to the allegation.[244] Thus a co-defendant named by an interviewee who gives a wholly exculpatory account of himself might properly seek its exclusion. However, since the introduction of the adverse inference from silence in interview under CJPOA 1994, s 34, it is likely that the interviewee would be allowed to rely upon a wholly self-serving statement.

---

237 For a comprehensive review of the subject see P Thornton 'The Prejudiced Defendant: Unfairness Suffered by a Defendant in a Joint Trial' [2003] Crim LR 433.

238 *R v Sharp* (1988) 86 Cr App R 274, CA.

239 *R v Gunawardene* (1951) Cr App R 80, CCA. Such exclusion would be subject to the right of the prosecution to use the edited extract in cross-examination should the interviewee give evidence.

240 The practice was adopted in *R v Silcott* [1987] Crim LR 765, CCC.

241 *Lobban v R* [1995] 2 Cr App R 573, [1995] Crim LR 881, PC following *R v Guneeardene* (1951) Cr App R 80, CCA.

242 [1995] 2 Cr App R 573, [1995] Crim LR 881, PC.

243 These included *R v Silcott* [1987] Crim LR 765 which was disapproved on the facts because the editing was not agreed by co-defendants. See also *R v Rogers and Tarran* [1971] Crim LR 413, *R v Matthias and others* [1988] Crim LR 64 and *R v Jefferson and others* [1988] 99 Cr App R 13.

244 *R v Sat-Bhambra* (1989) 88 Cr App R 55, CA; *R v Pearce* 69 Cr App R 365, CA.

10.146 One remedy to the prejudice of an identification in a co-defendant's interview is an order for separate trials, although judges are generally reluctant to direct severance when defendants face the same or closely associated charges.[245] Failing that, 'the most explicit directions by the trial judge to the effect that the statement of one co-defendant is not evidence against the other' should be given.[246] Unless the co-defendant has confirmed the evidence at trial, the prosecution may not cross-examine a defendant based upon the incriminatory parts of the interview of the co-defendant's interview.[247]

Sole or decisive hearsay evidence

10.147 *R v Dragic*[248] was an identification case considered under the previous hearsay legislation, CJA 1988, and before the incorporation of the ECHR. The defendant was charged with burglary. His defence was alibi. The prosecution hinged upon the identification by a witness who, in the event, was too ill to attend the trial. His statement was therefore read. It was argued on appeal that it had not been in the interests of justice to admit identification evidence which could not be challenged and which represented almost the totality of the evidence against the defendant. The Court of Appeal found otherwise. It was held that:

> 'The fact that there is no ability to cross-examine, that the witness who is absent is the only evidence against the accused and that his evidence is identification evidence is not sufficient to render the admission of written evidence from that witness contrary to the interests of justice or unfair to the defendant per se. What matters, in our judgment, is the content of the statement and the circumstances of the particular case, bearing in mind the considerations which section 26 require the judge to have in mind.'

10.148 Self-evidently, if a case depended upon an unsupported identification statement which was so tenuous that the jury could not convict, the statement should be excluded.[249] But in *R v Dragic* the identification evidence was said not to be weak and, as suggested in an alibi notice, the defendant and his witnesses were apparently able to controvert the statement. However, by reference to the right to a fair trial under ECHR, Article 6, there must be some doubt whether the judgment's reasoning would now be approved. Article 6(3) provides

> 'Everyone charged with a criminal offence has the following minimum rights:
>
> ...

---

245 *R v Christou* [1997] AC 117, HL. See P Thornton 'The Prejudiced Defendant: Unfairness Suffered by a Defendant in a Joint Trial' [2003] Crim LR 433 for a criticism of this judicial reluctance.

246 See **12.117** for summing up requirements.

247 *Lobban v R* [1995] 2 Cr App R 573, [1995] Crim LR 881, PC.

248 [1996] 2 Cr App R 232, CA, following *Scott and another v R* (1989) 89 Cr App R 153, PC.

249 *Scott and another v R* (1989) 89 Cr App R 153, PC.

(d) to have examined witnesses against him …'

10.149 In *R v Arnold*[250] the admission of a statement identifying the defendant was read after it was claimed that the witness had been intimidated and would not give evidence through fear. It was held that the convention right was not inflexible.[251] If it was so construed, the hearsay provisions might never apply. Nevertheless the Court of Appeal went on to hold that:

> 'Very great care must be taken in each and every case to ensure that attention is paid to the letter and spirit of the Convention and judges should not easily be persuaded that it is in the interests of justice to permit evidence to be read. Where that witness provides the sole or determinative evidence against the accused, permitting it to be read may well, depending on the circumstances, jeopardise infringing the defendant's Article 6(3)(d) right; even if it is not the only evidence, care must be taken to ensure that the ultimate aim of each and every trial, namely, a fair hearing, is achieved.'

10.150 The question considered by the European Court of Human Rights in *Al-Khawaja and Tahery v UK*[252] was whether a fair trial could be achieved if hearsay, introduced in breach of Article 6(3)(d), was the sole or decisive evidence which led to conviction. Save for witnesses who do not give evidence through fear induced by the defendants, 'in the absence of special circumstances, the Court doubts whether any counterbalancing factors would be sufficient to justify the introduction in evidence of an untested statement which was the sole or decisive basis for the conviction of an applicant'. That judgment was reviewed in *R v Horncastle and others* by a five-judge Court of Appeal[253] and a seven-judge Supreme Court.[254] It was held that Article 6(3)(d) was not a complete bar on calling hearsay even where it might be the sole or decisive evidence. Provided the hearsay was reliable or that its reliability could be properly tested a fair trial was possible if there were adequate counterbalancing factors in favour of a defendant, such as the opportunity to call evidence in rebuttal and appropriate jury directions.

Acts and words of identification

10.151 The act of a witness identifying someone may involve a gesture such as pointing in the person's direction. It will often be accompanied by words indicative of an identification which may lead to an arrest by a police officer. In many cases words alone might constitute an identification, such as the citation of a number at an identification procedure. The admissibility of such oral

---

250 [2004] EWCA Crim 1293, 148 SJ 660, following *R v M (KJ)* [2003] Cr App R 21, CA.

251 The judgment of *Luca v Italy* (2003) 36 EHRR 46, para 40 suggests that where a conviction is based solely or to a decisive degree on depositions made by a person who the accused has had no opportunity to have examined the rights of the defendant were restricted to an extent incompatible with the guarantees provided by Article 6.

252 (2009) 49 EHRR 1.

253 [2009] EWCA Crim 964, [2009] 2 Cr App R 15, following *R v Sellick and Sellick* [2005] EWCA Crim 651, [2005] 2 Cr App R 15.

254 [2009] UKSC 14.

identification evidence in the context of the hearsay rule has aroused considerable debate. It is now settled that words forming part of or constituting an identification are admissible. *R v Christie*[255] was a case which involved a street identification in the presence of others. It was held that the words 'that is the man' uttered by the victim shortly after the offence 'meant little, if anything, more than the act of touching the sleeve … or pointing'.[256] The victim gave evidence at trial that the defendant was his attacker but not of his identification of the defendant at the scene. However his mother and a police officer were permitted to give evidence of that verbal identification. So too in *R v Mckay*[257] the witness selected the suspect at an identification parade by announcing 'it is number eight'. At trial he gave evidence of the identification but could no longer recollect the number. The evidence was adduced through the identification officer. In former times the touching of a suspect's shoulder at a parade would have been part of the act of identification. The Court of Appeal could find no real distinction between that and the use of words to achieve the same effect. It accordingly held the officer's evidence of what the witness had said to be admissible. The court did not think it necessary to decide whether admissibility was on the basis that nomination by number was an act of identification and therefore a species of real evidence or whether it constituted an exception to the hearsay rule. However characterised, both pre CJA 2003 cases are plainly examples of what s 118 rule 4(b) intended to preserve as an exception to the hearsay rule: a 'statement accompanied by an act which can be properly evaluated as evidence only if considered in conjunction with the statement.'

10.152 More controversial is the question whether a description of the suspect's conduct by person when making the identification is admissible. That may be of importance where there are a number of people potentially concerned in an offence and the description relates to the role of the particular suspect. In *R v Christie* the victim's statement narrated by another witness went beyond identification and included an account of the offence. It was held that:

> '… to allow proof of statements made, narrating or describing events constituting the offence, on the ground that they form part of or explain the act of identification [would be] a dangerous extension of the law.'[258]

10.153 In *R v Lynch*,[259] the Court of Appeal confirmed the narrow confines of the common law exception. That was a case of violent disorder. After a witness had selected the defendant at an identification procedure she was asked to explain what exactly she had seen him do and did so. At trial she could no longer remember. The Court of Appeal rejected the proposition that the evidence fell within a common law exception to the hearsay rule. However, it agreed with the alternative route by which the trial judge had approved its

---

[255] [1914] AC 545, HL.
[256] See the speeches of Lord Reading and Lord Atkinson.
[257] (1990) 91 Cr App R 84, [1990] Crim LR 338, CA.
[258] Per Lord Reading.
[259] [2007] EWCA Crim 3035.

admission, namely 'in the interests of justice' under s 114(1)(d). That judgment was based in part upon the fact that the statement had been made in the formal setting of an identification procedure of which there was a contemporaneous and reliable written record.

10.154 It should also be observed that, in the context of a formal identification procedure of which a record is made, the witness may be permitted under CJA 2003 s 139, to use a memory refreshing document (including a recording) to recall both the identification and any narrative given at the time of the procedure.

Hearsay naming

10.155 The naming of a suspect or defendant by a witness generally causes little controversy because it is accepted that the witness knows and has correctly named the person. Where the issue is in dispute, it may be necessary to examine how the witness acquired the knowledge of the name in order to consider whether it amounts to hearsay evidence. At what stage that knowledge ceases to become hearsay and becomes a matter of first-hand knowledge is a matter of degree. It may depend upon the normal indications and acknowledgements by the named person of the correctness of his or her name; it may be derived from a familiarity developed on a number of occasions or over a period of time. When the issue arose in *R v Clarke and Baker*[260] the court approached it in the following way:

> 'During a period of four years school children, or others in comparable institutions for that matter, get to know who their fellows are, sometimes directly by some informal introduction or acknowledgment, but often because they are named by persons who know them with never a suggestion to the contrary. If one might take an extreme example if a man who reads little and whose only pastime is watching the endless football matches with which the television channels are saturated, if one were to ask him who it was that had just scored a goal for Manchester United wearing a number 5 on the back of his shirt, the reply would be instant and definite, tinged with doubtless contempt for one's ignorance, although the knowledge had only come from a series of commentators over the years. Thus, what once may have been hearsay to start with, after much uncontradicted repetition over a period of time becomes repute and common knowledge. To hold otherwise, in our judgment, must be an affront to common sense.'

10.156 In *R v Phillips*[261] the identification witness possessed a significant degree of familiarity with the defendant but had been later supplied with his surname. The court pointed out that the attribution of a surname was often based upon information supplied by others. It was held that the 'reputation' for identity was always a common law exception to the rule against hearsay and is preserved by s 118(1) and rule 3(c) of the CJA 2003.

---

[260] [2003] EWCA Crim 718.

[261] [2010] EWCA Crim 378.

10.157 By contrast, the victim in *R v Wood*[262] had very little knowledge of his alleged attacker. He had seen him on a few occasions over many years, had never spoken to him and had been told his name by a neighbour 12 years earlier. Evidence naming him was hearsay and not within the 'reputation' exception. Had the case been decided after the CJA 2003 hearsay provisions came into force it would now be open to the prosecution to have applied under s 114(1)(d), the 'interests of justice' gateway. In some cases it may be possible to call evidence from the third party who supplied the name to an identifying witness, thus making the link between the name and the offender.[263] That would plainly be one of the factors to be considered under s 114(2). In *R v Taylor*,[264] the decision to admit the hearsay naming evidence of two witnesses was upheld where the judge had given consideration to the relevant factors and the identification was buttressed by a considerable body of other evidence including that of two further witnesses who had named the defendant.

The self-naming conundrum

10.158 A different problem may arise if a witness's knowledge of a suspect's name emanates exclusively from the mouth of the suspect. A suspect giving the name of another person can hardly be said to be a rare occurrence. Strictly speaking such evidence is hearsay,[265] regardless of whether the defendant formally disputes being the person who provided the name or alleges that the person who provided it assumed his or her identity. It constitutes an out of court statement made by another person whose purpose was to cause the listener to believe in its truth, later tendered at trial for the purpose of proving its correctness. The point arose in *R v Ward, Andrews and Broadley,*[266] a pre CJA 2003 case concerning a conspiracy to steal cars. During the course of the conspiracy a vehicle was observed in suspicious circumstances and was stopped by the police. When asked by a police officer, a passenger gave his name as Michael Kevin Ward together with the correct date of birth and address for that person. It was submitted on behalf of the defendant Ward that the evidence of the officer was hearsay. The Court of Appeal accepted the proposition and considered whether the evidence might be admissible under the hearsay exception which allows confessions or admissions against interest to be adduced. The court found that such reasoning would be circular. An admission as to identity can only be made by the person who is in fact the bearer of that identity. If there is no evidence (other than the admission) that the person making the admission bore that identity, the admission becomes self-fulfilling. The court recognised the need for protection against the dangers of hearsay but found the proposition that a defendant might object to such evidence and refuse to enter the witness box unattractive. The conundrum was resolved by a pragmatic approach which turned upon the quality and accuracy of the

---

262 [2005] EWCA Crim 3018.

263 See for example *R v Elliot (Denrick)* [2000] Crim LR 51, CA.

264 [2006] EWCA Crim 260, [2006] 2 Cr App R 14.

265 *R v Glover* [1991] Crim LR 48, CA demonstrates how it may be admissible under the *res gestae* exception. See **10.166**.

266 [2001] Crim LR 316, CA.

'admission'. It was held that the fact that detailed particulars of Ward's identity were provided by the passenger together with the fact that Ward was a part-owner of the vehicle were sufficiently compelling to treat the statement as an admission. The court added that in such circumstances a jury should be directed to rely upon it only if sure from the content and other circumstances that the person who made the statement was the defendant.

10.159 Another way of analysing such evidence would have been to allow the words of the passenger in evidence, not for the purpose of proving their content but to establish the fact that they were uttered by someone with knowledge of the information. The jury could then have measured the passenger's knowledge of the defendant's personal details, together with other circumstances such as assuredness and spontaneity, against the possibility of someone other than the defendant having been able to recite them.[267] This approach can be inferred from *R v Lydon*.[268] Shortly after an armed robbery, scraps of paper bearing the words 'Sean rules' were discovered near to a gun allegedly used in the robbery. The paper and gun were scientifically linked to one another. The scraps of paper were admitted as real evidence, circumstantially pointing to the self-identification of the defendant whose name was Sean. It was a matter for the jury to determine whether the person who had been in possession of the paper had written his own name on the paper or some other first name. In any event there may be little doubt that a court now considering the conundrum posed in *R v Ward, Andrews and Broadley* would reach the same judgment in the interests of justice under s 114(1)(d), taking into account under s 114(2) the very factors, in particular reliability, it had regarded as decisive.

Res gestae

10.160 A statement made by a person participating in or observing an act might be so closely connected to the act that it forms part of the res gestae.[269] In certain circumstances the statement, which may include reference to the identity of someone involved in the act, will be admissible in the evidence of a third party despite the hearsay rule. Res gestae is a common exception to the statutory hearsay rule preserved by s 118 rule 4(a). The exception relates to a 'statement made by a person so emotionally overpowered by an event that the possibility of concoction or distortion can be disregarded'. That description does not purport to define res gestae, merely to describe the rule.

---

[267] The commentaries following the reports in the *Criminal Law Review* and in *Criminal Law Week* 2001/05/6 provide helpful analysis.

[268] (1987) Cr App R 221, CA.

[269] Literally translated means 'things done', the phrase is generally defined as 'the events at issue or others contemporaneous with them'. B A Garner *A Dictionary of Modern Legal Usage* (OUP, 2nd edn, 2001).

10.161 In the leading case of *R v Andrews*[270] the occupant of burgled premises was fatally injured. Police arrived within minutes. The victim, knowing the identity of his assailants, named them to the police. He died some weeks later. The evidence of the police officers who reported the deceased's naming was admitted and the ruling was upheld by the House of Lords. Lord Ackner summarised the criteria against which evidence might be admitted as res gestae:

> '(1) The primary question which the judge must ask himself is – can the possibility of concoction or distortion be disregarded?
> (2) To answer that question the judge must first consider the circumstances in which the particular statement was made, in order to satisfy himself that the event was so unusual or startling or dramatic as to dominate the thoughts of the victim, so that the utterance was an instinctive reaction to that event, thus giving no real opportunity for reasoned reflection. In such a situation the judge would be entitled to conclude that the involvement or the pressure of the event would exclude the possibility of concoction or distortion, providing that the statement was made in conditions of approximate but not exact contemporaneity.
> (3) In order for the statement to be sufficiently 'spontaneous' it must be so closely associated with the event which has excited the statement, that it can be fairly stated that the mind of the declarant was still dominated by the event. Thus the judge must be satisfied that the event, which provided the trigger mechanism for the statement, was still operative. The fact that the statement was made in answer to a question is but one factor to consider under this heading.
> (4) Quite apart from the time factor, there may be special features in the case, which relate to the possibility of concoction or distortion. In the instant appeal the defence relied upon evidence to support the contention that the deceased had a motive of his own to fabricate or concoct … The judge must be satisfied that the circumstances were such that having regard to the special feature of malice, there was no possibility of any concoction or distortion to the advantage of the maker or the disadvantage of the accused.
> (5) As to the possibility of error in the facts narrated in the statement, if only the ordinary fallibility of human recollection is relied upon, this goes to the weight to be attached to and not to the admissibility of the statement and is therefore a matter for the jury. However, here again there may be special features that may give rise to the possibility of error. In the instant case there was evidence that the deceased had drunk to excess … Another example would be where the identification was made in circumstances of particular difficulty or where the declarant suffered from defective eyesight. In such circumstances the trial judge must consider whether he can exclude the possibility of error.'

10.162 The test has been crystallised in *Phipson on Evidence*[271] as follows:

(1) Was the identification relevant?

(2) Was it spontaneous?

---

[270] [1987] 1 AC 281, (1987) 84 Cr App R 382, HL, following and applying *R v Ratten* [1972] AC 378, PC. See also (the other) *R v Turnbull* (1985) 80 Cr App R 104, CA.

[271] (Sweet & Maxwell, 17th edn, 2010) at para 31–18.

(3) Was there an opportunity for concoction?

(4) What risk was there of error?

Only if the answers are yes to the first question and no to the others would the evidence be admissible within the res gestae exception.[272]

10.163 Lord Ackner indicated that the use of a res gestae statement as a device to avoid calling the person who allegedly made the statement was to be deprecated. The point arose in unusual circumstances in *Attorney General's Reference (No 1 of 2003)*.[273] The defendant was charged with causing grievous bodily harm to his mother. She was heard to call out for help and identify her son as her attacker. She later maintained that her injures had been sustained accidentally. Consequently the prosecution did not propose to call her but sought leave to call the witnesses to give evidence as to what they had heard. The application was refused. Having no other evidence the case collapsed and the prosecution appealed. It was held that there was no rule of law which prohibits such evidence when the best evidence, that of the mother, was not to be called. Nevertheless the decision of the judge was upheld on the basis that he might in any event have excluded the evidence because the defence would have been unable to cross-examine the alleged victim.

10.164 The res gestae rule is also illustrated in *R v Elliot (Denrick)*,[274] which applied *R v Andrews*. Within a few minutes of an attack on him the deceased identified the defendant as his attacker. A police officer's evidence of the deceased's words was properly admitted as forming part of the res gestae of the offence. In *R v Nye and Loan*[275] an altercation between two motorists culminated in an assault. Police attended moments later and the injured victim, pointing at his assailant, said 'That man hit me in the face'. The evidence of identification, together with the account explaining how he came to be injured, were admitted as part of the res gestae. The Court of Appeal upheld the decision, commenting that it was difficult to imagine a more spontaneous identification and in the circumstances there was no realistic possibility of concoction or of error.

10.165 Provided the event dominates the mind of the speaker it is immaterial whether the words relied on were uttered before,[276] during or after the crime, though the more distant the statement, the less likely that it could be regarded as spontaneous. There could be little doubt in *R v West*[277] that the statement met this criterion as, during the course of a robbery, the victim was overheard by a neighbour to shout 'Fuck off Adrian' – the name of the alleged robber.

---

272 As to the necessary directions to the jury, see **12.102**.

273 [2003] Crim LR 547, CA.

274 [2000] Crim LR 51, CA.

275 (1978) 66 Cr App R 252; [1978] Crim LR 94, CA. See also *R v Watson* [2003] EWCA Crim 3795.

276 For example *R v Ratten* [1972] AC 378, PC.

277 (Unreported) 14 September 1999, CA.

However in *R v Newport*[278] where the deceased spoke to a friend prior to her fatal stabbing, the words spoken were found to be 'in no sense a spontaneous and unconsidered reaction to an immediately impending emergency'. The evidence ought not to have been admitted. The rigour of the rule was demonstrated in *Sparks v R*.[279] The defendant was accused of indecently assaulting a girl aged just under 4 years. Though she did not give evidence, her mother did. The Privy Council held that the mother's evidence of her child's remark that 'it was a coloured boy', in circumstances where the defendant was white, was not admissible under the res gestae exception to the hearsay rule. Being about an hour after the assault, the statement was not sufficiently associated with the assault in time, place or circumstances to be admissible.

10.166 The person whose words are repeated in court need not be the victim. A res gestae statement may be that of a witness who is affected by an observed or overheard incident.[280] In *R v Glover*[281] the defendant himself was the author of the reported statement. Immediately following a violent altercation the defendant was thoughtful enough to reveal his identity by saying 'I am David Glover ... we will not think twice of shooting you and your kids.' The spontaneity of the statement could not be denied and the opportunity for concoction was said to be so unlikely as to be excluded.

IDENTIFICATION BY ASSOCIATION WITH ACCOMPLICE

10.167 A defendant's association in time, distance or relationship with an accomplice may provide circumstantial evidence of his or her complicity in the offence. In *R v Grey*[282] observations were made of three people in the vicinity of burgled premises both before and immediately after the burglary. Fifteen minutes later the defendant and his two co-accused, all of similar appearance to the three observed earlier, were arrested half a mile away. Grey, who claimed not to know the others, and a second defendant contested the charge. The third, against whom there was shoeprint evidence, pleaded guilty. The defendant's link, if accepted, with a person proven to be one of the burglars at a time and place sufficiently proximate to the initial observations and burglary was probative of his guilt. In *R v O'Neil*,[283] a video recording showed two men committing a burglary in Leeds. The appellant's brother, who lived nearby, pleaded guilty to the offence. Police officers viewed the recording and purported to recognise the appellant as the other burglar. His defence was alibi. He claimed that he was in Carlisle where he lived at the material time. The

---

278 [1998] Crim LR 581, CA. See also *Teper v R* [1952] AC 48, PC.

279 [1964] AC 946, PC.

280 In *R v Ratten* [1972] AC 378, PC, Lord Wilberforce referred to a statement made 'either by the victim of an attack or by a bystander'.

281 [1991] Crim LR 48, CA.

282 (1989) 88 Cr App R 375, CA.

283 9 February 1998 (unreported), CA. Another example of the coincidence of identification and relationship with an accomplice may be found in *R v Williams* [2005] EWCA Crim 2332.

Court of Appeal held that the evidence of the relationship was relevant to explain the appellant's presence at the scene of a burglary a considerable distance from his home. The jury were entitled to consider the likelihood of a mistaken identification and the proven participation of the appellant's brother.

10.168 Evidence of association with gang members may be admissible to establish participation in an offence.[284] The association might be shown to have taken place both considerably before or after the offence. In *R v Davis and Murphy,*[285] Murphy was picked out by a witness at an identification parade as one of an armed gang involved in a post office robbery. Many weeks later, within a few hours of a second, similar fact post office robbery, he was stopped by police in a car containing Davis and two other participants in that offence. Murphy was not tried for the second robbery. Nevertheless because of his association with those others shortly after the second offence it was held that 'as a matter of common sense, the likelihood of [the witness's] identification of him being a true one was greatly increased'. The Court of Appeal found that the probative value of the evidence outweighed the potentially prejudicial effect of the association with the robbers of the second post office, if not the robbery itself. It should be noted that evidence of gang membership may require an application to introduce bad character.[286]

10.169 The guilt of the accomplice may be beyond dispute if he or she has been convicted, as in *R v Grey* and *R v O'Neil.* Where contested, the prosecution will need to establish guilt by other evidential means before an association with the defendant could be probative. If evidence of that guilt emanates from alleged admissions made by the accomplice, care must be taken not to rely upon them as probative of the case against the associate.[287] It is the guilt of the accomplice and not his admission to the crime which may be probative of a defendant's guilt. In *R v Hayter,*[288] the appellant's co-accused was alleged to have been recruited by him to commit a murder. The case against the co-accused was based exclusively on a disputed confession. The case against the appellant was founded substantially on their association together with, if proved, his co-accused's guilt. The judge invited the jury first to consider the co-accused's case based on his confession, instructing them to disregard its content so far as it might implicate the appellant; if guilty, they might then use that guilt as evidence which could be probative in deciding the appellant's case. The claim on appeal that the appellant's conviction was, in effect, based upon the hearsay confession of an accomplice was rejected by the House of Lords. It was immaterial whether the guilt of the co-accused was established by his

---

284 *R v Laidman and Agnew* [1992] Crim LR 428, *R v Lee* [1996] Crim LR 825 and *R v Brown and others* [1997] Crim LR 502.

285 56 Cr App R 249, CA.

286 For the bad character provisions see **10.96**.

287 *R v Daniel and Watson* [1973] Crim LR 628, CA; *R v Rhodes* (1959) 44 Cr App R 23, CA; *R v Munn* (unreported) 25 February 2002, CA. See **10.141** on the effect of a co-defendant's interview.

288 [2005] UKHL 6, [2005] 2 Cr App R 3.

confession, by an eyewitness, by scientific evidence or by his conviction at an earlier trial. It was the fact of guilt not the means by which it was established that was probative.

10.170 An accomplice's conviction may be adduced in evidence for the purpose of establishing the identification of a defendant. Before introducing it the requirement of relevance in PACE, s 74(1) must be established. It states that:

> 'In any proceedings the fact that a person other than the accused has been convicted of an offence … shall be admissible in evidence for the purpose of proving, where to do so is relevant to any issue in the proceedings, that that person committed the offence, whether or not any other evidence of his having committed the offence is given.'

10.171 Once admitted, the person convicted 'shall be taken to have committed the offence unless the contrary is proved'.[289] This is, in effect, a device excusing the prosecution from proving what has already been admitted by plea of guilty or established on conviction by a jury. The conviction proves, without other evidence, no more than the essential elements of the offence as against the person convicted, though other contextual evidence may buttress and explain it.

10.172 In considering the admissibility of an accomplice's conviction, a useful starting point is to consider its probative purpose. In some cases a conviction will serve to prove the fact that the offence was committed. So a thief's conviction will be introduced to settle the issue whether property in the defendant's possession was stolen. The term 'issue in the proceedings' is wide enough to encompass evidential issues raised by the case, such as the association of a defendant with a convicted co-defendant at around the time of a burglary.[290] However care should be taken to isolate precisely what the conviction establishes.[291] Where in reality a conviction has no or negligible probative purpose relative to an issue in the case it should not be admitted. It is insufficient to assert that a jury may wonder about an absent accomplice, especially if the admission of his conviction is capable of causing prejudice to a defendant on trial.[292]

10.173 Difficulty is sometimes encountered in determining the nature of factual inferences revealed by evidence of a conviction. The meaning of a conviction may be open to a number of different interpretations concerning the role of the convicted accomplice. For example offences may be committed in a variety of ways or in alternative states of mind, such as knowledge or suspicion. There may have been a basis of plea which reveals a factual scenario

---

289 PACE, s 74(2).

290 For example see *R v Grey* (1989) 88 Cr App R 375, CA and *R v O'Neil* (unreported) 9 February 1998, CA referred to in **10.167**.

291 *R v Downer* [2009] EWCA Crim 1361, [2009] 2 Cr App R 452.

292 *R v Girma* [2009] EWCA Crim 912.

inconsistent with that which the prosecution seek to advance at trial.[293] A conviction which might on the face of it tend to incriminate a defendant may be founded on admissions in interview which in fact exculpate the defendant. The introduction of a bare conviction, shorn of the evidence in support may accentuate the difficulty in interpretation. Such difficulties are particularly acute in conspiracy cases where the guilt of one conspirator inevitably connotes the complicity of at least one other person, often the guilt of the person standing trial. Where a conviction is to be admitted, but the discernment of its factual implications is speculative, fairness may demand that the prosecution allow the jury to judge the matter by calling the evidence establishing the guilt of a co-accused rather than relying upon the conviction alone.[294]

10.174 The Court of Appeal has held that PACE, s 74 should be used sparingly.[295] Even where admissible, the exclusionary power under PACE, s 78 should be exercised if the conviction, which by its nature cannot effectively be challenged, leads inexorably to a conclusion that the defendant must be guilty or tends to close off a legitimate line of defence. On the one hand the conviction may carry enormous weight in the minds of the jury while on the other it cannot properly be tested. The court must ask itself whether the conviction might carry a weight disproportionate to its probative value to the prosecution.[296] Indeed caution should be exercised where the conviction is reasonably capable of an interpretation which may not incriminate the defendant, especially on a plea of guilty. In *R v Lee*[297] the Court of Appeal, providing general guidance on the use of PACE, s 74 and its relationship with s 78, held:

> 'It is possible to envisage situations in which a co-defendant might plead guilty to a charge even though the evidence on that charge was far from conclusive against him. In such a case it could well be unfair to the remaining defendant or defendants to allow his conviction to be proved as evidence against them, for it might deprive them of the opportunity to challenge the evidence on which the conviction was based.'

TRANSFERRED RELIABILITY OF IDENTIFICATION

10.175 'Issue in the proceedings' in PACE, s 74 has been construed to include the accuracy and reliability of a witness's identification evidence. In *R v Castle*[298] the victim of a robbery attended an identification parade where he positively identified the defendant. He identified a friend of the defendant as only 'possibly' an assailant. The friend pleaded guilty whereas the defendant

---

293 See for example *R v Girma* [2009] EWCA Crim 912.

294 The argument was advanced in *R v Gummerson and Steadman* [1999] Crim LR 680, CA, unreported on this point.

295 *R v Robertson and Golder* (1987) 85 Cr App R 304, CA; *R v Curry* [1988] Crim LR 527, CA.

296 *R v Smith* (2007) [2007] EWCA Crim 2105, 151 SJLB 1260, followed in. *R v Girma* [2009] EWCA Crim 912.

297 [1996] Crim LR 825, CA.

298 [1989] Crim LR 567, CA. See also *R v Jones (Terrence)* [1992] Crim LR 356, CA.

contested the case. The defendant had admitted being in the company of the friend prior to the robbery but not at the time of its commission. It was held that the prosecution were entitled to rely upon the friend's plea of guilty on the ground that it demonstrated the correctness of the tentative identification of the defendant's friend which was relevant to the issue of the victim's reliability in his unqualified identification of the defendant. This strained interpretation of the phrase 'issue in those proceedings' has also been applied in a case of identification by voice recognition, *R v Gummerson and Steadman*.[299] The victim of an assault purported to recognise the voices of his masked attackers. The defence asserted that he would not have been able to recognise the voices of his assailants. The plea of guilty by one was adduced to promote the victim's reliability in identifying the others.

10.176 Where the conviction is used to support reliability of identification, it is essential that the jury are directed carefully as to its effect and are warned against being influenced by the mere fact of a defendant's association with a convicted party.[300] In *R v Wait*[301] the victim of a robbery purported to recognise and make a street identification of two of his assailants some days later. The conviction of one was held to have been correctly adduced as supporting the correctness of the identification of the appellant. However the Court of Appeal recognised the obvious danger that the identification of the appellant may have been influenced by his association with the other at the time of the street identification. It was held that the summing up had inadequately set out the limit of the purpose for which the plea of guilty had been admitted in evidence. It had tended to conflate the issues of accuracy of the identifying witness with the guilt of the defendant by association with the person convicted.

10.177 It is submitted that the principle that a correct identification of one offender can be used as a guide to the reliability of an identification of another is an approach which, though rationally sustainable, should be treated with caution. If the defence seek to impugn the reliability of eyewitness evidence, say by suggesting that the distance or some obstacle impeded a good view, the fact that the witness was able to observe another person sufficiently to make a correct identification may be relevant to the jury's inquiry. The danger lies in reliance upon an apparent infallibility of the witness. As 'a number of witnesses can all be mistaken', *(Turnbull)* so too can a single witness in respect of one of two identifications. Indeed it is far from uncommon for a witness to be correct at one identification procedure but select a volunteer at another. Hence it is of crucial importance to consider the circumstances of each observation before allowing a conviction to be used to enhance a witness's reliability. A recognition case, such as *R v Gummerson and Steadman,* may carry greater weight. By contrast the identification of one person who later pleads guilty to a public order offence involving a large number of people may provide little protection against the erroneous identification of others. Similarly the correct

---

[299] [1999] Crim LR 680, CA, not reported on this point.

[300] See **12.65**.

[301] [1998] Crim LR 68, CA, not reported on this point.

identification of a person of singular appearance may be of limited value in assessing the accuracy of an identification of someone with no outstanding features.

10.178 If the principle of transferred reliability of identification is valid, it is not logically dependant upon the conviction of the person correctly identified at all. On a trial of co-defendants, if a jury was satisfied that A's identification of X was correct, they might take it into account in assessing the accuracy of A's identification of Y. However, there appears to be no precedent for such an approach. Moreover in *R v El-Hannachi and others*[302] it was rejected on appeal. The Court of Appeal regarded:

> '... as erroneous the suggestion on behalf of the prosecution that [an appellant's] conviction should be regarded as safe because [a witness's] identification of the other three appellants resulted in safe convictions. This flies in the face of the principle that a jury must consider the case against each defendant separately.'

IDENTIFICATION BY ASSOCIATION WITH OBJECT

10.179 Articles in the possession of a defendant which are alleged to be the proceeds of crime, for example stolen goods,[303] or used in its commission, for example a weapon or tool, are all plainly admissible as direct evidence tending to identify the perpetrator of an offence. Possession of an object not directly connected to the offence may also be admissible where, despite its prejudicial effect, it is sufficiently coincidental to render it probative of the offence. In *R v Thompson*[304] a man committed acts of gross indecency with boys in a public urinal and arranged to meet them 3 days later. Police officers observed the rendezvous and arrested the defendant. He gave an innocent explanation for his association with them on that day and claimed to have an alibi for the period, 3 days earlier, when the offences were committed. In support of the identification made by the boys, evidence was adduced that on arrest he was found in possession of two powder puffs. A search of his home revealed a number of photographs of naked boys. The House of Lords upheld the decision to admit this evidence on the basis that both the perpetrator of the indecency and the defendant possessed a common 'abnormal propensity' and hence the articles found tended to confirm the identification made by the boys.

10.180 Factors such as the extent to which the article is in common use and the time between the commission of the offence and its seizure may be taken into account when considering the admission of this type of evidence. In offences of dishonesty a jury may be entitled to consider the likelihood of a

---

302 [1998] 2 Cr App R 226, CA. See also *R v Briant* [2006] EWCA Crim 2006 where, on an indictment alleging indecent assault, it was impermissible to rely upon the convictions of two men for unconnected sexual offences against the same complainant in order to bolster her credibility.

303 The doctrine of 'recent possession' of a stolen article shortly after a theft, burglary or robbery may tend to identify the person in possession as the offender.

304 [1918] AC 221, HL.

mistaken identification against the finding of tools of the nefarious trade. Clearly the objects must have sufficient probative nexus with the offence and not merely prove that the defendant has criminal propensity, unless the evidence is admissible under the bad character provisions of CJA 2003. In *R v Taylor*[305] for example. a jemmy should not have been admitted to prove that the defendant was responsible for a burglary where none was used in the breaking of a door.

10.181 By contrast, in *R v Reading and others,*[306] after two incidents of lorry 'hijacking' police found walkie talkies and a police style uniform. Though there was no evidence of the use of the walkie talkies or uniform in the offences they were held to have been correctly admitted to rebut the defence of mistaken identification and alibi. The connection was perhaps a little tenuous though they were found together with items similar to those stolen from one of the lorries. In *R v Mustaffa,*[307] the defendant was charged with obtaining goods by deception by means of a stolen credit card. At the defendant's address another stolen credit card was found together with paper showing attempts at copying the owner's signature. They were admitted to confirm the identity of the fraudulent user of the card with which the goods had been obtained. Though a pre-CJA 2003 'similar fact' case, that evidence would now doubtless have been admissible as bad character under s 101.

10.182 In *R v Clarke*[308] a bank robber wearing a baseball cap and scarf discharged a sawn-off shotgun. The defendant was later identified from CCTV still photographs by means of facial mapping. A witness's description of a getaway car was consistent with one driven by the defendant 2 months later. Discovered in a car at that time were a sawn-off shotgun, ammunition, facemask and surgeon's gloves. Although the 'robber's kit' could not be linked to the robbery it was held to be admissible to establish that it was the same robber's getaway car described by a witness. Plainly the evidence would have been admissible under the propensity gateway in CJA 2003.

ADVERSE INFERENCES

10.183 In a trial where the identity of the offender is the issue, evidence in support of a witness's identification often plays a crucial part. Under ss 34–37, support may be drawn from adverse inferences. Subject to the exclusionary power at common law or under PACE, s 78 once the relevant criteria have been satisfied, a failure to mention facts or to account for objects or presence at a particular place may be relied upon in deciding whether there is a case to answer, either at committal, dismissal or the close of the prosecution case.[309] A defendant who gives evidence at trial may be cross-examined on the default.

---

[305] (1923) Cr App R 109, CCA.

[306] 50 Cr App R 98, CA.

[307] 65 Cr App R 26, CA.

[308] [1995] 2 Cr App R 425, CA.

[309] See **11.15** for consideration of its effect on a submission of no case.

The provisions which permit adverse inferences, and any specific ramifications they may have upon identification evidence, are summarised below.

Failure to mention fact when questioned – CJPOA 1994, s 34

10.184 An adverse inference under CJPOA 1994, s 34 requires evidence that:[310]

(1) a person was questioned by a constable under caution;

(2) the constable was trying to discover whether or by whom an offence had been committed;

(3) the person failed to mention a fact later relied upon in his or her defence;

(4) the fact was one which, in the circumstances existing at the time of the questioning, the person could reasonably have been expected to mention when questioned; and

(5) the questioning took place before or upon charge or on being informed that he might be prosecuted for the offence.

10.185 It should be borne in mind that a fact later relied on in a defence is not limited to a statement made by a defendant in evidence at trial. It may include assertions of specific facts put to a prosecution witness which the defendant might have been expected to mention in interview, regardless of whether they are accepted by the witness and notwithstanding the defendant does not give evidence of them. It may also include a fact stated by a co-defendant which is subsequently adopted as part of a defendant's defence.[311]

Failure to account for objects – CJPOA 1994, s 36

10.186 The possession of an incriminating article or substance connected to the offence is admissible against a defendant. The adverse inference resulting from a failure to account for it merely adds weight to the evidence of its possession as against any later innocent explanation. The criteria for admission under CJPOA 1994, s 36, supplemented by Code C10.10 and 10.11 are:

(1) a person has been arrested by a constable,

(2) the person has:

   (a) on his person,
   (b) in or on his clothing or footwear,
   (c) otherwise in his possession,

---

[310] See *R v Argent* [1997] 2 Cr App R 27, CA.
[311] *R v Webber* [2004] UKHL 1, [2004] 1 Cr App R 40.

(d) in any place in which he is at the time of the arrest,

(3) an object, substance or mark, or object with any mark,

(4) the (or another) constable reasonably believes that the presence of the object, substance or mark may be attributable to the person's participation in the offence specified by the constable,

(5) the (or another) constable:

(a) so informs the person, and
(b) requests him to account for its presence, and
(c) explains the failure for doing so in ordinary language,

(6) the person fails to do so.

10.187 Unlike CJPOA 1994, s 34, no reference is made to the questioning being under caution. However, a caution is necessary on arrest. Moreover the circumstances in which questioning may take place outside a formal interview at a police station are circumscribed by Code C.[312]

10.188 In many cases an inference relating to an object will be available under CJPOA 1994, s 34. But the inference under s 36 is not dependant upon the defendant later relying on a fact in evidence. Thus the inference may be drawn if the defendant does not give evidence or gives no explanation for the object at trial. Further s 36, unlike s 34, makes no mention of the explanation being one which the defendant could reasonably have been expected to provide. A submission that the suspect could not reasonably have been expected to explain possession of the object is not precluded. Evidence of the failure may consequently be excluded; alternatively the jury will have to resolve the issue of reasonableness.

Failure to account for presence – CJPOA 1994, s 37

10.189 The presence of a person at a particular place may in itself be probative of guilt. The adverse inference derived from a failure to account for presence adds to its weight. The criteria for admission under CJPOA 1994, s 37, supplemented by Code C10.10 and 10.11 are:

(1) a person has been arrested by a constable,

(2) the person was found by the constable at a place at or about the time of the offence for which he was arrested was alleged to have been committed,

---

[312] See Code C10.1, 11.1A and 11.1. The words of the special caution for CJPOA 1994, s 36 are set out in Code C10.10.

(3) the (or another) constable reasonably believes that presence may be attributable to participation in the offence,

(4) the (or another) constable:

  (a) so informs the person,
  (b) requests him to account for his presence,
  (c) explains the failure for doing so in ordinary language,

(5) the person fails to do so.

The comments relating to CJPOA 1994, s 36 above apply equally to an inference under s 37.

Failure to consent to taking of intimate sample – PACE 1984, s 62(10)

10.190 An intimate sample can only be taken from a suspect if certain criteria are met, but may not be taken without consent.[313] Once the criteria have been met, a warning that refusal may harm the suspect's case at trial has been issued[314] and the suspect's consent is refused, 'such inferences from the refusal as appear proper' in determining guilt may be drawn if the suspect's refusal is 'without good cause'. The inference may bolster other evidence of identification.

Failures in disclosure of defence case, defence witnesses and alibi – CPIA 1996, s 11

10.191 The adverse inferences available as a result of defects or failures in disclosure within a defence case, a defence witness list or alibi notice are considered in Chapter 9 – Disclosure, at **9.30**.

---

313 PACE, s 62(1)(b). See **6.39**.

314 Code D6.3. See **6.48**.

Chapter 11

SUBMISSION OF NO CASE

INTRODUCTION

11.1 The jurisprudential starting point for any submission of 'no case to answer' at the close of the prosecution case is *R v Galbraith,*[1] in which the following guidelines were issued:

> 'How then should the judge approach a submission of 'no case'?
>
> (1) If there is no evidence that the crime alleged has been committed by the defendant there is no difficulty. The judge will of course stop the case.
> (2) The difficulty arises where there is some evidence but it is of a tenuous character, for example, because of inherent weakness or vagueness or because it is inconsistent with other evidence.
>   (a) Where the judge comes to the conclusion that the prosecution evidence, taken at its highest, is such that a jury properly directed could not properly convict on it, it is his duty, on a submission being made, to stop the case.
>   (b) Where however the prosecution evidence is such that its strength or weakness depends on the view to be taken of a witness's reliability, or other matters which are generally speaking within the province of the jury and where on one possible view of the facts there is evidence upon which a jury could properly come to the conclusion that the defendant is guilty, then the judge should allow the matter to be tried by the jury.'

THE *TURNBULL* GUIDELINE

11.2 The trial judge's duty to withdraw the case from the jury in an identification case is wider, and certainly more refined, than the general duty

---

1 (1981) 73 Cr App R 124, [1981] Crim LR 648, CA.

under *R v Galbraith*.[2] In *R v Turnbull*[3] 'the special need for caution' in identification cases was considered in the context of submissions of no case to answer. The following guidance was given.

> 'When, in the judgment of the trial judge, the quality of the identifying evidence is poor, as for example when it depends solely upon a fleeting glance or on a longer observation made in difficult conditions, the situation is very different. The judge should then withdraw the case from the jury and direct an acquittal unless there is other evidence which goes to support the correctness of the identification. This may be corroboration in the sense lawyers use the word; but it need not be so if its effect is to make the jury sure that there has been no mistaken identification: for example, X sees the accused snatch a woman's handbag; he gets only a fleeting glance of the thief's face as he runs off but he does see him entering a nearby house. Later he picks out the accused on an identity parade. If there was no more evidence than this, the poor quality of the identification would require the judge to withdraw the case from the jury; but this would not be so if there was evidence that the house into which the accused was alleged by X to have run was his father's … In our judgment odd coincidences can, if unexplained, be supporting evidence.'

11.3 This guidance 'acts as a special and necessary gloss on the determination of no case to answer … It is something additional to the duty of the judge as set out in the case of *R v Galbraith*'.[4] The duty of a judge to intervene arises even where no submission is made by the defence. The matter should be raised by the judge for discussion with counsel and if, after submissions, the judge remains of the opinion that no reasonable jury could safely convict, the case should be stopped. Moreover, this duty does not end at the close of the prosecution case. It continues to the conclusion of the evidence.[5]

GENERAL CONSIDERATIONS

11.4 In deciding whether the identification evidence falls beneath the required threshold, the court will have regard to those potential weaknesses which would require a jury direction: time, distance, lighting and so on. Contradictions and disparities must also be considered. The proposition that a mistaken witness may be a convincing witness should not be ignored by the judge. The test demands that the evidence is analysed objectively, not on an opinion as to the credibility of the witness based upon performance in the witness box. The jury should be prevented from 'acting upon the type of evidence which, even if believed, experience has shown to be a possible source of injustice'.[6] That was precisely the injustice visited upon the defendant in *R v Fergus*.[7] In common with many eyewitnesses, the victim of a robbery in that case 'displayed, and it is

---

2 *R v Ivan Fergus* (1994) Cr App R 313, CA. See *Daley v R* (1994) Cr App R 447, PC for a discussion of the relationship between *R v Turnbull and R v Galbraith*.

3 (1977) 63 Cr App R 132, [1977] 1 QB 224, [1976] Cr App R 565, CA.

4 *R v Sampson and Sampson* [2004] EWCA Crim 2171.

5 *R v Turnbull* (1977) 63 Cr App R 132; [1977] 1 QB 224; [1976] Cr App R 565, CA; *R v Ivan Fergus* (1994) Cr App R 313, CA; *R v Brown (Jamie)* [1998] Crim LR 196, CA.

6 *R v Daley* (1994) 98 Cr App R 447; [1994] Crim LR 931, PC.

7 (1994) Cr App R 313, CA.

plain, genuinely felt an invincible conviction in the correctness of his identification'. Seven months later the Court of Appeal declared the appellant 'wholly innocent of the offence'. The distinction is sometimes made between submissions based on the quality of identification evidence and those based on the credibility of witnesses. In the latter case it has been held that the evidence is pre-eminently a matter for the jury.[8] However, as *R v Fergus* demonstrates, credibility does not mean the witness's conviction or plausibility when giving evidence. A recognition case is not excluded from the principle in *R v Turnbull*. The degree of familiarity is a factor as relevant as the other circumstances of the observation[9], though naturally identification of a person known to the witness may be regarded as stronger than by someone unknown.[10]

11.5 If the prosecution case rests upon no more than a qualified identification the case will not be fit to go to the jury.[11] In *R v Dolive*[12] the only evidence identifying the defendant as one of two robbers was that of the victim. The circumstances were far from fleeting or in poor conditions, though there was no supporting evidence. At the identification procedure he vacillated between the defendant and another before selecting the defendant. In evidence he stated that he thought it 'more likely' that the robber was the person he had chosen but accepted it might have been the other candidate. He also accepted the possibility that he might have chosen a person he had seen in other, innocent, circumstances. In re-examination he stated that he was 'pretty confident' of his choice at the time. The Court of Appeal concluded that the terms in which he expressed himself were not capable of enabling a jury properly to convict.

11.6 Where evidence in support is relied upon, the judge may not abrogate responsibility to consider its weight. The *R v Turnbull* guideline is additional to the *R v Galbraith* test, not a substitute for it. *R v Galbraith* 'still requires a judge to consider whether the evidence is of a tenuous nature, for example because of inherent weakness or vagueness "or because it is inconsistent with other evidence"'. Accordingly 'it is wrong for a judge simply to identify a matter in support, however modest, without considering it in the context of the evidence as a whole at the end of the prosecution case.'[13] Where the case goes to the jury it is incumbent on the judge to analyse the detail of the evidence which the defendant faces and to set out the reasons for allowing the case to proceed,[14] not least so that it is properly susceptible to review on appeal.[15] Equally a ruling which results in a directed acquittal should explain the want of evidence in the event that the prosecution seek to appeal a terminating ruling.[16]

---

8 *R v McMath* [1997] Crim LR 586, CA; *R v Daley* (1994) 98 Cr App R 447; [1994] Crim LR 931, PC.
9 *R v Ley* [200] EWCA Crim 3063.
10 See for example *R v Aziz* [2008] EWCA Crim 2641.
11 *R v George* [2003] Crim LR 282, CA.
12 [2009] EWCA Crim 1144.
13 *R v Sampson and Sampson* [2004] EWCA Crim 2171.
14 *R v Shervington* [2008] EWCA Crim 658.
15 *R v Dolive* [2009] EWCA Crim 1144.
16 See for example *R v H* [2008] EWCA Crim 3284.

Visual identification

11.7 An example of the application of the 'fleeting glance' principle may be found in the Privy Council case of *Junior Reid and others v R.*[17] In the conjoined case of Errol Reece and Robert Taylor, a police officer attended identification parades and identified the appellants as participants in a gunfight six months earlier. He estimated that he had seen them for seven and four seconds respectively while lying flat on his chest trying to conceal himself from the very men he later purported to recognise. The Privy Council found that this was a 'classic case where uncorroborated identifying evidence was so poor, depending solely on fleeting glances and further made in difficult conditions, that the judge should have withdrawn the case from the jury'.

11.8 It has been said that the dicta in *R v Turnbull* was intended primarily to deal with fleeting glance cases.[18] However fleeting glances or observations in difficult conditions were cited in *R v Turnbull* as examples only of poor quality identification. The duty to withdraw a case arises where the identification evidence is either innately weak[19] or where its weakness derives from other evidence which undermines or contradicts it. Indeed inconsistency with other evidence remains a basis for a successful no case submission under *R v Galbraith. R v Fergus* (see **11.4**) was not a fleeting glance case at all. The victim of the robbery and the robber were at close quarters for some 20 minutes. Some weakness arose from the fact that it was starting to get dark and that the witness did not have very good eyesight. But of most significance was the witness's description of his assailant in which age, height, facial hair, skin colour and hairstyle were substantially different from the defendant's appearance. The Court of Appeal found that a proper analysis of the cumulative effect of the specific weaknesses in the identification ought to have brought the trial to an end with a directed acquittal.

11.9 In *R v Junior Reid*[20] the weakness in the identification was based upon its contradiction with evidence from an entirely different source. The witness to a murder purported to recognise the killer as someone she had known for 8 years, and indeed had seen daily while working at a restaurant. She named him as Junior Godfather and identified him at a parade. However her account of the incident, in which the assailant had approached a vehicle and shot the driver, was belied by the condition of the car. Most significantly, her evidence that the assailant had shot through the passenger window was irreconcilable with the medical evidence of the trajectory of the bullets entering the victim's body, indicative of a shooting from the other side of the car. In the circumstances the Privy Council held that the case should have been withdrawn from the jury.

---

17 [1990] 1 AC 363; (1990) 90 Cr App R 121, PC. See also *R v Roberts* (unreported) 3 July 1997, CA. For contrasting facts, see *Rose v R* [1995] Crim LR 939, PC.

18 *R v Beckles and Montague* [1999] Crim LR 148, CA.

19 See for example *R v Smith and Doe* (1987) 85 Cr App R 197, CA and *R v North* [2006] EWCA Crim 915.

20 [1990] 1 AC 363; (1990) 90 Cr App R 121, PC.

11.10 Common sense suggests that two or more identifications may support and strengthen one another provided they are independent of each other. In *R v Tyler and others*[21] a number of arrests were made during the course of a demonstration, resulting in a charge of riot. Two police officers gave evidence identifying Tyler as a participant who had thrown a rock at police. It was accepted that the observations were made in difficult circumstances. Had there been one identification the position might have been different. But the Court of Appeal held that two separate and independent identifications supported each other and that therefore the judge was under no duty to withdraw the case from the jury. In other circumstances identification evidence may be poor even though it is given by several witnesses.[22] A number of witnesses, as *R v Turnbull* points out, may all be mistaken. By contrast with *R v Tyler*, in *R v H*,[23] also a case of large scale public disorder, the prosecution unsuccessfully appealed a terminating ruling in which the judge decided that the identification was unfit to go to the jury. Two police officers gave evidence that the defendant arrested had been the ringleader. The judge analysed the various factors which affected the officers' visual observation and their deficiencies. He considered that there was an inherent danger that one officer's identification may have been influenced by the arrest made by the other, thus rendering it symbiotic not independent, and concluded that the identification was poor and flawed.

11.11 Where identification evidence is admitted despite a proven breach of Code D, a judge should have regard to the breach when considering the strength of a submission of no case if it potentially weakens the evidence.[24] In a fleeting glance case, other evidence which is compromised by being in breach of the Code may be incapable of providing the support necessary to establish a prima facie case.[25]

Voice identification

11.12 Voice identification is subject to the same general principles as visual identification. An example of their application is *R v Devlin*.[26] A robbery by two masked men took place in a shop. The evidence was based exclusively on that of the shopkeeper. He purported to recognise the voice of one of the robbers as a young man who had been a customer of the shop for some 8 years. The only words uttered by the robber were 'Money, money'. The shopkeeper also stated that the build and body shape of the robber, which were in no way unusual, were those of the defendant. Indeed, at a parade in which all those paraded wore masks, he identified the defendant by build. The Court of Appeal applied the guidance given in *Turnbull* and concluded 'without hesitation' that:

---

21 (1993) 96 Cr App R 332, CA.
22 *R v Weeder* (1980) 71 Cr App R 228, CA.
23 [2008] EWCA Crim 3284.
24 *R v Conway* (1990) 91 Cr App R 143, CA; *R v Hutton* [1999] Cr App R 74, CA.
25 *R v Bryne* [2004] EWCA Crim 979.
26 (Unreported) 14 March 1997, CA.

> 'Such evidence is, in our judgment, incapable of being described as being other than poor, and it is not made other than poor by the fact that when he turned round he observed that the attacker was a man of similar size and shape to the person whose voice he thought he had recognised.'

In the circumstances it was held that the judge ought to have acceded to the defence submission at trial and withdrawn the case from the jury.

11.13 Another masked man was the offender in *R v Johnson*.[27] He was responsible for committing an aggravated burglary and sexual offences. The only evidence of the defendant's culpability (other than similar fact evidence which ought not to have been admitted) was the voice identification parades of the two victims. Both positively identified the suspect's voice, though one had not been 100% sure at the time of the procedure. In the absence of any supporting evidence whatsoever the Court of Appeal volunteered an opinion as to the quality of the evidence, though it was not formally a ground of appeal. In the court's judgment:

> 'The prosecution case was, on any view, a most insubstantial one – indeed one that might well have been the subject of a submission at the close of the prosecution case.'

11.14 In *R v Roberts*[28] the defendant's guilt was almost exclusively dependant upon the victim of an attack who identified the defendant's voice in the course of a street identification. She was Polish and the defendant had an unexceptional London accent. The Court of Appeal quashed the conviction holding that the identification was not good enough to accept that the conviction was safe. Similarly the conviction in *R v O'Doherty*[29] could not be regarded as safe, based as it was on the recognition by a police officer of the defendant's voice on a poor quality recorded 16 second 999 call.

ADVERSE INFERENCE

11.15 An adverse inference under the Criminal Justice and Public Order Act (CJPOA) 1994[30] can never by itself provide the basis for a case to answer.[31] Moreover it is unlikely that identification evidence which fails to meet the required threshold could be supplemented by the drawing of an adverse inference from a failure to mention facts under CJPOA 1994, s 34. Though s 34(2)(c) contemplates the possibility by allowing the use of adverse inferences to a court 'determining whether there is a case to answer', the fact not mentioned must be one relied upon in the defendant's defence. At the close of the prosecution case no facts will have been relied upon in the defendant's

---

27 [1995] Cr App R 41, CA.
28 [2000] Crim LR 183, CA.
29 [2003] 1 Cr App R 5, [2002] Crim LR 766, NICA.
30 See **10.183–10.191** for the criteria for adverse inferences.
31 CJPOA 1994, s 38(3).

defence.[32] By contrast inferences might be drawn from the failure to account for objects, substances or marks under CJPOA 1994, s 36 or for presence at a particular place under s 37. These provisions do not impose the prerequisite of reliance upon facts in a defendant's defence. Both may be applied to the determination of a case to answer.[33] It may be assumed that possession of the object or presence at the place are themselves incriminating facts and to that extent form part of the evidence to be considered at the close of the prosecution case. The effect of an adverse inference is to add weight to those facts.

---

32 *R v Hart and Mclean* [1998] 6 *Archbold News* 1, CA.

33 CJPOA 1994, s 36(2)(c) and s 37(2)(c) respectively.

Chapter 12

JURY DIRECTIONS

INTRODUCTION

12.1 In March 2010 the Judicial Studies Board published the Crown Court Bench Book[1] to assist judges in the preparation and presentation of their jury directions. They were not at first intended to be a direct replacement for specimen directions. The purpose of the Bench Book is to identify in bullet point form necessary directions, explain their legal background and rationale

---

1 See www.judiciary.gov.uk/Resources/JCO/Documents.

and to provide practical illustrations of summings up on standard topics. They are a move away from the more formulaic specimen directions so familiar to practitioners and are intended to give the trial judge greater latitude in tailoring directions to the circumstances of the case.

12.2 The principal directions required in an identification case are the *Turnbull* directions. This chapter discusses the particular requirements imposed by that case and later authorities. It also considers directions that are commonly associated with identification, such as in alibi cases, and others which have a bearing on identification issues.

THE *TURNBULL* DIRECTION

Introduction

12.3 The nature of jury directions in visual identification cases is governed by *R v Turnbull*.[2] The case was decided following the wrongful convictions and imprisonment of two men whose cases became the subject of the Devlin report on 'Evidence of Identification in Criminal Cases'.[3] The report concluded that juries needed special instruction as to their approach to identification evidence. The rationale for such guidance is distilled in the dictum of the later and much approved Australian case of *R v Dickson*:[4]

> 'It is difficult to convey to the jury the reality of particular dangers which exist in the evidence without drawing to the attention of the jury two things which they are unlikely to know. The first is that experience in the courts over the years has shown that in a not insignificant number of cases erroneous identification evidence by apparently honest witnesses has led to wrong convictions. For this knowledge the judge draws on accumulated judicial experience … The second thing which the jury are unlikely to know is the substantial degree of risk that honest witnesses may be wrong in their evidence of identification. Jurors, who, unlike trial lawyers, have not given thought to the way in which evidence of visual identification depends on receiving, recording and recalling accurately a fairly subjective impression on the mind, are unlikely to be aware of the risk that honest and convincing witnesses may be mistaken, especially where their opportunities for observing a previously unknown offender were limited. The best way of explaining to the jury the extent of the risk is by explaining the reasons for there being the risk and that it is essential to distinguish between honesty and accuracy and not assume the latter because of belief in the former.'

12.4 The Devlin report recommended that where the evidence against a person was wholly or mainly eye-witness identification evidence, the jury should be directed that it would not be safe to convict unless the circumstances were exceptional or the identification was supported by substantial evidence of

---

2 (1976) 63 Cr App R 132, [1977] 1 QB 224, CA.

3 Report to the Secretary of State for the Home Department, 1976. The report is more fully considered at **1.7**.

4 [1983] 1 VR 227. Approved in *Reid v R* [1990] 1 AC 363, (1990) 90 Cr App R 121, PC and *R v Pattinson and Exley* [1996] 1 Cr App R 51, CA.

another sort.[5] However the Court of Appeal in *Turnbull* declined to adopt this formula because it would tend to create case law which fettered justice. Further, corroboration as a matter of law was not a requirement.[6] Nevertheless the Court issued firm advice to trial judges as to the approach to be taken in future and asserted its opinion that 'the danger of miscarriages of justice occurring can be much reduced if trial judges sum up to juries in the way indicated in this judgment'.

Turnbull guidelines

12.5 The *Turnbull* guidelines for summing up,[7] delivered by Lord Widgery, are as follows:

> 'First, whenever the case against an accused depends wholly or substantially on the correctness of one or more identifications of the accused which the defence alleges to be mistaken, the judge should warn the jury of the special need for caution before convicting the accused in reliance on the correctness of the identification or identifications. In addition he should instruct them as to the reason for the need for such a warning and should make some reference to the possibility that a mistaken witness can be a convincing one and that a number of such witnesses can all be mistaken. Provided this is done in clear terms the judge need not use any particular form of words.
>
> Secondly, the judge should direct the jury to examine closely the circumstances in which the identification by each witness came to be made. How long did the witness have the accused under observation? At what distance? In what light? Was the observation impeded in any way, as for example by passing traffic or a press of people? Had the witness ever seen the accused before? How often? If only occasionally, had he any special reason for remembering the accused? How long elapsed between the original observation and the subsequent identification to the police? Was there any material discrepancy between the description of the accused given to the police by the witness when first seen by them and his actual appearance? [The requirement for disclosure of first description.[8]] Finally, he should remind the jury of any specific weaknesses which had appeared in the identification evidence.'

Recognition may be more reliable than identification of a stranger; but even when the witness is purporting to recognise someone whom he knows, the jury should be reminded that mistakes in recognition of close relatives and friends are sometimes made.

12.6 After giving guidance on the withdrawal of the case from the jury and providing examples of what might amount to supporting evidence, the judgment continued:

---

5 Devlin Report, paras 4.55 and 8.4(a).

6 *Scott v R* [1989] AC 1242, (1989) 89 Cr App R 153, PC. It was stated that to require corroboration as a matter of law tilted the balance too far against the prosecution.

7 (1976) 63 Cr App R 132, at 137.

8 See **5.5** on the duty to take a first description from a witness, **5.31** on disclosure before a procedure and **9.7** on the prosecution duty of disclosure.

> 'The trial judge should identify to the jury the evidence which he adjudges is capable of supporting the identification. If there is any evidence or circumstances which the jury might think was supporting when it did not have this quality, the judge should say so.'

12.7 The *Turnbull* guidelines on summing up can be summarised as follows:

The general requirements

(i) the special need for caution;

(ii) the reason for the special need for caution: previous miscarriages of justice;

(iii) the possibility of a mistaken [and honest] witness being a convincing witness and that a number of witnesses can be mistaken;

(iv) the possibility of mistaken recognition, even of a close friend or relative (where applicable).

The specific requirements

(v) scrutiny of circumstances of the identification;

(vi) the weaknesses of the identification;

(vii) the evidence capable of supporting identification and the evidence not capable of supporting identification.

12.8 If a summing up adopts the guidelines issued by the Judicial Studies Board,[9] whether the specimen direction or its successor the Bench Book, it is likely to be unassailable in most cases. However, in the context of a *Turnbull* direction, it is the substance of the direction rather than its form that matters. In *R v Keane*[10] it was held that:

> 'It would be wrong to interpret or apply *Turnbull* inflexibly. It imposes no rigid pattern, establishes no catechism, which a judge in his summing up must answer if a verdict is to stand. But it does formulate a basic principle and sound practice. The principle is the special need for caution when the issue turns on evidence of visual identification: the practice has to be a careful summing up, which not only contains a warning but exposes to the jury the weaknesses and dangers of identification evidence both in general and in the circumstances of the particular case.'

12.9 While a judge must have sufficient latitude to express the *Turnbull* direction according to the facts of the case, as will be seen, care must be taken

---

9 See note 1.

10 (1977) 65 Cr App R 247, CA.

to ensure that the use of an alternative formula adequately explains the potential dangers in identification evidence. In *R v Pattinson and Exley*[11] the Court of Appeal agreed that *Turnbull* 'should not be read as though it were a statute, nor recited verbatim as though a mantra'. But the Court went on to insist that the trial judge:

> '... must ensure that the fundamental requirements laid down by *Turnbull* are met – and they will not be met simply by paying lip service to that judgment. This Court will look to see that the message of *Turnbull* has been made clear to the jury.'

12.10 The importance of imparting that message could not have been made clearer than in *Turnbull* itself which warned that a 'failure to follow these guidelines is likely to result in a conviction being quashed'. The infinite variety of circumstances thrown up by criminal trials will demand directions tailored to the facts of the case and, as is plain from many of the authorities discussed below, the standard direction may require modification to meet the needs of a particular scenario. The problem of imposing 'too rigid rules' was pointed out in *R v Bentley*[12] where it was said that:

> '... it is almost as important to avoid giving unnecessary or irrelevant advice as it is to give appropriate warning and directions, because if the judge gives irrelevant and inappropriate directions, the jury tend to 'switch off' and they do not pay attention to the parts of the direction which are important.'

12.11 Taken to extreme, a misconceived *Turnbull* direction may so distort the real issue in the case that a guilty verdict is rendered unsafe. In *R v Panesar*[13] it was the defence case that police officers had falsely colluded to implicate the defendant in the possession of a loaded firearm which had been found near the scene of a chase that had ended with his arrest. The judge wrongly treated the case as one of identification. The *Turnbull* direction and repeated emphasis on the issue of identification were inappropriate and misleading, giving rise to the real danger that the jury were distracted from considering the central issue of credibility, on which there was an absence of any significant direction. Though *Turnbull* was intended to minimise the risk of wrongful conviction, in *R v Birchwood*[14] a direction was applied to a defence witness who claimed to have seen the deceased after her alleged murder had taken place. It was held that the judge was entitled to restate the difficulties inherent in visual identification and point out weaknesses. The complaint on appeal that direction reversed the burden of proof was rejected.

12.12 In all cases in which a *Turnbull* direction may be required a discussion between counsel and the judge should take place in order to clarify the evidence

---

11 [1996] 1 Cr App R 51, CA.

12 (1994) 99 Cr App R 342, [1991] Crim LR 620, CA.

13 [2007] EWCA Crim 2510.

14 [2011] EWCA Crim 431.

which supports and undermines the identification of the defendant.[15] Such a discussion will ensure that the judge is alive to the relevant aspects of the evidence which he might be expected to draw to the jury's attention.

The general requirements

12.13 These general requirements are 'fundamental'.[16] A failure to give the general warning is likely to be fatal to the safety of a conviction.[17] In two of the appeals considered in *Reid and others v R*[18] the general warning was not given. It was held that only in the most exceptional circumstances could a conviction based upon uncorroborated identification evidence be sustained in the absence of the warning. Care must also be taken to give the general warning due emphasis. In *R v Keane*[19] the *Turnbull* direction was flawed because it was 'overlaid, and its effect weakened, by [the judge's] other comments'. *In R v Shervington*[20] the addition of a gloss to the standard direction by the suggestion that it should not allow an oversophisticated approach to identification evidence to become a mugger's charter was regarded as unwise.

12.14 A partial general direction is likely to be insufficient. In *R v Bentley*[21] the judge neglected to warn the jury either of the special need for caution, the reasons for it and that a mistaken witness may be a convincing witness. They were held to be material misdirections. In *R v Phillips*[22] the appellant's conviction was quashed after the judge had failed sufficiently to draw to the jury's attention the dangers of identification evidence in a case of purported recognition.

12.15 In *Farquharson v R*[23] the trial judge had stressed the crucial importance of the identification evidence and dealt fully with the circumstances of the different identifications including the opportunity for reliability. However this failed to remedy the omission of the general warning as to the special need for

---

15 *R v Stanton* [2004] EWCA Crim 490; *R v Delaney* [2004] EWCA Crim 3465; *R v Haynes* [2004] EWCA Crim 390.

16 *R v Pattinson and Exley* [1996] 1 Cr App R 51, CA.

17 *Rv Turnbull; R v Bentley* (1994) 99 Cr App R 342, [1991] Crim LR 620, CA; *Beckford v R* (1993) 97 Cr App R 409, [1993] Crim LR 944, PC; *Scott v R* (1989) 89 Cr App R 153, PC; *Pop v R* [2003] UKPC 40; *R v Johnson* [2001] 1 Cr App R 405, CA. Contrast *Freemantle v R* [1995] Cr App R 1, [1994] Crim LR 930, PC.

18 [1990] 1 AC 363, (1990) 90 Cr App R 121, PC. The appeals were those of Roy Dennis and Oliver Whylie.

19 (1977) 65 Cr App R 247, CA. See also the misdirection in *R v Preddie* [2011] EWCA Crim 312 in which parts of the *Turnbull* direction merely reflected a defence submission. The direction 'ought to be given with the imprimatur of the court and it ought to be made clear that that is a direction of law from the judge to the jury'.

20 [2008] EWCA Crim 658.

21 (1994) 99 Cr App R 342, [1991] Crim LR 620, CA.

22 [2007] EWCA Crim 1042.

23 (1994) Cr App R 398, PC.

caution. The direction in *Pattinson and Exley*[24] informed the jury that 'questions of identification give considerable concern to the courts, for obvious reasons … because undoubtedly however honest a person is, however truthful they may be, however genuine they may be, mistakes can and do happen with identification'. It was held to have 'failed adequately to deal either with the court's experience of the risk of miscarriages of justice or how convincing a mistaken witness can be'. Moreover the direction failed to point out that there had been miscarriages in cases where two or more witnesses had made positive identifications.

12.16 Similar criticism was levelled at the summing up in *R v Sutton and Kelly*[25] which omitted the special need for caution, the reason for it and that an honest witness may be mistaken. Likewise the directions in *R v McNally and Knox*[26] failed to bring home sufficiently to the jury the danger of an honest witness being mistaken or that honest and convincing witnesses have, in the courts' experience, been wrong and as a result people have been wrongly convicted. The 'jump in reasoning from honesty to accuracy is not permitted'.[27] These cases contrast with *Mills v R*[28] in which the trial judge omitted to state that a mistaken witness may be convincing or that a number of convincing witnesses may be mistaken. Neither did he direct the jury that a witness who identifies by recognition may be mistaken, though this was held to have been implied.[29] Notwithstanding the departures from the *Turnbull* requirements, the grounds of appeal were regarded as unmeritorious. It is submitted that *Mills v R* stands very much alone. Though, on the facts the conviction may not have been unsafe, these directions lie at the very heart of the guidance required to expose the dangers of a jury's unquestioned reliance upon visual identification.

12.17 The omission of a direction concerning the court's experience of wrongful convictions in the past was considered in *R v Nash*.[30] Following *R v Pattinson and Exley* (above) it was held that the JSB specimen was the briefest permissible summary of the dangers inherent in identification. In quashing the conviction the Court of Appeal stated:

> 'Of course, exact words do not matter, but the trial judge must ensure that the full force of the *Turnbull* direction is conveyed to the jury in whatever words are chosen. The direction given by the learned Recorder in this case does not do that,

---

24 [1996] 1 Cr App R 51, CA. See also *R v Wharton* [1998] Crim LR 668, CA, in which the omission of the miscarriages part of the direction was a misdirection; *R v Elliot* (unreported) 22 December 1997, CA.

25 (Unreported) 12 November 2002, CA.

26 (Unreported) 31 March 1999, CA.

27 *R v Fergus* (1994) 98 Cr App R 313, CA.

28 [1995] 1 WLR 511, [1995] Crim LR 884, PC. See also *Rose v R* [1995] Crim LR 939, PC.

29 In *Brown and Isaac v R,* (unreported) 29 January 2003, PC, the absence of a direction about mistaken recognition was dismissed as of no consequence because the warning about mistaken identification could only have applied to witnesses who purported to recognise the defendants.

30 [2004] EWCA Crim 2696, [2005] Crim LR 232. See also *R v Greenaway* [2006] EWCA Crim 1346 where the reference to previous miscarriages of justice was omitted. Though a defect, it was held the direction as a whole succeeded in bringing home to the jury the dangers inherent in identification evidence.

> because he does not make it clear that the special need for caution is rooted in the court's actual experience of miscarriages of justice. To that extent the jury were not exposed to the full impact of the *Turnbull* direction in a case where identification was the central issue.'

12.18 In the light of these authorities it is notable and perhaps surprising that the *Turnbull* requirements suggested by the Crown Court Bench Book abandon any reference to previous miscarriages of justice. The reason for the special need for caution is conflated with the court's past experience of an impressive and convinced witness being mistaken. The former JSB specimen direction in which the jury were warned of 'the risk of injustice ... such as has happened in some cases in the past', has not been adopted. It is arguable that the Bench Book guidance diminishes the impact of the direction, not least because the jury may not appreciate that some mistakes made by witnesses, of which the court had experience, had not been exposed at trial but discovered some time after conviction.

The specific requirements

12.19 Even in pre-*Turnbull* days it was recognised that a fair summing up should deal with the circumstances in which the identification was made and the weaknesses in it.[31] The weaknesses are those both in the original observation and in the identification itself.[32] The circumstances referred to in *Turnbull*, common to many cases are:

(i) Original observation:

- length of time;
- distance;
- light;
- impediment or obstruction to observation;
- suspect unknown to the witness or recognition;
- if recognition, degree of familiarity.

(ii) Identification:

- time lapse between observation and identification;
- comparison of witness's first description and suspect's appearance.

12.20 There are naturally an infinite variety of potentially relevant features and sources of weakness. Those apposite to the facts of a particular case should be included in the summing up. The weaknesses which need to be addressed as part of the *Turnbull* direction are those relative to the

---

31 *R v Long* (1973) 57 Cr App R 871; [1973] Crim LR 577, CA.
32 *R v Stanton* [2004] EWCA Crim 490.

identification evidence, not weaknesses concerning other aspects of the case.[33] The requirement to scrutinise the circumstances of the identification evidence might, of necessity, include the points of strength as well as weakness.[34] But the failure to expose the weaknesses may result in the quashing of a conviction as happened in *R v Keane*[35] where the judge had sought to 'soften their impact'. A recital of the relevant parts of the evidence without identifying them as weaknesses will not suffice. The jury's attention must be drawn to them as weaknesses.[36] A direction simply to consider the witness's powers of observation and reliability will be an insufficient substitute for references to the specific weaknesses.[37] Neither will it suffice to make a passing reference to the weaknesses identified by counsel in a closing speech. In *R v Fergus*[38] a street identification took place when it was starting to get dark. The witness, who did not have very good eyesight, had purported to describe the assailant's age, height, facial hair, skin colour and hairstyle which in fact substantially differed from the defendant's appearance. The judge went no further than to ask the jury to consider whether there were any material discrepancies, saying that they were important when considering weaknesses in the identification. The Court of Appeal was unimpressed:

> 'It is not good enough for a trial judge simply to refer the jury to counsel's submissions about specific weaknesses in the identification. Under *Turnbull*, he must fairly and properly summarise for the jury such specific weaknesses as arguably are exposed by the evidence. The judge never came near to doing so.'

12.21 As a result of the inadequate summing up in that case the jury were not invited to grapple with the problem created by the witness's confident identification on the one hand and the list of specific weaknesses on the other. What is required is an authoritative summary from the judge's position of neutrality. A mere reminder that a point was taken by counsel was found to be inadequate in *R v Ryan*.[39] The reason was that a reminder may appear to be little more than an acknowledgment of 'a point counsel wanted to make as opposed to a real potential weakness that the jury had to concentrate on'. The same concern was voiced by the Court of Appeal in *R v Elliot*[40] in which the expedient of referring to weaknesses in terms of arguments raised by counsel

---

33 *R v Docherty* [2006] EWCA Crim 1759. Exactly where the dividing line falls may be difficult to determine. May, for example, a failure of one witness to identify weaken the identification of another?

34 *R v Mussell and Dalton* [1995] Crim LR 887, CA; *R v Pattinson and Exley* [1996] 1 Cr App R 55, CA. See also *R v Yates* [2003] EWCA Crim 629, [2003] JCL 385.

35 (1977) 65 Cr App R 247, CA followed and applied in *R v Haynes* [2004] EWCA Crim 390. Other examples may be found in *R v Harper* [2005] EWCA Crim 2142; *R v Whyman and Garbutt* [2006] EWCA Crim 3656; *R v Irvin* [2007] EWCA Crim 2701; *R v Hughes* [2007] EWCA Crim 2938 and *R v Williams* [2010] EWCA Crim 2226.

36 *R v Ryan* (unreported) 24 November 2000, CA.

37 *R v Thornton* [1995] 1 Cr App R 578, CA.

38 (1994) 98 Cr App R 313, CA. In *R v Graham* [1994] Crim LR 414, CA the judge was found to have paid lip service to *Turnbull*, making no reference to the poor lighting conditions for the observation.

39 (Unreported) 24 November 2000, CA.

40 [1998] 1 *Archbold News* 2, CA.

left 'the jury with the impression that they are no more than that, as opposed to constituting matters which the judge considers the jury should weigh carefully in the course of their task'.

12.22 The Court of Appeal has considered a wide variety of approaches to the scheme of summing up identification weaknesses: as part of the *Turnbull* direction or in the summary of evidence; whether as a composite summary of weaknesses or witness by witness. What emerges is that the latitude a judge enjoys in tailoring the summing up to the type of case is subject to the overriding imperative of ensuring that the weaknesses are exposed in a coherent and meaningful manner with due emphasis.

12.23 In *R v Perry*[41] it was contended that the weaknesses should have been dealt with when giving the *Turnbull* direction. It was held that it was open to the judge, and in many cases more helpful to the jury, to conduct the exercise as part of the summary of each witness's evidence. This was an echo of *R v Mussell and Dalton*[42] in which the trial judge identified the weaknesses as he went through the evidence. The Court of Appeal held that though he might have conveniently marshalled them in one place, *R v Fergus* (see **12.20**) did not impose a mandatory requirement that they should have been included in an overall summary of weaknesses. In a lengthy summing up it was said that it might be more helpful to make the points when reviewing the evidence, witness by witness. In *R v Nyanateh*,[43] the case was based exclusively in the identification evidence of one witness who purported to observe the defendant almost continuously from the scene of a burglary to arrest. The Court of Appeal rejected the criticism that any potential weaknesses should have been drawn to the jury's attention as part of the *Turnbull* direction rather than, as was the case, while rehearsing the witness's cross examination.

12.24 By contrast the Court of Appeal in *R v Langley*[44] interpreted *R v Fergus* as requiring the weaknesses in the identification to be brought to the jury's attention in one place. In *R v Pattinson and Exley*[45] the judge recounted the evidence of each witness in turn. The Court of Appeal followed the reasoning in *R v Mussell and Dalton*. However in the circumstances of the case – nine identification witnesses were called by the prosecution – the Court went on to find that 'the summing up might have been better focused on the question of identification had all the evidence as to identification been dealt with as a discrete part of the evidence'. The effect of not doing so was that the jury would have 'had difficulty in disentangling identification evidence from the overall summary and in separately evaluating the quality of the opportunity of observation that witnesses had and the specific weaknesses as they emerged in

---

41 (Unreported) 6 November 1998, CA.

42 [1995] Crim LR 887, CA. See also *R v Perry, Tennant and Bridges* (unreported) 6 November 1998, CA.

43 [2005] EWCA Crim 686, [2005] Crim LR 651.

44 (Unreported) 21 January 2000, CA.

45 [1996] 1 Cr App R 51, CA followed in *R v Murrell* (unreported) 10 March 1998, CA. See also *R v Barnes* [1995] 2 Cr App R 491, CA. Both followed in *R v Qadir* [1998] Crim LR 828, CA.

evidence.' Consequently it was held that the summing up did not sufficiently expose to the jury the weaknesses of the identification evidence.

12.25 The summing up in *R v Elliot*[46] was subjected to similar criticism. It was held that:

> '… where issues of identification arise, which depend so often on an accumulation of detailed points, it is usually a desirable approach for the judge, at some stage, to put before the jury a coherent list of the points for the defence. If the exercise is conducted solely on the basis that individual points to be made will be dealt with in the course of recounting the evidence, it is perilously easy for the individual points to be overlooked.'

12.26 Likewise in *R v Ryan*[47] the summing up was defective because the judge had 'left it to the jury at each point to identify any weaknesses and to put them together. They were not put together in a coherent way at any point'. The mischief of that approach was that it 'may be the cumulative force of weaknesses which strikes most powerfully at the reliability of an identification'. In *R v Hughes*[48] the Court stated that where significant weaknesses may go to the heart of the matter they should be dealt with as part of the *Turnbull* direction. So too in *R v Sampson and Sampson*[49] it was held that the judge ought to have referred to specific weaknesses as part of the Turnbull direction. The Court stated that:

> 'It is no answer to [the judge's] failure to do so to observe that most, if not all, of them are recounted as items of evidence at a later stage in the summing-up. The whole point of the requirement of *Turnbull* that the judge identifies areas of specific weakness is that, by doing so, he gives judicial endorsement to the points no doubt made earlier by counsel and draws them together so that they can be considered as a totality of weaknesses or discrepancies, rather than being spread throughout the summing up in a way which may dissipate their combined force. That simply was not done in this case.'

12.27 A *Turnbull* direction requires guidance as to the evidence capable of supporting the identification evidence to be given. The supportive evidence may come from any manner of other sources including false alibis, lies, bad character, possession of an incriminating article, an admission or an adverse inference. The identification by one witness may support that of another[50] even if both are poor, provided of course that the warning that any number of witnesses can be mistaken is given. Formerly the Judicial Studies Board specimen direction contained no reference to evidence capable of supporting an identification and the Court of Appeal in *R v Sawoniuk*[51] indicated its

---

46 [1998] 1 *Archbold News* 2, CA.

47 (Unreported) 24 November 2000, CA.

48 [2007] EWCA Crim 2938.

49 [2004} EWCA Crim LR 2171. See also *R v Trower* [2004] EWCA Crim 1533.

50 *R v Weeder* (1980) 71 Cr App R 228, CA, *R v Breslin* (1984) 80 Cr App R 226, CA; *R v Tyler and others* (1993) 96 Cr App R 332, CA.

51 [2000] 2 Cr App R 220, CA.

experience that many *Turnbull* directions do not contain this feature. This lacuna has been remedied in the Judicial Studies Board Crown Court Bench Book. Where evidence capable of supporting an identification is specified, it must be made clear to the jury that it is a matter for them whether it does or does not do so.[52]

12.28 Where a street identification or an identification by photograph has occurred it is often argued that a subsequent video or other identification procedure in which the suspect is again selected is merely a repetition of the earlier identification, whether accurate or mistaken. *R v Forbes*[53] acknowledged this when holding that while the later identification may strengthen the first, it may also be appropriate 'to alert the jury to the possible risk that the eye-witness may have identified not the culprit who committed the crime but the suspect identified by the same witness on the earlier occasion'.

12.29 In *R v Ley*[54] it was argued that, but for the supporting evidence, the judge would have withdrawn the case from the jury at the close of the prosecution case. Accordingly it was submitted that the jury ought to have been directed that if they rejected that additional evidence they could not convict on the identification evidence alone. The Court of Appeal held that there was no such general rule of principle although there may be cases where, in the light of the evidence at the conclusion of the trial, the jury should be directed not to convict on the evidence of an identifying witness alone.

12.30 Of equal or greater importance is the *Turnbull* requirement of a warning about evidence not capable of providing support for an identification in situations where its probative effect might be misconstrued by a jury.[55] An example is evidence on one count which, in a multi-count indictment, cannot constitute support for identification evidence on another count.[56]

APPLICATION OF *TURNBULL*

12.31 In *R v Oakwell*[57] the Court of Appeal suggested that '*Turnbull* is intended primarily to deal with the ghastly risk run in cases of fleeting encounters'. This dictum has occasionally been cited as authority for the proposition that only in such cases is an appropriate warning necessary. That is a misconception. *Turnbull* uses the phrase 'fleeting glance' in the context of a case which ought to be withdrawn from the jury and not in relation to the

---

[52] *R v Akaidere* [1990] Crim LR 808, CA.

[53] [2001] 1 Cr App R 430, HL.

[54] [2007] 1 Cr App R 25, [2006] EWCA Crim 3063.

[55] See *R v Jamel* [1993] Crim LR 52, CA for a case in which the judge wrongly indicated evidence could be supportive.

[56] *R v Musquera* [1999] Crim LR 857, CA; *R v Dye* [2003] EWCA Crim 2424; (2003) SJLB 1088; *R v Wharton* [1998] Crim LR 668, CA.

[57] (1978) 66 Cr App R 174; [1978] Crim LR 168, CA. The case was one in which presence was admitted but participation denied: see **12.49**.

requirements of a summing up. In *R v Yates*[58] the judge, in his preamble to a *Turnbull* direction, indicated that it was meant to apply to fleeting glance identifications of total strangers. The Court of Appeal stated that 'it is perfectly clear that the direction specified by this Court in *Turnbull* applies to identification cases generally and not just to fleeting glance cases'.

12.32 The *Turnbull* guidance requires judges to administer the direction when the case against an accused 'depends wholly or substantially' on the correctness of identification evidence. However this quantitative threshold has not been construed literally; rather, it is common practice where there is any disputed visual identification evidence which forms a part of the prosecution case that a *Turnbull* warning is given, though possibly subject to appropriate modification. Thus in *R v Oakwell,*[59] even a 'minor identification problem' where there existed the possibility of mistake merited a passage in the summing up concerning the problems of identification evidence. Determining whether to give a warning according to relative weight of the identification evidence is arguably both wrong in principle and unworkable in practice. An identification is just as vulnerable to mistake whether it forms a substantial or modest part of the case, though if buttressed by a substantial body of other evidence it may more readily be accepted by a jury. Moreover the quantitative test would amount to a prediction of the relative impact of different sources of evidence on a jury. It is submitted that even where it appears that identification evidence forms an insubstantial part of the prosecution case, a *Turnbull* direction is not wasted and a decision not to give one would be regarded as imprudent.[60]

12.33 In *R v Collins and Keep,*[61] a police officer saw a man from a distance of some 50–75 yards for about five seconds near the scene of a kidnap. He thought the man was one of the defendants who he had known for 20 years. He said it looked like him but was not 100% sure. The trial judge directed the jury that this evidence did not amount to an identification and therefore declined to give a *Turnbull* direction. However he went on to suggest that the presence of a person resembling the defendant near the scene might support other evidence of his participation. The Court of Appeal found that the evidence was of identification and that the direction was necessary.

12.34 A street identification which has taken place principally on the basis of the clothing worn by the suspect is no less susceptible to the possibility of error and a *Turnbull* direction is required.[62] But if identification of a person occurs by a process of elimination of other people or suspects, there would generally

---

58 [2003] EWCA Crim 629, [2003] 67 JCL 385. See also *R v Bradley* [2004] EWCA Crim 1481.

59 (1978) 66 Cr App R 174; [1978] Crim LR 168, CA.

60 *R v Andrews* [1993] Crim LR 591, CA.

61 [2004] EWCA Crim 83.

62 *R v Haynes* [2004] EWCA Crim 390.

be no need for a *Turnbull* direction.[63] There are, however, a number of variant situations in which the question whether a *Turnbull* direction is necessary call for further consideration.

1 Recognition cases

2 Mistake and fabrication

3 Identification and participation

4 Identification of associate

5 Description

6 Sketches, photofits and e-fits

7 Identification from photographs and video recordings

8 Reliability of identification by police officers

9 Conviction of accomplice: transferred reliability of identification

10 Identification of clothing and other objects.[64]

Recognition cases

12.35 Though recognition is regarded as more reliable than identification of a stranger, a warning was considered necessary in *Turnbull* because 'mistakes in recognition of close relatives and friends are sometimes made'. This was amplified by Lane LCJ in *R v Bentley*:[65]

> 'Each of us, and no doubt everyone sitting in this Court, has had the experience of seeing someone in the street whom we know, only to discover later that it was not that person at all. The expression 'I could have sworn it was you' indicates the sort of warning which the judge should give, because that is exactly what the witness does. He swears that it was the person he thinks it was. He may nevertheless have been mistaken even where it is a case of recognition rather than one of identification.'

12.36 In recognition cases a further variable factor beyond those identified in *Turnbull* is introduced: the degree of acquaintance between the witness and person identified. This may be important in formulating the direction. An observation of someone extremely well-known to the witness but in difficult

63 *R v Kooistra* [2003] EWCA Crim 3686 and *R v Byron* (unreported) 12 February 1999, CA considered at **12.56**. But where the identification of the others is challenged, see *R v Bath* [1990] Crim L R 716, CA considered at **12.54**.

64 For example cars.

65 (1994) 99 Cr App R 342, [1991] Crim LR 620, CA.

conditions will need different guidance from that of an observation in perfect conditions but of someone that the witness had not seen for many years.

12.37 The recognition, for which a *Turnbull* direction is required, does not necessarily connote any significant degree of familiarity. It might be no more than the visual association of the person observed with another place, person or event (either before or even after the offence) by which the person observed may be identified. In *R v Wait*[66] the victim of an attack purported to recognise his attackers as young people he had seen in the area both before and on two occasions since the attack. Though 'not a classic recognition case' it was held that the warning ought to have been given. Recognition based upon body shape will require an appropriate direction.[67]

12.38 In *R v Bentley*[68] the victim of a 'glassing' in a club had known the defendant for a considerable time. He claimed that he had seen a blur like the defendant's arm rushing towards his face. The defendant admitted presence in the premises earlier but denied presence at the time of the offence. The appeal was allowed because the judge had failed to give a *Turnbull* direction. Others present might conceivably have been confused with the perpetrator and the jury should therefore have been alerted to 'the possibility of the honest mistake and to the dangers of identification evidence, and the reasons for those dangers'. In *R v Bowden*[69] a police officer who knew the defendant stated that he had observed him in the commission of a robbery and wounding. The jury were given no warning as to the special need for caution, the reasons for it or the fact that recognition, though more reliable, was also vulnerable to error. The lack of warning was a material misdirection resulting in the quashing of the conviction.

12.39 The need for a *Turnbull* direction in recognition cases was re-iterated by the Privy Council in *Pop v R*.[70] The witness to a murder purported to recognise the defendant, having known him by sight for some ten years. The trial judge pointed out the possibility of mistaken recognition. But he failed to direct the jury that a mistaken witness may be convincing; neither did he draw their attention to the circumstances of the observation and the weaknesses exposed by the differing accounts. The conviction was held to be unsustainable.

12.40 Even where the relationship between the witness and defendant is close and the opportunity of the former to observe the latter appears to preclude any mistake, a *Turnbull* direction should normally be given if the defence asserts that the identification was mistaken. Recognition cases in which the *Turnbull*

---

66 [1998] Crim LR 68, CA. See also *R v Thomas* [1994] Crim LR 128, CA.
67 *R v Phillips* [2007] EWCA Crim 1042.
68 (1994) 99 Cr App R 342, [1991] Crim LR 620, CA.
69 [1993] Crim LR 379, CA.
70 [2003] UKPC 40, (2003) 174 SJ 692.

warning 'can be entirely dispensed with must be wholly exceptional'.[71] That proposition applies also to some cases where the defence is one of fabricated identification (see below).

Mistake and fabrication

12.41 Cases in which defendants assert that their identification has been fabricated present a particular difficulty in the context of *Turnbull.* Usually there will be identification by way of recognition, where the central issue will be the truthfulness of the witness rather than the possibility of mistake; and on the face of it *Turnbull* is limited to cases of mistake. However a series of Privy Council cases has emphasised the need for a *Turnbull* direction, tailored to meet the circumstances of the case, where mistaken identification is not the line of defence taken at trial but is nevertheless a possibility even if an unlikely one.

12.42 The sole witness to a murder in *Beckford v R*[72] stated that the three defendants were well-known to him and that his observation was prolonged and in good conditions. In their Lordships' opinion:

> 'The need to give the general warning even in recognition cases where the main challenge is to the truthfulness of the witness should be obvious. The first question for the jury is whether the witness is honest. If the answer to that question is yes, the next question is the same as that which must be asked concerning every honest witness who purports to make an identification, namely, is he right or could he be mistaken.'

12.43 *Beckford v R* was followed in *Shand v R*[73] in which two witnesses independently identified the defendant as the person responsible for a murder. Though both were accused of deliberately lying, the *Turnbull* warning should have been given.

> 'The cases in which the warning can be entirely dispensed with must be wholly exceptional, even where credibility is the sole line of defence. In the latter type of case the judge should normally, and even in the exceptional case would be wise to, tell the jury in an appropriate form whether they are satisfied that the witness was not mistaken in view of the danger of mistake referred to in *Turnbull*.'

12.44 An example of the exceptional case in which a *Turnbull* direction would be redundant was given in *Beckford v R*:

> 'Of course no rule is absolutely universal. If, for example, the witness's identification evidence is that the accused was his workmate whom he has known for 20 years and that he was conversing with him for half an hour face to face in

---

71 *Shand v R* [1996] 2 Cr App R 204, PC. See also *Beckford v R* (1993) Cr App R 409, [1993] Crim LR 94, PC.

72 (1993) Cr App R 409, [1993] Crim LR 944, PC. See also *Freemantle v R* [1995] 1 Cr App R 1, [1994] Crim LR 930, PC; *Farquharson v R* (1994) 98 Cr App R 398, [1994] Crim LR 930, PC.

73 [1996] 2 Cr App R 204, PC. See also *R v Delaney and others* [2004] EWCA Crim 3465.

the same room and the witness is sane and sober, then if credibility is the issue, it will be the only issue. But cases like that will constitute a very rare exception to a strong general rule.'

12.45 In *R v Capron*[74] two witnesses identified the defendant as the person who shot and killed the deceased. The first had grown up with him and known him for 8 or 9 years, seeing him almost every day; the other had known him for 16 years and latterly would see him about three times a month. There was no dispute that the witnesses knew the defendant. His case was that they were lying in their identification. It was held to be unnecessary to give a full *Turnbull* direction. The direction given, that even if the jury rejected the defence of fabrication they had to be sure that the witnesses were not mistaken, was adequate. The complainant in *R v Giga*[75] was the subject of harassment and threats to kill in a sequence of events over a period of days. He claimed to have observed the defendant on several occasions and to have recognised him as the same person on each. It was contended by the defendant that the complainant was deliberately implicating a man he knew to be innocent. The Court of Appeal reviewed several of the authorities in point and noted that, unlike the present case, they were mostly concerned with a single observation. It was held that though it would have been preferable if a qualified *Turnbull* direction had been given, the failure to do so could not be characterised as misdirection.

12.46 Whether there is any real room for mistaken identification will often depend upon a combination of factors such as the relationship between the parties, the circumstances of the observation and whether presence is admitted. A factor which may militate against the need for a *Turnbull* direction is the extent to which the assertion of a fabricated identification is supported by a reason for doing so. In *R v Cape and others*[76] the defendants were convicted of grievous bodily harm with intent and violent disorder, largely upon the evidence of a publican in whose premises the offences had been committed. It was held, in respect of two of the appellants, that no *Turnbull* warning was appropriate. The issue had not been one of identification but whether, as the defence asserted, the publican was lying to avenge a loss he had sustained over a deal concerning stolen cigarettes.

12.47 Similarly in *R v Courtnell*[77] the defence to a charge of robbery of a publican was one of fabrication, not only as to identification but, apparently, as to the incident itself. The defence called evidence that suggested that the publican had previously talked of faking a robbery and another witness who asserted that on the morning following the alleged robbery he had pocketed some cash. In the circumstances it was held that no issue of mistaken identification arose.

74 [2006] UKPC 34. See also *R v Jastrzebski* [2008] EWCA Crim 1330 where the central issue was whether the complainant was telling the truth. Accordingly a very limited *Turnbull* direction sufficed.

75 [2007] Crim L R 571, [2007] EWCA Crim 345.

76 [1996] Cr App R 191, CA.

77 [1990] Crim LR 115, CA.

Identification and participation

12.48 It is commonplace, usually in an offence of violence, for a defendant to accept presence at the scene of the offence while denying being the perpetrator or a participant. Whether a *Turnbull* direction or a full *Turnbull* direction should be given will depend upon the circumstances of the case and in particular the extent to which a mistake might realistically have been made. Similar considerations arise in the analogous context of deciding if an issue is one of identification or participation for the purposes of whether an identification procedure under Code D is required.[78]

12.49 In *R v Oakwell*[79] a police officer intervened in a scene of group violence and was knocked to the ground. He purported to identify the defendant, who was next to him when he got to his feet, as his assailant. It was argued that a full warning ought to have been given since the officer may have confused the person who assaulted him with the person standing next to him as he rose. The Court of Appeal disagreed, holding that it was sufficient for the judge to have indicated that it was possible that a mistake might have been made. By contrast in *R v Andrews*[80] the defendant was alleged to have been one of three people participating in an affray. The evidence showed his presence and an association with the other two offenders, one of whom was his brother, but he denied participation. It was held that a *Turnbull* direction should have been given.[81]

12.50 *R v Thornton*[82] concerned a disturbance at a wedding reception in which the victim was assaulted by a group of people. The defendant was said to be a participant. He was described and then picked out at an identification parade by two witnesses. He did not dispute his presence at the material time but maintained that he was an observer who had in fact shouted at an attacker to stop and then intervened to help the victim to his feet. The Court of Appeal held that a full *Turnbull* direction should have been given because there were many other people present who were similarly dressed and therefore a mistake was 'clearly possible'. *R v Thornton* was distinguished in *R v Slater*[83] because in the latter case 'there was no basis for mistake'. The victim of an assault in a nightclub had suffered a broken jaw caused by a punch. The defendant admitted his presence and that an incident had taken place but denied that he was responsible for the blow. Evidence of his culpability lay in his 'wholly unusual size' which matched the identification evidence. There being no suggestion that there was anyone else remotely similar in height or build present, the Court of Appeal held that the case was not one of identification but of what the defendant had done. 'The possibility of mistake is a necessary prerequisite for an identification issue to arise such as to require a *Turnbull* direction' and, on the facts of the case, there was none.

---

78 See **3.78–3.84** above and the cases cited.

79 (1978) 66 Cr App R 174, [1978] Crim LR 168, CA.

80 [1993] Crim LR 590, CA. See the commentary for contrasting view.

81 *R v Graham* [1994] Crim LR 212, CA provides another example.

82 [1995] 1 Cr App R 578, CA.

83 [1995] 1 Cr App R 584, CA.

12.51 The Court of Appeal considered the identification/participation dichotomy, and which of *R v Slater* and *R v Thornton* to apply, in *R v O'Leary and Lloyd Evans*.[84] The victim and his friends became involved in a dispute with another group, of whom the defendants were members, over who had hailed a taxi. Violence ensued and the victim was subjected to a violent attack by members of the defendant's group. The victim later alleged that a group of five people had attacked him and that it was the same group of five who had been involved in the altercation over the taxi. An onlooker corroborated this. Three were identified in the street and at trial a *Turnbull* direction was given in respect of their identification. Of the other two, who became the appellants, one admitted being among the group involved in the initial argument but denied any participation in the attack, saying that after the argument he had gone to an off-licence. The other was silent throughout, though there was evidence that he too had been with the group initially. The Court of Appeal likened the case to *R v Thornton,* holding that the issue was one of identification of the appellants. Accordingly the jury should have been given a *Turnbull* direction. The Court noted the paradox of the three defendants against whom there was additional street identification evidence benefiting from a *Turnbull* direction whilst the appellants, against whom there was no such additional evidence, did not receive the protection of the direction.

12.52 An exclusive distinction between the issues of identification and participation is not always possible. In the attempt to distinguish the two, it may be easy to lose sight of the broader purpose of a *Turnbull* direction, namely the avoidance of a miscarriage of justice due to mistaken eyewitness testimony. An eyewitness might provide a perfect description of a suspect and later select the suspect at an identification procedure. However in a scene of torrid violence, the witness might confuse the suspect, who was admittedly present, with that of a participant. Though strictly speaking it could be said that the issue was one of participation, it might equally be said that the mistake goes to the identity of the participant in the violence. And in either case the reasons for the mistake may be precisely those to be considered under *Turnbull* such as period of observation, distance, light, obstruction and so on. Equally in either case an honest and convincing witness may be mistaken. It is therefore submitted that where it is possible that a person's actions have been mistakenly attributed to the defendant a *Turnbull* direction, adapted to the evidence, will be appropriate.[85]

12.53 If the offence takes place over a prolonged period and there is no impediment to observation, the full force of a *Turnbull* warning may be unnecessary. In *R v Beckles and Montague*[86] the victim of a robbery was held captive in a flat for three hours before being thrown through a fourth floor

---

84 [2002] EWCA Crim 2055, (2002) 67 JCL 115, CA.

85 See *Curry and Keble* [1983] Crim LR 737, CA and its commentary. For the purposes of Code D, an issue of mistaken participation would generally be regarded as one of identification rendering an identification procedure necessary. See **3.78–3.84**.

86 [1999] Crim LR 148, CA. See also *R v Chen and others* [2001] 5 *Archbold News* 3, CA for a similar situation, considered at **3.84**.

window. At first neither defendant admitted presence in the flat at the material time. However, following a video identification both did so. The trial judge gave an abbreviated warning, highlighting the importance of giving extra care to the evidence of identification and that honest witnesses can be mistaken which might lead to miscarriages of justice. It was held that the case 'was not an ordinary identification case with classic *Turnbull* dangers' because there had been ample opportunity for the victim to observe what was happening to him. The abbreviated warning was regarded by the Court of Appeal as adequate in the circumstances of the case.

Identification of associate

12.54 If the identification of an accomplice or associate of a defendant is probative of the defendant's guilt, it may be necessary to give a *Turnbull* warning where that identification is in dispute. In *R v Bath*[87] the defendant was alleged to have obtained money by deception from a shopkeeper to whom he had sold stolen goods. The shopkeeper purported to recognise a child who had accompanied the defendant. It was held that where the identity of the accused is at issue and there is strong evidence that the accused was with another at the relevant time, a purported identification of that other should, as a rule, be the subject of a *Turnbull* direction. However on the facts it was held that a direction was not required because there was no challenge to the correctness of the identification of the child.

Description

12.55 Where the identification evidence is that of an unchallenged description alone, the case is likely to be one to which a *Turnbull* direction has no application at all. In *R v Kelly*[88] the undisputed descriptions of an attacker matched that of the defendant, though there was no direct identification of him. The description was allied to other evidence from which it could be inferred that the defendant was the offender. It was held that the evidence identifying him was not dependant upon visual identification (indeed it was not even suggested that a *Turnbull* direction was required) but upon the basis of deduction from the primary facts.

12.56 *R v Kelly* was followed in *R v Byron*[89] where the evidence was of a witness who, from outside a house, observed a man inside striking two children with a stick. The description was of a man having a large tattoo on his upper left arm. The defendant and another person were the only males living in the house and the other did not have such a tattoo. The observation was unchallenged. Despite the defendant's denial that he was the person observed, the Court of Appeal did not regard the evidence of the tattoo as raising an

---

87 [1990] Crim LR 716, CA. Similarly in *R v White* (unreported) 19 April 2000, CA.

88 (Unreported) 10 February 1998, CA. See also *R v Gayle* [1999] 2 Cr App R 130, CA where a description, for the purposes of Code D, was not held to amount to an identification (see **3.52**).

89 (Unreported) 12 February 1999, CA.

identification issue requiring a *Turnbull* direction; rather it was a description which eliminated the only other candidate.[90]

12.57 The distinction between evidence of identification and description was revisited in *R v Murhaba*.[91] Descriptions of a man responsible for an assault were given by two witnesses, though no identification took place. The submission that the judge ought to have given a *Turnbull* warning was held by the Court of Appeal to be misconceived:

> 'No witness identified [the defendant] as the assailant … There is a difference between evidence *of identification of the defendant* for which a Turnbull direction is required, and evidence *of the description of the culprit* for which it is not, though in some cases – of which this was not one – a modified direction may be appropriate'

12.58 If the description of a witness is challenged or doubt is cast upon it by the adverse circumstances of the observation, a *Turnbull* direction will be appropriate, adapted to the facts of the case. A description which tends to implicate a defendant is no less vulnerable to a mistake resulting from poor visibility than an identification. In *R v Andrews*[92] one of three attackers was described as 'well built'. The defendant was arrested close to the scene of the attack and matched that description. He accepted that he had been with the other two defendants, one of whom was his brother, but claimed only to have been a bystander. It was held that the summing up effectively withdrew the question of the accuracy of the description and that it would have been prudent to have given a *Turnbull* direction. A modified direction was appropriately given in *R v Birmingham*[93] in which the appellant was one of three defendants accused of affray, of whom two were also charged with manslaughter. The prosecution was largely dependant upon descriptions of clothing worn by the principal attacker. It was held that, strictly speaking, there was no necessity for a *Turnbull* direction because the case rested on description, not identification. However there remained a need for caution where the points made on the observation evidence were closely analogous to those made by the Court in *Turnbull* in the context of identification, and thus the trial judge had sensibly given a modified direction.

Sketches, photofits and e-fits

12.59 A sketch, photofit or e-fit admitted as evidence of description[94] possesses the same quality as an oral description for the purpose of deciding whether a *Turnbull* direction is required. If there is no challenge to the accuracy of the image produced from the witness's description there is no need for a

---

90 See also *R v Kouistra* [2003] EWCA Crim 3686.

91 [2006] EWCA Crim 1491. See also *R v Thomas and others* [2010] EWCA Crim 148.

92 [1993] Crim LR 590, CA.

93 [2007] EWCA Crim 676.

94 See **10.12**.

Turnbull direction. In *R v Constantiniou*,[95] in which a photofit was adduced, the complaint about the failure to give one was rejected. The judge in fact described the circumstances of the witness's observation and indicated that the photofit was not a photograph of the offender but an attempt to reconstruct the features observed. The jury were further directed that it did not constitute an identification and that though the image was consistent with the defendant it was consistent with many other people. That direction was held to be appropriate to the circumstances. Where, on the other hand, the accuracy of the image is challenged, especially if the observation was in difficult circumstances, an adapted form of *Turnbull* direction may be appropriate.

Identification from photographs and video recordings

12.60 The permanence of a photograph or video can be contrasted with the transience of a live observation in allowing a witness to study the image. However, in other respects it is susceptible to mistake in the same way as identification from observation of the offence. Accordingly a *Turnbull* direction is necessary.[96] The general directions will be identical, though it may be necessary to consider particular additional factors. These may include warnings as to perspective, the position of the camera and its distance from the person recorded as well as the quality of the images and their duration. In the case of an identification from live or unrecorded images a further consideration will be the opportunity of the viewer to observe the screen.[97]

12.61 Additionally, if there are flaws or other weaknesses in either the viewing procedure or in its recording, they should be drawn to the jury's attention. The possibility of contamination may occur for example when witnesses identify a person having view images simultaneously or where the viewer has been told in advance of the viewing the identity of the person suspected to be depicted. Thus a warning that the name of the defendant had been put into the head of the identifying police officer was appropriately given in *R v Swinscoe*.[98] Similarly in *R v Tucker*,[99] the trial judge had given the jury a clear warning that when the police witness viewed the CCTV, having been told that the defendant was thought to be present, the officer was expecting to see him. A series of deficiencies in the recording of the circumstances of a viewing and the resultant identification were found in *R v Smith & others*.[100] The summing up made no reference to them. The Court of Appeal held that the judge 'ought to have directed the jury that by reason of the inadequacies of the procedure there was no objective standard or record against which to measure the reliability of [the officer's] assertion'.

---

95 (1990) 91 Cr App R 74, CA.

96 See *R v Ali* [2008] EWCA Crim 1522 where the failure to do so contributed to the conviction being unsafe and *R v Moss* [2011] EWCA Crim 252 in which appropriate warnings were endorsed.

97 *Taylor v Chief Constable of Cheshire* (1987) 84 Cr App R 191, DC.

98 [2005] EWCA Crim 1064.

99 [2008] EWCA Crim 3063, [2009] Crim LR 441.

100 [2008] EWCA Crim 1342, [2009] 1 Cr App R 521, [2009] Crim L R 440.

Reliability of identification by police officers

12.62 The Court of Appeal in *R v Ramsden*[101] upheld the trial judge's direction suggesting that a police officer might be more reliable than an ordinary witness in observation and identification. The issue at trial was the identity of the driver of a stolen vehicle. A police officer had been involved in a car chase and had made a concentrated effort to look at the driver for about three seconds at 10 yards. In so far as the direction was based upon the officer's evidence that he had made a deliberate attempt to observe the driver for identification purposes, it was unremarkable. It had been buttressed by an adequate *Turnbull* direction. However the Court of Appeal went further by adopting the proposition that honest police officers, being trained, were more likely to be reliable than the general public and less likely to have their observations and recollections affected by the excitement of the situation. Provided the usual warnings were given, this was regarded as a common sense approach. It was followed in *R v Tyler and others*[102] in which a similar direction was given in respect of identifications made by police officers when observing violence at a poll tax demonstration.

12.63 Those cases contrast with *R v Sutton and Kelly*.[103] There the Court of Appeal did not consider as appropriate the direction that 'lay people made mistakes, whereas police officers were trained and by implication less likely to do so' despite, it seems, evidence from the officer that he had had some form of training. In the case of *Reid and others v R*[104] the Privy Council went a step further. Considering the trial judge's direction concerning a police officer's superior ability to identify, it found that 'experience has undoubtedly shown that police identification can be just as unreliable' as that of a member of the public.

12.64 Whether any gloss to a standard *Turnbull* direction can properly be added must depend upon the circumstances of the particular identification. A police officer might credibly distinguish him or herself from a lay person by saying 'I paid special attention to the suspect's facial features and clothing in order to be able to recognise the person to make an arrest or prepare a note or give evidence'. However the abstract notion that a police officer's identification is more reliable than another person's identification tends to promote the fact of being a police officer into an objective feature of the observation such as length of time, distance and light. These of course are not improved by the fact that the observer is a police officer. Moreover unless there is in fact a comparative, such as a civilian standing next to the police officer observing the same incident, the direction in its abstract form is arguably meaningless. The mischief of a generic approach to police prowess in identification is that it will tend to magnify the danger of mis-identification in the case of an honest and convinced but mistaken police officer.

---

[101] [1991] Crim LR 295, CA.

[102] (1993) 96 Cr App R 332, CA.

[103] (Unreported), 12 November 2002, CA.

[104] [1990] 1 AC 363, (1990) 90 Cr App R 121, PC.

Conviction of accomplice: transferred reliability of identification

12.65 In some instances the conviction of one defendant identified by a witness has been used as support for the reliability of the witness's identification of another.[105] Cases in which this has been permitted are discussed at **10.176**. In such situations the jury must be clearly warned about the limitations of the evidence and given a full *Turnbull* direction. Where there is a danger that guilt might be inferred by the association of the defendant with the convicted person, the jury must be specifically disabused of that line of reasoning. In *R v Wait,*[106] some days after an attack the victim made a street identification of the defendant and a friend who were both arrested. The defendant's friend pleaded guilty and reliance was placed upon the correctness of the witness's identification of the friend as probative of his identification of the defendant on trial. The Court of Appeal found that the summing up fell some way short of a clear warning concerning the legitimate use of the guilt of the defendant's friend. The jury ought to have been directed in clear terms that they must be alive to the real possibility that the victim might have been correct about one identification and wrong about the other. Indeed in the circumstances it might be added there existed an added danger – that of the victim making a mistaken assumption based upon the defendant's association with his friend at the time of the later observation and arrest.

Identification of clothing and other objects

12.66 The identification of an object, such as clothing worn by an offender, a weapon or a car may be important incriminatory evidence. To what extent is any direction concerning the observation or recognition of it by a witness required? Where a person is identified by a witness as the result of recognition of clothing there will be a need for a full *Turnbull* direction. In *R v Haynes*[107] the driver of a car taken without consent was recognised and identified at a street procedure shortly after it had crashed. His identification was based upon the clothing worn by the defendant rather than any aspect of his personal features. His appeal was allowed because the judge failed to give a full *Turnbull* warning, omitting certain weaknesses in the identification evidence. Where, by contrast to *R v Haynes*, there is no identification but descriptive evidence of clothing alone, no *Turnbull* direction is necessary, though in some circumstances a modified warning may be appropriate. In *R v Hassan*[108] the defendant was incriminated by a description of clothing he was admittedly wearing at the time of a violent disorder. No *Turnbull* direction was needed.

---

105 *R v Castle* [1989] Crim LR 567; *R v Gummerson and Steadman* [1999] Crim LR 680, CA, not reported on this point.

106 [1998] Crim LR 68, CA, not reported on this point.

107 [2004] EWCA Crim 390. See also *R v McNeil* [2011] EWCA Crim 1243: 'This was an identification case. That the identification or recognition was of clothing rather than of a face does not alter the application of the general principles as carefully explained in Turnbull'.

108 [2004] EWCA Crim 1478. See also *R v Birmingham* [2007] EWCA Crim 676 at **12.58**.

12.67 The identification of a car was considered in *R v Browning*[109] where it was held that no general *Turnbull* direction was necessary. Though the judge was required to remind the jury of the circumstances of the identification, for example as the opportunity for observation, the witness's ability to distinguish between vehicles and whether the identification of make and model might have been influenced by other information, the general warning requirements were not necessary. This was followed and explained in *R v Hampton & Brown.*[110]

> 'No recognised basis exists for suggesting that this type of evidence needs to be approached with special caution: it has not been established that the introduction of evidence of this kind in the past has caused particular injustice or that witnesses mistaken as to this kind of detail can also be convincing in a special way that calls for a *Turnbull* type direction. A witness who gives evidence of the details of a number plate is performing exactly the same role as a witness who, for instance, describes the number of punches delivered during a fight, whether traffic lights were green or red before a collision, or whether there were four or five masked men present during an armed robbery.'[111]

12.68 The Court of Appeal considered that there was no reason to suppose that jurors may be unaware of or insufficiently understand the dangers of such identification. However the Court went on to approve the need to give a direction specific to the facts of the case where the evidence is questioned, disputed or otherwise open to doubt, and to consider whether a cautionary note may be appropriate in some cases.

> 'However, we stress it will usually be necessary for the judge to remind the jury of the circumstances in which the observation was made. Moreover he should set out the factors which might render the testimony less reliable than otherwise would have been the case. Further, we are not in any way seeking to restrict either the circumstances in which a judge may, as a matter of discretion, urge caution in regard to a particular witness when summing up to a jury, or the terms to be used when doing so. We fully recognise that in particular cases judges may consider that the facts merit giving a special warning, tailored to the requirements of the trial of the trial in question.'[112]

ALIBI

12.69 The rationale for a direction on an alibi defence was explained in the Devlin report:[113]

> 'It is quite possible that wrong convictions due to mis-identification have been caused not by the jury being over-impressed by the identification evidence, but by their being unfavourably impressed by the alibi.'

---

[109] (1992) 94 Cr App R 109.

[110] [2004] EWCA Crim 2139, [2006] Crim LR 60.

[111] Ibid, at [42].

[112] Ibid, at [50].

[113] Report to the Secretary of State for the Home Department 1976, para 4.75.

12.70 The report went on to consider the type of human frailties to which an alibi defence might succumb:

> 'It is more likely that as in Virag's case an alibi, which is true in essence, will contain minor inaccuracies or even be decorated by incidental lies. There are characters who, when in fear or under stress, find it difficult to stick to the unvarnished truth. Even a spotless character putting forward an unsupported alibi may be tempted to invent corroborative detail. The accused who are wrongly identified are hardly ever spotless characters; and the tendency to lie themselves out of a tight corner will be given just as free a rein when innocent as when they are guilty.'[114]

12.71 The alibi direction, the Judicial Studies Board model direction for which can be found at Appendix F, comprises two limbs:

(1) the burden of proof;

(2) the effect of a false alibi.

12.72 Lest a jury be misled into thinking that the burden has shifted to the defence to establish the defence of alibi, they should be reminded that it remains with the prosecution and that it is therefore for the prosecution to disprove the alibi and not for the defence to prove it. This direction should be specifically linked to the alibi defence as separate and distinct from the burden of proof direction.[115]

12.73 The second limb is concerned with the consequence of a finding that an alibi was false. The jury must be warned that such a finding does not itself prove the contested identification or establish guilt. There may be many reasons for a false alibi consistent with innocence as well as guilt. It may be a genuine mistake as to time or date. It may have been invented to bolster a true defence. It should only be taken into account if the jury are certain that the false alibi was intended and that it has no innocent connotation. The direction is closely associated with the direction concerning a defendant's lies, the *Lucas* direction. Much of the case-law relating to lies applies equally to alibi directions and the *Lucas* direction, considered further below at **12.87**, contains an elaboration of the second limb by giving examples of reasons why a defendant may have lied.

12.74 *Turnbull* provides the starting point for guidance on the second limb of the direction.

> 'Care should be taken by the judge when directing the jury about support for an identification which may be derived from the fact that they have rejected an alibi. False alibis may be put forward for many reasons; an accused, for example, who has only his own truthful evidence to rely on may stupidly fabricate an alibi and get lying witnesses to support it out of fear that his own evidence will not be enough. Further, alibi witnesses can make genuine mistakes about dates and

---

[114] Report to the Secretary of State for the Home Department 1976, para 4.76.

[115] *R v Anderson* [1991] Crim LR 361, CA; *R v Elliot* (unreported) 22 December 1997, CA.

> occasions like any other witnesses can. It is only when the jury is satisfied that the sole reason for the fabrication was to deceive them and there is no other explanation for its being put forward can fabrication provide any support for identification evidence. The jury should be reminded that proving the accused has told lies about where he was at the material time does not prove by itself that he was where the identifying witness says he was.'[116]

12.75 This dictum was reiterated in *R v Keane*[117] in which the jury had been told that if they found the alibi to be untrue it could be taken into account. This was a misdirection insofar as the jury were not reminded that they could rely upon it 'only if they were satisfied that the sole reason for the fabrication was to deceive them on the issue of identification.' The Court of Appeal has repeatedly regarded the omission of an alibi direction as a misdirection and, depending upon the other circumstances of the case, liable to render the conviction unsafe.[118]

12.76 The omission of an alibi direction in *R v Pemberton*[119] was regarded as a material irregularity which rendered the conviction unsafe. The defendant was alleged to have robbed a minicab driver. He was picked out at an identification parade by the victim as being the passenger who had robbed him. The defendant's grandmother, who alone gave evidence in his defence, stated that he was at home on the night of the attack. However the alibi collapsed in cross-examination when it became clear that she could not recall precisely the night to which she had been referring, either by day or date. Whether that was the result of deliberate lies or a poor memory the Court of Appeal could not say. However the Court was in no doubt as to its potential impact. The jury may have interpreted the evidence as supporting the identification evidence and therefore the jury ought to have been given proper directions as to their approach if the alibi evidence was rejected.

12.77 Whereas the guidance in *Turnbull* concerned the alibi direction in visual identification cases. In *R v Penman,*[120] the defendant was accused of burglary. The identification evidence was based exclusively upon a scientific link between the defendant and the scene of the offence – fragments of glass found on his shoes and socks consistent with a shattered window of the burgled premises. In his defence he claimed to have been with a girlfriend at the time of the burglary but had passed the premises on the way home. The complaint was made that the second limb of the alibi direction had not been given. The Court of Appeal pointed out that *Turnbull* was concerned with visual identification and did not accept that an alibi direction was necessary in every case where identity was in issue. It was held that the judge was justified in not giving the full direction. However current practice appears to be reflected in the Judicial Studies Board

---

116 (1976) 63 Cr App R 132, at 139, [1977] 1 QB 224, at 230.

117 (1977) 65 Cr App R 247, CA. See also *R v Baillie* [1995] 2 Cr App R 31, [1995] Crim LR 739.

118 *R v Duncan* (1992) *The Times* 24 July, CA; *R v Drake* [1996] Crim LR 109, CA; *R v Elliot* (unreported) 22 December 1997, CA; *R v Brown* [1998] Crim LR 196, CA; *R v Page* [2003] EWCA Crim 2388.

119 (1994) 99 Cr App R 228, CA.

120 (1985) 82 Cr App R 44, CA.

Crown Court Bench Book guidelines on direction on alibi.[121] It contains both limbs without distinction between cases of visual identification and those depending upon other evidence of identity. Indeed it was accepted in *R v Penman* that:

> '... the reasons which may cause a defendant to put forward a false alibi must be of general application. It would be absurd to suggest that those reasons exist only in cases where the evidence against the defendant consists wholly or mainly of evidence of visual identification.'[122]

12.78 The need to give an alibi direction does not depend upon the prosecution's reliance on the untruthfulness of the alibi but on whether the jury might draw an inference from it. In *R v Lesley*[123] the defendant was accused of a murder at a dance in a community hall. The evidence comprised, first, two eyewitnesses who purported to identify him and, secondly, his fingerprint on a beer bottle near to the scene of the shooting. Though the judge reminded the jury of the burden of proof in relation to alibi he failed to explain how to approach the consequences of a rejection of the defence. It was held that, subject to one exception, the direction should be given not only when reliance is placed on a false alibi by the prosecution but whenever there is a risk that a jury might conclude that a rejected alibi is probative of guilt.[124] The risk existed in that case because the jury might have taken his efforts to hide his presence at the dance as evidence of guilt. The Court added that the 'failed alibi direction is short and simple. It should routinely be given.'

12.79 The exception to which *R v Lesley* referred was the situation in which the rejection of the alibi 'almost necessarily leaves the jury with no choice but to convict as a matter of logic'.[125] Another way of viewing the exception is to ask whether the rejected alibi provides collateral or independent support for the identification or whether its failure is, in effect, only the counterpart to the successful identification evidence. The latter was the situation in *R v Harron*.[126] The defendant was accused of an assault in a nightclub. His defence was alibi. He was identified by two witnesses both of whom knew him well: the victim and a second witness who placed him at the premises though did not see the incident. The defendant's evidence was that he had not been in the premises that evening at all and, at the time of the incident, was at home. Two witnesses supported the alibi. The complaint that the second limb of the alibi direction

---

121 See note 1.

122 This case is perhaps best regarded as one in which the rejected alibi left the jury with little alternative but to infer guilt. See **12.79** for this exception to the alibi notice requirement.

123 [1996] 1 Cr App R 39, CA expressly disapproving *R v Penman* (1985) 82 Cr App R 44, CA, which had decided that an alibi direction was unnecessary unless the prosecution relied on its falsity. Neither *R v Francis* [1990] 91 Cr App R 271, CA nor *R v Anderson* [1991] Crim LR 361, CA, which both followed *R v Penman* can be regarded as good law on this point.

124 See also *R v Peacock* [1998] Crim LR 681, CA. By contrast in *R v Wharton* [1998] Crim LR 668, CA it was held that there was no danger that what was said by the defendant in interview would be regarded as probative of guilt and that a direction would have been harmful by highlighting the apparent lie.

125 This dictum is taken from the New Zealand case of *Dehar* [1969] NZLR 763.

126 [1996] 2 Cr App R 457, CA.

had not been given was rejected. The Court of Appeal distinguished *R v Lesley* on the basis that, unlike that case where the identification evidence was questionable, in the *Harron* case the central issue for the jury was whether the two prosecution witnesses were lying. The false alibi did not therefore support the identification by constituting a separate matter from their determination of the main issue which was the truthfulness of the witnesses. If the jury rejected the alibi evidence it could have been of no assistance to tell the jury there might be other reasons for the invention because there was no other defence that could have been bolstered.

12.80 *R v Harron* was followed in *R v Patrick,*[127] in which the defendant was accused of an arson attack in Lincolnshire. The case relied heavily on the identification evidence of the owner of the property attacked. He knew the defendant as the person he had previously identified as the perpetrator of a burglary of a neighbour. The defendant claimed to have been in Scotland at the material time and a substantial body of evidence elaborated upon his presence there for some days before and after the offence. At trial the jury were directed as to the prosecution's burden of disproof of the alibi but given no direction as to the effect of rejecting it. It was found that the possibility that the alibi was false and yet the witness was mistaken in his identification existed only in theory. As a matter of practical reality and common sense given the way that the case was presented, the only basis upon which the jury could have rejected the alibi was that they were satisfied that the identification was correct. There was no distinction between the issue of guilt and that of lies in relation to the alibi and accordingly there was no reason for the second limb of the alibi direction.

12.81 The opposite conclusion was reached in *R v Peacock*[128] albeit in the context of a *Lucas* direction. The central issue in the case was the identification of the defendant as a robber of a shop. A witness picked him out at a parade. In interview he claimed that he had been with his former partner at the time, but at trial said that he had been mistaken about the days and in fact was with his current girlfriend. The prosecution alleged that the account in interview was a deliberate lie which contaminated the later alibi. The Court of Appeal held that if they found it to be a deliberate lie the jury might well regard it as an additional ground for disbelieving the evidence of the defendant and his girlfriend. Accordingly a *Lucas* direction ought to have been given.

12.82 There may be no need for an alibi direction if an analysis of the defence reveals no more than an unsupported assertion of being absent from the place where the defence was committed. A statement such as 'I definitely wasn't there but I can't remember where I was' does not amount to an alibi. Whether unsupported claims such as 'I must have been at home at that time' or 'I was down the pub that afternoon' will warrant an alibi direction must depend upon the facts of each case.

---

[127] [1999] 6 *Archbold News* 4, CA.
[128] [1998] Crim LR 681, CA.

12.83 In *R v Mussell and Dalton*[129] the defendants were convicted of an armed robbery of a sub-post office. Both accepted that they were in a nearby public house for most of the afternoon of the robbery, one stating that he had not left until after the time of the robbery, the other that he had left the public house first to go to a betting shop and then for a walk. The standard alibi direction was not given though the judge, when referring to their evidence, stated that they did not have to prove their innocence but the prosecution had to prove their guilt. It was held that if, as here, the evidence amounted to little more than a denial of the crime, an alibi direction was not necessary. In the circumstances the jury could not have been misled into thinking the burden was on defendants to produce evidence supporting their movements. The judgment is consistent with the tenor of *Turnbull* whose reference to false alibis suggests some degree of substance to the defence. However the need for an alibi direction ultimately depends upon whether there is a danger that a jury may draw independent support from the rejection of an assertion of presence elsewhere. In some cases the very fact that the alibi is vague or unsubstantiated might provoke an adverse inference if it was thought that evidence which might have been available was not called.

12.84 The alibi direction is not dependant upon the service of an alibi notice.[130] It is the evidence given and the issues raised which determine the need for a direction and the failure to serve a notice will not obviate the need for a direction. In some cases it may be questionable whether as a matter of form the defence has been raised at all, for example where alibi has been raised but no evidence is called in support of it. In *R v Lesley*[131] it was held, notwithstanding that no alibi evidence was adduced, the issue had been canvassed by reference to the notice of alibi and a direction was necessary. Where a defence raised in interview is relied upon at trial in the absence of any evidence in support, it should generally be necessary for that defence to be summed up to the jury.[132] It is accordingly submitted that an alibi direction will be appropriate if there is a risk that a disbelieved claim of alibi in interview will be treated as independent support for visual identification.

12.85 An alibi direction is appropriate not only where evidence shows presence elsewhere at precisely the time of the offence but where it shows an unlikelihood of presence at the material time, for example presence 100 miles from the scene an hour before the offence.[133] What of the position when the alibi relates to incriminating conduct at a time other than that of the commission of the offence? If, on a charge of theft of a vehicle a witness claims to have observed the defendant driving it a week later and the defendant

---

129 [1995] Crim LR 887, CA.

130 See **9.16–9.18** for the requirement to serve a notice of alibi.

131 [1996] 1 Cr App R 39, CA.

132 *R v Holloran and Hughes* [2003] EWCA Crim 3282; *R v Bagga* [2002] EWCA Crim 1049; *R v Akhtar* [2000] 1 *Archbold News* 2, CA.

133 See **9.19–9.23**.

provides an alibi for that observation, the rationale in *Turnbull* for a warning would be exactly the same as if the identification and alibi related to the act of theft.

12.86 A jury may be predisposed to regard the alibi evidence of a close relative of a defendant with a certain suspicion. The Court of Appeal in *Turnbull* considered the impact of a summing up which asked rhetorically what the defendant's wife could have done other than back-up her husband, thereby giving an impression that her evidence was of little value. As the Court noted, if the defendant was indeed at home, who else could he have called. The Court went on to state that:

> 'In such circumstances it will almost certainly be present in the jury's mind that the witness is the defendant's wife and they will no doubt make what they think is the proper allowance for this fact. They should, however, be warned in most, if not all, similar cases that they should not necessarily regard the fact that the witness is the defendant's wife as derogating from the worth of her evidence when the nature and content of the defence is such that anyone would expect her to be called as a witness in any event.'[134]

LIES

12.87 If a defendant's lies, admitted or proven, might be regarded as evidence of guilt it may be necessary to give the jury a *Lucas* direction[135] as to the approach to be taken when considering those lies. The danger of the 'forbidden reasoning' which allows guilt to be assumed from a defendant's lie, and its remedy, were described in *Broadhurst v R*[136] by Lord Devlin:

> 'It is very important that a jury should be carefully directed upon the effect of a conclusion, if they reach it, that the accused is lying. There is a natural tendency for a jury to think that if an accused is lying it must be because he is guilty, and accordingly convict him without more ado. It is the duty of the judge to make it clear to them that this is not so.'

12.88 In *R v Burke and Pegg*[137] the Court of Appeal identified four situations (which may overlap) in which a *Lucas* direction 'is usually required':

(1) Where the defence relies on an alibi (see above).

(2) Where the judge considers it necessary or desirable to suggest that the jury should look for support or corroboration of one piece of evidence from other evidence in the case, and among that other evidence draws attention to lies told, or allegedly told by the defendant.

---

134 (1976) 63 Cr App R 132, at 143, [1977] 1 QB 224, at 230.

135 *R v Lucas* (1981) 73 Cr App R 159, CA. The direction was originally concerned with the former common law requirement of corroboration.

136 [1964] AC 441, HL.

137 [1996] 1 Cr App R 163, CA.

(3) Where the prosecution seek to show that something said, whether in or out of court, in relation to a separate and distinct issue was a lie, and to rely on that lie as evidence of guilt in relation to the charge which is sought to be proved.

(4) Where, although the prosecution have not adopted the approach in (3) above, the judge reasonably envisages that there is a real danger that the jury may do so.

12.89 The Court stated that the direction should to be tailored to the particular circumstances of the case but needed to make two basic points:

(1) that the lie must be admitted or proved beyond reasonable doubt; and

(2) the mere fact that the defendant lies is not in itself evidence of guilt since the defendant may lie for innocent reasons, so only if the jury is sure that the defendant did not lie for an innocent reason can a lie support the prosecution case.

12.90 Examples of innocent reasons for a lie include those intended to bolster a true defence, to protect somebody else, to conceal other discreditable conduct or out of panic or confusion. It is not necessary for the direction to list all conceivable reasons for a lie, only those which might reasonably arise on the evidence or which are specifically relied upon by a defendant. The Judicial Studies Board Crown Court Bench Book[138] approves the continued use of the specimen direction.[139]

12.91 As with the alibi direction, a direction as to lies will be unnecessary if the exposure of the lie leaves the jury with no choice but to convict.[140] In *R v Peacock*[141] the Court of Appeal considered the test in the following way:

> 'The general principle is that a *Lucas* direction is not necessary when the lie in question [will not be treated] as additional proof of the defendant's guilt, but is merely the obverse of the allegation that the defendant is guilty. In other words, the jury cannot decide whether he is lying, without first being satisfied on the central issue of guilt.'

12.92 If there is no risk that the lie will be regarded as collateral evidence of guilt no direction is called for. In *R v Middleton*[142] the defendant raised alibi in respect of a burglary. He was stopped by police driving a car stolen from outside the burgled house and items stolen from within the house were found at his mother's address. He gave an innocent explanation of these facts. The common sense view taken by the Court of Appeal was that if he was lying the

---

138 See note 1.

139 Bench Book, Appendix 1.

140 *R v Burke and Pegg*, citing *R v Dehar* [1969] NZLR 763; *R v Landon* [1995] Crim LR 338, CA; and *R v Patrick* [1999] 6 *Archbold News* 4, CA considered above at **12.80**.

141 *R v Peacock* [1998] Crim LR 681, CA.

142 [2001] Crim LR 251, CA.

obvious inference was that he had done so to conceal guilt. Though this was an inference for the jury to draw if they saw fit, the Court held that an embellishment of the summing up with a *Lucas* direction would only have served to confuse and complicate an essentially simple issue.

12.93 In *R v Goodway*[143] the alleged lie was capable of providing collateral support for identification evidence. The defendant was convicted of a murder which arose from a confrontation between two groups of people. The prosecution relied on identification evidence supported by the defendant's lies in interview that he had not been close to the victim during the violence. He contended that the person responsible was another member of his group. In view of the conflicting identification evidence and the fact that the other person resembled the defendant, the Court of Appeal held that failure to direct the jury as to how to approach the defendant's lies was a material misdirection. The lie did not inexorably denote guilt. It may well have been told to bolster a true defence.

IDENTIFICATION BY JURY FROM PHOTOGRAPHS AND VIDEO RECORDINGS

12.94 Photographs or video recordings of an incident may be exhibited at trial as evidence of the offence or to establish a witness's identification from the image. They may co-incidentally allow a jury to compare the person depicted with the defendant in the dock or indeed be produced for that very purpose.[144] In some cases a jury will be asked to compare such an image with another, contemporary image of the defendant. If the images are too poor for comparison a jury should be told not to attempt the task.[145] If they are introduced for the purpose only of presenting evidence of the crime and a jury is neither invited to make a comparison, nor is there any risk that they will, no *Turnbull* direction is required.[146] However, where the jury may compare the image with the defendant and it is disputed that the defendant is the person depicted, it has been held that a quasi *Turnbull* direction is appropriate.[147]

12.95 The warning necessary was explained in *R v Dodson and Williams*[148] in which the following guidance was issued:

> 'It is, however, imperative that a jury is warned by a judge in summing up of the perils of deciding whether by this means alone or with some form of supporting evidence a defendant has committed the crime alleged. According to the quality of the photographs, change in appearance in a defendant and other considerations which may arise in a trial, the jury's task may be rendered difficult or simple in

---

143 (1994) 98 Cr App R 11, CA. See also *R v Peacock* [1998] Crim LR 681, CA at **12.81** for the facts.

144 See **10.15** for admissibility.

145 *R v Faraz Ali* [2008] EWCA Crim 1522, [2009] Crim LR 40.

146 *R v Williams* [2005] EWCA Crim 2332.

147 *R v Blenkinsop* [1995] 1 Cr App R 7, CA, *R v Moss* [2011] EWCA Crim 252.

148 (1984) 79 Cr App R 220, CA.

> bringing about a decision either in favour or against a defendant. So long as the jury having been brought face to face with these perils are firmly directed that to convict they must be sure that the man in the dock is the man in the photograph, we envisage no injustice arising from this manner of evaluating evidence with the aids of what the jurors' eyes tell them is a fact which they are sure exists.'

12.96 The Court of Appeal found those perils to have been admirably addressed by the trial judge, who invited the jury to bear in mind the dangers and difficulties of identification and that photographs may give false impressions. The Court went on to indicate that:

> 'What is of the utmost importance … is that the quality of the photographs, the extent of the exposure of the facial features of the person photographed, evidence, or the absence of it, of a change in the defendant's appearance and the opportunity a jury has to look at a defendant in the dock and over what period of time are factors, among other matters of relevance … which the jury must receive guidance upon from the judge …'

There is no particular formula for the direction; the extent to which a detailed direction will be required will depend upon the particular identification difficulties in the case.

12.97 In *R v Downey*[149] the Court of Appeal rejected the suggestion that *R v Dodson and Williams* 'intended to lay down an invariable rule that something must be said in every case, however obvious and even banal it might be'. *R v Dodson and Williams* was distinguished because in that case there had been no witness identification evidence and thus no general warning as to the dangers of identification in accordance with *Turnbull* whereas in *R v Downey* there had been a *Turnbull* direction. In *R v Blenkinsop*[150] the Court of Appeal appeared to retreat towards *R v Dodson and Williams.* It was held that though the guidelines in that case did not have to be applied rigidly in every case, there was an underlying requirement of a direction according to the principle in *R v Dodson and Williams*. In particular there is:

> '… a general and invariable requirement that the jury shall be warned of the risk of mistaken identification, and of the need to exercise particular care in any identification which they make for themselves.'

12.98 In *R v Faraz Ali*[151] CCTV images were of sufficiently poor quality to cause the Court of Appeal to doubt whether even the clearest images were capable of permitting jury identification. However, the trial judge, having invited the jury to 'use your own eyes' when comparing them to the defendant, failed to give a careful and full direction as to the dangers of mistaken identification. The case had demanded one and accordingly the conviction was regarded as unsafe.

---

149 [1995] Cr App R 547, CA.
150 [1995] 1 Cr App R 7, CA.
151 [2008] EWCA Crim 1522, [2009] Crim LR 40.

VOICE IDENTIFICATION

12.99 The essential elements of an adapted *Turnbull* direction will be necessary in a case of voice identification. In *R v Hersey*[152] it was held that:

> 'A judge should tailor his directions to the jury on the lines indicated by this court and in the specimen directions issued by the Judicial Studies Board in respect of visual recognition or identification. The judge should follow, suitably adapted, the guidelines laid down in *R v Turnbull* and the cases which have followed. Above all, it is vital that a judge should spell out to the jury the risk of mistaken identification, the reason why a witness may be mistaken, pointing out that a truthful witness may yet be a mistaken witness, and dealing with the particular strengths and weaknesses of the identification in the instant case.'

12.100 In *R v Roberts*[153] research into voice identification presented to the Court of Appeal indicated that voice identification is more likely to be wrong than visual and there existed an even greater danger of the witness believing himself or herself to be right when in fact mistaken. The research, which commended itself to the Court, concluded that the warning to jurors should be even more stringent than in relation to the evidence of eyewitnesses.[154]

12.101 These potential weaknesses should be tailored to the nature and circumstances of the identification. They may include:

- audibility and clarity of speech heard at time of offence;
- amount and variety of speech;
- interference by extraneous noise and other environmental factors;
- degree of the witness's familiarity with the suspect's voice;
- whether offender's speech/voice/accent has positive or lack of distinguishing features;
- witness's familiarity with language and ability to distinguish accent;
- witness's hearing disability, whether natural or induced by intoxication;
- discrepancy between first or other description and offender's voice;
- lapse of time between offence and identification procedure.

---

152 [1998] Crim LR 281, CA. Followed in *R v Gummerson and Steadman* [1999] Crim LR 680, CA and *R v Phillips* [2007] EWCA Crim 1042.

153 [2000] Crim LR 183, CA. See also *R v Flynn & St John* [2008] EWCA Crim 970, [2008] 2 Cr App R 266 and **10.64** for a discussion of the dangers.

154 This appeared to have been accepted in *R v Chenia* [2003] 2 Cr App R 83(6), CA.

12.102 The jury will require a further direction where they are in a position to seek to make their own identification, either by comparison of recordings or from the voice of the defendant in the witness box.[155] If not permitted, they should be directed accordingly.[156] If the judge permits the jury to form their own judgement, it was held in *R v O'Doherty*[157] that further guidance was necessary:

> '[T]here should be a specific warning given to jurors of the dangers of relying on their own untrained ears, when they do not have the training or equipment of an auditory phonetician or the training or equipment of an acoustic phonetician, in conditions which may be far from ideal, in circumstances in which they are asked to compare the voice of one person, the defendant, with the voice on the tape, in conditions in which they may have been listening to the defendant give evidence and concentrating on what he was saying, not comparing it with the voice on the tape at that time and in circumstances in which they may have a subconscious bias because the defendant is in the dock. We do not seek to lay down precise guidelines as to the appropriate warning. Each case will be governed by its own set of circumstances. But the authorities to which we have referred emphasise the need to give a specific warning to the jurors themselves.'

12.103 Where expert or lay listener (eg police recognition) evidence comparing recorded voices of offenders with those of defendants is relied upon, the jury should be permitted to make the comparison themselves. However, in doing so the judge should direct the jury that they should be guided by the evidence of the voice identification witnesses.[158]

DOCK IDENTIFICATION

12.104 The propriety of dock identification evidence is considered at **10.83**. If it is accepted that the defendant is well known to the identifying witness no harm is done and there is no need for any jury direction.[159] Where a trial continues after an accidental dock identification, the jury should usually be instructed to ignore it completely. It may be prudent to issue a warning immediately. It is not a matter which can be ignored in the hope that by doing so the jury too may ignore it.[160] At the very least the judge must give a direction to the jury warning of its dangers, the reasons for those dangers and an instruction to exercise great caution. In the Privy Council case of *R v Williams*[161] defence counsel had not apparently sought a re-trial when a police officer identified the defendant for the first time at trial. Neither had he requested a direction that the evidence be disregarded. The jury were told of the undesirability of such evidence, that the proper means of identification was

---

155 See **10.78**.
156 *R v Chenia* [2003] 2 Crim App R 83(6), CA.
157 [2003] 1 Cr App R 5, NICA.
158 *R v Flynn and St John* [2008] EWCA Crim 970, [2008] 2 Cr App R 266.
159 *Capron v R* [2006] UKPC 34.
160 *R v Tricoglus* (1977) 65 Cr App R 16, CA.
161 [1997] 1 WLR 548, PC.

a parade and that there was no explanation for the failure to hold one. They were warned to treat it with great caution. In the circumstances it was held that the trial judge had said all that could reasonably have been expected of him. The Privy Council went a step further in *Edwards v R*[162] by stating that the jury should be directed that dock identification evidence carried little or no weight. Simply pointing out to a jury that the practice was unfair because there was no choice has been held to be insufficient.[163] The necessity of a proper and full direction was confirmed in *Tido v The Queen*[164] in which it was held that it should comprise warnings both that the defendant had been deprived of the opportunity of an exculpatory parade and of the danger that that he had been identified by virtue of being in the dock.

CODE D: BREACHES

12.105 In *R v Quinn*[165] there were a series of breaches of the Code relating to the conduct of an identification parade in which the defendant was selected. The trial judge allowed the identification evidence to be adduced but failed to invite the jury to consider whether the breaches could have affected the identifications made. The Court of Appeal found that the judge was wrong to have neglected to direct the jury to consider whether the breaches caused doubt about the safety or reliability of the identification evidence.

12.106 The House of Lords gave their attention to the direction appropriate to breaches of Code D in *R v Forbes.*[166] The following guidance was given:

> 'It is in our judgment important that the position should be clear. In any case where a breach of Code D has been established but the trial judge has rejected an application to exclude evidence to which the defence objected because of that breach, the trial judge should in the course of the summing up to the jury: (a) explain that there has been a breach of the Code and how it has arisen, and (b) invite the jury to consider the possible effect of the breach. The Court of Appeal has so ruled on many occasions, and we approve of those rulings: see, for example *Quinn*. The terms of the appropriate direction will vary from case to case and breach to breach. But if the breach is a failure to hold an identification parade when required by D2.3 [now Code D3.12], the jury should ordinarily be told that

162 [2006] UKPC 23.

163 *R v Thomas* [1994] Crim LR 128, CA. See also *R v Conibeer* [2002] EWCA Crim 2059; and *R v Howick* [1970] Crim LR 403, CA, for a case in which the conviction was quashed after no warning was given at all.

164 [2011] UKPC 16.

165 [1995] 1 Cr App R 480, at 490F, CA. See also *R v Graham* [1994] Crim LR 212, CA; *R v Allen* [1995] Crim LR 643, CA; *R v McMath* [1997] Crim LR 586, CA; *R v Wait* [1998] Crim LR 68, CA; *R v Skeetes* (unreported) 5 February 1998, CA; *R v Harris* [2003] EWCA Crim 174; (2003) SJ 237, *R v Preddie* [2011] EWCA Crim 312.

166 [2001] 1 Cr App R 430, HL. Followed in *R v Harris* [2003] EWCA Crim 174; (2003) SJ 237 and *R v Brennan* [2005] EWCA Crim 438. In *R v Gojra and Dhir* [2010] EWCA Crim 1939 the suggestion that an identification procedure 'might have been desirable' when the failure to hold one had been a breach of the Code was a misdirection which rendered the conviction unsafe. That defence counsel had addressed the matter in a closing speech was no answer; the appellant was entitled to the imprimatur of the court.

an identification parade enables a suspect to put the reliability of an eyewitness's identification to the test, that the suspect has lost the benefit of that safeguard and that the jury should take account of that fact in its assessment of the whole case, giving it such weight as it thinks fair.'

12.107 Two aspects of this guidance deserve closer attention. First, the proposition that the duty to warn the jury arises from a submission to exclude evidence which has been rejected. It is submitted that if a breach is established, the need to give an appropriate direction is not precluded simply because no application has been made to exclude the evidence. No submission may have been made for tactical reasons, or because the prejudice was regarded as insufficient to warrant exclusion. The breach may have emerged only when the evidence of the procedure was given. Provided there is some prejudice or potential prejudice caused by an established breach a direction should be given regardless of whether it has been the subject of an application to exclude evidence.

12.108 The second aspect concerns a ruling that no breach of the Code has occurred which is based upon a finding of fact by the judge. What direction, if any, should the jury be given if the issue of fact is rehearsed before the jury? For example, a defendant alleges that a police officer has improperly directed a witness's attention to him or her during the course of a street identification or witnesses at a video identification have been allowed to discuss the procedure after one of them has made an identification. If the trial judge, after hearing evidence in the jury's absence, rules that no breach has been established, the jury may yet reach the opposite view. It is submitted that it may be appropriate to direct the jury, in the event they make a finding in favour of the defendant, that the evidence should be ignored completely if exclusion would have been the consequence of the judge making the same finding; alternatively a conditional direction in accordance with *Quinn* to consider the impact of the breach upon the safety of the identification should be given.

PARTIAL, QUALIFIED AND NON-IDENTIFICATION

12.109 If a witness fails to identify the defendant at a formal procedure it is generally improper to direct the jury that the witness may have been mistaken. In *R v Speede*[167] four witnesses at an identification parade failed to pick out the defendant while another four asserted that he was not the robber. The Court of Appeal criticised the direction in which it was said that it was just as possible to mistakenly fail to identify someone as to wrongly identify a person. However it may be permissible to remind the jury of the practical difficulties in a witness's observation where they are relied upon to provide a possible reason for the witness's later failure to identify at a formal procedure.

---

[167] (1991) *The Times*, 3 April, CA.

12.110 In *R v Trew*[168] two women were robbed of handbags in similar circumstances. At later identification parades each picked a volunteer. The summing up pointed out the deficiencies in lighting and the short period of observation, which rendered the possibility of mistake in selection at a parade more likely. The Court of Appeal found that the jury were entitled to consider the possibility, provided the summing up dealt properly with the weaknesses in the prosecution case. A similar conclusion was reached in *R v George*.[169] The case centred upon the admissibility of qualified identification evidence and the difficulties due to the lapse in time and the change in the suspect's appearance between the offence and the identification procedure. The Court of Appeal held that in some instances such evidence was admissible subject to the jury receiving appropriate warnings. In particular the Court warned against reasoning from which a non- or qualified identification could be transformed into a positive identification by the evidence of such difficulties. This error is evident in *R v Barrowes*.[170] The victim of a theft selected a volunteer at an identification procedure. Before making the selection he had indicated that two of those paraded resembled the thief, the defendant and the volunteer eventually chosen. The jury were directed on the one hand that the prosecution relied upon identification evidence, buttressed by a *Turnbull* direction, and on the other that it would be dangerous to rely on the victim's dalliance with the image of the defendant because he did not in fact identify him. The effect of these contradictory directions was to render the guilty verdict unsafe. It was not an identification case at all. Where circumstances do require a *Turnbull* direction, it should be modified in such a way as not to elevate a non-identification case to the status of an identification case.[171] If an identification of which the jury have heard is retracted as mistaken by the person responsible for making it, unless the witness is treated as hostile and the prosecution seek to rely on the earlier statement, there is no occasion for a *Turnbull* direction.[172]

BAD CHARACTER DIRECTIONS

12.111 Whether a direction is necessary once bad character evidence is adduced and if so, its nature, will depend upon its evidential purpose. Where admitted to establish an important matter in issue under CJA 2003, s 101(1)(d), the matter in issue may be the identity of the perpetrator, the accused's propensity to commit offences of the kind charged which lends support of other identification evidence or combination of both. (See **10.03** for a discussion of the distinction.)

12.112 If bad character evidence is adduced to prove that a defendant's propensity to commit like offences makes it more probable that he has been

---

168 [1996] Crim LR 441, CA.
169 [2003] Crim LR 282, CA. See **10.29–10.33** for a discussion of the case.
170 [2010] EWCA Crim 1293.
171 *R v Gray* [2005] EWCA Crim 3564.
172 *R v Davis* [2006] EWCA Crim 2015.

correctly identified by other evidence, a propensity direction must be given. In *R v Hanson*[173] the Court of Appeal stated that the jury should be warned against placing undue reliance on previous convictions.

> 'The jury should be directed: that they should not conclude that the defendant is guilty ... merely because he has these convictions; that although the convictions may show a propensity, this does not mean that he has committed this offence ... that whether they in fact show a propensity is for them to decide; that they must take into account what the defendant has said about the previous conviction; and that, although they are entitled, if they find propensity is shown, to take this into account when determining guilt, propensity is only one relevant factor and they must assess its significance in the light of all the other evidence.'

12.113 But if the evidence of other offences is not deployed to demonstrate propensity, it follows that no propensity direction will be required. That will be the situation where other offences, often counts on the same indictment, have a nexus circumstantially probative in pointing the finger of guilt towards the same perpetrator. Such evidence may cumulatively tend to show that the defendant is that person.[174] Though a bad character direction will be redundant, the judge will nevertheless be required to explain how the evidence should be treated.[175] In some cases it will be appropriate to ask:

(1) By their connection or similarity has it been shown that both offence A and offence B appear to have been committed by the same person?

(2) If so, does the evidence of both taken together identify the defendant as the perpetrator?

Under the old 'similar fact' rules certain situations called for further cautionary directions. For example it might be necessary to balance a direction concerning connections between offences with references to dissimilarities tending to show that the offences might not have been committed by the same person.[176] If it has been suggested that the similar fact evidence has been brought about by collusion between prosecution witnesses, the jury must be directed to consider that assertion and to proceed to rely upon the evidence only if sure that there has been none.[177] There is no reason to suppose that in appropriate circumstances, such directions will not continue to be apposite.

HEARSAY DIRECTIONS

12.114 The multiple grounds on which hearsay may be admitted are set out in **10.135**. It is not possible to be prescriptive about the nature of a hearsay

173 [2005] EWCA Crim 824, [2005] 2 Cr App 21.

174 *R v Wallace* [2007] EWCA Crim 1760, [2007] 2 Cr App R 30 and *R v Freeman; R v Crawford* [2008] EWCA Crim 1863, [2009] 1 Cr App R 15.

175 See Judicial Studies Board Bench Book, chapter 12 on cross admissibility.

176 *R v Miller* [2003] EWCA Crim 2840, CA. See also *R v Johnson* [1995] 2 Cr App R 41, CA.

177 *R v Ryder* (1994) 98 Cr App R 242, CA.

direction; much will depend upon the reason for the absence of the witness. In most cases it will be necessary to warn the jury of the potential risks of reliance on a statement which has not been verified on oath and whose maker has not been seen by the jury nor tested in cross examination. The following matters, if relevant and particularly where the subject of proper or identifiable concern or challenge, are likely to form part of a direction:

(1) the circumstances in which the statement was made;

(2) the reliability of the maker of the statement;

(3) the reliability of the person or thing recording the statement;

(4) the apparent reliability of the statement, eg whether supported or contradicted by other evidence and the scope for error;

(5) the degree of difficulty a defendant will have in contradicting the statement.

12.115 The need for a forceful direction in an identification case where the evidence of the maker of the statement is central was made plain in *R v McCoy*.[178] The Court of Appeal held that:

> 'If a statement of a critical witness is to be read to the jury, perhaps especially in an alibi case where identification is the true issue, it must be incumbent on the trial judge to ensure that the jury realise the drawbacks which are imposed on the defence if the prosecution statement is read to them. It is not enough simply to say that counsel has not had the opportunity of cross-examining. The lay jury may not appreciate the significance of that fact. The judge must at least explain that it means that they may feel quite unable to attach anything like as much weight to the evidence in the statement, as they might if it were tested in cross-examination; and where appropriate it would be necessary, certainly desirable, for the judge to indicate to the jury by way of illustration the sort of matters that might well be put in cross-examination in the particular case.'

12.116 If an out-of-court statement is admitted under the res gestae[179] exception to the hearsay rule the jury should also be directed:

> '… that it is for them to decide what was said and to be sure that the witnesses were not mistaken in what they believed had been said to them. Further, they must be satisfied that the declarant did not concoct or distort to his advantage or the disadvantage of the accused the statement relied upon and where there is material to raise the issue, that he was not activated by any malice or ill will.'[180]

---

178 [2000] 6 *Archbold News* 2, CA.

179 See **10.160** for admissibility.

180 *R v Andrews* [1987] 1 AC 281, (1987) 84 Cr App R 382, CA.

DIRECTIONS CONCERNING ACCOMPLICES AND CO-ACCUSED

12.117 A co-defendant's interview or other out-of-court statement (apart from one in furtherance of the offence) which incriminates or identifies another is not evidence against that other. Accordingly, unless it has been admitted as hearsay under CJA 2003[181] the jury must be directed to disregard it entirely in the case of that other defendant.[182] To assist the jury in achieving that potentially difficult task it may be sensible to invite them to consider the case of the incriminated defendant first.[183]

12.118 Where a co-defendant or accomplice gives evidence at trial against another defendant it is admissible like any other incriminating evidence. However, it may be appropriate to give the jury a warning as to how it should be treated. The former common law obligation to give an 'accomplice warning' was abolished by Criminal Justice and Public Order Act 1994 s32, but a discretion to do so still exists. The Court of Appeal in *R v Makanjuola*[184] considered that the discretion to give a warning and its content depended upon the circumstances of the case, the issues raised and the quality of the accomplice's evidence. Often no warning would be necessary, but where there is some evidential basis for regarding the witness as unreliable the judge may consider it necessary to urge caution before placing reliance on it. In more extreme cases a stronger warning should be given and the jury advised to look for supporting evidence before acting on it. The Court went on to suggest that the warning should be given as part of the review of the evidence rather than a set piece direction. Where one defendant has given evidence against another, even where defendants are running mutual cut-throat defences, it will generally be necessary, in exercising the discretion to give a direction, at least to issue a warning to examine the evidence with care because the defendant may have a personal interest to serve.[185]

ADVERSE INFERENCE DIRECTIONS

12.119 An adverse inference under the Criminal Justice and Public Order Act (CJPOA) 1994 might be drawn against a defendant if he has failed:

(1) to mention any fact later relied upon in his defence;[186]

---

[181] See **10.141**.

[182] *R v Gunewardene* (1951) 35 Cr App R 80, CA.

[183] *R v Hickey and Robinson* [1997] 8 *Archbold News* 3, CA.

[184] [1995] 2 Cr App R 469, CA. This was a case concerning the corroboration warning in sexual cases whose judgment considered the effect of CJPOA 1994, s 32 for accomplice cases also.

[185] *R v Jones and Jenkins* [2003] EWCA Crim 1966 following *Knowlden and Knowlden* 77 CR App R 94, CA and *R v Cheema* (1994) 98 Cr App R 195, CA.

[186] CJPOA 1994, s 34.

(2) to account for the presence of any object in his possession or at the place of arrest or any substance or mark on his person or clothing;[187]

(3) to account for his presence at a particular place;[188]

(4) to give evidence at trial.[189]

12.120 The first three of these are considered at **10.184–10.189**. The jury directions applicable in identification cases are no different from those in any other case. The Judicial Studies Board Crown Court Bench Book guidance on these adverse inferences is set out in Appendix F. It approves the specimen direction under CJPOA 1994. It is important to note that, in respect of the failure to mention a fact when questioned under that section, the judge must identify to the jury precisely which facts are capable of leading to the inference.[190] Generally the nature of the adverse inference will be that the defendant has fabricated the fact since the time when questioned about it, but it is not the only inference the jury are entitled to draw.[191] In some cases a defendant will resile from something said in interview and advance an alternative fact at trial. In those circumstances it may be appropriate to give a *Lucas* direction in relation to the content of the interview as well as a direction under CJPOA 1994 s34.[192] If a defendant's silence is not capable of yielding an adverse inference the jury should be directed in accordance with the common law principle that they must not draw any adverse inference.[193]

12.121 Adverse inferences under the Criminal Procedure and Investigations Act (CPIA) 1996 may be drawn from the failures:

(5) to disclose the defence case in the defence statement and particulars of defence witnesses;[194]

(6) to disclose particulars of alibi and alibi witnesses.[195]

12.122 The various failures by a defendant from which an inference might be drawn are considered at **9.30** above. The nature of the inference will depend upon the particular failure alleged. The jury should be reminded of the

---

187 CJPOA 1994 s 36.

188 CJPOA 1994, s 37.

189 CJPOA 1994, s 35.

190 *R v Webber* [2004] UKHL 1, [2004] 1 Cr App R 101. See also *R v Lewis* [2003] EWCA Crim 223. Simply to ask rhetorically why the defendant did not provide 'all this information' was held to be inadequate.

191 *R v Daniel* [1998] 2 Cr App R 373, [1998] Crim LR 818, CA; *R v Beckles and Montague* [1999] Crim LR 148, CA.

192 *R v O(A)* [2000] Crim LR 617, CA.

193 *R v McGarry* [1999] 1 Cr App R 377, [1999] Crim LR 316, CA. The direction spoke of a defendant's 'right to silence' when interviewed. Though this aspect of it is not specifically mentioned in the judgment, the Court accepted the propriety of an 'old-style' direction.

194 CPIA 1996, s 11.

195 CPIA 1996, s 11.

explanation given for the failure and directed not to draw the inference unless the explanation is rejected. The jury would also be required to consider any evidence of legal advice to the defendant as to the content of the statement or notice. CPIA 1996, s 11 provides that, in addition to the adverse inferences that might be drawn by a jury, a court 'may make such comment as appears appropriate'.

12.123 An adverse inference may also be drawn under the Police and Criminal Evidence Act 1984 from the failure:

(7) to consent to the taking of an intimate sample.[196]

12.124 The circumstances in which the inference may be drawn are considered at **10.190**. It would appear that the adverse inference available to the jury is the defendant's fear that the sample would match a sample taken from the victim or scene of the crime. However, before it might be available, the jury would need to be satisfied that the correct procedure for the request had been complied with and directed to consider the explanation for the failure, including the implications of any legal advice received.

---

[196] PACE, s 62(10).

Part III

SCIENTIFIC EVIDENCE

Chapter 13

DNA PROFILING

INTRODUCTION TO DNA AND ITS USE IN FORENSIC SCIENCE

What is DNA?

13.1 In the human body, there are billions of cells that are the building blocks of our tissues and organs which are only visible under a microscope. Cells are, in turn, comprised of even smaller structures that allow them to perform particular functions. One such structure is the nucleus (plural, nuclei). The nucleus of each cell, with the notable exception of red blood cells, contains DNA (Deoxyribonucleic acid). DNA is therefore a material present in almost every part of everyone.

13.2 This DNA is referred to as 'nuclear DNA' and is considered unique to each individual (except for genetically identical twins). There is a second variety of DNA that is not contained within the nucleus, but within another sub-cellular structure called the mitochondrion (plural, mitochondria), and this DNA is referred to as mitochondrial DNA (mtDNA). Unlike the nucleus, there are many mitochondria within each cell.

13.3 Cells, containing DNA, can be shed and become deposited upon surfaces. These cells can be recovered, the DNA extracted, analysed and statistics provided to aid identification of the potential donor. This is forensic DNA profiling.

Types of crime stains

13.4 Nuclear DNA is the form traditionally associated with forensic DNA analysis, as it is detectable in blood, spermatozoa (sperm cells) in semen, hair roots, nasal secretions and epithelial cells. Sperm cells have a 'head' and a 'tail', but only the head contains DNA. Semen is a liquid comprising sperm cells and seminal fluid. Although it is the sperm cells that provide results for DNA profiling, it is the seminal fluid that is detected in the chemical test for semen. Thus not all suspected semen stains will produce DNA profiles as no sperm cells may be present (perhaps as a result of a medical condition or vasectomy). Epithelial cells are surface cells many of which are in contact with the external physical environment, thereby comprising all surfaces of the body, including our skin and orifices, such as mouth, anus, vagina etc. For example, epithelial cells from the mouth are the source of DNA in saliva and those from the scalp comprise dandruff.

13.5 Mitochondrial DNA profiling is most often used for crime stains from which nuclear DNA would be very difficult and usually impossible to detect, eg faeces, hair and bone. There are some biological materials from which DNA is hard to detect due to the paucity of epithelial cells present, such as urine and sweat.

13.6 The success of a DNA analysis is dependent upon many factors, including the quantity (the more the better) and quality (lack of degradation, contaminants, etc) of DNA present, and the methods employed. The amount of DNA present and available for recovery can depend upon the nature of the DNA containing material. In general terms blood and semen, are good sources of DNA. Hairs must have root material present in order to provide a nuclear DNA profile (the shafts contain mitochondrial DNA). The root cells are normally present because the hair has been pulled from the head, rather than being naturally shed. Thus hair samples suitable for nuclear DNA profiling are usually associated with forceful contacts such as would be expected during an assault. Although a reference buccal swab taken directly from the inside surface of the cheek will be packed full with lots of DNA-containing epithelial cells, the recovery of DNA from saliva is unpredictable. This is due to variation in the amount of epithelial cells present in saliva, as a result of many factors, such as drinking, eating, or a high abundance of oral bacteria that can cause degradation of the DNA.

Recovery of crime stains for DNA analysis

13.7 Only specific areas of nuclear DNA are tested in DNA profiling, described at **13.11–13.14**. DNA is contained in cells in a series of long strands (chromosomes). After cell death, the strands are broken into shorter pieces. If the DNA has broken at the areas of interest for profiling those areas will not be detected because the detection process depends on the length of the strand. When this happens, the DNA is referred to as being degraded. DNA can be degraded by a number of environmental factors including heat, humidity, light (particularly ultra violet light that is present in sunlight), bacteria and some chemicals. Crime stains must therefore be recovered as soon as possible by a method that will yield as much DNA as possible and stored in a manner which guards against degradation.

13.8 The best recovery method, where possible, is to submit the entire item to the laboratory (eg garments, bottles, weapons). Wet stains, such as blood, should be air-dried prior to packaging or immediately following recovery (heat must not be used to accelerate drying and the location of drying must be secure and monitored to prevent contamination). For DNA on non-transportable surfaces (eg walls, doors, windows), recovery is performed using wet and dry swabs (a swab is essentially the same as a cotton bud) or pieces of sticky tape. Within the laboratory, sticky tape is used as a particularly efficient means of recovering skin cells from garments. Whatever method is used, it is essential that the packaging is clearly labelled and that the integrity of the contents can be demonstrated. The packaging must be securely sealed with no gaps or holes, which could allow accidental contamination. Issues of continuity and contamination are considered at **13.66**. Items must never be stored in damp or warm conditions where bacterial growth could occur. Items bearing dried stains do not need to be frozen but all other items, such as swabs, should be frozen as soon as possible.

13.9 Freezing samples immediately after recovery will prevent any further degradation; however, the conditions to which a sample of DNA may have been exposed prior to recovery cannot be known. There may be factors that accelerated or prevented degradation, or that reduced the amount of DNA present. Thus, it is never possible to draw inferences from the condition or quantity of DNA observed in a DNA profile obtained. Depending on the specific conditions, DNA may degrade in a matter of hours, or last for thousands of years. A DNA profile is evidence of possible association between a person and a surface, not of contact, and cannot be evidence of the time of deposition of the DNA. Issues relating to the quality of DNA profiles and DNA transfer are discussed at **13.62–13.65**.

Methods of DNA profiling

13.10 Although a relatively large quantity of DNA is required to produce a DNA profile, the majority of crime stains submitted to the forensic laboratory contain extremely small amounts of DNA (at trace levels) insufficient for the procedure. In the past this hindered the applicability of DNA profiling, as the original method of restriction fragment length polymorphism (RFLP) required this large amount of DNA to be available within the crime stain. As technology has advanced, a method of copying DNA, the polymerase chain reaction (PCR), has been devised that allows small amounts to be increased to the required amount (see **13.18–13.20**). Scientists were therefore able to advance from requiring large stains for RFLP to requiring increasingly smaller sample sizes with improved discrimination between individuals (determined by statistical analysis, see **13.36–13.48**). The sensitivity of the standard nuclear DNA profiling method can be increased to enable DNA profiling from only a few cells, see **13.30–13.35**. The methods employed to profile mtDNA and also to obtain DNA specific for male donors are described at **13.49–13.56**.

NUCLEAR DNA PROFILING

13.11 Although the DNA in the nuclei of cells is considered unique for each individual (with the exception of identical twins), the vast majority of our DNA is the same for all humans. It is therefore only a very small proportion of our DNA that actually differs among us. Some areas of this variable DNA, termed 'junk DNA' as it does not 'code' or instruct any bodily process, are used in forensic DNA profiling techniques to distinguish between different individuals.

13.12 The number of these areas tested during DNA profiling depends on the kit employed. Each area is called a locus (plural: loci). At these areas the DNA molecule contains a number of identical repeating units, similar to carriages in a train. It is the number of repeats that can differ between us (i e the number of carriages on the train making it longer or shorter). These repeats are known as 'short tandem repeats' or STRs. For each locus, there exist a number of possible STRs of different length available. These pieces of DNA of specific but varying lengths, are collectively known as 'alleles' (pronounced al-eels), although for simplicity they are sometimes referred to as DNA components.

13.13 For DNA of one individual, a maximum of two alleles is present at each locus. We receive one allele from each parent; although the received allele may be the same from both parents. If we have a different allele from each parent at a particular area of DNA, then two components are observed at this locus, which is described as 'heterozygous' (hetero meaning different). If, at another locus, the same allele is received from both parents, then only one component is observed and the locus is described as 'homozygous' (homo meaning the same).

13.14 Each allele is not in itself unique, but only some people in the population will have it. It is the combination of components across all the loci tested that can be used to distinguish between individuals. This is what constitutes a DNA profile. The following stages are required to generate a DNA profile from cellular material.

DNA extraction

13.15 DNA is extracted from a sample by breaking up the cells present to release the DNA, and then separating the DNA from other cellular material and any debris from the sample (such as, fabric, cigarette butt, etc). There are a number of extraction methods (many available as automated kits) and the most appropriate method has to be selected with consideration of type and quantity of cells present.

13.16 For semen-stained samples, DNA can be extracted separately from sperm and non-sperm cells to give 'seminal' and 'cellular' fractions, respectively. This is known as differential or preferential DNA extraction and is useful in sexual assault cases, since DNA from the seminal fraction can be attributed to the sperm cells and hence indicates the source of that sperm. Where DNA of interest is present on a heavily contaminated surface (eg fabric containing strong dyes) a combination of extraction methods may be applied to 'clean-up' the DNA extract. 'Clean-up' and concentration of DNA can also be performed by the use of specialist filters.

DNA quantification

13.17 To generate a good quality DNA profile, it is important to add an appropriate amount of DNA within the approved detection limits of the equipment. Too much or too little DNA can result in the signal being outside (above or below) the detectable range or could increase the number of artefacts generated (see below). Artefacts can make it difficult to interpret the DNA profile. The extracted DNA is therefore quantified before proceeding on to the next stage. An optimal amount of DNA for the kit that is most commonly used in the UK is in the range of 0.5 to 2 nanograms (ng, 10^{-9}g), although DNA profiles can be obtained down to approximately 0.2 ng.

DNA amplification

13.18 As mentioned above, only specific areas of the extracted DNA are tested. These areas are specifically targeted and repeatedly copied, producing many copies of only the STR alleles. This separates these alleles from the rest of the DNA. Remembering that the alleles differ in length due to varying number of repeating units, the alleles can be separated (described at **13.21–13.22**).

13.19 This multiplication (or more commonly termed, amplification) is done by a chemical reaction called the polymerase chain reaction (PCR). The number of copies of the alleles made depends on the number of multiplications, or cycles, in the PCR. Making many copies allows a small amount of starting material to be amplified to an amount that can be detected and visualised in a DNA profile. Increasing the number of cycles in the PCR results in more copies being made, which allows an even smaller amount of starting material to be used. This technique is discussed at **13.30–13.35**.

13.20 DNA amplification is generally performed using a manufactured kit, such as the AmpF*l*STR® SGM Plus® and Identifiler® PCR Amplification kits (simply referred to as SGM Plus and Identifiler). Both are made by Applied Biosystems to test 10 and 15 STR loci, respectively. The former is predominantly used in the UK and the latter in the US. In addition to testing the STR loci, these kits also test the amelogenin locus, which allows the sex of the DNA to be determined: X,X female, X,Y male. Other kits are available from other manufacturers such as Promega.

DNA separation and profile generation

13.21 In order to determine the size of the alleles amplified by the PCR, the alleles are separated according to their size. This is done by flowing them through a narrow tube containing a porous gel; smaller alleles are able to move through the pores quicker than the larger ones. A size standard (a set of DNA pieces of known sizes) is run through the tube at the same time as each sample. The size of the alleles in each sample can then be determined by comparison to the size standard. To determine the number of repeats that make up each allele, the size of an allele is compared to a series of alleles of known repeat numbers, known as an allelic ladder.

13.22 The determinations of the size and repeat number of each allele are performed by computer software, which then presents the data as a DNA profile graph (called an 'epg' or electrophoretogram). Such a graph looks like a series of peaks with some 'noise' at the baseline (Figure 1). A peak represents a DNA component if it is above a certain height (threshold), or can be clearly distinguished from the baseline noise, and cannot be attributed to known artefacts of the DNA profiling technique. Peaks that are identified as alleles are labelled by the computer software with their repeat number (Figure 1).

DNA profile interpretation

13.23 When a DNA profile has been generated by the computer software, the peaks that have been labelled as peaks are first verified to ensure that no artefactual peaks have been incorrectly labelled as alleles. The size, shape and position of the majority of these artefactual peaks make them easily distinguishable from allele peaks. However, artefactual peaks known as 'stutter' peaks can interfere with interpretation. A stutter peak is one repeat shorter than an allele and occurs adjacent to an allele peak (Figure 1). In standard DNA profiling, these stutter peaks are usually identified as being below 15% of the height of the adjacent allele peak. However, a peak at a stutter position may be caused by a stutter, or an allele, or a stutter and an allele, and these must be taken into consideration.

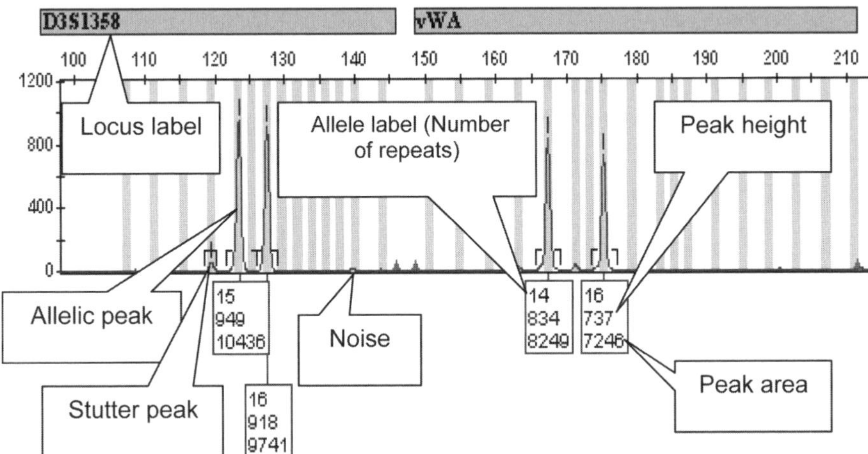

Figure 1: *Illustration of different parts of a section of an epg (DNA profile graph, as described in the text)*

Single-source DNA profiles

13.24 Once the allele peaks have been verified, the minimum number of people that could have contributed DNA to the DNA profile is determined. Each person can contribute a maximum of two alleles at each locus. This means that if there are no more than two alleles at each locus, the DNA profile probably came from one individual and is termed a 'single-source' DNA profile. If there are peaks at every locus, and any single peaks are above a certain height, then the DNA profile is considered to be a 'full' profile. If, however, some peaks are missing from some loci, then it is considered to be a 'partial' profile. When a single source DNA profile is obtained from a crime stain, it can be directly compared to a DNA profile from an individual. If the corresponding alleles in both profiles match at *all* available loci, then the crime stain DNA profile could have come from the suspect. The significance of such a match can be determined statistically and will be affected by whether the crime stain profile is a partial or full profile (see **13.36–13.48**).

13.25 If there are DNA components that do not match between the two profiles, then this person must be excluded as having contributed to the crime stain. If no suspect DNA profile is known, then any single source DNA profile inferred from a crime stain can be loaded onto the National DNA Database (NDNAD) to search for individuals who might have a matching DNA profile. The NDNAD was set up in 1995 and contains the DNA profiles of persons suspected, cautioned or convicted of a recordable offence, unsolved crime samples, some missing persons and unaccounted crime profiles. It is important to note that the AmpF*l*STR® SGM Plus® DNA profiling method that is now routinely employed in the UK was only brought into use in 1999. From the beginning of the NDNAD until then, a method called SGM was employed that only tested six areas of DNA. Consequently, if SGM DNA profiles produce a database hit during cold case reviews, then further work is required to provide a full SGM Plus® DNA profile that tests all ten areas. The intelligence provided by the NDNAD extends beyond only those persons profiled. A person who is not part of the database can also be identified through profiles of direct family members, such as parents, children or siblings, who may be on the database. This is possible due to a process called familial searching.

Mixed DNA profiles

13.26 It is common for DNA profiles obtained from casework samples to be 'mixed' DNA profiles, that is, more than one person has contributed to the profile. The easiest way to assess the number of contributors to a DNA profile is to count the number of allele peaks at each DNA area tested. If there are three alleles at any locus, this indicates the presence of DNA from at least two people, five alleles indicates at least three, and so on. In standard DNA profiling, there is another way in which to assess the number of contributors.

13.27 Two different alleles *at a specific locus* that originate from one individual are expected to produce peaks of similar height. This is because a single donor will have contributed both in equal amounts. Variations during the DNA amplification process, however, mean that two peaks can be accepted as being from a single person although they have different heights. If the height difference of the two peaks is beyond the laboratory's acceptable height difference (each laboratory should establish the limits for their technique, but this is usually when one peak is more than twice the size of the other) the peaks are considered to be 'imbalanced' (the phenomenon is referred to as 'heterozygote-imbalance'). Such an imbalance suggests that the two alleles are from two different people and thereby indicates that there is more than one contributor to the DNA profile even though there may be no more than two alleles at each locus.

13.28 Individual DNA profiles can often, although not always, be distinguished from within a mixed profile. This is possible where one contributor is known and can be subtracted to leave the second (eg victim/perpetrator mix) or where there is a marked difference in the amount of DNA donated by each contributor (represented by peak heights). The larger peak can be considered to come from a 'major' contributor and the smaller peak from a 'minor' contributor. With a mixed DNA profile, if this major/minor designation can be made at every locus, then it may be possible to infer two separate DNA profiles: a major and a minor DNA profile.

13.29 There remain some mixed DNA profiles from which individual contributors cannot be reliably distinguished. When there are more than two indistinguishable DNA contributors (no major/minor) in one profile it is generally considered uninterpretable and no meaningful information can be gained. Where there are apparently only two indistinguishable DNA contributors in a mixed profile, however, statistical methods can be applied to allow its comparison to the DNA profile of a suspect; these are discussed at **13.36–13.48**.

LOW TEMPLATE DNA PROFILING

13.30 It is sometimes necessary to obtain a DNA profile from a crime stain that contains less DNA than that recommended for the standard DNA profiling methods. Modifications to the DNA amplification stage, or just after DNA amplification, can be employed to increase the sensitivity of standard DNA profiling methods and allow smaller amounts of starting material to be used. Methods employing these modifications are collectively known as low template DNA (LT-DNA) profiling techniques and are designed to analyse DNA of amounts below 200 picograms (pg, 10^{-12}g).

13.31 The first LT-DNA technique developed, commonly referred to as Low Copy Number (LCN), involved increasing the number of cycles in the PCR to increase the number of copies of the alleles made. Twenty-eight PCR cycles are used in standard DNA profiling, whereas 34 cycles were used in LCN. Other LT-DNA techniques, known as 'enhancement', use specialist filters after the PCR to clean-up the amplified alleles. This is to remove any contaminants from the crime stain and chemicals from the PCR process that may affect the next stages in the generation of a DNA profile. The use of LT-DNA techniques result in higher peaks in the DNA profile than those that would be generated in standard profiling from the same amount of starting DNA. This therefore allows the detection of peaks that would not normally be detected.

13.32 On the one hand, this is a good thing, as more alleles from a crime stain can be detected. However, on the other, this increases the chance of detecting alleles not associated with the crime stain, known as 'drop-in' alleles, for example as a result of contamination. When testing very low amounts of DNA, a number of random effects can occur that may complicate the interpretation of the DNA profiles generated. These are known as stochastic effects; the occurrence of drop-in alleles is one such effect. Other effects include the observations of larger stutter peaks relative to their adjacent alleles (stutters with peak heights of up to 40% of their adjacent alleles have been reported[1]), increased heterozygote-imbalance, and allele 'drop-out'. Since LT-DNA techniques are usually only employed when there is a very low amount of DNA available for testing, only a few copies of each allele may be present. This means that the chemistry of the kit used to profile the DNA may not detect all of the copies, such that some alleles may be better at being seen than others. This can be reflected in the heights of the allele peaks. If, at a heterozygous locus, more of one allele is detected than the other, then its peak is bigger, making the two peaks imbalanced. When testing very low amounts of DNA, peak height imbalance can therefore no longer be used to indicate whether a second contributor is present. In extreme situations, this effect can result in only one allele of the two being detected, such that a heterozygote appears as a homozygote. This is known as allele drop-out, as one of the alleles present in the original crime stain has not been detected.

13.33 These four effects can, alone or in combination, cause stochastic variation between different analyses (runs) of the same crime stain. The lower the amount of DNA, the more likely the effects are to occur, leading to stochastic variation and poor reproducibility of the DNA profiles. However, the same amount of DNA in different samples does not necessarily entail the same degree of stochastic variation. It is the presence of the effects, not the amount of DNA that tells us whether the reliability of the interpretation is likely to be affected.

13.34 Interpretation guidelines have been developed in an attempt to overcome the poor reproducibility in DNA profiles that exhibit stochastic effects. These include the use of:

- higher stutter percentages than the 15% routinely used in standard DNA profiling to help distinguish between stutter and true allelic peaks;
- a 'consensus' or biological method, in which a sample is profiled at least twice and only alleles that occur in at least two of the replicates are reported in a 'consensus' profile.[2] This is proposed to resolve the issues of allele drop-in and drop-out.

13.35 However, no guidelines have been universally accepted on how to deal with stutter in DNA profiles generated by LT-DNA techniques. A range of views can be found in the scientific literature on whether stutter percentage actually does increase,[3] and if so, what is an appropriate threshold percentage

---

1 J Whitaker, E Cotton and P Gill 'A Comparison of the Characteristics of Profiles Produced with the AMPFlSTR® SGM Plus™ Multiplex System for both Standard and Low Copy Number (LCN) STR DNA Analysis' (2001) 123 *Forensic Science International* 215–223.

2 P Gill, J Whitaker, C Flaxman, N Brown and J Buckleton 'An Investigation of the Rigor of Interpretation Rules for STRs Derived from Less than 100 pg of DNA' (2000) 112 *Forensic Science International* 17–40.

3 T Caragine, R Mikulasovich, J Tamariz, E Bajda, J Sebestyen, H Baum and M Prinz

to apply for interpretation.[4] Likewise, although the consensus method is now routinely employed to interpret DNA profiles obtained from LT-DNA techniques, there is still debate in the scientific literature as to the number of replicates that are sufficient to resolve drop-out as well as drop-in. It is generally accepted that the more replicates run the better, but this has to be offset against the amount of crime stain available, which is usually limited in cases where LT-DNA techniques are required. It was originally proposed that a statistical method would be more appropriate for the interpretation of LT-DNA profiles than the biological method. However, over ten years on, although various statistical methods are in progress, none is yet routinely accepted and applied.

STATISTICAL ANALYSES

13.36 Once a DNA profile has been obtained from a crime stain, it can be compared to the DNA profiles of any persons of interest to see whether there is a potential match. Establishing a 'match' between DNA profiles from a crime stain and from an individual follows the same principles as establishing a match between any other characteristic linking a person to a crime. For example, if the offender is reported to have brown hair and the suspect has brown hair, then this is a match. However, many people in the general population have brown hair, and as such, we would put little weight on this match. But, if we did not know that having brown hair is a common characteristic in the general population, then we would not know how much weight to place on the observation of this match. It is therefore essential to know how common a characteristic is in the general population to be able to establish how much evidential weight, or significance, to place on a match. In DNA profiling, it is the alleles that create the match.

13.37 Because alleles are not visible in the same way that, for example, hair colour is, we cannot rely on our everyday experience to establish how significant a match is between DNA profiles. Studies are performed on populations to estimate the frequency of each allele in the population. Different populations may have different allelic frequencies. These frequencies are used to calculate the significance of a match using a number of statistical methods. Here, we will only present the two most common methods used in the UK: the determinations of a random match probability (RMP) for a single-source DNA profile and of a likelihood ratio (LR) for mixed DNA profiles.

'Validation of Testing and Interpretation Protocols for Low Template DNA Samples using AmpFlSTR Identifiler', (2009) 50 *Croatian Medical Journal* 250–267.

4 S Petricevic, J Whitaker, J Buckleton, S Vintiner, J Patel, P Simon, H Ferraby, W Hermiz and A Russell 'Validation and Development of Interpretation Guidelines for Low Copy Number (LCN) DNA Profiling in New Zealand using the AmpF/STR® SGM Plus™ multiplex' (2010) 4 *Forensic Science International: Genetics* 305–310.

Random match probability (RMP)

13.38 A DNA profile of interest could be directly obtained from a crime stain or inferred from a mixed DNA profile. As previously described (at 13.11–13.29), there are two ways in which to infer a single-source profile from a mixed profile:

- a major or minor DNA profile from one individual may be inferred from a mixed profile based on allele peak heights;
- in some mixed profiles, one of the contributors is known. For example, a vaginal swab would be expected to give the DNA profile of the woman from whom the swab was taken. Her DNA profile can be determined from her single source reference buccal swab. The alleles determined as originating from own DNA can then be subtracted from the mixed profile obtained from her vaginal swab. The remaining 'foreign' alleles may constitute a single source profile of the second contributor (or a new mixture if there is more than one additional contributor). The remaining alleles may be associated with the offender and can be compared to the DNA profile of any suspects or a single source profile could be uploaded to the NDNAD.

13.39 If just one allele within the profile of interest differs from the DNA profile of the suspect, then that person is conclusively excluded as the person who deposited the DNA. If, however, all of the alleles detected match that of the suspect, there are two possible explanations: either the DNA of interest matches the profile of the suspect because that DNA has originated from them, or the DNA belongs to another person but matches simply by chance. In *R v Doheny & Adams*,[5] the Court of Appeal held that the expert should not offer an opinion that DNA had come from a specific person, but that he should consider only the probability that it had come from another person (see **13.70–13.73**).

13.40 The probability of finding one allele is not influenced by the presence of any other allele, ie the presence of each allele is an independent event. This allows a very simple calculation to be performed, termed 'the product rule', which states that the probability of a series of independent events is the product of the probability of each occurring. Thus we can essentially multiply together the probabilities of randomly finding a person with each of the alleles observed to provide the probability of randomly finding a person within the population who by chance has all of these alleles – the DNA profile (this does not however consider related persons).

13.41 Whilst we do not know the DNA profile of every individual in the population, it is possible to use the frequencies of alleles in the population to provide an estimate of the chance of finding a particular DNA profile in that

---

5 [1996] EWCA Crim 728.

population. The estimated frequency of any profile within a population equates to the probability of randomly selecting a person from that population who has that profile.

13.42 The correct reporting of these is of the form, 'The probability of finding this profile by chance, in an unknown, unrelated, individual is 1 in x', where x may be up to a billion (1,000 million).

13.43 The more complete the DNA profile of interest (the greater the amount of alleles), and the rarer the alleles are, the more discriminating the profile is. The chance of randomly finding it within the population is reduced and the RMP will be low (note that as these likelihoods are simply fractions 1 in a million is larger than 1 in a billion). For example, for a match with a full DNA profile (which would have a maximum of 22 alleles if generated by the SGM Plus system), the RMP is in the order of one in several billion, but is conventionally reported as one in a billion to ensure that the evidence is not overstated and to acknowledge that there is always the possibility of a chance match. Conversely when fewer (as in a partial profile) or more common alleles are present, there is less discrimination and a greater number of people could match by chance, hence there will be a higher RMP. The RMP is not the probability that a person with a DNA profile matching the profile of interest (ie a crime stain) is responsible for that stain, it simply indicates how discriminating the DNA profile can be, hence whether or not many people could be expected to match by chance.

13.44 The meaning of this random match probability is easily confused. One common error is where the condition upon which the probability is calculated is changed (transposed conditional). In terms of reporting a DNA profile this would be when the statistic calculated is no longer reported as the frequency of occurrence of a person's DNA profile, rather the statistic is used to indicate the probability of guilt. For example, if there is expected to be a one in one billion probability of a chance match to the crime stain DNA profile, the wording might be changed such that because the person's DNA matched the crime stain, there is a billion to one probability that they are responsible for the crime stain. Although this may sound logical, it is statistically incorrect. The change of subject for which the DNA statistic has been calculated overestimates the strength of the evidence. It is therefore known as the Prosecutor's Fallacy (see **13.70–13.73**).

13.45 Similarly there is a Defence Attorney's Fallacy where evidence is underestimated as the RMP is applied to the population of a location to try and indicate how many others could be responsible. For example, if the probability of a chance occurrence was 1 in 100,000 and the crime occurred in a city with a population of 5 million, the defence attorney may incorrectly assert that there is a 1 in 50 chance that the defendant is guilty because there may be 49 other people with that profile. Champod and Evett, for example, provide further explanations of these fallacies.[6]

Likelihood Ratio (LR)

13.46 A likelihood ratio (LR) is a method of comparing the probability of two things by simply dividing one by the other. In horse racing, if one horse is 10–1 and another is 50–1, then the LR is 5 (=50/10) that the outcome will be the former horse will win rather than the latter, and 1/5 (=10/50=0.2) that the outcome will be that the latter will win rather than the former. Note that the LR compares only those two in this instance. An LR of greater than 1 (>1) favours the 'top line' (numerator) outcome, whereas an LR less than 1 (<1) favours the 'bottom line' (denominator) outcome. It is simply a means of measuring how much more likely one thing is compared to another.

13.47 In DNA profiling, an LR can be used to establish the significance of observing alleles in a mixture that match corresponding alleles in a suspect's DNA profile. Mixtures can only be evaluated in this manner when it is assumed that only DNA from two contributors is present in the mixture, that is, when there is no evidence of DNA from a third contributor. This is crucial as the LR employed in evaluating the significance of mixtures compares the following two alternative hypotheses:

- that the DNA profile of interest comes from the suspect plus an unknown and unrelated individual;
- that the DNA profile of interest comes from two unknown and unrelated individuals.

The probabilities of the evidence (the mixed DNA profile) given each of these hypotheses are determined using the product rule with the frequencies of the alleles observed, in a similar manner to that described above. The LR is then calculated by dividing the probability of the crime stain DNA profile given hypothesis A by the probability of the evidence given by hypothesis B. If the resulting number is greater than one, then the evidence supports hypothesis A. For example, if the LR is calculated to be 1,000, then this means that the crime stain DNA profile observed is a thousand times more likely to have originated from the suspect plus an unknown and unrelated individual, than from two unknown and unrelated individuals. Alternatively, if the LR is less that one, then the evidence supports hypothesis B.

Effect of genetic relatedness

13.48 The use of the statistical analyses discussed above is based on assessing how likely it is that a suspect's DNA profile matches a crime stain DNA profile

---

6 C Champod and I Evett in A Jamieson and A Moenssens (eds) *Wiley Encyclopedia of Forensic Science* (Wiley, 2009).

by chance. This does not include a consideration of individuals that are genetically related to the suspect. When two DNA profiles come from related individuals, then there is a greater chance that they will have some matching alleles than if the individuals are not related. The chance of matching alleles increases with increasing genetic relatedness. For example, DNA profiles from two brothers are more likely to have shared alleles than DNA profiles from two cousins. If this is a relevant issue in a particular case, then it would need to be taken into consideration when calculating the LR or RMP. A RMP for siblings is in the order of 1 in 10,000, whereas an RMP for first cousins is in the order of 1 in 100 million.[7]

OTHER DNA PROFILING TECHNIQUES

Mitochondrial DNA profiling

13.49 Unlike nuclear DNA, mitochondrial DNA is not inherited from both parents; it is of maternal inheritance only. A mother will pass the same mtDNA to all of her children and her daughters will pass this same mtDNA to their children. The mtDNA of siblings does not differ although their nuclear DNA does. Mitochondrial DNA also has a much shorter structure than nuclear DNA, it is in fact circular. Being the same for all maternal relatives, it is much less discriminating than nuclear DNA, but still has forensic applications.

13.50 Mitochondrial DNA is most useful for crime stains from which only very small amounts of nuclear DNA can be extracted: tissues such as bone, teeth and hair, and also environmentally damaged or old degraded samples. There are two main reasons for this. First, there is much more mtDNA per cell than nuclear DNA. There are two 'copies' (one from each parent) of nuclear DNA contained in the nucleus and only one nucleus per cell. However, there are around five copies of mtDNA in each mitochondrion, and each cell can have hundreds of mitochondria present, giving an average of around 500 copies of mtDNA per cell. Secondly, the mitochondrion is enclosed by two walls and its DNA molecule is circular, both of which make it less susceptible to degradation and breakdown. Thus enough intact mtDNA can remain available for profiling after nuclear DNA has perished. Extreme vigilance is required, however, as this also means that mtDNA is much more susceptible to contamination.

13.51 Mitochondrial DNA is rarely applied to routine criminal casework. The properties of this substance however, have rendered it a useful form of identification for very old remains, and particularly in disasters that result in a large number of deaths. The maternal lineage means that reference samples can be readily obtained for many of the deceased persons, and the durability of

---

[7] L Foreman and I Evett 'Statistical Analyses to Support Forensic Interpretation for a New Ten-Locus STR Profiling System' (2001) 114 *International Journal of Legal Medicine* 147–155.

mtDNA allows its detection from poor quality samples that could result from disasters, in which bodies may have been badly damaged by fire, submersion, or simply by a long delay in recovery.

13.52 The analysis of mtDNA is termed sequencing. Unlike nuclear DNA profiling, which tests several areas of the nuclear DNA (for example, 10 or 15), only two areas of mtDNA are tested. These areas are known to be very variable and can differ between different individuals. All DNA is composed of strings of nucleotide units containing one of only four possible bases; adenine (A), thymine (T), cytosine (C) or guanine (G). Sequencing effectively lists the order in which these units are present at the two areas tested. The sequence produced is compared to an appropriate reference sequence, such as the revised Cambridge Reference Sequence. Any differences are noted, and it is these that effectively form the mtDNA profile.

13.53 Mitochondrial DNA sequencing can be complex and at present it is not possible to provide any interpretation from mixtures. Difficulties arising, even when there is a single source, include the possibility of mutation from mother to child or difficulties with the sequencing chemistry causing some bases to be unspecified. The analyst must perform a careful interpretation of the sequencing results. One of three conclusions will be reported:

- *Exclusion*: the sequences have two or more differences and therefore do not belong to the same family.
- *Inconclusive*: there is one difference between the sequences
- *Cannot exclude*: the samples cannot be excluded as originating from the same maternal linage as there are no apparent differences in the mtDNA sequences.

13.54 A frequency statistic is provided but this is dependant upon the size of the database used by the analyst (and whether this is representative of the population). Mitochondrial DNA profiles are not compatible with the National DNA Database; it is therefore not possible to search for the identity of an unknown mtDNA profile.

Y-STR DNA profiling

13.55 Y-STR profiling, a form of nuclear DNA profiling, involves the analysis of STRs. Rather than looking at regions of DNA across many different chromosomes, Y-STR analysis is applied to a number of regions on only one chromosome. This is the Y-chromosome that is only present in males. The analytical method employed in Y-STR profiling is the same as that applied to nuclear DNA profiling (described at **13.11–13.29**), although different pieces of DNA are targeted. In a similar manner to mtDNA profiling, a Y-STR DNA profile does not contain information from both parents. As it focuses on a male only chromosome, it provides information of DNA that is passed from father to son. Furthermore, because it is only present in male individuals, analysis of the DNA of the Y-chromosome is particularly useful in forensic science in situations where it is desired to isolate information of a male perpetrator from a male/female mixture; usually in crimes of sexual assault. This is especially useful where a male does not produce sperm cells (due to vasectomy or medical condition). In such a situation, there may be some male epithelial cells from the penis present in the seminal fluid, but these would be so few that detection would be unlikely as they would be swamped by female cells. Specific targeting of the Y-chromosome means that there is no interference from the large concentration of female cells, such that the perpetrator's DNA can often be distinguished.

13.56 Matches from Y-STR profiling are not as discriminating as those from nuclear DNA profiling. The commercial kit routinely used in Y-STR DNA profiling in the UK (AmpFISTR® Yfiler® PCR Amplification Kit made by Applied Biosystems) identifies alleles at 16 areas of the Y-chromosome. This results in a DNA profile of 17 alleles, as only one of the areas tested will show two alleles. Although more loci are tested than for nuclear DNA profiling, they all originate from the same long strand of DNA, the Y-Chromosome. The Scientific Working Group on DNA Analysis Methods (SWGDAM) specifies 12 areas (plus amelogenin) that ought to be included in a Y-STR DNA profile. Databases that contain Y-STR DNA profiles for frequency information, however, may not contain all 12 SWGDAM recommended loci. The result of Y-STR DNA comparisons are exclusion, inconclusive (where there has been insufficient or ambiguous data) or cannot be excluded. When it is not possible to exclude, a figure for the probability of a chance match is required. There are various methods available to calculate this which are complex.

FACTORS AFFECTING THE EVALUATION OF DNA EVIDENCE

13.57 When a DNA profile from a crime stain has been matched to that from a suspect, and the significance of the match has been established, the meaning of the presence of the DNA should be evaluated. This is important since the finding of DNA does not necessarily infer that the donor of that DNA was involved in the criminal act. Such an evaluation requires a consideration of the following factors:

- Can the cellular source of the DNA be identified and, as a result, can the DNA be associated with a particular event?

- Has the DNA been deposited directly or indirectly?

- Has the continuity of the crime stain from which the DNA was obtained been maintained?

- Is there any possibility for contamination?

Cellular source of DNA

13.58 In order to attempt to establish the cellular source of any DNA found in a crime stain, tests can be conducted to identify the type of cellular material present. Presumptive tests are commonly used to indicate the possible presence of particular body fluids, such as blood, saliva and semen. Presumptive tests are not conclusive (hence the name). It is possible to confirm the presence of semen by microscopic examination (its presence is also supported by successful differential extraction). There is no further work possible to confirm the presence of blood or saliva. It is therefore generally assumed that a single source DNA profile generated from a visible red/brown which is presumptive positive for blood, has in fact originated from blood. Saliva is slightly more complex as most often there will not be a visible stain. A single source DNA profile obtained from a presumptive saliva positive area will usually be thought to have originated from saliva, although this must be treated with some caution. Caution is also required when mixed profiles are generated from body fluid stains.

13.59 Identifying the type of cellular material from which the DNA originated can assist in establishing how the DNA came to be present in the crime stain. For example, if the DNA originated from a blood stain on a T-shirt, then interpretation of the pattern of that blood stain can assist in identifying the types of events that may have caused the blood stain, such as being in close proximity to airborne blood. Likewise, if the DNA can be attributed to sperm from a semen stain, then its presence is a result of deposition from an ejaculation at some point in time. With respect to semen stains on vaginal and anal swabs, the number of sperm present, rather than the presence of DNA, can then be used to indicate the time since ejaculation.[8] Further consideration of these matters is outside the scope of this chapter.

13.60 Although a positive presumptive test for a particular body fluid can indicate that the DNA detected has originated from that body fluid, caution in drawing this conclusion must be taken when the quantity of DNA detected is very low. In such cases, it has been observed that the DNA recovered has not originated from the body fluid detected, but from other cellular material present.[9] For example, a crime stain may be composed of a blood stain and epithelial cells from skin, such that the stain tests positive for blood, but the DNA actually originates from the skin cells.

13.61 DNA may also be detected from a crime stain that tests negative for a body fluid, and as such, cannot be attributed to a particular body fluid. In such cases, it is generally assumed that the DNA has originated from epithelial cells,

---

8 A Davies and E Wilson 'The Persistence of Seminal Constituents in the Human Vagina', (1974) 3 *Forensic Science* 45–55; J Allard 'The Collection of Data from Findings in Cases of Sexual Assault and the Significance of Spermatozoa on Vaginal, Anal and Oral Swabs' (1997) 37 *Science & Justice* 99–108.

9 C Peel and P Gill 'Attribution of DNA Profiles to Body Fluid Stains' (2004) 1261 *International Congress Series* 53–55.

although the source of those cells, whether from skin, mouth, vagina, etc, cannot currently be determined. Such DNA moves independently, and often readily, and its transfer is not fully understood.

Transfer of DNA

13.62 As DNA-bearing cellular material from an individual can come to be present on an object through a variety of mechanisms, including touching, but also talking or sneezing within the vicinity, the detection of a DNA profile on a surface should not be considered evidence of contact. Various transfer mechanisms are generally described as being either direct or indirect. Direct transfer occurs when an individual has touched an object with, for example, bare hands. Indirect transfer of DNA is when DNA from an individual is deposited on an object without the individual having touched that object. For example, if DNA is transferred from the individual to another individual and subsequently to the object in question. Such transfer has been demonstrated by a number of studies, albeit to varying degrees. Most crucially, it has been demonstrated that a full DNA profile of an individual can be recovered from an object that they have not touched, while the profile of the individual that has touched the object is not recovered.[10]

13.63 Research has demonstrated that the quality of DNA profiles recovered from items that have been touched (ie whether the profiles are full or partial profiles) is a complex issue that is dependent on a number of factors. These factors include: the ability of an individual to deposit DNA, the time since they washed their hands, the type of surface that is touched,[11] and the method employed to swab the touched object.[12] The nature and duration of direct contact also affect the recovery of DNA, for example, it is believed that increased pressure and/or friction during contact may increase the amount of DNA deposited. Since indirect DNA transfer requires DNA to be initially deposited onto an intermediary surface, these factors may also explain the varying results obtained in studies on indirect transfer. DNA transfer can also be significantly influenced by the nature of the cellular material from which the DNA originated, and the nature of the surfaces that the DNA is transferred between.

13.64 Based on the published scientific research that has identified all these many factors affecting the deposition and transfer of DNA, it is not possible to infer from the amount of DNA detected whether it has resulted from direct or indirect transfer. Likewise, even if the DNA has been deposited by direct

---

10 A Lowe, C Murray, J Whitaker, G Tully and P Gill 'The Propensity of Individuals to Deposit DNA and Secondary Transfer of Low Level DNA from Individuals to Inert Surfaces' (2002) 129 *Forensic Science International* 25–34.

11 M Goray, E Eken, R Mitchell and R van Oorschot 'Secondary DNA Transfer of Biological Substances under Varying Test Conditions' (2010) 4 *Forensic Science International: Genetics* 62–67.

12 R van Oorschot, D Phelan and S Furlong 'Are You Collecting all the Available DNA from Touched Objects?' (2003) 1239 *International Congress Series* 803–807.

transfer, it is not possible to infer that the DNA has originated from the longest, strongest, or most recent contact. Furthermore, in the current scientific research, it is widely acknowledged that further research into DNA transfer is required, such that a full understanding of the methods of and factors affecting indirect DNA transfer is still far off. In a recent paper, it was suggested that,

> 'The lack of knowledge relating to secondary [indirect] DNA transfer can limit the acquisition of useful genetic profiles and restrict the ability of investigators, as well as the judiciary, to make reasonable evaluations of the likelihood of alternative crime scene scenarios.'[13]

13.65 This has been acknowledged by some forensic practitioners who suggest that, when a low level DNA profile is recovered from an item, no inferences about the means of deposition can be made.[14] Consider, for example, the finding of a DNA profile on the inside of the collar and cuffs of a jacket. These areas are commonly tested to identify the regular wearer of the jacket and as such it is believed that the person from whom that DNA originated probably wore the jacket at some point. Based on the published research available on DNA transfer, the view commonly expressed by forensic practitioners is that it is not possible to say when the 'wearer' wore the jacket, or whether they were the last, or indeed the only, person to wear it.

Contamination and continuity

13.66 With the advances in DNA profiling (particularly with the LT-DNA techniques), sensitivity to any contamination present is heightened and can increase interference with the DNA profile of interest. In order to avoid contamination and accidental mix-ups, strict quality control procedures are necessary at the crime scene and within the laboratory. Appropriate protective clothing (gloves, masks, goggles, mob caps) must be worn and reference and crime stain samples must be analysed at different locations within the laboratory. These areas are routinely monitored to ensure that they are free of DNA.

13.67 Positive and negative controls must also be applied at various stages of the analysis. A negative control is taken whenever a new set of reagents are introduced (ie at the scene swab, extraction and PCR stages) and should always be 'blank', that is, no DNA is detected. These controls are intended to demonstrate that any DNA detected has originated from the sample of interest and has not been introduced during the recovery or analysis. It is good practice to also recover a 'background control' to indicate any DNA which may have already been present upon a surface prior to the incident of interest. For example, where a blood stain on a garment is of interest as it is believed to be the blood of an injured party, an area adjacent to the stain can be sampled and profiled to provide an indication of the background DNA present on the item, possibly from the wearer. Positive controls are simply to demonstrate that the

---

13 M Goray et al, op cit, note 11, at 66.

14 T Caragine et al, op cit, note 3.

processes applied during the DNA analysis have been successful. If a crime stain does not produce a DNA profile, but the positive control does, it is therefore possible to confidently conclude that the crime stain did not contain any detectable DNA.

13.68 To ensure that it can be asserted that any DNA profile obtained from a crime stain is actually from the stain, and not from any possible contamination, it is essential that records of the continuity of the crime stain are maintained. These records should demonstrate the complete process of the crime stain, from its recovery at the crime scene to when a DNA profile is obtained from it. Any break in this continuity can undermine whether a DNA profile can be linked with a particular crime stain or to a particular crime scene.

DNA EVIDENCE AT TRIAL

13.69 The evidence that a scientist might give about a DNA match, and its probative implications, was scrutinised in *R v Doheny and Adams.*[15] The first task of the expert at trial is to explain the nature of the DNA match between the scene of crime sample and that of the defendant. The next step is to provide the match probability, that is, frequency with which the matching DNA characteristics are likely to be found in the population at large.[16] This may be refined by estimating the number of people with matching DNA within a sub-group such as a geographical area or by age group. What the expert may not do is to give an opinion as to the likelihood that it was the defendant who left the incriminating crime scene sample nor use terminology which may lead the jury to believe that such an opinion is being expressed.[17] Once the jury have heard the statistical evidence it is for them to decide, bearing in mind the other evidence, whether the defendant or someone else left the crime scene sample.

Random match probabilities and the prosecutor's fallacy

13.70 The error into which some experts, advocates and judges have fallen is to deploy reasoning known as 'the prosecutor's fallacy'. This was recognised in *R v Deenin,*[18] in which two distinct questions were considered:

(1) What was the probability that an individual would match the DNA profile from the crime sample given that he was innocent?

---

[15] [1997] Cr App R 369, CA.

[16] The Crown should serve on the defence details of how the calculations have been carried out and, on request, make available to the defence expert the databases upon which the statistical calculations have been made.

[17] See *Pringle v R* [2003] UKPC 17, PC, as an example of an expert wrongly giving such an opinion.

[18] (1994) *The Times*, 10 January, CA. See D Balding and P Donnelly 'The Prosecutor's Fallacy and DNA Evidence' [1994] Crim LR 711; G Cooke 'Are We Still Misusing DNA Evidence?' [2003] 3 *Archbold News* 4.

(2) What was the probability that an individual was innocent, given that he matched the DNA profile from the crime sample?

13.71 The fallacy consists of giving the answer to the first question as the answer to the second. In other words it would be correct to say that one innocent person in a million would have matching DNA. However the statistic should not be used to suggest that there is a million to one chance that the defendant is innocent. The innocence of a defendant is a matter for the jury based upon all the evidence. The use to which the statistic may be put was considered by Phillips LJ in *R v Doheny and Adams.*[19]

> 'If one person in a million has a DNA profile which matches that obtained from the crime stain, then the suspect will be 1 of perhaps 26 men in the United Kingdom who share that characteristic. If no fact is known about the defendant, other than he was in the United Kingdom at the time of the crime the DNA evidence tells us no more than there is a statistical probability that he was the criminal of 1 in 26.
>
> The significance of the DNA evidence will depend critically upon what else is known about the suspect. If he has a convincing alibi at the other end of the United Kingdom at the time of the crime, it will appear highly improbable that he can have been responsible for the crime, despite his matching profile. If, however, he was near the scene of the crime when it was committed, or he has been identified as a suspect because of other evidence which suggests that he may have been responsible for the crime, the DNA evidence becomes very significant. The possibility that two of the only 26 men in the United Kingdom with the matching DNA should have been in the vicinity of the crime will seem almost incredible and a comparatively slight nexus between the defendant and the crime, independent of the DNA, is likely to suffice to present an overall picture to the jury that satisfies them of the defendant's guilt.'

13.72 In summing up the case, Phillips LJ held that the trial judge should explain the relevance of the match probability and draw attention to the extraneous evidence, which provides the context that gives the frequency its significance and that which conflicts with the conclusion that the defendant was responsible for the crime stain.

13.73 The database from which the statistical analysis is performed provides a guide only. If a database of first names showed that 0.2% of the male population have the first name Miles, it is likely that in a mixed sex school of 1,000 pupils there will only be one boy of that name. However it would come as no real surprise if in one school no boys bore that name while in another three did. The advances in DNA analysis increasingly lead to statistical calculations of say 1 in 1,000 million or smaller. That in turn will suggest that no other person in the population (or, in pure mathematical terms, a small fraction of a person) bears the crime stain DNA characteristics. This may be misleading, for

---

19 [1997] Cr App R 369, CA.

the database upon which the calculation is based cannot preclude the possibility that, of the loci examined in the profile, at least one other person has matching DNA characteristics.[20]

Bayes theorem

13.74 In *R v Adams*[21] the defence introduced the 'Bayes theorem' by which numerical probability weighting to other pieces of evidence was calculated in evaluating the likelihood that the defendant left the crime stain. The Court of Appeal deprecated this exercise suggesting that it would plunge 'the jury into inappropriate and unnecessary realms of theory and complexity deflecting them from their proper task'. This view was endorsed in *R v Doheny and Adams*[22] and *R v Adams (No 2)*,[23] in the latter of which cases it was held that, lacking special features, 'expert evidence should not be admitted to induce juries to attach mathematical values to probabilities arising from non-scientific evidence at the trial'.

Low copy number (low template) DNA analysis

13.75 The target of the most recent challenge to the admissibility DNA evidence has been the reliability of LCN DNA analysis (the technique is described at **13.30** et seq). Doubt was cast on the reliability of the technique in *R v Hoey*,[24] a first instance decision in Northern Ireland. Experts called by the defence gave evidence that although standard DNA analysis was the subject of internationally agreed validation guidelines and definitions, no such agreement had been reached in respect of LCN DNA analysis. 'Validation' is defined in the existing guidelines as 'the process whereby the scientific community acquires the necessary information to: (i) assess the ability of a procedure to obtain reliable results, (ii) determine the conditions under which such results can be obtained, and (iii) define the limitations of the procedure'.[25]

13.76 In view of the risk of stochastic effects (see **13.32–13.35**), it was suggested by the defence experts that 'reproduceability' should be considered a very important determinant of reliability. If the same test is repeated a number of times, and the same result is achieved in each test, replication of outcome would suggest that the result is accurate. Evidence was given that standard practice in the Forensic Science Service laboratory in which the test on the DNA in *Hoey* was carried out, was to conduct two tests. The defence pointed out that this genetic material had in fact been subjected to three tests in the FSS

---

20 The term 'random occurrence ratio' was used in *R v Doheny and Adams*. However, scientists tend to use the term 'random match probability' as more accurately reflecting the statistic presented to the court. For a critique of the presentation of profile evidence at trial see I Evett et al 'DNA Profiling: A Discussion of the Issues Relating to the Reporting of Very Small Match Probabilities' [2000] Crim LR 341.

21 [1996] 2 Cr App R 467, CA.

22 [1997] 1 Cr App R 369, CA.

23 [1998] 1 Cr App R 377, CA.

24 [2007] NICC 49.

25 Ibid, at [62].

laboratory and that while a consensus was produced by the first two tests, a third test had produced a result that differed. As the integrity of the samples had been compromised by the manner in which they had been handled, packaged, transported and stored (see **13.66**), the trial judge found it unnecessary to make any ruling on the reliability of the technique. However, the judgment contained a note of concern over the reliability for evidential purposes of the science and methodology associated with LCN DNA analysis.

13.77 The admissibility of LCN DNA analysis in England and Wales was considered subsequently in *R v Reed & Reed*.[26] The Court noted that prior to the challenge to the admissibility of LCN DNA analysis in *Hoey*, the Home Office had established a review of the validity of the technique.[27] The authors of the report, which was published after the judgment in *Hoey* had been delivered, concluded that the various techniques used for LCN DNA analysis on amounts of DNA that fell below the threshold of 100–200 picograms, at which stochastic effects may occur, were valid. The Court of Appeal held that where the quantity of DNA was above this threshold the results of the technique are capable of reliable interpretation and, in the absence of new scientific evidence, a challenge to the validity of the LCN process should no longer be permitted in criminal trials. However, it also concluded that where the quantity of DNA analysed is below the stochastic threshold of 100–200 picograms range, it would be necessary for the party seeking to rely on evidence of such analysis to adduce expert evidence as to whether a reliable interpretation could be made in the particular case. Such evidence ought to be provided by persons with sufficient expertise in the science of DNA, and be supported by the latest research on the subject.

13.78 The admissibility of evidence of LCN Analysis conducted on quantities of DNA that fall below the stochastic threshold of 100–200 picograms was given further consideration in *R v Broughton*.[28] It was observed that there was nothing in the judgment in *Reed & Reed* that suggested evidence of such analysis was inadmissible. There would be occasions where profiles generated using LCN DNA techniques are 'wholly and obviously unreliable', and it was to be expected that the Crown would not seek to adduce evidence of analysis conducted on such profiles. However, in cases where the probative value of the profiles was more debatable, it may properly be adduced with the issues of reliability and weight to be addressed by traditional forensic adversarial techniques.

13.79 In *R v C*,[29] at issue was the admissibility of LCN DNA analysis conducted in relation to a profile that was below 50 picograms, in respect of which it was accepted that the risk of stochastic effects was likely to be considerable. The court noted that it was made clear in *Broughton* and *Reed &*

---

26 [2009] EWCA Crim 2698.

27 B Caddy, G Taylor and A Linacre *A Review of the Science of Low Template DNA Analysis* (Home Office, 2008).

28 [2010] EWCA Crim 549.

29 [2010] EWCA Crim 2578.

Reed that profiles obtained from less than 200 picograms of DNA material could be reliable. It concluded that where reliability is in issue it is the quality of the profile rather than the quantity of material that is relevant to the consideration of stochastic effects. A reliable profile could be produced notwithstanding that it is derived from a low quantity of genetic material. The court suggested that quality could be established by reproducibility of results in separate tests. In *Broughton*, the scientist that conducted the LCN DNA analysis used two separate tests and considered only those alleles that appeared in both sets of results for the purpose of conducting a random match probability. However, it should be noted that the reliability of this procedure was challenged by the experts called by the defence, who pointed out that the occurrence of stochastic effects across the two tests indicated that they were unreliable.

13.80 In the absence of clearly defined and adequately validated criteria for evaluating the reliability of LCN DNA analysis carried out on profiles derived from very small amounts of DNA the reliability of the technique appears to remain open to challenge. More needs to be known about the occurrence of stochastic effects.

Transfer of DNA

13.81 DNA might be transferred from a person to an object in various ways (see **13.62–13.65**). In *Reed & Reed* it was acknowledged that while some research has been conducted on this subject, 'much remains to be done'.[30] Notwithstanding the paucity of research, the court concluded that it was permissible for an expert to enumerate the possible mechanisms of transfer of DNA from a person to the object on which it was found:

> 'Even though the scientific knowledge is plainly incomplete, we consider the underlying science is sufficiently reliable for a range of possibilities to be enumerated as to the circumstances of transfer, including the mechanisms and timing, provided the limitations are made clear.'[31]

Accordingly, the court held that a forensic science officer with scenes of crime experience may use knowledge of the scene of the crime, his or her experience, and the scientific research that had been undertaken, to evaluate the possible means of transfer where the quantity of DNA analysed was within the 100–200 picograms range when there was a sufficient evidential basis for it to be done.

13.82 The admissibility of this form of expert opinion was the subject of renewed challenge in *R v Weller*.[32] The appellant submitted that if a proper review of the available scientific literature relating to transfer of DNA were to be undertaken, it would show the state of the scientific knowledge to be such that no evaluative judgment on the possible means of transfer could be made.

---

30 [2009] EWCA Crim 2698, at [60].

31 Ibid, at [119].

32 [2010] EWCA Crim 1085.

In rejecting this submission, the Court of Appeal suggested that an expert's practical experience could provide 'a sufficiently reliable scientific basis for a forensic science officer to give evidence of the evaluation of the possibilities of transfer' in the circumstances of a particular case.[33] However, in reasoning that has attracted significant criticism,[34] the court provided little explanation as to what the qualities of the 'day-to-day experience of forensic science work' were that transformed that experience into scientific knowledge, or how that could provide a sufficiently reliable basis for the evaluative opinions that were expressed.

DNA evidence and the Criminal Procedure Rules

13.83 In *Reed & Reed*,[35] the court reiterated the importance of compliance with the Criminal Procedure Rules in respect of expert evidence relating to DNA. It stated that a challenge should only be permitted where new scientific evidence was properly put before the trial court at a Plea and Case Management Hearing (PCMH) or other pre-trial hearing for detailed consideration by the judge. Part 33 of the Rules sets out the procedure through which the court controls expert evidence in the developing science of DNA. Sub-paragraphs (f) and (g) of r 33.3(1) require each expert to indicate whether there is a range of opinion on the matters dealt with in his or her report. If so, the expert has to summarise the scope of that opinion and provide reasons for his or her opinion. Where an expert cannot provide an unqualified opinion, the qualification must be stated. The importance of compliance with this obligation, the court observed, is that it will identify for the other party an area where there was a range of opinion. It was said, to be particularly important that the rule be followed in the expert report obtained by the Crown.

13.84 Compliance with the rule will enable clear identification of what is in issue before the trial begins. Rule 33.6(2) provides the judge with a power to direct experts to prepare a statement for the court concerning matters on which they agreed and disagreed, and to provide their reasons. If an expert does not comply with any such direction, that party cannot call the expert to give evidence without the permission of the court.[36]

13.85 In relation to cases involving DNA evidence, it provided the following guidance:[37]

> 'i) It is particularly important to ensure that the obligation under Rule 33.3(1)(f) and (g) is followed and also that, where propositions are to be advanced as part of an evaluative opinion, that each proposition is spelt out with precision in the expert report.

---

33 [2010] EWCA Crim 1085, at [34].

34 A Jamieson and G Meakin 'Experience is the Name that Everyone Gives to Their Mistakes' (2011) 45 *The Barrister Magazine;* N Rudin and K Inman (2010) *The CACNews*, 4th Quarter; Editorial (2010) 50 *Science and Justice* 111–112.

35 [2009] EWCA Crim 2698.

36 Criminal Procedure Rules 2010, SI 2010/60, r 33.6(4).

37 [2009] EWCA Crim 2698, at [131].

ii) Expert reports must, after each has been served, be carefully analysed by the parties. Where a disagreement is identified, this must be brought to the attention of the court.

iii) If the reports are available before the PCMH, this should be done at the PCMH; but if the reports have not been served by all parties at the time of the PCMH (as may often be the case), it is the duty of the Crown and the defence to ensure that the necessary steps are taken to bring the matter back before the judge where a disagreement is identified.

iv) It will then in the ordinary case be necessary for the judge to exercise his powers under Rule 33.6 and make an order for the provision of a statement.

v) We would anticipate, even in such a case, that, as was eventually the position in the present appeal, much of the science relating to DNA will be common ground. The experts should be able to set out in the statement under Rule 33.6 in clear terms for use at the trial the basic science that is agreed, in so far as it is not contained in one of the reports. The experts must then identify with precision what is in dispute – for example, the match probability, the interpretation of the electrophoretograms or the evaluative opinion that is to be given.

vi) If the order as to the provision of the statement under Rule 33.6 is not observed and in the absence of a good reason, then the trial judge should consider carefully whether to exercise the power to refuse permission to the party whose expert is in default to call that expert to give evidence. In many cases, the judge may well exercise that power. A failure to find time for a meeting because of commitments to other matters, a common problem with many experts as was evident in this appeal, is not to be treated as a good reason.’

Chapter 14

FINGERPRINT AND OTHER SKIN IMPRESSION EVIDENCE

INTRODUCTION

14.1 Fingerprint evidence has been given in court for over a century.[1] It can be used to provide specific links to scenes of crimes, to items recovered from scenes or to items alleged to be related to a criminal event. Fingerprint comparisons can also be used to eliminate from enquiries legitimate contacts, suspects, police and support personnel. The orthodox view among those working in this branch of the forensic sciences is that each person's fingerprints are unique. According to this orthodoxy, where a person's fingerprints are found to match a latent fingerprint discovered at a crime scene, it can be concluded that the person was the unique source of that fingerprint. However, in recent years the validity of this claim has been challenged (see **14.38**).

DEVELOPMENT OF RIDGE CHARACTERISTICS

14.2 Finger, palm and footprints are developed in the womb. During the fourth week of foetal development the limb buds start to form. During the fifth week the first traces of the hands and the feet can be seen. By the eighth week

---

1 *R v Castleton* 3 Cr App R 74, CCA.

the distinction between the arm and forearm, the thigh and lower leg is apparent as well as the interdigital clefts. At 10 to 11 weeks localised proliferations occur in the epidermis that eventually develop into primary ridges. Between 10 to 16 weeks the primary ridges continue to grow in an unpredictable fashion. Surface furrows begin to form. Between 16 and 24 weeks secondary ridges (also known as incipient or immature ridges) start to form. Various stresses cause unpredictable buckling of the ridges. No new primary ridges now form, the ridges are set for life and they continue to grow and mature. Barring injury, such as burning or dermal-deep scarring, fingerprints will remain unchanged for life.

BASIC PATTERN-TYPES

14.3 The skin found on the underside of the fingers, the palm, the underside of the toes and the soles of the feet differ from the rest of the skin in that it possesses ridges, the raised lines that can be seen on fingertips. A range of fingerprint pattern-types can be found, from simple *arches, loops* and *whorls* to more complex patterns. Both loop formations and whorls possess *cores* and *deltas*. The core is found approximately at the centre of the pattern area. The delta is formed from two ridgelines that diverge and surround the core. Loops have only one delta whereas whorls have two or more. Arches tend to lack deltas. There are many variations of pattern-type that fall between and partially overlap these types while others may possess complex mixtures of pattern-types. There can be a wealth of variation even among the basic pattern-types allowing for almost infinite classification categories. An individual's fingers may all have the same pattern-type or they may be different.

14.4 In basic terms the major pattern-types can be described as follows.

14.5 Arches are the simplest pattern-type. They possess ridges that flow from one side of the pattern area rising shallowly or sharply to an apex falling again to the opposite side to form a gentle upward swell or a more pronounced arching or tenting of the ridges. They may be plain, tented, ulna, radial. Arch patterns tend to lack deltas. See figure 1 below.

Figure 1: arch

14.6 Loop patterns possess ridges that fold back over themselves resulting in a hairpin or loop formation. They may be simple loops, almost circular, oval or complex in formation. They possess one delta and one core area. They may have an ulnar or radial slant. Double loop formations may occur in one pattern-type. In computer terms these are classified as whorls. See figure 2 below.

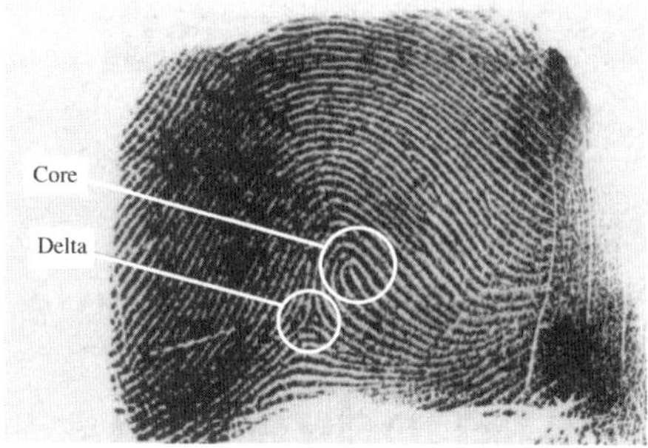

Figure 2: loop

14.7 Whorls have ridges formed in a circular, oval or elliptical fashion that complete a 360 degree circuit and pass in front of both deltas. They may be plain, central pocket, double loop or accidental. In computer terms any pattern that does not conform to any other pattern-type is classified as a whorl. See figure 3 below.

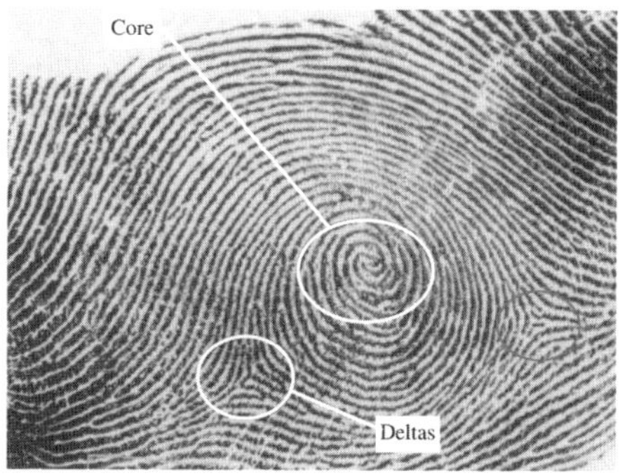

Figure 3: whorl

CLASSIFICATION

14.8 Fingerprints are classified in order to make the task of searching a database to find a match among fingerprint form records possible. The standard manual classification system, the Henry system, provided 1024 primary classifications. However, as 55% of all fingerprint forms fall into one of 16 primary classification 'bins', the more populous bins are further subdivided to provide many thousands of secondary, tertiary, major and minor sub-classifications. This helps to illustrate that while there are many variations within fingerprints there are also many similarities. The manual system is complex, permitting great power of discrimination.

14.9 For computer classification purposes, the classification system is simplified and more computer-friendly. Ten-finger fingerprint forms are divided into major classes by pattern-type then subdivided into a number of sub-classes. Added sub-classifications further divide the collection. The classification system results in many thousands of classification groupings being possible. Scene marks are then searched against the force database. Initially each police force or small consortia of forces developed their own computerised systems eventually leading to a nationwide integrated system.

NATIONAL AUTOMATED FINGERPRINT RECOGNITION SYSTEM

14.10 The National Computerised Automatic Fingerprint Recognition System (NAFIS) and reference database has been developed since the 1980s. In essence ten-print fingerprint forms are manually loaded onto a database and the fingerprints are classified. This database runs into millions of sets of prints. These ten-print forms can be used to check the identity of detained persons, prison inmates, or persons suspected of being involved in criminal activity. They can also be used to help identify finger and palm prints recovered from scenes of crime, unidentified dead or injured individuals, corpses or body parts from major incidents such as vehicular crashes or bombing, etc.

14.11 When finger, palm or footprints are recovered from scenes they are initially examined to determine if they are suitable for further examination and whether they have sufficient clarity of detail to be scanned into the computer. If possible they are classified by pattern-type, eg loop, whorl, and the most probable area of print detail, eg right fore finger, left middle finger, palm, foot. They can be further classified by a number of means depending on the quality, clarity and proportion of print available. The degree of classification and, therefore, discrimination possible with one fingerprint is necessarily less than can be applied to ten print forms. If the scene marks are suitable they are scanned onto the computer. A number of key features and possible/probable pattern-types are indicated to the computer. The computer determines geographical references between the key features indicated. It can then be asked to search the reference database for possible matches to characteristics disclosed on the ten-print forms.

14.12 The computer looks for geographical similarities between points of reference available in both the scene mark and the ten-print forms in the database. These points of reference can be programmed into the computer manually or determined by the computer itself.

14.13 When searches are made, the computer produces a candidate list of any possible matches that it finds, in order of probability as determined by the computer. This does not mean that the match with the highest probability is an identification – often this will be found not to be the case when checked manually. However, a match is commonly found within the candidate ten-print forms indicated by the computer. If no match or 'hit' is found, the latent mark will be inserted into the 'Unsolved Latent' database for future searches.

LIVESCAN

14.14 Livescan is a computerised method of capturing a person's fingerprint images without the use of ink. It uses an electro-optical computerised device that can immediately transmit for processing on the NAFIS system. It is less messy and theoretically improves the chances of obtaining good quality fingerprint forms first time. The computer should reject any forms where the finger/palm impressions are of poor quality. The device has a facility to indicate when the captured print is of poor quality. However the operator may ignore and override this advice. Fingerprint Bureau staff later assess the forms and check that the quality of the prints is acceptable. Rejected forms may be returned to forces for monitoring purposes. In reality around 2 to 5 per cent of forms may be rejected due to poor quality and clarity, with approximately half requiring reprinting. Hand-held computer terminals can be used by police at scenes or at the roadside to check the identity of individuals. The images may be transmitted via telephone. The Livescan system has been gradually introduced throughout England, Scotland, Wales and Northern Ireland. If a corresponding fingerprint form is held on file, identity can normally be confirmed in less than 2 hours. Palm print capture and searching is now available to all forces in England and Wales.

DEPOSIT OF FINGERPRINTS

14.15 Ridged skin possesses sweat glands that excrete sweat through the pores of the skin. This sweat travels along the ridges and when a person touches a surface the sweat is left behind causing the deposit of a latent (hidden or unseen) finger or palm print. Alternatively the fingers may pick up material from the surface touched, again causing the deposit of latent marks. The fingers or the surface may be contaminated with other types of bodily secretions or miscellaneous substances, for example dust, grease or paint.

14.16 There are three types of sweat gland:

- Eccrine – found on the underside of the hands and feet.
- Sebaceous – Sebum secreting glands found in association with hair follicles, for example on the head and face area.
- Apocrine – found in the armpits, groin, hairy areas and become active around puberty.

14.17 Each type of sweat gland excretes different compounds in an aqueous base. The aqueous component (water) will not be detectable once it has evaporated. However fatty, sticky or sugary compounds may remain on a surface for a considerable period. Latent fingerprints may also be deposited as imprints left in a wet or deformable substance such as blood, putty or paint, or material may be picked up from the surface touched leaving a negative impression where the material has been removed. In other words transfer may be in both directions.

14.18 Fingerprint impressions may be found on a variety of surfaces or substrates. These include:

- Smooth non-porous surfaces such as glass, paint, hard plastic mouldings, varnished surfaces, wax or waxed surfaces.

- Rough non-porous surfaces such as grained plastic mouldings, plastics, untreated metals.

- Porous surfaces such as paper, cardboard, matt emulsion painted surfaces, wood, fabric.

- Plastic extrusions of many varieties such as plastic bags, telephones, sports bags, polystyrene foam.

- Adhesive-coated surfaces such as sellotape, duct tape.

14.19 The condition of the item, the degree of handling or contact, the environmental conditions in which the items are found or have previously encountered and the manner in which they are retrieved will affect the extent to which the item holds latent marks well, poorly or not at all. For example, paper is potentially a good medium for the retention of latent fingerprints. However if the paper is recycled paper it will disintegrate when treated. Conversely fingerprints can be recovered from some types of paper even after it has been submerged in water for periods of time, depending on a variety of unknown variables. However if paper has been heavily handled or roughly treated it may not be possible to recover useful latent marks.

14.20 Wet surfaces are less likely to retain latent impressions depending on what has moistened the surface. For example, if the surface is wet with blood or body fluids it is possible to remove the wet substance from the surface still leaving recoverable and identifiable latent marks.

14.21 China and glass are potentially good surfaces for the recovery of latent impressions. However if the item was very dusty or the surface was crazed, dirty or smeared it may not be possible to recover latent marks. As a general rule each item should be examined individually to determine its suitability for testing.

14.22 Theoretically latent marks can persist indefinitely if undisturbed by desiccation, frictional contact or adverse environmental conditions. If the marks are deposited in a deformable material, such as clay, metal, paint, etc, they can persist until the material is destroyed or removed. They tend not to persist on the outside surfaces of, for example, in-use vehicles, exposed outside glazing or certain types of hard plastics. They can last for many months on, for example, glass, painted surfaces and plastic bags.

RECOVERY OF LATENT FINGERPRINTS

14.23 Different recovery strategies have been developed over the years, from simple powdering techniques to a series of physical, chemical and visual treatments. The final visualised marks are usually captured by photography. The type of treatment used is dependent upon the substrate being examined. Much research is available on the most appropriate treatment for various types of substrates and various types of sweat constituents.

14.24 The treatments can be broadly categorised as:

- *Visual* – simple lighting techniques can be utilised to look for fingerprints in substances such as blood, paint and putty. The marks can often be captured photographically without further treatment. Subsequent physical or chemical treatments may be applied in an attempt to enhance the prints.

- *Physical* – including powdering (smooth surfaces), casting (prints found in deformable materials such as blood or putty), ESDA[2] (paper items), light excitation (including UV light in combination with the use of dyes) or photography (visible marks).

- *Chemical* – including, to name but a few, superglue fuming (nonporous surfaces), ninhydrin (porous surfaces), amido black (blood marks), fluorescent dyes (subsequent to superglue fuming). Ninhydrin reacts with types of protein found in sweat. Amido black reacts with types of protein found in blood. All these techniques can cross-react with other substances.

IDENTIFICATION: THE ACE – V PROTOCOL

14.25 The ACE – V protocol is a procedure that examiners follow for the purposes of examining friction ridge impressions to establish whether or not there is a match.[3] The acronym describes four cognitive processes that are undertaken: Analysis, Comparison, Evaluation and Validation.[4]

---

2 Electrostatic Detection Apparatus.

3 C Champod 'Fingerprint examination: towards more transparency' (2007) 6 *Law Probability and Risk* 111.

4 For a detailed exposition of the elements of the protocal see National Academy of Sciences

Analysis

14.26 The first process undertaken is one in which the fingerprint examiner studies the latent fingerprint and considers whether the quality and quantity of detail in the print is such that further examination would be of forensic value.

Comparison

14.27 If the examiner concludes that the print may be of value, he or she will manually compare the fingerprints on a fresh fingerprint form obtained from the suspected individual and the latent mark from the crime scene (or other situation). Manual identification is carried out using a side-by-side image of the fingerprint of the suspect and that from the crime scene displayed on a computer workstation. This enables the examiner to identify similar features in both impressions and decide whether or not a match exists.

14.28 The examiner compares the flow of the individual ridges combined with the pattern-type, shape and the relationship and geography of ridge endings, bifurcations and divergences that individualise each finger impression.

14.29 A significant factor in the comparison will be the quality of the impressions taken from the scene. When the print to be compared and the reference impressions are of good quality and clarity, it is very unlikely that another fingerprint examiner's opinion would differ. However latent fingerprint, palmprint, or footprints recovered from scenes are often incomplete and may be of poor quality or clarity. The prints may be smeared or smudged to a greater or lesser degree. Certain areas of ridge skin, such as the delta, possess greater similarities than others. Therefore there are greater chances of mistaken identification occurring if only such areas of finger, palm, or footprints are recovered and/or the prints are of poor quality. The corollary is also true: a non-match does not necessarily equate to the mark having been placed by another person. Matching detail may not be available on the relevant finger or palm print forms or the detail may be distorted or smeared preventing a match being achieved.

14.30 One facet of the quality of the print is the quality of the skin leaving it. As a person matures, the skin ages and the ageing process can be accelerated if the skin is subjected to harsh environmental factors or substances. For example, persons handling wood, stone, metal or chemicals on a daily basis will develop dry or damaged skin. Skin elasticity reduces and various creases develop and deepen. This has the effect of increasing 'interference' of the fingerprint and loss of fine detail resulting in their prints being harder to compare.

Strengthening Forensic Science in the United States: A Path Forward (Washington D.C, National Academies Press, 2009). These are also described by L Haber and R Haber 'Scientific validation of fingerprint evidence under Daubert', (2007) 6 *Law, Probability and Risk* 87, who also provide critical analysis of the validity of the processes that comprise the protocol. See also, Champod, op cit, for observations on the critique offered by these authors.

Evaluation

14.31 The examiner will evaluate any similarities that are found. There is no scientific formula by which an examiner may deduce with certainty a match.[5] Fingerprint identification ultimately relies upon the expertise of the examiner judging that, in their opinion, one image of a finger/palm/foot print closely resembles that of another reference impression to the exclusion of all others. That the matter is one of opinion could not be better demonstrated than in the case of *R v McNamee*.[6] The appellant had been convicted of conspiracy to cause explosions. A thumb mark was found on a battery connected with a bomb. On appeal no less than 14 fingerprint experts were called, occupying seven full days of evidence. Most of the witnesses had well in excess of 20 years' experience, some 30 years. Several were heads of fingerprint departments in regional constabularies. They came to a wide variety of different conclusions both as to the number and positions of matching ridge characteristics. Though the majority concluded there were sufficient characteristics for a match, some found that the print on the battery was not sufficiently identifiable.

14.32 The position and orientation of a recovered mark can provide further intelligence regarding how or when it arrived on the substrate from which it was recovered. Where matches are made but events are disputed or allegations denied, the siting of the fingerprints may reveal information relating to the position or actions of the person to whom the print belongs or the position of an object allegedly held by that person.

Verification

14.33 In larger laboratories and in the fingerprint branches of all police forces in England and Wales, where the examiner concludes that the similarities are such that the crime scene print can be 'individuated' to the suspect, ie that the similarities identify the suspect as the source of the crime scene print to the exclusion of all other persons, verification of the conclusion is required by two further examiners.

ADMISSIBILITY

14.34 For many years a standard of 16 matching ridge characteristics was required as evidence of a conclusive match. Where a second print was found, ten ridge characteristics from each were deemed sufficient.[7] However those standards were questioned by experts, some of whom suggested that as few as eight ridge characteristics on a single print would provide a complete

---

5 Following the Court of Appeal's decision in *R v Buckley* (1999) 163 JP 561 the Association of Chief Police Officers formally adopted a non-numerical standard in 2001 (adopted in Northern Ireland in 2006). Rather than focusing on the number of similarities, fingerprint experts now justify their conclusions by reference to various distinctive features.

6 17 December 1998 (unreported), CA.

7 Fingerprint Bureau and Home Office protocol, 1953.

safeguard. Others maintained that there was no scientific, logical or statistical basis for the retention of any numerical standard;[8] rather the evidence could be expressed by degrees of opinion.

14.35 *R v Buckley*[9] considered the history of fingerprint evidence standards and recommendations of a body of experts.[10] The Court of Appeal pointed out that:

> 'Fingerprint evidence, like any other evidence, is admissible as a matter of law, if it tends to prove the guilt of an accused. It may so tend, even if there are only a few similar ridge characteristics but it may, in such a case, have little weight. It may be excluded in the exercise of judicial discretion, if its prejudicial effect outweighs its probative value.'

14.36 In the current state of knowledge and expertise the Court proffered the following guidance to the prosecution and judges:

> 'If there are fewer than eight similar ridge characteristics, it is highly unlikely that a judge will exercise his discretion to admit such evidence and, save in wholly exceptional circumstances, the prosecution should not seek to adduce such evidence. If there are eight or more ridge characteristics, a judge may or may not exercise his or her discretion in favour of admitting the evidence. How the discretion is exercised will depend upon all the circumstances of the case, including in particular:
>
> (i) the experience and expertise of the witness;
> (ii) the number of ridge characteristics;
> (iii) whether there are dissimilar characteristics;
> (iv) the size of the print relied on, in that the number of ridge characteristics may be more compelling in a fragment of print than in an entire print; and
> (v) the quality and clarity of the print on the item relied on, which may involve, for example, consideration of possible injury to the person who left the print, as well as factors such as smearing or contamination.
>
> In every case where fingerprint evidence is admitted, it will generally be necessary, as in relation to all expert evidence, for the judge to warn the jury that it is evidence [of] opinion only, that the expert's opinion is not conclusive and that it is for the jury to determine whether guilt is proved in the light of all the evidence.'

14.37 In *R v Smith*,[11] the Court of Appeal, deprecated both the fingerprints expert's failure to keep adequate notes regarding his conclusion that the appellant was the source of a fingerprint found at the scene of a murder, and the refusal of those responsible for administering the National Automated

---

8 Eg M Leadbetter 'Fingerprint evidence in England and Wales' (2005) 45 *Medicine, Science and the Law* 1.

9 (1999) 163 JP 561, CA following *R v Giles* 13 February 1998 (unreported), CA and *R v Charles* 17 December 1998 (unreported), CA.

10 For an account of the move from the 16 point standard to a non-numeric standard, see Leadbetter, op cit.

11 [2011] EWCA Crim 1296.

Fingerprint Recognition System to download digital images of fingerprints for the court to view on its screens. Noting that there had been very few cases in which fingerprint evidence had been challenged at trial, the Court made a number of important (and largely critical) observations concerning the methods used by the fingerprint examiner in the case and the state of the discipline more generally:[12]

> 'i) Most forensic science services have for some time been provided by organisations wholly independent of police forces. There are also a number of private providers of forensic science services. In contradistinction, fingerprint experts are organised in Fingerprint Bureaux which fall within the organisational structure of each police force. This may be a distinction that is justified; it may be possible for independence to be assured by strict standards of control on quality and by accountability.
>
> ii) There is no opportunity for a person outside a police Fingerprint Bureau to become fully qualified as a fingerprint expert by training in England and Wales or for having that person's competence recognised by the police forces.
>
> iii) Police forces do not recognise the qualifications or competence of those who have obtained these overseas. It is for a judge to decide whether a person is a competent expert, not the police. Because of the course the trial took, the judge did not have to rule on whether [the expert instructed by the defence], who obtained qualifications overseas, was a competent expert.
>
> iv) It is essential for the proper administration of justice that there are independent persons expert in fingerprint examination; almost all who do this are retired from police Fingerprint Bureaux. The position is in marked contrast to other forensic science disciplines. There may be good reason for this distinction; for example the fingerprint bureau of other forces may be able to provide expert evidence for the defence.
>
> v) No competent forensic scientist in other areas of forensic science these days would conduct an examination without keeping detailed notes of his examination and the reasons for his conclusions. That universal practice of other forensic scientists was not followed by the … Fingerprint Bureau [that provided the evidence relied upon by the prosecution]. There may be reasons for this, but they were not explained to us.
>
> vi) As neither the original examiner nor those who confirmed his examination made any notes of their reasons and did not identify the points of comparison contemporaneously on a chart, it was not possible to see whether their reasoning was the same. We were told that this was not done because those who made the subsequent identification should make that identification without knowing the views of those who had previously examined the print. Although we accept that identification by two other persons who do not know the conclusions of the original examiner or the other examiner form an important safeguard, we do not understand that reasoning. There would be nothing to prevent the earlier examiners sealing their conclusions until the completion of all the examinations. We do not know whether there is any other justification for examiners not making detailed contemporaneous notes that can be the subject of transparent examination in court where the identification of the mark is in issue.
>
> vii) The quality of the reports provided by the … Fingerprint Bureau [that provided evidence relied upon by the prosecution] for the trial reflected

[12] At [61].

standards that existed in other areas of forensic science some years ago and not the vastly improved standards expected in contemporary forensic science.

viii) The presentation of the evidence to the jury made no attempt to use modern methods of presentation. The presentation to this court was similar; a large amount of time was wasted because of this. It was incomprehensible to us why digital images were not provided to the jury; the refusal of NAFIS … to permit a digital image to be supplied to the court was a further example of the lack of a contemporary approach to the presentation of evidence. The presentation to the jury must be done in such a way that enables the jury to determine the disputed issues.'

14.38 It might transpire that the judgment in *Smith* marks the beginning of a process that will lead to significant changes in the way that fingerprint experts reach conclusions and also subsequently present them in court. ACPO and the Forensic Regulator have established a Fingerprint Quality Standards Specialist Group to evaluate the adequacy existing quality standards and consider whether present arrangements are sufficiently robust and accountable. The extent to which this initiative will address the growing body of criticism that has been directed at the forensic discipline of fingerprint examination and the way in which fingerprint evidence is presented in court (see **14.40-14.45**) remains to be seen.

EAR AND OTHER PRINTS

14.39 A variety of different types of marks such as ear prints, lip prints and nose prints may be left at scenes of crimes or on items under investigation. Ear print identification alone has been scrutinised by the Court of Appeal. The science is in its early stages of development and there are relatively few practitioners. Nevertheless, its admissibility was confirmed in *R v Dallagher*.[13] In that case an ear print was deposited on glass adjacent to a window that had been forced open. The inference that the person responsible for leaving it was the murderer of the occupier of the premises was undeniable. Two experts called by the prosecution compared the mark left with ear impressions of the defendant. Both stated that no two ear prints were alike in all respects. However, they accepted that research was in its infancy and that the assumption that no two ears are the same was based upon limited experience. Further research, they agreed, would be useful to discover whether two different ears could, on deposit, produce prints showing similarities. Despite those empirical shortcomings, the first expert concluded with certainty that the defendant was responsible. He would generally look for five or six points when making a comparison, and found there to be seven points of similarity and two differences for which he was able to account. The second expert, though questioning the use of measurements because of the possibility of distortion when pressed against a hard surface, found that the likelihood of another person having left the ear prints to be remote. The jury were directed that if

---

13 [2003] 1 Cr App R 12, [2002] Crim LR 821, CA. It was followed in *R v Kempster* [2003] EWCA Crim 3555.

they accepted the evidence of the first expert witness they could convict on it alone. On appeal against the conviction, the Court of Appeal heard evidence from other experts, the impact of which was to suggest that the paucity of research and scientific peer review rendered reliance upon identification by ear print alone unsafe. The assumption that nature does not repeat itself was also questioned, given the small size of the database available. The Court of Appeal held that the expert ear identification was admissible but that, had the jury heard evidence of the misgivings expressed by the further experts, they may not have reached the same conclusion. The conviction was accordingly quashed.[14] The further ground of appeal, that the experts should have limited their evidence to comparison and not to opinion as to probability or, in effect, guilt was rejected.

CHALLENGES TO THE ORTHODOXY

14.40 Although in many jurisdictions fingerprint evidence has been accepted in criminal proceedings for over a century, there has in recent years been a sustained challenge to the validity and reliability of the incriminating opinions offered by expert fingerprint examiners. Saks and Koehler have observed of forensic identification science generally, that it involves two fundamental steps, which have been described above.[15] The first involves comparison of an exemplar form of a known source with an item of evidence. In the case of fingerprints, this is a comparison of the fingerprints taken from the suspect with a latent fingerprint impression found at a crime scene. The second step involves some assessment of the meaning or significance of a reported match. In other words, 'in view of the similarities, what is the probability that the print recovered from the crime scene belongs to the suspect?'[16]

14.41 There are risks associated with both of these steps. Some have suggested that the risk of error when comparing fingerprint impressions is due, in part, to the fact that the criteria for establishing fingerprint identification are 'ill-defined, flexible and explicitly subjective'.[17] It has been suggested that some form of 'blind' testing,[18] using latent impressions belonging to a known donor,

---

14 The concerns raised about the propriety and accuracy of ear print identification were later justified when the re-trial was abandoned because it had emerged that a DNA profile from the print established that it could not have been left by the defendant.

15 M Saks and J Koehler 'The individualization fallacy in forensic science evidence', (2008) *Vanderbilt Law Review* 199.

16 Ibid.

17 D Stoney 'Measurement of fingerprint individuality' in H Lee and R Gaensslen (eds) *Advances in Fingerprint Technology* (CRC Press, 2nd edn, 2001), at p 329.

18 Such testing would involve presenting the fingerprint examiner with the kind of single latent fingerprint impression that might be obtained from a crime scene , the donor of which is known to the person conducting the test but not the examiner. The examiner would be provided with a set of ten fingerprints taken from a subject (who may or may not be the donor) and asked to express an opinion on whether or not the crime scene print and the set of ten prints originated from the same source. The frequency of false positives and negatives, i e incorrect identifications and rejections, found in such tests would provide some indication of the error rate of the techniques employed and judgments made by fingerprint examiners.

might provide some indication of the error rate associated with the techniques that are employed and judgments that are made by fingerprint examiners. Some have called for such testing to be 'closed' or covert, so that when tests are conducted fingerprint examiners are not aware that they are being tested.[19] However, it appears forensic science providers, or those who oversee its provision, have undertaken little, if any, of this kind of testing.[20] The relatively small number of independent studies that have been conducted suggest that there is significant variation in examiners' abilities to perceive pattern variability and the thresholds at which they are willing to declare a match.[21] Moreover, there is empirical research that demonstrates how fingerprint examiners' judgments may be influenced by the acquisition of extraneous information.

14.42 In a study conducted by Dror et al,[22] five expert fingerprint examiners were provided with fingerprints and informed that they were the prints from a case of erroneous identification that had attracted significant publicity. The implication was that the fingerprints ought to be excluded. The fingerprint examiners were asked to compare the 'crime scene prints' with a set of fingerprints that they were told had been taken from the suspects. In fact, the examiners had been presented with sets of fingerprints that they had compared around 5 years earlier as part of their own caseloads and in respect of which they had found a match. When presented with these pairs of fingerprints along with the misleading information during the study, only one of the experts reached a conclusion that was consistent with his previous decision; that there was a match. Three experts concluded that the sets of prints were not matches, and the other took the view that there was insufficient detail to make a match. In other words, when provided with misleading erroneous contextual information, four of the five experts reached a conclusion that contradicted their earlier conclusions on the same sets of prints.

14.43 In a subsequent similar study,[23] six fingerprint examiners, each with at least 5 years' experience, were provided with eight pairs of prints. Each set of

---

19 Saks and Koehler, op cit, note 15. As Dror and Charlton have pointed out: 'If you want to know how people drive, then their performance during a driving test is not very insightful and revealing, neither is their driving when they know they are near speed cameras or radars. One must try to observe and examine performance as well as collect data in the normal routine setting with minimal (or no) knowledge of the people involved'; I Dror and D Charlton 'Why experts make errors' 56 *Journal of Forensic Identification* 600, at p 604.

20 J Mnookin et al 'The need for a research culture in the forensic sciences' (2011) 58 *UCLA Law Review* 725, at pp 737–738 suggest that little testing of this kind is conducted by forensic science providers or those who oversee its provision. One response to such criticism might be that decisions that are reached using the ACE – V protocol will be verified by other examiners. However, it has been argued that because the current verification processes which take place within a fingerprint department or laboratory are 'non-blind' contamination and biases reduce the chance of errors being detected; Haber & Haber, op cit, note 4, at p 97.

21 See V Phillips et al 'The application of signal detection theory to decision-making in forensic science', (2001) *Journal of Forensic Sciences* 294.

22 I Dror, D Charlton and A Peron 'Contextual information renders experts vulnerable to making erroneous identifications' (2006) 156 *Forensic Science International* 74.

23 Dror and Charlton, op cit note 19.

prints included four pairs of prints that the examiners had previously judged to be individualisations (prints belonging to the same person), and four sets of prints that had previously been considered exclusions (prints that did not originate from the same person). Four pairs of the prints were used as controls and no contextual information was provided in relation to them. Contextual information provided to the examiners regarding the other four pairs of prints included that the suspect was in police custody when the prints were taken, that he had confessed etc. Two-thirds of examiners reached some conclusions that were inconsistent with their previous decisions about the prints. Moreover, some inconsistencies were found in decisions that were made in relation to the control set of prints, in respect of which no contextual information had been provided to the examiners. Dror and Charlton point out that these errors do not constitute a scientific flaw, nor should they be considered the fault of the individual practitioners. Rather they are evidence of problems associated with human memory and cognition[24] that have been widely acknowledged in other forensic contexts, e g eyewitness's attempts at identification. Our understanding of the vulnerabilities and shortcomings of the cognitive processes involved in forensic comparison of patterns and impressions is limited and there have been calls for more research.[25]

14.44 The target of a second broad challenge to fingerprint evidence concerns the significance of the similarities found in a fingerprint recovered from a crime scene, and fingerprints belonging to a suspect. The assertion that it is possible on the basis of such similarities to prove that a suspect was the unique source of the crime scene print, to the exclusion of all other persons (so-called individualisation), has been the subject of significant criticism.[26] Critics point to the lack of empirical foundation for claims of individualisation.[27] As Balding has pointed out, 'It is impossible to prove any human characteristic to be distinct in each individual without checking every individual, which has not been done.'[28] In the absence of such universal study, conclusions about the significance of similarities in ridge patterns can properly only take the form of probability statements.[29] There has also been judicial doubt as to the validity of

---

24 Ibid, at p 602.

25 I Dror and S Cole 'The vision in "blind" justice: expert perception, judgment, and visual cognition in forensic pattern recognition' (2010) 17 *Psychonomic Bulletin and Review* 161.

26 'Individualization' is 'absolute specificity and absolute identification'; D Stoney 'What made us ever think we could individualise using statistics?', (1991) 31 *Journal of the Forensic Science Society* 197.

27 See e g C Champod 'Fingerprint examination: towards more transparency', (2007) 6 *Law Probability and Risk* 111 at p 114: 'At present, my opinion is that only random match probabilities in the order of one in a billion or larger can be justified through systematic research. Articulating any smaller probability (down to the probability of zero) is nothing more than a leap of faith or playing God.'

28 D Balding, *Weight-of-Evidence for Forensic DNA Profiles* (Chichester: Wiley, 2005), at p 148, cited by Saks and Kohler, op cit, note 15.

29 See Saks and Koehler, ibid, at p 211, who argue that claims of individualisation are illogical and unscientific. For similar critical comment see C Champod and I Evett 'Commentary, a probabilistic approach to fingerprint evidence' along with the misleading information(2001) 51 *Journal of Forensic Identification* 101. For suggestions as to how conclusions ought to be expressed see Saks and Koehler, op cit, note 15 at pp 216–217.

claims of individualisation. In a dissenting judgment in *US v Crisp*,[30] Michael J noted that although the error rate in fingerprint identification may in fact be low, this must be demonstrated by reliable scientific studies rather than assumption, and observed that:

> 'Fingerprint identification may also be seen as reliable because the examination community prevents its experts from testifying to a match unless they are certain of the match. Fingerprint experts, in other words, refuse to hedge their testimony in terms of probability. This practice seems to have hastened the technique's acceptance by courts, which have been attracted to its seeming infallibility. Professions of absolute certainty by an expert witness, however, seem out of place in today's courtroom. Even DNA match has a small chance of being an error.'

14.45 A move to conclusions that take the form of meaningful probabalistic statements would present the community of fingerprint examiners with significant challenges. It would require the development of some method of measuring the types of patterns that are compared, and the collection of data on how frequently variations in those patterns are found in the general population.[31] Statistical models would have to be developed for calculating the match probabilities in particular cases, and these would have to be explained to judges and juries.[32] There is, therefore, good reason to presume that such a move will be resisted by those working in the field.

---

30 (2003) 324 F.3 261.

31 Saks and Koehler, op cit, note 15.

32 Ibid.

Chapter 15

HUMAN IMAGE COMPARISON

INTRODUCTION

15.1 The term 'face mapping' was first coined by the Press, and should more correctly be referred to as 'image comparison of the face'. In fact even that may be misleading because image comparison for the purposes of identification may include far more than analysis of the face alone. In many instances the process will comprise analysis of the build and height of an individual, as well as of their sex which is not always a foregone conclusion. The study of hands, clothing and occasionally jewellery or weapons may also be conducted by the techniques of an expert. The exercise will generally involve a comparison of the image of an offender, usually at the time of the offence, with a known image of the suspect. On some occasions it may involve the comparison of two images of an offender.

15.2 In the years since the development of image comparison as a forensic science for evidential use, it has been realised that proof of non-identity was the only conclusion that could be arrived at with absolute certainty. Proof of identity is much more problematic. The fact that the two images appear to look identical cannot establish beyond doubt, in strict scientific terms, that they are the same person. This is because one cannot prove that there is not another person in existence who, if recorded under exactly the same circumstances as the offender, would appear indistinguishable from the defendant.

15.3 Experts in the field tend to be drawn either from people associated with medicine such as medical physicists, pathologists, anatomists and medical artists used to studying the structure and form of the human body or from image analysts whose expertise is derived from image technology. The lay person, though used to the everyday commodity of photographs, may not appreciate the nuances of ears, hairlines, the significance of the small folds and creases, or indeed the overall proportions of the body and particularly the face.

The expert, on the other hand, when making his or her analysis, is largely unconcerned with the superficial similarity, but will be looking for specific features to confirm or deny a proposed similarity.

IMAGES

15.4 The extent to which images may be studied and compared by an expert depends entirely on the quality of the images available. If the images to be compared are of high quality, for example studio portraits from a family album, they are unlikely to require the attentions of an expert. It is those images which have been captured under less than perfect conditions that require the opinion of an expert; for example, where there is a marked difference between the camera angles; where the movement of an individual causes image blur; where the image is taken from a great distance as is frequently the case with certain surveillance images of crowds, demonstrations and street crime; or in situations where the features are partially obscured, for example by wearing a mask or stocking (see Figure 1). Under such circumstances the expert will seek to obtain, wherever possible, suitable images of the individual to be compared with the suspect.

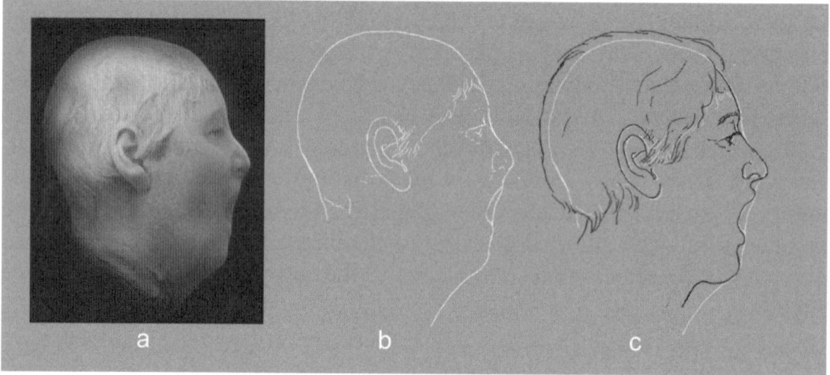

Figure 1a: Photograph of a man in a 'stocking mask'.

Figure 1b: An outline of the photograph 'a'.

Figure 1c: Outline 'b' superimposed over an outline of the man in the 'stocking mask'

15.5 The simplest and most straightforward image comparison occurs when comparing like with like, for example passport photographs, identity card images or photographs that have been made on formal social occasions, such as weddings. These images are always taken in a very similar manner – a full face view with the camera at eye level. Carefully compared, such images can provide very powerful support to an allegation, or may prove the allegation to be totally unfounded.

15.6 Still images can provide a great deal of detail, generally at a considerably higher definition than the images available from a surveillance or security camera. However, there is often the disadvantage that there are far fewer images taken of an event and the ones that might have proved most useful may not necessarily have been captured on film. By contrast images captured by video or digital technology can provide continuous recording. But the disadvantage of surveillance cameras is their perspective – they are almost always mounted well above eye level. Under such circumstances it is important to ensure that the individual to be compared is recorded in a manner that mimics these conditions as closely as possible. In some instances the individual concerned will be quite willing to assist fully with this exercise. Where impracticable, comparison of images obtained in different circumstances may be less fruitful.

15.7 A video image is not captured and displayed at one time but is made up of a number of lines of information running from left to right and from the top to the bottom of the screen. In the PAL video system used in the UK there are 625 of these lines of which only 576 contain picture information. The situation is further complicated because a video frame is split into two fields, one containing the odd lines followed by the other field showing the even lines. Video severely limits the smallest detail that can be determined and is expressed as the system resolution. It also means that 'small' picture information is just not captured in the video image. Poor imaging can limit the opportunity to detect a significant difference, which would allow items or people to be positively differentiated.

15.8 Where comparable images are not immediately available it will be necessary for the expert to trawl through negatives or, more usually, videotape to locate and capture stills of the views of the alleged offender which match as closely as possible the available views of the suspect. Such a trawl frequently results in finding a number of reasonably well-matched views. Although each one by itself may provide relatively little information, collectively they can be most revealing.

15.9 The importance of access to the original material rather than copies cannot be over-emphasised. This is particularly true of videotape where the original recording may itself have been made using old tape. However, in the case of material that has been recorded in digital form, copies, unlike videotape, do not suffer image degradation or loss of resolution if made correctly. In the case of photographs which have not been recorded digitally, the negatives should be made available whenever possible.

15.10 The technique employed to transform the imagery evidence into a format suitable for comparison is largely dependent on the format of the evidence to be examined. The importance of maintaining compatibility of images produced, using digital and analogue technology is essential and may require the additional skills of an image technology expert to carry out the transfer of imagery from one format to another and to ensure continuity, integrity and the maintenance of the correct aspect ratios. Failure to adopt the correct techniques for opening certain digital packages by using the 'extraction software', which will only be available from the manufacturers of the system being used, may result in gross distortions appearing within the image, which in turn may invalidate the results of a comparison.

EXAMINATION OF IMAGES

15.11 The objective of the comparison exercise is to identify both similarities and differences between images. It is accepted that many people share the same facial proportions and that some will have similar features. But as already noted similarities do not prove identity whereas differences may prove non-identity. Even differences may not be conclusive of non-identity because two images of the same person will rarely be exactly the same. Changes of lighting, movement, expression and situation are some of the factors that will affect a person's appearance from one moment to the next.

15.12 The detection of similarities and differences by detailed examination of facial and other images can be conducted in two complementary ways. Initially a proportional comparison of the face or body and their features will be carried out. If it is found that there are no demonstrable differences that cannot be explained, the comparison will proceed to consider the morphology. This exercise concentrates upon the form and shape of the head, facial features such as mouth, nose and ears, and the body shape and other body parts such as hands. Scars, tattoos, piercings and associated 'body furniture' may be examined. Skin and hair colour are included in this examination and racial origin may be referred to, but generally only in the broadest terms such as Caucasian, Mongoloid or Negroid.

Proportional comparison

15.13 Proportional comparison, referred to by some practitioners as photogrammetry involves:

(1) comparison of proportional measurements of distance and/or angles between morphological landmarks; and/or

(2) comparison of horizontal and vertical facial proportions.

15.14 The proportional measurement may be of a person's profile as well as frontal view. In order to conduct these proportional studies, the images must contain a comparable facial view taken from a camera perspective of comparable height and distance from the subject. A variance of up to about 7% in angle will not make a significant difference. The measurement of distances and angles demands images of superior resolution and quality. Comparison of the horizontal and vertical proportions of the two faces can generally be carried out using images containing less definition.

15.15 Of the numerous methods and techniques that have been adopted to carry out proportional examinations, the most straightforward, and in many ways the most difficult to achieve, is superimposition. This technique requires that the images to be compared are recorded from a very similar angle and viewpoint. The size and orientation of the images may then be adjusted to approximately the same size while maintaining their aspect ratio. Horizontal lines can then be taken through specific anatomical points on one image to the corresponding anatomical points upon the other. Careful adjustments to the sizes of the two images can be made to check for differences and similarities of both the vertical and horizontal proportions. In a situation where seven anatomical points are selected on image A, should two of the points be sized to match the corresponding points on image B, the other five points should also match their corresponding points for consistency to be demonstrated. When one or more of the other five points do not match for reasons other than that of physiological changes to the features of the face there exists an inconsistency (see Figure 2). Ideally, the exercise of checking the vertical and horizontal proportions should be undertaken on more than one set of images. The use of a grid used in conjunction with the placing of these lines assists with objectivity.

15.16 Perhaps the simplest method of superimposition is by the creation of an outline around each of the images, either by tracing or using one of the find-edge tools on a computer graphics programme. Having made the necessary adjustments to the scale of the outlines, one can be superimposed upon the other (see Figure 3). This technique starkly demonstrates where the differences and similarities lie. Furthermore, it may demonstrate both proportional and morphological similarities (see Figure 4).

15.17 Using video techniques, the same superimposition can be carried out by slowly reducing and then increasing the opacity of one image over the other. It may also be carried out by taking 'wipes', in which the underlying image is slowly revealed as the upper image is slowly wiped away. It is then possible to see edges and features appearing as the overlying image disappears. Such techniques require the use of sophisticated video technology. Another method frequently used during examination of image is the 'flicker' technique in which the images, having been superimposed, change rapidly from one to the other. However, while useful for examination, it is virtually impossible to demonstrate this technique in court.

15.18 One of the more esoteric forms of comparison involves the scanning of a suspect's face by using a sophisticated laser scanning device which plots the coordinates of the face digitally and which, when processed, allows the entire head to be rotated in any direction. This allows the practitioner to modify the position of the defendant's head to match the exact viewpoint of the suspect. A specialised and extremely useful facility; it demands the suspect's co-operation in the digital recording.

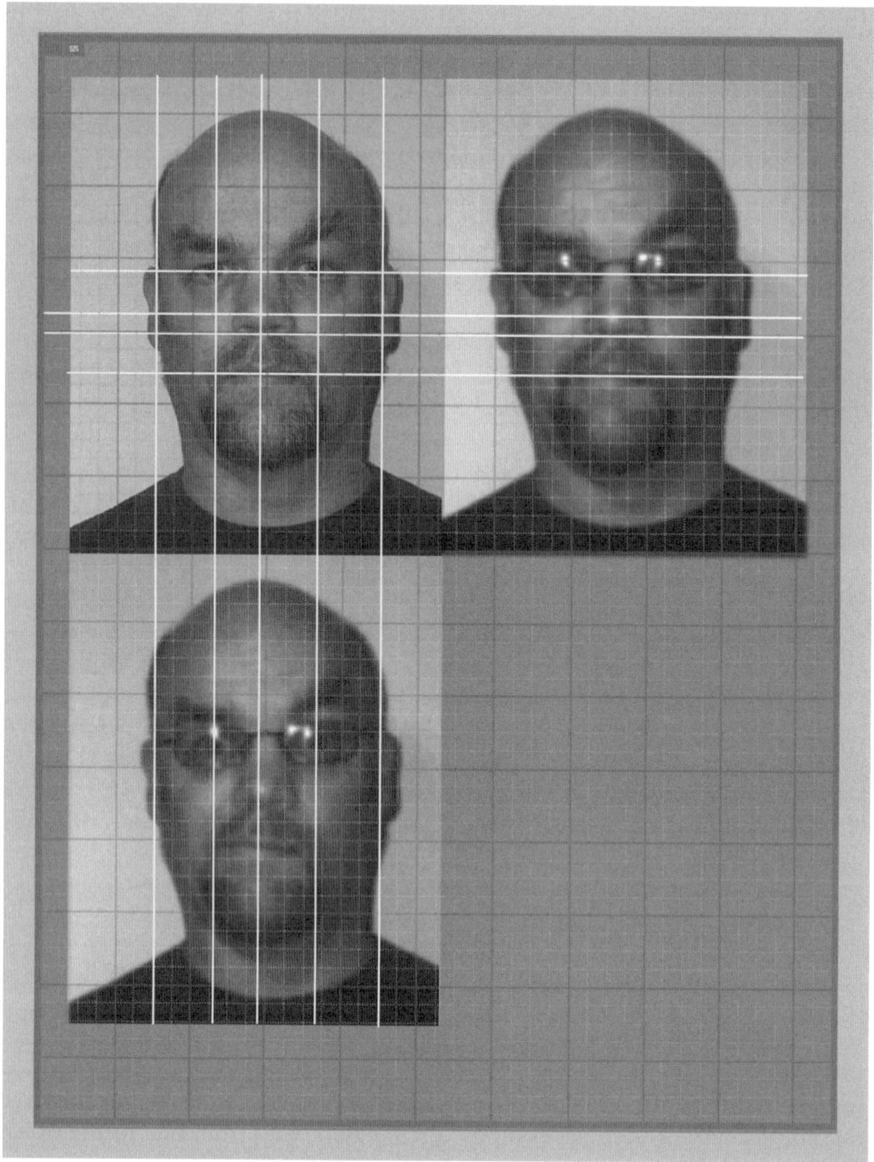

Figure 2: Images scaled by the drawing of vertical and horizontal lines through the anatomical features on each image and adjusting the sizes as necessary whilst maintaining the aspect ratio.

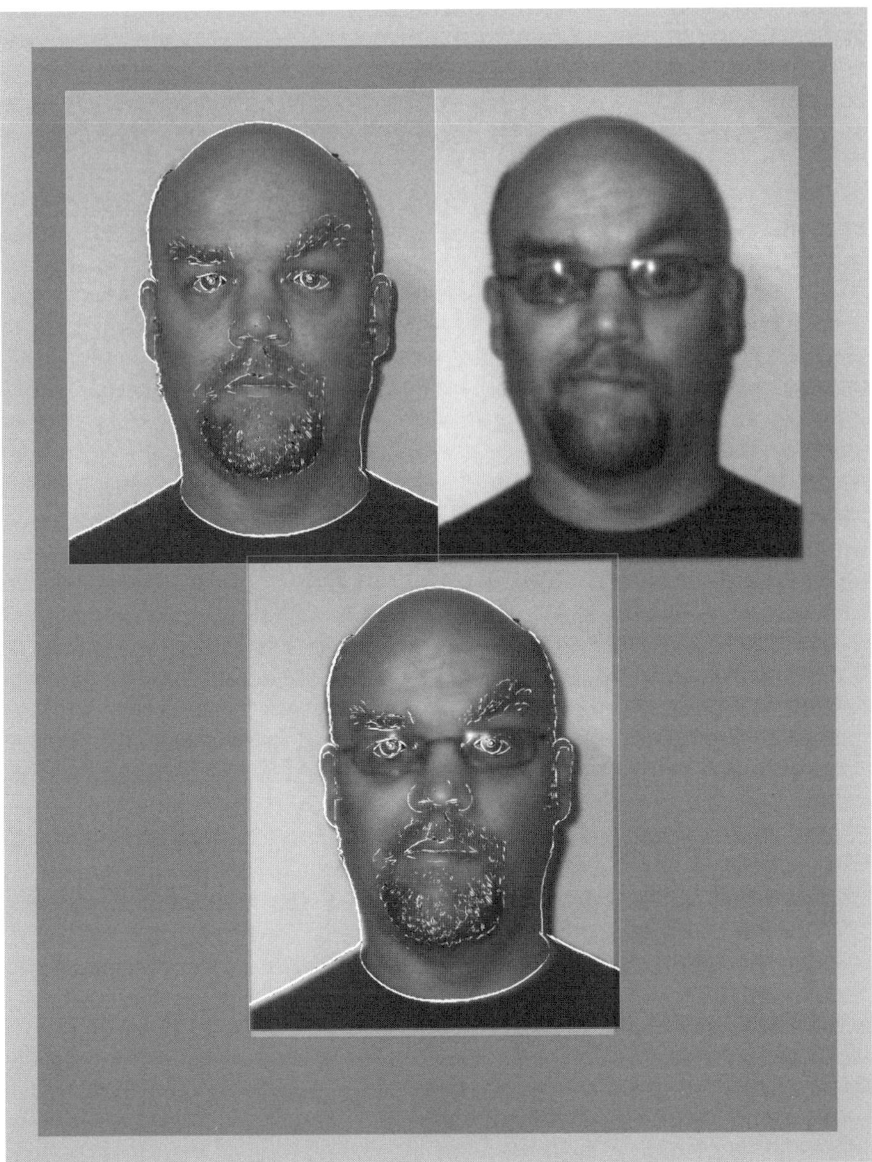

Figure 3: Superimposition of one image over another can demonstrate similarities and differences or proportion and morphology.

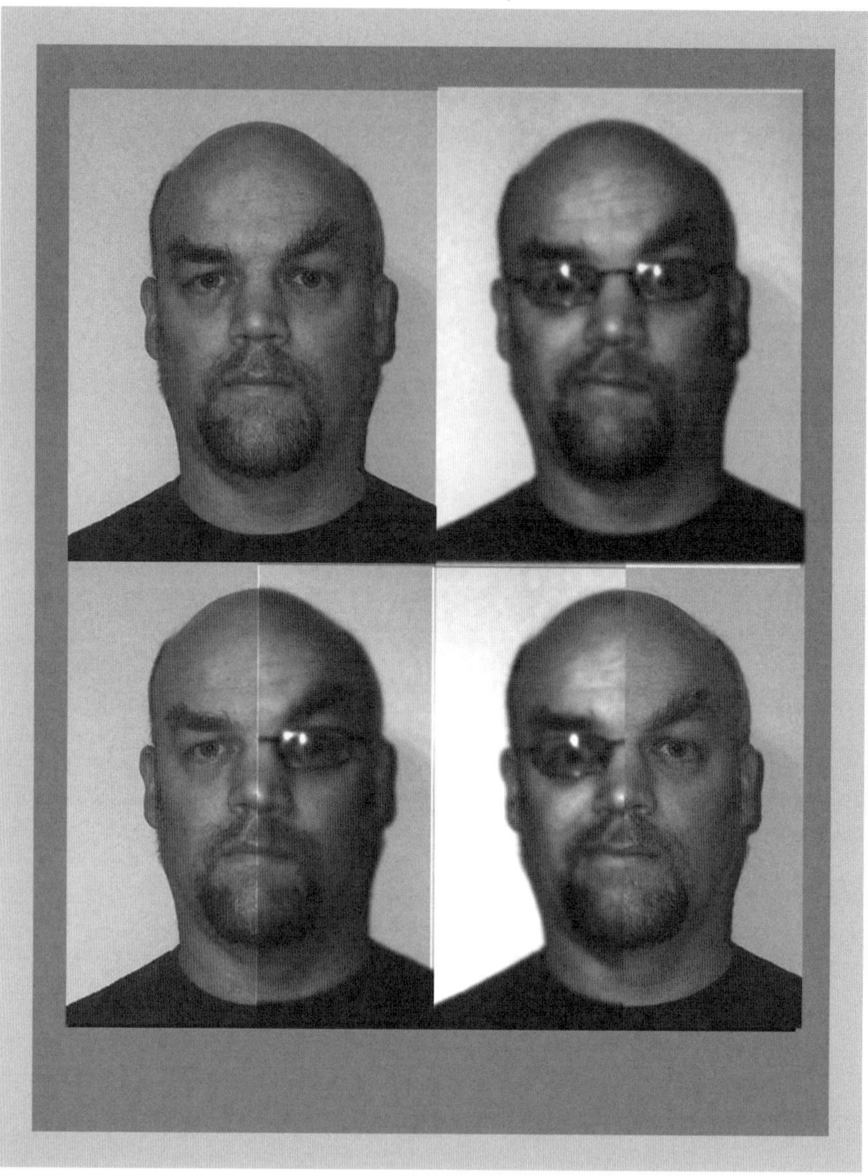

Figure 4: Split image technique in which left half of one image is merged with right half of another and vice versa.

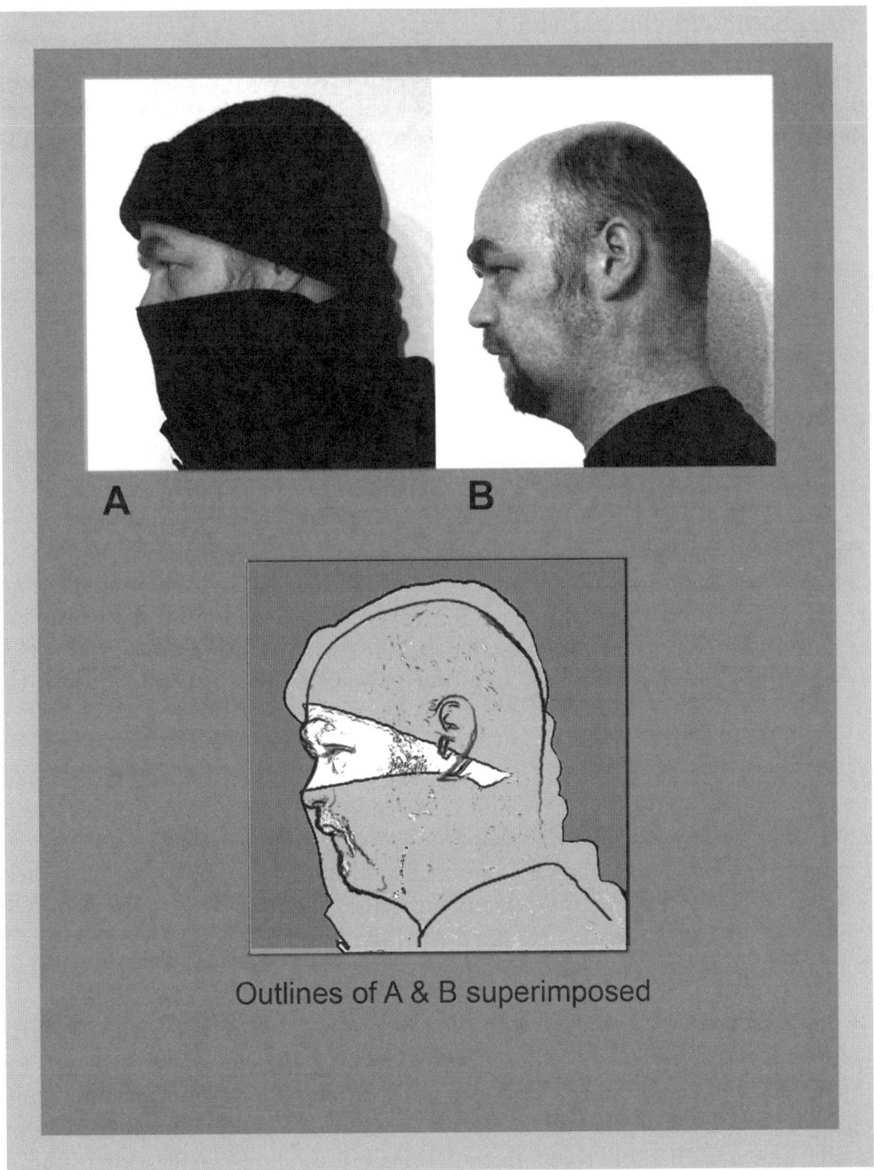

Figure 5: Outlines of A & B superimposed.

Morphological comparison

15.19 The study of the facial morphology involves a detailed examination of the shape and form of each facial feature. There are in the region of 93 different terms that can be used to describe different features of the face. These include features such as:

- the fullness of the apex of the nose;
- the individual features of the ear such as the tragus, antitragus and helix;
- the adherence or non-adherence of the lobe of the ear;
- the prominence or otherwise of the supraorbital margin;
- the form of the philtrum.

15.20 Examination should also identify the absence and presence of folds and creases, for example the creases upon the forehead, be they vertical or horizontal, and the various folds and creases that form around the mouth. In addition scars, spots or other visible features can be compared. Indeed the examination may extend to non-morphological features found on the photographic images, such as tattoos, jewellery and even clothing.

15.21 The correct use of the morphological lexicon is necessary to describe facial features in fine detail so as to be understood by other experts and ultimately the court. General terminology such as 'the nostril' may lead to confusion or misunderstanding. An example would be a reference to the nostril when in fact the feature being described is the ala; the nostril being the hole which in turn is surrounded by the nostril margin and the nostril sill; the ala being the outer part of the nose.

15.22 The precision of the expert's observations will be dependent upon the quality of the material available for examination. Though a comparison can be undertaken where the images are from quite different angles and positions, the effects of perspective may be a relevant factor when giving an opinion about similarities and dissimilarities. In the absence of suitable images for use in a proportional comparison, the morphological exercise may alone be conducted.

15.23 Morphology and proportion can be demonstrated simultaneously using the 'split image' technique whereby the left hand side of the offender's face is replaced by the left hand side of the defendant's face and vice versa. Where the two images are of different people the inconsistencies become very clear. Inconsistencies nevertheless have to be considered against the fact that very few individuals have completely symmetrical faces or bodies, for example one side may be smaller, an eye higher, a nose off centre or ears may be at different heights. This technique may be useful despite the fact that the image resolution of the offender image is quite limited. It is rendered much more intelligible when juxtaposed with a good quality image of the defendant.

ADMISSIBILITY

15.24 In *R v Stockwell*[1] the appeal turned on the admissibility of expert facial mapping evidence. It was argued that the jury should have been left to decide, unaided by expert evidence, whether the offender depicted in a video recording of a building society robbery was the defendant based upon their own observations of the image and the defendant. In that case the difficulty presenting itself was that the defendant had grown a beard shortly before arrest and it was suggested that the robber was wearing spectacles and a wig. The Court of Appeal held that:

> 'In such circumstances we can see no reason why expert evidence, if it can provide the jury with information and assistance they would otherwise lack, should not be given. In each case it must be for the judge to decide whether the issue is one on which the jury could be assisted by expert evidence.'

15.25 *R v Stockwell* was followed by *R v Clarke*[2] in which the comparison was made between the images of a bank robber taken by camera at the bank and police photographs of the defendant. The court acknowledged that photographs and video recordings are regularly placed before juries without expert evidence but held that:

> '… if that real evidence is not sufficiently intelligible to the jury without expert evidence, it has always been accepted that it is possible to place before the jury the opinion of an expert in order to assist them in their interpretation of the real evidence.'

15.26 Provided an expert is suitably qualified and his opinion is neither so outlandish or tentative as to render it ineffectual, the judge's role in determining the admissibility of expert evidence is circumscribed. Hence in *R v Ciantar*,[3] the identification evidence of a prosecution expert was properly left to the jury, notwithstanding the opinions of defence experts, of whom one cast doubt on whether the images examined were of sufficient quality for comparison, while the other stated that its quality positively prevented comparison.

THE EXPERT'S CONCLUSION AND OPINION

15.27 The principal objective of the expert's evidence is the identification of points of proportional and morphological consistency and inconsistency between images. The expert should explain, preferably in detail, the similarities

---

1 (1993) 97 Cr App R 260, CA.
2 [1995] 2 Cr App R 425, CA.
3 [2005] EWCA Crim 3559.

and differences and the methods by which they were revealed. Copies of the images used, marked where appropriate, and a video recording which displays the method of wiping or fading of images will assist the lay person in their comprehension.

15.28 It is recognised that there are occasions when images of two different people can appear so similar as to be indistinguishable. Hence similarities cannot scientifically prove identity. By contrast unexplained differences may prove non-identity. Moreover a single significant difference between two objects outweighs any number of similarities between them. When considering a difference, possible explanations such as changes of expression, lighting and movement must be taken into consideration. The limitations of a comparison based upon a partial facial view must also be recognised. In the absence of inconsistency, as the number of similarities increases, the number of people who share that particular combination of features and proportions decreases. Ultimately, the evidential weight to be given to consistency of characteristics is for the jury to decide.

15.29 To what extent may the expert express an opinion as to the strength of evidential support that the comparison can provide in support of the proposition that the suspect is the offender? That question was addressed in *R v Gray*[4] where it was said that in the absence of a database comprising the frequency of occurrence of combinations of facial or other characteristics, or of any mathematical formula for evaluating probability, the expert should not proffer an opinion beyond the consistency of characteristics. However that part of the judgment in *R v Grey* was obiter and the approach taken in it has been expressly disapproved in *R v Atkins*.[5] In that case a sliding scale ranging from 'lends no support' to 'lends powerful support' was used by the prosecution expert. Having identified particular features of similarity he concluded that they were at the top end of 'lends support' into 'lends strong support'. The challenge to this means of assessment was rejected by the Court of Appeal. It did 'not agree that the absence of a database means that no opinion can be expressed by the witness beyond rehearsing his examination of the photographs'. The Court held that:

> 'An expert who spends years studying this kind of comparison can properly form a judgment as to the significance of what he has found in a particular case. It is a judgment based upon his experience. A jury is entitled to be informed of his assessment. The alternative, of simply leaving the jury to make up its own mind about the similarities and dissimilarities, with no assistance at all about their significance, would be to give the jury the raw material with no means of evaluating it. It would be as likely to result in over-valuation of the evidence as under-valuation. It would be more, not less, likely to result in an unsafe conclusion than providing the jury with the expert's opinion, properly debated through cross examination and, if not shared by another expert, countered by contrary evidence.'

---

4 [2003] EWCA Crim 1001.

5 [2009] EWCA Crim 1876, [2010] 1 Cr App R 8, CA.

Chapter 16

HANDWRITING

INTRODUCTION

16.1 The forensic science of identification of a person by their writing or signature concentrates upon the analysis of the results of an event in which the writer has participated. It is thus distinguishable from the analysis of fingerprints or DNA profiling which are personal characteristics that can be expected to remain constant. A person's handwriting may be subject to natural variation or even wilful alteration.

16.2 Forensic document examiners assert that, given enough handwriting, the writings of two individuals can be distinguished from one another. The key notions are the sufficiency of the amount of writing and its distinctiveness; depending upon the variation in style the less text available the more difficult it becomes to discriminate between writings. Similarly, with sufficient material to assimilate their likenesses, two writings by the same person can be identified as having common authorship. An expert document examiner will express an opinion by degrees of probability. Though the opinion might strongly support common authorship, analysis cannot provide conclusive proof.

DEVELOPMENT AND STYLE OF HANDWRITING

16.3 A person's writing will generally combine both class characteristics derived from cultural and educational background and individual characteristics forming the basis of a personally developed style. The origin of the features in writing that discriminate between people lies in the way in which children are taught to write, their own mental ability and manual dexterity in using a writing implement and their educational and cultural backgrounds. The teaching of handwriting varies from country to country (even those using the same alphabet), within regions of some countries, from school to school and even from teacher to teacher. Teaching can be based on a number of resources such as set published texts, so-called copy book styles, which have been generally developed by educationalists for either their ease of learning or their aesthetic appeal.

16.4 During the years in which a child's writing improves and alters, there may be a number of cultural factors which in turn play their part in moulding the final, mature writing. These include parental or peer influences and the practical needs of writing more quickly as the child moves through school and as note-taking and examination pressures build. These elements reflect the different strategies children adopt to optimise their writing in terms of how they hold the pen, the geometrical relationship between the paper, the desk, their body and the pen, and what letter forms they find easiest or quickest to execute. Further, the timing of some of these changes can, particularly in the teenage years, be very rapid as they learn to play with their writing, altering it almost at will, until such time as the final, mature style emerges. It follows that the writings of adolescents can often vary significantly over short periods of time. It is the development away from the taught style that produces the features that define a person's writing style and their individual characteristics. Generally, most handwriting experts would not expect that an individual's writing had fully formed and matured until around the age of 20 or even later. By that age the style of writing will usually have settled for their adult life with only relatively minor changes thereafter.

16.5 At the other end of the age spectrum, those heading towards old age may tend to start to lose their ability to write, though this varies considerably between individuals. It is a reflection, in the absence of a specific illness, of a generalised loss of coordination. Illness, however, also often plays a significant role in the loss of writing ability in later years. Diseases such as Parkinson's disease, with its associated tremor, or strokes, with associated loss of mental or movement capability depending on the site in the brain affected, can radically affect both the physical ability to write and also the mental capacity to know what to write. The traumatic nature of some disease processes is such that the effect on the writing of a given person may be sudden and dramatic. This has important consequences when examining the handwriting of the elderly.

16.6 The dexterity of individuals varies quite considerably. The learning process in the brain produces a series of highly automated actions that produce fine and fast movement of the relevant bones and muscles of the arm, wrist, hand and fingers. Such is the complexity of these anatomical interactions, that it is impossible for an individual, no matter how hard they may try, to produce two pieces of writing that are absolutely identical in any meaningful sense. This is supported by the anecdotal experience of anyone that realises, for instance, that their signature varies every time they write it. This is particularly striking because, as we shall see later, the signature is probably the most highly learned writing act that an individual can make.

16.7 For many, education and work and the consequential extent to which writing is either an everyday event or a rare activity is influential in their dexterity with a writing implement. Some may have difficulties caused by an underlying problem with body coordination. Another influence that may occasionally affect writing is intoxication or the use of mood altering drugs, prescribed or otherwise. The effect on the brain may alter the ability to coordinate movement generally and the fine movement control needed for writing in particular. When intoxication is a potential factor in the execution of a piece of writing, the document examiner will consider, not so much alteration in letter construction, but the more general properties of the writing such as its size, positioning on the paper and its fluency.

MATERIALS FOR COMPARISON

16.8 The handwriting whose authorship is the subject of the identification exercise is commonly known as the 'questioned writing'. It is compared to 'known writing' which may comprise pre-existing examples of writing whose authorship is known or deliberately procured specimens. The scope for an effective examination can be limited by factors such as:

(i) The availability of original documents. Detailed examination of writing is best done from original documents, not copies such as photocopies, carbon copies and facsimiles. Fine detail of construction and the fluency of pen movement often cannot be adequately discerned from the poorer clarity of the copy document.

(ii) The amount of questioned writing and known writing available. Comparison may be hindered if only a small number of characters are available.

(iii) The contemporaneity of the documents being compared. This is particularly important when examining writings of children and older people because their writings are prone to change over short time periods.

(iv) Whether the known handwriting was produced naturally in the course of the writer's daily life or is a specially drafted specimen for the purpose of the examination. The latter is susceptible to either deliberate or unconscious alteration and it may therefore be of more limited value.

COMPARISON

16.9 Handwriting identification is largely an exercise in pattern recognition and comparison. The forensic handwriting expert makes a visual examination of the writings, using low power magnification where necessary to determine the fine detail of construction. The first part of the examination is to build up a representative picture of the range of variation in a piece of writing or in a series of writings that may be in dispute. While the writings of a given person vary in their fine detail from occasion to occasion, they generally fall within the range of natural variation of that person's writing. Establishing this for all of the various letters, both upper and lower case, numerals and even other marks such as commas and question marks, is a central part of the process of determining authorship. Once this has been determined for, say, the questioned writing, a similar exercise is carried out for the specimen or known writings of a particular person.

16.10 The features to which the expert pays particular attention are the construction of letters and other characters, the way in which letters relate to one another both in joining and their proportions, and the path that the pen follows to produce them. For example, when writing the frequently used letter pairing 'th'. Figure 1 shows a number of variations which might be encountered.

16.11 The determination of the structure of written characters can often be made by the unaided eye. However, where pen lines overlap and intersect for example, it may well be necessary to use magnification from a hand lens or a stereo microscope. The direction of pen movement of a ballpoint pen can often be determined by microscopic examination of the inkline for what are generally termed 'striations'. Figure 2 shows photomicrographs of striations from lines going in clockwise and anticlockwise directions. Information of this kind may be useful in determining one of the general features of handwriting, namely handedness. A significant proportion of left-handed writers write the letter O in a clockwise direction, whereas this is rarely encountered in the writings of right-handers. Other writing features may also be indicative of handedness, such as the left-to-right (right-handed trait) or right-to-left (left-handed trait) of writing the **t** crossbar.

16.12 Given the considerable variation that can be found in just the 'th' letter pairing that can be seen in Figure 1, the scope for variation is multiplied when all letters (upper and lower case), letter combinations (or at least those generally encountered), numerals and other marks are taken into account.

16.13 The questioned and specimen writings are compared on a like-with-like basis; a letter A is compared with a letter A, a letter B with a letter B and so on. A comparison may produce a number of features which are shared by the two writings, a number of features which fundamentally differ, which may differ slightly in some fine detail or are simply absent. Interpretation of the evidence available is dependant upon a number of factors and upon the limitations described above. However, most importantly it is the distinctiveness of the writings that plays the major part in the assessment of significance of the available evidence. It follows from this, that in order to identify someone whose writing is not very distinctive, it requires more of their writing to be examined

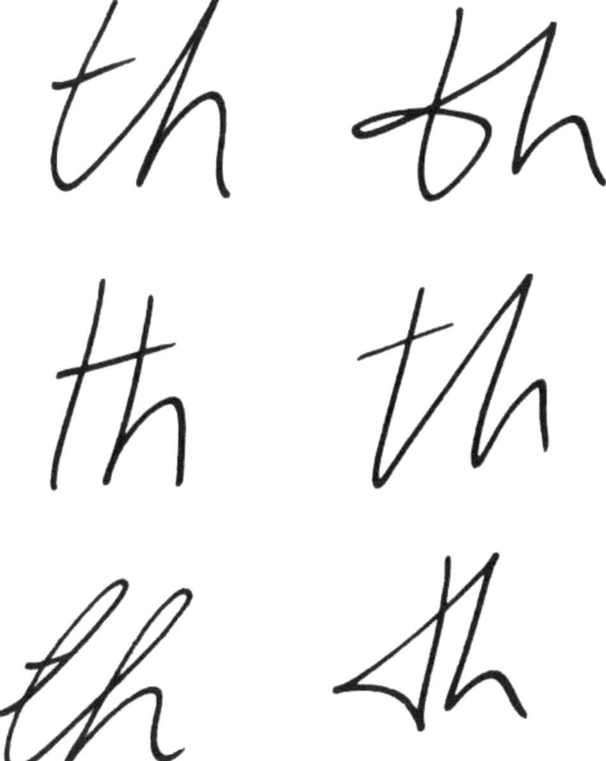

Figure 1: Even something as simple as the frequently used t-h join can be written in many ways, some of which are shown here.

to distinguish it from that of others who write in a generally similar style. By contrast, someone who has very unusual letter forms may be readily identified as the writer even from a small sample of writing.

Figure 2a: The letter O on the left has been written anticlockwise, as can be seen from the striations indicated going from the inside to the outside of the written line.

Figure 2b: In contrast, the letter O on the right has been written clockwise.

SIGNATURES

16.14 The comparison exercise may be limited to a signature alone, as for example where the remainder of a document is typed. Signatures can be written in many different styles depending upon the idiosyncrasies of the writer. Some are little more than a version of the writer's name in their normal writing, perhaps with some embellishment such as an underline. Others are more stylised with unusual letter forms or proportions. At the extreme, a signature may contain no recognisable letter forms and be completely indecipherable. Nonetheless, the principles for the examination of signatures are just the same as for normal writing of text. Because of the particular function that the signature fulfils, namely as a mark of identification, signatures are prone to an additional problem not generally encountered with other writings: forgery.

FORGERY

16.15 The forger can adopt one of two main strategies when attempting to copy the handwriting or signature of another: either simulation of the detail or fluency. Concentration on detail usually suffers from slower and therefore less fluent penlines. This can be particularly noticeable with magnification, a fluent penline having a smooth appearance and a variable ink deposit along its length as the pen speeds up and slows down, whereas a line of poor fluency may be shaky and show even inking caused by less variation in pen speed. If the forger seeks fluency, the detail is likely to be less well executed, although practice may help. The detection of forgery, as with handwriting comparison generally, is affected by distinctiveness of the writing and the amount of it. Another factor to be considered when examining for forgery is the possible use of guidelines. This can generally be observed because the writing has become a drawing rather than a writing exercise, and there tends to be a loss of fluency. Further, physical evidence of the guidelines is likely to be detected; for instance carbon copy tracings or an indented impression in the paper surface subsequently inked-in (see Figure 3 below). Detection of guidelines may require the use of specialised equipment to detect differences between writing media. Such machines use various light sources, optical filters and imaging technology to discriminate between, for example, inks that have different properties.

OTHER WRITING SYSTEMS

16.16 Since the examiner is searching for pattern comparison, the examination of other writing systems is carried out using the same principles. However, a document examiner may encounter difficulty in knowing whether or not a like-with-like comparison is being made. A further difficulty is that of distinguishing between class characteristics (such as those derived from the taught styles) which are of less evidential value and individual characteristics which define the uniqueness of that person's writing. For example, a British handwriting expert will be familiar with other writings of those in the UK and take into account their diverse cultural origins. However the examination of

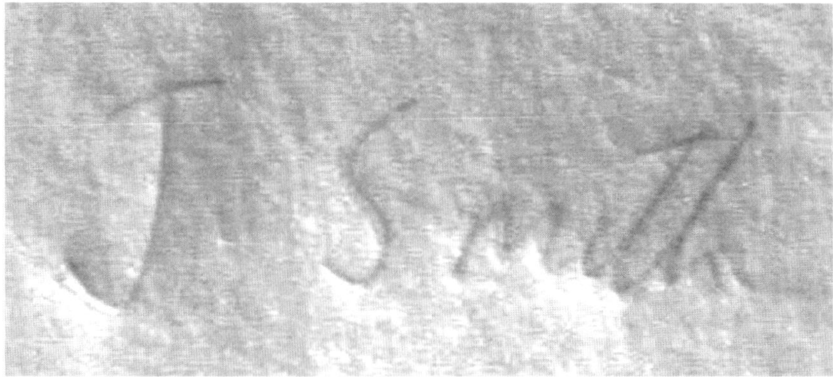

Figure 3: This shows a signature illuminated by oblique light which reveals the impression associated with it that has been used as a guideline.

writing in Arabic poses problems in knowing how unusual certain writing characteristics are and whether they are class or individual characteristics. Thus familiarity with the writings of an expert's own population does not necessarily equip the document examiner with expertise in writings in other populations.

THE EXPERT'S CONCLUSIONS

16.17 Once the handwriting has been analysed most experts endeavour to express their opinion as to authorship on a scale of certainty with only a few points on it. This varies among experts, but in general it is a reflection of the limitations of the material in a given case and the constraint this puts on the reliability of the opinion that can be expressed. For example, in a case with plenty of reliable known specimens and questioned writings which match closely and are distinctively written, the expert may be able to express a strong opinion of authorship. If, however, there are limitations that preclude such an opinion, such as unnatural questioned writing or only a small amount of specimen writing, then a weaker opinion will be more likely. In some cases the evidence available is either so flimsy or so difficult to interpret reliably, that the expert cannot justify the expression of any conclusion.

THE USE OF COMPUTERS IN HANDWRITING COMPARISONS

16.18 Increasingly powerful computer technology has opened up the possibility of studying the complexities of handwriting using image analysis and appropriate algorithms to describe letter forms in mathematical terms. In turn, this has the potential to enable a comparison between handwritings based upon a comparison of the derived mathematical descriptors. This approach has achieved success in some areas, such as in the automatic recognition of handwriting. However, in forensic work, its potential value is more as an aid to document examiners, informing in a mathematical framework on the degree of similarity and difference between writings, rather than as a replacement for their interpretive skills which require experience and a knowledge of what can and cannot be achieved by individual writers.

ADMISSIBILITY AND JURY DIRECTIONS

16.19 Handwriting evidence is admissible by virtue of the Criminal Procedure Act 1865, s 8 which provides:

> Comparison of a disputed writing with any writing proved to the satisfaction of the judge to be genuine shall be permitted to be made by witnesses and such writings, and the evidence of witnesses respecting the same, may be submitted to the court and jury as evidence of the genuineness of the writing in dispute.

16.20 Thus where there is an issue as to the authorship of the allegedly 'known writing' the trial judge must first rule on admissibility according to whether the prosecution have established that it genuinely belongs to the defendant. The standard to be applied is the criminal standard.[1] On the substantive issue of whether there is common authorship, expert evidence should provide an explanation for an opinion that two writings share authorship.[2] The judge should refrain from purporting to have expertise and expressing an opinion.[3] Neither should the exercise of comparison be carried out by a jury unaided by expert evidence.[4] Indeed in the absence of expert evidence the jury should be directed that it is impermissible for them to conduct their own analysis to reach a conclusion about authorship.[5]

HANDWRITING OBSERVATION AND RECOGNITION

16.21 An exception to the rule requiring expert evidence for determination of authorship is the case of a witness who testifies to having observed the writing of the document or who has sufficient knowledge and experience of a person's handwriting to be able to recognise it.[6]

---

1 *R v Eweng* (1983) 77 Cr App R 47, CA.

2 *R v Hipson* [1969] Crim LR 85, CA.

3 *R v Simbodyal* (1991) *The Times* October 10, CA.

4 *R v Tilley and Tilley* (1961) 45 Cr App R 360, CCA.

5 *R v O'Sullivan* (1969) 53 Cr App R 274, CA.

6 *R v O'Brien* (1912) 7 Cr App R 29, CCA; *R v Rickard* (1919) 13 Cr App R 140, CCA.

Chapter 17

VOICE

INTRODUCTION

17.1 A voice expert is likely to be consulted in the course of an investigation when a tape recording of the perpetrator of an offence is available to be compared with a recording of the known voice of a suspect. A record of an offender's voice may have been made, for example, during a hoax emergency call, a bomb threat, kidnap negotiations or as the result of covert police recordings. An expert should also be used when the police decide to carry out a police voice identification procedure.[1] The expert is usually a phonetician, a scientist who has speech as his or her central focus.[2]

17.2 Unlike everyday speaker identification in which there generally exist contextual clues in addition to familiarity with the voice in question, the task of comparing recordings of two unknown voices to discover whether they must have been made by the same speaker and not by any other speaker in the relevant population is extremely challenging. In fact the task, stated like that in absolute terms, cannot be achieved. It is not possible to use voice samples to establish identity with anything like the reliability of fingerprints or DNA.

17.3 There are many reasons for this. Whereas an individual's fingerprints and DNA are invariable physical characteristics, a person's voice is far from constant. It is determined by two mechanisms with considerable scope for variation: the speech organs and the language used.

---

1 See Chapter 8.
2 A Code of Practice for experts has been produced by the International Association for Forensic Phonetics and Acoustics.

VARIATION IN SPEECH PRODUCTION

17.4 The various speech organs have to be flexible to carry out their primary function of eating and breathing as well as their secondary function of speech, and the complexity of the structure and control of the speech organs results in a high number of degrees of freedom in the 'machine' producing speech. These degrees of freedom may be manipulated at will, as when someone 'puts on a voice', or may be subject to variation due to external factors such as stress, fatigue, and health. The result of this 'plasticity' of the vocal organs is that no two utterances from the same individual are ever, strictly speaking, identical in a physical sense.

17.5 The linguistic mechanism which drives the vocal mechanism is also far from invariant. The change in a person's 'tone of voice' is a common experience. The loudness, pitch, emphasis, and rate of utterances may vary. Moreover style, pronunciation, and to some extent dialect can change according to the social context in which the person is speaking. A further reason why identification cannot be stated in absolute terms is that adequate population statistics do not exist to determine whether a particular sound, or a given measured acoustic value, is rare or common in the relevant speech community.

COMPARISON OF SPEECH SAMPLES

17.6 Subject to those limitations the phonetician can uncover features of otherwise very similar sounding samples which consistently differentiate them, thus eliminating a suspect to a fairly high level of reliability. Similarities, too, can be demonstrated and quantified which, in the absence of significant differences, make the two samples compatible with the hypothesis that they were spoken by the same person. And an informed opinion can be offered as to how rare the kind of similarities found might be in the population as a whole, and hence how significant an indicator that the speaker might be the same.

17.7 Phoneticians rely on two broadly complementary approaches. One, the auditory approach, involves detailed listening and analysis in terms of a framework for describing pronunciation. This kind of analysis is best at capturing the 'accent' of speakers. The other involves acoustic analysis, usually by computer. The acoustic features quantified in this way will reflect both a speaker's accent and also his or her vocal anatomy and habits of forming sounds. These two approaches are discussed in more detail in the next two sections, but it should be appreciated that the two kinds of analysis normally proceed hand-in-hand.[3] For instance an auditory observation of a potentially unusual or unexpected pronunciation can be followed up by acoustic measurements to help confirm or controvert the auditory impression, and to reveal cues to whether the same vocal tract is the source of both samples.

---

[3] See D Ormerod 'Sounding Out Expert Voice Identification' [2002] Crim LR 771 for a critique of both methods of analysis.

AUDITORY ANALYSIS

17.8 Phoneticians are trained to analyse sounds by ear using a framework which is based on how sounds are produced. In the word 'tin', the first sound is a 'voiceless aspirated alveolar plosive'. This means that the sound is produced by using the tongue to make a closure just behind the teeth ('alveolar') and letting air pressure build up before releasing the closure ('plosive') while the vocal cords are separated so they do not vibrate ('voiceless'), and stay apart for a brief time after the lip closure is released ('aspirated') allowing a puff of air to escape before the vocal cord vibration for the vowel starts.

17.9 There is not a lot of scope for variation in how the English 't' is produced at the beginning of a word such as 'tin' (although speakers of some dialects may lack the aspiration), but in other positions considerable variation is possible. In a phrase like 'What a fat beetle!', there could be various pronunciations of the sounds written as 't'. All of them might be more or less the kind of plosive described above. All of them might be 'glottal stops', where instead of using the tongue to cut off the airflow the vocal cords are closed ('Wha' a fa' bee'le'). Alternatively the first 't', at the end of 'what', but not the others, could be pronounced rather like an 'r' ('Whar a fa' bee'le') – this is frequent in many northern accents of England. Again, the first and last of the 't' sounds could be pronounced like 'd', as standard in American English but more sporadic in British English. It is also possible to combine the plosive 't' with a glottal stop. As is evident from 't' alone, the sounds produced by speech may be broken down into a multitude of variants which a phonetician would be able to describe with precision.

17.10 Once it is possible to identify fine variants of pronunciation for 't', and for many other sounds, it becomes clear that there are many ways for speakers to differ. One speaker may never use a glottal stop in this phrase, one may use it only at the end of 'what', and another may use for all occurrences of 't' in this phrase. The pattern of usage will be largely determined by the dialect of the speaker, but there may be some room for idiosyncrasy, particularly as many speakers are influenced by a number of dialects. So a speaker from the north of England who had lived in America might use a 'd'-like sound in 'beetle', but retain an 'r'-like sound in 'What a', which would be a rare combination. Clearly if two samples showed internally consistent but contrasting patterns for a sound this must weigh against the samples being from the same speaker.

17.11 The picture is a little more complicated than that might imply, however, because speech samples are often not consistent in their patterns, reflecting the fact that speakers vary their pronunciations. Many speakers who would readily use a glottal stop in 'What a …' when speaking informally would instead use an alveolar plosive in their more formal styles. This of course would be relevant if the samples to be compared were spoken in different styles. But even within one style it is normal for speakers to vary, so finding the glottal stop does not guarantee that the next utterance of (even) the same phrase will not have an alveolar plosive. It is part of the expertise required for the comparison of speech samples not only to describe sounds, but also to be familiar with and understand the patterns of variation within the relevant dialect. The discovery of different sounds in the two samples will not necessarily lead to the elimination of the suspect if the variants are explicable by a coherent model of variation, frequently a sociolinguistic or a stylistic one.

17.12 This extended example has focused on the detail of one consonant, but it can easily be seen that the alternative pronunciations in the samples of the 20 or so vowels of English and 24 consonants will potentially provide a complex network of data for interpretation by the expert. These fine details of pronunciation can be described using the categories of the International Phonetic Alphabet, which provides a comprehensive framework for the sounds of human languages.[4] The more extensive the recorded speech available, the greater the ability of the expert to describe the range of an individual's speech patterns. A word such as 'that' may be uttered in a number of different ways by the same speaker, thus in ideal circumstances the phonetician would have many examples to analyse.

17.13 The expert's ability to judge by auditory analysis is necessarily limited to some extent by his or her familiarity with the dialect being considered. Thus an English phonetician would have to be cautious conducting a voice analysis of North American samples without prior familiarity with the variety in question. Academic texts may assist this task. However even in parts of the United Kingdom the nuances of sub-dialects may be so refined as to render a sample identifiable as coming from a particular part of a county and distinguishable from another part of the county 10 or 20 miles away. Attempting a voice identification analysis on samples in a foreign language unknown to the phonetician, certainly without the assistance of a linguistically-aware native speaker, would be thoroughly ill-advised.

17.14 At the same time as making observations on individual sounds the experts will be 'learning' the voice or voices heard on the sample, and forming a general perceptual impression of what might be termed broadly 'voice quality', including aspects of the speaker's pitch level and melody. There exists a framework for voice quality analysis[5] which captures long-term tendencies in speech such as a whispery voice or heavy nasality. It is beginning to be used by some forensic phoneticians, but is not widely used. Phoneticians generally do not treat voice quality in as analytic a way as individual sounds, and the distorting effect of the variable quality of samples, particularly if one sample and not the other is recorded over the telephone, means that impressions of voice quality have to be treated cautiously. Speech rate and loudness are factors which are extremely susceptible to contextually-induced variation from which it is unlikely that much, if any, assistance in identification will be gained. Similarly fluency or hesitation are, except perhaps in extreme cases such as a

---

4 See the 'IPA Chart' at para 17.28.

5 J Laver *The Phonetic Description of Voice Quality* (Cambridge University Press, 1980).

stutter, an unreliable guide to identity. Nonetheless the overall impression of the voice or voices heard will be taken into account.

ACOUSTIC ANALYSIS

17.15 Acoustic analysis is carried out with the aid of a computer. One of the most important kinds of analysis and most revealing ways of visualising the acoustics of speech is the spectrogram. Figure 1 shows spectrograms of the utterance 'We were relying on a milliner' spoken by two young men with similar accents. The spectrogram shows how much energy there is at each frequency (darker means more energy; low frequencies are at the bottom of the pattern and high at the top). The evolution of the energy pattern over the time course of the utterance is shown from left to right. Particularly important are the thick dark bands that vary higher and lower over the course of the utterance. These result from the resonances of the vocal tract, and they reflect the shape of the vocal tract at any moment in time and therefore for many sounds they define the sound for our perception (the lowest three are the most important). But as well as being determined by the sound being produced, they also reflect the dimensions of the vocal tract. The smaller the vocal tract, the higher the resonance will be. The pattern of resonances in a sound therefore encodes information about the sound (including its precise pronunciation) and also about the speaker. For this reason the measurement of formant frequencies is considered by many to be the single most important part of acoustic analysis for speaker identification.

17.16 Looking at the spectrograms from these two speakers it is possible both to see the ways in which the patterns are equivalent (they are of the same utterance) and to obtain a global impression of the between-speaker differences. However this requires careful skilled interpretation, since the global appearance of a speaker on a spectrogram can vary dramatically. As a pertinent example, if these speakers had also been recorded over the telephone, there would now be no meaningful marking on the spectrogram above about 3000 Hz (less than half way-up the patterns) and below 300Hz (the boxes on the spectrograms show schematically all the spectral information that would be left after telephone transmission). This is because the telephone transmits only the part of the speech signal most important for understanding the content. The telephone and 'direct' spectrogram of the same speech event by the same speaker would look dramatically different to superficial inspection.

17.17 In fact a diversity of factors affect the global appearance of a spectrogram and therefore it cannot be regarded as analogous to the visual examination of the detail of a fingerprint. Instead the expert will seek to identify linguistically equivalent events – for instance the same vowel, with the same degree of stress, between the same consonants (since the pattern of resonances for a sound is greatly affected by adjacent sounds, because in the articulation of speech one sound flows into the next). As noted above, the spectrograms in Figure 1 represent the same utterance by two different

Figure 1: Spectrograms of two speakers (top and bottom) saying 'We were relying on a milliner'. The approximate time-alignment of the sounds with the acoustic signal is shown in the transcript. The arrow points to the third resonance in the 'r' of 'relying'. The box shows the information that would be reliably transmitted by the telephone, ie the 'telephone bandwidth'

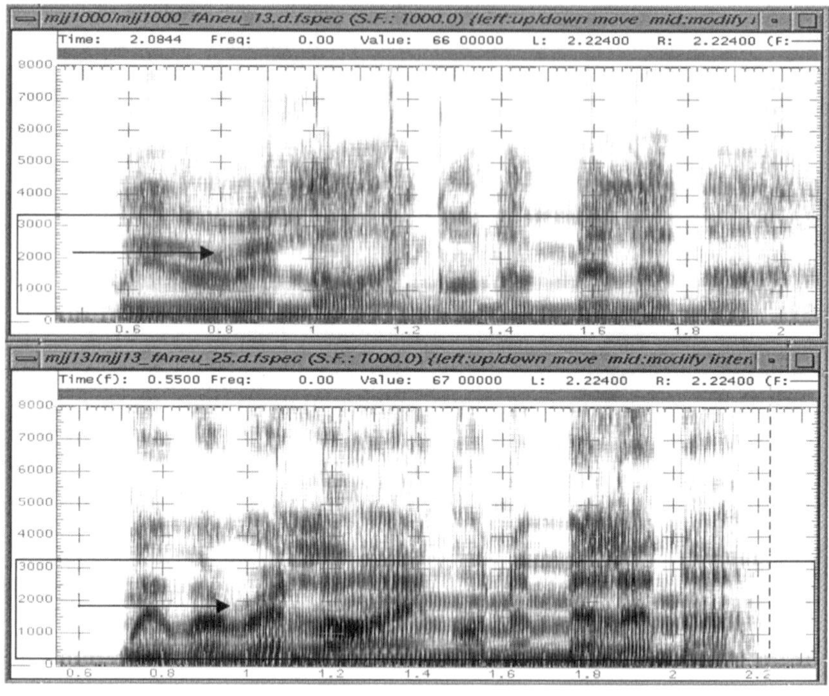

we w erer e l y i ng o n a mi ll i n er

speakers. As an example of a linguistically equivalent event, the arrows point to the third resonance in the centre of the 'r' at the start of 'relying'. Both speakers' 'r' is characterised by a dipping of the second and third resonance, but the lower speaker's resonance dips further (and becomes much weaker), going below 2000 Hz rather than staying above. Nothing worthwhile could be inferred on the basis of this one difference. However, by measuring a whole series of equivalent 'r' sounds, all of which would be slightly different because speakers are not machines, plotting the values on the same graph might reveal two fairly distinct clusters of points corresponding to the two recordings. That would weigh in the balance in favour of the recordings being from different speakers. By contrast, clusters which overlapped to a significant degree would be a factor suggesting that the recordings might be from the same speaker, though it could in no sense be regarded as conclusive.

17.18 The expert will do this kind of analysis for as many sounds as are available in sufficient numbers. Where, as is often the case, recordings are of degraded quality, the opportunities for comparison may be limited.

17.19 The expert may also look at the overall frequency favoured by different resonances; if the long-term average of resonant frequencies is higher in one recording than the other, or some resonances are higher and others lower, this suggests different sizes and/or shapes of vocal tract which points strongly in favour of different speakers.

17.20 In addition, experts will often compute the fundamental frequency of the sample, that is the acoustic result of the rate of vibration of the vocal cords which we perceive as the pitch of the voice. The statistics derived from the computation, such as the mean fundamental frequency of the voice and its standard deviation, will correspond fairly closely to the perceived pitch level of the voice as high or low and its pitch range – how monotonous or varied the pitch of the voice sounds. As with all aspects of forensic speaker identification, however, very careful interpretation of such values is needed. An important reason for this is that both pitch level and pitch range are highly variable. The mere fact of 'speaking up' in a noisy environment will cause both pitch level and pitch range to increase significantly. The expert will look not only at the values but also try to construe their significance given the circumstances in which the recordings were made.

REACHING A CONCLUSION

17.21 In the course of the analysis the phonetician will have built up as comprehensive a picture as the samples allow of the voice of the perpetrator and the suspect. The picture will consist of the auditory categorisation of particular sounds, analysis of their patterns of occurrence with reference to the linguistic patterns of the relevant dialect or dialects, acoustic measurements of various dimensions of the voice, and an overall impression of the voice or voices acquired through repeated listening. Rarely will all factors point unambiguously in the same direction. The expert will therefore have to use his or her judgment to determine the balance between factors which point to identity and those which suggest two different speakers.

17.22 There are a number of factors which may inhibit examination and comparison and thus the weight of any opinion advanced. They include the quality of recording and the length of the recorded segments of speech. Quality may be poor where the voice is recorded on a telephone answering service because of the frequency limitations of the telephone medium described at **17.16**. It may also be adversely affected by inferior quality of the recording device, where its speed calibration is incorrect or, if tape is used, it has been degraded by constant use. Quality may also be adversely affected by extraneous noise such as traffic or television. The speech itself may be short and have limited linguistic content on which to base an opinion. The emotional state of the speaker can also make comparison more difficult. At one extreme the material of a brief 999 telephone call in which the anxious speaker says only that there is a fire at a certain address may reveal little. At the other extreme, the phonetician may have many hours of good quality covert recordings in which the speaker is talking perfectly naturally.

17.23 Until recently most experts expressed their conclusion on a likelihood scale, for instance 'almost certainly/very likely/likely/possibly the same; no decision; possibly/likely/very likely/almost certainly different'. The number of points on the scale and the terms used differ, but the principle was generally the same. However, it should be understood that phonetics experts were not basing their opinion on quantified statistical likelihood, save in vary rare situations, but on informed estimates. One problem with such scales is that they allowed the phonetician to concentrate on similarities (and differences) between samples, while giving too little prominence to the distribution of similarities in the population as a whole.

17.24 Forensic phoneticians have taken note of the application of Bayesian statistics in other areas of evidence such as DNA. In this approach, the two crucial questions are 'how likely is the evidence on the hypothesis that the suspect left it', and 'how likely is the evidence on the alternative hypothesis' – which can be as general as 'someone else left it'. Some phoneticians advocate a quantitative evaluation of this 'likelihood ratio' in speaker comparison. In the UK, practitioners active in forensic phonetics have felt that, in the absence as yet of population data for the majority of phonetic features, a numerical likelihood ratio would give a spuriously quantitative air to an analysis which still relies heavily on judgment. Instead, a two-part verbal format within a broadly Bayesian conceptual framework was agreed,[6] and has been widely adopted in the UK. First, the two samples are judged 'consistent' or 'not consistent' with having been spoken by the same speaker – the latter if there are observed differences which cannot be explained by sociolinguistic/stylistic variation or other contextual factors. If the samples are 'consistent', then the common features are rated on a five-point scale from 'not distinctive' to 'exceptionally distinctive'.

17.25 Thus, where two samples show no crucial differences, but (say) a run-of-the-mill Manchester accent, with pitch and formant frequencies around the average for the relevant population, the common features would be 'not distinctive', and (quite correctly) add little weight to the case for a suspect having spoken the incriminating sample. On the other hand a mixed Manchester-and-Scottish accent with pitch in the lowest 5 per cent of the population range and formant frequencies in the upper quartile, combined with a lisp and a specific stutter, would be 'exceptionally distinctive', and potentially lend considerable weight. The new formulation is less direct than a conclusion in terms of an impressionistic probability. However it highlights, appropriately, the fact that forensic speaker identification can only contribute to the overall probabilities in the case in conjunction with other evidence. It cannot properly determine with certainty the positive identification of a suspect. The debate

6 J P French and P Harrison 'Position statement concerning use of impressionistic likelihood terms in forensic speaker comparison cases' (2007) 14 *Int Journal of Speech, Language and the Law* 137–144.

about the most appropriate way to state conclusions continues[7] and will be shaped by advances in forensic phonetics.

ADMISSIBILITY

17.26 The admission of evidence of voice comparison by auditory analysis was recognised in *R v Robb*.[8] However, with advances in technology most experts now use acoustic as well as auditory analysis. In *R v O'Doherty*[9] the Northern Ireland Court of Appeal, having accepted the limitations of auditory analysis alone and the significant discriminatory information that acoustic techniques can reveal, held that:

> '... in the present state of scientific knowledge no prosecution should be brought in Northern Ireland in which one of the planks is voice identification given by an expert which is solely confined to auditory analysis. There should be expert evidence of acoustic analysis such as is used by Dr Nolan, Dr French and all but a small percentage of experts in the United Kingdom and by experts in the rest of Europe ...'

17.27 To that general rule there were said to be three exceptions. First, where the voices are of speakers who comprise a known group and the task is narrowed to the distinction between the voices. This exception does not appear to contemplate the presence of two people with very similar accents and speech patterns. The second was where there exist rare characteristics which render the speaker identifiable, although as was recognised by the court, this may beg the question rather than answer it. The third exception was said to be where the issue relates to the accent or dialect of the speaker. However, in *R v Flynn & St John*[10] the Court of Appeal considered that it was 'neither possible nor desirable to go as far as the Northern Ireland Court of Criminal Appeal in *O'Doherty*'. If proffered by a properly qualified expert, evidence of auditory analysis which is unsupported by acoustic analysis is admissible in England and Wales.

---

7 P Rose and G Morrison 'A response to the UK Position Statement on forensic speaker comparison' (2009)16 *Int Journal of Speech, Language and the Law* 139–163. See also J P French, F Nolan, P Foulkes, P Harrison amd K McDougall 'The UK Position Statement on forensic speaker comparison: a rejoinder to Rose and Morrison' (2010) 17 *Int Journal of Speech, Language and the Law* 143–152.

8 [1991] Crim LR 539, CA.

9 [2003] 1 Cr App R 5, NICA.

10 [2008] EWCA Crim 970.

17.28

Symbols of the International Phonetic Alphabet

THE INTERNATIONAL PHONETIC ALPHABET (revised to 2005)

CONSONANTS (PULMONIC)

	Bilabial	Labiodental	Dental	Alveolar	Postalveolar	Retroflex	Palatal	Velar	Uvular	Pharyngeal	Glottal
Plosive	p b			t d		ʈ ɖ	c ɟ	k ɡ	q ɢ		ʔ
Nasal	m	ɱ		n		ɳ	ɲ	ŋ	ɴ		
Trill	ʙ			r					ʀ		
Tap or Flap		ⱱ		ɾ		ɽ					
Fricative	ɸ β	f v	θ ð	s z	ʃ ʒ	ʂ ʐ	ç ʝ	x ɣ	χ ʁ	ħ ʕ	h ɦ
Lateral fricative				ɬ ɮ							
Approximant		ʋ		ɹ		ɻ	j	ɰ			
Lateral approximant				l		ɭ	ʎ	ʟ			

Where symbols appear in pairs, the one to the right represents a voiced consonant. Shaded areas denote articulations judged impossible.

CONSONANTS (NON-PULMONIC)

Clicks		Voiced implosives		Ejectives	
ʘ	Bilabial	ɓ	Bilabial	ʼ	Examples:
ǀ	Dental	ɗ	Dental/alveolar	pʼ	Bilabial
ǃ	(Post)alveolar	ʄ	Palatal	tʼ	Dental/alveolar
ǂ	Palatoalveolar	ɠ	Velar	kʼ	Velar
ǁ	Alveolar lateral	ʛ	Uvular	sʼ	Alveolar fricative

VOWELS

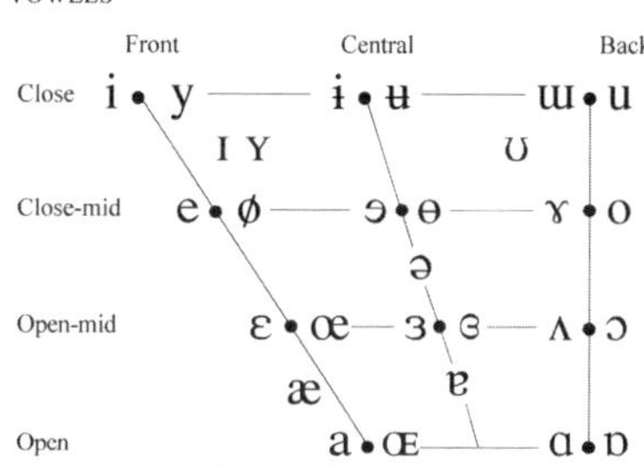

Where symbols appear in pairs, the one to the right represents a rounded vowel.

OTHER SYMBOLS

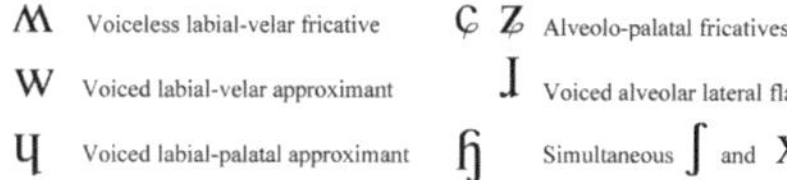

ʍ Voiceless labial-velar fricative

w Voiced labial-velar approximant

ɥ Voiced labial-palatal approximant

ʜ Voiceless epiglottal fricative

ʢ Voiced epiglottal fricative

ʡ Epiglottal plosive

ɕ ʑ Alveolo-palatal fricatives

ɺ Voiced alveolar lateral flap

ɧ Simultaneous ʃ and x

Affricates and double articulations can be represented by two symbols joined by a tie bar if necessary. k͡p t͡s

SUPRASEGMENTALS

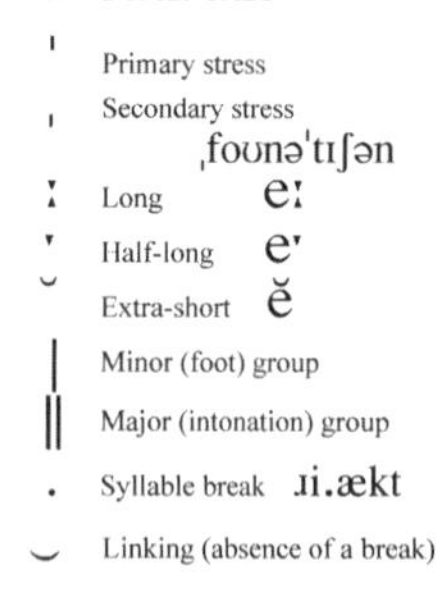

ˈ Primary stress

ˌ Secondary stress ˌfoʊnəˈtɪʃən

ː Long eː

ˑ Half-long eˑ

˘ Extra-short ĕ

| Minor (foot) group

‖ Major (intonation) group

. Syllable break ɹi.ækt

‿ Linking (absence of a break)

DIACRITICS Diacritics may be placed above a symbol with a descender, e.g. ŋ̊

̥	Voiceless	n̥ d̥	̤	Breathy voiced	b̤ a̤	̪	Dental	t̪ d̪
̬	Voiced	s̬ t̬	̰	Creaky voiced	b̰ a̰	̺	Apical	t̺ d̺
ʰ	Aspirated	tʰ dʰ	̼	Linguolabial	t̼ d̼	̻	Laminal	t̻ d̻
̹	More rounded	ɔ̹	ʷ	Labialized	tʷ dʷ	̃	Nasalized	ẽ
̜	Less rounded	ɔ̜	ʲ	Palatalized	tʲ dʲ	ⁿ	Nasal release	dⁿ
̟	Advanced	u̟	ˠ	Velarized	tˠ dˠ	ˡ	Lateral release	dˡ
̠	Retracted	e̠	ˤ	Pharyngealized	tˤ dˤ	̚	No audible release	d̚
̈	Centralized	ë	̴	Velarized or pharyngealized	ɫ			
̽	Mid-centralized	e̽	̝	Raised	e̝		(ɹ̝ = voiced alveolar fricative)	
̩	Syllabic	n̩	̞	Lowered	e̞		(β̞ = voiced bilabial approximant)	
̯	Non-syllabic	e̯	̘	Advanced Tongue Root	e̘			
˞	Rhoticity	ɚ a˞	̙	Retracted Tongue Root	e̙			

TONES AND WORD ACCENTS

LEVEL			CONTOUR		
e̋ or	˥	Extra high	ě or	˩˥	Rising
é	˦	High	ê	˥˩	Falling
ē	˧	Mid	e᷄	˦˥	High rising
è	˨	Low	e᷅	˩˨	Low rising
ȅ	˩	Extra low	e᷈	˧˦˧	Rising-falling
↓		Downstep	↗		Global rise
↑		Upstep	↘		Global fall

Chapter 18

DOG TRACKING

INTRODUCTION

18.1 Dogs are capable of tracking a person's scent and can thereby indicate the route taken by that person. If the route leads to the source of the scent, the person whose scent was followed will be identified as having been present at the position from which the scent was first picked up. It is important to recognise that tracking as evidence of identification is inferential. The skill has an element of canine subjectivity, the possibility of error and the impossibility of exposing the error by questioning of the dog. Care must therefore be taken in analysing the tracking, the prevailing circumstances which might render it unreliable and the expertise of dog and handler.

THE TRACKING DOG

18.2 *Canis familiaris* or the domestic dog is a sub-family of the family *Canidae*, a group of foxlike animals. There are over 300 breeds of dog spread throughout the world and about 170 are recognised in this country. The inherited characteristics of *Canis familiaris*, especially those pertaining to the hunt for food, make it ideally suited to tracking.

18.3 Domestication has altered some dogs' physical and mental characteristics far from their wild ancestors. However, with very few exceptions dogs have inherited their predecessor's natural ability to hunt and kill. Domestication has in most cases, through the selective breeding for physical or temperamental changes, suppressed the killing instinct. The ability and instinct to hunt remains very strong and is encouraged in many breeds. It is the utilisation of this skill that is developed in the search and tracking exercises.

18.4 For the purpose of tracking the properties required in a dog are those of an acute sense of smell, a good conformation, fitness, stamina, intelligence and preferably a good temperament. These elements should produce an animal that can without difficulty detect, identify and make use of scents, while travelling at a reasonable pace over varying terrains. A good tracking dog is capable of tracking for several miles and, depending upon the prevailing conditions, follow a scent deposited more than a day earlier.

18.5 General police dogs in the United Kingdom have a multi-disciplinary use. Tracking is only one of the disciplines taught. Others include crowd control and searching for persons. The dog will be trained, among other things, in obedience, agility, criminal work or searching as well as tracking. (Drugs and explosive detection require more specialised training.) Being only a part of the general police dog's role, the ability to track is therefore only a contributory part in the selection process for a suitable dog for police training. The most suitable breed, possessing all the attributes for general purpose police work is the German Shepherd or Alsatian as it is sometimes called. These represent the vast majority of general purpose police dogs. Some of the other breeds that are occasionally used are the Rottweiler, Doberman, Labrador, Weimaraner, Giant Schnauzer and Belgian Shepherd Dog. However the breed recognised as the most suitable for specialist tracking is the Bloodhound because of its acute sense of smell. Some police forces have trained general police dogs to 'trail' (see below) as well as track; some employ Bloodhounds specifically and solely trained to track and trail.

SENSE OF SMELL

18.6 When a dog breathes or smells it draws air in at the nostrils. This air is warmed, filtered free of particles and bacteria, and moistened almost to saturation point. The nasal cavity is simply a bony shell, which is split into two separate chambers. The size of these chambers varies considerably between the breeds. Each chamber is a series of air-conducting passages containing a meshwork of bones. Thus, air breathed in is effectively broken up, warmed, filtered and humidified. The ability to sense odours is highly developed in the dog, and it is within the deeper parts of the nose that the olfactory hair-like sensors lie. The act of 'sniffing', in the case of the dog, simply ensures that the odour particles are rapidly and forcibly drawn upwards into the nose. The fact that they are warmed and moistened gives the dog the immeasurably keener sense to smell than that of the human. Use of this ability is the means by which a dog can follow a track or trail.

TRACKING AND TRAILING

18.7 The term 'tracking' is generally accepted to mean the locating and following of a scent pattern different to that of the immediate surrounding area. The track to be followed is located by the dog through searching a dictated area of ground. The dog identifies the unique area of ground and air disturbance and follows the track through its varying compositions, across differing terrain and distractions to its termination.

18.8 'Trailing' is generally accepted to mean the following of a trail that carries a specific scent or odour that has been introduced to the dog at the commencement of the search. For police purposes this would normally be an article of clothing, which absorbs the body scent, that had been worn by the person to be trailed. Plastic or metal objects held by a person are less likely to be suitable because of their non-absorbent nature. This method of tracking is also known as the 'Scent Article Method'. The trail to be followed is identified by the dog at the start by searching for an area of ground and/or air whose scent matches that of the article.

THE TRACK

18.9 A person's scent is considered to be extremely distinctive. It varies, among other things, according to race, gender, and biological make up. Additional factors that will vary the scent patterns include the type of footwear and clothing worn, occupational or leisure smells such as food, alcohol, perfume and chemical or plant material carried by the person.

18.10 The ability of a dog successfully to track or trail is dependent upon and complicated by a number of factors. These include:

(1) The training, experience, hunting instinct and temperament of the dog.

(2) The training and experience of its handler together with his or her understanding of the dog.

(3) The weather prevailing at the time of day. When first laid the track can be detected quite clearly as ground disturbance and air scent, but the weather conditions may move the scent or cause it to become mixed with and contaminated by other scents. The wind can blow and disperse the scent in the air or rising from the ground for a considerable distance from the track. Sun and warm weather enhance evaporation and accelerate scent dissipation. Heavy or prolonged rainfall may wash away odours whereas light rainfall before the trail is made can assist in the retention of odours. Odours are more likely to be retained if the ground temperature is higher than that of the air, which is more likely to occur at nighttime.

(4) The type of terrain. In general, surfaces such as pavements and roads hold scents for much shorter periods than those of grass and vegetation.

(5) Odours given off by the earth, for example the crushing and breaking of the ground, vegetation, insects and worms, may affect the scent pattern.

(6) Activity on or over the track or trail. Animal, pedestrian or vehicle movements may cover, scatter or change the odours of a trail.

(7) The amount of time elapsed between the trail being made and when it is followed. Time will allow a scent pattern to spread out or disperse. Scents do not significantly reduce or disappear over a period of time if unexposed to the above variable factors. However when affected by all or some of them, they will deteriorate, dissipate and eventually disappear.

(8) The speed at which the dog is worked may affect its accuracy.

HOW A DOG TRACKS

18.11 The dog and handler are a team; the handler uses the dog's abilities and assists it through logic and reasoning. A dog tracks by finding a scent that is different to that of the surrounding area. It then searches for other instances of this scent and if it finds them, follows it through the 'corridor' formed within the area as it hunts for the source. The dog is worked by 'casting' it on the line, that is to say by allowing it to run around at the distance allowed by the length of the line in order to search for the scent. If it finds it, the handler can follow the dog as it follows the scent trail. If not then the handler can systematically work an area by moving about it and allowing the dog to cast. It follows that if there is more than one scent in the vicinity one of which has been left by a suspect and another by someone unconnected with an offence the handler will not know which the dog is following.

18.12 Most dogs track naturally and easily follow any scent trail to find prey, be it an animal or person. They normally do this at a speed far in excess of the natural human gait. If it is necessary to keep sight of the dog as it would be in the case of a police officer following a suspect then a means of contact and control must be established. This can be achieved by stopping the dog through an obedience command when it is about to leave the handler's sight or control and joining it before continuing (a method frequently used when the dog is tracking while searching) or by placing the dog on a harness and line. The harness allows the animal to work without any physical restriction and the line keeps the dog within a manageable distance normally up to about 10 metres.

18.13 If the dog has lost the track in a garden then the handler can work the dog round the perimeter in an attempt to recover it. When tracking or trailing a dog may overshoot a turn. A dog normally indicates this by raising its head and starting to turn, although different terrains and conditions may alter this. In this case the handler should stand still and allow the dog to cast around until the track or trail is picked up again. If not then the handler can retrace the route to search by casting the dog on either side of the route taken. If a tracking dog is prevented from continuing due to an obstacle, for example a high fence or wall, then the handler can take the dog to the other side and cast around the adjoining area.

18.14 It is important to note that once a dog has picked up a track there may be no absolute certainty that a dog has followed the same scent throughout the tracking. If there is a break in continuity such as a fence or a busy road, the later track may not be the same as that first followed. Similarly where the paths of two scents have crossed or the wind has caused two scents to merge it is possible for a dog to switch from one to another. The same might apply to a scent left by one person along a path which is overlaid by the scent of a second person along the same path. The dog might begin to track the first on to the path but, scenting both on the path, follow the second when the scents finally diverge, especially if the second scent is the stronger. Whether the dog maintains the path of a single scent may depend upon the training, experience and age of the dog. The behaviour of the dog, purposeful or hesitant, may indicate to its handler whether there has been any corruption to the tracking of a single scent. The difficulties associated with tracking a single scent should not apply to a dog which is trailing by the scent article method. It will have identified the specific scent it is to follow and remain undistracted by other scents.

18.15 When trailing a scent introduced by an article, such as clothing, it is necessary for evidential purposes that the article carries only the scent of the track layer because the dog can give no indication or evidence as to what scent it is following. Thus if it is contaminated by other people or exhibits the exercise may become flawed. It is therefore preferable to preserve the item by picking it up with tongs or plastic gloves and placing it into a non-absorbent plastic rather than paper bag. The article is presented to the dog generally by wrapping it round the dog or holding it to its nose. Once the specific scent has been introduced the animal will be instructed to follow the trail. This is normally done by placing a harness on the dog and giving a verbal command. Not only does it 'key' the dog into the exercise but also allows the handler to maintain contact with the dog.

TRAINING AND CERTIFICATION

18.16 The training of a dog is carried out with its handler. Thereafter they act as a team and dogs and handlers are not generally interchangeable. The Home Office Standing Advisory Committee on Police Dogs (HOSAC) has set out a number of requirements in relation to the assessment of general purpose police dogs of which tracking is one. Licensing should take place annually. In between licensing each team should be given the number of training days as recommended by HOSAC. This is a minimum of 16 continuation/refresher training days for dogs under 6 years of age, while for dogs over 6 years of age the requirement is for a minimum of 10 days per annum. Tracking on various terrains is an area of assessment recommended by HOSAC, though it is recognised that each constabulary may have varying local practices. There is at present no specific testing requirement for trailing.

18.17 The continuation training dates should be noted in the handler's training records by the continuation training instructor. All training records should be maintained showing the level of attainment of the dog. However the training records, which should also disclose any weaknesses of the dog, are often only as good as the records kept by the handler. All work carried out by the dog should also be recorded in operational records. To monitor its performance, these should include not only the successes but any failures by the dog in tracking exercises together with reasons, if known. As with training records, these are matters of judgement for the handler.

EVIDENCE, ADMISSIBILITY AND JURY DIRECTION

18.18 The evidence of the dog handler should feature the complete history of the tracking or trailing procedure. It may often require a plan of the area showing the track followed, any break in continuity as well as any preliminary casting in which no scent was detected. The handler should record the time, weather conditions including temperature, wind and recent rain, the terrain covered and any other factor which might affect the ability of the dog to follow a scent. The reaction of the dog itself, such as purposefulness or hesitance, may assist in indicating the reliability of the tracking. Where a scented article has been introduced, evidence as to its finding and preservation should be recorded.

18.19 The admissibility of dog tracking evidence and the approach to it by a jury were considered in *R v Pieterson and Holloway*.[1] Evidence of tracking by a dog is admissible provided that a dog handler can establish that the dog has been properly trained and that over a period of time the dog's reactions indicate that it is a reliable pointer to the existence of a scent from a particular individual. Detailed evidence establishing the reliability of the dog in question is an essential requirement. The trial judge must, in addition, direct the jury to consider the evidence as to the conduct of the dog carefully and with circumspection, since the dog may not always be reliable and cannot be cross-examined.

---

1 [1995] 2 Cr App R 11, CA followed in *R v Sykes* [1997] Crim LR 752, CA.

Appendix A

PACE CODE D: CODE OF PRACTICE FOR THE IDENTIFICATION OF PERSONS BY POLICE OFFICERS

FIRST DESCRIPTION OF SUSPECTS GIVEN BY WITNESSES

1 Introduction

1.1 This Code of Practice concerns the principal methods used by police to identify people in connection with the investigation of offences and the keeping of accurate and reliable criminal records. The powers and procedures in this code must be used fairly, responsibly, with respect for the people to whom they apply and without unlawful discrimination. The Equality Act 2010 makes it unlawful for police officers to discriminate against, harass or victimise any person on the grounds of the 'protected characteristics' of age, disability, gender reassignment, race, religion or belief, sex and sexual orientation, marriage and civil partnership, pregnancy and maternity when using their powers. When police forces are carrying out their functions they also have a duty to have regard to the need to eliminate unlawful discrimination, harassment and victimisation and to take steps to foster good relations.

1.2 In this code, identification by an eye-witness arises when a witness who has seen the offender committing the crime and is given an opportunity to identify a person suspected of involvement in the offence in a video identification, identification parade or similar procedure. These eye-witness identification procedures (see Part A of section 3 below) are designed to:

- test the witness' ability to identify the suspect as the person they saw on a previous occasion
- provide safeguards against mistaken identification.

While this Code concentrates on visual identification procedures, it does not preclude the police making use of aural identification procedures such as a "voice identification parade", where they judge that appropriate.

1.2A In this code, separate provisions in Part B of section 3 below apply when any person, including a police officer, is asked if they recognise anyone they see in an image as being someone they know and to test their claim that they recognise that person as someone who is known to them. Except where stated, these separate provisions are not subject to the eye-witnesses identification procedures described in paragraph 1.2.

1.3 Identification by fingerprints applies when a person's fingerprints are taken to:

- compare with fingerprints found at the scene of a crime
- check and prove convictions
- help to ascertain a person's identity.

1.3A Identification using footwear impressions applies when a person's footwear impressions are taken to compare with impressions found at the scene of a crime.

1.4 Identification by body samples and impressions includes taking samples such as blood or hair to generate a DNA profile for comparison with material obtained from the scene of a crime, or a victim.

1.5 Taking photographs of arrested people applies to recording and checking identity and locating and tracing persons who:

- are wanted for offences
- fail to answer their bail.

1.6 Another method of identification involves searching and examining detained suspects to find, e.g., marks such as tattoos or scars which may help establish their identity or whether they have been involved in committing an offence.

1.7 The provisions of the Police and Criminal Evidence Act 1984 (PACE) and this Code are designed to make sure fingerprints, samples, impressions and photographs are taken, used and retained, and identification procedures carried out, only when justified and necessary for preventing, detecting or investigating crime. If these provisions are not observed, the application of the relevant procedures in particular cases may be open to question.

2 General

2.1 This Code must be readily available at all police stations for consultation by:

- police officers and police staff
- detained persons
- members of the public

2.2 The provisions of this Code:

- include the *Annexes*
- do not include the *Notes for guidance.*

2.3 Code C, paragraph 1.4, regarding a person who may be mentally disordered or otherwise mentally vulnerable and the *Notes for guidance* applicable to those provisions apply to this Code.

2.4 Code C, paragraph 1.5, regarding a person who appears to be under the age of 17 applies to this Code.

2.5 Code C, paragraph 1.6, regarding a person who appears to be blind, seriously visually impaired, deaf, unable to read or speak or has difficulty communicating orally because of a speech impediment applies to this Code.

2.6 In this Code:

- 'appropriate adult' means the same as in Code C, paragraph 1.7
- 'solicitor' means the same as in Code C, paragraph 6.12

and the *Notes for guidance* applicable to those provisions apply to this Code.

- where a search or other procedure under this code may only be carried out or observed by a person of the same sex as the person to whom the search or procedure applies, the gender of the detainee and other persons present should be established and recorded in line with Annex F of Code A.

2.7 References to custody officers include those performing the functions of custody officer, see *paragraph 1.9* of Code C.

2.8 When a record of any action requiring the authority of an officer of a specified rank is made under this Code, subject to *paragraph 2.18,* the officer's name and rank must be recorded.

2.9 When this Code requires the prior authority or agreement of an officer of at least inspector or superintendent rank, that authority may be given by a sergeant or chief inspector who has been authorised to perform the functions of the higher rank under PACE, section 107.

2.10 Subject to *paragraph 2.18*, all records must be timed and signed by the maker.

2.11 Records must be made in the custody record, unless otherwise specified. References to 'pocket book' include any official report book issued to police officers or police staff.

2.12 If any procedure in this Code requires a person's consent, the consent of a:

- mentally disordered or otherwise mentally vulnerable person is only valid if given in the presence of the appropriate adult
- juvenile is only valid if their parent's or guardian's consent is also obtained unless the juvenile is under 14, when their parent's or guardian's consent is sufficient in its own right. If the only obstacle to an identification procedure in *section 3* is that a juvenile's parent or guardian refuses consent or reasonable efforts to obtain it have failed, the identification officer may apply the provisions of *paragraph 3.21.* See *Note 2A*

2.13 If a person is blind, seriously visually impaired or unable to read, the custody officer or identification officer shall make sure their solicitor, relative, appropriate adult or some other person likely to take an interest in them and not involved in the investigation is available to help check any documentation. When this Code requires written consent or signing, the person assisting may be asked to sign instead, if the detainee prefers. This paragraph does not require an appropriate adult to be called solely to assist in checking and signing documentation for a person who is not a juvenile, or mentally disordered or otherwise mentally vulnerable (see *Note 2B* and Code C *paragraph 3.15*).

2.14 If any procedure in this Code requires information to be given to or sought from a suspect, it must be given or sought in the appropriate adult's presence if the suspect is mentally disordered, otherwise mentally vulnerable or a juvenile. If the appropriate adult is not present when the information is first given or sought, the procedure must be repeated in the presence of the appropriate adult when they arrive. If the suspect appears deaf or there is doubt about their hearing or speaking ability or ability to understand English, and effective communication cannot be established, the information must be given or sought through an interpreter.

2.15 Any procedure in this Code involving the participation of a suspect who is mentally disordered, otherwise mentally vulnerable or a juvenile must take place in the presence of the appropriate adult. See Code C paragraph 1.4.

2.15A Any procedure in this Code involving the participation of a witness who is or appears to be mentally disordered, otherwise mentally vulnerable or a juvenile should take place in the presence of a pre-trial support person unless the witness states that they do not want a support person to be present. A support person must not be allowed to prompt any identification of a suspect by a witness. See *Note 2AB*.

2.16 References to:

- 'taking a photograph', include the use of any process to produce a single, still or moving, visual image
- 'photographing a person', should be construed accordingly
- 'photographs', 'films', 'negatives' and 'copies' include relevant visual images recorded, stored, or reproduced through any medium
- 'destruction' includes the deletion of computer data relating to such images or making access to that data impossible

2.17 Except as described, nothing in this Code affects the powers and procedures:

(i) for requiring and taking samples of breath, blood and urine in relation to driving offences, etc, when under the influence of drink, drugs or excess alcohol under the:

- Road Traffic Act 1988, sections 4 to 11
- Road Traffic Offenders Act 1988, sections 15 and 16
- Transport and Works Act 1992, sections 26 to 38;

(ii) under the Immigration Act 1971, Schedule 2, paragraph 18, for taking photographs and fingerprints from persons detained under that Act, Schedule 2, paragraph 16 (Administrative Controls as to Control on Entry etc.); for taking fingerprints in accordance with the Immigration and Asylum Act 1999; sections 141 and 142(3), or other methods for collecting information about a person's external physical characteristics provided for by regulations made under that Act, section 144;

(iii) under the Terrorism Act 2000, Schedule 8, for taking photographs, fingerprints, skin impressions, body samples or impressions from people:

- arrested under that Act, section 41,
- detained for the purposes of examination under that Act, Schedule 7, and to whom the Code of Practice issued under that Act, Schedule 14, paragraph 6, applies ('the terrorism provisions')

See *Note 2C*;

(iv) for taking photographs, fingerprints, skin impressions, body samples or impressions from people who have been:

- arrested on warrants issued in Scotland, by officers exercising powers under the Criminal Justice and Public Order Act 1994, section 136(2)
- arrested or detained without warrant by officers from a police force in Scotland exercising their powers of arrest or detention under the Criminal Justice and Public Order Act 1994, section 137(2), (Cross Border powers of arrest etc.).

Note: In these cases, police powers and duties and the person's rights and entitlements whilst at a police station in England and Wales are the same as if the person had been arrested in Scotland by a Scottish police officer.

2.18 Nothing in this Code requires the identity of officers or police staff to be recorded or disclosed:

(a) in the case of enquiries linked to the investigation of terrorism;

(b) if the officers or police staff reasonably believe recording or disclosing their names might put them in danger.

In these cases, they shall use warrant or other identification numbers and the name of their police station. *See Note 2D*

2.19 In this Code:

(a) 'designated person' means a person other than a police officer, designated under the Police Reform Act 2002, Part 4, who has specified powers and duties of police officers conferred or imposed on them;

(b) any reference to a police officer includes a designated person acting in the exercise or performance of the powers and duties conferred or imposed on them by their designation.

2.20 If a power conferred on a designated person:

(a) allows reasonable force to be used when exercised by a police officer, a designated person exercising that power has the same entitlement to use force;

(b) includes power to use force to enter any premises, that power is not exercisable by that designated person except:

(i) in the company, and under the supervision, of a police officer; or

(ii) for the purpose of:

- saving life or limb; or
- preventing serious damage to property.

2.21 Nothing in this Code prevents the custody officer, or other officer given custody of the detainee, from allowing police staff who are not designated persons to carry out individual procedures or tasks at the police station if the law allows. However, the officer remains responsible for making sure the procedures and tasks are carried out correctly in accordance with the Codes of Practice. Any such person must be:

(a) a person employed by a police authority maintaining a police force and under the control and direction of the Chief Officer of that force;

(b) employed by a person with whom a police authority has a contract for the provision of services relating to persons arrested or otherwise in custody.

2.22 Designated persons and other police staff must have regard to any relevant provisions of the Codes of Practice.

Notes for guidance

2A For the purposes of paragraph 2.12, the consent required from a parent or guardian may, for a juvenile in the care of a local authority or voluntary organisation, be given by that authority or organisation. In the case of a juvenile, nothing in paragraph 2.12 requires the parent, guardian or representative of a local authority or voluntary organisation to be present to give their consent, unless they are acting as the appropriate adult under paragraphs 2.14 or 2.15. However, it is important that a parent or guardian not present is fully informed before being asked to consent. They must be given the same information about the procedure and the juvenile's suspected involvement in the offence as the juvenile and appropriate adult. The parent or guardian must also be allowed to speak to the juvenile and the appropriate adult if they wish. Provided the consent is fully informed and is not withdrawn, it may be obtained at any time before the procedure takes place.

2AB The Youth Justice and Criminal Evidence Act 1999 guidance "Achieving Best Evidence in Criminal Proceedings" indicates that a pre-trial support person should accompany a vulnerable witness during any identification procedure unless the witness states that they do not want a support person to be present. It states that this support person should not be (or not be likely to be) a witness in the investigation.

2B People who are seriously visually impaired or unable to read may be unwilling to sign police documents. The alternative, i.e. their representative signing on their behalf, seeks to protect the interests of both police and suspects.

2C Photographs, fingerprints, samples and impressions may be taken from a person detained under the terrorism provisions to help determine whether they are, or have been, involved in terrorism, as well as when there are reasonable grounds for suspecting their involvement in a particular offence.

2D The purpose of paragraph 2.18(b) is to protect those involved in serious organised crime investigations or arrests of particularly violent suspects when there is reliable information that those arrested or their associates may threaten or cause harm to the officers. In cases of doubt, an officer of inspector rank or above should be consulted.

3 Identification and recognition of suspects

(A) Identification of a suspect by an eye-witness

3.0 This part applies when an eye-witness has seen the offender committing the crime or in any other circumstances which tend to prove or disprove the involvement of the person they saw in the crime, for example, close to the scene of the crime, immediately before or immediately after it was committed. It sets out the procedures to be used to test the ability of that eye-witness to identify a person suspected of involvement in the offence as the person they saw on the previous occasion. Except where stated, this part does not apply to the procedures described in Part B and *Note 3AA.*

3.1 A record shall be made of the suspect's description as first given by a potential witness. This record must:

(a) be made and kept in a form which enables details of that description to be accurately produced from it, in a visible and legible form, which can be given to the suspect or the suspect's solicitor in accordance with this Code; and

(b) unless otherwise specified, be made before the witness takes part in any identification procedures under *paragraphs 3.5 to 3.10, 3.21 or 3.23.*

A copy of the record shall where practicable, be given to the suspect or their solicitor before any procedures under *paragraphs 3.5* to *3.10, 3.21 or 3.23* are carried out. See *Note 3E*

(a) Cases when the suspect's identity is not known

3.2 In cases when the suspect's identity is not known, a witness may be taken to a particular neighbourhood or place to see whether they can identify the person they saw on a previous occasion. Although the number, age, sex, race, general description and style of clothing of other people present at the location and the way in which any identification is made cannot be controlled, the principles applicable to the formal procedures under *paragraphs 3.5* to *3.10* shall be followed as far as practicable. For example:

(a) where it is practicable to do so, a record should be made of the witness' description of the suspect, as in paragraph 3.1 (a), before asking the witness to make an identification*;*

(b) care must be taken not to direct the witness' attention to any individual unless, taking into account all the circumstances, this cannot be avoided. However, this does not prevent a witness being asked to look carefully at the people around at the time or to look towards a group or in a particular direction, if this appears necessary to make sure that the witness does not overlook a possible suspect simply because the witness is looking in the opposite direction and also to enable the witness to make comparisons between any suspect and others who are in the area; See *Note 3F*

(c) where there is more than one witness, every effort should be made to keep them separate and witnesses should be taken to see whether they can identify a person independently;

(d) once there is sufficient information to justify the arrest of a particular individual for suspected involvement in the offence, e.g., after a witness makes a positive identification, the provisions set out from paragraph 3.4 onwards shall apply for any other witnesses in relation to that individual.;

(e) the officer or police staff accompanying the witness must record, in their pocket book, the action taken as soon as, and in as much detail, as possible. The record should include: the date, time and place of the relevant occasion the witness claims to have previously seen the suspect; where any identification was made; how it was made and the conditions at the time (e.g., the distance the witness was from the suspect, the weather and light); if the witness's attention was drawn to the suspect; the reason for this; and anything said by the witness or the suspect about the identification or the conduct of the procedure.

3.3 A witness must not be shown photographs, computerised or artist's composite likenesses or similar likenesses or pictures (including 'E-fit' images) if the identity of the suspect is known to the police and the suspect is available to take part in a video identification, an identification parade or a group identification. If the suspect's identity is not known, the showing of such images to a witness to obtain identification evidence must be done in accordance with *Annex E*.

(b) Cases when the suspect is known and available

3.4 If the suspect's identity is known to the police and they are available, the identification procedures set out in paragraphs 3.5 to 3.10 may be used. References in this section to a suspect being 'known' mean there is sufficient information known to the police to justify the arrest of a particular person for suspected involvement in the offence. A suspect being 'available' means they are immediately available or will be within a reasonably short time and willing to take an effective part in at least one of the following which it is practicable to arrange:

- video identification;
- identification parade; or
- group identification.

Video identification

3.5 A 'video identification' is when the witness is shown moving images of a known suspect, together with similar images of others who resemble the suspect. Moving images must be used unless:

- the suspect is known but not available (see paragraph 3.21 of this Code); or
- in accordance with paragraph 2A of Annex A of this Code, the identification officer does not consider that replication of a physical feature can be achieved or that it is not possible to conceal the location of the feature on the image of the suspect.

  The identification officer may then decide to make use of video identification but using **still** images.

3.6 Video identifications must be carried out in accordance with *Annex A*.

Identification parade

3.7 An 'identification parade' is when the witness sees the suspect in a line of others who resemble the suspect.

3.8 Identification parades must be carried out in accordance with *Annex B*.

Group identification

3.9 A 'group identification' is when the witness sees the suspect in an informal group of people.

3.10 Group identifications must be carried out in accordance with *Annex C*.

Arranging eye-witness identification procedures

3.11 Except for the provisions in *paragraph 3.19*, the arrangements for, and conduct of, the identification procedures in paragraphs 3.5 to 3.10 and circumstances in which an identification procedure must be held shall be the responsibility of an officer not below inspector rank who is not involved with the investigation, 'the identification officer'. Unless otherwise specified, the identification officer may allow another officer or police staff, see *paragraph 2.21*, to make arrangements for, and conduct, any of these identification procedures. In delegating these procedures, the identification officer must be able to supervise effectively and either intervene or be contacted for advice. No officer or any other person involved with the investigation of the case against the suspect, beyond the extent required by these procedures, may take any part in these procedures or act as the identification officer. This does not prevent the identification officer from consulting the officer in charge of the investigation to determine which procedure to use. When an identification procedure is required, in the interest of fairness to suspects and witnesses, it must be held as soon as practicable.

Circumstances in which an eye-witness identification procedure must be held

3.12 Whenever:

(i) an eye witness has identified a suspect or purported to have identified them prior to any identification procedure set out in paragraphs 3.5 to 3.10 having been held; or

(ii) there is a witness available who expresses an ability to identify the suspect, or where there is a reasonable chance of the witness being able to do so, and they have not been given an opportunity to identify the suspect in any of the procedures set out in paragraphs 3.5 to 3.10,

and the suspect disputes being the person the witness claims to have seen, an identification procedure shall be held unless it is not practicable or it would serve no useful purpose in proving or disproving whether the suspect was involved in committing the offence, for example:

- where the suspect admits being at the scene of the crime and gives an account of what took place and the eye-witness does not see anything which contradicts that.
- when it is not disputed that the suspect is already known to the witness who claims to have recognised them when seeing them commit the crime.

3.13 An eye-witness identification procedure may also be held if the officer in charge of the investigation considers it would be useful.

Selecting an eye-witness identification procedure

3.14 If, because of paragraph 3.12, an identification procedure is to be held, the suspect shall initially be offered a video identification unless:

(a) a video identification is not practicable; or

(b) an identification parade is both practicable and more suitable than a video identification; or

(c) paragraph 3.16 applies.

The identification officer and the officer in charge of the investigation shall consult each other to determine which option is to be offered. An identification parade may not be practicable because of factors relating to the witnesses, such as their number, state of health, availability and travelling requirements. A video identification would normally be more suitable if it could be arranged and completed sooner than an identification parade. Before an option is offered the suspect must also be reminded of their entitlement to have free legal advice, see Code C, *paragraph 6.5*.

3.15 A suspect who refuses the identification procedure first offered shall be asked to state their reason for refusing and may get advice from their solicitor and/or if present, their appropriate adult. The suspect, solicitor and/or appropriate adult shall be allowed to make representations about why another procedure should be used. A record should be made of the reasons for refusal and any representations made. After considering any reasons given, and representations made, the identification officer shall, if appropriate, arrange for the suspect to be offered an alternative which the officer considers suitable and practicable. If the officer decides it is not suitable and practicable to offer an alternative identification procedure, the reasons for that decision shall be recorded.

3.16 A group identification may initially be offered if the officer in charge of the investigation considers it is more suitable than a video identification or an identification parade and the identification officer considers it practicable to arrange.

Notice to suspect

3.17 Unless *paragraph 3.20* applies, before a video identification, an identification parade or group identification is arranged, the following shall be explained to the suspect:

(i) the purposes of the video identification, identification parade or group identification;

(ii) their entitlement to free legal advice; see Code C, paragraph 6.5;

(iii) the procedures for holding it, including their right to have a solicitor or friend present;

(iv) that they do not have to consent to or co-operate in a video identification, identification parade or group identification;

(v) that if they do not consent to, and co-operate in, a video identification, identification parade or group identification, their refusal may be given in evidence in any subsequent trial and police may proceed covertly without their consent or make other arrangements to test whether a witness can identify them, see *paragraph 3.21;*

(vi) whether, for the purposes of the video identification procedure, images of them have previously been obtained, see *paragraph 3.20*, and if so, that they may co-operate in providing further, suitable images to be used instead;

(vii) if appropriate, the special arrangements for juveniles;

(viii) if appropriate, the special arrangements for mentally disordered or otherwise mentally vulnerable people;

(ix) that if they significantly alter their appearance between being offered an identification procedure and any attempt to hold an identification procedure, this may be given in evidence if the case comes to trial, and the identification officer may then consider other forms of identification, see *paragraph 3.21* and *Note 3C*;

(x) that a moving image or photograph may be taken of them when they attend for any identification procedure;

(xi) whether, before their identity became known, the witness was shown photographs, a computerised or artist's composite likeness or similar likeness or image by the police, see *Note 3B;*

(xii) that if they change their appearance before an identification parade, it may not be practicable to arrange one on the day or subsequently and, because of the appearance change, the identification officer may consider alternative methods of identification, see *Note 3C;*

(xiii) that they or their solicitor will be provided with details of the description of the suspect as first given by any witnesses who are to attend the video identification, identification parade, group identification or confrontation, see paragraph 3.1.

3.18 This information must also be recorded in a written notice handed to the suspect. The suspect must be given a reasonable opportunity to read the notice, after which, they should be asked to sign a second copy to indicate if they are willing to co-operate with the making of a video or take part in the identification parade or group identification. The signed copy shall be retained by the identification officer.

3.19 The duties of the identification officer under *paragraphs 3.17* and *3.18* may be performed by the custody officer or other officer not involved in the investigation if:

(a) it is proposed to release the suspect in order that an identification procedure can be arranged and carried out and an inspector is not available to act as the identification officer, see *paragraph 3.11*, before the suspect leaves the station; or

(b) it is proposed to keep the suspect in police detention whilst the procedure is arranged and carried out and waiting for an inspector to act as the identification officer, see *paragraph 3.11,* would cause unreasonable delay to the investigation.

The officer concerned shall inform the identification officer of the action taken and give them the signed copy of the notice. See *Note 3C*

3.20 If the identification officer and officer in charge of the investigation suspect, on reasonable grounds that if the suspect was given the information and notice as in *paragraphs 3.17* and *3.18*, they would then take steps to avoid being seen by a witness in any identification procedure, the identification officer may arrange for images of the suspect suitable for use in a video identification procedure to be obtained before giving the information and notice. If suspect's images are obtained in these circumstances, the suspect may, for the purposes of a video identification procedure, co-operate in providing new images which if suitable, would be used instead, see *paragraph 3.17(vi).*

(c) Cases when the suspect is known but not available

3.21 When a known suspect is not available or has ceased to be available, see *paragraph 3.4*, the identification officer may make arrangements for a video identification (see Annex A). If necessary, the identification officer may follow the video identification procedures but using still images. Any suitable moving or still images may be used and these may be obtained covertly if necessary. Alternatively, the identification officer may make arrangements for a group identification. See *Note 3D*. These provisions may also be applied to juveniles where the consent of their parent or guardian is either refused or reasonable efforts to obtain that consent have failed. (see *paragraph 2.12*).

3.22 Any covert activity should be strictly limited to that necessary to test the ability of the witness to identify the suspect.

3.23 The identification officer may arrange for the suspect to be confronted by the witness if none of the options referred to in paragraphs 3.5 to 3.10 or 3.21 are practicable. A "confrontation" is when the suspect is directly confronted by the witness. A confrontation does not require the suspect's consent. Confrontations must be carried out in accordance with Annex D.

3.24 Requirements for information to be given to, or sought from, a suspect or for the suspect to be given an opportunity to view images before they are shown to a witness, do not apply if the suspect's lack of co-operation prevents the necessary action.

(d) Documentation

3.25 A record shall be made of the video identification, identification parade, group identification or confrontation on forms provided for the purpose.

3.26 If the identification officer considers it is not practicable to hold a video identification or identification parade requested by the suspect, the reasons shall be recorded and explained to the suspect.

3.27 A record shall be made of a person's failure or refusal to co-operate in a video identification, identification parade or group identification and, if applicable, of the grounds for obtaining images in accordance with *paragraph 3.20*.

(e) Showing films and photographs of incidents and information released to the media

3.28 Nothing in this Code inhibits showing films, photographs or other images to the public through the national or local media, or to police officers for the purposes of recognition and tracing suspects. However, when such material is shown to obtain evidence of recognition, the procedures in Part B will apply. See *Note 3AA.*

3.29 When a broadcast or publication is made, see *paragraph 3.28*, a copy of the relevant material released to the media for the purposes of recognising or tracing the suspect, shall be kept. The suspect or their solicitor shall be allowed to view such material before any eye-witness identification procedures under *paragraphs 3.5* to *3.10*, *3.21* or *3.23* of Part A are carried out, provided it is practicable and would not unreasonably delay the investigation. Each eye-witness involved in the procedure shall be asked, after they have taken part, whether they have seen any film, photograph or image relating to the offence or any description of the suspect which has been broadcast or published in any national or local media or on any social networking site and if they have, they should be asked to give details of the circumstances, such as the date and place as relevant. Their replies shall be recorded. This paragraph does not affect any separate requirement under the Criminal Procedure and Investigations Act 1996 to retain material in connection with criminal investigations.

(f) Destruction and retention of photographs taken or used in eye-witness identification procedures

3.30 PACE, section 64A, see *paragraph 5.12*, provides powers to take photographs of suspects and allows these photographs to be used or disclosed only for purposes related to the prevention or detection of crime, the investigation of offences or the conduct of prosecutions by, or on behalf of, police or other law enforcement and prosecuting authorities inside and outside the United Kingdom or the enforcement of a sentence. After being so used or disclosed, they may be retained but can only be used or disclosed for the same purposes.

3.31 Subject to *paragraph 3.33,* the photographs (and all negatives and copies), of suspects not taken in accordance with the provisions in *paragraph 5.12* which are taken for the purposes of, or in connection with, the identification procedures in *paragraphs 3.5* to *3.10, 3.21 or 3.23* must be destroyed unless the suspect:

(a) is charged with, or informed they may be prosecuted for, a recordable offence;

(b) is prosecuted for a recordable offence;

(c) is cautioned for a recordable offence or given a warning or reprimand in accordance with the Crime and Disorder Act 1998 for a recordable offence; or

(d) gives informed consent, in writing, for the photograph or images to be retained for purposes described in *paragraph 3.30.*

3.32 When *paragraph 3.31* requires the destruction of any photograph, the person must be given an opportunity to witness the destruction or to have a certificate confirming the destruction if they request one within five days of being informed that the destruction is required.

3.33 Nothing in *paragraph 3.31* affects any separate requirement under the Criminal Procedure and Investigations Act 1996 to retain material in connection with criminal investigations.

(B) Evidence of recognition by showing films, photographs and other images

3.34 This Part of this section applies when, for the purposes of obtaining evidence of recognition, any person, including a police officer:

(a) views the image of an individual in a film, photograph or any other visual medium; and

(b) is asked whether they recognise that individual as someone who is known to them.

See *Notes 3AA* and *3G*

3.35 The films, photographs and other images shall be shown on an individual basis to avoid any possibility of collusion and to provide safeguards against mistaken recognition (see *Note 3G*), the showing shall as far as possible follow the principles for video identification if the suspect is known, see *Annex A*, or identification by photographs if the suspect is not known, see *Annex E*.

3.36 A record of the circumstances and conditions under which the person is given an opportunity to recognise the individual must be made and the record must include:

(a) Whether the person knew or was given information concerning the name or identity of any suspect.

(b) What the person has been told *before* the viewing about the offence, the person(s) depicted in the images or the offender and by whom.

(c) How and by whom the witness was asked to view the image or look at the individual.

(d) Whether the viewing was alone or with others and if with others, the reason for it.

(e) The arrangements under which the person viewed the film or saw the individual and by whom those arrangements were made.

(f) Whether the viewing of any images was arranged as part of a mass circulation to police and the public or for selected persons.

(g) The date time and place images were viewed or further viewed or the individual was seen.

(h) The times between which the images were viewed or the individual was seen.

(i) How the viewing of images or sighting of the individual was controlled and by whom.

(j) Whether the person was familiar with the location shown in any images or the place where they saw the individual and if so, why.

(k) Whether or not on this occasion, the person claims to recognise any image shown, or any individual seen, as being someone known to them, and if they do:

(i) the reason

(ii) the words of recognition

(iii) any expressions of doubt

(iv) what features of the image or the individual triggered the recognition.

3.37 The record under paragraph 3.36 may be made by:

- the person who views the image or sees the individual and makes the recognition.
- the officer or police staff in charge of showing the images to the person or in charge of the conditions under which the person sees the individual.

Notes for guidance

3AA The eye-witness identification procedures in Part A should not be used to test whether a witness can recognise a person as someone they know and would be able to give evidence of recognition along the lines that "On (describe date, time location) I saw an image of an individual who I recognised as AB." In these cases, the procedures in Part B shall apply.

3A Except for the provisions of Annex E, paragraph 1, a police officer who is a witness for the purposes of this part of the Code is subject to the same principles and procedures as a civilian witness.

3B When a witness attending an identification procedure has previously been shown photographs, or been shown or provided with computerised or artist's composite likenesses, or similar likenesses or pictures, it is the officer in charge of the investigation's responsibility to make the identification officer aware of this.

3C The purpose of paragraph 3.19 is to avoid or reduce delay in arranging identification procedures by enabling the required information and warnings, see sub-paragraphs 3.17(ix) and 3.17(xii), to be given at the earliest opportunity.

3D Paragraph 3.21 would apply when a known suspect deliberately makes themselves 'unavailable' in order to delay or frustrate arrangements for obtaining identification evidence. It also applies when a suspect refuses or fails to take part in a video identification, an identification parade or a group identification, or refuses or fails to take part in the only practicable options from that list. It enables any suitable images of the suspect, moving or still, which are available or can be obtained, to be used in an identification procedure. Examples include images from custody and other CCTV systems and from visually recorded interview records, see Code F Note for Guidance 2D.

3E *When it is proposed to show photographs to a witness in accordance with Annex E, it is the responsibility of the officer in charge of the investigation to confirm to the officer responsible for supervising and directing the showing, that the first description of the suspect given by that witness has been recorded. If this description has not been recorded, the procedure under Annex E must be postponed. See Annex E paragraph 2*

3F *The admissibility and value of identification evidence obtained when carrying out the procedure under paragraph 3.2 may be compromised if:*

(a) before a person is identified, the witness' attention is specifically drawn to that person; or

(b) the suspect's identity becomes known before the procedure.

3G *The admissibility and value of evidence of recognition obtained when carrying out the procedures in Part B may be compromised if before the person is recognised, the witness who has claimed to know them is given or is made, or becomes aware of, information about the person which was not previously known to them personally but which they have purported to rely on to support their claim that the person is in fact known to them.*

4 Identification by fingerprints and footwear impressions

(A) Taking fingerprints in connection with a criminal investigation

(a) General

4.1 References to 'fingerprints' means any record, produced by any method, of the skin pattern and other physical characteristics or features of a person's:

(i) fingers; or

(ii) palms.

(b) Action

4.2 A person's fingerprints may be taken in connection with the investigation of an offence only with their consent or if *paragraph 4.3* applies. If the person is at a police station consent must be in writing.

4.3 PACE, section 61, provides powers to take fingerprints without consent from any person over the age of ten years:

(a) under section 61(3), from a person detained at a police station in consequence of being arrested for a recordable offence, see *Note 4A*, if they have not had their fingerprints taken in the course of the investigation of the offence unless those previously taken fingerprints are not a complete set or some or all of those fingerprints are not of sufficient quality to allow satisfactory analysis, comparison or matching.

(b) under section 61(4), from a person detained at a police station who has been charged with a recordable offence, see *Note 4A*, or informed they will be reported for such an offence if they have not had their fingerprints taken in the course of the investigation of the offence unless those previously taken fingerprints are not a complete set or some or all of those fingerprints are not of sufficient quality to allow satisfactory analysis, comparison or matching.

(c) under section 61(4A), from a person who has been bailed to appear at a court or police station if the person:

(i) has answered to bail for a person whose fingerprints were taken previously and there are reasonable grounds for believing they are not the same person; or

(ii) who has answered to bail claims to be a different person from a person whose fingerprints were previously taken;

and in either case, the court or an officer of inspector rank or above, authorises the fingerprints to be taken at the court or police station (an inspector's authority may be given in writing or orally and confirmed in writing, as soon as practicable);

(ca) under section 61(5A) from a person who has been arrested for a recordable offence and released if the person:

(i) is on bail and has not had their fingerprints taken in the course of the investigation of the offence, or;

(ii) has had their fingerprints taken in the course of the investigation of the offence, but they do not constitute a complete set or some, or all, of the fingerprints are not of sufficient quality to allow satisfactory analysis, comparison or matching.

(cb) under section 61(5B) from a person not detained at a police station who has been charged with a recordable offence or informed they will be reported for such an offence if they have not had their fingerprints taken in the course of the investigation or their fingerprints have been taken in the course of the investigation of the offence, but they do not constitute a complete set or some, or all, of the fingerprints are not of sufficient quality to allow satisfactory analysis, comparison or matching.

(d) under section 61(6), from a person who has been:

(i) convicted of a recordable offence;

(ii) given a caution in respect of a recordable offence which, at the time of the caution, the person admitted; or

(iii) warned or reprimanded under the Crime and Disorder Act 1998, section 65, for a recordable offence,

if, since their conviction, caution, warning or reprimand their fingerprints have not been taken or their fingerprints which have been taken since then do not constitute a complete set or some, or all, of the fingerprints are not of sufficient quality to allow satisfactory analysis, comparison or matching, and in either case, an officer of inspector rank or above, is satisfied that taking the fingerprints is necessary to assist in the prevention or detection of crime and authorises the taking;

(e) under section 61(6A) from a person a constable reasonably suspects is committing or attempting to commit, or has committed or attempted to commit, any offence if either:

- the person's name is unknown and cannot be readily ascertained by the constable; or
- the constable has reasonable grounds for doubting whether a name given by the person is their real name.

Note: fingerprints taken under this power are not regarded as having been taken in the course of the investigation of an offence.

[See *Note 4C*]

(f) under section 61(6D) from a person who has been convicted outside England and Wales of an offence which if committed in England and Wales would be a qualifying offence as defined by PACE, section 65A (see *Note 4AB*) if:

(i) the person's fingerprints have not been taken previously under this power or their fingerprints have been so taken on a previous occasion but they do not constitute a complete set or some, or all, of the fingerprints are not of sufficient quality to allow satisfactory analysis, comparison or matching; and

(ii) a police officer of inspector rank or above is satisfied that taking fingerprints is necessary to assist in the prevention or detection of crime and authorises them to be taken.

4.4 PACE, section 63A(4) and Schedule 2A provide powers to:

(a) make a requirement (in accordance with Annex G) for a person to attend a police station to have their fingerprints taken in the exercise of certain powers in paragraph 4.3 above when that power applies at the time the fingerprints would be taken in accordance with the requirement. Those powers are:

(i) section 61(5A) – Persons arrested for a recordable offence and released, see paragraph 4.3(ca): The requirement may not be made more than six months from the day the investigating officer was informed that the fingerprints previously taken were incomplete or below standard.

(ii) section 61(5B) – Persons charged etc. with a recordable offence, see paragraph 4.3(cb): The requirement may not be made more than six months from:

- the day the person was charged or reported if fingerprints have not been taken since then; or
- the day the investigating officer was informed that the fingerprints previously taken were incomplete or below standard.

(iii) section 61(6) – Person convicted, cautioned, warned or reprimanded for a recordable offence in England and Wales, see paragraph 4.3(d): Where the offence for which the person was convicted etc is also a qualifying offence (see *Note 4AB*), there is no time limit for the exercise of this power. Where the conviction etc. is for a recordable offence which is not a qualifying offence, the requirement may not be made more than two years from:

- the day the person was convicted, cautioned, warned or reprimanded, or the day Schedule 2A comes into force (if later), if fingerprints have not been taken since then; or
- the day an officer from the force investigating the offence was informed that the fingerprints previously taken were incomplete or below standard or the day Schedule 2A comes into force (if later).

(v) section 61(6D) – A person who has been convicted of a qualifying offence (see *Note 4AB*) outside England and Wales, see paragraph 4.3(g): There is no time limit for making the requirement.

Note: A person who has had their fingerprints taken under any of the powers in section 61 mentioned in paragraph 4.3 on two occasions in relation to any offence may not be required under Schedule 2A to attend a police station for their fingerprints to be taken again under section 61 in relation to that offence, unless authorised by an officer of inspector rank or above. The fact of the authorisation and the reasons for giving it must be recorded as soon as practicable.

(b) arrest, without warrant, a person who fails to comply with the requirement.

4.5 A person's fingerprints may be taken, as above, electronically.

4.6 Reasonable force may be used, if necessary, to take a person's fingerprints without their consent under the powers as in *paragraphs 4.3* and *4.4*.

4.7 Before any fingerprints are taken:

(a) without consent under any power mentioned in *paragraphs 4.3* and *4.4* above, the person must be informed of:

(i) the reason their fingerprints are to be taken;

(ii) the power under which they are to be taken; and

(iii) the fact that the relevant authority has been given if any power mentioned in *paragraph 4.3(c), (d)* or *(f)* applies

(b) with or without consent at a police station or elsewhere, the person must be informed:

(i) that their fingerprints may be subject of a speculative search against other fingerprints, see *Note 4B*; and

(ii) that their fingerprints may be retained in accordance with *Annex F, Part (a)* unless they were taken under the power mentioned in paragraph 4.3(e) when they must be destroyed after they have being checked (See *Note 4C*).

(c) Documentation

4.8A A record must be made as soon as practicable after the fingerprints are taken, of:

- the matters in paragraph 4.7(a)(i) to (iii) and the fact that the person has been informed of those matters; and
- the fact that the person has been informed of the matters in paragraph 4.7(b) (i) and (ii).

The record must be made in the person's custody record if they are detained at a police station when the fingerprints are taken.

4.8 If force is used, a record shall be made of the circumstances and those present.

4.9 Not used

(B) Taking fingerprints in connection with immigration enquiries

Action

4.10 A person's fingerprints may be taken and retained for the purposes of immigration law enforcement and control in accordance with powers and procedures other than under PACE and for which the UK Border Agency (not the police) are responsible. Details of these powers and procedures which are under the Immigration Act 1971, Schedule 2 and Immigration and Asylum Act 1999, section 141, including modifications to the PACE Codes of Practice are contained in Chapter 24 of the Operational Instructions and Guidance manual which is published by the UK Border Agency (See *Note 4D).*

4.11 *Not used*

4.12 *Not used*

4.13 *Not used*

4.14 *Not used*

4.15 *Not used*

(C) Taking footwear impressions in connection with a criminal investigation

(a) Action

4.16 Impressions of a person's footwear may be taken in connection with the investigation of an offence only with their consent or if *paragraph 4.17* applies. If the person is at a police station consent must be in writing.

4.17 PACE, section 61A, provides power for a police officer to take footwear impressions without consent from any person over the age of ten years who is detained at a police station:

(a) in consequence of being arrested for a recordable offence, see *Note 4A*; or if the detainee has been charged with a recordable offence, or informed they will be reported for such an offence; and

(b) the detainee has not had an impression of their footwear taken in the course of the investigation of the offence unless the previously taken impression is not complete or is not of sufficient quality to allow satisfactory analysis, comparison or matching (whether in the case in question or generally).

4.18 Reasonable force may be used, if necessary, to take a footwear impression from a detainee without consent under the power in *paragraph 4.17.*

4.19 Before any footwear impression is taken with, or without, consent as above, the person must be informed:

(a) of the reason the impression is to be taken;

(b) that the impression may be retained and may be subject of a speculative search against other impressions, see *Note 4B*, unless destruction of the impression is required in accordance with *Annex F, Part (a)*; and

(c) that if their footwear impressions are required to be destroyed, they may witness their destruction as provided for in *Annex F, Part (a).*

(b) Documentation

4.20 A record must be made as soon as possible, of the reason for taking a person's footwear impressions without consent. If force is used, a record shall be made of the circumstances and those present.

4.21 A record shall be made when a person has been informed under the terms of *paragraph 4.19(b),* of the possibility that their footwear impressions may be subject of a speculative search.

Notes for guidance

4A References to 'recordable offences' in this Code relate to those offences for which convictions, cautions, reprimands and warnings may be recorded in national police records. See PACE, section 27(4). The recordable offences current at the time when this Code was prepared, are any offences which carry a sentence of imprisonment on conviction (irrespective of the period, or the age of the offender or actual sentence passed) as well as the non-imprisonable offences under the Vagrancy Act 1824 sections 3 and 4 (begging and persistent begging), the Street Offences Act 1959, section 1 (loitering or soliciting for purposes of prostitution), the Road Traffic Act 1988, section 25 (tampering with motor vehicles), the Criminal Justice and Public Order Act 1994, section 167 (touting for hire car services) and others listed in the National Police Records (Recordable Offences) Regulations 2000 as amended.

4AB A qualifying offence is one of the offences specified in PACE, section 65A. These indictable offences which concern the use or threat of violence or unlawful force against persons, sexual offences and offences against children include, for example, murder, manslaughter, false imprisonment, kidnapping and other offences such as:

- *sections 4, 16, 18, 20 to 24 or 47 of the Offences Against the Person Act 1861;*
- *sections 16 to 18 of the Firearms Act 1968;*
- *sections 9 or 10 of the Theft Act 1968 or under section 12A of that Act involving an accident which caused a person's death;*
- *section 1 of the Criminal Damage Act 1971 required to be charged as arson;*
- *section 1 of the Protection of Children Act 1978 and;*
- *sections 1 to 19, 25, 26, 30 to 41, 47 to 50, 52, 53, 57 to 59, 61 to 67, 69 and 70 of the Sexual Offences Act 2003.*

4B Fingerprints, footwear impressions or a DNA sample (and the information derived from it) taken from a person arrested on suspicion of being involved in a recordable offence, or charged with such an offence, or informed they will be reported for such an offence, may be subject of a speculative search. This means the fingerprints, footwear impressions or DNA sample may be checked against other fingerprints, footwear impressions and DNA records held by, or on behalf of, the police and other law enforcement authorities in, or outside, the UK, or held in connection with, or as a result of, an investigation of an offence inside or outside the UK. Fingerprints, footwear impressions and samples taken from a person suspected of committing a recordable offence but not arrested, charged or informed they will be reported for it, may be subject to a speculative search only if the person consents in writing. The following is an example of a basic form of words:

> *"I consent to my fingerprints, footwear impressions and DNA sample and information derived from it being retained and used only for purposes related to the prevention and detection of a crime, the investigation of an offence or the conduct of a prosecution either nationally or internationally.*
>
> *I understand that my fingerprints, footwear impressions or DNA sample may be checked against other fingerprint, footwear impressions and DNA records held by or on behalf of relevant law enforcement authorities, either nationally or internationally.*
>
> *I understand that once I have given my consent for my fingerprints, footwear impressions or DNA sample to be retained and used I cannot withdraw this consent."*

See Annex F regarding the retention and use of fingerprints and footwear impressions taken with consent for elimination purposes.

4C The power under section 61(6A) of PACE described in paragraph 4.3(e) allows fingerprints of a suspect who has not been arrested to be taken in connection with any offence (whether recordable or not) using a mobile device and then checked on the street against the database containing the national fingerprint collection. Fingerprints taken under this power cannot be retained after they have been checked. The results may make an arrest for the suspected offence based on the name condition unnecessary (See Code G paragraph 2.9(a)) and enable the offence to be disposed of without arrest, for example, by summons/charging by post, penalty notice or words of advice. If arrest for a non-recordable offence is necessary for any other reasons, this power may also be exercised at the station. Before the power is exercised, the officer should:

- *inform the person of the nature of the suspected offence and why they are suspected of committing it.*
- *give them a reasonable opportunity to establish their real name before deciding that their name is unknown and cannot be readily ascertained or that there are reasonable grounds to doubt that a name they have given is their real name.*
- *as applicable, inform the person of the reason why their name is not know and cannot be readily ascertained or of the grounds for doubting that a name they have given is their real name, including, for example, the reason why a particular document the person has produced to verify their real name, is not sufficient.*

4D Powers to take fingerprints without consent for immigration purposes are given to police and immigration officers under the:

(a) Immigration Act 1971, Schedule 2, paragraph 18(2), when it is reasonably necessary for the purposes of identifying a person detained under the Immigration Act 1971, Schedule 2, paragraph 16 (Detention of person liable to examination or removal), and

(b) Immigration and Asylum Act 1999, section 141(7) when a person:

- *fails without reasonable excuse to produce, on arrival, a valid passport with a photograph or some other document satisfactorily establishing their identity and nationality;*
- *is refused entry to the UK but is temporarily admitted if an immigration officer reasonably suspects the person might break a residence or reporting condition;*

- *is subject to directions for removal from the UK;*
- *has been arrested under the Immigration Act 1971, Schedule 2, paragraph 17;*
- *has made a claim for asylum*
- *is a dependant of any of the above.*

The Immigration and Asylum Act 1999, section 142(3), also gives police and immigration officers power to arrest without warrant, a person who fails to comply with a requirement imposed by the Secretary of State to attend a specified place for fingerprinting.

5 Examinations to establish identity and the taking of photographs

(A) Detainees at police stations

(a) Searching or examination of detainees at police stations

5.1 PACE, section 54A(1), allows a detainee at a police station to be searched or examined or both, to establish:

(a) whether they have any marks, features or injuries that would tend to identify them as a person involved in the commission of an offence and to photograph any identifying marks, see *paragraph 5.5*; or

(b) their identity, see *Note 5A*.

A person detained at a police station to be searched under a stop and search power, see Code A, is not a detainee for the purposes of these powers.

5.2 A search and/or examination to find marks under section 54A (1) (a) may be carried out without the detainee's consent, see *paragraph 2.12*, only if authorised by an officer of at least inspector rank when consent has been withheld or it is not practicable to obtain consent, see *Note 5D.*

5.3 A search or examination to establish a suspect's identity under section 54A (1) (b) may be carried out without the detainee's consent, see *paragraph 2.12*, only if authorised by an officer of at least inspector rank when the detainee has refused to identify themselves or the authorising officer has reasonable grounds for suspecting the person is not who they claim to be.

5.4 Any marks that assist in establishing the detainee's identity, or their identification as a person involved in the commission of an offence, are identifying marks. Such marks may be photographed with the detainee's consent, see *paragraph 2.12*; or without their consent if it is withheld or it is not practicable to obtain it, see *Note 5D.*

5.5 A detainee may only be searched, examined and photographed under section 54A, by a police officer of the same sex.

5.6 Any photographs of identifying marks, taken under section 54A, may be used or disclosed only for purposes related to the prevention or detection of crime, the investigation of offences or the conduct of prosecutions by, or on behalf of, police or other law enforcement and prosecuting authorities inside, and outside, the UK. After being so used or disclosed, the photograph may be retained but must not be used or disclosed except for these purposes, see *Note 5B.*

5.7 The powers, as in *paragraph 5.1,* do not affect any separate requirement under the Criminal Procedure and Investigations Act 1996 to retain material in connection with criminal investigations.

5.8 Authority for the search and/or examination for the purposes of *paragraphs 5.2* and *5.3* may be given orally or in writing. If given orally, the authorising officer must confirm it in writing as soon as practicable. A separate authority is required for each purpose which applies.

5.9 If it is established a person is unwilling to co-operate sufficiently to enable a search and/or examination to take place or a suitable photograph to be taken, an officer may use reasonable force to:

(a) search and/or examine a detainee without their consent; and

(b) photograph any identifying marks without their consent.

5.10 The thoroughness and extent of any search or examination carried out in accordance with the powers in section 54A must be no more than the officer considers necessary to achieve the required purpose. Any search or examination which involves the removal of more than the person's outer clothing shall be conducted in accordance with Code C, Annex A, paragraph 11.

5.11 An intimate search may not be carried out under the powers in section 54A.

(b) Photographing detainees at police stations and other persons elsewhere than at a police station

5.12 Under PACE, section 64A, an officer may photograph:

(a) any person whilst they are detained at a police station; and

(b) any person who is elsewhere than at a police station and who has been:

(i) arrested by a constable for an offence;

(ii) taken into custody by a constable after being arrested for an offence by a person other than a constable;

(iii) made subject to a requirement to wait with a community support officer under paragraph 2(3) or (3B) of Schedule 4 to the Police Reform Act 2002;

(iiia) given a direction by a constable under section 27 of the Violent Crime Reduction Act 2006.

(iv) given a penalty notice by a constable in uniform under Chapter 1 of Part 1 of the Criminal Justice and Police Act 2001, a penalty notice by a constable under section 444A of the Education Act 1996, or a fixed penalty notice by a constable in uniform under section 54 of the Road Traffic Offenders Act 1988;

(v) given a notice in relation to a relevant fixed penalty offence (within the meaning of paragraph 1 of Schedule 4 to the Police Reform Act 2002) by a community support officer by virtue of a designation applying that paragraph to him;

(vi) given a notice in relation to a relevant fixed penalty offence (within the meaning of paragraph 1 of Schedule 5 to the Police Reform Act 2002) by an accredited person by virtue of accreditation specifying that that paragraph applies to him; or

(vii) given a direction to leave and not return to a specified location for up to 48 hours by a police constable (under section 27 of the Violent Crime Reduction Act 2006).

5.12A Photographs taken under PACE, section 64A:

(a) may be taken with the person's consent, or without their consent if consent is withheld or it is not practicable to obtain their consent, see *Note 5E*; and

(b) may be used or disclosed only for purposes related to the prevention or detection of crime, the investigation of offences or the conduct of prosecutions by, or on behalf of, police or other law enforcement and prosecuting authorities inside and outside the United Kingdom or the enforcement of any sentence or order made by a court when dealing with an offence. After being so used or disclosed, they may be retained but can only be used or disclosed for the same purposes. See *Note 5B.*

5.13 The officer proposing to take a detainee's photograph may, for this purpose, require the person to remove any item or substance worn on, or over, all, or any part of, their head or face. If they do not comply with such a requirement, the officer may remove the item or substance.

5.14 If it is established the detainee is unwilling to co-operate sufficiently to enable a suitable photograph to be taken and it is not reasonably practicable to take the photograph covertly, an officer may use reasonable force, see *Note 5F*.

(a) to take their photograph without their consent; and

(b) for the purpose of taking the photograph, remove any item or substance worn on, or over, all, or any part of, the person's head or face which they have failed to remove when asked.

5.15 For the purposes of this Code, a photograph may be obtained without the person's consent by making a copy of an image of them taken at any time on a camera system installed anywhere in the police station.

(c) Information to be given

5.16 When a person is searched, examined or photographed under the provisions as in *paragraph 5.1* and *5.12*, or their photograph obtained as in *paragraph 5.15*, they must be informed of the:

(a) purpose of the search, examination or photograph;

(b) grounds on which the relevant authority, if applicable, has been given; and

(c) purposes for which the photograph may be used, disclosed or retained.

This information must be given before the search or examination commences or the photograph is taken, except if the photograph is:

(i) to be taken covertly;

(ii) obtained as in *paragraph 5.15*, in which case the person must be informed as soon as practicable after the photograph is taken or obtained.

(d) Documentation

5.17 A record must be made when a detainee is searched, examined, or a photograph of the person, or any identifying marks found on them, are taken. The record must include the:

(a) identity, subject to paragraph 2.18, of the officer carrying out the search, examination or taking the photograph;

(b) purpose of the search, examination or photograph and the outcome;

(c) detainee's consent to the search, examination or photograph, or the reason the person was searched, examined or photographed without consent;

(d) giving of any authority as in *paragraphs 5.2* and *5.3*, the grounds for giving it and the authorising officer.

5.18 If force is used when searching, examining or taking a photograph in accordance with this section, a record shall be made of the circumstances and those present.

(B) Persons at police stations not detained

5.19 When there are reasonable grounds for suspecting the involvement of a person in a criminal offence, but that person is at a police station **voluntarily** and not detained, the provisions of *paragraphs 5.1* to *5.18* should apply, subject to the modifications in the following paragraphs.

5.20 References to the 'person being detained' and to the powers mentioned in *paragraph 5.1* which apply only to detainees at police stations shall be omitted.

5.21 Force may not be used to:

(a) search and/or examine the person to:

(i) discover whether they have any marks that would tend to identify them as a person involved in the commission of an offence; or

(ii) establish their identity, see *Note 5A*;

(b) take photographs of any identifying marks, see *paragraph 5.4*; or

(c) take a photograph of the person.

5.22 Subject to *paragraph 5.24*, the photographs of persons or of their identifying marks which are not taken in accordance with the provisions mentioned in *paragraphs 5.1* or *5.12*, must be destroyed (together with any negatives and copies) unless the person:

(a) is charged with, or informed they may be prosecuted for, a recordable offence;

(b) is prosecuted for a recordable offence;

(c) is cautioned for a recordable offence or given a warning or reprimand in accordance with the Crime and Disorder Act 1998 for a recordable offence; or

(d) gives informed consent, in writing, for the photograph or image to be retained as in *paragraph 5.6*.

5.23 When *paragraph 5.22* requires the destruction of any photograph, the person must be given an opportunity to witness the destruction or to have a certificate confirming the destruction provided they so request the certificate within five days of being informed the destruction is required.

5.24 Nothing in *paragraph 5.22* affects any separate requirement under the Criminal Procedure and Investigations Act 1996 to retain material in connection with criminal investigations.

Notes for guidance

5A The conditions under which fingerprints may be taken to assist in establishing a person's identity, are described in Section 4.

5B Examples of purposes related to the prevention or detection of crime, the investigation of offences or the conduct of prosecutions include:

(a) checking the photograph against other photographs held in records or in connection with, or as a result of, an investigation of an offence to establish whether the person is liable to arrest for other offences;

(b) when the person is arrested at the same time as other people, or at a time when it is likely that other people will be arrested, using the photograph to help establish who was arrested, at what time and where;

(c) when the real identity of the person is not known and cannot be readily ascertained or there are reasonable grounds for doubting a name and other personal details given by the person, are their real name and personal details. In these circumstances, using or disclosing the photograph to help to establish or verify their real identity or determine whether they are liable to arrest for some other offence, e.g. by checking it against other photographs held in records or in connection with, or as a result of, an investigation of an offence;

(d) when it appears any identification procedure in section 3 may need to be arranged for which the person's photograph would assist;

(e) when the person's release without charge may be required, and if the release is:

(i) on bail to appear at a police station, using the photograph to help verify the person's identity when they answer their bail and if the person does not answer their bail, to assist in arresting them; or

(ii) without bail, using the photograph to help verify their identity or assist in locating them for the purposes of serving them with a summons to appear at court in criminal proceedings;

(f) *when the person has answered to bail at a police station and there are reasonable grounds for doubting they are the person who was previously granted bail, using the photograph to help establish or verify their identity;*

(g) *when the person arrested on a warrant claims to be a different person from the person named on the warrant and a photograph would help to confirm or disprove their claim;*

(h) *when the person has been charged with, reported for, or convicted of, a recordable offence and their photograph is not already on record as a result of (a) to (f) or their photograph is on record but their appearance has changed since it was taken and the person has not yet been released or brought before a court.*

5C *There is no power to arrest a person convicted of a recordable offence solely to take their photograph. The power to take photographs in this section applies only where the person is in custody as a result of the exercise of another power, e.g. arrest for fingerprinting under PACE, section 27.*

5D *Examples of when it would not be practicable to obtain a detainee's consent, see paragraph 2.12, to a search, examination or the taking of a photograph of an identifying mark include:*

- *(a)* *when the person is drunk or otherwise unfit to give consent;*
- *(b)* *when there are reasonable grounds to suspect that if the person became aware a search or examination was to take place or an identifying mark was to be photographed, they would take steps to prevent this happening, e.g. by violently resisting, covering or concealing the mark etc and it would not otherwise be possible to carry out the search or examination or to photograph any identifying mark;*
- *(c)* *in the case of a juvenile, if the parent or guardian cannot be contacted in sufficient time to allow the search or examination to be carried out or the photograph to be taken.*

5E *Examples of when it would not be practicable to obtain the person's consent, see paragraph 2.12, to a photograph being taken include:*

- *(a)* *when the person is drunk or otherwise unfit to give consent;*
- *(b)* *when there are reasonable grounds to suspect that if the person became aware a photograph, suitable to be used or disclosed for the use and disclosure described in paragraph 5.6, was to be taken, they would take steps to prevent it being taken, e.g. by violently resisting, covering or distorting their face etc, and it would not otherwise be possible to take a suitable photograph;*

(c) *when, in order to obtain a suitable photograph, it is necessary to take it covertly; and*

(d) *in the case of a juvenile, if the parent or guardian cannot be contacted in sufficient time to allow the photograph to be taken.*

5F *The use of reasonable force to take the photograph of a suspect elsewhere than at a police station must be carefully considered. In order to obtain a suspect's consent and co-operation to remove an item of religious headwear to take their photograph, a constable should consider whether in the circumstances of the situation the removal of the headwear and the taking of the photograph should be by an officer of the same sex as the person. It would be appropriate for these actions to be conducted out of public view.*

6 Identification by body samples and impressions

(A) General

6.1 References to:

(a) an 'intimate sample' mean a dental impression or sample of blood, semen or any other tissue fluid, urine, or pubic hair, or a swab taken from any part of a person's genitals or from a person's body orifice other than the mouth;

(b) a 'non-intimate sample' means:

(i) a sample of hair, other than pubic hair, which includes hair plucked with the root, see Note 6A;

(ii) a sample taken from a nail or from under a nail;

(iii) a swab taken from any part of a person's body other than a part from which a swab taken would be an intimate sample;

(iv) saliva;

(v) a skin impression which means any record, other than a fingerprint, which is a record, in any form and produced by any method, of the skin pattern and other physical characteristics or features of the whole, or any part of, a person's foot or of any other part of their body.

(B) Action

(a) Intimate samples

6.2 PACE, section 62, provides that intimate samples may be taken under:

(a) section 62(1), from a person in police detention only:

(i) if a police officer of inspector rank or above has reasonable grounds to believe such an impression or sample will tend to confirm or disprove the suspect's involvement in a recordable offence, see *Note 4A*, and gives authorisation for a sample to be taken; and

(ii) with the suspect's written consent;

(b) section 62(1A), from a person not in police detention but from whom two or more non-intimate samples have been taken in the course of an investigation of an offence and the samples, though suitable, have proved insufficient if:

(i) a police officer of inspector rank or above authorises it to be taken; and

(ii) the person concerned gives their written consent. See *Notes 6B* and *6C*

(c) section 62(2A), from a person convicted outside England and Wales of an offence which if committed in England and Wales would be qualifying offence as defined by PACE, section 65A (see *Note 4AB*) from whom two or more non-intimate samples taken under section 63(3E) (see paragraph 6.6(h) have proved insufficient if:

(i) a police officer of inspector rank or above is satisfied that taking the sample is necessary to assist in the prevention or detection of crime and authorises it to be taken; and

(ii) the person concerned gives their written consent.

6.2A PACE, section 63A(4) and Schedule 2A provide powers to:

(a) make a requirement (in accordance with Annex G) for a person to attend a police station to have an intimate sample taken in the exercise of one of the following powers in paragraph 6.2 when that power applies at the time the sample is to be taken in accordance with the requirement or after the person's arrest if they fail to comply with the requirement:

(i) section 62(1A) – Persons from whom two or more non-intimate samples have been taken and proved to be insufficient, see paragraph 6.2(b): There is no time limit for making the requirement.

(ii) section 62(2A) – Persons convicted outside England and Wales from whom two or more non-intimate samples taken under section 63(3E) (see paragraph 6.6(h) have proved insufficient, see *paragraph 6.2(c)*: There is no time limit for making the requirement.

6.3 Before a suspect is asked to provide an intimate sample, they must be:

(a) informed:

(i) of the reason, including the nature of the suspected offence (except if taken under *paragraph 6.2(c)* from a person convicted outside England and Wales.

(ii) that authorisation has been given and the provisions under which given;

(iii) that a sample taken at a police station may be subject of a speculative search;

(b) warned that if they refuse without good cause their refusal may harm their case if it comes to trial, see *Note 6D*. If the suspect is in police detention and not legally represented, they must also be reminded of their entitlement to have free legal advice, see Code C, *paragraph 6.5*, and the reminder noted in the custody record. If *paragraph 6.2(b)* applies and the person is attending a station voluntarily, their entitlement to free legal advice as in Code C, *paragraph 3.21* shall be explained to them.

6.4 Dental impressions may only be taken by a registered dentist. Other intimate samples, except for samples of urine, may only be taken by a registered medical practitioner or registered nurse or registered paramedic.

(b) Non-intimate samples

6.5 A non-intimate sample may be taken from a detainee only with their written consent or if *paragraph 6.6* applies.

6.6 a non-intimate sample may be taken from a person without the appropriate consent in the following circumstances:

(a) under section 63(2A) from a person who is in police detention as a consequence of being arrested for a recordable offence and who has not had a non-intimate sample of the same type and from the same part of the body taken in the course of the investigation of the offence by the police or they have had such a sample taken but it proved insufficient.

(b) Under section 63(3) from a person who is being held in custody by the police on the authority of a court if an officer of at least the rank of inspector authorises it to be taken. An authorisation may be given:

(i) if the authorising officer has reasonable grounds for suspecting the person of involvement in a recordable offence and for believing that the sample will tend to confirm or disprove that involvement, and

(ii) in writing or orally and confirmed in writing, as soon as practicable;

but an authorisation may not be given to take from the same part of the body a further non-intimate sample consisting of a skin impression unless the previously taken impression proved insufficient

(c) under section 63(3ZA) from a person who has been arrested for a recordable offence and released if the person:

(i) is on bail and has not had a sample of the same type and from the same part of the body taken in the course of the investigation of the offence, or;

(ii) has had such a sample taken in the course of the investigation of the offence, but it proved unsuitable or insufficient.

(d) under section 63(3A), from a person (whether or not in police detention or held in custody by the police on the authority of a court) who has been charged with a recordable offence or informed they will be reported for such an offence if the person:

(i) has not had a non-intimate sample taken from them in the course of the investigation of the offence;

(ii) has had a sample so taken, but it proved unsuitable or insufficient, see *Note 6B*; or

(iii) has had a sample taken in the course of the investigation of the offence and the sample has been destroyed and in proceedings relating to that offence there is a dispute as to whether a DNA profile relevant to the proceedings was derived from the destroyed sample.

(e) under section 63(3B), from a person who has been:

(i) convicted of a recordable offence;

(ii) given a caution in respect of a recordable offence which, at the time of the caution, the person admitted; or

(iii) warned or reprimanded under the Crime and Disorder Act 1998, section 65, for a recordable offence, if, since their conviction, caution, warning or reprimand a non-intimate sample has not been taken from them or a sample which has been taken since then has proved to be unsuitable or insufficient and in either case, an officer of inspector rank or above, is satisfied that taking the fingerprints is necessary to assist in the prevention or detection of crime and authorises the taking;

(f) under section 63(3C) from a person to whom section 2 of the Criminal Evidence (Amendment) Act 1997 applies (persons detained following acquittal on grounds of insanity or finding of unfitness to plead).

(g) under section 63(3E) from a person who has been convicted outside England and Wales of an offence which if committed in England and Wales would be a qualifying offence as defined by PACE, section 65A (see *Note 4AB*) if:

(i) a non-intimate sample has not been taken previously under this power or unless a sample was so taken but was unsuitable or insufficient; and

(ii) a police officer of inspector rank or above is satisfied that taking a sample is necessary to assist in the prevention or detection of crime and authorises it to be taken.

6.6A PACE, section 63A(4) and Schedule 2A provide powers to:

(a) make a requirement (in accordance with Annex G) for a person to attend a police station to have a non-intimate sample taken in the exercise of one of the following powers in paragraph 6.6 when that power applies at the time the sample would be taken in accordance with the requirement:

(i) section 63(3ZA) – Persons arrested for a recordable offence and released, see paragraph 6.6(c): The requirement may not be made more than six months from the day the investigating officer was informed that the sample previously taken was unsuitable or insufficient.

(ii) section 63(3A) – Persons charged etc. with a recordable offence, see paragraph 6.6(d): The requirement may not be made more than six months from:

- the day the person was charged or reported if a sample has not been taken since then; or
- the day the investigating officer was informed that the sample previously taken was unsuitable or insufficient.

(iii) section 63(3B) – Person convicted, cautioned, warned or reprimanded for a recordable offence in England and Wales, see paragraph 6.6(e): Where the offence for which the person was convicted etc is also a qualifying offence (see *Note 4AB*), there is no time limit for the exercise of this power. Where the conviction etc was for a recordable offence that is not a qualifying offence, the requirement may not be made more than two years from:

- the day the person was convicted, cautioned, warned or reprimanded, or the day Schedule 2A comes into force (if later), if a samples has not been taken since then; or
- the day an officer from the force investigating the offence was informed that the sample previously taken was unsuitable or insufficient or the day Schedule 2A comes into force (if later).

(iv) section 63(3E) – A person who has been convicted of qualifying offence (see *Note 4AB*) outside England and Wales, see paragraph 6.6(h): There is no time limit for making the requirement.

Note: A person who has had a non-intimate sample taken under any of the powers in section 63 mentioned in paragraph 6.6 on two occasions in relation to any offence may not be required under Schedule 2A to attend a police station for a sample to be taken again under section 63 in relation to that offence, unless authorised by an officer of inspector rank or above. The fact of the authorisation and the reasons for giving it must be recorded as soon as practicable.

(b) arrest, without warrant, a person who fails to comply with the requirement.

6.7 Reasonable force may be used, if necessary, to take a non-intimate sample from a person without their consent under the powers mentioned in *paragraph 6.6*.

6.8 Before any non-intimate sample is taken:

(a) without consent under any power mentioned in paragraphs 6.6 and 6.6A, the person must be informed of:

(i) the reason for taking the sample;

(ii) the power under which the sample is to be taken;

(iii) the fact that the relevant authority has been given if any power mentioned in *paragraph 6.6(b), (e)* or *(h)* applies;

(b) with or without consent at a police station or elsewhere, the person must be informed:

(i) that their sample or information derived from it may be subject of a speculative search against other samples and information derived from them, see *Note 6E* and

(ii) that their sample and the information derived from it may be retained in accordance with Annex F, Part (a).

(c) Removal of clothing

6.9 When clothing needs to be removed in circumstances likely to cause embarrassment to the person, no person of the opposite sex who is not a registered medical practitioner or registered health care professional shall be present, (unless in the case of a juvenile, mentally disordered or mentally vulnerable person, that person specifically requests the presence of an appropriate adult of the opposite sex who is readily available) nor shall anyone whose presence is unnecessary. However, in the case of a juvenile, this is subject to the overriding proviso that such a removal of clothing may take place in the absence of the appropriate adult only if the juvenile signifies in their presence, that they prefer the adult's absence and they agree.

(c) Documentation

6.10 A record must be made as soon as practicable after the sample is taken of:

- The matters in paragraph 6.8(a)(i) to (iii) and the fact that the person has been informed of those matters; and
- The fact that the person has been informed of the matters in paragraph 6.8(b)(i) and (ii).

6.10A If force is used, a record shall be made of the circumstances and those present.

6.11 A record must be made of a warning given as required by *paragraph 6.3*.

6.12 *Not used*

Notes for guidance

6A When hair samples are taken for the purpose of DNA analysis (rather than for other purposes such as making a visual match), the suspect should be permitted a reasonable choice as to what part of the body the hairs are taken from. When hairs are plucked, they should be plucked individually, unless the suspect prefers otherwise and no more should be plucked than the person taking them reasonably considers necessary for a sufficient sample.

6B (a) *An insufficient sample is one which is not sufficient either in quantity or quality to provide information for a particular form of analysis, such as DNA analysis. A sample may also be insufficient if enough information cannot be obtained from it by analysis because of loss, destruction, damage or contamination of the sample or as a result of an earlier, unsuccessful attempt at analysis.*

(b) *An unsuitable sample is one which, by its nature, is not suitable for a particular form of analysis.*

6C *Nothing in paragraph 6.2 prevents intimate samples being taken for elimination purposes with the consent of the person concerned but the provisions of paragraph 2.12 relating to the role of the appropriate adult, should be applied. Paragraph 6.2(b) does not, however, apply where the non-intimate samples were previously taken under the Terrorism Act 2000, Schedule 8, paragraph 10.*

6D *In warning a person who is asked to provide an intimate sample as in paragraph 6.3, the following form of words may be used:*

> *'You do not have to provide this sample/allow this swab or impression to be taken, but I must warn you that if you refuse without good cause, your refusal may harm your case if it comes to trial.'*

6E *Fingerprints or a DNA sample and the information derived from it taken from a person arrested on suspicion of being involved in a recordable offence, or charged with such an offence, or informed they will be reported for such an offence, may be subject of a speculative search. This means they may be checked against other fingerprints and DNA records held by, or on behalf of, the police and other law enforcement authorities in or outside the UK or held in connection with, or as a result of, an investigation of an offence inside or outside the UK. Fingerprints and samples taken from any other person, e.g. a person suspected of committing a recordable offence but who has not been arrested, charged or informed they will be reported for it, may be subject to a speculative search only if the person consents in writing to their fingerprints being subject of such a search. The following is an example of a basic form of words:*

> *"I consent to my fingerprints/DNA sample and information derived from it being retained and used only for purposes related to the prevention and detection of a crime, the investigation of an offence or the conduct of a prosecution either nationally or internationally.*
>
> *I understand that this sample may be checked against other fingerprint/DNA records held by or on behalf of relevant law enforcement authorities, either nationally or internationally.*

I understand that once I have given my consent for the sample to be retained and used I cannot withdraw this consent."

See Annex F regarding the retention and use of fingerprints and samples taken with consent for elimination purposes.

6F Samples of urine and non-intimate samples taken in accordance with sections 63B and 63C of PACE may not be used for identification purposes in accordance with this Code. See Code C note for guidance 17D.

Annex A - Video identification

(a) General

1. The arrangements for obtaining and ensuring the availability of a suitable set of images to be used in a video identification must be the responsibility of an identification officer, who has no direct involvement with the case.

2. The set of images must include the suspect and at least eight other people who, so far as possible, resemble the suspect in age, general appearance and position in life. Only one suspect shall appear in any set unless there are two suspects of roughly similar appearance, in which case they may be shown together with at least twelve other people.

2A If the suspect has an unusual physical feature, e.g., a facial scar, tattoo or distinctive hairstyle or hair colour which does not appear on the images of the other people that are available to be used, steps may be taken to:

(a) conceal the location of the feature on the images of the suspect and the other people; or

(b) replicate that feature on the images of the other people.

For these purposes, the feature may be concealed or replicated electronically or by any other method which it is practicable to use to ensure that the images of the suspect and other people resemble each other. The identification officer has discretion to choose whether to conceal or replicate the feature and the method to be used. If an unusual physical feature has been described by the witness, the identification officer should, if practicable, have that feature replicated. If it has not been described, concealment may be more appropriate.

2B If the identification officer decides that a feature should be concealed or replicated, the reason for the decision and whether the feature was concealed or replicated in the images shown to any witness shall be recorded.

2C If the witness requests to view an image where an unusual physical feature has been concealed or replicated without the feature being concealed or replicated, the witness may be allowed to do so.

3. The images used to conduct a video identification shall, as far as possible, show the suspect and other people in the same positions or carrying out the same sequence of movements. They shall also show the suspect and other people under identical conditions unless the identification officer reasonably believes:

(a) because of the suspect's failure or refusal to co-operate or other reasons, it is not practicable for the conditions to be identical; and

(b) any difference in the conditions would not direct a witness' attention to any individual image.

4. The reasons identical conditions are not practicable shall be recorded on forms provided for the purpose.

5. Provision must be made for each person shown to be identified by number.

6. If police officers are shown, any numerals or other identifying badges must be concealed. If a prison inmate is shown, either as a suspect or not, then either all, or none of, the people shown should be in prison clothing.

7. The suspect or their solicitor, friend, or appropriate adult must be given a reasonable opportunity to see the complete set of images before it is shown to any witness. If the suspect has a reasonable objection to the set of images or any of the participants, the suspect shall be asked to state the reasons for the objection. Steps shall, if practicable, be taken to remove the grounds for objection. If this is not practicable, the suspect and/or their representative shall be told why their objections cannot be met and the objection, the reason given for it and why it cannot be met shall be recorded on forms provided for the purpose.

8. Before the images are shown in accordance with *paragraph 7,* the suspect or their solicitor shall be provided with details of the first description of the suspect by any witnesses who are to attend the video identification. When a broadcast or publication is made, as in *paragraph 3.28*, the suspect or their solicitor must also be allowed to view any material released to the media by the police for the purpose of recognising or tracing the suspect, provided it is practicable and would not unreasonably delay the investigation.

9. The suspect's solicitor, if practicable, shall be given reasonable notification of the time and place the video identification is to be conducted so a representative may attend on behalf of the suspect. The suspect may not be present when the images are shown to the witness(es). In the absence of the suspect's solicitor, the viewing itself shall be recorded on video. No unauthorised people may be present.

(b) Conducting the video identification

10. The identification officer is responsible for making the appropriate arrangements to make sure, before they see the set of images, witnesses are not able to communicate with each other about the case, see any of the images which are to be shown, see, or be reminded of, any photograph or description of the suspect or be given any other

indication as to the suspect's identity, or overhear a witness who has already seen the material. There must be no discussion with the witness about the composition of the set of images and they must not be told whether a previous witness has made any identification.

11. Only one witness may see the set of images at a time. Immediately before the images are shown, the witness shall be told that the person they saw on a specified earlier occasion may, or may not, appear in the images they are shown and that if they cannot make a positive identification, they should say so. The witness shall be advised that at any point, they may ask to see a particular part of the set of images or to have a particular image frozen for them to study. Furthermore, it should be pointed out to the witness that there is no limit on how many times they can view the whole set of images or any part of them. However, they should be asked not to make any decision as to whether the person they saw is on the set of images until they have seen the whole set at least twice.

12. Once the witness has seen the whole set of images at least twice and has indicated that they do not want to view the images, or any part of them, again, the witness shall be asked to say whether the individual they saw in person on a specified earlier occasion has been shown and, if so, to identify them by number of the image. The witness will then be shown that image to confirm the identification, see *paragraph 17.*

13. Care must be taken not to direct the witness' attention to any one individual image or give any indication of the suspect's identity. Where a witness has previously made an identification by photographs, or a computerised or artist's composite or similar likeness, the witness must not be reminded of such a photograph or composite likeness once a suspect is available for identification by other means in accordance with this Code. Nor must the witness be reminded of any description of the suspect.

14. After the procedure, each witness shall be asked whether they have seen any broadcast or published films or photographs, or any descriptions of suspects relating to the offence and their reply shall be recorded.

(c) Image security and destruction

15. Arrangements shall be made for all relevant material containing sets of images used for specific identification procedures to be kept securely and their movements accounted for. In particular, no-one involved in the investigation shall be permitted to view the material prior to it being shown to any witness.

16. As appropriate, *paragraph 3.30 or 3.31* applies to the destruction or retention of relevant sets of images.

(d) Documentation

17. A record must be made of all those participating in, or seeing, the set of images whose names are known to the police.

18. A record of the conduct of the video identification must be made on forms provided for the purpose. This shall include anything said by the witness about any identifications or the conduct of the procedure and any reasons it was not practicable to comply with any of the provisions of this Code governing the conduct of video identifications.

Annex B - Identification parades

(a) General

1. A suspect must be given a reasonable opportunity to have a solicitor or friend present, and the suspect shall be asked to indicate on a second copy of the notice whether or not they wish to do so.

2. An identification parade may take place either in a normal room or one equipped with a screen permitting witnesses to see members of the identification parade without being seen. The procedures for the composition and conduct of the identification parade are the same in both cases, subject to *paragraph 8* (except that an identification parade involving a screen may take place only when the suspect's solicitor, friend or appropriate adult is present or the identification parade is recorded on video).

3. Before the identification parade takes place, the suspect or their solicitor shall be provided with details of the first description of the suspect by any witnesses who are attending the identification parade. When a broadcast or publication is made as in *paragraph 3.28*, the suspect or their solicitor should also be allowed to view any material released to the media by the police for the purpose of recognising or tracing the suspect, provided it is practicable to do so and would not unreasonably delay the investigation.

(b) Identification parades involving prison inmates

4. If a prison inmate is required for identification, and there are no security problems about the person leaving the establishment, they may be asked to participate in an identification parade or video identification.

5. An identification parade may be held in a Prison Department establishment but shall be conducted, as far as practicable under normal identification parade rules. Members of the public shall make up the identification parade unless there are serious security, or control, objections to their admission to the establishment. In such cases, or if a group or video identification is arranged within the establishment, other inmates may participate. If an inmate is the suspect, they are not required to wear prison clothing for the identification parade unless the other people taking part are other inmates in similar clothing, or are members of the public who are prepared to wear prison clothing for the occasion.

(c) Conduct of the identification parade

6. Immediately before the identification parade, the suspect must be reminded of the procedures governing its conduct and cautioned in the terms of Code C, paragraphs 10.5 or 10.6, as appropriate.

7. All unauthorised people must be excluded from the place where the identification parade is held.

8. Once the identification parade has been formed, everything afterwards, in respect of it, shall take place in the presence and hearing of the suspect and any interpreter, solicitor, friend or appropriate adult who is present (unless the identification parade involves a screen, in which case everything said to, or by, any witness at the place where the identification parade is held, must be said in the hearing and presence of the suspect's solicitor, friend or appropriate adult or be recorded on video).

9. The identification parade shall consist of at least eight people (in addition to the suspect) who, so far as possible, resemble the suspect in age, height, general appearance and position in life. Only one suspect shall be included in an identification parade unless there are two suspects of roughly similar appearance, in which case they may be paraded together with at least twelve other people. In no circumstances shall more than two suspects be included in one identification parade and where there are separate identification parades, they shall be made up of different people.

10. If the suspect has an unusual physical feature, e.g., a facial scar, tattoo or distinctive hairstyle or hair colour which cannot be replicated on other members of the identification parade, steps may be taken to conceal the location of that feature on the suspect and the other members of the identification parade if the suspect and their solicitor, or appropriate adult, agree. For example, by use of a plaster or a hat, so that all members of the identification parade resemble each other in general appearance.

11. When all members of a similar group are possible suspects, separate identification parades shall be held for each unless there are two suspects of similar appearance when they may appear on the same identification parade with at least twelve other members of the group who are not suspects. When police officers in uniform form an identification parade any numerals or other identifying badges shall be concealed.

12. When the suspect is brought to the place where the identification parade is to be held, they shall be asked if they have any objection to the arrangements for the identification parade or to any of the other participants in it and to state the reasons for the objection. The suspect may obtain advice from their solicitor or friend, if present, before the identification parade proceeds. If the suspect has a reasonable objection to the arrangements or any of the participants, steps shall, if practicable, be taken to remove the grounds for objection. When it is not practicable to do so, the suspect shall be told why their objections cannot be met and the objection, the reason given for it and why it cannot be met, shall be recorded on forms provided for the purpose.

13. The suspect may select their own position in the line, but may not otherwise interfere with the order of the people forming the line. When there is more than one witness, the suspect must be told, after each witness has left the room, that they can, if they wish, change position in the line. Each position in the line must be clearly numbered, whether by means of a number laid on the floor in front of each identification parade member or by other means.

14. Appropriate arrangements must be made to make sure, before witnesses attend the identification parade, they are not able to:

    (i) communicate with each other about the case or overhear a witness who has already seen the identification parade;

    (ii) see any member of the identification parade;

    (iii) see, or be reminded of, any photograph or description of the suspect or be given any other indication as to the suspect's identity; or

    (iv) see the suspect before or after the identification parade.

15. The person conducting a witness to an identification parade must not discuss with them the composition of the identification parade and, in particular, must not disclose whether a previous witness has made any identification.

16. Witnesses shall be brought in one at a time. Immediately before the witness inspects the identification parade, they shall be told the person they saw on a specified earlier occasion may, or may not, be present and if they cannot make a positive identification, they should say so. The witness must also be told they should not make any decision about whether the person they saw is on the identification parade until they have looked at each member at least twice.

17. When the officer or police staff (see paragraph 3.11) conducting the identification procedure is satisfied the witness has properly looked at each member of the identification parade, they shall ask the witness whether the person they saw on a specified earlier occasion is on the identification parade and, if so, to indicate the number of the person concerned, see *paragraph 28*.

18. If the witness wishes to hear any identification parade member speak, adopt any specified posture or move, they shall first be asked whether they can identify any person(s) on the identification parade on the basis of appearance only. When the request is to hear members of the identification parade speak, the witness shall be reminded that the participants in the identification parade have been chosen on the basis of physical appearance only. Members of the identification parade may then

be asked to comply with the witness' request to hear them speak, see them move or adopt any specified posture.

19. If the witness requests that the person they have indicated remove anything used for the purposes of *paragraph 10* to conceal the location of an unusual physical feature, that person may be asked to remove it.

20. If the witness makes an identification after the identification parade has ended, the suspect and, if present, their solicitor, interpreter or friend shall be informed. When this occurs, consideration should be given to allowing the witness a second opportunity to identify the suspect.

21 After the procedure, each witness shall be asked whether they have seen any broadcast or published films or photographs or any descriptions of suspects relating to the offence and their reply shall be recorded.

22. When the last witness has left, the suspect shall be asked whether they wish to make any comments on the conduct of the identification parade.

(d) Documentation

23. A video recording must normally be taken of the identification parade. If that is impracticable, a colour photograph must be taken. A copy of the video recording or photograph shall be supplied, on request, to the suspect or their solicitor within a reasonable time.

24. As appropriate, *paragraph 3.30* or *3.31*, should apply to any photograph or video taken as in *paragraph 23*.

25. If any person is asked to leave an identification parade because they are interfering with its conduct, the circumstances shall be recorded.

26. A record must be made of all those present at an identification parade whose names are known to the police.

27. If prison inmates make up an identification parade, the circumstances must be recorded.

28. A record of the conduct of any identification parade must be made on forms provided for the purpose. This shall include anything said by the witness or the suspect about any identifications or the conduct of the procedure, and any reasons it was not practicable to comply with any of this Code's provisions.

Annex C - Group identification

(a) General

1. The purpose of this Annex is to make sure, as far as possible, group identifications follow the principles and procedures for identification parades so the conditions are fair to the suspect in the way they test the witness' ability to make an identification.

2. Group identifications may take place either with the suspect's consent and co-operation or covertly without their consent.

3. The location of the group identification is a matter for the identification officer, although the officer may take into account any representations made by the suspect, appropriate adult, their solicitor or friend.

4. The place where the group identification is held should be one where other people are either passing by or waiting around informally, in groups such that the suspect is able to join them and be capable of being seen by the witness at the same time as others in the group. For example people leaving an escalator, pedestrians walking through a shopping centre, passengers on railway and bus stations, waiting in queues or groups or where people are standing or sitting in groups in other public places.

5. If the group identification is to be held covertly, the choice of locations will be limited by the places where the suspect can be found and the number of other people present at that time. In these cases, suitable locations might be along regular routes travelled by the suspect, including buses or trains or public places frequented by the suspect.

6. Although the number, age, sex, race and general description and style of clothing of other people present at the location cannot be controlled by the identification officer, in selecting the location the officer must consider the general appearance and numbers of people likely to be present. In particular, the officer must reasonably expect that over the period the witness observes the group, they will be able to see, from time to time, a number of others whose appearance is broadly similar to that of the suspect.

7. A group identification need not be held if the identification officer believes, because of the unusual appearance of the suspect, none of the locations it would be practicable to use, satisfy the requirements of *paragraph 6* necessary to make the identification fair.

8. Immediately after a group identification procedure has taken place (with or without the suspect's consent), a colour photograph or video should be taken of the general scene, if practicable, to give a general impression of the scene and the number of people present. Alternatively, if it is practicable, the group identification may be video recorded.

9. If it is not practicable to take the photograph or video in accordance with *paragraph 8,* a photograph or film of the scene should be taken later at a time determined by the identification officer if the officer considers it practicable to do so.

10. An identification carried out in accordance with this Code remains a group identification even though, at the time of being seen by the witness, the suspect was on their own rather than in a group.

11. Before the group identification takes place, the suspect or their solicitor shall be provided with details of the first description of the suspect by any witnesses who are to attend the identification. When a broadcast or publication is made, as in *paragraph 3.28*, the suspect or their solicitor should also be allowed to view any material released by the police to the media for the purposes of recognising or tracing the suspect, provided that it is practicable and would not unreasonably delay the investigation.

12. After the procedure, each witness shall be asked whether they have seen any broadcast or published films or photographs or any descriptions of suspects relating to the offence and their reply recorded.

(b) Identification with the consent of the suspect

13. A suspect must be given a reasonable opportunity to have a solicitor or friend present. They shall be asked to indicate on a second copy of the notice whether or not they wish to do so.

14. The witness, the person carrying out the procedure and the suspect's solicitor, appropriate adult, friend or any interpreter for the witness, may be concealed from the sight of the individuals in the group they are observing, if the person carrying out the procedure considers this assists the conduct of the identification.

15. The person conducting a witness to a group identification must not discuss with them the forthcoming group identification and, in particular, must not disclose whether a previous witness has made any identification.

16. Anything said to, or by, the witness during the procedure about the identification should be said in the presence and hearing of those present at the procedure.

17. Appropriate arrangements must be made to make sure, before witnesses attend the group identification, they are not able to:

(i) communicate with each other about the case or overhear a witness who has already been given an opportunity to see the suspect in the group;

(ii) see the suspect; or

(iii) see, or be reminded of, any photographs or description of the suspect or be given any other indication of the suspect's identity.

18. Witnesses shall be brought one at a time to the place where they are to observe the group. Immediately before the witness is asked to look at the group, the person conducting the procedure shall tell them that the person they saw may, or may not, be in the group and that if they cannot make a positive identification, they should say so. The witness shall be asked to observe the group in which the suspect is to appear. The way in which the witness should do this will depend on whether the group is moving or stationary.

Moving group

19. When the group in which the suspect is to appear is moving, e.g. leaving an escalator, the provisions of *paragraphs 20* to *24* should be followed.

20. If two or more suspects consent to a group identification, each should be the subject of separate identification procedures. These may be conducted consecutively on the same occasion.

21. The person conducting the procedure shall tell the witness to observe the group and ask them to point out any person they think they saw on the specified earlier occasion.

22. Once the witness has been informed as in *paragraph 21* the suspect should be allowed to take whatever position in the group they wish.

23. When the witness points out a person as in *paragraph 21* they shall, if practicable, be asked to take a closer look at the person to confirm the identification. If this is not practicable, or they cannot confirm the identification, they shall be asked how sure they are that the person they have indicated is the relevant person.

24. The witness should continue to observe the group for the period which the person conducting the procedure reasonably believes is necessary in the circumstances for them to be able to make comparisons between the suspect and other individuals of broadly similar appearance to the suspect as in *paragraph 6*.

Stationary groups

25. When the group in which the suspect is to appear is stationary, e.g. people waiting in a queue, the provisions of *paragraphs 26* to *29* should be followed.

26. If two or more suspects consent to a group identification, each should be subject to separate identification procedures unless they are of broadly similar appearance when they may appear in the same group. When separate group identifications are held, the groups must be made up of different people.

27. The suspect may take whatever position in the group they wish. If there is more than one witness, the suspect must be told, out of the sight and hearing of any witness, that they can, if they wish, change their position in the group.

28. The witness shall be asked to pass along, or amongst, the group and to look at each person in the group at least twice, taking as much care and time as possible according to the circumstances, before making an identification. Once the witness has done this, they shall be asked whether the person they saw on the specified earlier occasion is in the group and to indicate any such person by whatever means the person conducting the procedure considers appropriate in the circumstances. If this is not practicable, the witness shall be asked to point out any person they think they saw on the earlier occasion.

29. When the witness makes an indication as in *paragraph 28,* arrangements shall be made, if practicable, for the witness to take a closer look at the person to confirm the identification. If this is not practicable, or the witness is unable to confirm the identification, they shall be asked how sure they are that the person they have indicated is the relevant person.

All cases

30. If the suspect unreasonably delays joining the group, or having joined the group, deliberately conceals themselves from the sight of the witness, this may be treated as a refusal to co-operate in a group identification.

31. If the witness identifies a person other than the suspect, that person should be informed what has happened and asked if they are prepared to give their name and address. There is no obligation upon any member of the public to give these details. There shall be no duty to record any details of any other member of the public present in the group or at the place where the procedure is conducted.

32. When the group identification has been completed, the suspect shall be asked whether they wish to make any comments on the conduct of the procedure.

33. If the suspect has not been previously informed, they shall be told of any identifications made by the witnesses.

(c) Identification without the suspect's consent

34. Group identifications held covertly without the suspect's consent should, as far as practicable, follow the rules for conduct of group identification by consent.

35. A suspect has no right to have a solicitor, appropriate adult or friend present as the identification will take place without the knowledge of the suspect.

36. Any number of suspects may be identified at the same time.

(d) Identifications in police stations

37. Group identifications should only take place in police stations for reasons of safety, security or because it is not practicable to hold them elsewhere.

38. The group identification may take place either in a room equipped with a screen permitting witnesses to see members of the group without being seen, or anywhere else in the police station that the identification officer considers appropriate.

39. Any of the additional safeguards applicable to identification parades should be followed if the identification officer considers it is practicable to do so in the circumstances.

(e) Identifications involving prison inmates

40. A group identification involving a prison inmate may only be arranged in the prison or at a police station.

41. When a group identification takes place involving a prison inmate, whether in a prison or in a police station, the arrangements should follow those in *paragraphs 37* to *39*. If a group identification takes place within a prison, other inmates may participate. If an inmate is the suspect, they do not have to wear prison clothing for the group identification unless the other participants are wearing the same clothing.

(f) Documentation

42. When a photograph or video is taken as in *paragraph 8* or *9,* a copy of the photograph or video shall be supplied on request to the suspect or their solicitor within a reasonable time.

43. *Paragraph 3.30* or *3.31*, as appropriate, shall apply when the photograph or film taken in accordance with *paragraph 8* or *9* includes the suspect.

44. A record of the conduct of any group identification must be made on forms provided for the purpose. This shall include anything said by the witness or suspect about any identifications or the conduct of the procedure and any reasons why it was not practicable to comply with any of the provisions of this Code governing the conduct of group identifications.

Annex D - Confrontation by a witness

1. Before the confrontation takes place, the witness must be told that the person they saw may, or may not, be the person they are to confront and that if they are not that person, then the witness should say so.

2. Before the confrontation takes place the suspect or their solicitor shall be provided with details of the first description of the suspect given by any witness who is to attend. When a broadcast or publication is made, as in *paragraph 3.28*, the suspect or their solicitor should also be allowed to view any material released to the media for the purposes of recognising or tracing the suspect, provided it is practicable to do so and would not unreasonably delay the investigation.

3. Force may not be used to make the suspect's face visible to the witness.

4. Confrontation must take place in the presence of the suspect's solicitor, interpreter or friend unless this would cause unreasonable delay.

5. The suspect shall be confronted independently by each witness, who shall be asked "Is this the person?". If the witness identifies the person but is unable to confirm the identification, they shall be asked how sure they are that the person is the one they saw on the earlier occasion.

6. The confrontation should normally take place in the police station, either in a normal room or one equipped with a screen permitting a witness to see the suspect without being seen. In both cases, the procedures are the same except that a room equipped with a screen may be used only when the suspect's solicitor, friend or appropriate adult is present or the confrontation is recorded on video.

7. After the procedure, each witness shall be asked whether they have seen any broadcast or published films or photographs or any descriptions of suspects relating to the offence and their reply shall be recorded.

Annex E - Showing photographs

(a) Action

1. An officer of sergeant rank or above shall be responsible for supervising and directing the showing of photographs. The actual showing may be done by another officer or police staff, see *paragraph 3.11*.

2. The supervising officer must confirm the first description of the suspect given by the witness has been recorded before they are shown the photographs. If the supervising officer is unable to confirm the description has been recorded they shall postpone showing the photographs.

3. Only one witness shall be shown photographs at any one time. Each witness shall be given as much privacy as practicable and shall not be allowed to communicate with any other witness in the case.

4. The witness shall be shown not less than twelve photographs at a time, which shall, as far as possible, all be of a similar type.

5. When the witness is shown the photographs, they shall be told the photograph of the person they saw may, or may not, be amongst them and if they cannot make a positive identification, they should say so. The witness shall also be told they should not make a decision until they have viewed at least twelve photographs. The witness shall not be prompted or guided in any way but shall be left to make any selection without help.

6. If a witness makes a positive identification from photographs, unless the person identified is otherwise eliminated from enquiries or is not available, other witnesses shall not be shown photographs. But both they, and the witness who has made the identification, shall be asked to attend a video identification, an identification parade or group identification unless there is no dispute about the suspect's identification.

7. If the witness makes a selection but is unable to confirm the identification, the person showing the photographs shall ask them how sure they are that the photograph they have indicated is the person they saw on the specified earlier occasion.

8. When the use of a computerised or artist's composite or similar likeness has led to there being a known suspect who can be asked to participate in a video identification, appear on an identification parade or participate in a group identification, that likeness shall not be shown to other potential witnesses.

9. When a witness attending a video identification, an identification parade or group identification has previously been shown photographs or computerised or artist's composite or similar likeness (and it is the responsibility of the officer in charge of the

investigation to make the identification officer aware that this is the case), the suspect and their solicitor must be informed of this fact before the identification procedure takes place.

10. None of the photographs shown shall be destroyed, whether or not an identification is made, since they may be required for production in court. The photographs shall be numbered and a separate photograph taken of the frame or part of the album from which the witness made an identification as an aid to reconstituting it.

(b) Documentation

11. Whether or not an identification is made, a record shall be kept of the showing of photographs on forms provided for the purpose. This shall include anything said by the witness about any identification or the conduct of the procedure, any reasons it was not practicable to comply with any of the provisions of this Code governing the showing of photographs and the name and rank of the supervising officer.

12. The supervising officer shall inspect and sign the record as soon as practicable.

Annex F - Fingerprints, footwear impressions and samples - destruction and speculative searches

(a) Fingerprints, footwear impressions and samples taken in connection with a criminal investigation from a person suspected of committing the offence under investigation.

1. The retention and destruction of fingerprints, footwear impressions and samples taken in connection with a criminal investigation from a person suspected of committing the offence under investigation is subject to PACE, section 64.

(b) Fingerprints, footwear impressions and samples taken in connection with a criminal investigation from a person not suspected of committing the offence under investigation.

2. When fingerprints, footwear impressions or DNA samples are taken from a person in connection with an investigation and the person is not suspected of having committed the offence, see *Note F1*, they must be destroyed as soon as they have fulfilled the purpose for which they were taken unless:

   (a) they were taken for the purposes of an investigation of an offence for which a person has been convicted; and

   (b) fingerprints, footwear impressions or samples were also taken from the convicted person for the purposes of that investigation.

   However, subject to *paragraph 2*, the fingerprints, footwear impressions and samples, and the information derived from samples, may not be used in the investigation of any offence or in evidence against the person who is, or would be, entitled to the destruction of the fingerprints, footwear impressions and samples, see *Note F2.*

3. The requirement to destroy fingerprints, footwear impressions and DNA samples, and information derived from samples, and restrictions on their retention and use in *paragraph 1* do not apply if the person gives their written consent for their fingerprints, footwear impressions or sample to be retained and used after they have fulfilled the purpose for which they were taken, see *Note F1.*

4. When a person's fingerprints, footwear impressions or sample are to be destroyed:

   (a) any copies of the fingerprints and footwear impressions must also be destroyed;

   (b) the person may witness the destruction of their fingerprints, footwear impressions or copies if they ask to do so within five days of being informed destruction is required;

(c) access to relevant computer fingerprint data shall be made impossible as soon as it is practicable to do so and the person shall be given a certificate to this effect within three months of asking; and

(d) neither the fingerprints, footwear impressions, the sample, or any information derived from the sample, may be used in the investigation of any offence or in evidence against the person who is, or would be, entitled to its destruction.

5. Fingerprints, footwear impressions or samples, and the information derived from samples, taken in connection with the investigation of an offence which are not required to be destroyed, may be retained after they have fulfilled the purposes for which they were taken but may be used only for purposes related to the prevention or detection of crime, the investigation of an offence or the conduct of a prosecution in, as well as outside, the UK and may also be subject to a speculative search. This includes checking them against other fingerprints, footwear impressions and DNA records held by, or on behalf of, the police and other law enforcement authorities in, as well as outside, the UK.

(b) Fingerprints taken in connection with Immigration Service enquiries

6. See *paragraph 4.10.*

Notes for guidance

F1 Fingerprints, footwear impressions and samples given voluntarily for the purposes of elimination play an important part in many police investigations. It is, therefore, important to make sure innocent volunteers are not deterred from participating and their consent to their fingerprints, footwear impressions and DNA being used for the purposes of a specific investigation is fully informed and voluntary. If the police or volunteer seek to have the fingerprints, footwear impressions or samples retained for use after the specific investigation ends, it is important the volunteer's consent to this is also fully informed and voluntary.

Examples of consent for:

- *DNA/fingerprints/footwear impressions - to be used only for the purposes of a specific investigation;*
- *DNA/fingerprints/footwear impressions - to be used in the specific investigation and retained by the police for future use.*

To minimise the risk of confusion, each consent should be physically separate and the volunteer should be asked to sign each consent.

(a) *DNA:*

(i) *DNA sample taken for the purposes of elimination or as part of an intelligence-led screening and to be used only for the purposes of that investigation and destroyed afterwards:*

"I consent to my DNA/mouth swab being taken for forensic analysis. I understand that the sample will be destroyed at the end of the case and that my profile will only be compared to the crime stain profile from this enquiry. I have been advised that the person taking the sample may be required to give evidence and/or provide a written statement to the police in relation to the taking of it".

(ii) *DNA sample to be retained on the National DNA database and used in the future:*

"I consent to my DNA sample and information derived from it being retained and used only for purposes related to the prevention and detection of a crime, the investigation of an offence or the conduct of a prosecution either nationally or internationally."

"I understand that this sample may be checked against other DNA records held by, or on behalf of, relevant law enforcement authorities, either nationally or internationally".

"I understand that once I have given my consent for the sample to be retained and used I cannot withdraw this consent."

(b) *Fingerprints:*

(i) *Fingerprints taken for the purposes of elimination or as part of an intelligence-led screening and to be used only for the purposes of that investigation and destroyed afterwards:*

"I consent to my fingerprints being taken for elimination purposes. I understand that the fingerprints will be destroyed at the end of the case and that my fingerprints will only be compared to the fingerprints from this enquiry. I have been advised that the person taking the fingerprints may be required to give evidence and/or provide a written statement to the police in relation to the taking of it."

(ii) *Fingerprints to be retained for future use:*

"I consent to my fingerprints being retained and used only for purposes related to the prevention and detection of a crime, the investigation of an offence or the conduct of a prosecution either nationally or internationally".

"I understand that my fingerprints may be checked against other records held by, or on behalf of, relevant law enforcement authorities, either nationally or internationally."

"I understand that once I have given my consent for my fingerprints to be retained and used I cannot withdraw this consent."

(c) *Footwear impressions:*

(i) *Footwear impressions taken for the purposes of elimination or as part of an intelligence-led screening and to be used only for the purposes of that investigation and destroyed afterwards:*

"I consent to my footwear impressions being taken for elimination purposes. I understand that the footwear impressions will be destroyed at the end of the case and that my footwear impressions will only be compared to the footwear impressions from this enquiry. I have been advised that the person taking the footwear impressions may be required to give evidence and/or provide a written statement to the police in relation to the taking of it."

(ii) *Footwear impressions to be retained for future use:*

"I consent to my footwear impressions being retained and used only for purposes related to the prevention and detection of a crime, the investigation of an offence or the conduct of a prosecution, either nationally or internationally".

"I understand that my footwear impressions may be checked against other records held by, or on behalf of, relevant law enforcement authorities, either nationally or internationally."

"I understand that once I have given my consent for my footwear impressions to be retained and used I cannot withdraw this consent."

F2 *The provisions for the retention of fingerprints, footwear impressions and samples in paragraph 1 allow for all fingerprints, footwear impressions and samples in a case to be available for any subsequent miscarriage of justice investigation.*

Annex G –Requirement for a person to attend a police station for fingerprints and samples.

1. A requirement under Schedule 2A for a person to attend a police station to have fingerprints or samples taken:

   (a) must give the person a period of at least seven days within which to attend the police station; and

   (b) may direct them to attend at a specified time of day or between specified times of day.

2. When specifying the period and times of attendance, the officer making the requirements must consider whether the fingerprints or samples could reasonably be taken at a time when the person is required to attend the police station for any other reason. See Note G1.

3. An officer of the rank of inspector or above may authorise a period shorter than 7 days if there is an urgent need for person's fingerprints or sample for the purposes of the investigation of an offence. The fact of the authorisation and the reasons for giving it must be recorded as soon as practicable.

4. The constable making a requirement and the person to whom it applies may agree to vary it so as to specify any period within which, or date or time at which, the person is to attend. However, variation shall not have effect for the purposes of enforcement, unless it is confirmed by the constable in writing.

Notes for Guidance

G1 The specified period within which the person is to attend need not fall within the period allowed (if applicable) for making the requirement.

G2 To justify the arrest without warrant of a person who fails to comply with a requirement, (see paragraph 4.4(b) above), the officer making the requirement, or confirming a variation, should be prepared to explain how, when and where the requirement was made or the variation was confirmed and what steps were taken to ensure the person understood what to do and the consequences of not complying with the requirement.

Appendix B

HISTORY OF CODE D

1st Version	In force: 1 January 1986

The Police and Criminal Evidence Act 1984 (Codes of Practice) (No 1) Order 1985, SI 1985/1937

2nd Version	In force: 1 April 1991

The Police and Criminal Evidence Act 1984 (Codes of Practice) (No 2) Order 1990, SI 1990/2580

3rd Version	In force: 10 April 1995

The Police and Criminal Evidence Act 1984 (Codes of Practice) (No 3) Order 1995, SI 1995/450

Temporary modifications to 3rd Version	In force: 1 April 2002

The Police and Criminal Evidence Act 1984 (Codes of Practice) (Temporary Modifications to Code D) Order 2002, SI 2002/615

4th Version	In force: 1 April 2003

The Police and Criminal Evidence Act 1984 (Codes of Practice) (Codes B to E) (No 2) Order 2003, SI 2003/703

5th Version	In force: 1 August 2004

The Police and Criminal Evidence Act 1984 (Codes of Practice) Order 2004, SI 2004/1887

6th Version	In force: 31 January 2008

The Police and Criminal Evidence Act 1984 (Codes of Practice) Order 2008, SI 2008/167

7th Version	In force: 7 March 2011

Police and Criminal Evidence Act 1984 (Codes of Practice) (Revision of Codes A, B and D) Order 2011, SI 2011/412

Appendix C

PRO FORMA NOTICE TO SUSPECT AND IDENTIFICATION PROCEDURE RECORDS

FIRST DESCRIPTION OF SUSPECTS GIVEN BY WITNESSES

RESTRICTED

METROPOLITAN POLICE SERVICE **Form 620**

IDENTIFICATION PROCEDURES – NOTICE TO SUSPECT

(Part 1 of 2 parts) (from 01/04/2003)

> You will be given reasonable opportunity to read this form and asked to sign to indicate whether or not you are willing to take part in an identification procedure.
>
> You are entitled to free legal advice before making any decisions regarding the identification procedures proposed. This includes the right to speak to a solicitor on the telephone.
>
> The procedures outlined in this Notice are detailed in the 'Code of Practice (D) for the Identification of Persons by Police Officers' in section 3 (Identification by witnesses) which you may consult.
>
> You will be given a copy of both parts of this Notice.

1. The purpose of an identification procedure is to test the ability of a witness to pick out from a set of images or group of similar looking people, the person they say they saw on a specified occasion, if that person is present

2. A police officer of the rank of inspector or above who is not involved in the investigation is responsible for the arrangements and conduct of identification procedures. This officer is called the "identification officer". The officer may allow another officer or civilian support staff, who is not involved in the investigation to make arrangements for, and conduct, any of these identification procedures. In delegating these procedures, the identification officer must be able to supervise effectively and either intervene or be contacted for advice.

3. If it is proposed to hold an identification procedure, you will initially be offered a video identification unless: (a) a video identification is not practicable; or (b) an identification parade is both practicable and more suitable than a video identification or (c) a group identification is initially offered because police consider it is more suitable than a video identification or an identification parade and the identification officer considers it is practicable to arrange. The identification officer and the officer in charge of the investigation shall consult each other to determine which option is to be offered. An identification parade may not be practicable because of factors relating to the witnesses, such as their number, state of health, availability and travelling requirements. A video identification would normally be more suitable if it could be arranged and completed sooner than an identification parade. If you refuse the procedure you are first offered, you will be asked to state why and you may obtain advice from your solicitor and/or if present, the appropriate adult. You and your solicitor and appropriate adult will be allowed to make representations about why another procedure should be used. Your reasons for refusing and any representations made will be recorded. After considering any reasons given, and representations made, the identification officer will, if appropriate, arrange for you to be offered an alternative which the officer considers suitable and practicable in your case. If the officer decides it is not suitable and practicable to offer an alternative, the reasons for that decision will be recorded.

4. **If you significantly alter your appearance between being offered an identification procedure and any attempt to hold an identification procedure, this may be given in evidence if the case comes to trial and the identification officer may then consider other forms of identification.**

5. A video (moving image) or photograph may be taken of you when you attend for any identification procedure.

6. You or your solicitor will be given details of the description of the suspect as first given by any witnesses who are to attend the video identification, identification parade, group identification, or confrontation. You or your solicitor will also be allowed, provided it is practicable to do so and would not unreasonably delay the investigation, to view any material which police have released to the media for the purpose of recognising or tracing suspects in connection with your case. You will also be informed whether a witness has been shown any photograph, photofit, identikit or similar photographs by the police.

7. **If you change your appearance before an identification parade, it may not be practicable to arrange one on the day in question or subsequently and because of your change of appearance, the identification officer may then consider alternative methods of identification.**

8. If you or your solicitor have a reasonable objection to any other participants in an identification procedure, or to any of the arrangements, you or your solicitor will be asked to state the reasons for the objection. Steps shall, if practicable, be taken to remove the grounds for objection. If this is not practicable you or your solicitor will be told why and the objection, the reasons for it and why it cannot be met will be recorded. Such objections should be directed to the identification officer or person conducting the procedure.

9. At the conclusion of a procedure, you can make any comments you wish and these will be recorded.

10. If you have not been detained, photographs of you (and the negatives and all copies thereof) taken for the purposes of, or in connection with, identification procedures will be normally be destroyed unless you are (a) charged with, or informed you may be prosecuted or are prosecuted for a recordable offence; (b) cautioned or (if aged under 18) given a warning or reprimand for a recordable offence; or (c) give your informed written consent for them to be retained and used for purposes related to the prevention or detection of crime, the investigation of offences or the conduct of prosecutions by or on behalf of police or other law enforcement and prosecuting authorities inside and outside the United Kingdom. If destruction is required, you may witness this if you so request within five days of being informed that destruction is required. The above also applies to moving images of you (and copies) whether or not you have been detained.

RESTRICTED

IDENTIFICATION PROCEDURES

Video Identification

11. The witness is shown a video or set of other images which must include you and at least eight other people who as far as practicable resemble you in age, height, general appearance and position in life. These persons will be pre-selected and identified by a number.

12. Both you and the others shall as far as possible be shown in the same positions or carrying out the same activities and under identical conditions. The conditions need not be identical however if this is not practicable provided that any differences in the conditions do not direct a witness's attention to you or any other person.

13. You or your solicitor will be given a reasonable opportunity to view the images before they are shown to any witness.

14. You or your solicitor will, if practicable, be given a reasonable notification of the time and place that the images will be shown to witnesses. You yourself may not be present but your solicitor or other representative may. If your solicitor or representative is not present, the showing of the images to witnesses will be recorded on video.

15. Only one witness will see the set of images at a time and the witness will not be told who is the suspect.

16. If the identification officer has images of you, taken or obtained before you were given this notice you will be told and asked if you wish to co-operate in providing further suitable images which will be used in place of those previously taken or obtained.

Identification Parade

17. You will be asked to stand in a line with at least eight other pre-selected people who, so far as practicable, are of similar age, height and general appearance to you. Each person's position will be clearly numbered. You may stand in any position in the line you wish but may not otherwise interfere with the order of others forming the line.

18. An identification parade may take place either in a normal room or in one equipped with a screen permitting witnesses to see its members without being seen. The procedures for the composition and conduct of an identification parade are the same whether or not a screen is used but a parade which uses a screen may take place only if your solicitor, friend or appropriate adult is present or a video recording is made.

19. The parade will be inspected by the witness. If there is more than one witness, each will be brought in separately.

20. If you have an unusual physical feature, for example, a facial scar or tattoo or distinctive hairstyle or hair colour which cannot be replicated on other members of the identification parade steps may be taken to conceal the location of that feature on you and the other members of the identification parade, if you agree. An example would be the use of a plaster or a hat, so that all members of the identification parade resemble each other in general appearance. Should a witness request the removal of this article in order to confirm an identification then that witness should be asked whether they can positively identify any person on the basis of what they can see and their reply should be noted. A request for the article to be removed may then be made.

21. You will be allowed to change your position in the line after each witness has left. The witness will not be told who is the suspect.

Group Identification

22. A group identification should be held in a place other than a police station, but may be held in a police station when the identification officer considers it not practicable to hold it elsewhere.

23. The identification officer will determine the location of a group identification and the method by which it will be carried out. You will be invited to join a group of people who may be stationary or moving. The officer will consider the general appearance and numbers of people likely to be present at the location and select one where it is reasonably expected that the witness will see others who are broadly similar in appearance to you.

SOLICITORS, APPROPRIATE ADULTS AND OTHER REPRESENTATIVES

24. You will be given a reasonable opportunity to have a solicitor and an appropriate adult or friend present and you will be asked to indicate on Part 2 of this Notice whether or not you so wish.

25. If you are aged under 17 or are mentally disordered or otherwise mentally vulnerable, your participation in an identification procedure must take place in the presence of an appropriate adult.

CONSENT

26. You do not have to consent to or co-operate in a video identification, identification parade or a group identification.

27. If you do not consent to or co-operate in a video identification, identification parade or group identification, your refusal may be given in evidence in any subsequent trial and police may proceed covertly without your consent or make other arrangements to test whether a witness can identify you.

28. You are asked to sign this form to indicate whether you are willing to take part in a video identification, identification parade or group identification. If you refuse to consent, you are not obliged to give your reasons.

RESTRICTED

METROPOLITAN POLICE SERVICE **Form 620A**

Notice to Suspect (Part 2 of 2 parts)

Station/Branch: .... Date: .... Case Ref.: ....

Suspect's name: .... Address: ....

....

Suspect's Declaration

I am aged 17 years or over ☐ I am under 17 years of age ☐ tick one box

The Notice has been given to me and I have been informed that .... witness(es) who are to take part in the video identification / identification parade / group identification* have been shown photographs, photofit, identikit or similar pictures by police. *insert "No" or number as appropriate*

I am willing ☐ not willing ☐ to take part in a video identification tick one box

I am willing ☐ not willing ☐ to take part in an identification parade tick one box

I am willing ☐ not willing ☐ to take part in a group identification tick one box

My reasons for not wanting to take part are **(Note: You do not have to give any reasons for your decisions but if you do these reasons may be given in evidence in any subsequent court proceedings):-**

....

....

....

I would ☐ would not ☐ like my solicitor or other representative to attend the identification procedures.

Name of Solicitor/Representative*: .... Address: ....

....

Signature of suspect: .... Date: .... Time: ....

Appropriate adult present when form served on, and consent given by, a person under 17 or a person who is mentally disordered or otherwise mentally vulnerable. *Note: an appropriate adult can only given consent on behalf of a person under 17 if they are also that person's parent or guardian. [see Code D2.12 and *Note 2A*]

Name of Appropriate adult: .... Address: ....

....

Status/Relationship to suspect: .... Age: ....

Signature of Parent/
Guardian/Appropriate Adult*: .... Date: .... Time: ....

If suspect under 17 and consent of parent/guardian not given above, show when, where and by whom obtained

Date: .... Time: .... Place: .... by : ....
or enter '*REFUSED*' as applicable

Declaration of person serving notice (identification officer, [+]custody officer or [+]other not involved in the investigation)
[[+]A person other than the identification officer must inform the identification officer of the action taken and give them the signed copy of the notice.]

I certify that I have explained the contents of this Notice and served the suspect with a copy.

Name: .... Rank/Grade: .... Station: ....

Signature: .... Date: .... Time: ....

**Delete as appropriate*

RESTRICTED

Description of Exhibit: ....
....
....
On date: ....
From place/person: ....
....
I identify this item as Exhibit Identity Number:
[ ]
Signature(s)
....
....
....
....
....
Court Exhibit No. ....

WITNESS STATEMENT

(CJ Act 1967, s.9; MC Act 1980, ss.5A(3) (a) and 5B; MC Rules 1981, r.70)

Statement of: ....

Age if under 18: .... (if over 18 insert 'over 18') Occupation: ....

At (time): .... on (date): .... at (location): ....

I served Form 620 (Notice to suspect) on (suspect's name): ....

and I produce Form 620A (Signed copy of the Notice to suspect) marked Exhibit No.:

This statement is true to the best of my knowledge and belief and I make it knowing that, if it is tendered in evidence, I shall be liable to prosecution if I have wilfully stated in it anything which I know to be false or do not believe to be true.

Dated the .... day of .... 20..........

Signature: .... Signature witnessed by: ....

Retention period: 7 years
MP 1418/04

NOTICE TO SUSPECT

RESTRICTED

Form 620X

METROPOLITAN
POLICE
Working together for a safer London

METROPOLITAN POLICE SERVICE

Police and Criminal Evidence Act 1984 Codes of Practice Code D para. 3.0
Provision of details of first description of suspects given by witnesses

Police station:	Code:	Other Refs.:	Custody No.:

Name: *(full name of suspect)* Date of birth: ☐

A. Details of First Description (to be completed by the officer in the case)

I hereby certify that the details of the descriptions set out below are an accurate copy of the recorded details of the description(s) of the above name as first given by witness(es) who are to attend an identification procedure under code D 3.1 (i.e. video identification parade, live parade, group identification, confrontation) involving the above named.

Witness (1): (To correspond with Form 650A) "First Description (as given at scene or from MG11 if no scene description).

Witness (2): (To correspond with Form 650A) "First Description (as given at scene or from MG11 if no scene description).

Witness (3): (To correspond with Form 650A) "First Description (as given at scene or from MG11 if no scene description).

Further witnesses in this case: ☐ No ☐ Yes If yes use additional form(s) Place cross in one box

Totals: Number of witnesses: Number of forms used:

Name: Rank: Station:

Signature: .... (date): (time):

B. Details provided to suspect/solicitor
A copy of this form containing the above details was given to:-

(i) the above named

(ii) the solicitor for the above named, as follows:-

Person to whom the form given (name): Status:

Name of Firm:

Address:

(iii) Signature of recipient ....

Signature of Appropriate Adult ....

C. Officer supplying details

Name: Rank: Station:

Signature: .... (date): (time):

1. The officer in the case must inform the identification officer that the details of the first description given by each witness have been provided BEFORE any procedure in Code D 3.1 can take place and give the identification officer a copy of this form.
2. A copy of the completed form(s) must be attached to the relevant identification procedure report.

Retention period: 7 years
MP 220/07

RECORD OF VIDEO FILM IDENTIFICATION

RESTRICTED

Identification Parades – Incident Details

Name of witness (Please indicate if there are anonymity issues relating to the identification of the witness) Each witness must correspond to the running order on Form 620X	Day, date, time and place saw suspect	Question to be asked of the witness, e.g. the man who robbed you - or, the person you saw running away from the house
	Day Date Time Place	
	Day Date Time Place	
	Day Date Time Place	
	Day Date Time Place	
	Day Date Time Place	
	Day Date Time Place	

Retention period: 7 years
MP 1131/07

Form 650A

VIDEO FILM IDENTIFICATION

Individual reference no for this suspect ---------------------------

RESTRICTED

METROPOLITAN POLICE

Working together for a safer London

Form 621M

Location:

Date of viewing:

CRIS No.:

Custody No.:

METROPOLITAN POLICE SERVICE

Viewing of Video ID parades involving multiple suspects and witnesses
(consult ID Insp before using this set of forms.)

Description of Exhibit:
Record of video identification procedure involving .... witness(es)
(Insert number)

Date:
Suspect: Name

Individual reference no for this suspect ---------------------------

I identify this item as Exhibit Identity Number:

Signature(s)

Court Exhibit No.:

In terrorism cases police officer's names may be replaced by warrant numbers.

Identification Inspector(name):

Officer in charge of arrangements, etc.
The arrangements for, and conduct of, this identification procedure shall be the responsibility of an officer not below the rank of inspector who is not involved with the investigation ("the identification officer"). Arranging, supervising and directing the making and showing of a video film to be used in a video identification must be the responsibility of an identification officer or identification officers who have no direct involvement with the relevant case. (From Code D Annex A Para. 1)

1. Officer in the case (name):

   Station/Branch: Rank:

Individual reference no for this suspect ----------------------------

RESTRICTED

Not to be present: No officer involved with the investigation of the case against the suspect may take part in these procedures. (From Code D 3.11)

2. Location of the viewing:

3. Details of the suspect(s) – must not be present at this procedure
Name:
Date of birth:

4. Details of solicitor/representative .
Name and address of solicitor/representative :

Has the suspect/solicitor been shown the video ID parade?

Yes/No--if no, consult ID Insp before proceeding.

NOTE:
The suspect or their solicitor, friend or appropriate adult must be given a reasonable opportunity to see the complete film before it is shown to the witnesses. (From Code D Annex A Para. 7)

If solicitor/representative is not present.

Has the suspect or solicitor been notified of date and time of showing?
If so, by whom and when..
if not, consult ID Insp before proceeding.

NOTE:The suspect's solicitor, or where one is not instructed the suspect themselves, where practicable shall be given reasonable notification of the time and place that it is intended to conduct the video identification in order that a representative may attend on behalf of the suspect. The suspect may not be present when the film is shown to the witness(es). No unauthorised people may be present. (From Code D Annex A Para. 9)

5 Details of service of the first description/media release on suspect/solicitor

NOTE: First descriptions and other material

Before the video identification takes place the suspect or his solicitor shall be provided with details of the first description of the suspect, as given by any witnesses who are to attend the identification. The suspect or his/her solicitor should also be allowed to view any material released to the media by the police for the purpose of recognising or tracing the suspect, provided it is practicable to do so and would not unreasonably delay the investigation.
(Code D Annex A Para. 8)

Details of the first description(s) of this suspect, given by the witnesses to view this parade, and/or media release provided to suspect/solicitor (delete as appropriate)
On (date):
By (name):

Individual reference no for this suspect ---------------------------

RESTRICTED

6. Is the viewing being video-recorded? Yes ☐ No ☐
   NOTE:
   In the absence of a person representing the suspect the viewing itself shall be recorded on video. (From Code D Annex A Para. 9)
   Name of video operator:

7. Where witnesses situated prior to viewing:

8 Police officer/staff posted with them:

NOTE:The identification officer is responsible for ensuring that, before they see the film, witnesses are not able to communicate with each other about the case or overhear a witness who has seen the film. He or she must not discuss with the witness the composition of the film and must not disclose whether a previous witness has made any identification. Only one witness may see the film at a time. (Code D Annex A pares. 9 and 10)
Witnesses will be kept in a place where they cannot see or hear any of the proceedings, and while waiting to enter the viewing room must not communicate with each other about the case.
Witnesses are not to see or be reminded of any photographs or descriptions of the suspect or be given any other indication of his/her identity.
Witnesses will be introduced one at a time. On leaving they will not be allowed to communicate with witnesses still waiting to see the video film.

9. Time procedure begins: ☐

10. Persons other than Identification officer and representatives present in viewing room.

    Show who is present and why. No officer involved in the investigation of the case to be present.

IF NO REPRESENTATIVE PRESENT THEN GO TO SECTION 13

11. Question to representative(s)
    "Do you object to any of the persons present or to any of the arrangements for the procedure today?"
    Reply by suspect's representative:

    Inform ID Inspector then record steps taken to comply with any objection or reasons why objection cannot be resolved:

Individual reference no for this suspect ----------------------------

RESTRICTED

12. Address to solicitor or representative
"The purpose of the video identification procedure today is to show to the witness(es) for identification purposes a video parade of:

(insert suspect's name)
and eight other persons in relation to an offence(s) of:

committed on:

The video parade which was viewed by:

on (date):

was compiled into nine different versions, with the suspect in position 1 on parade 1, through to position 9 on parade 9. Prior to the/ each witness entering the viewing room you will be given the opportunity to select a compilation to be shown to the witness(es). Do you understand?"
Reply by suspect's representative:

13. Removal of the CD/DVD from sealed property bag

Seal number: Exhibit No.:

Open the sealed bag in the presence of the representative(s) or where no representative present ensure removal is recorded on video.

QUESTIONS/ACTIONS 14 to 28 FOR EACH WITNESS VIEWING THIS PARADE MUST BE RECORDED SEPARATELY SO THEY CAN BE GIVEN TO THE ESCORTING/RECEIVING OFFICER TO ALLOW A STATEMENT TO BE TAKEN IMMEDIATELY AFTER THE VIEWING

Individual reference no for this suspect ----------------------------

RESTRICTED

14 WITNESS-SURNAME:

Forename(s):

If under 17 show age:

How arrived at viewing location:

If brought, by whom:

Time of arrival:

If witness is under 17 or is mentally disordered or mentally handicapped an appropriate adult must attend the viewing process, but must not be allowed to prompt any identification by the witness.

Appropriate adult (full name):

Status to witness: Age:

If witness (or appropriate adult for witness) requires an interpreter record details here.

Interpreters name

Contact details

15. Before the witness is ushered in
"Please state the compilation number that you wish to be shown to the witness."
Reply by suspect's representative:

This compilation will show the suspect at position: [ ]

Turn over page before witness enters viewing room

Individual reference no for this suspect ---------------------------

RESTRICTED

17. Address to the witness by officer undertaking showing

You are being asked if you can identify the person/ one of the persons* that you saw on

On (Date)..

At (Place)..

Who..
...

I am going to show you a film of nine people. The person/one of the persons* you saw may or may not be on this film. Please view the film twice before you make any decision. After this, you may see the film or any part of it as many times as you like. At any point, you may ask to see a particular part of the set of images or have a particular image frozen to study. When you have finished I will ask you if you can make an identification. If you cannot make a positive identification you should say so. Do you understand?

Witness reply

18 Showing of the parade:
Describe what the witness does and says during the showing: All comments must be recorded verbatim.

19. Question to witness after parade viewed at least twice

"Do you want to see the film again or any individual images?"

Individual reference no for this suspect ----------------------------

RESTRICTED

Witness reply:

Show what action taken in response to request by witness to view all or part again:

NOTE If the witness requests to view an image where an unusual physical feature has been concealed or replicated without the feature being concealed or replicated, the witness may be allowed to do so. Code D Annex A 2C

20. Question to witness

"If the person that you are here to identify was shown on that film, please state the number that was on the screen when that person was displayed."
Witness reply:

NOTE:
Where the response to question 20 is unambiguous or clear then further questioning about the identification should not take place. e.g. "It's number 2", "He's not there" "I can't make an identification", etc

Where, however, the response is qualified or ambiguous, e.g. "I'm not sure", "I can't be certain", "I'm not 100% ", I think it's no.5 but I'm not sure",
Then further questions can be asked to clarify.

The questions must be open and non-leading
e.g. "Why can you not be certain?" "Why are you not sure?"

You must be careful not to nudge, prompt, or encourage a witness [whether unwittingly or otherwise] to make a more positive identification of a suspect.

All questions and responses must be recorded verbatim. Additionally and as soon as possible afterwards, an MG11 must be taken from the witness to reflect the observations they made in response to questioning.

Individual reference no for this suspect ----------------------------

RESTRICTED

21 Record details of any questions and answers below.

22. Identification NOT made
Go to question 26.

23. Identification made- Number identified……..
Confirmation of identification. I showed the witness image no.: ☐

24 **"Is this the person that you are identifying?"**

Witness reply:

25 Question to witness- (not necessary in some cases-consult ID Insp)

"What did you see this person do?"

Witness reply:

Signature of witness……………………………………………………………………….
Date………/………/………. Time………………..

Signature of app. adult…………………………………………………..………………..
Date………/………/………. Time………………..

26. Question to witness
"Have you seen any broadcasts or published films or photographs or any description of suspects relating to this offence?"

Individual reference no for this suspect ----------------------------

RESTRICTED

Witness reply:

27. Witness leaves viewing room
    Where witness taken after viewing :

    Escorting officer:
    Staff receiving witness(es):

28 Remarks e.g. if procedure aborted for any reason:

Individual reference no for this suspect ---------------------------

RESTRICTED

29. Question to representative after last witness has left
"Do you wish to make any comments on the conduct of the identification procedure today?
Reply by suspect's representative:

Bring any comments to the attention of the Identification Inspector.

30. Sealing of CD/DVD in bag
Place CD/DVD in bag and seal in presence of suspect's representative. Where there is no representative present ensure that the sealing of the bag is recorded on video. .
Seal number(s) Exhibit No.:
NB Retains original exhibit no.

31. Time procedure ends: [ ]

32. Seal number(s) of recording of viewing process
Seal No

33. I certify that this identification procedure took place in accordance with Code D of the Codes of Practice to the Police and Criminal Evidence Act 1984. I am not involved with the investigation of this case.

Name (BLOCK CAPITALS):

Signature...
Date........./........./.................... Time.......................................

IDENTIFICATION OFFICER

34. I confirm I was the Identification officer responsible for the conduct of these identification procedures.
I personally supervised these procedures.*
I delegated supervision of these procedures to*.............
Delete as appropriate

Name and signature
....

Date........./........./.................... Time...................................

Individual reference no for this suspect ---------------------------

RESTRICTED

Retention period: 7 years

Appendix D

POLICE AND CRIMINAL EVIDENCE ACT 1984

****

PART III

27 Fingerprinting of certain offenders

(1) (*repealed*)

(1A) (*repealed*)

(1B) (*repealed*)

(2) (*repealed*)

(3) (*repealed*)

(4) The Secretary of State may by regulations make provision for recording in national police records convictions for such offences as are specified in the regulations.

(4A) (*repealed*)

(5) Regulations under this section shall be made by statutory instrument and shall be subject to annulment in pursuance of a resolution of either House of Parliament.

Amendments- Crime and Security Act 1010, s 6(3).

****

PART V

****

54A Searches and examination to ascertain identity

(1) If an officer of at least the rank of inspector authorises it, a person who is detained in a police station may be searched or examined, or both—

(a) for the purpose of ascertaining whether he has any mark that would tend to identify him as a person involved in the commission of an offence; or

(b) for the purpose of facilitating the ascertainment of his identity.

(2) An officer may only give an authorisation under subsection (1) for the purpose mentioned in paragraph (a) of that subsection if—

(a) he appropriate consent to a search or examination that would reveal whether the mark in question exists has been withheld; or
(b) it is not practicable to obtain such consent.

(3) An officer may only give an authorisation under subsection (1) in a case in which subsection (2) does not apply if—

(a) the person in question has refused to identify himself; or
(b) the officer has reasonable grounds for suspecting that that person is not who he claims to be.

(4) An officer may give an authorisation under subsection (1) orally or in writing but, if he gives it orally, he shall confirm it in writing as soon as is practicable.

(5) Any identifying mark found on a search or examination under this section may be photographed—

(a) with the appropriate consent; or
(b) if the appropriate consent is withheld or it is not practicable to obtain it, without it.

(6) Where a search or examination may be carried out under this section, or a photograph may be taken under this section, the only persons entitled to carry out the search or examination, or to take the photograph, are constables.

(7) A person may not under this section carry out a search or examination of a person of the opposite sex or take a photograph of any part of the body of a person of the opposite sex.

(8) An intimate search may not be carried out under this section.

(9) A photograph taken under this section—

(a) may be used by, or disclosed to, any person for any purpose related to the prevention or detection of crime, the investigation of an offence or the conduct of a prosecution; and
(b) after being so used or disclosed, may be retained but may not be used or disclosed except for a purpose so related.

(10) In subsection—

(a) the reference to crime includes a reference to any conduct which—
   (i) constitutes one or more criminal offences (whether under the law of a part of the United Kingdom or of a country or territory outside the United Kingdom); or
   (ii) is, or corresponds to, any conduct which, if it all took place in any one part of the United Kingdom, would constitute one or more criminal offences;

and

(b) the references to an investigation and to a prosecution include references, respectively, to any investigation outside the United

Kingdom of any crime or suspected crime and to a prosecution brought in respect of any crime in a country or territory outside the United Kingdom.

(11) In this section—

(a) references to ascertaining a person's identity include references to showing that he is not a particular person; and
(b) references to taking a photograph include references to using any process by means of which a visual image may be produced, and references to photographing a person shall be construed accordingly.

(12) In this section "mark" includes features and injuries; and a mark is an identifying mark for the purposes of this section if its existence in any person's case facilitates the ascertainment of his identity or his identification as a person involved in the commission of an offence.

(13) Nothing in this section applies to a person arrested under an extradition arrest power.

Amendments-Anti-terrorism, Crime and Security Act 2001, s 90(1); Police Reform Act 2002, s 107(1), Sch 7, para 9(2); Extradition Act 2003, s 169(1), (2).

****

61 Fingerprinting

(1) Except as provided by this section no person's fingerprints may be taken without the appropriate consent.

(2) Consent to the taking of a person's fingerprints must be in writing if it is given at a time when he is at a police station.

(3) The fingerprints of a person detained at a police station may be taken without the appropriate consent if—

(a) he is detained in consequence of his arrest for a recordable offence; and
(b) he has not had his fingerprints taken in the course of the investigation of the offence by the police.

(3A) Where a person mentioned in paragraph (a) of subsection (3) or (4) has already had his fingerprints taken in the course of the investigation of the offence by the police, that fact shall be disregarded for the purposes of that subsection if—

(a) the fingerprints taken on the previous occasion do not constitute a complete set of his fingerprints; or
(b) some or all of the fingerprints taken on the previous occasion are not of sufficient quality to allow satisfactory analysis, comparison or matching (whether in the case in question or generally).

(4) The fingerprints of a person detained at a police station may be taken without the appropriate consent if—

(a) he has been charged with a recordable offence or informed that he will be reported for such an offence; and
(b) he has not had his fingerprints taken in the course of the investigation of the offence by the police.

(4A) The fingerprints of a person who has answered to bail at a court or police station may be taken without the appropriate consent at the court or station if—

(a) the court, or
(b) an officer of at least the rank of inspector,

authorises them to be taken.

(4B) A court or officer may only give an authorisation under subsection (4A) if—

(a) the person who has answered to bail has answered to it for a person whose fingerprints were taken on a previous occasion and there are reasonable grounds for believing that he is not the same person; or
(b) the person who has answered to bail claims to be a different person from a person whose fingerprints were taken on a previous occasion.

(5) An officer may give an authorisation under subsection (4A) above orally or in writing but, if he gives it orally, he shall confirm it in writing as soon as is practicable.

(5A) The fingerprints of a person may be taken without the appropriate consent if (before or after the coming into force of this subsection) he has been arrested for a recordable offence and released and—

(a) in the case of a person who is on bail, he has not had his fingerprints taken in the course of the investigation of the offence by the police; or
(b) in any case, he has had his fingerprints taken in the course of that investigation but subsection (3A)(a) or (b) above applies.

(5B) The fingerprints of a person not detained at a police station may be taken without the appropriate consent if (before or after the coming into force of this subsection) he has been charged with a recordable offence or informed that he will be reported for such an offence and—

(a) he has not had his fingerprints taken in the course of the investigation of the offence by the police; or
(b) he has had his fingerprints taken in the course of that investigation but subsection (3A)(a) or (b) above applies.

(6) Subject to this section, the fingerprints of a person may be taken without the appropriate consent if (before or after the coming into force of this subsection)—

(a) he has been convicted of a recordable offence,
(b) he has been given a caution in respect of a recordable offence which, at the time of the caution, he has admitted, or

(c) he has been warned or reprimanded under section 65 of the Crime and Disorder Act 1998 for a recordable offence, and

either of the conditions mentioned in subsection (6ZA) below is met.

(6ZA) The conditions referred to in subsection (6) above are–

(a) the person has not had his fingerprints taken since he was convicted, cautioned or warned or reprimanded;
(b) he has had his fingerprints taken since then but subsection (3A)(a) or (b) above applies.

(6ZB) Fingerprints may only be taken as specified in subsection (6) above with the authorisation of an officer of at least the rank of inspector.

(6ZC) An officer may only give an authorisation under subsection (6ZB) above if the officer is satisfied that taking the fingerprints is necessary to assist in the prevention or detection of crime.

(6A) A constable may take a person's fingerprints without the appropriate consent if—

(a) the constable reasonably suspects that the person is committing or attempting to commit an offence, or has committed or attempted to commit an offence; and
(b) either of the two conditions mentioned in subsection (6B) is met.

(6B) The conditions are that—

(a) the name of the person is unknown to, and cannot be readily ascertained by, the constable;
(b) the constable has reasonable grounds for doubting whether a name furnished by the person as his name is his real name.

(6C) The taking of fingerprints by virtue of subsection (6A) does not count for any of the purposes of this Act as taking them in the course of the investigation of an offence by the police.

(6D) Subject to this section, the fingerprints of a person may be taken without the appropriate consent if—

(a) under the law in force in a country or territory outside England and Wales the person has been convicted of an offence under that law (whether before or after the coming into force of this subsection and whether or not he has been punished for it);
(b) the act constituting the offence would constitute a qualifying offence if done in England and Wales (whether or not it constituted such an offence when the person was convicted); and
(c) either of the conditions mentioned in subsection (6E) below is met.

(6E) The conditions referred to in subsection (6D)(c) above are—

(a) the person has not had his fingerprints taken on a previous occasion under subsection (6D) above;

(b) he has had his fingerprints taken on a previous occasion under that subsection but subsection (3A)(a) or (b) above applies.

(6F) Fingerprints may only be taken as specified in subsection (6D) above with the authorisation of an officer of at least the rank of inspector.

(6G) An officer may only give an authorisation under subsection (6F) above if the officer is satisfied that taking the fingerprints is necessary to assist in the prevention or detection of crime.

(7) Where a person's fingerprints are taken without the appropriate consent by virtue of any power conferred by this section–

(a) before the fingerprints are taken, the person shall be informed of–
  (i) the reason for taking the fingerprints;
  (ii) the power by virtue of which they are taken; and
  (iii) in a case where the authorisation of the court or an officer is required for the exercise of the power, the fact that the authorisation has been given; and
(b) those matters shall be recorded as soon as practicable after the fingerprints are taken.

(7A) If a person's fingerprints are taken at a police station, or by virtue of subsection (4A), (6A) at a place other than a police station, whether with or without the appropriate consent—

(a) before the fingerprints are taken, an officer (or, where by virtue of subsection (4A), (6A) or (6BA) the fingerprints are taken at a place other than a police station, the constable taking the fingerprints) shall inform him that they may be the subject of a speculative search; and
(b) the fact that the person has been informed of this possibility shall be recorded as soon as is practicable after the fingerprints have been taken.

(8) If he is detained at a police station when the fingerprints are taken, the matters referred to in subsection (7)(a)(i) to (iii) above and, in the case falling within subsection (7A) above, the fact referred to in paragraph (b) of that subsection] shall be recorded on his custody record.

(8A) *(repealed)*

(8B) The power to take the fingerprints of a person detained at a police station without the appropriate consent shall be exercisable by any constable.

(9) Nothing in this section—

(a) affects any power conferred by paragraph 18(2) of Schedule 2 to the Immigration Act 1971; or
(b) applies to a person arrested or detained under the terrorism provisions.

(10) Nothing in this section applies to a person arrested under an extradition arrest power.

Amendments- Criminal Justice Act 2003, s 9(1), (2); Criminal Justice and Police Act 2001, s 78(3); Policing and Crime Act 2009, s 116(6)(a); Terrorism Act 2000, s 125(1), Sch 15, para 5(1), (7). Crime and Security Act 2010, ss 2(1)–(4), 3(1), 4(1)–(3).

62 Intimate samples

(1) Subject to section 63B below, an intimate sample may be taken from a person in police detention only—

- (a) if a police officer of at least the rank of inspector authorises it to be taken; and
- (b) if the appropriate consent is given.

(1A) An intimate sample may be taken from a person who is not in police detention but from whom, in the course of the investigation of an offence, two or more non-intimate samples suitable for the same means of analysis have been taken which have proved insufficient—

- (a) if a police officer of at least the rank of inspector authorises it to be taken; and
- (b) if the appropriate consent is given.

(2) An officer may only give an authorisation under subsection (1) or (1A) above if he has reasonable grounds—

- (a) for suspecting the involvement of the person from whom the sample is to be taken in a recordable offence; and
- (b) for believing that the sample will tend to confirm or disprove his involvement.

(2A) An intimate sample may be taken from a person where—

- (a) two or more non-intimate samples suitable for the same means of analysis have been taken from the person under section 63(3E) below (persons convicted of offences outside England and Wales etc) but have proved insufficient;
- (b) a police officer of at least the rank of inspector authorises it to be taken; and
- (c) the appropriate consent is given.

(2B) An officer may only give an authorisation under subsection (2A) above if the officer is satisfied that taking the sample is necessary to assist in the prevention or detection of crime.

(3) An officer may give an authorisation under subsection (1) or (1A) or (2A) above orally or in writing but, if he gives it orally, he shall confirm it in writing as soon as is practicable.

(4) The appropriate consent must be given in writing.

(5) Before an intimate sample is taken from a person, an officer shall inform him of the following—

- (a) the reason for taking the sample;

(b) the fact that authorisation has been given and the provision of this section under which it has been given; and
(c) if the sample was taken at a police station, the fact that the sample may be the subject of a speculative search.

(6) The reason referred to in subsection (5)(a) above must include, except in a case where the sample is taken under subsection (2A) above, a statement of the nature of the offence in which it is suspected that the person has been involved.

(7) After an intimate sample has been taken from a person, the following shall be recorded as soon as practicable—

(a) the matters referred to in subsection (5)(a) and (b) above;
(b) if the sample was taken at a police station, the fact that the person has been informed as specified in subsection (5)(c) above; and
(c) the fact that the appropriate consent was given.

(8) If an intimate sample is taken from a person detained at a police station, the matters required to be recorded by subsection (7) above shall be recorded in his custody record.

(9) In the case of an intimate sample which is a dental impression, the sample may be taken from a person only by a registered dentist.

(9A) In the case of any other form of intimate sample, except in the case of a sample of urine, the sample may be taken from a person only by–

(a) a registered medical practitioner; or
(b) a registered health care professional.

(10) Where the appropriate consent to the taking of an intimate sample from a person was refused without good cause, in any proceedings against that person for an offence—

(a) the court, in determining—
    (i) whether to commit that person for trial; or
    (ii) whether there is a case to answer; and
(aa) a judge, in deciding whether to grant an application made by the accused under—
    (i) section 6 of the Criminal Justice Act 1987 (application for dismissal of charge of serious fraud in respect of which notice of transfer has been given under section 4 of that Act); or
    (ii) paragraph 5 of Schedule 6 to the Criminal Justice Act 1991 (application for dismissal of charge of violent or sexual offence involving child in respect of which notice of transfer has been given under section 53 of that Act); and

paragraph 2 of Schedule 3 to the Crime and Disorder Act 1998 (applications for dismissal); and

(b) the court or jury, in determining whether that person is guilty of the offence charged,

may draw such inferences from the refusal as appear proper

(11) Nothing in this section applies to the taking of a specimen for the purposes of any of the provisions of sections 4 to 11 of the Road Traffic Act 1988 or of sections 26 to 38 of the Transport and Works Act 1992.

(12) Nothing in this section applies to a person arrested or detained under the terrorism provisions; and subsection (1A) shall not apply where the non-intimate samples mentioned in that subsection were taken under paragraph 10 of Schedule 8 to the Terrorism Act 2000.

Amendments-Criminal Justice and Public Order Act 1994, ss 54(2), 168(2), Sch 10, paras 57(a), 62(4)(a); Terrorism Act 2000, s 125(1), Sch 15, para 5(1), (8); Criminal Justice and Court Services Act 2000, s 74, Sch 7, Pt II, paras 76, 78; Criminal Justice and Police Act 2001, s 80(1); Police Reform Act 2002, s 53(2)(b); Road Traffic (Consequential Provisions) Act 1988, s 4, Sch 3, para 27.

63 Other samples

(1) Except as provided by this section, a non-intimate sample may not be taken from a person without the appropriate consent.

(2) Consent to the taking of a non-intimate sample must be given in writing.

(2A) A non-intimate sample may be taken from a person without the appropriate consent if two conditions are satisfied.

(2B) The first is that the person is in police detention in consequence of his arrest for a recordable offence.

(2C) The second is that—

- (a) he has not had a non-intimate sample of the same type and from the same part of the body taken in the course of the investigation of the offence by the police, or
- (b) he has had such a sample taken but it proved insufficient.

(3) A non-intimate sample may be taken from a person without the appropriate consent if—

- (a) he is being held in custody by the police on the authority of a court; and
- (b) an officer of at least the rank of inspector authorises it to be taken without the appropriate consent.

(3ZA) A non-intimate sample may be taken from a person without the appropriate consent if (before or after the coming into force of this subsection) he has been arrested for a recordable offence and released and—

- (a) in the case of a person who is on bail, he has not had a non-intimate sample of the same type and from the same part of the body taken from him in the course of the investigation of the offence by the police; or
- (b) in any case, he has had a non-intimate sample taken from him in the course of that investigation but–
  - (i) it was not suitable for the same means of analysis, or
  - (ii) it proved insufficient.

(3A) A non-intimate sample may be taken from a person (whether or not he is in police detention or held in custody by the police on the authority of a court) without the appropriate consent if he has been charged with a recordable offence or informed that he will be reported for such an offence and—

(a) he has not had a non-intimate sample taken from him in the course of the investigation of the offence by the police; or
(b) he has had a non-intimate sample taken from him in the course of that investigation but–
    (i) it was not suitable for the same means of analysis, or
    (ii) it proved insufficient; or
(c) he has had a non-intimate sample taken from him in the course of that investigation and–
    (i) the sample has been destroyed pursuant to section 64ZA below or any other enactment, and
    (ii) it is disputed, in relation to any proceedings relating to the offence, whether a DNA profile relevant to the proceedings is derived from the sample.

(3B) Subject to this section, a non-intimate sample may be taken from a person without the appropriate consent if (before or after the coming into force of this subsection)—

(a) he has been convicted of a recordable offence,
(b) he has been given a caution in respect of a recordable offence which, at the time of the caution, he has admitted, or
(c) he has been warned or reprimanded under section 65 of the Crime and Disorder Act 1998 for a recordable offence, and

either of the conditions mentioned in subsection (3BA) below is met.

(3BA) The conditions referred to in subsection (3B) above are—

(a) a non-intimate sample has not been taken from the person since he was convicted, cautioned or warned or reprimanded;
(b) such a sample has been taken from him since then but–
    (i) it was not suitable for the same means of analysis, or
    (ii) it proved insufficient.

(3BB) A non-intimate sample may only be taken as specified in subsection (3B) above with the authorisation of an officer of at least the rank of inspector.

(3BC) An officer may only give an authorisation under subsection (3BB) above if the officer is satisfied that taking the sample is necessary to assist in the prevention or detection of crime.

(3C) A non-intimate sample may also be taken from a person without the appropriate consent if he is a person to whom section 2 of the Criminal Evidence (Amendment) Act 1997 applies (persons detained following acquittal on grounds of insanity or finding of unfitness to plead).

(a) under the law in force in a country or territory outside England and Wales the person has been convicted of an offence under that law (whether before or after the coming into force of this subsection and whether or not he has been punished for it);

(b) the act constituting the offence would constitute a qualifying offence if done in England and Wales (whether or not it constituted such an offence when the person was convicted); and

(c) either of the conditions mentioned in subsection (3F) below is met.

(3E) Subject to this section, a non-intimate sample may be taken without the appropriate consent from a person if—

(a) under the law in force in a country or territory outside England and Wales the person has been convicted of an offence under that law (whether before or after the coming into force of this subsection and whether or not he has been punished for it);

(b) the act constituting the offence would constitute a qualifying offence if done in England and Wales (whether or not it constituted such an offence when the person was convicted); and

(c) either of the conditions mentioned in subsection (3F) below is met.

(3F) The conditions referred to in subsection (3E)(c) above are—

(a) the person has not had a non-intimate sample taken from him on a previous occasion under subsection (3E) above;

(b) he has had such a sample taken from him on a previous occasion under that subsection but–

(i) the sample was not suitable for the same means of analysis, or

(ii) it proved insufficient.

(3G) A non-intimate sample may only be taken as specified in subsection (3E) above with the authorisation of an officer of at least the rank of inspector.

(3H) An officer may only give an authorisation under subsection (3G) above if the officer is satisfied that taking the sample is necessary to assist in the prevention or detection of crime.

(4) An officer may only give an authorisation under subsection (3) above if he has reasonable grounds—

(a) for suspecting the involvement of the person from whom the sample is to be taken in a recordable offence; and

(b) for believing that the sample will tend to confirm or disprove his involvement.

(5) An officer may give an authorisation under subsection (3) above orally or in writing but, if he gives it orally, he shall confirm it in writing as soon as is practicable.

(5A) An officer shall not give an authorisation under subsection (3) above for the taking from any person of a non-intimate sample consisting of a skin impression if—

(a) a skin impression of the same part of the body has already been taken from that person in the course of the investigation of the offence; and

(b) the impression previously taken is not one that has proved insufficient.

(6) Where a non-intimate sample is taken from a person without the appropriate consent by virtue of any power conferred by this section–

(a) before the sample is taken, an officer shall inform him of–
  (i) the reason for taking the sample;
  (ii) the power by virtue of which it is taken; and
  (iii) in a case where the authorisation of an officer is required for the exercise of the power, the fact that the authorisation has been given; and
(b) those matters shall be recorded as soon as practicable after the sample is taken.

(7) The reason referred to in subsection (6)(a)(i) above must include, except in a case where the non-intimate sample is taken under subsection (3B) or (3E) above, a statement of the nature of the offence in which it is suspected that the person has been involved.

(8) (*repealed*)

(8A) (*repealed*)

(8B) If a non-intimate sample is taken from a person at a police station, whether with or without the appropriate consent—

(a) before the sample is taken, an officer shall inform him that it may be the subject of a speculative search; and
(b) the fact that the person has been informed of this possibility shall be recorded as soon as practicable after the sample has been taken.

(9) If a non-intimate sample is taken from a person detained at a police station, the matters required to be recorded by subsection (6) or (8B) above shall be recorded in his custody record.

(9ZA) The power to take a non-intimate sample from a person without the appropriate consent shall be exercisable by any constable.

(9A) Subsection (3B) above shall not apply to—

(a) any person convicted before 10th April 1995 unless he is a person to whom section 1 of the Criminal Evidence (Amendment) Act 1997 applies (persons imprisoned or detained by virtue of pre-existing conviction for sexual offence etc)[; or
(b) a person given a caution before 10th April 1995.

(10) Nothing in this section applies to a person arrested or detained under the terrorism provisions.

(11) Nothing in this section applies to a person arrested under an extradition arrest power.

Amendments-Criminal Justice and Public Order Act 1994, s 168(2), Sch 10, para 62(4)(b); Extradition Act 2003, s 169(1), (4); Criminal Justice Act 2003, s 10(1), (2); Policing and Crime Act 2009, s 116(6)(a); Criminal Justice and Police Act 2001, s 80(1); Crime and Security Act 2010, ss 2(5)-(8), 3(4), 4(7)-(8).

63A Fingerprints and samples: supplementary provisions

(1) Where a person has been arrested on suspicion of being involved in a recordable offence or has been charged with such an offence or has been informed that he will be reported for such an offence, fingerprints, impressions of footwear or samples or the information derived from samples taken under any power conferred by this Part of this Act from the person may be checked against—

(a) other fingerprints, impressions of footwear or samples to which the person seeking to check has access and which are held by or on behalf of any one or more relevant law-enforcement authorities or which are held in connection with or as a result of an investigation of an offence;
(b) information derived from other samples if the information is contained in records to which the person seeking to check has access and which are held as mentioned in paragraph (a) above

(1ZA) Fingerprints taken by virtue of section 61(6A) above may be checked against other fingerprints to which the person seeking to check has access and which are held by or on behalf of any one or more relevant law-enforcement authorities or which are held in connection with or as a result of an investigation of an offence.

(1A) In subsection (1) and (1ZA) above "relevant law-enforcement authority" means—

(a) a police force;
(b) the Serious Organised Crime Agency;
(d) a public authority (not falling within paragraphs (a) to (c)) with functions in any part of the British Islands which consist of or include the investigation of crimes or the charging of offenders;
(e) any person with functions in any country or territory outside the United Kingdom which—
 (i) correspond to those of a police force; or
 (ii) otherwise consist of or include the investigation of conduct contrary to the law of that country or territory, or the apprehension of persons guilty of such conduct;
(f) any person with functions under any international agreement which consist of or include the investigation of conduct which is—
 (i) unlawful under the law of one or more places,
 (ii) prohibited by such an agreement, or
 (iii) contrary to international law,

or the apprehension of persons guilty of such conduct.

(1B) The reference in subsection (1A) above to a police force is a reference to any of the following—

(a) any police force maintained under section 2 of the Police Act 1996 (c 16) (police forces in England and Wales outside London);
(b) the metropolitan police force;
(c) the City of London police force;

(d) any police force maintained under or by virtue of section 1 of the Police (Scotland) Act 1967 (c 77);
(e) the Police Service of Northern Ireland;
(f) the Police Service of Northern Ireland Reserve;
(g) the Ministry of Defence Police;
(h) the Royal Navy Police;
(i) the Royal Military Police;
(j) the Royal Air Force Police;
(k) (*repealed*)
(l) the British Transport Police;
(m) the States of Jersey Police Force;
(n) the salaried police force of the Island of Guernsey;
(o) the Isle of Man Constabulary.

(1C) Where—

(a) fingerprints, impressions of footwear or samples have been taken from any person in connection with the investigation of an offence but otherwise than in circumstances to which subsection (1) above applies, and
(b) that person has given his consent in writing to the use in a speculative search of the fingerprints, of the impressions of footwear or of the samples and of information derived from them,

the fingerprints or impressions of footwear or, as the case may be, those samples and that information may be checked against any of the fingerprints[, impressions of footwear], samples or information mentioned in paragraph (a) or (b) of that subsection.

(1D) A consent given for the purposes of subsection (1C) above shall not be capable of being withdrawn.

(1E) Where fingerprints or samples have been taken from any person under section 61(6) or 63(3B) above (persons convicted etc), the fingerprints or samples, or information derived from the samples, may be checked against any of the fingerprints, samples or information mentioned in subsection (1)(a) or (b) above.

(1F) Where fingerprints or samples have been taken from any person under section 61(6D), 62(2A) or 63(3E) above (offences outside England and Wales etc), the fingerprints or samples, or information derived from the samples, may be checked against any of the fingerprints, samples or information mentioned in subsection (1)(a) or (b) above.

(2) Where a sample of hair other than pubic hair is to be taken the sample may be taken either by cutting hairs or by plucking hairs with their roots so long as no more are plucked than the person taking the sample reasonably considers to be necessary for a sufficient sample.

(3) Where any power to take a sample is exercisable in relation to a person the sample may be taken in a prison or other institution to which the Prison Act 1952 applies.

(3A) Where—

(a) the power to take a non-intimate sample under section 63(3B) above is exercisable in relation to any person who is detained under Part III of the Mental Health Act 1983 in pursuance of—
    (i) a hospital order or interim hospital order made following his conviction for the recordable offence in question, or
    (ii) a transfer direction given at a time when he was detained in pursuance of any sentence or order imposed following that conviction, or

(b) the power to take a non-intimate sample under section 63(3C) above is exercisable in relation to any person,

the sample may be taken in the hospital in which he is detained under that Part of that Act.

Expressions used in this subsection and in the Mental Health Act 1983 have the same meaning as in that Act.

(3B) Where the power to take a non-intimate sample under section 63(3B) above is exercisable in relation to a person detained in pursuance of directions of the Secretary of State under section 92 of the Powers of Criminal Courts (Sentencing) Act 2000 the sample may be taken at the place where he is so detained.

(4) Schedule 2A (fingerprinting and samples: power to require attendance at police station) shall have effect.

(5) (*repealed*)

(6) (*repealed*)

(7) (*repealed*)

(8) (*repealed*)

Amendments-Criminal Justice and Public Order Act 1994, s 56; Criminal Evidence (Amendment) Act 1997, s 4; Powers of Criminal Courts (Sentencing) Act 2000, s 165(1), Sch 9, para 97; Serious Organised Crime and Police Act 2005, s 118(1), (3)(b)(iv), s59, s117 (5) (a), (b); Armed Forces Act 2006, s 378, Sch 16, para 100(b), Sch 17; Criminal Justice and Police Act 2001, s 81(2); Crime and Security Act 2010, ss 5(1), 6(1).

64 Destruction of fingerprints and samples

(1A) Where—

(a) fingerprints, impressions of footwear or samples are taken from a person in connection with the investigation of an offence, and

(b) subsection (3) below does not require them to be destroyed,

the fingerprints, impressions of footwear or samples may be retained after they have fulfilled the purposes for which they were taken but shall not be used by any person except for purposes related to the prevention or detection of crime, the investigation of an offence, the conduct of a prosecution or the identification of a deceased person or of the person from whom a body part came .

(1B) In subsection (1A) above—

- (a) the reference to using a fingerprint or an impression of footwear includes a reference to allowing any check to be made against it under section 63A(1) or (1C) above and to disclosing it to any person;
- (b) the reference to using a sample includes a reference to allowing any check to be made under section 63A(1) or (1C) above against it or against information derived from it and to disclosing it or any such information to any person;
- (c) the reference to crime includes a reference to any conduct which—
  - (i) constitutes one or more criminal offences (whether under the law of a part of the United Kingdom or of a country or territory outside the United Kingdom); or
  - (ii) is, or corresponds to, any conduct which, if it all took place in any one part of the United Kingdom, would constitute one or more criminal offences;

and

- (d) the references to an investigation and to a prosecution include references, respectively, to any investigation outside the United Kingdom of any crime or suspected crime and to a prosecution brought in respect of any crime in a country or territory outside the United Kingdom.

(1BA) Fingerprints taken from a person by virtue of section 61(6A) above must be destroyed as soon as they have fulfilled the purpose for which they were taken.

(3) If—

- (a) fingerprints , impressions of footwear or samples are taken from a person in connection with the investigation of an offence; and
- (b) that person is not suspected of having committed the offence,

they must, except as provided in the following provisions of this section, be destroyed as soon as they have fulfilled the purpose for which they were taken.

(3AA) Samples, fingerprints and impressions of footwear are not required to be destroyed under subsection (3) above if—

- (a) they were taken for the purposes of the investigation of an offence of which a person has been convicted; and
- (b) a sample, fingerprint, (or as the case may be) an impression of footwear was also taken from the convicted person for the purposes of that investigation.

(3AB) Subject to subsection (3AC) below, where a person is entitled under subsection (1BA) or (3) above to the destruction of any fingerprint , impression of footwear or sample taken from him (or would be but for subsection (3AA) above), neither the fingerprint , nor the impression of footwear, nor the sample, nor any information derived from the sample, shall be used—

(a) in evidence against the person who is or would be entitled to the destruction of that fingerprint , impression of footwear or sample; or
(b) for the purposes of the investigation of any offence;

and subsection (1B) above applies for the purposes of this subsection as it applies for the purposes of subsection (1A) above.

(3AC) Where a person from whom a fingerprint , impression of footwear or sample has been taken consents in writing to its retention—

(a) that fingerprint, impression of footwear or sample need not be destroyed under subsection (3) above;
(b) subsection (3AB) above shall not restrict the use that may be made of the fingerprint , impression of footwear or sample or, in the case of a sample, of any information derived from it; and
(c) that consent shall be treated as comprising a consent for the purposes of section 63A(1C) above;

and a consent given for the purpose of this subsection shall not be capable of being withdrawn.

This subsection does not apply to fingerprints taken from a person by virtue of section 61(6A) above.

(3AD) For the purposes of subsection (3AC) above it shall be immaterial whether the consent is given at, before or after the time when the entitlement to the destruction of the fingerprint , impression of footwear or sample arises.

(4) (*repealed*)

(5) If fingerprints or impressions of footwear are destroyed—

(a) any copies of the fingerprints or impressions of footwear shall also be destroyed; and
(b) any chief officer of police controlling access to computer data relating to the fingerprints or impressions of footwear shall make access to the data impossible, as soon as it is practicable to do so.

(6) A person who asks to be allowed to witness the destruction of his fingerprints or impressions of footwear or copies of them shall have a right to witness it.

(6A) If—

(a) subsection (5)(b) above falls to be complied with; and
(b) the person to whose fingerprints or impressions of footwear the data relate asks for a certificate that it has been complied with,

such a certificate shall be issued to him, not later than the end of the period of three months beginning with the day on which he asks for it, by the responsible chief officer of police or a person authorised by him or on his behalf for the purposes of this section.

(6B) In this section—

"the responsible chief officer of police" means the chief officer of police in whose [police] area the computer data were put on to the computer.

(7) Nothing in this section—

- (a) affects any power conferred by paragraph 18(2) of Schedule 2 to the Immigration Act 1971 or section 20 of the Immigration and Asylum Act 1999 (c 33) (disclosure of police information to the Secretary of State for use for immigration purposes); or
- (b) applies to a person arrested or detained under the terrorism provisions.

Amendments-Criminal Justice and Police Act 2001, s 82(1), (2), (6); Serious Organised Crime and Police Act 2005, s 118(1), (4)(a); Serious Organised Crime and Police Act 2005, ss 117(6)-(9), (10)(a), (b), 118(1), (4)(b); Criminal Justice and Public Order Act 1994, s 57(2); Criminal Justice and Police Act 2001, s 82(1), (3); Sub-sections (3AA)–(3AD): substituted, for sub-sections (3A), (3B) (as inserted by the Criminal Justice and Public Order Act 1994, s 57(3)), by the Criminal Justice and Police Act 2001, s 82(1), (4), (6).

64A Photographing of suspects etc

(1) A person who is detained at a police station may be photographed—

- (a) with the appropriate consent; or
- (b) if the appropriate consent is withheld or it is not practicable to obtain it, without it.

(1A) A person falling within subsection (1B) below may, on the occasion of the relevant event referred to in subsection (1B), be photographed elsewhere than at a police station—

- (a) with the appropriate consent; or
- (b) if the appropriate consent is withheld or it is not practicable to obtain it, without it.

(1B) A person falls within this subsection if he has been—

- (a) arrested by a constable for an offence;
- (b) taken into custody by a constable after being arrested for an offence by a person other than a constable;
- (c) made subject to a requirement to wait with a community support officer under paragraph 2(3) or (3B) of Schedule 4 to the Police Reform Act 2002 ("the 2002 Act");
- (ca) given a direction by a constable under section 27 of the Violent Crime Reduction Act 2006;
- (d) given a penalty notice by a constable in uniform under Chapter 1 of Part 1 of the Criminal Justice and Police Act 2001, a penalty notice by a constable under section 444A of the Education Act 1996, or a fixed penalty notice by a constable in uniform under section 54 of the Road Traffic Offenders Act 1988;

(e) given a notice in relation to a relevant fixed penalty offence (within the meaning of paragraph 1 of Schedule 4 to the 2002 Act) by a community support officer by virtue of a designation applying that paragraph to him;

(f) given a notice in relation to a relevant fixed penalty offence (within the meaning of paragraph 1 of Schedule 5 to the 2002 Act) by an accredited person by virtue of accreditation specifying that that paragraph applies to him; or

(g) given a notice in relation to a relevant fixed penalty offence (within the meaning of Schedule 5A to the 2002 Act) by an accredited inspector by virtue of accreditation specifying that paragraph 1 of Schedule 5A to the 2002 Act applies to him.

(2) A person proposing to take a photograph of any person under this section—

(a) may, for the purpose of doing so, require the removal of any item or substance worn on or over the whole or any part of the head or face of the person to be photographed; and

(b) if the requirement is not complied with, may remove the item or substance himself.

(3) Where a photograph may be taken under this section, the only persons entitled to take the photograph are constables.

(4) A photograph taken under this section—

(a) may be used by, or disclosed to, any person for any purpose related to the prevention or detection of crime, the investigation of an offence or the conduct of a prosecution or to the enforcement of a sentence; and

(b) after being so used or disclosed, may be retained but may not be used or disclosed except for a purpose so related.

(5) In subsection (4)—

(a) the reference to crime includes a reference to any conduct which—

 (i) constitutes one or more criminal offences (whether under the law of a part of the United Kingdom or of a country or territory outside the United Kingdom); or

 (ii) is, or corresponds to, any conduct which, if it all took place in any one part of the United Kingdom, would constitute one or more criminal offences;

and

(b) the references to an investigation and to a prosecution include references, respectively, to any investigation outside the United Kingdom of any crime or suspected crime and to a prosecution brought in respect of any crime in a country or territory outside the United Kingdom; and

(c) "sentence" includes any order made by a court in England and Wales when dealing with an offender in respect of his offence.

(6) References in this section to taking a photograph include references to using any process by means of which a visual image may be produced; and references to photographing a person shall be construed accordingly.

(6A) In this section, a "photograph" includes a moving image, and corresponding expressions shall be construed accordingly.

(7) Nothing in this section applies to a person arrested under an extradition arrest power.

Amendments-Anti-terrorism, Crime and Security Act 2001, s 92; Police Reform Act 2002, s 107(1), Sch 7, para 9(5); Extradition Act 2003, s 169(1), (5); Serious Organised Crime and Police Act 2005, s 116(1), (5); Police and Justice Act 2006, s 52, Sch 14, para 11; Violent Crime Reduction Act 2006, s 27(7).

65 Part V—supplementary

(1) In this Part of this Act—

'analysis', in relation to a skin impression, includes comparison and matching;

'appropriate consent' means—

(a) in relation to a person who has attained the age of 17 years, the consent of that person;
(b) in relation to a person who has not attained that age but has attained the age of 14 years, the consent of that person and his parent or guardian; and
(c) in relation to a person who has not attained the age of 14 years, the consent of his parent or guardian;

'extradition arrest power' means any of the following–

(a) a Part 1 warrant (within the meaning given by the Extradition Act 2003) in respect of which a certificate under section 2 of that Act has been issued;
(b) section 5 of that Act;
(c) a warrant issued under section 71 of that Act;
(d) a provisional warrant (within the meaning given by that Act);

'fingerprints', in relation to any person, means a record (in any form and produced by any method) of the skin pattern and other physical characteristics or features of–

(a) any of that person's fingers; or
(b) either of his palms;

'intimate sample' means–

(a) a sample of blood, semen or any other tissue fluid, urine or pubic hair;
(b) a dental impression;
(c) a swab taken from any part of a person's genitals (including pubic hair) or from a person's body orifice other than the mouth;

'intimate search' means a search which consists of the physical examination of a person's body orifices other than the mouth;

'non-intimate sample' means–

(a) a sample of hair other than pubic hair;
(b) a sample taken from a nail or from under a nail;
(c) a swab taken from any part of a person's body other than a part from which a swab taken would be an intimate sample;
(d) saliva;
(e) a skin impression;

'offence', in relation to any country or territory outside England and Wales, includes an act punishable under the law of that country or territory, however it is described;

'registered dentist' has the same meaning as in the Dentists Act 1984;

'registered health care professional' means a person (other than a medical practitioner) who is–

(a) a registered nurse; or
(b) a registered member of a health care profession which is designated for the purposes of this paragraph by an order made by the Secretary of State;

'skin impression', in relation to any person, means any record (other than a fingerprint) which is a record (in any form and produced by any method) of the skin pattern and other physical characteristics or features of the whole or any part of his foot or of any other part of his body;

'speculative search', in relation to a person's fingerprints or samples, means such a check against other fingerprints or samples or against information derived from other samples as is referred to in section 63A(1) above;

'sufficient' and 'insufficient', in relation to a sample, means [(subject to subsection (2) below) sufficient or insufficient (in point of quantity or quality) for the purpose of enabling information to be produced by the means of analysis used or to be used in relation to the sample;

'the terrorism provisions' means section 41 of the Terrorism Act 2000, and any provision of Schedule 7 to that Act conferring a power of detention; and

'terrorism' has the meaning given in section 1 of that Act;

(1A) A health care profession is any profession mentioned in section 60(2) of the Health Act 1999 (c 8) other than the profession of practising medicine and the profession of nursing.

(1B) An order under subsection (1) shall be made by statutory instrument and shall be subject to annulment in pursuance of a resolution of either House of Parliament.

(2) References in this Part of this Act to a sample's proving insufficient include references to where, as a consequence of—

(a) the loss, destruction or contamination of the whole or any part of the sample,

(b) any damage to the whole or a part of the sample, or
(c) the use of the whole or a part of the sample for an analysis which produced no results or which produced results some or all of which must be regarded, in the circumstances, as unreliable,

the sample has become unavailable or insufficient for the purpose of enabling information, or information of a particular description, to be obtained by means of analysis of the sample.

(3) For the purposes of this Part, a person has in particular been convicted of an offence under the law of a country or territory outside England and Wales if—

(a) a court exercising jurisdiction under the law of that country or territory has made in respect of such an offence a finding equivalent to a finding that the person is not guilty by reason of insanity; or
(b) such a court has made in respect of such an offence a finding equivalent to a finding that the person is under a disability and did the act charged against him in respect of the offence.

Amendments-Criminal Justice and Police Act 2001, s 80(5); Drug Trafficking Offences Act 1986, s 32(3); Proceeds of Crime Act 2002, s 457, Sch 12; Extradition Act 2003, s 169(1), (6); Criminal Justice and Police Act 2001, s 78(8); Criminal Justice and Public Order Act 1994, s 58(1), (2); Serious Organised Crime and Police Act 2005, s 119(1), (3) (54) (3); Criminal Justice and Public Order Act 1994, s 58(1), (4); Police Reform Act 2002, s 54(2); Terrorism Act 2000, s 125(1), Sch 15, para 5(1), (10); Crime and Security Act 2010, s 3(5), (6).

65A Qualifying offence

(1) In this Part, 'qualifying offence' means—

(a) an offence specified in subsection (2) below, or
(b) an ancillary offence relating to such an offence.

(2) The offences referred to in subsection (1)(a) above are—

(a) murder;
(b) manslaughter;
(c) false imprisonment;
(d) kidnapping;
(e) an offence under section 4, 16, 18, 20 to 24 or 47 of the Offences Against the Person Act 1861;
(f) an offence under section 2 or 3 of the Explosive Substances Act 1883;
(g) an offence under section 1 of the Children and Young Persons Act 1933;
(h) an offence under section 4(1) of the Criminal Law Act 1967 committed in relation to murder;
(i) an offence under sections 16 to 18 of the Firearms Act 1968;
(j) an offence under section 9 or 10 of the Theft Act 1968 or an offence under section 12A of that Act involving an accident which caused a person's death;
(k) an offence under section 1 of the Criminal Damage Act 1971 required to be charged as arson;

(l) an offence under section 1 of the Protection of Children Act 1978;
(m) an offence under section 1 of the Aviation Security Act 1982;
(n) an offence under section 2 of the Child Abduction Act 1984;
(o) an offence under section 9 of the Aviation and Maritime Security Act 1990;
(p) an offence under any of sections 1 to 19, 25, 26, 30 to 41, 47 to 50, 52, 53, 57 to 59, 61 to 67, 69 and 70 of the Sexual Offences Act 2003;
(q) an offence under section 5 of the Domestic Violence, Crime and Victims Act 2004;
(r) an offence for the time being listed in section 41(1) of the Counter-Terrorism Act 2008.

(3) The Secretary of State may by order made by statutory instrument amend subsection (2) above.

(4) A statutory instrument containing an order under subsection (3) above shall not be made unless a draft of the instrument has been laid before, and approved by resolution of, each House of Parliament.

(5) In subsection (1)(b) above 'ancillary offence', in relation to an offence, means—

(a) aiding, abetting, counselling or procuring the commission of the offence;
(b) an offence under Part 2 of the Serious Crime Act 2007 (encouraging or assisting crime) in relation to the offence (including, in relation to times before the commencement of that Part, an offence of incitement);
(c) attempting or conspiring to commit the offence.

Amendment–Inserted by the Crime and Security Act 2010, s 7.

Appendix E

ADVICE ON THE USE OF VOICE IDENTIFICATION PARADES (HOME OFFICE CIRCULAR 57/2003)

1. Further consideration has been given to the scope for developing voice identification procedures for use by police forces in England & Wales. Currently, Code D, paragraph 1.2, of the Codes of Practice under the Police & Criminal Evidence Act (PACE) 1984 allows for such procedures to be used, but does not specify which procedures must be followed.

2. This work to develop reliable procedures for voice identification, which may ultimately go forward for inclusion in Code D of the PACE Codes of Practice is on-going in consultation with relevant stakeholders. However, as there will continue to be cases from time to time where the police may wish to use such procedures, this Circular seeks to offer advice to forces through an example of good practice.

3. The procedures set out below for establishing a voice identification parade and generating admissible evidence were devised by DS McFarlane (Metropolitan Police) in order to bring a case to the Central Criminal Court in December 2002 (*R v. Khan & Bains*). The case was successful and both men were convicted, in small part, due to the voice identification evidence submitted, which was in turn commended by the trial Judge.

4. The Home Secretary has agreed that slightly amended procedures can be promulgated to forces, as an example of good practice, which have been tried and tested in the Courts and can be safely applied in similar, relevant circumstances.

5. The purpose of this Circular therefore, is to offer forces an example of good practice for advice and guidance. The procedures set out here are not mandatory, but it is recommended they be followed closely, as appropriate in the circumstances, where a voice identification parade is to be held by the force.

PREPARATION OF MATERIAL

6. The identification officer in charge should obtain a detailed statement from the witness. This should contain as much detail and description of the voice as is possible (and should follow the guidelines handed down in *R v TURNBULL 1977)*. All descriptions of the voice given by the witness must be included in the

material supplied to the relevant forensic phonetics/linguistics expert. The statement and any 'first description' of the suspect's voice should also be the subject of disclosure to the suspect/solicitor prior to any identification procedure.

7. Under no circumstances should an attempt be made to conduct a live voice identification procedure, using live suspect and foils.

8. The identification officer should obtain a representative sample of the suspect's voice. A suitable source may be the police recorded interview tapes, during which the suspect is speaking naturally, responding to questions (although experts have advised the voice can be affected by stress). The suspect should be informed at the beginning of the interview that a sample of their recorded interview may be used for identification purposes and asked to give their consent. Experts in the field state clearly that under no circumstances should the suspect be invited to read any set text, as the speech/rhythm/tone may be unnatural and may well be altered by a person reading aloud from prescribed written material.

9. The identification officer should obtain no less than 20 samples of speech, from persons of similar age and ethnic, regional and social background as the suspect. A suitable source of such material may be other police recorded interview tapes from unconnected cases, either in-force or from other appropriate forces, e.g. where there is a strong regional accent.

10. The identification officer should ensure that all the work can be undertaken and completed within a reasonable time. It is advised that these procedures should be undertaken within 4-6 weeks of the incident in question, as memory degradation or 'fade' on the part of the witness has been identified as a critical factor by experts in the field.

11. The identification officer should request the services of a force approved expert witness in phonetics/ linguistics, for example, a Member of the International Association of Forensic Phonetics, to ensure the final selection and compilation of sample voices and match with the suspect's is as accurate and balanced as possible.

EXPERT WITNESS

12. The tape containing the sample of the suspect's voice, together with the batch of 'similar voices' tapes should be passed to the commissioned expert witness. The identification officer should ensure that the suspect's tape is clearly marked as such. The remaining tapes should be marked, with the surname or custody reference number of the individual/ case concerned.

13. The expert should be commissioned to take selected samples of speech from the batch of tape sources. These should each be about one minute long, and

may comprise various fragments of speech and/or continuous speech. It is irrelevant that each sample will contain different words or topics. A total of nine samples should be selected (i.e. the suspect's plus 8 others).

14. These 9 speech samples should be recorded onto three video cassettes, each of which should have the samples in a different, random order. The samples should be numbered, with a visual (video) display of the number to accompany the sample. The identification officer must prepare an index for each video, detailing the name/reference of each sample and the allocated number. The three videos prepared should clearly be marked A, B and C. The reference number for each sample must be displayed on screen throughout the playing time of that particular sample. Each tape should contain three cycles of the samples.

15. The identification officer is responsible for ensuring, as far as is reasonable, that there is nothing within the selected samples which would lead to the identification of any individual or the offence which they were being questioned about. Each of the eight foil samples must be examined to ensure that the accent, inflection, pitch, tone and speed of the speech used, provides a fair example for comparison against the suspect.[1]

16. It is strongly advised that the expert and identification officer conduct a number of test hearings, utilising mock witnesses, who are neither police officers nor connected with the suspect, where possible. These individuals should be given a brief resumé of the case. They should then be asked to listen to the series of samples under controlled conditions and asked to try and pick out the suspect for the offence (which they will only be able to do on a random basis or if there is a bias).

17. A further examination of all the samples against the results of the tests should be made to ensure that:

i. There is nothing contained in the words spoken, which would lead to an unfair assumption that one or other of the samples was that of the suspect;

ii. There is nothing in the manner of the speech, which would lead to an unfair assumption that one or other of the samples was that of the suspect.

18. These test results should form part of the evidence offered by the expert witness, demonstrating the objectivity of the procedures and the careful, balanced manner in which the procedures have been carried out.

---

[1] However, it should be noted that these procedures do not offer any opportunity for the suspect to review/reject any of the foil samples – but ref. Paragraphs 22 and 23.

19. The nine selected sample audio tapes should be sealed in one bag whilst the indices, placed in an envelope, should be placed in a separate sealed bag. Each bag must be signed and dated and an expert witness statement prepared, detailing the work undertaken in relation to the preparation of the material. The expert must present all the completed material, in sealed bags to the identification officer.

20. On completion of the preparation of the three sample video tapes and related indices, these must be sealed in police evidence bags by the commissioned expert carrying out the work.

21. The identification officer is responsible for the security and integrity of the material throughout the identification procedure process.

CONDUCT OF AUDIO/VOICE PROCEDURE

22. The suspect's solicitor must be given the opportunity to be present when the voice identification procedure is conducted. The seal on the bag of tapes must only be broken in the presence of the solicitor, if present, and the witness and the identification officer.

23. The identification procedure should be videotaped and the suspect given the opportunity to review at a suitable time after the procedure has taken place.

24. The solicitor should be given the opportunity to select the sample tape to be played (i.e. A, B or C). Throughout the process only the clearly marked identification letter will be used to refer to the samples.

25. The witness must be instructed by the identification officer that the voice of the suspect may, or may not be on one of the samples played during the procedure. The witness must be instructed to listen to each tape at least once before he/she makes a selection. The witness must be allowed to listen to any or all the samples as many times as they wish.

26. The identification officer must make a complete record of any comments or selections made by the witness.

27. Following the procedure a statement must be taken from the witness, recording the events and their selection. Once the witness has left the room the procedures were conducted in, the videotape should be left in the VCR machine/running. The identification officer should only then open the sealed bag and envelope, containing the index relating to the tapes and allow the solicitor the opportunity to record the details shown.

28. All materials relating to the procedure should be retained by the identification officer, for use in court.

These procedures are based upon procedures conceived originally by Detective Sergeant John McFarlane, Metropolitan Police Service, and are extended to all forces in England & Wales as an example of good practice, which has been tested and commended in court (Central Criminal Court, December 2002).

PLPU

Home Office

December 2003

Appendix F

CRIMINAL JUSTICE ACT 2003

PART 11
EVIDENCE

Chapter 1
Evidence of Bad Character

Introductory

98 Bad character

References in this Chapter to evidence of a person's "bad character" are to evidence of, or of a disposition towards, misconduct on his part, other than evidence which –

(a) has to do with the alleged facts of the offence with which the defendant is charged, or
(b) is evidence of misconduct in connection with the investigation or prosecution of that offence.

99 Abolition of common law rules

(1) The common law rules governing the admissibility of evidence of bad character in criminal proceedings are abolished.

(2) Subsection (1) is subject to section 118(1) in so far as it preserves the rule under which in criminal proceedings a person's reputation is admissible for the purposes of proving his bad character.

Persons other than defendants

100 Non-defendant's bad character

(1) In criminal proceedings evidence of the bad character of a person other than the defendant is admissible if and only if –

(a) it is important explanatory evidence,
(b) it has substantial probative value in relation to a matter which –
   (i) is a matter in issue in the proceedings, and
   (ii) is of substantial importance in the context of the case as a whole, or
(c) all parties to the proceedings agree to the evidence being admissible.

(2) For the purposes of subsection (1)(a) evidence is important explanatory evidence if –

(a) without it, the court or jury would find it impossible or difficult properly to understand other evidence in the case, and
(b) its value for understanding the case as a whole is substantial.

(3) In assessing the probative value of evidence for the purposes of subsection (1)(b) the court must have regard to the following factors (and to any others it considers relevant) –

(a) the nature and number of the events, or other things, to which the evidence relates;
(b) when those events or things are alleged to have happened or existed;
(c) where –
 (i) the evidence is evidence of a person's misconduct, and
 (ii) it is suggested that the evidence has probative value by reason of similarity between that misconduct and other alleged misconduct,

 the nature and extent of the similarities and the dissimilarities between each of the alleged instances of misconduct;
(d) where –
 (i) the evidence is evidence of a person's misconduct,
 (ii) it is suggested that that person is also responsible for the misconduct charged, and
 (iii) the identity of the person responsible for the misconduct charged is disputed,

 the extent to which the evidence shows or tends to show that the same person was responsible each time.

(4) Except where subsection (1)(c) applies, evidence of the bad character of a person other than the defendant must not be given without leave of the court.

Defendants

101 Defendant's bad character

(1) In criminal proceedings evidence of the defendant's bad character is admissible if, but only if –

(a) all parties to the proceedings agree to the evidence being admissible,
(b) the evidence is adduced by the defendant himself or is given in answer to a question asked by him in cross-examination and intended to elicit it,
(c) it is important explanatory evidence,
(d) it is relevant to an important matter in issue between the defendant and the prosecution,
(e) it has substantial probative value in relation to an important matter in issue between the defendant and a co-defendant,
(f) it is evidence to correct a false impression given by the defendant, or
(g) the defendant has made an attack on another person's character.

(2) Sections 102 to 106 contain provision supplementing subsection (1).

(3) The court must not admit evidence under subsection (1)(d) or (g) if, on an application by the defendant to exclude it, it appears to the court that the admission of the evidence would have such an adverse effect on the fairness of the proceedings that the court ought not to admit it.

(4) On an application to exclude evidence under subsection (3) the court must have regard, in particular, to the length of time between the matters to which that evidence relates and the matters which form the subject of the offence charged.

102 Important explanatory evidence

For the purposes of section 101(1)(c) evidence is important explanatory evidence if –

(a) without it, the court or jury would find it impossible or difficult properly to understand other evidence in the case, and
(b) its value for understanding the case as a whole is substantial.

103 Matter in issue between the defendant and the prosecution

(1) For the purposes of section 101(1)(d) the matters in issue between the defendant and the prosecution include –

(a) the question whether the defendant has a propensity to commit offences of the kind with which he is charged, except where his having such a propensity makes it no more likely that he is guilty of the offence;
(b) the question whether the defendant has a propensity to be untruthful, except where it is not suggested that the defendant's case is untruthful in any respect.

(2) Where subsection (1)(a) applies, a defendant's propensity to commit offences of the kind with which he is charged may (without prejudice to any other way of doing so) be established by evidence that he has been convicted of –

(a) an offence of the same description as the one with which he is charged, or
(b) an offence of the same category as the one with which he is charged.

(3) Subsection (2) does not apply in the case of a particular defendant if the court is satisfied, by reason of the length of time since the conviction or for any other reason, that it would be unjust for it to apply in his case.

(4) For the purposes of subsection (2) –

(a) two offences are of the same description as each other if the statement of the offence in a written charge or indictment would, in each case, be in the same terms;
(b) two offences are of the same category as each other if they belong to the same category of offences prescribed for the purposes of this section by an order made by the Secretary of State.

(5) A category prescribed by an order under subsection (4)(b) must consist of offences of the same type.

(6) Only prosecution evidence is admissible under section 101(1)(d).

[(7) Where –

(a) a defendant has been convicted of an offence under the law of any country outside England and Wales ("the previous offence"), and
(b) the previous offence would constitute an offence under the law of England and Wales ("the corresponding offence") if it were done in England and Wales at the time of the trial for the offence with which the defendant is now charged ("the current offence"),

subsection (8) applies for the purpose of determining if the previous offence and the current offence are of the same description or category.

(8) For the purposes of subsection (2) –

(a) the previous offence is of the same description as the current offence if the corresponding offence is of that same description, as set out in subsection (4)(a);
(b) the previous offence is of the same category as the current offence if the current offence and the corresponding offence belong to the same category of offences prescribed as mentioned in subsection (4)(b).

(9) For the purposes of subsection (10) "foreign service offence" means an offence which –

(a) was the subject of proceedings under the service law of a country outside the United Kingdom, and
(b) would constitute an offence under the law of England and Wales or a service offence ("the corresponding domestic offence") if it were done in England and Wales by a member of Her Majesty's forces at the time of the trial for the offence with which the defendant is now charged ("the current offence").

(10) Where a defendant has been found guilty of a foreign service offence ("the previous service offence"), for the purposes of subsection (2) –

(a) the previous service offence is an offence of the same description as the current offence if the corresponding domestic offence is of that same description, as set out in subsection (4)(a);
(b) the previous service offence is an offence of the same category as the current offence if the current offence and the corresponding domestic offence belong to the same category of offences prescribed as mentioned in subsection (4)(b).

(11) In this section –

"Her Majesty's forces" has the same meaning as in the Armed Forces Act 2006;

"service law", in relation to a country outside the United Kingdom, means the law governing all or any of the naval, military or air forces of that country.]

Amendment: Coroners and Justice Act 2009, s 144, Sch 17, para 1(1), (2).

104 Matter in issue between the defendant and a co-defendant

(1) Evidence which is relevant to the question whether the defendant has a propensity to be untruthful is admissible on that basis under section 101(1)(e) only if the nature or conduct of his defence is such as to undermine the co-defendant's defence.

(2) Only evidence –

- (a) which is to be (or has been) adduced by the co-defendant, or
- (b) which a witness is to be invited to give (or has given) in cross-examination by the co-defendant,

is admissible under section 101(1)(e).

105 Evidence to correct a false impression

(1) For the purposes of section 101(1)(f) –

- (a) the defendant gives a false impression if he is responsible for the making of an express or implied assertion which is apt to give the court or jury a false or misleading impression about the defendant;
- (b) evidence to correct such an impression is evidence which has probative value in correcting it.

(2) A defendant is treated as being responsible for the making of an assertion if –

- (a) the assertion is made by the defendant in the proceedings (whether or not in evidence given by him),
- (b) the assertion was made by the defendant –
  - (i) on being questioned under caution, before charge, about the offence with which he is charged, or
  - (ii) on being charged with the offence or officially informed that he might be prosecuted for it,

  and evidence of the assertion is given in the proceedings,
- (c) the assertion is made by a witness called by the defendant,
- (d) the assertion is made by any witness in cross-examination in response to a question asked by the defendant that is intended to elicit it, or is likely to do so, or
- (e) the assertion was made by any person out of court, and the defendant adduces evidence of it in the proceedings.

(3) A defendant who would otherwise be treated as responsible for the making of an assertion shall not be so treated if, or to the extent that, he withdraws it or disassociates himself from it.

(4) Where it appears to the court that a defendant, by means of his conduct (other than the giving of evidence) in the proceedings, is seeking to give the court or jury an impression about himself that is false or misleading, the court may if it appears just to do so treat the defendant as being responsible for the making of an assertion which is apt to give that impression.

(5) In subsection (4) "conduct" includes appearance or dress.

(6) Evidence is admissible under section 101(1)(f) only if it goes no further than is necessary to correct the false impression.

(7) Only prosecution evidence is admissible under section 101(1)(f).

106 Attack on another person's character

(1) For the purposes of section 101(1)(g) a defendant makes an attack on another person's character if –

- (a) he adduces evidence attacking the other person's character,
- (b) he (or any legal representative appointed under section 38(4) of the Youth Justice and Criminal Evidence Act 1999 (c 23) to cross-examine a witness in his interests) asks questions in cross-examination that are intended to elicit such evidence, or are likely to do so, or
- (c) evidence is given of an imputation about the other person made by the defendant –
  - (i) on being questioned under caution, before charge, about the offence with which he is charged, or
  - (ii) on being charged with the offence or officially informed that he might be prosecuted for it.

(2) In subsection (1) "evidence attacking the other person's character" means evidence to the effect that the other person –

- (a) has committed an offence (whether a different offence from the one with which the defendant is charged or the same one), or
- (b) has behaved, or is disposed to behave, in a reprehensible way;

and "imputation about the other person" means an assertion to that effect.

(3) Only prosecution evidence is admissible under section 101(1)(g).

107 Stopping the case where evidence contaminated

(1) If on a defendant's trial before a judge and jury for an offence –

- (a) evidence of his bad character has been admitted under any of paragraphs (c) to (g) of section 101(1), and
- (b) the court is satisfied at any time after the close of the case for the prosecution that –
  - (i) the evidence is contaminated, and
  - (ii) the contamination is such that, considering the importance of the evidence to the case against the defendant, his conviction of the offence would be unsafe,

the court must either direct the jury to acquit the defendant of the offence or, if it considers that there ought to be a retrial, discharge the jury.

(2) Where –

(a) a jury is directed under subsection (1) to acquit a defendant of an offence, and
(b) the circumstances are such that, apart from this subsection, the defendant could if acquitted of that offence be found guilty of another offence,

the defendant may not be found guilty of that other offence if the court is satisfied as mentioned in subsection (1)(b) in respect of it.

(3) If –

(a) a jury is required to determine under section 4A(2) of the Criminal Procedure (Insanity) Act 1964 (c 84) whether a person charged on an indictment with an offence did the act or made the omission charged,
(b) evidence of the person's bad character has been admitted under any of paragraphs (c) to (g) of section 101(1), and
(c) the court is satisfied at any time after the close of the case for the prosecution that –
 (i) the evidence is contaminated, and
 (ii) the contamination is such that, considering the importance of the evidence to the case against the person, a finding that he did the act or made the omission would be unsafe,

 the court must either direct the jury to acquit the defendant of the offence or, if it considers that there ought to be a rehearing, discharge the jury.

(4) This section does not prejudice any other power a court may have to direct a jury to acquit a person of an offence or to discharge a jury.

(5) For the purposes of this section a person's evidence is contaminated where –

(a) as a result of an agreement or understanding between the person and one or more others, or
(b) as a result of the person being aware of anything alleged by one or more others whose evidence may be, or has been, given in the proceedings,

the evidence is false or misleading in any respect, or is different from what it would otherwise have been.

108 Offences committed by defendant when a child

(1) Section 16(2) and (3) of the Children and Young Persons Act 1963 (c 37) (offences committed by person under 14 disregarded for purposes of evidence relating to previous convictions) shall cease to have effect.

(2) In proceedings for an offence committed or alleged to have been committed by the defendant when aged 21 or over, evidence of his conviction for an offence when under the age of 14 is not admissible unless –

(a) both of the offences are triable only on indictment, and
(b) the court is satisfied that the interests of justice require the evidence to be admissible.

[(2A) Subsection (2B) applies where –

(a) the defendant has been convicted of an offence under the law of any country outside England and Wales ("the previous offence"), and
(b) the previous offence would constitute an offence under the law of England and Wales ("the corresponding offence") if it were done in England and Wales at the time of the proceedings for the offence with which the defendant is now charged.

(2B) For the purposes of subsection (2), the previous offence is to be regarded as triable only on indictment if the corresponding offence is so triable.]

(3) Subsection (2) applies in addition to section 101.

Amendment: Coroners and Justice Act 2009, s 144, Sch 17, para 1(1), (3).

General

109 Assumption of truth in assessment of relevance or probative value

(1) Subject to subsection (2), a reference in this Chapter to the relevance or probative value of evidence is a reference to its relevance or probative value on the assumption that it is true.

(2) In assessing the relevance or probative value of an item of evidence for any purpose of this Chapter, a court need not assume that the evidence is true if it appears, on the basis of any material before the court (including any evidence it decides to hear on the matter), that no court or jury could reasonably find it to be true.

110 Court's duty to give reasons for rulings

(1) Where the court makes a relevant ruling –

(a) it must state in open court (but in the absence of the jury, if there is one) its reasons for the ruling;
(b) if it is a magistrates' court, it must cause the ruling and the reasons for it to be entered in the register of the court's proceedings.

(2) In this section "relevant ruling" means –

(a) a ruling on whether an item of evidence is evidence of a person's bad character;
(b) a ruling on whether an item of such evidence is admissible under section 100 or 101 (including a ruling on an application under section 101(3));
(c) a ruling under section 107.

111 Rules of court

(1) Rules of court may make such provision as appears to the appropriate authority to be necessary or expedient for the purposes of this Act; and the appropriate authority is the authority entitled to make the rules.

(2) The rules may, and, where the party in question is the prosecution, must, contain provision requiring a party who –

(a) proposes to adduce evidence of a defendant's bad character, or
(b) proposes to cross-examine a witness with a view to eliciting such evidence,

to serve on the defendant such notice, and such particulars of or relating to the evidence, as may be prescribed.

(3) The rules may provide that the court or the defendant may, in such circumstances as may be prescribed, dispense with a requirement imposed by virtue of subsection (2).

(4) In considering the exercise of its powers with respect to costs, the court may take into account any failure by a party to comply with a requirement imposed by virtue of subsection (2) and not dispensed with by virtue of subsection (3).

(5) The rules may –

(a) limit the application of any provision of the rules to prescribed circumstances;
(b) subject any provision of the rules to prescribed exceptions;
(c) make different provision for different cases or circumstances.

(6) Nothing in this section prejudices the generality of any enactment conferring power to make rules of court; and no particular provision of this section prejudices any general provision of it.

[(7) In this section "prescribed" means prescribed by rules of court.]

Amendment: SI 2004/2035, art 3, Schedule, paras 45, 49.

112 Interpretation of Chapter 1

(1) In this Chapter –

"bad character" is to be read in accordance with section 98;
"criminal proceedings" means criminal proceedings in relation to which the strict rules of evidence apply;
"defendant", in relation to criminal proceedings, means a person charged with an offence in those proceedings; and "co-defendant", in relation to a defendant, means a person charged with an offence in the same proceedings;
"important matter" means a matter of substantial importance in the context of the case as a whole;
"misconduct" means the commission of an offence or other reprehensible behaviour;
"offence" includes a service offence;

"probative value", and "relevant" (in relation to an item of evidence), are to be read in accordance with section 109;
"prosecution evidence" means evidence which is to be (or has been) adduced by the prosecution, or which a witness is to be invited to give (or has given) in cross-examination by the prosecution;
["service offence" has the same meaning as in the Armed Forces Act 2006;]
"written charge" has the same meaning as in section 29 and also includes an information.

(2) Where a defendant is charged with two or more offences in the same criminal proceedings, this Chapter (except section 101(3)) has effect as if each offence were charged in separate proceedings; and references to the offence with which the defendant is charged are to be read accordingly.

(3) Nothing in this Chapter affects the exclusion of evidence –

(a) under the rule in section 3 of the Criminal Procedure Act 1865 (c 18) against a party impeaching the credit of his own witness by general evidence of bad character,
(b) under section 41 of the Youth Justice and Criminal Evidence Act 1999 (c 23) (restriction on evidence or questions about complainant's sexual history), or
(c) on grounds other than the fact that it is evidence of a person's bad character.

Amendment: Armed Forces Act 2006, s 378(1), Sch 16, para 215.

113 Armed forces

Schedule 6 (armed forces) has effect.

Chapter 2
Hearsay Evidence

Hearsay: main provisions

114 Admissibility of hearsay evidence

(1) In criminal proceedings a statement not made in oral evidence in the proceedings is admissible as evidence of any matter stated if, but only if –

(a) any provision of this Chapter or any other statutory provision makes it admissible,
(b) any rule of law preserved by section 118 makes it admissible,
(c) all parties to the proceedings agree to it being admissible, or
(d) the court is satisfied that it is in the interests of justice for it to be admissible.

(2) In deciding whether a statement not made in oral evidence should be admitted under subsection (1)(d), the court must have regard to the following factors (and to any others it considers relevant) –

(a) how much probative value the statement has (assuming it to be true) in relation to a matter in issue in the proceedings, or how valuable it is for the understanding of other evidence in the case;
(b) what other evidence has been, or can be, given on the matter or evidence mentioned in paragraph (a);
(c) how important the matter or evidence mentioned in paragraph (a) is in the context of the case as a whole;
(d) the circumstances in which the statement was made;
(e) how reliable the maker of the statement appears to be;
(f) how reliable the evidence of the making of the statement appears to be;
(g) whether oral evidence of the matter stated can be given and, if not, why it cannot;
(h) the amount of difficulty involved in challenging the statement;
(i) the extent to which that difficulty would be likely to prejudice the party facing it.

(3) Nothing in this Chapter affects the exclusion of evidence of a statement on grounds other than the fact that it is a statement not made in oral evidence in the proceedings.

115 Statements and matters stated

(1) In this Chapter references to a statement or to a matter stated are to be read as follows.

(2) A statement is any representation of fact or opinion made by a person by whatever means; and it includes a representation made in a sketch, photofit or other pictorial form.

(3) A matter stated is one to which this Chapter applies if (and only if) the purpose, or one of the purposes, of the person making the statement appears to the court to have been –

(a) to cause another person to believe the matter, or
(b) to cause another person to act or a machine to operate on the basis that the matter is as stated.

Principal categories of admissibility

116 Cases where a witness is unavailable

(1) In criminal proceedings a statement not made in oral evidence in the proceedings is admissible as evidence of any matter stated if –

(a) oral evidence given in the proceedings by the person who made the statement would be admissible as evidence of that matter,
(b) the person who made the statement (the relevant person) is identified to the court's satisfaction, and
(c) any of the five conditions mentioned in subsection (2) is satisfied.

(2) The conditions are –

(a) that the relevant person is dead;
(b) that the relevant person is unfit to be a witness because of his bodily or mental condition;
(c) that the relevant person is outside the United Kingdom and it is not reasonably practicable to secure his attendance;
(d) that the relevant person cannot be found although such steps as it is reasonably practicable to take to find him have been taken;
(e) that through fear the relevant person does not give (or does not continue to give) oral evidence in the proceedings, either at all or in connection with the subject matter of the statement, and the court gives leave for the statement to be given in evidence.

(3) For the purposes of subsection (2)(e) "fear" is to be widely construed and (for example) includes fear of the death or injury of another person or of financial loss.

(4) Leave may be given under subsection (2)(e) only if the court considers that the statement ought to be admitted in the interests of justice, having regard –

(a) to the statement's contents,
(b) to any risk that its admission or exclusion will result in unfairness to any party to the proceedings (and in particular to how difficult it will be to challenge the statement if the relevant person does not give oral evidence),
(c) in appropriate cases, to the fact that a direction under section 19 of the Youth Justice and Criminal Evidence Act 1999 (c 23) (special measures for the giving of evidence by fearful witnesses etc) could be made in relation to the relevant person, and
(d) to any other relevant circumstances.

(5) A condition set out in any paragraph of subsection (2) which is in fact satisfied is to be treated as not satisfied if it is shown that the circumstances described in that paragraph are caused –

(a) by the person in support of whose case it is sought to give the statement in evidence, or
(b) by a person acting on his behalf,

in order to prevent the relevant person giving oral evidence in the proceedings (whether at all or in connection with the subject matter of the statement).

117 Business and other documents

(1) In criminal proceedings a statement contained in a document is admissible as evidence of any matter stated if –

(a) oral evidence given in the proceedings would be admissible as evidence of that matter,
(b) the requirements of subsection (2) are satisfied, and
(c) the requirements of subsection (5) are satisfied, in a case where subsection (4) requires them to be.

(2) The requirements of this subsection are satisfied if –

(a) the document or the part containing the statement was created or received by a person in the course of a trade, business, profession or other occupation, or as the holder of a paid or unpaid office,
(b) the person who supplied the information contained in the statement (the relevant person) had or may reasonably be supposed to have had personal knowledge of the matters dealt with, and
(c) each person (if any) through whom the information was supplied from the relevant person to the person mentioned in paragraph (a) received the information in the course of a trade, business, profession or other occupation, or as the holder of a paid or unpaid office.

(3) The persons mentioned in paragraphs (a) and (b) of subsection (2) may be the same person.

(4) The additional requirements of subsection (5) must be satisfied if the statement –

(a) was prepared for the purposes of pending or contemplated criminal proceedings, or for a criminal investigation, but
(b) was not obtained pursuant to a request under section 7 of the Crime (International Co-operation) Act 2003 (c 32) or an order under paragraph 6 of Schedule 13 to the Criminal Justice Act 1988 (c 33) (which relate to overseas evidence).

(5) The requirements of this subsection are satisfied if –

(a) any of the five conditions mentioned in section 116(2) is satisfied (absence of relevant person etc), or
(b) the relevant person cannot reasonably be expected to have any recollection of the matters dealt with in the statement (having regard to the length of time since he supplied the information and all other circumstances).

(6) A statement is not admissible under this section if the court makes a direction to that effect under subsection (7).

(7) The court may make a direction under this subsection if satisfied that the statement's reliability as evidence for the purpose for which it is tendered is doubtful in view of –

(a) its contents,
(b) the source of the information contained in it,
(c) the way in which or the circumstances in which the information was supplied or received, or
(d) the way in which or the circumstances in which the document concerned was created or received.

118 Preservation of certain common law categories of admissibility

(1) The following rules of law are preserved.

‘Public information etc

1 Any rule of law under which in criminal proceedings –

(a) published works dealing with matters of a public nature (such as histories, scientific works, dictionaries and maps) are admissible as evidence of facts of a public nature stated in them,
(b) public documents (such as public registers, and returns made under public authority with respect to matters of public interest) are admissible as evidence of facts stated in them,
(c) records (such as the records of certain courts, treaties, Crown grants, pardons and commissions) are admissible as evidence of facts stated in them, or
(d) evidence relating to a person’s age or date or place of birth may be given by a person without personal knowledge of the matter.

Reputation as to character

2 Any rule of law under which in criminal proceedings evidence of a person’s reputation is admissible for the purpose of proving his good or bad character.

Note: The rule is preserved only so far as it allows the court to treat such evidence as proving the matter concerned.

Reputation or family tradition

3 Any rule of law under which in criminal proceedings evidence of reputation or family tradition is admissible for the purpose of proving or disproving –

(a) pedigree or the existence of a marriage,
(b) the existence of any public or general right, or
(c) the identity of any person or thing.

Note: The rule is preserved only so far as it allows the court to treat such evidence as proving or disproving the matter concerned.

Res gestae

4 Any rule of law under which in criminal proceedings a statement is admissible as evidence of any matter stated if –

(a) the statement was made by a person so emotionally overpowered by an event that the possibility of concoction or distortion can be disregarded,
(b) the statement accompanied an act which can be properly evaluated as evidence only if considered in conjunction with the statement, or
(c) the statement relates to a physical sensation or a mental state (such as intention or emotion).
(d) evidence relating to a person’s age or date or place of birth may be given by a person without personal knowledge of the matter.

Confessions etc

5 Any rule of law relating to the admissibility of confessions or mixed statements in criminal proceedings.

Admissions by agents etc

6 Any rule of law under which in criminal proceedings –

(a) an admission made by an agent of a defendant is admissible against the defendant as evidence of any matter stated, or
(b) a statement made by a person to whom a defendant refers a person for information is admissible against the defendant as evidence of any matter stated

Common enterprise

7 Any rule of law under which in criminal proceedings a statement made by a party to a common enterprise is admissible against another party to the enterprise as evidence of any matter stated.

Expert evidence

8 Any rule of law under which in criminal proceedings an expert witness may draw on the body of expertise relevant to his field.'

(2) With the exception of the rules preserved by this section, the common law rules governing the admissibility of hearsay evidence in criminal proceedings are abolished.'

119 Inconsistent statements

(1) If in criminal proceedings a person gives oral evidence and –

(a) he admits making a previous inconsistent statement, or
(b) a previous inconsistent statement made by him is proved by virtue of section 3, 4 or 5 of the Criminal Procedure Act 1865 (c 18),

the statement is admissible as evidence of any matter stated of which oral evidence by him would be admissible.

(2) If in criminal proceedings evidence of an inconsistent statement by any person is given under section 124(2)(c), the statement is admissible as evidence of any matter stated in it of which oral evidence by that person would be admissible.

120 Other previous statements of witnesses

(1) This section applies where a person (the witness) is called to give evidence in criminal proceedings.

(2) If a previous statement by the witness is admitted as evidence to rebut a suggestion that his oral evidence has been fabricated, that statement is admissible as evidence of any matter stated of which oral evidence by the witness would be admissible.

(3) A statement made by the witness in a document –

(a) which is used by him to refresh his memory while giving evidence,
(b) on which he is cross-examined, and
(c) which as a consequence is received in evidence in the proceedings,

is admissible as evidence of any matter stated of which oral evidence by him would be admissible.

(4) A previous statement by the witness is admissible as evidence of any matter stated of which oral evidence by him would be admissible, if –

(a) any of the following three conditions is satisfied, and
(b) while giving evidence the witness indicates that to the best of his belief he made the statement, and that to the best of his belief it states the truth.

(5) The first condition is that the statement identifies or describes a person, object or place.

(6) The second condition is that the statement was made by the witness when the matters stated were fresh in his memory but he does not remember them, and cannot reasonably be expected to remember them, well enough to give oral evidence of them in the proceedings.

(7) The third condition is that –

(a) the witness claims to be a person against whom an offence has been committed,
(b) the offence is one to which the proceedings relate,
(c) the statement consists of a complaint made by the witness (whether to a person in authority or not) about conduct which would, if proved, constitute the offence or part of the offence,
(d)…
(e) the complaint was not made as a result of a threat or a promise, and
(f) before the statement is adduced the witness gives oral evidence in connection with its subject matter.

(8) For the purposes of subsection (7) the fact that the complaint was elicited (for example, by a leading question) is irrelevant unless a threat or a promise was involved.

Amendment: Coroners and Justice Act 2009, ss 112, 178, Sch 23, Pt 3.

Supplementary

121 Additional requirement for admissibility of multiple hearsay

(1) A hearsay statement is not admissible to prove the fact that an earlier hearsay statement was made unless –

(a) either of the statements is admissible under section 117, 119 or 120,
(b) all parties to the proceedings so agree, or
(c) the court is satisfied that the value of the evidence in question, taking into account how reliable the statements appear to be, is so high that the interests of justice require the later statement to be admissible for that purpose.

(2) In this section "hearsay statement" means a statement, not made in oral evidence, that is relied on as evidence of a matter stated in it.

122 Documents produced as exhibits

(1) This section applies if on a trial before a judge and jury for an offence –

(a) a statement made in a document is admitted in evidence under section 119 or 120, and
(b) the document or a copy of it is produced as an exhibit.

(2) The exhibit must not accompany the jury when they retire to consider their verdict unless –

(a) the court considers it appropriate, or
(b) all the parties to the proceedings agree that it should accompany the jury.

123 Capability to make statement

(1) Nothing in section 116, 119 or 120 makes a statement admissible as evidence if it was made by a person who did not have the required capability at the time when he made the statement.

(2) Nothing in section 117 makes a statement admissible as evidence if any person who, in order for the requirements of section 117(2) to be satisfied, must at any time have supplied or received the information concerned or created or received the document or part concerned –

(a) did not have the required capability at that time, or
(b) cannot be identified but cannot reasonably be assumed to have had the required capability at that time.

(3) For the purposes of this section a person has the required capability if he is capable of –

(a) understanding questions put to him about the matters stated, and
(b) giving answers to such questions which can be understood.

(4) Where by reason of this section there is an issue as to whether a person had the required capability when he made a statement –

(a) proceedings held for the determination of the issue must take place in the absence of the jury (if there is one);
(b) in determining the issue the court may receive expert evidence and evidence from any person to whom the statement in question was made;
(c) the burden of proof on the issue lies on the party seeking to adduce the statement, and the standard of proof is the balance of probabilities.

124 Credibility

(1) This section applies if in criminal proceedings –

(a) a statement not made in oral evidence in the proceedings is admitted as evidence of a matter stated, and

(b) the maker of the statement does not give oral evidence in connection with the subject matter of the statement.

(2) In such a case –

(a) any evidence which (if he had given such evidence) would have been admissible as relevant to his credibility as a witness is so admissible in the proceedings;
(b) evidence may with the court's leave be given of any matter which (if he had given such evidence) could have been put to him in cross-examination as relevant to his credibility as a witness but of which evidence could not have been adduced by the cross-examining party;
(c) evidence tending to prove that he made (at whatever time) any other statement inconsistent with the statement admitted as evidence is admissible for the purpose of showing that he contradicted himself.

(3) If as a result of evidence admitted under this section an allegation is made against the maker of a statement, the court may permit a party to lead additional evidence of such description as the court may specify for the purposes of denying or answering the allegation.

(4) In the case of a statement in a document which is admitted as evidence under section 117 each person who, in order for the statement to be admissible, must have supplied or received the information concerned or created or received the document or part concerned is to be treated as the maker of the statement for the purposes of subsections (1) to (3) above.

125 Stopping the case where evidence is unconvincing

(1) If on a defendant's trial before a judge and jury for an offence the court is satisfied at any time after the close of the case for the prosecution that –

(a) the case against the defendant is based wholly or partly on a statement not made in oral evidence in the proceedings, and
(b) the evidence provided by the statement is so unconvincing that, considering its importance to the case against the defendant, his conviction of the offence would be unsafe,

the court must either direct the jury to acquit the defendant of the offence or, if it considers that there ought to be a retrial, discharge the jury.

(2) Where –

(a) a jury is directed under subsection (1) to acquit a defendant of an offence, and
(b) the circumstances are such that, apart from this subsection, the defendant could if acquitted of that offence be found guilty of another offence,

the defendant may not be found guilty of that other offence if the court is satisfied as mentioned in subsection (1) in respect of it.

(3) If –

(a) a jury is required to determine under section 4A(2) of the Criminal Procedure (Insanity) Act 1964 (c 84) whether a person charged on an indictment with an offence did the act or made the omission charged, and
(b) the court is satisfied as mentioned in subsection (1) above at any time after the close of the case for the prosecution that –
  (i) the case against the defendant is based wholly or partly on a statement not made in oral evidence in the proceedings, and
  (ii) the evidence provided by the statement is so unconvincing that, considering its importance to the case against the person, a finding that he did the act or made the omission would be unsafe,

the court must either direct the jury to acquit the defendant of the offence or, if it considers that there ought to be a rehearing, discharge the jury.

(4) This section does not prejudice any other power a court may have to direct a jury to acquit a person of an offence or to discharge a jury.

126 Court's general discretion to exclude evidence

(1) In criminal proceedings the court may refuse to admit a statement as evidence of a matter stated if –

(a) the statement was made otherwise than in oral evidence in the proceedings, and
(b) the court is satisfied that the case for excluding the statement, taking account of the danger that to admit it would result in undue waste of time, substantially outweighs the case for admitting it, taking account of the value of the evidence.

(2) Nothing in this Chapter prejudices –

(a) any power of a court to exclude evidence under section 78 of the Police and Criminal Evidence Act 1984 (c 60) (exclusion of unfair evidence), or
(b) any other power of a court to exclude evidence at its discretion (whether by preventing questions from being put or otherwise).

Miscellaneous

127 Expert evidence: preparatory work

(1) This section applies if –

(a) a statement has been prepared for the purposes of criminal proceedings,
(b) the person who prepared the statement had or may reasonably be supposed to have had personal knowledge of the matters stated,
(c) notice is given under the appropriate rules that another person (the expert) will in evidence given in the proceedings orally or under section 9 of the Criminal Justice Act 1967 (c 80) base an opinion or inference on the statement, and

(d) the notice gives the name of the person who prepared the statement and the nature of the matters stated.

(2) In evidence given in the proceedings the expert may base an opinion or inference on the statement.

(3) If evidence based on the statement is given under subsection (2) the statement is to be treated as evidence of what it states.

(4) This section does not apply if the court, on an application by a party to the proceedings, orders that it is not in the interests of justice that it should apply.

(5) The matters to be considered by the court in deciding whether to make an order under subsection (4) include –

(a) the expense of calling as a witness the person who prepared the statement;
(b) whether relevant evidence could be given by that person which could not be given by the expert;
(c) whether that person can reasonably be expected to remember the matters stated well enough to give oral evidence of them.

(6) Subsections (1) to (5) apply to a statement prepared for the purposes of a criminal investigation as they apply to a statement prepared for the purposes of criminal proceedings, and in such a case references to the proceedings are to criminal proceedings arising from the investigation.

(7) The appropriate rules are [Criminal Procedure Rules made by virtue of] –

(a) section 81 of the Police and Criminal Evidence Act 1984 (advance notice of expert evidence in Crown Court), or
(b) section 20(3) of the Criminal Procedure and Investigations Act 1996 (c 25) (advance notice of expert evidence in magistrates' courts).

Amendment: SI 2004/2035, art 3, Schedule, paras 45, 50(a), (b) and (c).

128 Confessions

(1) In the Police and Criminal Evidence Act 1984 (c 60) the following section is inserted after section 76 –

> **"76A Confessions may be given in evidence for co-accused**
>
> (1) In any proceedings a confession made by an accused person may be given in evidence for another person charged in the same proceedings (a co-accused) in so far as it is relevant to any matter in issue in the proceedings and is not excluded by the court in pursuance of this section.
>
> (2) If, in any proceedings where a co-accused proposes to give in evidence a confession made by an accused person, it is represented to the court that the confession was or may have been obtained –
>
> (a) by oppression of the person who made it; or
> (b) in consequence of anything said or done which was likely, in the circumstances existing at the time, to render unreliable any confession which might be made by him in consequence thereof,

the court shall not allow the confession to be given in evidence for the co-accused except in so far as it is proved to the court on the balance of probabilities that the confession (notwithstanding that it may be true) was not so obtained.

(3) Before allowing a confession made by an accused person to be given in evidence for a co-accused in any proceedings, the court may of its own motion require the fact that the confession was not obtained as mentioned in subsection (2) above to be proved in the proceedings on the balance of probabilities.

(4) The fact that a confession is wholly or partly excluded in pursuance of this section shall not affect the admissibility in evidence –

(a) of any facts discovered as a result of the confession; or
(b) where the confession is relevant as showing that the accused speaks, writes or expresses himself in a particular way, of so much of the confession as is necessary to show that he does so.

(5) Evidence that a fact to which this subsection applies was discovered as a result of a statement made by an accused person shall not be admissible unless evidence of how it was discovered is given by him or on his behalf.

(6) Subsection (5) above applies –

(a) to any fact discovered as a result of a confession which is wholly excluded in pursuance of this section; and
(b) to any fact discovered as a result of a confession which is partly so excluded, if the fact is discovered as a result of the excluded part of the confession.

(7) In this section "oppression" includes torture, inhuman or degrading treatment, and the use or threat of violence (whether or not amounting to torture)."

(2) Subject to subsection (1), nothing in this Chapter makes a confession by a defendant admissible if it would not be admissible under section 76 of the Police and Criminal Evidence Act 1984 (c 60).

(3) In subsection (2) "confession" has the meaning given by section 82 of that Act.

129 Representations other than by a person

(1) Where a representation of any fact –

(a) is made otherwise than by a person, but
(b) depends for its accuracy on information supplied (directly or indirectly) by a person,

the representation is not admissible in criminal proceedings as evidence of the fact unless it is proved that the information was accurate.

(2) Subsection (1) does not affect the operation of the presumption that a mechanical device has been properly set or calibrated.

130 Depositions

In Schedule 3 to the Crime and Disorder Act 1998 (c 37), sub-paragraph (4) of paragraph 5 is omitted (power of the court to overrule an objection to a deposition being read as evidence by virtue of that paragraph).

131 Evidence at retrial

For paragraphs 1 and 1A of Schedule 2 to the Criminal Appeal Act 1968 (c 19) (oral evidence and use of transcripts etc at retrials under that Act) there is substituted–

> **"1 Evidence**
>
> (1) Evidence given at a retrial must be given orally if it was given orally at the original trial, unless –
>
> (a) all the parties to the retrial agree otherwise;
> (b) section 116 of the Criminal Justice Act 2003 applies (admissibility of hearsay evidence where a witness is unavailable); or
> (c) the witness is unavailable to give evidence, otherwise than as mentioned in subsection (2) of that section, and section 114(1)(d) of that Act applies (admission of hearsay evidence under residual discretion).
>
> (2) Paragraph 5 of Schedule 3 to the Crime and Disorder Act 1998 (use of depositions) does not apply at a retrial to a deposition read as evidence at the original trial."

General

132 Rules of court

(1) Rules of court may make such provision as appears to the appropriate authority to be necessary or expedient for the purposes of this Chapter; and the appropriate authority is the authority entitled to make the rules.

(2) The rules may make provision about the procedure to be followed and other conditions to be fulfilled by a party proposing to tender a statement in evidence under any provision of this Chapter.

(3) The rules may require a party proposing to tender the evidence to serve on each party to the proceedings such notice, and such particulars of or relating to the evidence, as may be prescribed.

(4) The rules may provide that the evidence is to be treated as admissible by agreement of the parties if –

(a) a notice has been served in accordance with provision made under subsection (3), and
(b) no counter-notice in the prescribed form objecting to the admission of the evidence has been served by a party.

(5) If a party proposing to tender evidence fails to comply with a prescribed requirement applicable to it –

(a) the evidence is not admissible except with the court's leave;

(b) where leave is given the court or jury may draw such inferences from the failure as appear proper;
(c) the failure may be taken into account by the court in considering the exercise of its powers with respect to costs.

(6) In considering whether or how to exercise any of its powers under subsection (5) the court shall have regard to whether there is any justification for the failure to comply with the requirement.

(7) A person shall not be convicted of an offence solely on an inference drawn under subsection (5)(b).

(8) Rules under this section may –

(a) limit the application of any provision of the rules to prescribed circumstances;
(b) subject any provision of the rules to prescribed exceptions;
(c) make different provision for different cases or circumstances.

(9) Nothing in this section prejudices the generality of any enactment conferring power to make rules of court; and no particular provision of this section prejudices any general provision of it.

[(10) In this section "prescribed" means prescribed by rules of court]

Amendment: SI 2004/2035, art 3, Schedule, paras 45, 51.

133 Proof of statements in documents

Where a statement in a document is admissible as evidence in criminal proceedings, the statement may be proved by producing either –

(a) the document, or
(b) (whether or not the document exists) a copy of the document or of the material part of it,

authenticated in whatever way the court may approve.

134 Interpretation of Chapter 2

(1) In this Chapter–

"copy", in relation to a document, means anything on to which information recorded in the document has been copied, by whatever means and whether directly or indirectly;
"criminal proceedings" means criminal proceedings in relation to which the strict rules of evidence apply;
"defendant", in relation to criminal proceedings, means a person charged with an offence in those proceedings;
"document" means anything in which information of any description is recorded;
"oral evidence" includes evidence which, by reason of any disability, disorder or other impairment, a person called as a witness gives in writing or by signs or by way of any device;

"statutory provision" means any provision contained in, or in an instrument made under, this or any other Act, including any Act passed after this Act.

(2) Section 115 (statements and matters stated) contains other general interpretative provisions.

(3) Where a defendant is charged with two or more offences in the same criminal proceedings, this Chapter has effect as if each offence were charged in separate proceedings.

INDEX

References are to paragraph numbers.